Encyclopedia of
Contemporary Christian Music

Encyclopedia of
Contemporary Christian Music

Pop, Rock, and Worship

Don Cusic, Editor

GREENWOOD PRESS
An Imprint of ABC-CLIO, LLC

A B C C L I O

Santa Barbara, California • Denver, Colorado • Oxford, England

Library of Congress Cataloging-in-Publication Data

Encyclopedia of contemporary Christian music : pop, rock, and worship / Don Cusic,
editor.
    p. cm.
  Includes bibliographical references and index.
  ISBN 978-0-313-34425-1 (hard copy : alk. paper) — ISBN 978-0-313-34426-8 (ebook)
  1. Contemporary Christian music—Bio-bibliography—Dictionaries. I. Cusic, Don.
  ML105.E52   2010
  782.25–dc22

                                  2009029545

14   13   12   11   10   1   2   3   4   5

This book is also available on the World Wide Web as an eBook.
Visit www.abc-clio.com for details.

ABC-CLIO, LLC
130 Cremona Drive, P.O. Box 1911
Santa Barbara, California 93116-1911

This book is printed on acid-free paper ∞

Manufactured in the United States of America

Contents

List of Entries

Guide to Related Topics

Biographical Information on Key Executives

Contemporary Christian Music: Definition and Background

Jesus Music

Religious Music in America, a History

Contemporary Christian Music and Other Genres

Black Gospel and Contemporary Christian Music

Catholics and Contemporary Christian Music

Instrumentalists in Contemporary Christian Music

Southern Gospel and Contemporary Christian Music

Contemporary Christian Music and Popular Culture

Christian Culture

Godspell

Jesus Christ Superstar

Politics and Contemporary Christian Music

Popular Music and Contemporary Christian Music

Television and Contemporary Christian Music

Marketing of Contemporary Christian Music

Christian Artists Seminar in the Rockies

Christian Booksellers Association

Christian Radio and Contemporary Christian Music

Dove Award

Festivals

Gospel Grammy Awards

Gospel Music Association

Gospel Music Hall of Fame

Praise and Worship Music

Record Labels

Retail and Contemporary Christian Music

Zondervan

Preface

"Contemporary Christian music is part of the music business, but not really."
"There's no such thing as Christian music; there are only Christian songs."

Those two statements show the enigma that is Christian and gospel music. First, contemporary Christian music (CCM) is part of the music industry because it uses the tools of that industry; artists record in some of the same studios that secular artists use; their recordings have been pressed on records, tapes, and CDs and are now downloaded to electronic listening devices; the publishing and record companies operate under the same copyright laws as secular companies; and these recordings are sold in stores, just like secular artists. The difference is that the secular industry sees itself as part of the entertainment industry; the Christian industry, for the most part, sees itself as a ministry.

This ministry is dedicated to supporting, encouraging, and upholding the beliefs of Christians as well as seeking to convert non-Christians to embrace Christianity. As to the idea of there being no such thing as Christian music, that statement simply means that Christian artists use all types of music—rock, pop, country, hip hop, and whatever else—to convey the Christian message. The difference in Christian music is found in the lyrics of the song, which convey a Christian belief or are written by a Christian who acknowledges his or her faith in a straightforward manner so that everything they write reflects or embodies their Christian belief.

The secular, or non-Christian, world has, to a large extent, ignored contemporary Christian music and, as a result, very little has been written about contemporary Christian music outside the realm of Christian publications. This book is written for those in the secular world who want information about Christian artists and Christian music presented in an objective, straightforward way. It is especially intended for academics and general music critics who seek a reference work on contemporary Christian music. We hope this work will also reach the friends, fans, and participants in Christian music who need a reference book for key people, trends, and background for Christian music.

This volume has 204 entries, and most of them are biographical entries of artists, like those found in any other encyclopedic work on a musical genre. It also contains entries on Jesus music, the forerunner to contemporary Christian music; a history of contemporary Christian music; and a historical overview of religious music in America. This encyclopedia also includes topics as they relate to contemporary Christian music such as record labels, major executives, politics, and the Christian culture. The artists and topics were chosen by a group of key executives, writers, and others involved in Christian music. Entries cite works for further reading and often include discographies and lists of awards for major artists. The encyclopedia closes with a bibliography and an extensive index.

This book is organized in alphabetical order, so if you're looking for a particular artist it is easy to find them; for example, if you're looking for the entry on Amy Grant, then look under "G" for Grant, Amy. There are also longer entries on the history of contemporary Christian music, Christian radio, festivals, and articles on politics, black gospel, and southern gospel as they relate to contemporary Christian music. This book is not in chronological order; it is meant to be "dipped into" for information on various aspects of contemporary Christian music.

I would like to thank Mike Curb and the Mike Curb Family Foundation for supporting me with a professorship at Belmont University, which enables me to tackle projects such as this. Mike has been involved in contemporary Christian music for almost 40 years—back to the days when he was president of MGM Records and signed Larry Norman and Second Chapter of Acts to that label for their early recordings. More recently, Curb Records has Christian artists Natalie Grant, Michael English, Fernando Ortego, and Selah on their roster.

I would like to give a special thanks to my assistant Molly Shehan, who is invaluable to me in so many ways, including working on pictures for this encyclopedia. I can never thank her enough. I would also like to thank George Butler, who took over from Kristi Ward in the midst of this project and carried it through to completion. Kristi moved up to a new position and George did a great job of seeing this through.

A

ADAMS, YOLANDA

Yolanda Adams (b. August 27, 1962, in Houston, Texas) is an African American artist who comes from a family of six children; her father died when she was 13 and her grandfather died shortly afterward. Her mother introduced her children to gospel music as well as jazz and classical, and Yolanda first toured with the Southeast Inspirational Choir when she was 13. A former elementary school teacher, 6'1" Yolanda wanted to become a model before she recorded her first album, *Just As I Am* (1987), a collection of traditional spirituals, produced by Thomas Whitfield. Her songs address social issues; her vocal style, reminiscent of Whitney Houston, ranges from traditional gospel to rhythm and blues (R&B) and jazz. Adams is involved in several children's charities, including Operation Rebound, dedicated to inner-city children. Adams won Gospel Music Association Dove Awards for "Traditional Gospel Album of the Year" for her album *Through the Storm* in 1992 and "Traditional Gospel Song of the Year" for "Is Your All on the Altar" in 1999. She won Grammys for "Best Contemporary Soul Gospel Album" for *Mountain High . . . Valley Low* in 1999 and *The Experience* in 2001; at the 2005 Grammys she won "Best Gospel Song" for "Be Blessed." Her album *Mountain High . . . Valley Low* was certified platinum.

Don Cusic

For Further Reading

Carpenter, Bil. *Uncloudy Days: The Gospel Music Encyclopedia.* San Francisco: Backbeat, 2005.

Cusic, Don. *The Sound of Light: A History of Gospel and Christian Music.* New York: Hal Leonard, 2002.

Darden, Bob. *People Get Ready!: A New History of Black Gospel Music.* New York: Continuum, 2005.

Jackson, Jerma A. *Singing in My Soul: Black Gospel Music in a Secular Age.* Chapel Hill: University of North Carolina Press, 2004.

McNeil, W. K., ed. *Encyclopedia of American Gospel Music.* New York: Routledge, 2005.

Powell, Mark Allen. *Encyclopedia of Contemporary Christian Music.*

Gospel music recording artist Yolanda Adams poses for photographers at a party celebrating the first anniversary of Oprah Winfrey's O *magazine on April 17, 2001, in New York. (AP Photo/Mark Lennihan)*

Peabody, Mass.: Hendrickson Publishers, Inc., 2002.

Young, Alan. *Woke Me Up This Morning: Black Gospel Singers and the Gospel Life*. Jackson: University Press of Mississippi, 1997.

Zolten, Jerry. *Great God A'Mighty: The Dixie Hummingbirds: Celebrating the Rise of Soul Gospel Music*. New York: Oxford University Press, 2003.

AGAPE

Agape was one of the pioneers in Jesus Rock; formed in 1968 after the conversion of lead singer Fred Caban at a coffeehouse in Huntington Beach,

California, the group, whose hard rock sound was reminiscent of Grand Funk Railroad, performed regularly at the Salt Company Christian Coffeehouse in Hollywood. Their name comes from the Greek word meaning "divine love." The original featured female bass player Lonnie Campbell, who was replaced by Jason Peckhart before their first album. Keyboardist Jim Hess joined the group for their second album but died shortly after the band's breakup. Their third bass player, Richard Greenburg, later recorded as solo act. Agape, influenced by Grand Funk, Cream, and Jimi Hendrix, was one of the first Jesus music acts to play hard rock. Based in Azusa, California, the band's followers evolved into the International Agape Ministries. The band broke up in 1974.

Don Cusic

For Further Reading

Alfonso, Barry. *The Billboard Guide to Contemporary Christian Music*. New York: Billboard Books/Watson-Guptill, 2002.

Powell, Mark Allen. *Encyclopedia of Contemporary Christian Music*. Peabody, Mass.: Hendrickson Publishers, Inc., 2002.

Thompson, John J. *Raised by Wolves: The Story of Christian Rock and Roll*. Toronto, Ontario: ECW Press, 2000.

ALTAR BOYS, THE

Mike Stand, vocals, guitar
Ric Alba, bass, keyboard
Jeff Crandall, drums
Steve Panier, guitar (until 1984, rejoined in 1989)

Mike Stand formed this punk rock group in 1982. Inspired by the Ramones, the group's high energy music turned off many traditional fans although the lyrics were decidedly evangelical. After the breakup of the group, Mike Stand, from Clash of Symbols, received a degree from California State, Fullerton and joined the staff as worship leader at Calvary Church, Santa Ana. Jeff Crandall became worship pastor at High Desert Church in Victorville, California; Mark Robertson moved to Chicago and formed This Train; Steve Panier formed Fourth Watch and then formed a landscaping business; Ric Alba formed Chef's Hat Boxing and became active in working with organizations fighting AIDs.

Don Cusic

For Further Reading

Powell, Mark Allen. *Encyclopedia of Contemporary Christian Music*. Peabody, Mass.: Hendrickson Publishers, Inc., 2002.

Thompson, John J. *Raised by Wolves: The Story of Christian Rock and Roll*. Toronto, Ontario: ECW Press, 2000.

ANDRUS, BLACKWOOD AND COMPANY

Sherman Andrus, vocals
Terry Blackwood, vocals
Karen Voegtin, vocals
Bill Egtlin, keyboards and vocals
Bob Villareal, guitar and vocals
Tim Marsh, drums
Rocky Laughlin, bass

Sherman Andrus and Terry Blackwood were in the Imperials when they decided to form Andrus, Blackwood and Company in 1976. Terry Blackwood is the son of Doyle Blackwood, one of the original members of the Blackwood Brothers Quartet; Sherman Andrus was an original member of Andrae Crouch and the Disciples. In 1967, because of Jake Hess's health problems, he handed over the reins of the Imperials to Armond Morales, Jim Murray, and Joe Moscheo. The group hired Terry Blackwood as lead singer; in 1971 the Imperials hired Andrus Blackwood and became the first interracial group in southern gospel music. The Imperials, with Andrus and Blackwood both singing lead, released six albums between 1972 and 1976 before Andrus and Blackwood left to form their own group. Andrus, Blackwood and Company stayed together for nine years, then Blackwood and Andrus each pursued a solo career.

Since both Terry Blackwood and Sherman Andrus were with the Imperials during the period when group sang with Elvis, the two have been involved in Elvis memorial concerts and tributes.

Don Cusic

For Further Reading

McNeil, W. K., ed. *Encyclopedia of American Gospel Music*. New York: Routledge, 2005.

Powell, Mark Allen. *Encyclopedia of Contemporary Christian Music*. Peabody, Mass.: Hendrickson Publishers, Inc., 2002.

ARCHERS, THE

Steve Archer, vocals
Tim Archer, vocals

Nancy Short, vocals (until 1976)
Janice Archer, vocals (from 1976)

The Archers were a young, traditional gospel group at the beginning of the Jesus movement; their sound progressed to harmonies sung to a pop/rock backing. The group began in the San Joaquin Valley of northern California where their father was a pastor. The first version of the group, the Archer Brothers, was made up of brothers Gary, Tim, and Steve Archer, who sang in churches in the northern California area. During the late 1960s, Gary left the group to go into artist management, and Tim and Steve added vocalist Nancye Short, drummer Fred Satterfield, and guitarist Billy Rush Master to their group, known now as the Archers. In 1977, sister Janice Archer joined the group after Short departed.

They recorded their first album in 1972 for their own Charisma Records label; the following year the Benson Company in Nashville purchased Charisma and released this album. They continued to record for Benson labels and toured heavily, playing numerous Jesus festivals. In 1975, they switched to Light Records after coming to the attention of Andrae Crouch and Ralph Carmichael.

After their 1984 album *All Systems Go*, the members pursued solo projects. In 1985, they hosted a TV show on the Trinity Broadcasting Network. In 1991, they regrouped and recorded their last album, *Colors of Your Love*, toured together, and then disbanded in 1993.

Steve Archer has had a successful solo recording career beginning in 1982 with his album *Solo*.

Don Cusic

For Further Reading

Cusic, Don. *The Sound of Light: A History of Gospel and Christian Music.* New York: Hal Leonard, 2002.

McNeil, W. K., ed. *Encyclopedia of American Gospel Music.* New York: Routledge, 2005.

Powell, Mark Allen. *Encyclopedia of Contemporary Christian Music.* Peabody, Mass.: Hendrickson Publishers, Inc., 2002.

ASLAN

There have been several different groups named Aslan (after the lion in C. S. Lewis's *Chronicles of Narnia*).

The first group, active with the Maranatha group from Calvary Chapel, began as In His Name before taking the name Aslan and consisted of Jim Abdo, vocals, guitar, keyboard; Rick Conklin, vocals, bass; Johnnie Graves, drums; Mike Holmes, vocals, guitar, bass; Bill Hoppe, keyboard; and Toni McWilliams, vocals, violin. They were active in the California Christian scene from 1972 to 1978. This group never recorded an album but had a track on the *Maranatha Six: A Family Portrait* album.

The next group named Aslan consisted of Greg Buick, keyboard; Ted Kallman, guitar, vocals; Linda Kendall, vocals; Jeff Roley, guitar, vocals; Scott Roley, guitar, vocals; and Martin Vipond, bass. In 1974, this group changed its name to Stillwaters to avoid confusion with the Maranatha group. As Aslan, this group recorded one album.

A third group named Aslan consisted of Mike Bizanovich, guitar; Mike

Coates, keyboard; Tony Congi, vocals, guitar; Bill McCoy, vocals, guitar; Brain O'Konski, vocals, bass (until 1997); and Dan Sewell, bass (from 1997). This group worked with the Young Life organization and recorded one album, released on their own independent label.

A fourth group named Aslan is a non-Christian rock band from Dublin, Ireland, which began in 1986; group members include (past and present) Christy Dignam, Joe Jewell, Tony McGuinness, Billy McGuinness, Alan Downey, Rodney O'Brien, and Eamo Doyle.

Don Cusic

For Further Reading

Powell, Mark Allen. *Encyclopedia of Contemporary Christian Music*. Peabody, Mass.: Hendrickson Publishers, Inc., 2002.

Thompson, John J. *Raised by Wolves: The Story of Christian Rock and Roll*. Toronto, Ontario: ECW Press, 2000.

AUDIO ADRENALINE

Mark Stuart, vocals
Will McGinniss, bass
Bob Herdman, keyboards (until 2001)
Barry Blair, guitar, vocals (until 1998)
Tyler Burkum, guitar (from 1998)
Ben Cissel, drums (from 1998)

During the 1990s, Audio Adrenaline dominated Christian rock with their hit singles, high energy stage shows, and relentless touring. The band was unabashedly Christian and aimed their music for the Christian audience; during their career they had 18 number one songs on Christian radio charts.

The band began at Kentucky Christian College in Grayson, Kentucky. Brothers Mark and David Stuart were putting together a rock band; Will McGinniss's mother told Mark about her son, David. The Stuart brothers, McGinniss, and Barry Blair formed A-180 in 1991 and recorded two independent albums. McGinniss wrote a song, "My God," which they recorded with Bob Herdman on keyboards; that single reached Toby McKeehan with DC Talk and he brought them to the attention of ForeFront Records.

The members of the group were education and ministry majors, studying to be teachers and youth pastors, and initially thought they should play rock 'n' roll during the summers when they weren't teaching; however, they realized that the recording contract with ForeFront was a rare opportunity, so they signed with the label and moved to Nashville in 1991.

The group took the name Audio Adrenaline in 1992 and released their first album, self-titled, with singles "My God" and "DC-10." Their second album, *Don't Censor Me*, was produced by the Gotee Brothers, which included Toby McKeehan. Their album *Hit Parade*, a greatest hits collection, sold more than a million copies.

Through the years, the group had some personnel changes. In 1994, drummer Greg Harrington, formerly with Geoff Moore and the Distance, replaced their original drummer, then Ben Cissel replaced Harrington. In 1998, guitarist Barry Blair left and was replaced by Tyler Burkum.

Lead singer Mark Stuart was raised in Haiti, the son of missionaries, and the group committed to building a home for orphans in Haiti, the Hands and Feet Project. The group also

Members of the Christian rock group Audio Adrenaline accept the award for best rock gospel album for Until My Heart Caves In *at the 48th annual Grammy Awards on February 8, 2006, at the Staples Center in Los Angeles. (AP Photo/Mark J. Terrill)*

compiled a book *Some Kind of Journey: On the Road with Audio Adrenaline—7 Days, 7 Issues, 7 Souls* that profiled seven young people and their struggles with moral issues.

The group disbanded in 2005 after a farewell tour because lead singer Mark Stuart was in danger of losing his voice if he continued to sing.

Group members Herdman, McGinniss, and Stuart formed a record label, Flicker Records, and signed Riley Armstrong and Pillar; they sold that company to Provident Music and McGinniss and Stuart worked for the label in A&R.

Don Cusic

Discography

Audio Adrenaline (1992)

Don't Censor Me (1993)

Live Bootleg (1995)

Bloom (1996)

Some Kind of Zombie (1997)

Underdog (1999)

Hit Parade (2001)

Lift (2001)

Worldwide (2003)

Until My Heart Caves In (2005)

Adios: Their Greatest Hits (2006)

Gospel Music Association Dove Awards

1996   Long Form Music Video: *Big House* by Audio Adrenaline; Producers and Directors: Clarke Gallivan, Cindy Montano, Kari Reeves; Jeffrey

Phillips, Thom Oliphant;
Label: ForeFront

1998   Alternative/Modern Rock
Recorded Song: "Some Kind
of Zombie" Written by Mark
Stuart, Barry Blair, Will
McGinniss, Bob Herman;
Recorded by Audio Adrena-
line; Label: ForeFront

2000   Rock Recorded Song: "Get
Down" Written by Mark
Stuart, Bob Herdman, Will
McGinniss, Ben Cissell,
Tyler Burkum; Recorded by
Audio Adrenaline; Label:
ForeFront

2003   Rock Album of the Year: *Lift;*
Audio Adrenaline; Producers:
Mark Stuart, Will McGinnis,
Ben Cissell, Tyler Burkam;
ForeFront

2008   Long Form Music Video of the
Year: *Live from Hawaii*; Audio
Adrenaline; Mark McCallie;
Forefront Records

Grammy Awards

2003   46th Grammy Awards: Best
Rock Gospel Album:
Worldwide

2005   48th Grammy Awards: Best
Rock or Rap Gospel Album:
Until My Heart Caves In

For Further Reading

Alfonso, Barry. *The Billboard Guide to Contemporary Christian Music*. New York: Billboard Books/Watson-Guptill, 2002.

Powell, Mark Allen. *Encyclopedia of Contemporary Christian Music*. Peabody, Mass.: Hendrickson Publishers, Inc., 2002.

AYALA, BOB

Los Angeles native Bob Ayala grew up in the Jesus movement and began performing at the Salt Company Coffeehouse in Hollywood in 1969. A genetic eye disease blinded him but did not stop him from touring; during the Jesus movement he toured with his wife, Pam, performing folk-based songs. Ayala's debut album was *Joy by Surprise* (1976), which was followed by *Wood Between the Worlds* (1978), *Journey* (1980), and *Rescued* (1986). Active in anti-abortion rallies, Ayala became involved in Keith Green's Last Days Ministries after Green's death.

Don Cusic

For Further Reading

Powell, Mark Allen. *Encyclopedia of Contemporary Christian Music*. Peabody, Mass.: Hendrickson Publishers, Inc., 2002.

B

BAILEY, PHILIP

A member of the Rock and Roll Hall of Fame from his work with the seminal jazz/rock group Earth, Wind and Fire, Philip Bailey's four-octave range was featured on EWF's hits "Shining Star," "Sing a Song," and "After the Love Is Gone." During his time with EWF, Bailey's faith led him to record several solo Christian albums.

Born on May 8, 1985, in Denver, Colorado, Bailey was first interested in percussion and was originally recruited to join Earth, Wind and Fire as a drummer. EWF opened for Santana during a European tour in 1994 and Santana's lead singer, Leon Patillo, led him to a full Christian commitment through Bible studies.

Although Bailey has had success in the gospel and Christian market, his commitment is to the jazz/pop/funk group Earth, Wind and Fire.

Don Cusic

For Further Reading

Powell, Mark Allen. *Encyclopedia of Contemporary Christian Music.* Peabody, Mass.: Hendrickson Publishers, Inc., 2002.

BANNISTER, BROWN

One of the premier producers in Christian music, Brown Bannister has produced albums for Amy Grant, David Meece, Debby Boone, Farrell and Farrell, Michael W. Smith, Chris Eaton, the Imperials, Kim Hill, White Heart, Bruce Carroll, PFR, Petra, Steven Curtis Chapman, and Avalon.

A college buddy of Chris Christian, Bannister got his start working as an engineer at Christian's studio. During the mid-1970s, Bannister led a high school church group that included Amy Grant. He took Grant into the studio to record some of her songs for her friends; this led to a recording contract and Grant's illustrious career.

In addition to serving as engineer and producer, Bannister is also known as the songwriter of "Old Man's Rubble," "Faith Walkin' People," "Look What Has Happened to Me," "Angels," and "In a Little While" for

Grant; and "Praise the Lord" for the Imperials and "Stubborn Love" for Kathy Troccoli.

Bannister only recorded one album as an artist, *Talk to One Another* (1981).

Don Cusic

For Further Reading

Alfonso, Barry. *The Billboard Guide to Contemporary Christian Music.* New York: Billboard Books/ Watson-Guptill, 2002.

Cusic, Don. *The Sound of Light: A History of Gospel and Christian Music.* New York: Hal Leonard, 2002.

McNeil, W. K., ed. *Encyclopedia of American Gospel Music.* New York: Routledge, 2005.

Powell, Mark Allen. *Encyclopedia of Contemporary Christian Music.* Peabody, Mass.: Hendrickson Publishers, Inc., 2002.

BECKER, MARGARET

Margaret Becker (b. July 17, 1959, in Bayshore, New York) was a female rocker whose Catholic background raised some eyebrows in contemporary Christian music circles until she took some time off, regrouped, and began writing books and doing acoustic-based music.

Becker grew up in an Irish/German Catholic home, the youngest of four children, and showed an interest in music early in life, learning the violin when she was a child. When she was a teenager, Becker began playing guitar, which led to her writing songs that reflected her Christian values. Becker's family was very supportive of her

interest in music as she played various venues in the area. In 1985, she moved to Nashville, Tennessee, and discovered there was a whole industry that focused on gospel and Christian music. Becker went to Sparrow Records hoping to become a demo singer for the Christian label—someone who records demonstration records for the label's songwriters to play to artists who might record them—but the person she met there liked her songs and signed her to a publishing deal as a songwriter. She had songs recorded by Steve Camp ("One on One"), Sandi Patti ("Exalt Thy Name"), and Steven Curtis Chapman ("Wait"). Becker also worked as a background singer for Christian artist Rick Cua.

In 1987, she signed an artist recording contract with Sparrow and had numerous radio hits, including "Never for Nothing," "Just Come In," "Say the Name," "This I Know," and "Clay and Water." In 1992 she won the Dove Award for "Rock Recorded Song of the Year" and "Rock Album of the Year" for her song "Simple House" and album of the same name.

Becker's early material was rock oriented, but as her career developed she moved toward more R&B and pop sounds. Becker recorded ten albums with Sparrow, but her career was not without controversy. Some in the Christian industry did not look with favor on her Catholic background; others said some of the songs she wrote were not Christ-based; still others criticized her clothing style and her stage show. In 1999, Becker took a three-year break from the business and explored what she wanted to do with her life. She explored other forms of expression, which turned into cowriting a children's series with a scriptwriter and writing for several different magazines. Once word was out that Becker wrote material other than songs, Harvest House approached her about writing a book. She was already working on a collection of essays and they became *With New Eyes,* her first effort in publishing. Becker did not ignore her songwriting and found time to cowrite with other people in the industry

After her break, Becker asked to be released from her contract with Sparrow and signed with Cross Driven Records. She released new material for her audience that was acoustic based, more in line with the shows she had been performing for a number of years. She also devoted time to mentoring new talent that she felt had potential in the music industry. Becker became involved in World Vision, an international Christian relief and development organization whose goal is to work for the well-being of all people, especially children.

Vernell Hackett

For Further Reading

Becker, Margaret. *With New Eyes: Fresh Vision for the Soul.* Harvest House, 1998.

Becker, Margaret. *Growing Up Together*, Harvest House, 2000.

Becker, Margaret. *Coming Up for Air: Simple Acts to Redefine Your Life.* Eugene, Ore.: Harvest House, 2006.

BEVILL, LISA

Lisa Bevill (b. June 24, 1968, in North Carolina) grew up in Nashville, where she attended Belmont University, then went on the road as a background singer for Russ Taff and David Meece. She worked as a session singer and was on albums by Amy Grant, Michael W. Smith, Carman, Rich Mullins, Petra, and Russ Taff as well as country artists Wynonna Judd, Reba McEntire, and Vince Gill; she also sang commercials for McDonald's, Chevrolet, and Domino's Pizza. She signed with Vireo, a label owned by Brown Bannister and distributed by Sparrow and released her first single, "Place in the Sun." She began as a spokesperson for True Love Waits, which promotes abstinence before marriage, then, in the summer of 1995, she started a girls camp, Place in the Sun, in Bowling Green, Kentucky, for teenage girls wrestling with self-esteem, suicide, and other issues, an outgrowth of her involvement with Focus on the Family. Her debut album, *My Freedom* (1992), was followed by *All Because of You* (1994), *Love of Heaven* (1996), and *Lisa Bevill* (2000) before she stopped recording to focus on her family; she returned to the contemporary Christian music field in 2008 with her album *When the Healing Starts.*

Don Cusic

For Further Reading

Alfonso, Barry. *The Billboard Guide to Contemporary Christian Music.* New York: Billboard Books/Watson-Guptill, 2002.

Powell, Mark Allen. *Encyclopedia of Contemporary Christian Music.* Peabody, Mass.: Hendrickson Publishers, Inc., 2002.

BIBLE, THE, AND CONTEMPORARY CHRISTIAN MUSIC

Christianity and contemporary Christian music is anchored in the Bible, which believers accept as the Word of God. The biblical justification for contemporary Christian music is demonstrated throughout the Bible, which shows songs and singing as an important part of religious life. Music is used in religious services, in secular celebrations, in wars, as private prayer, as a means of offering thanksgiving and praise to God, to record events, in apocalyptic visions of the final days of earth, and in visions of life in heaven where songs will be used as a way to honor God with praise and thanksgiving, expressing awe and wonder.

The first mention of songs in the Bible is in Genesis, Chapter 31, when Jacob leaves Laban. Jacob and Rachel flee early one morning to return to Canaan, the land of his father and grandfather (Isaac and Abraham) without telling Laban, who they had been visiting. However, Laban, learning Jacob has left, pursues him for seven days, finally overtaking him and asking, "What have you done, that you have cheated me, and carried away my daughters like captives of the sword? Why did you flee secretly, and cheat me, and did not tell me, so that I might have sent you away with mirth and songs, with tambourine and lyre?" (vv. 26–27). It is clear that even at this early time, music was part of the culture, used in this case for festive occasions.

The first mention of singing in a religious context is in Exodus, Chapter 15. Moses has crossed the Red Sea after the sea had been rolled back for the Israelites but then closed on Pharaoh's army, ensuring the Israelites' safety. Moses and the people of Israel sing a song of thanksgiving to the Lord for their deliverance; the song begins, "I will sing to the Lord, for he has triumphed gloriously; the horse and his rider he has thrown into the sea," and then continues with a description of what happened at the Red Sea and how the Lord had defeated his enemies. This was topical and apparently composed on the spot, probably by Moses who, if this is true, would be the first acknowledged gospel songwriter.

This first biblical song lasts 18 verses and is a celebration of praise and appreciation for what God has done. Although it is not safe to assume that other biblical characters before Moses—Adam, Noah, Abraham, Isaac, Jacob, Joseph, and so on—never sang, there is at least no mention of their doing so. It is also significant to note that a song of thanksgiving was established as an important part of the religious life of the new nation forming under the leadership of Moses.

From the earliest establishment of Israel as the nation of God and the Jews as the people of God in the Old Testament, singing was a vital part of communication with God. When the people were in the wilderness with Moses, without food and water, suffering from their rebellion, they reconciled themselves with God by singing and He provided water.

In establishing the nation of Israel, God commanded Moses to "write this song, and teach it to the people of Israel; put it in their mouths, that this song may be a witness for me against the people of Israel. For when I have brought them into the land flowing with milk and honey, which I swore to give to their fathers, and they have eaten and full and grown fat they will turn to other gods and serve them, and break my covenant. And when many evils and troubles have come upon them, this song shall confront them as a witness (for it will live unforgotten in the mouths of their descendants); for I know the purposes which they are already forming, before I had brought them into the land that I swore to give." Moses writes this song that very same day and teaches it to the people of Israel (Deut. 31:19–22).

The song itself is Chapter 32 of Deuteronomy and tells the story of the formation of Israel, admonishing the people not to forget that God brought them to Israel to be a special nation, and warning of the wrath and vengeance of God should they forget their heritage. After singing the song, Moses commands the people to "lay to heart all the words which I enjoin upon you this day, that you may command them to your children, that they may be careful to do all the words of this law. For it is no trifle for you, but it is your life, and thereby you shall live long in the land which you are going over the Jordan to possess" (Deut. 32:45–47).

The Psalms, which are essentially a collection of songs from around the time of David, contain an abundance of references to songs and singing, with the emphasis being on communicating with God through singing. Many of the Psalms urge the people of God to sing as an expression of their faith with passages like "Come into his presence with singing" (100:2) and "I will praise the name of God with a song" (69:30). The Psalms also demonstrate

that singing and songs are part of everyday life—not just life in the assembly of worship or churches—but a continuous outpouring of faith and praise. There is also encouragement to compose new songs expressing faith; the passage "Sing to the Lord a new song" is found in several Psalms.

There are not a large number of examples of songs in the New Testament; still, it is obvious that singing and songs were considered an important part of the religious life of the early Christian. It was a way of communicating with God as well as sharing a sense of togetherness among believers.

Perhaps the most significant mention of a song in the New Testament is after the last supper when Jesus and his disciples sing a hymn before retiring to the Mount of Olives where he spends his last free moments with the group who has been the core of his earthly followers. There is no record of what they sang, but the implication is that the song was known by all of them and that they had sung together before, thus implying that singing was a part of the spiritual life of Jesus and his disciples.

A significant example of the power of singing in the New Testament comes in Acts, Chapter 16, where Paul and Silas have been thrown in jail in Philippi after casting an evil spirit from a prophetess. It states, "About midnight, Paul and Silas were praying and singing hymns to God, and the prisoners were listening to them, and suddenly there was a great earthquake, so that the foundations of the prison were shaken; and immediately all the doors were opened and every one's fetters were unfastened" (vv. 25–26). Clearly, singing was considered part of spiritual life, and the New Testament proves this by providing examples of both Jesus and Paul, his chief apostle, singing. Once again, the song Paul sang was not mentioned, but the implication is that it was a known hymn.

Later, in his letters, Paul exhorts new believers to "be filled with the Spirit, addressing one another in psalms, and hymns and spiritual songs, singing and making melody to the Lord with all your heart, always and for everything giving thanks in the name of our Lord Jesus Christ to God the Father" (Ephesians 5:19–20) and to "let the word of Christ dwell in you richly, teach and admonish one another in all wisdom, and sing psalms and hymns and spiritual songs with thankfulness in your hearts to God" (Colossians 3:16).

The Apostle Paul, in these two passages, cites "psalms, hymns, and spiritual songs" as three kinds of songs, but never defines the difference. It may be surmised, however, that the psalms and hymns were known songs while spiritual songs might have been sung "in the spirit" or extemporaneously and in an improvisational and personal manner, thereby encouraging believers to create their own songs. This implication sets the stage for Christianity to continually produce new songs that fit the changing times and spiritual revivals.

Not only are songs important in this world, they are also an important and a vital part of the next world, according to Revelation. In the apocalyptic vision, a "new song" is sung (Rev. 5:9–10) at the final moment. During the last days, as the scroll of life is opened, a song will be sung about the Savior: "Worthy art thou to take the scroll and to open its seals for thou was slain and by thy blood didst ransom men for God from every tribe and tongue and people and nation, and hast made them a kingdom and priests of our God, and they shall reign on earth." There are also passages (14:3) where Jesus will stand on Mount Zion on the final day and the 144,000 who are chosen to be saved will learn a "new song" that "no one else could learn" (15:3). Also, the song of Moses will be sung during this time as well as the song of the Lamb, which says, "Great and wonderful are thy deeds, O Lord God Almighty! Just and true are thy ways, O King of the ages! Who shall not fear and glorify thy name, O Lord? For thou alone are holy. All nations shall come and worship thee, for thy judgments have been revealed" (15:3–5).

Contemporary Christian music is not just songs about the Jesus born two thousand years ago, but about the God of eternity. The Jewish roots have been Christianized and the branches run through the ages, a testament to the timeless spiritual thread that runs through the history of mankind. Contemporary gospel music is really a circle with the Bible as both the starting and ending point. The history of gospel music may be seen as a series of circles that has continually grown larger as the music has become more diverse and encompassed more styles and roles in the lives of believers and nonbelievers. Thus, the history of gospel music is also the history of Christianity, particularly in the United States, where music has played such a vital role in Christian revivals throughout the life of the country.

Don Cusic

For Further Reading

Cusic, Don. *The Sound of Light: A History of Gospel and Christian Music*. New York: Hal Leonard, 2002.

BLACK GOSPEL AND CONTEMPORARY CHRISTIAN MUSIC

The church world is divided along black and white lines; there are black congregations and there are white congregations, with very little integration in most churches. This has been reflected in the emergence of contemporary Christian music, which has appealed primarily to a white audience. There are African American performers in contemporary Christian music, but they generally sing to a white audience; white contemporary Christian artists see few African Americans in their audiences.

The history of black gospel has shown it to be a music that spoke to African Americans. During the 19th century, the Fisk Jubilee Singers performed old spirituals, but in a European style, very formal, standing erect, singing with trained voices. The mainline Baptist and Methodist churches were emblems of social respectability, and gave their congregants the dignity of a formal worship service. But the Holiness movement challenged this formality and threatened the mainline churches with a service heavy on emotion and physical release. The music provided a release from troubles, rather than the quiet, inner strength to tame the spirit that mainline churches sought to impart.

The conflict between the Holiness and mainline churches was played out over a number of years, with the Azusa Street Revival as the major catalyst for changes in African American worship services and, ultimately, in the development of a distinctive sound for black gospel music.

The black gospel quartet has its roots in Fisk University in Nashville. In 1905, Fisk made a decision to feature a male quartet instead of a mixed choir of Jubilee Singers. The school led the way for mixed choirs with the Fisk Jubilee Singers; they had been followed by "Jubilee singers" from Hampton, Tuskegee, Utica, Mississippi, and Wilberforce Universities, which also developed singing groups.

The first quartets were formed at black universities and generally operated as clubs, electing officers, paying dues, wearing uniforms and singing formal arrangements at concerts that were prearranged. These quartets were primarily Baptists, who generally ridiculed the Holiness singers and their improvisation, emotionalism, and untrained singing; the Baptists preferred trained voices, singing the melody in a concert demeanor—standing erect, with proper enunciation, in a formal, reserved style. This, they felt, elevated the music and themselves. The Holiness singers, on the other hand, sang spontaneously during a church service, as audience participants rather than special guests. Gradually, the quartets began borrowing some of the emotional style of singing from the Holiness singers. The quartets became so popular that members of a community or church, not a university, began forming four-man groups.

A major difference between the university quartets and the quartets formed in communities and churches was the untrained voice. Rhythmically more free, the quartets moved on stage and used gestures with their hands, such as patting their thighs and swaying back and forth.

Although these quartets were influenced by the Holiness movement, they did not use instruments but sang a cappella. Although the Baptist and Methodist sects grew, particularly as large numbers of blacks left the South and moved north during the World War I era and joined these established churches, the Holiness movement expanded by planting churches—finding a community and setting up a storefront church. Music was an important part of the Holiness churches, which appealed to the less educated and those who wanted to feel a connection to their southern roots.

The Holiness singers wanted to have a piano accompany their singing. The first-known gospel pianist was Arizona Dranes, a blind woman, from Dallas, Texas. Dranes introduced the "gospel beat" to the piano—adding a syncopated rhythm akin to ragtime, with a heavy left hand driving the rhythm. She sang in a high, nasal voice and was an effective song leader.

In 1921, the National Baptist Convention published a hymnal, *Gospel Pearls*, edited by Willa A. Townsend, who worked at Roger Williams University in Nashville. There were 163 songs in the book, which contained many standard Protestant hymns; however, *Gospel Pearls* broadened the style of music available to Baptists and led to the formation of several important groups.

The worlds of blues and gospel were, literally, worlds apart. Gospel music was for the church and blues was for the honkytonks and dives; blues appealed to man's carnal nature and gospel sought to purify and elevate the soul. Blues was aligned with "the Devil" and those who sang gospel did

"God's work." Still, the popularity and commercial success of blues recordings during the 1920s helped black gospel because the recording companies saw both as music for the African American market.

The key figure in black gospel songwriting and publishing is Thomas Dorsey, who became known as a great personality, composer, publisher, performer, teacher, choir director, and organizer as well as minister of music for the Pilgrim Baptist Church in Chicago. More than any other individual, Dorsey defined contemporary black gospel music, even though he was not the first African American to have his songs published. But it was Dorsey himself as well as his songs that unified the movement which became black gospel, giving a definition to the music that survived throughout the 20th century.

Dorsey, of course, was a gigantic figure in gospel music outside his publishing. He trained and accompanied countless singers and fought for recognition with ministries and church musicians who were opposed to adding his songs to church services. Finally, the National Baptist Convention (Negro), which convened in Chicago in 1930, allowed the performance of two Dorsey songs, "How about You" and "Did You See My Savior." The positive reaction from delegates charted the direction for black gospel.

Throughout the 1920s Dorsey was a prolific composer of blues songs. He was initially "saved" through a song, "I Do, Don't You" at a Baptist convention in 1921. During the following years, he kept a foot in both worlds— gospel and blues—and performed all kinds of music. He always returned to the church after recovering from a grave illness, but the demands to support his wife led to his continued involvement in the blues field.

In gospel, Thomas Dorsey found his calling and his true genius took root and flourished. As director of the gospel choir at Pilgrim Baptist Church in Chicago, Dorsey helped a number of singers and had a forum for writing and experimenting with new songs he composed. He was heavily influenced by preachers, and he composed for those who used his songs as a minisermon, singing a line, then expounding while the audience shouted. The choir joined on the chorus while Dorsey played the accompaniment on the piano.

Dorsey's new songs ushered in a new era for black gospel at the same time some great gospel singers emerged, most of whom came out of choirs (often Dorsey's) as soloists. As black gospel was recorded and released, these singers established national reputations and influenced others who never saw or heard them otherwise. This served to unify black gospel and increasingly brought it to the attention of white churches and singers, who were influenced by the style and rhythms and often copied some of the songs and bought the records.

During the 1930s there was a widening gap between mainline churches and the Holiness/Pentecostal denominations that were creating a new style, music, language, and behavior in their services. Further, the Holiness/Pentecostals were more interested in personal salvation—"heaven or hell" was their rallying cry—than in assimilation. Their services were filled with emotional ecstasy, with members giving dramatic testimonies, clapping their hands, stomping their feet, singing forcefully, and making music with drums, tambourines, guitars, pianos or any other instruments they could find. The music was loud, rhythmic, and jubilant, and a song, accompanied by a "shouting session," could last half an hour or more. Women fainted and men jumped during these services; it was not uncommon for someone to be "slain in the spirit"—or "knocked out cold" for God—or for someone to be seen dancing in the aisle, oblivious to anything else.

The reserved sense of decorum, the withholding of emotion in order to present a dignified appearance, that was part of the mainline services was ejected from the Pentecostal service. The stoic demeanor was replaced with an emotional release that proclaimed joy, strength, and jubilation.

One of the keys to Dorsey's success was finding key collaborators, and he found his best in Sallie Martin, Roberta Martin (no relation), and Mahalia Jackson. In 1932 Dorsey organized a gospel choir at the Pilgrim Baptist Church in Chicago; Roberta Martin was his first choir director and Sallie Martin was a principal soloist who also became a business partner.

Thomas Dorsey toured throughout America between 1932 and 1944, performing concerts of the new gospel music he called "Evenings with Dorsey." The singers included Sallie Martin, Mahalia Jackson, Roberta Martin, Theodore Frye, and others he had trained. Admission was nominal and sheet music was sold at the concerts for a nickel a song. It proved to be an effective way of building a publishing company as well as promoting the songs because he left copies of the songs at churches for others to perform wherever he went. In many ways, this sense and knack for self-promotion was as great a gift as the songs themselves.

A key in the evolution of Thomas Dorsey from choir director and songwriter into the "Father of Black Gospel" was his formation, in 1933, of the National Convention of Gospel Choirs and Choruses. Along with several associates, Dorsey held these conventions in various cities, attracting choirs and soloists he instructed. They also learned his songs. The National Baptist Convention was another key for Dorsey; this annual convention drew thousands of black Baptists from all over the country. In 1935, his song "Take My Hand, Precious Lord" was sung four times; it was the first step toward this song becoming a gospel standard.

Throughout the 1930s, Mahalia Jackson sang at Dorsey's church; Dorsey accepted her as a gospel singer and gave her a "gospel home" whenever she was in Chicago. Mahalia's first recording was "God's Gonna Separate the Wheat from the Tares" in 1937 backed with "Keep Me Every Day." This first record brought her national recognition and made her name equal to that of the other great soloists in Chicago during that time: Willie Mae Ford Smith, Sallie Martin, Madame Lula Mae Hurst, Mary Johnson Davies, Roberta Martin, and Louise Lemon. It was a rich time for female soloists and Mahalia was just one of many, but her strong southern influence, which manifested itself in the moaning, growling, strutting, and skipping stage performances, soon caused her talent to be at the forefront of all the rest.

Unlike many other forms of gospel music, black gospel has a distinctive, identifiable sound. Thomas Dorsey was a leader in introducing jazz rhythms and blues singing in the church, adding gospel lyrics to the blues tradition.

The emotional impact of black gospel came from the Holiness Church and from southern singers who moved north. There, they found the opportunity to connect with a large African American community. Although the mainstream churches in this community originally rejected the Holiness sound, in time they embraced it as black gospel developed its own unique sound, rooted in the black experience in the United States which came from a deep-felt emotionalism anchored in a certain hopelessness about their earthly life balanced by a shining hopefulness about the Heavenly life to come.

The golden age for black gospel was during the 20 years following World War II. Mahalia Jackson joined forces with Thomas Dorsey in the early 1940s, creating more national attention as Dorsey toured the nation. She sang such songs of his as "Precious Lord" and "If You See My Savior" in a way that was distinctively hers, changing the melody and meter, stretching out the song, slurring her words, and projecting an image that was both spirit-filled and sexy at the same time. By 1945, she was famous in the black churches. Dorsey became firmly established as the "Father of Black Gospel" and Mahalia became the most famous gospel singer of her time. Black gospel quartets also experienced a golden age from 1945 to 1965. They were aided by the fact that a number of independent labels were formed to market music to the black audience.

Black gospel was more influential than white gospel in providing a "sound" and performers for rock 'n' roll, although most of the mainstream churches found the new music disturbing, to say the least.

The 1930s was the age of white southern gospel on radio, but the period after World War II brought black gospel to the airwaves. The sound of the black gospel quartet was four men and a piano. The groups were sharp dressers, choreographed their moves on stage, and developed the "swinging lead" where two men traded the lead vocal, as well as a soaring tenor—which often reached into falsetto—with smooth harmonies on the chorus. Increasingly, the music had a driving beat and, because the Holiness/Pentecostals demanded an emotional service, the music often brought crowds to their feet.

During World War II several important groups, first formed before the war, developed into full-time, professional groups. Archie Brownlee and the Original Five Blind Boys of Mississippi were first formed in 1932; Clarence Fountain and the Five Blind Boys of Alabama were formed in 1937; in 1936 Joe Johnson formed the Pilgrim Travelers; in 1938 the Swan Silvertones were formed; in 1945 the Highway QCs, a "farm team" for the Soul Stirrers, was organized.

Groups and singers popular during the decade after World War II include the Dixie Hummingbirds, the Nightingales, the Famous Davis Sisters from Philadelphia, the Royal Sons Quintet (which recorded secular music as the Five Royales), the Golden Gate Quartet, Swan Silvertones, the Soul Stirrers, Wings Over Jordan Choir, Southernaires, Sonny Til and the Orioles, Delloreese Patricia Early (later known as

Della Reese) in the group Meditation Singers, Gospel Harmonettes, Dorothy Love Coates, the Clara Ward Singers, the Angelic Gospel Singers, Aretha Franklin, and the Drinkard Singers, whose members included Cissy Houston, mother of Whitney, and Marcel Warwick, father of Dionne. The Mighty Clouds of Joy were formed in 1959 in Los Angeles; by 1962 they were one of the leading quartets in gospel music.

During the 1950s Albertina Walker and the Caravans produced more gospel stars than any other group or choir; they were, in essence, an ensemble of soloists. Singers who came out of the Caravans include Bessie Griffin, Shirley Caesar, Inez Andrews, Cassietta George, Dorothy Norwood, and Albertina Walker.

Numerous R&B groups were influenced by the Soul Stirrers, Pilgrim Travelers, and Dixie Hummingbirds, whose charismatic singers were combined with tight harmony background singing; many of these individuals and groups began in gospel, then shifted to R&B.

Although Ray Charles, James Brown, and Little Richard were all influenced by gospel music, borrowing songs and styles, none of them was ever a gospel singer. The first singer who proved that gospel could be the training ground for a pop star was Sam Cooke.

Cooke was certainly not the first singer to leave gospel for pop music. Dinah Washington had done it years before and Ray Charles, only a year older than Cooke but already a veteran in the recording studio (he had begun recording in 1948 when he was 18), had shown the powerful appeal inherent in gospel music when he took a traditional gospel song, put some secular lyrics to it, and delivered it with the gusto and delivery of a sanctified holiness preacher, resulting in the hit "I Got a Woman" in 1953.

Other precedents for black success in the white market were quartets like the Mills Brothers, the Ink Spots, and the Orioles, who presented a supper-club type harmony on songs like "Crying in the Chapel." The key year is 1954, when Elvis Presley made his first recordings in Memphis for Sun Records, Roy Hamilton had a pop hit with the gospel song, "You'll Never Walk Alone," and Ray Charles had a pop hit with a gospel-influenced performance of the bawdy "I Got a Woman." Then in 1955 and 1956, a succession of black acts, beginning with Little Richard, Chuck Berry, Fats Domino, the Coasters, and the Platters, opened the path in the musical world for black artists to appeal to white audiences. It was a world ripe for Sam Cooke, but he was hesitant and did not make his move until 1957.

Sam Cooke was the first gospel sex symbol and brought young people in the droves to gospel concerts, proving that the music could have an appeal for the young as well as the old. Too, he showed that a performer with gospel roots could have a major effect on the pop world, that the talent of gospel performers was first rate, and that the church—via musicians and singers who received their early training and experience there—would be a major influence on pop music in the rock 'n' roll revolution from the mid-1950s through the 1960s. Because the rise of soul music paralleled the rise of the civil rights movement, this places the career of Sam Cooke in the strategic center

where gospel, soul, and social activism all fused to bring about a major social revolution.

During the 1950s, Mahalia Jackson was promoted by Columbia Records as the "World's Greatest Gospel Singer." In 1956, she became involved in the civil rights movement when she went to Alabama and sang for free in support of the Montgomery bus boycott. From this point forward she became a regularly featured performer at civil rights seminars and rallies and played a major role in bringing the world of black gospel into the civil rights movement. This movement redefined life for African Americans in the United States during the 1960s.

Since music is a key focal point for the black church, it is logical that black gospel music would play a pivotal role in the civil rights movement. Although there are a number of television clips of people singing "We Shall Overcome," "Blowin' in the Wind," and other songs while their arms are locked together, it was the old black gospel standards that provided the foundation for that movement.

Black gospel in the latter part of the 20th century split into two different camps called traditional and contemporary. The traditional artists had their roots in the church choir and, musically, in blues and the older R&B. Contemporary artists were influenced by the contemporary R&B sound, the Motown influences, jazz, and disco—or dance—music heard on the radio. The contemporary sound generally appealed to younger audiences whose ties to the church were not as strong; the traditional sound appealed to older audiences and those who grew up with strong ties to the church.

Although those two paths existed in black gospel, they were not two totally separate roads but rather close, intertwining paths. Often played on the same gospel radio programs, often back to back, the two types of black gospel were sold together in record bins at retail outlets. The difference was mostly a matter of attitude, on the part of artists as well as the audiences, which manifested itself in music that either scorned pop (traditional) or embraced it (contemporary).

Within black gospel during the mid-1980s was a move toward a smoother sound that appealed to the white audience. It was this smoother sound that permeated the white gospel market and provided the initial impetus for traditionally white gospel labels to embrace this music and sell it through the Christian bookstores.

The term crossover generally means a music that appeals to several different audiences and can appear on several different charts—country and pop, R&B and pop, jazz and R&B, rock and easy listening—and therefore can sell in much greater numbers. Within black gospel, the term crossover has a two-fold meaning. First, there was the crossover into the pop market and, second, the crossover into the white gospel market. The crossover into the pop market had generally come from artists who went from being black gospel artists to pop artists. These artists had to abandon gospel to cross over. Once these artists switched they were not considered gospel anymore.

The crossover into the white gospel market became a much more lucrative and viable alternative for the black gospel artist because it allowed them to expand their market while staying true to their Christian commitment. Too, the white audience was generally receptive to African American artists whose music was smoother and pop-influenced.

Black gospel was generally sold in independently owned retail record stores (mom and pop stores) or in chain stores located in the black sections of a city. The albums were located in the same bins as R&B, soul, dance, and secular music. It did not sell in huge numbers but, with production costs kept low, promotion limited by the number of radio stations who played it, and tour support and other record company financial amenities virtually nonexistent, a label could produce a profit. If artists consistently sold 40,000–50,000 albums, they were considered highly successful and major stars.

Most black gospel was heard on African American radio stations that play an hour or two of gospel each day. Programs were generally funded by brokers, who paid for the time and then either sold ads or gained revenue from promoting concerts or other related activities. About 40 percent of black gospel was heard this way. There were only a handful (12 to 15) of radio stations that programmed black gospel full time. The remainder of radio airplay for this music came from Sunday programs provided by black radio stations and a few white contemporary stations who programmed a black contemporary artist.

The church is still the center of black gospel music, although artists performing in concerts and making studio records have become the centerpieces. The market for African American gospel music has created a steady demand for the choirs that record for black gospel labels, although most of these albums sell better regionally than they do nationally.

For their part, black gospel artists are faithful to gospel music, to the church, and to their audiences. They are rewarded by having audiences who are faithful to them for years.

For black gospel, one era ended and another began during the early 1990s. In February 1991, James Cleveland died; in January 1993, Thomas Dorsey, the "Father of Black Gospel," died. But in 1993, Kirk Franklin released his debut album, *God's Property*, and it went platinum. The album was released on a label begun by Puff Daddy (Sean Combs) and Russell Simmons, whose Def Jam label had popularized hip hop. They knew how to market to the black community in a way that also reached the white community.

Kirk Franklin, along with BeBe and CeCe Winans, Tramaine Hawkins, Yolanda Adams, and others proved that gospel music could sell in big numbers. This wasn't exactly contemporary Christian music, but the contemporary Christian audience bought it.

Don Cusic

For Further Reading

Boyer, Horace Clarence, text, Lloyd Yearwood, photography. *How Sweet the Sound: The Golden Age of Gospel*. Washington D.C.: Elliott and Clark, 1995.

Carpenter, Bil. *Uncloudy Days: The Gospel Music Encyclopedia*. San Francisco: Backbeat, 2005.

Cone, James H. *The Spirituals and the Blues: An Interpretation*. New York: Seabury, 1972.

Cusic, Don. *The Sound of Light: A History of Gospel and Christian Music*. New York: Hal Leonard, 2002.

Darden, Bob. *People Get Ready!: A New History of Black Gospel Music*. New York: Continuum, 2005.

Harris, Michael W. *The Rise of Gospel Blues: The Music of Thomas Andrew Dorsey in the Urban Church*. New York: Oxford University Press, 1992.

Heilbut, Tony. *The Gospel Sound: Good News and Bad Times*. New York: Simon and Schuster, 1971.

Jackson, Irene. *Afro-American Religious Music*. Westport, Conn.: Greenwood Press, 1979.

Jackson, Jerma A. *Singing in My Soul: Black Gospel Music in a Secular Age*. Chapel Hill: University of North Carolina Press, 2004.

Johnson, James Weldon, ed. *The Second Book of Negro Spirituals*. New York: Viking, 1926.

Marsh, J. B. T. *The Story of the Jubilee Singers; with Their Songs*. Boston: Houghton, Mifflin and Company, 1881.

Johnson, James Weldon, and J. Rosamond Johnson. *American Negro Spirituals*. New York: Viking, 1925.

Oliver, Paul, Max Harrison, and William Bolcom. *The New Grove Gospel, Blues and Jazz*. New York: W. W. Norton, 1986.

Pike, G. D. *Jubilee Singers, and their Campaign for Twenty Thousand Dollars*. New York: AMS Press, Inc., 1974, reprinted from edition from Boston: Lee and Shepard, Publishers; New York: Lee, Shepard and Dillingham, 1873.

Reagon, Bernice Johnson, and Linn Shapiro, eds. *Roberta Martin and the Roberta Martin Singers: The Legacy and the Music.* Washington D.C.: Smithsonian, 1982.

Salvatore, Nick. *Singing in a Strange Land: C. L. Franklin, the Black Church, and the Transformation of America.* New York: Little, Brown and Company, 2005.

Wald, Gayle F. *Shout, Sister, Shout!: The Untold Story of Rock-and-Roll Trailblazer Sister Rosetta Tharpe.* Boston: Beacon Press, 2007.

Ward, Andrew. *Dark Midnight When I Rise: The Story of the Jubilee Singers Who Introduced the World to the Music of Black America.* New York: Farrar, Straus and Giroux, 2000.

Witter, Evelyn. *Mahalia Jackson.* Milford, Mich.: Mott Media, 1985.

Work, John W. ed. *American Negro Songs and Spirituals.* New York: Bonanza, 1940.

Work, John Wesley. *Folk Song of the American Negro.* 1915. Reprint. New York: Negro Universities Press, 1969.

Young, Alan. *The Pilgrim Jubilees.* Jackson: University Press of Mississippi, 2001.

Young, Alan. *Woke Me Up This Morning: Black Gospel Singers and the Gospel Life.* Jackson: University Press of Mississippi, 1997.

Zolten, Jerry. *Great God A'Mighty: The Dixie Hummingbirds: Celebrating the Rise of Soul Gospel Music.* New York: Oxford University Press, 2003.

BOLTZ, RAY

Ray Boltz grew up in Muncie, Indiana, and graduated from Ball State University in that city with a degree in business and marketing. In high school and college he began his ministry during Sunday night services, at youth meetings, in prisons, and at evangelistic services. A talented songwriter, he wrote the anti-abortion song, "What Was I Supposed to Be?"

Boltz has long been active in Mission of Mercy, which provides food and sponsorship for children in Calcutta, India; the organization also sponsors the New Life Home for Abandoned Babies in Kenya. Boltz has also worked with Teen Mania, helping organize and sponsor mission trips for teenagers.

In 2001 he founded Spindust Records; their first signing was the grunge/metal band GS Megaphone.

Don Cusic

For Further Reading

Powell, Mark Allen. *Encyclopedia of Contemporary Christian Music.* Peabody, Mass.: Hendrickson Publishers, Inc., 2002.

BOONE, DEBBY

Debby Boone's song, "You Light Up My Life," is sometimes considered the first contemporary Christian "hit" song. The song debuted on the *Billboard* pop chart on September 3, 1977, and rose to number one, where it remained for ten consecutive weeks and came at a time when Jesus music was evolving into contemporary Christian music. The event that marks the "official" beginning of CCM was the publication of *Contemporary Christian Music* magazine, which debuted in July

Singer Debby Boone on November 11, 1977. (AP Photo/Nick Ut)

1978 with the Boone Girls on the cover. That cover story was a direct result of Debby's success with "You Light Up My Life" and was the first national story where Debby discussed her Christian beliefs.

Debby Boone (b. September 22, 1956) comes from a long line of music legends; her father is Pat Boone, who began his career as a teen idol in the 1950s, and her grandfather is Red Foley, a member of the Country Music Hall of Fame, whose career goes back to the National Barn Dance in Chicago during the 1930s. Debby's grandmother, who recorded under the name Judy Martin, was also a star with her sisters, the Overstake Sisters, on the National Barn Dance. Her aunt, Jenny Lou Carson, is a member of the Nashville Songwriters Hall of Fame; she wrote "Don't Rob Another Man's

Castle" and "Lovebug Itch" for Eddy Arnold, "You Two-Timed Me One Time Too Often" and "Jealous Heart" for Tex Ritter, and co-wrote the pop hit "Let Me Go, Lover."

Debby and her sisters Cherry, Linda, and Laura toured with their parents Pat and Shirley Boone and performed with them beginning in 1969; in 1970 they toured in Japan with the Osmonds.

The four sisters appeared on the first issue of *Contemporary Christian Music* magazine. They recorded their first album, *Glass Castle*, for Lamb and Lion Records, the label owned by their father and Mike Curb. Originally known as the Boone Girls, they changed their name to the Boones as they grew. Their pop-type harmonies made them a popular album group in early contemporary Christian music. The success of Debby Boone caused her to launch a solo career, and the marriages and families of the other three caused the group to disband as they pursued separate careers. Laurie Boone continued her career with her husband, Harry Browning; Lindy sang with the Cordettes, a 1940s-type dance band; Cherry became a writer and worked with victims of anorexia nervosa, a disability she overcame during the late 1970s.

"You Light Up My Life" was in a movie, *Sessions*, that Mike Curb saw; Curb had previously been president of MGM Records and had formed a production company and thought the song had potential. Curb spoke with Debby and her parents about Debby recording the song as a solo artist and she agreed. The film was retitled *You Light Up My Life*, but the song in the movie was sung by Cissy Kasyck, the original singer.

The success of "You Light Up My Life"—it was the most popular song of the 1970s, based on *Billboard* chart activity—led to Debby Boone receiving the Grammy for "Best New Artist" and her debut album sold more than two million units.

Debby Boone's follow-up singles never achieved close to the level of success of her debut single; "California" reached number 50 and "God Knows" reached number 74 on the pop charts. However, she had 13 records on the country charts, including a number 1 hit with "Are You on the Road to Lovin' Me Again" in 1980.

Debby Boone married Gabriel Ferrer, son of actor Jose Ferrer and singer Rosemary Clooney, on September 1, 1979. She sang the theme song for the movie *The Magic of Lassie* in 1978 and returned to Christian music in 1980 with her album *With My Song*, produced by Brown Bannister; on that album she recorded the Bob Dylan song, "What Can I Do for You." In 1985 she released the Christian album *Friends for Life*.

Boone has starred in the musicals *Seven Brides for Seven Brothers, The Sound of Music* (as Maria), *Meet Me in St. Louis, Camelot, Mississippi Love, The King and I, The Human Comedy* and *South Pacific*, made two made-for-TV movies, *The Gift of the Magi* and *Sins of the Past*, and appeared on the TV series "Baywatch Nights."

Debby Boone's major contribution to contemporary Christian music is that she showed the secular world that a Christian artist could achieve mainstream success without compromising her beliefs. She is a pioneer because her song "You Light Up My Life" brought attention to Christian music at a time when contemporary Christian music was beginning to emerge as a major genre in the music industry.

For Further Reading

Boone, Debby, and Dennis Baker. *Debby Boone So Far*. Nashville, Tenn.: Thomas Nelson, 1981.

Cusic, Don. *The Sound of Light: A History of Gospel and Christian Music.* New York: Hal Leonard, 2002.

McNeil, W. K., ed. *Encyclopedia of American Gospel Music*. New York: Routledge, 2005.

Powell, Mark Allen. *Encyclopedia of Contemporary Christian Music*. Peabody, Mass.: Hendrickson Publishers, Inc., 2002.

Discography

You Light Up My Life (1977)

Midstream (1978)

The Promise (1979)

Love Has No Reason (1980)

With My Song . . . I Will Praise Him (1980)

Savin' It Up (1981)

Surrender (1983)

Choose Life (1984)

Friends for Life (1987)

Reflections (1988)

Be Thou My Vision (1989)

Home for Christmas (1989)

The Best of Debby Boone (1990)

Greatest Hymns (2000)

You Light Up My Life: Greatest Inspirational Songs (2001)

Reflections of Rosemary (2005)

Gospel Music Association Dove Awards

1980   Album by a Secular Artist:
        With My Song by Debby Boone
        (Producer: Brown Bannister;
        Label: Lamb and Lion)

1983   Album by a Secular Artist:
        Surrender by Debby Boone
        (Producer: Brown Bannister;
        Label: Lamb and Lion)

Grammy Awards

1977   20th Grammy Awards: Best
        New Artist.

1980   23rd Grammy Awards: Best
        Inspirational Performance:
        Debby Boone: *With My Song
        I Will Praise Him*

1984   27th Grammy Awards: Best
        Gospel Performance by a Duo
        or Group: Debby Boone and
        Phil Driscoll "Keep the Flame
        Burning"

Discography: The Boones

Glass Castle (1976)

The Boone Girls (1977)

First Class (1978)

Heavenly Love (1979)

Highlights (1980)

BOONE, PAT

Pat Boone (b. Charles Eugene Patrick
Boone, June 1, 1934) may be the most
underappreciated artist in the history of
popular and Christian music. He has
not been acknowledged for his role in

Pat Boone arrives at the MusiCares Person of
the Year tribute honoring Neil Diamond on
February 6, 2009, in Los Angeles. (AP Photo/
Chris Pizzello)

helping to break down the barriers
between R&B and pop music during
the 1950s; instead, he has become the
whipping boy for writers of the history
of rock 'n' roll for covering Little
Richard's records. Boone came along
at a time when black artists did not
receive airplay on mainstream radio; he
covered a number of early R&B hits
("Two Hearts" by the Charms, "Ain't
That a Shame" by Fats Domino, "I'll
Be Home" by the Flamingos, "I
Almost Lost My Mind" by Ivory Joe
Hunter, "Chains of Love" by Joe
Turner, "Gee Whittaker" by the Five
Keys, and "Tutti Frutti" and "Long
Tall Sally" by Little Richard).

These songs received pop airplay
because Boone recorded them; at that
time a black artist could never receive
the airplay that Boone received. In
doing this during the early to mid-
1950s, Boone helped break down barriers in pop radio, which led to black
artists receiving airplay. These cover
records came along at a time when
America was segregated and there were
barriers erected against blacks in
numerous endeavors. That might not
have been the way it should have been

but it was the way it was. Instead of being acknowledged for helping break down those barriers—like Elvis was when he recorded "That's All Right Mama" or when Bill Haley recorded "Shake, Rattle and Roll"—Boone has been castigated by rock writers who have generally felt his contributions to rock music were not worthy of their respect.

Part of the problem may have been Pat Boone's faith. Boone did not embrace or represent the teenage rebellion and bad boy image of the early rock stars; instead he was a "goody two-shoes" who made no secret of his Christian faith. Still, if you examine Pat Boone during the era of his early success you will find that he was a teen idol covering early R&B hits before Elvis recorded his first cover of an R&B hit. Boone's first chart record, "Two Hearts," entered the charts in April 1955, eight months after Bill Haley and the Comets hit with "Shake, Rattle and Roll," a cover of Joe Turner's R&B hit. White artists covering R&B hits were a product of the time. Further, cover records were nothing new; in 1955 the hit "Ballad of Davy Crockett" was covered by four different artists. Black artists covered white hits as well; Fat's Domino's hit "Blueberry Hill" in 1956 was a cover of the 1940 hit by Glenn Miller and Gene Autry; the Platters hit "Smoke Gets in Your Eyes" was a cover of a record from Paul Whiteman's Orchestra in 1934. There are other examples as well but the point is this: artists during the 1940s and 1950s regularly covered recordings by other artists in an attempt to get a hit record. This had been a continuing practice in the music industry long before white artists covered the R&B hits of early African American artists during the mid-1950s.

By the end of the 20th century, people had forgotten how popular Pat Boone was during the rock 'n' roll era; during the late 1950s he outsold every artist except Elvis. Although it is not advertised today, the fact remains that Pat Boone remained the most popular and "favorite" artist of a number of teenagers during the early rock era because he was a clean-cut young man, a shining example of what a young man should be. He was admired and emulated; although the history of rock 'n' roll as written by the majority of rock writers reinforces the notion that Elvis totally dominated that era, there were a number of young people who disliked Elvis and were turned off by his recordings. Those young people loved Pat Boone and bought his records.

During the period 1955–1962, Pat Boone had 56 records on the *Billboard* Pop charts; 17 were top ten and six reached number one. One of his songs, "A Wonderful Time Up There," aka "Gospel Boogie," was a gospel song originally recorded by the Statesmen (it reached number four in 1958).

Pat Boone achieved his greatest success with ballads; "Love Letters in the Sand" was number one for seven weeks and "April Love" was number one for six weeks, both in 1957.

Pat Boone may have been the very first contemporary Christian artist, although that term was not used to describe the music until 1978. However, Boone made no secret of his Christian faith; he was a family man who would not kiss a woman who was not his wife in a movie (he turned down a film role with Marilyn Monroe because a kiss was called for), at the height of his career he finished his college degree, and his image was always one of a clean-cut, nonrebellious young man.

Pat Boone grew up in Nashville and began singing when he was ten; he appeared on "The Ted Mack Amateur Hour" and "Arthur Godfrey's Talent Scouts," and married his high school sweetheart, Shirley Foley, in 1953. His first recordings were on the Nashville-based Republic label but none of them charted. Pat and Shirley moved to Denton, Texas, where he attended North Texas State University and signed with Nashville-based Dot Records. His first single, "Two Hearts," a cover of the R&B hit from the Charms, charted and his second single, a cover of Fats Domino's "Ain't That a Shame" became number one on the pop chart. This led to a career of consistent hits on the pop charts, TV and movie appearances, including hosting his own TV show, "The Pat Boone Chevy Showroom" 1957–1960, and then as an author who wrote several books and a businessman who owned record labels.

Although Pat Boone began as a pop artist during the rock era and as a teen idol was considered part of the rock 'n' roll movement during the 1950s, by the 1970s he was a gospel/Christian artist.

Although Boone was considered "wholesome," he also had his share of controversy with the church audience. In 1956, a number of churches organized boycotts of his records because they felt that by recording R&B cover songs he was a tool of the NAACP to destroy the morals of white youths. During the late 1960s he began speaking in tongues and was expelled from the Church of Christ (the denomination

he was raised in) and churches often boycotted his personal appearances.

Pat Boone should be considered one of the pioneers of the contemporary Christian music movement because he recorded an album, *Pat Boone Sings the New Songs of the Jesus People*, in 1972 when CCM was known as Jesus music. On that album, he recorded the Larry Norman classic, "I Wish We'd All Been Ready," Children of the Day's "For Those Tears I Died," as well as a song by Love Song. His 1975 album, *Something Supernatural*, featured the title song written by Chuck Girard as well as "You Were on His Mind" by Myron LeFevre, "Fool's Wisdom" by Malcolm and Alwyn, Annie Herring's "You'll Start Falling in Love," Randy Matthew's "Didn't He," and "Lord" by Michael Omartian.

These should have brought the early Jesus songs to a wide public acceptance—and should be acknowledged by those in contemporary Christian music—but Pat Boone's image had been tarnished to the point where he just could not be considered "cool" by young people at that point.

Despite his long history with contemporary Christian music (he started the label Lamb and Lion that signed DeGarmo and Key and others and gave Larry Norman and Randy Stonehill $3,000 to begin their One Way label) he is most often viewed as a relic of the past, someone that young people can't relate to and someone so hopelessly "un-hip" that a young CCM crowd could never relate to or acknowledge as part of their youth-oriented music.

Still, regardless of his image and what rock critics say, the proof is there for all to see: Pat Boone was into Jesus when Jesus wasn't cool and he was aware of and involved in the contemporary Christian movement before it became a well-known genre. That view was perpetuated when he recorded an album of heavy metal songs, *Metal Mood*, that included covers of songs by Guns 'N Roses, AC/DC, Deep Purple, Ozzy Osbourne, Led Zeppelin, Alice Cooper, and Jimi Hendrix.

Although he seemed a solid part of the older, conservative generation of Christians, he lost his TV show on the Trinity Broadcast Network when he released his heavy metal album. For someone who is not considered "controversial," Pat Boone has certainly stirred up more than his share of controversy within the Christian world.

Don Cusic

For Further Reading

Boone, Pat. *A New Song*. Lake Mary, Fla: Charisma House, 1988.

Boone, Pat. *Pat Boone's America*. Nashville, Tenn.: BandH Publishing Group, 2006.

Davis, Paul. *Pat Boone: The Authorized Biography: April Love: The Early Days of Rock 'n' Roll*. Grand Rapids, Mich.: Zondervan, 2001.

Powell, Mark Allen. *Encyclopedia of Contemporary Christian Music*. Peabody, Mass.: Hendrickson Publishers, Inc., 2002.

Discography

Pat Boone (1956)

Howdy! (1956)

Pat (1957)

Pat Boone Sings Irving Berlin (1957)

Hymns We Love (1957)

Star Dust (1958)

Yes Indeed! (1958)

White Christmas (1959)

He Leadeth Me (1959)

Pat Boone Sings (1959)

Great Millions (1959)

Tenderly (1959)

Hymns We Have Loved (1960)

Moonglow (1960)

This and That (1960)

Moody River (1961)

Great! Great! Great! (1961)

My God and I (1961)

I'll See You in My Dreams (1962)

Pat Boone Reads from the Holy Bible (1962)

Pat Boone Sings Guess Who? (1963)

I Love You Truly (1963)

The Star Spangled Banner (1963)

Days of Wine and Roses (1963)

Tie Me Kangaroo Down (1963)

Sing Along Without (1963)

Touch of Your Lips (1963)

Pat Boone (1964)

Ain't That a Shame (1964)

Lord's Prayer and Other Great Hymns (1964)

Boss Beat (Dot, 1964)

True Love: My Tenth Anniversary with Dot Records (1964)

Near You (1965)

Blest Be Thy Name (1965)

Golden Era of Country Hits (1965)

Pat Boone 1965 (1965)

Great Hits of '65 (1966)

Memories (1966)

Pat Boone Sings Winners of the Readers Digest Poll (1966)

Wish You Were Here, Buddy (1966)

Christmas Is a Comin' (1966)

How Great Thou Art (1967)

I Was Kaiser Bill's Batman (1967)

Look Ahead (1968)

Departure (1969)

The Pat Boone Family in the Holy Land (1972)

The New Songs of the Jesus People (1972)

I Love You More and More Each Day (1973)

Born Again (1973)

S.A.V.E.D. (1973)

The Family Who Prays (1973)

All in the Boone Family (1973)

The Pat Boone Family (1974)

Songs from the Inner Court (1974)

Something Supernatural (1975)

Texas Woman (1976)

Country Love (1977)

The Country Side of Pat Boone (1977)

Just the Way I Am (1981)

Songmaker (1981)

Whispering Hope (1982)

Pat Boone Sings Golden Hymns (1984)

Jivin' Pat (1986)

Let's Get Cooking, America (1987)

Tough Marriage (1987)

With the First Jesus Band (1988)

Pat Boone in a Metal Mood: No More Mr. Nice Guy (1997)

Pat Boone: The Fifties Complete 12-CD Box Set (1998)

Books

Boone, Pat. *A New Song*

Boone, Pat. *Together: 25 Years with the Boone Family*

Filmography

Bernadine (1957)

April Love (1957)

Mardi Gras (1958)

Journey to the Center of the Earth (1959)

All Hands on Deck (1961)

State Fair (1962)

The Main Attraction (1962)

The Yellow Canary (1963)

The Horror of It All (1963)

Goodbye Charlie (1964)

Never Put It in Writing (1964)

The Greatest Story Ever Told (1965)

The Perils of Pauline (1967)

The Cross and the Switchblade (1972)

Roger and Me (1989)

In a Metal Mood (1996)

The Eyes of Tammy Faye (2000)

BOYCE, KIM

Beauty queen Kim Boyce's (b. c. 1961 in Winter Haven, Florida) first albums in the 1980s reflected the trend in dance music in the pop world; however, by the end of the 1990s she was more comfortable with the sounds of adult contemporary Christian music.

Kim Boyce grew up singing with her younger sister and mother; she received a degree in broadcasting at the University of South Florida. During her college years she was voted Miss Florida and placed in the top ten at the 1984 Miss America Pageant; the following year she moved to Nashville for a career in contemporary Christian music. In Nashville, she found work singing backup for Christian artists Carman and the Joe English Band. Embarking on her own career, she developed a high energy show filled with choreography.

During a tour with Russ Taff she met Taff's backup singer, Gary Koreiba; the two were married in 1990 and currently live in Branson, Missouri, with their two children. Koreiba performs with the Branson vocal group Pierce Arrow, which allows them to stay home as a family rather than constantly touring.

Boyce is the author of several books, including *Beauty to Last a Lifetime, Touched by Kindness, Dreams I'm Dreamin': Devotions for Mothers of Young Children* as well as a series of devotional books.

Boyce is a national spokesperson for Bee Alive nutritional products and has worked with Compassion International.

Don Cusic

For Further Reading

Alfonso, Barry. *The Billboard Guide to Contemporary Christian Music*. New York: Billboard Books/Watson-Guptill, 2002.

Powell, Mark Allen. *Encyclopedia of Contemporary Christian Music*. Peabody, Mass.: Hendrickson Publishers, Inc., 2002.

BRIDE

Bride is a Christian heavy metal band formed by brothers Dale and Troy Thompson in Louisville, Kentucky, in 1986. They were originally a southern gospel group, the Hillville Lads, but added drummer Stephen Rolland and bassist Scott Hall and changed their name to Matrix as they toured Christian rock venues.

In 1987, they signed with Refuge Records, changed their name to Bride, and released their debut album, *Show No Mercy*. Later they moved to Star Song Records and bassist Rick Foley replaced Hall and drummer Jerry McBroom replaced Roland. In 2001, they added a new drummer and bassist, Mike Loy and Lawrence Bishop, respectively, and released *Fist Full of Bees* on a new label, Absolute.

For three consecutive years, Bride won the Dove Award for "Hard Music Songs." For 1992 the song was "Everybody Knows My Name," for 1993 it was "Rattlesnake," and for 1994 it was "Psychedelic Super Jesus." Bride won the 1995 Dove for "Hard Music Album" for their album *Scarecrow Messiah* on Star Song produced by John and Dino Elefante.

Don Cusic

For Further Reading

Alfonso, Barry. *The Billboard Guide to Contemporary Christian Music*. New York: Billboard Books/Watson-Guptill, 2002.

Powell, Mark Allen. *Encyclopedia of Contemporary Christian Music*. Peabody, Mass.: Hendrickson Publishers, Inc., 2002.

Thompson, John J. *Raised by Wolves: The Story of Christian Rock and Roll*. Toronto, Ontario: ECW Press, 2000.

BROWN, SCOTT WESLEY

Singer/songwriter Scott Wesley Brown's career goes back to the days of the Jesus movement, when the Washington, D.C., native began as a folk singer. Known for his social conscience and concern for social justice, Brown founded I Care Ministries and took a number of trips to the former Soviet Union during the Cold War days. An advocate for the poor and hungry, Brown moved to Nashville in 1981 and developed his career.

Brown's classic song is "I'm Not Religious (I Just Love the Lord)"; however, he has written a number of chart topping hits for himself as well as songs for Sandi Patty, Amy Grant, Bruce Carroll, Pat Boone, the Imperials, Petra, and even opera star Placido Domingo, who recorded his song "My Treasure."

As Brown's career progressed, he moved away from the simple, folk-based sound to one where he used a band and even an orchestra on some of his recordings.

Brown has been involved with a number of organizations; he has been with Promise Keepers, Campus Crusade for Christ, and Youth With a Mission as a featured performer at their conferences and involved with the U.S. Center for World Missions, the Lausanne Committee on World Evangelization, and Advancing Churches in Missions Commitment (ACMC).

Brown was ordained by the Southern Baptist Convention and lives in San Diego, where he is worship and missions pastor at North Coast Presbyterian Church; he also serves as worship pastor at Scottsdale Bible Church in Phoenix.

Don Cusic

For Further Reading

Brown, Scott Wesley. *Keeping the Gospel in Gospel Music*. Nashville, Tenn.: American Christian Writers, 1998.

Cusic, Don. *The Sound of Light: A History of Gospel and Christian Music*. New York: Hal Leonard, 2002.

Powell, Mark Allen. *Encyclopedia of Contemporary Christian Music*. Peabody, Mass.: Hendrickson Publishers, Inc., 2002.

BURNETT, T BONE

T Bone Burnett (b. Joseph Henry Burnett, January 14, 1948, in St. Louis, Missouri) is best known as the producer of the soundtrack to *O Brother Where Art Thou* and other projects. However, Burnett also established himself as a contemporary Christian artist in the early 1980s with a series of albums beginning with *Truth Decay* (Takoma, 1980) and including *Behind the Trap Door* (EP) (Warner Brothers, 1982) and *Proof Through the Night* (Warner Brothers, 1983). During the early 1980s, Burnett wrote a series of editorials for *Contemporary Christian Music* magazine.

Burnett had a spiritual awakening when he was 11 and has said his ministry "is to make doubters out of unbelievers." Even though Burnett was in the contemporary Christian music industry—albeit on the fringes—he was never of that culture because he was always more comfortable living his Christianity in the world at large.

Burnett produced projects for Bruce Cockburn, Elvis Costello, Roy Orbison, Los Lobos, the Wallflowers, Counting Crows, the BoDeans, Jackson Browne, the Call, Marshall Crenshaw, Leo Kottke, Tonio K., Delbert McClinton, Maria Muldaur, Nitty Gritty Dirt Band, and Gillian Welch. He produced Christian artist Leslie Phillips and later married her; she now records as Sam Phillips.

T Bone Burnett won the Grammy Award for "Producer of the Year" for 2001.

Don Cusic

For Further Reading

Alfonso, Barry. *The Billboard Guide to Contemporary Christian Music.* New York: Billboard Books/Watson-Guptill, 2002.

McNeil, W. K., ed. *Encyclopedia of American Gospel Music.* New York: Routledge, 2005.

Powell, Mark Allen. *Encyclopedia of Contemporary Christian Music.* Peabody, Mass.: Hendrickson Publishers, Inc., 2002.

C

CAEDMON'S CALL

Danielle Glenn Young, vocals
Cliff Young, vocals, guitar
Derek Webb, vocals, guitar
Aric Nitzberg, bass (till 2000)
Randy Holsapple, keyboard (1999–2000)
Todd Bragg, drums
Garett Buell, percussion

Caedmon's Call was a well-known unsigned band, selling their custom albums to college audiences before they signed with Warner Alliance and then Essential. The group began at Texas Christian University in Fort Worth when students Cliff Young and Aaron Tate began writing songs. In 1992, the two moved to Houston where singer Danielle Glenn, singer/guitarist Derek Webb, and drummer Todd Bragg joined. Tate was not an official member of the group but continued to write songs with singer/guitarist Young. The line-up for Caedmon's Call was completed when bassist Aric Nitzberg, keyboardist Randy Holsapple, and percussionist Garett Buell joined. Later, Josh Moore replaced Holsapple on keyboards. They chose their name from the 7th-century monk, Caedmon, who wrote religious poetry.

Caedmon's Call became a favorite band on the college circuit and in 1996 *Musician* magazine voted the group one of America's best unsigned bands. They sold 25,000 copies of their custom albums before recording their first album for Warner Alliance through the help of Wayne Watson. Their debut label album consisted of cuts from their indie releases as well as some new songs. In an attempt to reach the general audience, the group initially resisted being labeled a contemporary Christian group but eventually accepted that mantle as their albums sold well to the Christian audience.

The group signed with Essential after Warner Alliance folded and in 1997 formed Caedmon's Guild, an annual weekend retreat, and sponsored a songwriting contest. Later, Cliff Young formed Watershed Records and that label released albums by Bebo Norman and Andrew Peterson.

Caedmon's Call is involved in Compassion International and two ministries in India: The Dalit Freedom Network (involved with the lowest caste) and

Peace Gospel Ministries. Caedmon's Call's foundation is Share the Well Foundation.

Don Cusic

Discography

My Calm/Your Storm (1994)

Just Don't Want Coffee (1995)

Caedmon's Call (1997)

Intimate Portrait (1997)

The Guild Collection, Vol. 1 (1997)

The Guild Collection, Vol. 2 (1998)

40 Acres (1999)

Back Home (1999)

Long Line of Leavers (2000)

In the Company of Angels: A Call to Worship (2002)

The Guild Collection (2001)

Chronicles (2004)

Share the Well (2004)

Great and Mighty (2006)

Overdressed (2007)

For Further Reading

Alfonso, Barry. *The Billboard Guide to Contemporary Christian Music.* New York: Billboard Books/Watson-Guptill, 2002.

Powell, Mark Allen. *Encyclopedia of Contemporary Christian Music.* Peabody, Mass.: Hendrickson Publishers, Inc., 2002.

CAESAR, SHIRLEY

Known as the "First Lady of Gospel Music," Shirley Caesar (b. October 13, 1938, in Durham, North Carolina) comes from a family of 13 children whose father, James Caesar, was a member of the Just Come Four Quartet. Shirley began singing with the Caesar Singers, made up of her and her siblings, when she was eight. At 12, she sang with the Mt. Calvary Holy Church Choir and the Charity Singers and toured with soloist Leroy Johnson. At 13, she was a member of Thelma Bumpass and the Royalettes, then attended North Carolina College for a year before she joined Albertina Walker's Caravans where she sang for eight years (1958–1966). During her time with that group she became a lead vocalist and featured soloist before striking out on her own as a singing evangelist.

Caesar has never been identified as a contemporary Christian singer; instead she gained her fame in traditional black gospel. However, she reached a large interracial audience as she became a premier gospel singer and was the first black gospel singer to win a Grammy. Active as a civic and community leader in Durham, North Carolina, in addition to being a singer and pastor, Caesar re-enrolled in college during the 1970s and in 1984 received a degree in business administration from Shaw University.

Caesar appeared in the film *Why Do Fools Fall in Love?* with Halle Berry and was on the soundtrack to the Whitney Houston movie *The Preacher's Wife.* She continues to pastor a North Carolina church and published her autobiography in 1998.

Don Cusic

For Further Reading

Carpenter, Bil. *Uncloudy Days: The Gospel Music Encyclopedia.* San Francisco: Backbeat, 2005.

Gospel singer Shirley Caesar sings "Oh Happy Day" at the Gospel Music Hall of Fame induction program on October 30, 2000, in Franklin, Tennessee. (AP Photo/Mark Humphrey)

Cusic, Don. *The Sound of Light: A History of Gospel and Christian Music.* New York: Hal Leonard, 2002.

Darden, Bob. *People Get Ready!: A New History of Black Gospel Music.* New York: Continuum, 2005.

Jackson, Jerma A. *Singing in My Soul: Black Gospel Music in a Secular Age.* Chapel Hill: University of North Carolina Press, 2004.

McNeil, W. K., ed. *Encyclopedia of American Gospel Music.* New York: Routledge, 2005. Powell, Mark Allen. *Encyclopedia of Contemporary Christian Music.* Peabody, Mass.: Hendrickson Publishers, Inc., 2002.

Young, Alan. *Woke Me Up This Morning: Black Gospel Singers and the Gospel Life.* Jackson: University Press of Mississippi, 1997.

Zolten, Jerry. *Great God A'Mighty: The Dixie Hummingbirds: Celebrating the Rise of Soul Gospel Music.* New York: Oxford University Press, 2003.

CALL, THE

Michael Been, vocals, guitar, bass
Tom Ferrier, guitar
Scott Musick, drums
Greg Freeman, bass (until 1984)
Jim Good, keyboard (since 1984)

Group founder Michael Been played bass on 2nd Chapter of Acts "Easter Song" and then in 1979 formed Motion Pictures with drummer Scott Musick, bassist Gregg Freeman, and guitarist Tom Ferrier in Santa Cruz, California; they later changed their name to the

Call. The group has sought to be an American version of U2, tackling social and cultural themes from a group of Christians for the general market. They have recorded on secular labels (Mercury, Elektra, and MCA), and the Christian audience has generally been wary of the group's socially progressive messages. Their debut album featured Garth Hudson, former member of the Band, on several tracks. In the early 1990s the group disbanded, then regrouped by the end of the decade.

Been appeared in the movie *The Last Temptation of Christ* (he played John the Apostle), which caused controversy in the Christian market; the Call's recordings were banned on most Christian radio stations because the movie was considered blasphemous by many in the Christian community.

During the 2000 presidential campaign, the Call's song "Let the Day Begin" became Al Gore's theme song.

Don Cusic

For Further Reading

Powell, Mark Allen. *Encyclopedia of Contemporary Christian Music*. Peabody, Mass.: Hendrickson Publishers, Inc., 2002.

Thompson, John J. *Raised by Wolves: The Story of Christian Rock and Roll*. Toronto, Ontario: ECW Press, 2000.

CAMP, STEVE

Steve Camp (b. April 13, 1955, in Wheaton, Illinois) grew up in Wheaton and formed his first band in the sixth grade. At an early age he became involved in Christian music and sang with the Campus Life Singers in high school before enrolling at Roosevelt University in Chicago, where he studied music composition. Camp's role model was Keith Green and, like Green, he has often appeared abrasive while presenting a message that has been described as "self-righteous and judgmental." However, it is obvious that Camp is sincere in his beliefs and convictions and abhors compromise. In 1998 he founded ACCT (AIDs Crisis and Christianity Today) and that same year published 107 theses, "A Call for Reformation in the Contemporary Christian Music Industry." He hosted a radio talk show, "No Compromise with Steve Camp," from 1995 to 1997.

After some time spent in Nashville as part of the contemporary Christian community (he organized CAUSE—Christian Artists United to Save the Earth—a one time event in 1985), he moved to Sun Valley, California, where he pastors Grace Community Church.

Don Cusic

For Further Reading

Alfonso, Barry. *The Billboard Guide to Contemporary Christian Music*. New York: Billboard Books/Watson-Guptill, 2002.

Cusic, Don. *The Sound of Light: A History of Gospel and Christian Music*. New York: Hal Leonard, 2002.

McNeil, W. K., ed. *Encyclopedia of American Gospel Music*. New York: Routledge, 2005.

Powell, Mark Allen. *Encyclopedia of Contemporary Christian Music*. Peabody, Mass.: Hendrickson Publishers, Inc., 2002.

CANDLE AKA AGAPE FORCE

Agape Force was an evangelistic ministry founded in California; Candle was the Arts and Music division of Agape and Silverwind was the music ministry. Candle released children's albums of praise and worship; the most successful were *The Music Machine* and *Bullfrogs and Butterflies* featuring Barry McGuire, which sold several million records. The Chief Musician albums are praise and worship albums. The group left California and moved to Lindale, Texas.

Don Cusic

For Further Reading

Powell, Mark Allen. *Encyclopedia of Contemporary Christian Music*. Peabody, Mass.: Hendrickson Publishers, Inc., 2002.

CARD, MICHAEL

Michael Card (b. April 11, 1957, in Madison, Tennessee) is the son of a doctor and grandson of a Baptist minister who grew up in Nashville near Earl Scruggs's family. The legendary banjo player's sons, Randy, Gary, and Steve, were friends of Card, who attended Western Kentucky University and received his bachelor's and master's degrees in biblical studies. During his time at Western Kentucky, Card taught physics and astronomy as a grad student. While in college Card began writing songs, using his theological studies to dramatize scripture and accompany the sermons of Professor William Lane; his most commercially successful song is "El Shaddai," recorded by Amy Grant on her landmark *Age to Age* album.

Musically, Card's songs fall into the folk/pop category; his debut album was produced by Randy Scruggs. Because of his theological studies, Card's lyrics tend to have a theological depth beyond most contemporary Christian music.

Cards hosts a radio program, "In the Studio with Michael Card," and has written 16 books.

Don Cusic

For Further Reading

Alfonso, Barry. *The Billboard Guide to Contemporary Christian Music*. New York: Billboard Books/Watson-Guptill, 2002.

Cusic, Don. *The Sound of Light: A History of Gospel and Christian Music*. New York: Hal Leonard, 2002.

Powell, Mark Allen. *Encyclopedia of Contemporary Christian Music*. Peabody, Mass.: Hendrickson Publishers, Inc., 2002.

CARLISLE, BOB

Bob Carlisle (b. September 29, 1956, in Los Angeles, California) is best known for his song "Butterfly Kisses" (written with Randy Thomas), which became a number one song on the adult contemporary chart and a top ten pop hit in 1997. The song was written for Carlisle's daughter, Brookeon, for her 16th birthday. Originally titled "Shades of Grace," the song was featured on Oprah Winfrey's Father's Day special and went on to become one of the top-selling Christian songs of all time.

Carlisle grew up in Santa Ana, California, and began playing guitar at seven; at 16 he joined Good News (with Billy Batstone, David Diggs, and Erick Nelson) and then Psalm 150, both Christian groups, before he became the lead singer for the Allies. During this period he met his future songwriting partner, Randy Thomas. An excellent vocalist, Carlisle worked as a background singer in Los Angeles studios, singing on projects by Poison, Barry Manilow, Pat Benatar, Juice Newton, and REO Speedwagon.

In addition to "Butterfly Kisses," Carlisle and Thomas also wrote the Dolly Parton country hit "Why'd You Come in Here Lookin' Like That?" and "Father's Love" for the soundtrack of the film *Jack Frost*.

Don Cusic

For Further Reading

Alfonso, Barry. *The Billboard Guide to Contemporary Christian Music*. New York: Billboard Books/Watson-Guptill, 2002.

Powell, Mark Allen. *Encyclopedia of Contemporary Christian Music*. Peabody, Mass.: Hendrickson Publishers, Inc., 2002.

CARMAN

Carman—one of the few artists in any genre who is known by a single name—was one of the most versatile and commercially successful Christian artists in the 1980s and 1990s; he released nine albums that were gold and platinum and his concerts overflowed with fans.

Born Carmen Dominic Licciardello on January 19, 1956, in Trenton, New Jersey, the singer came from an Italian home and played drums and guitar in local bands in the New Jersey/Philadelphia area before moving to Las Vegas. His conversion experience came during an Andrae Crouch concert, and he then moved to Tulsa, Oklahoma, where he developed a ministry. In 1982 he released his debut album, *Some-O-Dat* with the hit single "Sunday's on the Way." His first gold album, *The Champion*, was released in 1986; after that *Live: Radically Saved, Revival in the Land, Addicted to Jesus, The Absolute Best, The Standard, R.I.O.T, I Surrender All: 30 Classic Hymns*, and *Heart of a Champion* have all been certified gold or platinum.

Musically, Carman has shown immense versatility, recording everything from rap to hymns to black gospel; he has also shown his versatility as a writer, penning novels and screenplays, and has been involved in acting and as a TV talk show host on the TBN network.

Don Cusic

For Further Reading

Alfonso, Barry. *The Billboard Guide to Contemporary Christian Music*. New York: Billboard Books/Watson-Guptill, 2002.

McNeil, W. K., ed. *Encyclopedia of American Gospel Music*. New York: Routledge, 2005.

Powell, Mark Allen. *Encyclopedia of Contemporary Christian Music*. Peabody, Mass.: Hendrickson Publishers, Inc., 2002.

CARMICHAEL, RALPH

Ralph Carmichael (b. May 27, 1927) was in his 40s when the Jesus movement hit and in his 50s when contemporary Christian music exploded, but he managed to become a leader in these youth-oriented movements through his songwriting ("He's Everything to Me") and by forming Light Records, which signed artists Andrae Crouch, the Winans, Walter and Tramaine Hawkins, Reba Rambo, Rez Band, and Bryan Duncan.

The son of a pastor, Carmichael grew up in North Dakota; in his teen years, he moved to California with his family. His father loved music and insisted on musical lessons for Ralph; at four he began violin lessons, then moved on to piano, trumpet, and vocal lessons. He committed his life to Christ in 1944 when he was 17, and after high school he entered Southern California Bible College (now Vanguard University), where he found outlets for his love of traditional church music as well as big band music—the most popular music of his formative years.

Carmichael was musical director at a Baptist church in Los Angeles, then began composing film scores for Billy Graham's film company, World Wide Pictures.

Carmichael's big break in pop music came when Capitol Records hired him to do the arrangements for a Nat King Cole album, *The Magic of Christmas*, released in 1960. This led to Carmichael working as an arranger on Cole's sessions until the singer's death in early 1965. Carmichael also wrote orchestral arrangements for Bing Crosby, Peggy Lee, Ella Fitzgerald, Al Martino, Julie London, and Stan Kenton. Carmichael's long-time collaboration with pianist Roger Williams produced the single "Born Free," a top ten hit in 1966.

Carmichael became musical director for the "I Love Lucy Show" during its final years, wrote "Reach Out to Jesus," which was recorded by Elvis Presley, and was the musical director for the touring Christian musical "Young Messiah."

In the late 1960s, Carmichael formed Light Records and Lexicon Publishing as a joint venture with Word Records. This label became one of the premier labels in contemporary Christian music through pioneering artists like Andrae Crouch and Walter Hawkins.

A former president of the Gospel Music Association, Carmichael was elected to the Gospel Music Hall of Fame in 1985.

Don Cusic

Discography

102 Strings (1958)

Man with a Load of Music (1968)

I Looked for Love (1969)

Electric Symphony (1970)

Sometimes I Just Feel It This Way (1970)

Tell It Like It Is: A Folk Musical about God (1970)

Cross and the Switchblade (1971)

Centurion (1971)

My Little World (1971)

Natural High (1971)

Have a Nice Day (1971)

The Savior Is Waiting (1975)

Rhapsody in Sacred Music (1976)

102 Strings Vol. 1 (1976)

Portrait (1977)

The Best of Ralph Carmichael (1981)

Big Band Christmas (1988)

Big Band Gospel Classics (1999)

For Further Reading

Alfonso, Barry. *The Billboard Guide to Contemporary Christian Music*. New York: Billboard Books/Watson-Guptill, 2002.

Carmichael, Ralph. *He's Everything to Me*. Waco, Tex.: Word Books, 1986.

Cusic, Don. *The Sound of Light: A History of Gospel and Christian Music*. New York: Hal Leonard, 2002.

McNeil, W. K., ed. *Encyclopedia of American Gospel Music*. New York: Routledge, 2005.

Powell, Mark Allen. *Encyclopedia of Contemporary Christian Music*. Peabody, Mass.: Hendrickson Publishers, Inc., 2002.

CASH, JOHNNY

Johnny Cash is an American icon: he is considered one of the greatest country music artists of all time. His connection with contemporary Christian music is tenuous, although he loved gospel music and recorded a number of gospel albums. Cash was the headline act at Explo '72, which was one of the most significant events in the history of contemporary Christian music. Cash's love of gospel music and his commitment to the Christian life played a role in Americans' appreciation of gospel music, and his movie, *The Gospel Road*, brought the gospel message to millions, but the contemporary Christian culture identified more with rock than country.

Johnny Cash (b. February 26, 1932, in Kingsland, Arkansas) was the grandson of a Baptist preacher. Cash's older brother, Jack, was killed in a sawmill accident when John was 12 and his death haunted Cash his entire life. The Cash family was deeply religious, and Cash grew up in a Pentecostal church in Dyess, Arkansas, where he accepted Jesus at the age of 12 as the congregation sang "Just As I Am."

Cash struggled with his faith his entire life; although he was a Bible-believing Christian, the temptations of the flesh and drugs pulled him away from his childhood faith. He signed with Sun Records and his recording of "I Walk the Line" was both a pop and country hit in 1956. Cash then signed with Columbia Records because they allowed him to record gospel material.

During the 1960s, Cash suffered from alcohol and drug abuse but in 1967 cleaned up his act; in early 1968 he recorded a breakthrough album, *Live at Folsom Prison* and the success of this album led to him obtaining a television show in Fall 1969.

In 1971 Cash recommitted his life to Jesus after answering an altar call at Evangel Temple in Nashville. In 1973 his movie *The Gospel Road* was released, and he appeared regularly on Billy Graham's Crusades.

Cash was more at home in the country music world than the world of contemporary Christian music; still his albums *The Gospel Road* (1973), *A Believer Sings the Truth* (Cachet, 1979), *I Believe* (1984), *Believe in Him* (1985), and *Goin' by the Book* (1990) demonstrated the strong commitment Johnny Cash had to Christianity and gospel music.

Don Cusic

Musician Johnny Cash in 1977. (AP Photo/File)

For Further Reading

Cash, Johnny, with Patrick Carr. *Cash: The Autobiography*. San Francisco: HarperSanFrancisco, 1997.

Cash, Johnny. *Man in Black*. Grand Rapids, Mich.: Zondervan, 1975.

Cash, June Carter. *Among My Klediments*. Grand Rapids, Mich.: Zondervan, 1979.

Conn, Charles Paul. *The New Johnny Cash*. Old Tappan, N.J.: Spire, 1976.

Cusic, Don. *Johnny Cash: The Songs*. New York: Thunder's Mouth, 2006.

McNeil, W. K., ed. *Encyclopedia of American Gospel Music*. New York: Routledge, 2005.

Powell, Mark Allen. *Encyclopedia of Contemporary Christian Music*. Peabody, Mass.: Hendrickson Publishers, Inc., 2002.

CASTING CROWNS

Mark Hall, vocals
Hector Cervantes, guitar
Juan DeVevo, guitar
Melodee DeVevo, violin
Megan Garrett, keyboard, vocals
Chris Huffman, bass
Andy Williams, drums

Casting Crowns has been one of the most successful and influential praise and worship bands in contemporary

Christian music. Mark Hall (b. September 14, 1970, in McDonough, Georgia), a youth pastor at First Baptist Church in Daytona Beach, began the group in 1999 as a way to reach the church youth he worked with; also in the group were Juan DeVevo, Melodee DeVevo, Hector Cervantes and Darren Hughes. In 2001 Hall and the group moved to Eagle's Landing First Baptist Church in McDonough, Georgia, where Chris Huffman, Megan Garrett, and Andy Williams were added to the group. They recorded two albums on their own and distributed them in the Atlanta area. The CDs came to the attention of Steven Curtis Chapman and Mark Miller, lead singer for the country group Sawyer Brown, who coproduced their first commercial label release. Casting Crowns was an immediate hit; their singles and album topped the

Christian charts with a music aimed directly at the Christian audience in an attempt to "disciple the body."

Mark Hall is the major songwriter and lead singer for the group and remains youth pastor at the Eagle's Landing First Baptist Church; the other members of the group also serve at the church. Although the group tours, they are at their home church most of the time, working with youth and leading worship.

Casting Crowns won the Dove for "Group of the Year" in 2005, 2006, and 2008. Their song "Voice of Truth" won the Dove for "Inspirational Recorded Song of the Year" and their song "Who Am I" won the Dove for "Pop/Contemporary Recorded Song of the Year" for 2005. The 2006 Dove for "Pop/Contemporary Album of the Year" was awarded to their album *Lifesong*.

Mark Hall, right, and the rest of the members of Casting Crowns accept the Dove Award for group of the year on April 25, 2007, in Nashville. (AP Photo/Mark Humphrey)

Their song "Praise You in this Storm" won the 2007 Dove for "Pop/Contemporary Recorded Song of the Year." At the 2008 Dove Awards, they received top honors for their song "East to West," which captured Doves for both "Song of the Year" and "Pop/Contemporary Recorded Song of the Year." That song came from their album *The Altar and the Door*, which won the Dove for "Pop/Contemporary Album of the Year."

Casting Crowns won the Grammy for their 2005 album *Lifesong* in the "Best Pop/Contemporary Gospel Album" category.

Don Cusic

For Further Reading

Hall, Mark. *Lifestories*. Nashville, Tenn.: Brentwood Music, 2006.

CATHOLICS AND CONTEMPORARY CHRISTIAN MUSIC

The Catholics were the first denomination to have contemporary music in their services, but that music was rooted in the urban folk revival of the 1960s and was tied to the liturgy. Although the Catholics were the first to have music that was contemporary and Christian, musically they did not progress to the pop and rock sounds of the later 1960s onward. However, the major changes brought about by Vatican II in the 1960s were felt by American Catholicism and musically led the way toward introducing contemporary music into their religion through the folk masses of the mid-1960s. This introduction of folk music into the church service preceded the introduction of contemporary music into Protestant churches. With this move—and their overtures to Protestants to unite under the banner of Christianity—the American Catholic church for the first time affected a major Christian revival: the Jesus revolution of the late 1960s and early 1970s. Too, John Kennedy became the first Catholic president in 1960, challenging many of the traditional fears and superstitions held by American Protestants about Catholics.

Vatican II was convened in 1962 by Pope John XXIII and completed under his successor, Pope Paul VI, in 1965. The most significant results of this church council, held in three different sessions, were that the Latin Mass was discarded and replaced by the vernacular or local language and that the laity was encouraged to participate more fully in the Mass and take initiative in both religious and temporal affairs. These sessions also sought to end the isolationism of Catholicism by embracing all of Christianity and, indeed, all the peoples of the Earth as God's creatures.

Musically, Vatican II meant the introduction of a whole new set of songs in the Mass and the encouragement of individuals writing songs for the services. The folk mass led to a musical movement in the Catholic Church that embraced the popular music of the day, using it for church, and in turn paved the way for the Jesus movement in the late 1960s, which also took popular music and used it to celebrate faith, making it relevant to contemporary youth. The first folk mass, *Mass for Young Americans*, was produced by Ray Repp in 1964.

Ray Repp is the John the Baptist of contemporary Christian music, and his primary work is tied to a publishing company, Friends of the English Liturgy (FEL), founded in 1963 by David Fitzpatrick as a response to Vatican II. Their first release was the album *Glory Bound* by Paul Quinlan in 1964; in 1965 they released Repp's *Mass for Young Americans*.

Repp was a seminarian at the time, studying for the priesthood, when he wrote this liturgical service. Influenced heavily by the folk sounds of groups like Peter, Paul, and Mary, the New Christy Minstrels and the Kingston Trio and songs such as "Kum Ba Ya" and "He's Got the Whole World in His Hands," Repp's songs included "Clap Your Hands," "Here We Are," "Allelu," "Hear, O Lord," "Shout from the Highest Mountain," and "Come Away."

FEL published *Hymnal for Young Christians*, which was the first youth-oriented songbook for mainline churches and Repp's best known song "I Am the Resurrection" from his album *Come Alive* was included. These early albums were marketed to youth pastors and camp counselors who needed songs for youth to sing in their church groups. The focus was on group singing and the albums were, essentially, teaching tools.

The result of this movement within the Catholic organization was a charismatic renewal in which many individual Catholics felt they could develop a direct personal relationship with Christ and the Mass became more people-oriented. This, in turn, resulted in a demand for liturgical music as almost overnight every Catholic church in America had to have songbooks, songs, and books of readings to accompany the new Mass. This led to the formation of Catholic groups and songwriters who wrote this material for the Mass. Perhaps the most influential group was the St. Louis Jesuits.

The St. Louis Jesuits were all Jesuit priests who first united at St. Louis University, where they met while pursuing their studies. Individually, they were known as Bob Dufford, Dan Schutte, John Foley, Roc O'Connor. and Tim Manion, and they began composing and developing their music in the early 1970s.

The first among the group to begin composing music for liturgical use was John Foley. Foley and John Davanaugh met at the Jesuit novitiate in Florissent, Missouri, in the 1960s and inspired each other with their folk-guitar compositions for the liturgy. Both arrived in St. Louis in the mid-1960s to study philosophy, and during this time they wrote numerous compositions. Foley's music and reputation soon spread, and by the time he left St. Louis for a teaching position in Denver in 1967 his music had already become popular within Jesuit circles.

Bob Dufford was familiar with Foley and his music because he too had studied in St. Louis and been involved with the choir there. When Dufford left for Omaha, Nebraska, to teach high school, he too began to compose songs.

Dufford met Dan Schutte when he visited the Jesuit Novitiate in St. Bonifacius, Minnesota, in the spring of 1968. Schutte had written several songs for the congregation there on guitar and John Foley's songs had begun to filter into the novitiate. Roc O'Connor was in the same novitiate in Minnesota with Schutte and offered his skills as an accomplished guitarist to the choral groups that Schutte and others organized for their community liturgies.

Dufford and Schutte arrived in St. Louis in 1970 and began working with Roc O'Connor and John Foley on providing music for the group who worshipped on Sundays at Fusz Memorial, the Jesuit house of studies. Word of their music soon spread and they were besieged with requests to perform. Meanwhile, Tim Manion arrived in St. Louis in 1971 from the novitiate in Florissant, Missouri. Tim had been a part of the liturgy music in Missouri and was familiar with the music of Dufford, Schutte, and Foley.

Over the next two years, this group began to investigate ways to publish their music. Discouraged and disheartened after their contact with religious music publishers, they decided to produce and publish a collection of 57 songs on their own and record a set of albums, which aided the performance of their songs. In the midst of this project, the young priests were approached by a relative newcomer in the field of Catholic publishing, North American Liturgy Resources (NALR), who made them an offer to record and publish their music. Impressed that NALR could do far more than the Jesuits could on their own, and flattered by NALR's interest and desire to work with them, the group agreed to the offer. Their first project, *Neither Silver Nor Gold*, was issued in June 1974.

In 1975 the Jesuits (except for Tim Manion) all left St. Louis to be scattered in Omaha, Berkeley, Calif., and Toronto. They continued to collaborate, though, and spent a summer together in Berkeley composing new music for their second collection. The result was *Earthen Vessels*, released in December 1975, which sold more than half a million units.

The success of the St. Louis Jesuits parallels the success of Catholic music. The fact that it has grown since the mid-1960s is well documented; however, for those not in Catholic circles, this growth, music, and influence has gone largely unknown. In fact, most of those involved in the contemporary Christian music world are not even aware of Catholic music, although an occasional act appears on the charts. Perhaps the best-known act producing music for Catholics is John Michael Talbot, a contemporary Christian musician who became a third order Franciscan monk and whose albums reached both the Catholic and contemporary Christian markets, giving the Christian mainstream a taste of liturgy music.

There are almost 19,000 Catholic parishes in the United States administered by nearly 200 dioceses. All of these parishes, or churches, need hymn books, song sheets, and chorus scores since the Mass was changed into English. This fact, along with the spiritual renewal in the Catholic charismatic movement—paralleling the charismatic and evangelical Christian movement in America since the Jesus revolution of the late 1960s—has been responsible for the tremendous growth of the Catholic music market.

Don Cusic

For Further Reading

Cusic, Don. *The Sound of Light: A History of Gospel and Christian Music.* New York: Hal Leonard, 2002.

CHAPMAN, GARY

Gary Chapman (b. August 19, 1957, in Waurika, Oklahoma) is known as a songwriter, TV talk show host, and former husband of Amy Grant. He penned "My Father's Eyes," the title track to Amy Grant's second album. He co-wrote "Tennessee Christmas" with Amy Grant; she and the group Alabama had hits with this song. He also wrote "Finally" for T. G. Sheppard, a number one hit for him, as well as songs recorded by Vanessa Williams, Alabama, Lee Greenwood, Kenny Rogers, Steve Wariner, Barbara Mandrell, Kathy Troccoli, and Russ Taff.

Chapman was raised in DeLeon, Texas, where his father was a minister. He attended Southwestern Assemblies of God College in Waxahachie, Texas, but dropped out to join the Downings, a southern gospel group, as a guitar player. After the Downings, Chapman joined the band of Buck and Dottie Rambo; while playing guitar for the Rambos, Gary was influenced by Dottie's songwriting, which inspired him to try his hand at writing songs.

In 1980, Chapman was the opening act for Amy Grant on a tour. The two began dating and because of a rule imposed by Grant's manager, he had to leave the concert package. However, the two later married (1982), toured together, and had three children; later they divorced and each remarried.

Chapman received the Dove Award for "Songwriter of the Year" for 1981 and was voted "Male Vocalist of the Year" for 1996; his 1998 album *Hymns from the Ryman* received the 1998 Dove for "Country Album."

In 1996 Chapman hosted "Prime Time Country" on the Nashville Network (TNN), replacing Tom Wopat. The show ended in 1999. Chapman was a founder of "Sam's Place," a Sunday evening gospel show at the Ryman Auditorium. He also served as host of "CCM Countdown with Gary Chapman," which was broadcast on 200 radio stations.

In 2005 Chapman began his involvement in TV production with several CMT shows, including specials on "The Music Mafia," and a concert featuring Big and Rich, Gretchen Wilson, Hank Williams Jr., and Kid Rock.

Don Cusic

For Further Reading

Alfonso, Barry. *The Billboard Guide to Contemporary Christian Music*. New York: Billboard Books/Watson-Guptill, 2002.

Cusic, Don. *The Sound of Light: A History of Gospel and Christian Music*. New York: Hal Leonard, 2002.

McNeil, W. K., ed. *Encyclopedia of American Gospel Music*. New York: Routledge, 2005.

Powell, Mark Allen. *Encyclopedia of Contemporary Christian Music*. Peabody, Mass.: Hendrickson Publishers, Inc., 2002.

CHAPMAN, STEVEN CURTIS

Steven Curtis Chapman (b. November 1, 1962) is Christian music's most awarded artist with 53 Gospel Music Association Dove Awards and five Grammy awards to his credit. Chapman became a pillar of the exponential growth of contemporary Christian music in the eighties and continued to be a dominant force 20 years after his 1987 Sparrow Records debut, *First Hand*. His 16 studio albums and multiple Christmas albums have sold more than 10 million records and produced 44 number one radio singles. Chapman became an advocate for adoption following his own family's adoption of Shohannah Hope from China. In 2000 Steven and his wife Mary Beth established Shohannah's Hope, an agency providing financial grants to qualified families in the process of adoption. As Chapman's star rose in CCM he became an inspiration to many aspiring artists and is credited with introducing Casting Crowns, serving as producer and musical collaborator on their debut release. A prolific songwriter, Chapman's record-setting Dove Award count includes nine as "Songwriter of the Year."

As a child, Chapman spent much of his time at his father's music store and learned to play the guitar and piano at an early age. He continued to develop his musical skills throughout high school and also began writing songs. With aspirations of becoming a doctor, Chapman pursued pre-med studies at Anderson College in Indiana. It wasn't long before his love of music took him to Nashville, where he found work at the Opryland U.S.A. theme park performing in a country music variety show. Chapman briefly attended Belmont University and continued to develop his songwriting skills, and soon found his songs being recorded by prominent Christian artists, including the Imperials and Sandi Patty.

Chapman's songwriting success brought interest from many Christian music publishers and he inked a deal to write songs for Sparrow Records. The label initially had rejected Chapman as an artist but his vocal work on demo recordings for another songwriter caught the ear of company chief Billy Ray Hearn when he overheard a recording in the Los Angeles office. As Hearn passed by the publishing manager's office, he inquired who the singer was, and when he found out it was Chapman he decided to take another look at him as an artist. The subsequent decision to sign the young singer to the label became a successful choice.

Teaming with producer Phil Naish, Chapman released his debut album, *First Hand*, with his first single, "Weak Days," rising to number two on the Christian music radio charts in 1987. The following year Chapman's sophomore release, *Real Life Conversations*, included four radio hits including the number one, "His Eyes." The song

Steven Curtis Chapman performs at the Dove Awards on April 25, 2007, in Nashville. (AP Photo/Mark Humphrey)

earned Chapman his first Gospel Music Association Dove Award in 1989 in the "Contemporary Recorded Song of the Year" category, an honor he shared with cowriter James Isaac Elliott. Chapman took home a second Dove Award that year as "Songwriter of the Year."

Chapman's next album, *More to This Life*, produced four number one radio singles and ten nominations at the 1990 Dove Awards. Chapman took home five Doves that year, including top honors as "Artist of the Year" and "Male Vocalist of the Year." His other three awards were for "Inspirational Song of the Year" ("His Strength Is Perfect"), "Southern Gospel Song of the Year" ("I Can See the Hand" recorded by the Cathedrals), and "Songwriter of the Year."

Chapman continued his reign as the Gospel Music Association's "Artist and Songwriter of the Year" the following year on the heels of his album *For the Sake of the Call* and its five number one singles. The set also earned Chapman his first Grammy Award in the "Best Pop Gospel Album" category.

The major EMI label acquired Sparrow Records in 1992, giving Chapman wider distribution for his next album, *The Great Adventure*. It also marked Chapman's first music video for the title track, which received airplay on cable channels TNN and CMT. The video also earned Chapman a Dove Award for "Short Form Music Video of the Year." He also picked up Dove Awards for "Album of the Year" and "Contemporary Recorded Song of the Year" for "The Great Adventure."

Another benefit of the partnership with a major label was that *The Great Adventure* was distributed to major retailers, helping the album pass the 500,000 sales mark, earning Chapman his first gold album. The album also was named "Best Pop Gospel Album" in 1993, marking Chapman's second Grammy Award.

Chapman's extensive tour to promote his gold selling disk resulted in a live album and video set called *The Live Adventure*. Named the "Best Pop Gospel Album" at the 1994 Grammy Awards, the album was also named "Long Form Music Video of the Year" at the Dove awards.

Released in 1994, *Heaven in the Real World* produced five number one radio singles and was honored with both the Dove Award for "Contemporary Album of the Year" and Grammy Award for "Best Pop/Contemporary Gospel Album" in 1995. The album was also a commercial success, earning the singer a gold album. Chapman's 1990 album, *For the Sake of the Call*, also passed the 500,000-unit mark in 1995, bringing him his third gold album award.

Chapman released his first collection of Christmas music titled *The Music of Christmas* in 1995. The album earned him another gold album and a number one radio single with "Christmas Is All in the Heart" featuring vocals by CeCe Winans. The album was reissued in 2003 as *Christmas Is All in the Heart* in a special version available for sale only in Hallmark stores.

The five songs released to Christian radio from Chapman's next album, *Signs of Life*, all went to number one. The disk was certified gold in 1997, and Chapman also received his first platinum award for sales of 1 million copies of *Heaven in the Real World*.

Chapman made national news in 1997 when he returned to his

hometown of Paducah, Kentucky, to support the community reeling from the school shooting that left three students dead. He composed "With Hope" for one of the funerals and included the song on his *Speechless* album. A few years later Steven was invited to testify on school violence before a Congressional committee.

Chapman's 1997 gold selling *Greatest Hits* collection was followed by the platinum selling *Speechless*. Released in 1999, the album produced seven number one singles and was named "Pop/Contemporary Album of the Year" at the 2000 Dove Awards. Chapman also picked up his fourth Grammy Award for *Speechless* in the "Best Pop/Contemporary Gospel Album" category. The following year his *Declaration* album yielded three number one radio singles and brought Chapman another gold album sales award. In 2002 the album won a Dove Award for "Pop/Contemporary Album of the Year." Later that year Chapman's 1989 *More to This Life* achieved enough sales to earn him another gold album award. Steven's wife, Mary Beth, served as the executive producer for his 2003 *All about Love* album. While always counting on her for a sounding board for his songs, Steven wanted his wife to have a voice in the selection of songs for the project. In a rare move for Chapman, he recorded two songs for the album that he didn't write: "I'm Gonna Be (500 Miles)" recorded by the Scottish duo the Proclaimers, and "I'll Take Care of You," originally performed by Ronnie Milsap. The two number one radio singles from the album were both written by Steven: "All about Love," and "Moment Made for Worshiping." Steven recorded his

next album, *All Things New*, in Los Angeles with musicians noted for their studio and touring with the likes of John Mayer, Alanis Morriset, and Jane's Addiction. Guest instrumentalists and vocalists on the album included Jonny Lang and Jason Wade from Lifehouse. The album yielded three number one radio singles, including the title track. Chapman also picked up his fifth Grammy Award for the album in 2005. Steven released his second Christmas album in 2005 titled *All I Really Want for Christmas*, which featured adopted daughter Shohannah opening the album with her version of the Christmas story from Luke 2:7–14. The album cover featured a photo of Steven and Shohannah.

After many years of working with noted record producer Brown Bannister, Chapman teamed with Matt Brownlee to record his 2007 release *This Moment*. Noted for his work with Leeland and Rebecca St. James, Brownlee and Chapman recorded the new collection of songs in Los Angeles with a studio band whose combined credits included Paul McCartney, Sheryl Crow, and Sting. The album included the radio hit "Cinderella" and the modern worship song "Yours," cowritten with Matt Redman.

Steven Curtis Chapman has always included his family in his music. From the early love ballad "I Will Be Here" written for his wife Mary Beth to "Finger Prints of God" written for teenage daughter Emily to "Cinderella," inspired by his three young adopted daughters. Steven's sons Caleb and Will Franklin became part of his touring band in 2007, playing guitar and drums, respectively.

In addition to his own albums, Steven Curtis Chapman has contributed songs to several special projects and a series of motion pictures. He earned Dove Awards for his contributions to *My Utmost for His Highest* (1996), *God with Us* (1998), *The Passion of the Christ: Songs* (2005), *Songs Inspired by the Chronicles of Narnia: The Lion, the Witch, and the Wardrobe* (2006), and *Glory Revealed* (2008). Academy Award winner actor Robert Duvall recruited Steven Curtis Chapman to compose the song "I Will Not Go Quietly" for his film *The Apostle*. The song was also included on the movie soundtrack and was a number one single on Christian radio. Chapman filmed a music video of the song that featured Robert Duvall.

Encouraged by his daughter Emily, Steven and wife, Mary Beth, adopted a young girl from China named Shohannah in 2000. His celebrity status brought much media attention to the new member of the Chapman family. The Congressional Coalition recognized Steven and Mary Beth's work on behalf of orphans and presented them with the Angel in Adoption award in 2001. The Chapman's adopted two more girls, Stevie Joy and Maria Sue, and became strong adoption advocates, leading to the founding of Shohannah's Hope, an agency providing financial assistance to adoptive families. Chapman has traveled to China many times, including month-long stretches in 2006 and 2007 to work at Chinese orphanages.

In early 2008 Chapman traveled to Perthshire, Scotland, to take part in an International Songwriters retreat with fellow artists Michael W. Smith, Chris Tomlin, Darlene Zschech, Matt and Beth Redman, Tim Hughes, Paul Baloche, Israel Houghton, Graham Kendrick, Andy Park, Martin Smith, and Stu Garrard. The goal of the week-long retreat was to write songs with all the proceeds given to Compassionart, a charity based in Littlehampton, England, whose mission is to see works of art generate income to help the poorest of the poor. The retreat produced 22 new songs, and the writers and artists recorded 12 of them at London's Abbey Road Studio.

Tragedy stuck the Chapman family on May 21, 2008, when adopted daughter Maria was struck in the driveway of the Chapman home in Franklin, Tennessee. Maria died of her injuries, and the Chapman's established Maria's Miracle Fund at Shohannah's Hope as a memorial to her. The outpouring of love and support for the Chapman family was widespread, and within weeks of her death more than $425,000 was contributed to Maria's Miracle Fund at Shohannah's Hope.

Chapman is the author of two books with his Pastor Scotty Smith, *Speechless* (1999) and *Restoring Broken Things* (2005). Steven and his wife Mary Beth have written three children's books, beginning with *Shaoey and Dot: Bug Meets Bundle* in 2004. The book celebrates the adoption of their daughter Shohannah and features illustrations by Mary Beth's brother, Jim Chapman. The Chapmans followed their first book with *Shaoey and Dot: The Christmas Miracle* in 2005 and *Shaoey and Dot: A Thunder and Lightning Bug Story* in 2006.

In addition to his myriad Dove and Grammy Awards, Steven also won an American Music Award in 2003 as "Favorite Inspiration Artist" and in 2008 was inducted into the Music City Walk of Fame in Nashville, Tennessee.

James Elliott

Discography

First Hand (1987)

Real Life Conversations (1988)

More to This Life (1989)

For the Sake of the Call (1990

The Great Adventure (1992)

The Live Adventure (1993)

Heaven in the Real World (1994)

The Music of Christmas (1995)

Signs of Life (1996)

Greatest Hits (1997)

Speechless (1999)

Declaration (2001)

All about Love (2003)

Christmas Is All in the Heart (Hall-mark) (2003)

All Things New (2004)

All I Really Want for Christmas (2005)

This Moment (2007)

Gospel Music Association Dove Awards

2008   Inspirational Recorded Song of the Year, "By His Wounds," *Glory Revealed*

2008   Special Event Album of the Year, *Glory Revealed*

2006   Special Event Album of the Year (for *Songs Inspired By the Chronicles of Narnia: The Lion, the Witch, and the Wardrobe*)

2005   Inspirational Recorded Song of the Year (for "Voice of Truth" *Casting Crowns*, producer)

2005   Special Event Album of the Year (for *The Passion of the Christ: Songs*)

2002   Pop/Contemporary Album of the Year, *Declaration*, Artist and Producer

2001   Male Vocalist of the Year

2000   Male Vocalist of the Year

2000   Artist of the Year

2000   Pop/Contemporary Recorded Song of the Year ("Dive")

2000   Pop/Contemporary Album of the Year (*Speechless*)

2000   Inspirational Life Awards (INSP Channel): Inspirational Pop/Contemporary Album of the Year (*Speechless*)

1999   Long Form Video of the Year (for his participation in *My Utmost for His Highest—The Concert*)

1998   Male Vocalist of the Year

1998   Songwriter of the Year

1998   Pop/Contemporary Recorded Song of the Year: "Let Us Pray" (songwriter)

1998   Pop/Contemporary Recorded Song of the Year: "Let Us Pray" (performer)

1998   Special Event Album of the Year (for his contribution to *God with Us*)

1997   Artist of the Year

1997   Male Vocalist of the Year

1997   Songwriter of the Year

1997   Pop/Contemporary Album of the Year: *Signs of Life*

1996   Special Event Album of the Year: *My Utmost for His Highest*

1995   Artist of the Year

1995   Male Vocalist of the Year

1995   Songwriter of the Year

1995	Contemporary Album of the Year: *Heaven in The Real World*
1995	Contemporary Recorded Song of the Year: "Heaven in the Real World"
1995	Praise and Worship Album of the Year: *Coram Deo II*
1994	Songwriter of the Year
1994	Contemporary Recorded Song of the Year: "Go There with You"
1994	Long Form Music Video of the Year: "The Live Adventure"
1993	Artist of the Year
1993	Songwriter of the Year
1993	Song of the Year: "The Great Adventure"
1993	Contemporary Recorded Song of the Year: "The Great Adventure"
1993	Contemporary Album of the Year: *The Great Adventure*
1993	Short Form Music Video of the Year: *The Great Adventure*
1992	Songwriter of the Year
1992	Contemporary Album of the Year: *For the Sake of the Call*
1991	Artist of the Year
1991	Songwriter of the Year
1991	Male Vocalist of the Year
1990	Artist of the Year
1990	Songwriter of the Year
1990	Male Vocalist of the Year
1990	Inspirational Recorded Song of the Year: "His Strength Is Perfect"
1990	Southern Gospel Recorded Song of the Year: "I Can See the Hand of God" (by the Cathedrals)
1989	Songwriter of the Year
1989	Contemporary Recorded Song of the Year: "His Eyes"

Grammy Awards

2005	Best Pop/Contemporary Gospel Album: *All Things New*
1999	Best Pop Gospel Album: *Speechless*
1994	Best Pop Gospel Album: *The Live Adventure*
1993	Best Pop Gospel Album: *The Great Adventure*
1992	Best Pop Gospel Album: *For the Sake of the Call*

For Further Reading

Alfonso, Barry. *The Billboard Guide to Contemporary Christian Music.* New York: Billboard Books/Watson-Guptill, 2002.

Cusic, Don. *The Sound of Light: A History of Gospel and Christian Music.* New York: Hal Leonard, 2002.

Powell, Mark Allen. *Encyclopedia of Contemporary Christian Music.* Peabody, Mass.: Hendrickson Publishers, Inc., 2002.

CHILDREN OF THE DAY

Marsha Carter Stevens, vocals, guitar
Wendy Carter Fremin, vocals, guitar
Russ Stevens, vocals, bass
Peter Jacobs, guitar, keyboard, vocals (until 1979)

Jeff Crandall, guitar, vocals (from 1979)

Children of the Day was the first successful Jesus music group whose debut album mirrored the pop music of that time. This is the album "that defined the Jesus movement" and became one of the most influential albums in early Christian music. With this album, a musical revolution began where young Christians embraced contemporary music with Christian lyrics in order to spread their message via pop culture to a young Christian audience as well as the audience of nonbelievers who found in this music a hip alternative to the old hymns of their parent's generation.

The urban folk revival was a major influence on '60s music; the lyric-dominated folk songs allowed songwriters to address issues such as the atomic bomb, civil rights, the Vietnam War, and societal ills, and artists such as Peter, Paul, and Mary used harmonies to make the hard-hitting lyrics palatable to a wide audience. Christian music often reflects the sounds of pop music about five years previous; the musical paths are usually blazed by pop and rock artists, and after their sounds are accepted by a large audience Christian groups will take these musical sounds and insert Christian lyrics so a young contemporary audience can better relate to the message.

Children of the Day had three members playing acoustic guitars and one acoustic stand-up bass; in terms of sound they are close to Peter, Paul, and Mary. The roots of the group go to Marsha Carter, a 16-year-old Southern California girl who had a "born again" experience. She witnessed to her 14-year-old sister, Wendy, who also converted. The two other members of the group, Peter Jacobs and Russ Stevens, were members of the Peter Jacobs Quartet, an instrumental jazz group. The four of them came together as Children of the Day and began writing songs.

Their most well-known song, "For Those Tears I Died," was written by Marsha Carter and was featured on *The Everlastin' Living Jesus Music Concert* album (1971), the most important album of early Christian music. The group—and that album—was connected to Calvary Chapel in Costa Mesa. That debut album was released on the Maranatha label in 1971. After the album was released, Marsha married Russ Stevens.

The group members attended Azusa Pacific University and joined the madrigal choir. They toured a great deal and recorded five more albums in addition to having featured tracks on Maranatha compilation albums as their sound evolved to embrace a more adult contemporary sound with the aid of additional instruments. There was a personnel change as Jeff Crandall replaced Peter Jacobs; Crandall later became drummer for the Altar Boys.

After seven years of marriage, Russ and Marsha Stevens divorced after Marsha announced she was gay. This created a scandal in the Maranatha and Calvary Church community as the group broke up and Marsha Stevens pursued a solo career.

After Marsha came out as a lesbian, the Christian church ostracized her although she continued to produce worship-oriented albums and founded the company Born Again Lesbian Music (BALM), which ministered to gays and lesbians. Since she became the first and only Jesus music singer to publicly identify herself with contemporary Christian music, her recordings are not carried in Christian bookstores, none of her songs are played on Christian radio, and she has been excluded from the Christian media. Still, she embraces a biblical, evangelical Christianity and feels called to a ministry of carrying the message of Christ to the gay and lesbian community even though the Christian community has condemned her.

Don Cusic

For Further Reading

Powell, Mark Allen. *Encyclopedia of Contemporary Christian Music*. Peabody, Mass.: Hendrickson Publishers, Inc., 2002.

Discography: Children of the Day

Come to the Waters (1971)

With All Our Love (1973)

Where Else Would I Go (1975)

Christmas Album (1975)

Never Felt So Free (1977)

Butterfly (1979)

Discography: Marsha Stevens

Free to Be (with Ken Caton and LeRoy Dystart) (1991)

The Best Is Yet to Come (1991)

I Still Have a Dream (1993)

I Will Not Behave Like Prey (1995)

For Those Who Know It Best (1995)

Hymns for the Church (1995)

No Matter What Way (1997)

The Gift Is on the Inside (1998)

Christian Music and Meditation #1 (1998)

Joy (1998)

Christian Music and Meditation #2 (1998)

The Waiting's Over (1999)

In Retrospect: A Double CD Collection (2000)

Is This the Real You? (2001)

Songs of Praise from a Strange Land (2003)

In Retrospect (2003)

You Called Us Good (2005)

CHOIR, THE

Derri Daugherty, vocals, guitar
Steve Hindalong, drums, percussion
Mike Sauerbrey, bass (until 1986, from 1990 to 1993)
Tim Chandler, bass (1986–1989; since 1993)
Robins Spurs, bass, vocals (1989–1993)
Dan Michaels, sax, lyricon (since 1986)

The Youth Choir was formed by Derri Daugherty and Steve Hindalong in 1984; they added bassist Mike Sauerbrey to make the group a trio. They recorded their first two albums with this line-up, then added Tim Chandler on bass and Dan Michaels on saxophone and lyricon in 1986 and changed their name to the Choir. Chandler and Daugherty had gotten their start in Christian music playing in evangelist Dwight Thompson's TBN-TV band; Chandler was a member of another alternative Christian band, Daniel Amos. Robin Spurs, who performed with the band from 1989 to 1993 had been a member of the Toasters; after leaving the Choir she formed Rachel Rachel.

Their dreamy, spacey sound made them a popular alternative band in Christian music during the 1990s and they toured extensively. However, in the mid-1990s the individuals in the group went off in different directions. Daugherty moved to Nashville and opened Neverland Recording Studio; he also cofounded the Lost Dogs. Chandler continued to perform with Daniel Amos and Michaels performed with Adam Again, Crystal Lewis, Bryan Duncan, and Larry Norman.

The rest of the group moved to Nashville in 1994. They formed Glasshouse Records and released projects by Ric Alba, John Austin, Rev. Dan Smith, and the Throes; they also released a worship series, *At the Foot of the Cross*. Daugherty and Hindalong have concentrated on studio work, producing Prayer Chain, the Throes, Hoi Polloi, Between Thieves, Common Children, Christine Glass, and others; Dan Michaels is an executive with INO Records and heads the indie label Galaxy 21.

Don Cusic

For Further Reading

Alfonso, Barry. *The Billboard Guide to Contemporary Christian Music*. New York: Billboard Books/Watson-Guptill, 2002.

Powell, Mark Allen. *Encyclopedia of Contemporary Christian Music*. Peabody, Mass.: Hendrickson Publishers, Inc., 2002.

Thompson, John J. *Raised by Wolves: The Story of Christian Rock and Roll*. Toronto, Ontario: ECW Press, 2000.

CHRISTIAN, CHRIS

Chris Christian (b. Lon Christian Smith, 1951, in Abilene, Texas) moved to Los Angeles after graduating from Abilene Christian College in the 1970s and became part of the group Cotton, Lloyd and Christian (with Daryl Cotton and Michael Lloyd); they released one album. Christian then moved to Nashville where he became a songwriter and publisher, writing songs recorded by Elvis Presley and Olivia Newton-John. His big break in Christian music came when he produced B. J. Thomas's debut Christian album, *Home Where I Belong*. Christian recorded the album in a studio he built in his home. This album, released in 1976, became a gold album. Around the same time he signed Amy Grant to a production and publishing deal and arranged for her recording contract with Myrrh Records. He also recorded his debut album and founded Home Sweet Home Records.

Through the years Christian has produced albums for Eric Champion, White Heart, the Imperials, Marilyn McCoo, Dan Peek, and B. W. Stevenson and written songs for the Imperials, B. J. Thomas, Steve Archer, Pat Boone, the Carpenters, Sheena Easton, the Gaither Vocal Band, Dan Peek, B. W. Stevenson, and Dionne Warwick. Christian has often been instrumental in launching the career of contemporary Christian artists through his production and publishing companies.

Christian left Nashville and moved his base of operations to Dallas, where he owns CC Entertainment, which produced commercials for Coca-Cola, GMC, Frito-Lay, McDonald's, and Stouffers. He wrote songs and scored for the children's TV show "Gerbert" and has scored music for several CBS Sports broadcasts, including the Masters Golf Tournament, the Super Bowl, the U.S. Open Tennis Championship, and the NFL Today.

Don Cusic

For Further Reading

Alfonso, Barry. *The Billboard Guide to Contemporary Christian Music*. New York: Billboard Books/Watson-Guptill, 2002.

Cusic, Don. *The Sound of Light: A History of Gospel and Christian Music*. New York: Hal Leonard, 2002.

Powell, Mark Allen. *Encyclopedia of Contemporary Christian Music*. Peabody, Mass.: Hendrickson Publishers, Inc., 2002.

CHRISTIAN ARTISTS SEMINAR IN THE ROCKIES

The Christian Artists Seminar in the Rockies was an influential gathering of Christian artists and those involved in the Christian music industry. Formed by Cam Floria in 1975, it was held annually in Estes Park, Colorado, at the YMCA campground. The seminar consists of a series of seminars and showcases for Christian artists and addresses various issues in the Christian music industry. The talent shows have been the springboard for several Christian acts to be noticed by the Christian music industry and go on to have successful careers. Among those who have benefited from either the showcases or talent shows are Point of Grace, Mark Lowry, Jaci Valesquez, Michael W.

Smith, Staci Orico, Rachel Lampa, Babbie Mason, and Carman. In Spring 2000, the Christian Artists Seminar was purchased by the Gospel Music Association. Beginning in July 2009, the Christian Artists Seminar is held in Nashville, Tennessee, on the campus of Belmont University.

Don Cusic

For Further Reading

Alfonso, Barry. *The Billboard Guide to Contemporary Christian Music*. New York: Billboard Books/Watson-Guptill, 2002.

Baker, Paul. *Contemporary Christian Music: Where It Came from S What It Is, Where It's Going*. Westchester, Ill.: Crossway, 1985.

Cusic, Don. *The Sound of Light: A History of Gospel and Christian Music*. New York: Hal Leonard, 2002.

Granger, Thom, ed. *CCM Presents the 100 Greatest Albums in Christian Music*. Eugene, Ore.: Harvest House, 2001.

McNeil, W. K., ed. *Encyclopedia of American Gospel Music*. New York: Routledge, 2005.

Powell, Mark Allen. *Encyclopedia of Contemporary Christian Music*. Peabody, Mass.: Hendrickson Publishers, Inc., 2002.

Styll, John W., ed. *The Heart of the Matter: The Best of CCM Interviews, Volume 1*. Nashville, Tenn.: Star Song, 1991.

Thompson, John J. *Raised by Wolves: The Story of Christian Rock and Roll*. Toronto, Ontario: ECW Press, 2000.

CHRISTIAN BOOKSELLERS ASSOCIATION

The Christian Booksellers Association (CBA), based in Colorado Springs, Colorado, is the trade organization for Christian retailers who distribute more than half of all Christian products, including Bibles, Christian books, music, videos, gifts, and apparel. The CBA represents more than 1,000 retailers, including independent retailers (55 percent of the total), chain stores (31 percent), and church, camp, or campus bookstores (14 percent).

In 2006, Christian products sold by CBA members accounted for $4.63 billion in sales. Christian books account for approximately 35.6 percent of products sold in Christian bookstores, with Bibles accounting for 19.3 percent, which means a combined total of almost 55 percent. Gifts account for 19.3 percent, music 16.2 percent, and "other" 9.2 percents of products sold.

The major convention for the CBA takes place each summer when they host their International Christian Retail Show. At this event, new product is introduced, retailers place orders, and seminars are held on retail-related issues such as advertising and marketing.

The CBA began in 1950 in Chicago with offices at Moody Press. Under president William Moore, the first convention was held at the Hotel LaSalle in Chicago. In 1952 they began publication of their periodicals *Advance* (later renamed *Bookstore Journal*), *CBA Marketplace*, and *Aspiring Retail*. In 1955 they held their first convention outside Chicago; their convention in Washington, D.C., introduced their first national ad campaign, Why You Should Buy at Your Christian Bookstore. At that convention it was announced that a Christian bookstore in Boston became the first Christian retailer with more than $1 million in sales.

In 1959 Bill Moore became the CBA's first full-time executive secretary, and the organization moved into their own offices in Chicago. In 1960 the CBA convention featured performances by singer Rudy Atwood, Frank Boggs, and the Blackwood Brothers Quartet. In 1965 John Bass replaced Bill Moore as CBA executive secretary, and a survey showed that the average Christian bookstore/manager was 54 years old.

In 1966 the CBA moved their headquarters from Chicago to Homewood, Illinois, and the Imperials performed at the Chicago convention. In 1968 the CBA publication *Advance* was renamed *Bookstore Journal* and George Beverly Shea performed. In 1969 The Peterson Trio and Ray Hildebrand performed at the convention.

In 1970 the CBA moved to Colorado Springs, and in 1971 Dino and Doug Oldham performed at their convention. That year *The Living Bible* was published with a first printing of 500,000; the following year *Publishers Weekly* announced that *The Living Bible* was the fastest selling book in the United States.

In 1974 the first contemporary Christian music acts appeared at the CBA convention when 2nd Chapter of Acts, Evie Tornquist, and Anita Bryant performed. In 1975 Johnny Cash performed at the CBA Convention and the best-selling book of the year was *Angels* by Billy Graham.

In 1978 the CBA moved into new headquarters in Colorado Springs; in 1980 CBA installed its own computer system and George Gallup spoke at the closing banquet, offering results from his polling of Christians and Christianity in America. In 1982 Sandi Patty performed at the CBA convention, and Debby Boone performed at the 1984 convention.

Bill Anderson was named president of CBA in 1985 and Gary Foster was named president of CBA Service Corporation. In 1986 John Bass retired as executive secretary of CBA and *Publishers Weekly* began reprinting the *Bookstore Journal's* best-selling book lists, letting secular bookstores know about the top-selling Christian titles. During that convention it was announced that Amy Grant, Steve Green, Sandi Patty, Michael W. Smith, and Petra were the best-selling Christian artists. The CBA also established a Hall of Honor that year with John and Betty Bass as the first inductees.

Sandi Patty, Twila Paris, and Steve Green performed at the 39th annual CBA Convention, held in Dallas in 1988. In 1989 the CBA Convention attracted more than 10,000 in attendance for the first time. In 1990 it was announced that the average age of a Christian bookstore owner/manager was 37, and the following year the publication *Current Christian Books* listed more than 40,000 titles from 22,000 authors and 480 publishers. In 1993 the CBA announced that the Christian industry accounted for more than $3 billion in annual sales.

SoundScan, which tracks sales of recordings, was launched in Christian retail stores in 1994, allowing the sales of Christian music to be counted on *Billboard*'s weekly top selling charts. The Christian African American

Booksellers Association was incorporated that year.

Jars of Clay, Point of Grace, and the Imperials performed at the CBA convention in Anaheim, California, in 1996; that convention attracted more than 13,000 attendees and it was announced that the *Veggie Tales* series was the top-selling videos for the year.

In 1997 *The Bookstore Journal* was renamed *CBA Marketplace* and CBA launched its *CBA Frontline* magazine and CBA Frontline Training Videos.

In 1999 the CBA broke ground on a new headquarters in Colorado Springs and moved in the following year. In 2002 it was announced that 42 percent of the American population purchased a Christian product; that year more than 70,000 publishers presented 135,000 new titles.

CBA's publication *CBA Marketplace* was renamed *Aspiring Retail* in 2005, and the Christian Trade Association was formed to develop Christian trade globally. The following year they held their first Marketsquare Europe trade show in Amsterdam.

Through the years Christian book stores have accounted for the bulk of sales of Christian music; however, during the 1990s mass merchandisers such as Wal-Mart and Target, warehouse clubs, and big box bookstores increasingly accounted for a significant portion of the sales of contemporary Christian music.

Don Cusic

For Further Reading

Cusic, Don. *The Sound of Light: A History of Gospel and Christian Music.* New York: Hal Leonard, 2002.

CHRISTIAN CULTURE

The Christian culture—although sociologists would label it the Christian subculture—is united nationally by books, recordings, and the Christian media. There are Christian television programs, even Christian channels, and Christian radio stations. The Christian culture includes a number of periodicals, many connected to denominations, but others offering a Christian version of those found on the newsstands. They are an important line of communication to Christian consumers as Christian celebrities, authors, singers, and speakers maintain their base of support through exposure in these publications.

In education, there are a large number of Christian colleges, most affiliated with a denomination, which offer students courses in Bible and ministry-related studies as well as degrees in business, the liberal arts, and sciences. This network provides an outlet for speakers, musicians, and authors who wish to penetrate the Christian market. It is not unusual for a youth to be educated in Christian schools his or her whole life, from kindergarten through postgraduate studies, receive Christian periodicals in the home, buy Christian books at a Christian bookstore, listen to Christian albums at home, and tune into Christian radio and Christian TV regularly. For a job, he or she may work in a Christian organization that markets Christian products or at least be involved in a number of organizations that center their activities and purposes around Christian ideals. The Christian culture is a whole network of like-minded people connected to each other by their church, the Christian bookstores, and the Christian media. It is a culture that is insular and self-perpetuating and has made its influence felt in the political, social, and cultural arena.

A large, strong Christian culture had emerged by 1985. The cornerstones were the Christian bookstores and the church. Evangelical Christians were actively involved in their church on a full-time basis. In addition to Sunday services, there might be Bible classes, men's groups, women's groups, outside speakers, seminars, and community outreach opportunities during the week. The church might have a softball team, or a gym where children played in a basketball league. The youth minister would have activities planned—from campouts to lock-ins (overnight stays that featured a short sermon along with fun and games)—and so would the music minister, who rehearsed and conducted a choir. There was something going on at an evangelical church almost every night of the week, appealing to the entire family.

Next to church, the other cornerstone in the Christian culture is the Christian bookstore. Believers find books, recordings, wall plaques, and gifts that proclaim, support, encourage, and affirm their faith. They also find books, recordings, and gifts that will "reach out" to unbelievers as aids for conversions. The atmosphere transmits a shared worldview to evangelical Christians.

The Christian culture in 1985 was predominantly white. Although there were some African American Christian speakers, authors, and TV personalities, the major bond between black and white Christianity was music. Musicians, songwriters, and singers from both fields influenced one another. Still, there was a radical difference between black gospel for the black audience and white gospel for the white audience. The end result was that black gospel artists did not benefit from the Christian bookstore network to any great degree.

In a world dominated by celebrities and celebrity consciousness, the Christian culture has generated its own coterie of celebrities who remain basically unknown outside Christian circles. There are Christian superstars who remain virtually anonymous in the secular culture. There are even circles within circles, and gospel music is an industry similar to the secular music industry in that it produces recordings and gets them played on radio and sold; however, it is vastly different in numerous other ways, including the way recordings are sold, how the artists reach their public, and even why the recordings are made.

White gospel is divided into several camps. First, there is the inspirational market where choirs and soloists perform primarily for churches. Then there's southern gospel, which is akin to country music in its sound, and finally there is contemporary Christian music, which is pop music—everything from heavy metal and hard rock to soft rock—with Christian lyrics. Within contemporary Christian is praise and worship music, which is primarily aimed for church worship.

The differences in musical tastes are often differences in the self-image of the consumer. On the whole, gospel music views itself as a ministry rather than entertainment, having a message the world needs to hear, serving God instead of man, and representing God's point of view.

Within Christianity, the fundamentalist counterculture entered the mainstream in 1976 when Jimmy Carter, a born again evangelical, was elected president; it became more prominent during the presidency of Ronald Reagan. This brought an immense amount of media coverage to the evangelical movement in the United States. In a 1976 survey, the Gallup Poll found that one out of every three Americans considered themselves a born again Christian; that same year, for the first time since World War II, church attendance increased rather than decreased.

Christian bookstores moved into malls, Christian books proliferated, and Christian music became widely accepted. The Christian culture became big business as it moved from retail outlets into homes via recordings, books, and assorted trinkets and artifacts worn or hung on walls, in addition to increased church growth. Television evangelists became leading populist figures and magazines by, about, and for Christians delivered their messages straight to the living room.

In a study conducted by the Cooperative Institutional Research Program of UCLA in the early 1980s, there were major differences between students at religious schools and their counterparts. For instance, the religious college student tended to view himself as "conservative," was less likely to drink beer or smoke, and was more likely to be against abortion, couples living together outside marriage, premarital sex, and homosexuality. These students tended to be higher achievers than the nonreligious college students, more involved with extracurricular activities, and more likely to take tranquilizers.

Overall, these students said that raising a family was more important than influencing social values and that getting a job was the primary reason for going to college (as opposed to preparing graduates for a life of involved and committed citizenship).

The emphasis on a personal faith reflected in the public arena influenced both politics and churches. During the 1970s, a number of young people attended churches but not necessarily the established denominations. Instead, independent churches were formed with no denominational affiliation and they incorporated music into their services.

The music sung by church choirs on Sundays and special programs during the week reaches more people directly than any other outlet for gospel music. Publishing this music has long been a major source of income for the industry; it accounted for about a fourth of the total income of the gospel music world in the mid-1980s. This publishing industry includes not only songs on records and the spin-off songbooks but a whole portfolio of material aimed directly at choirs in the form of octavos, cantatas, musicals, collected works, compilations, instrumental sheet music, and hymnals.

The music ministers of churches are reached primarily through workshops staged by different publishing companies for choral readings and the exposure of new material. At these workshops, the music ministers are usually given a sample kit of music as they gather together to sing through some of the works. From this experience, they decide whether they would like to purchase music for their church. Since these ministers purchase large quantities of each work for their choir, these seminars and workshops are an extremely important link between the music minister and the publisher, who benefits financially if the ministers like the material.

Still, the church publishing industry and the Christian music industry are two different worlds. Although there is some overlap—choirs may want to perform a hit song from an album, or a musical may be a successful record as well as a sheet music collection—they generally remain in two distinct camps. Because the church remains the basic foundation for the Christian culture, reaching that audience has been essential for the Christian music industry, which began to turn inward and direct its music more toward the church as it entered the 1980s. This is where the Christian record buying consumers were.

The question that hovers over all of this handwringing is, "Does this music produce results?" Results are defined as the conversion of nonbelievers, or perceived nonbelievers, to the criteria evangelists have established that define whether or not someone is a Christian. These criteria are (1) belief that the Bible is the unerring word of God; (2) belief in the divinity of Jesus Christ; and (3) belief in Jesus and his resurrection as the salvation of a person's soul. There are other criteria as well, criteria that are not an outcome of belief, but a precondition to it: the person must not smoke, drink, support abortion, swear, gamble, approve of homosexuality, or be politically liberal.

Evangelicals, broadly defined, are conservative Protestants who have been "born again," or converted to Christ, believe in the authority of the Bible, and share their faith with others, hoping to convert them into evangelicals as well.

Contemporary Christian music is a demanding music. It differs from secular or nongospel music in that Christian artists demand the audience agree with them. Further, the audience demands the artist agree with them. No other form of music is like this. In rock or pop or country or R&B, the artist may want the audience to be entertained, or get their money's worth, or leave satisfied, but they are not concerned about the individual religious beliefs of the members of the audience. The audience for secular music demands music that touches them, demands it be worth the money spent and that the time spent at the show is worthwhile. The artist's personal religious beliefs are generally irrelevant.

In contemporary Christian music, the song cannot stand alone. What is judged is the writer or the performer or both: Do they truly believe and profess fundamental, evangelical Christianity? That is the major criterion in the world of contemporary Christian music.

Further, in Christian music the artist and the songs must be produced, manufactured, distributed, and sold by a Christian organization. A rigid set of defining criteria must be met. If the song is marketed by a secular organization, it is suspect; if the artist appears before non-Christians—especially if they only sing and do not give a testimony—then they are suspect.

Although early Jesus music and contemporary Christian music were often created to evangelize, during the 1980s praise and worship music became a prominent part of the Christian culture. The purpose of this music is to worship God and many claim that the worship of God is the prime duty of the Christian life and hence the prime focus of a church service. This is a music for believers, intended to strengthen their Christian faith.

The Christian culture in America encompasses a marketing network that generates billions of dollars in business each year, and the development of its own media (and media stars) allows it to communicate to fellow believers and affect issues in the world at large. It provides a base of support for those involved in entertainment and has given Christian music in the latter part of the 20th and early 21st centuries the ways and means to reach a like-minded audience and provides entertainment with a message compatible with the audience's beliefs. Although it may be argued that the role of Christian music is to evangelize and attract new believers—and some musicians claim that as their purpose—in reality, the thrust of the Christian industry is "music for the saints" and it provides this service through the church, the Christian bookstores, and the Christian media.

In both the white and African American communities, conferences, or gatherings of believers, are major events. Promise Keepers and Women of Faith in the white market and the Full Gospel Baptist Church Fellowship Conference and annual COGIC conference, as well as a number of others, draw believers together. Music and musical acts are important parts of these conferences, which serve as a showcase for these performers. These conferences also serve as retailers as acts bring their recordings and sell them to attendees at the convention. From the mid-1980s on through the 1990s, these conferences became a key vehicle of exposure for religious music.

During the first half of the 1980s, the biggest "stars" of the white Christian culture were the televangelists;

however, during the 1990s a number of African American evangelists like Bishop Noel Jones from Los Angeles, Carlton Pearson, Bishop T. D. Jakes from Dallas, and Shirley Caesar attracted attention. During the 2000s, evangelists such as Joel Osteen as well as authors such as Max Lucado and contemporary Christian artists such as Michael W. Smith, Steven Curtis Chapman, and Amy Grant were the major celebrities of the Christian culture.

Don Cusic

For Further Reading

Baker, Paul. *Contemporary Christian Music: Where It Came from, What It Is, Where It's Going.* Westchester, Ill.: Crossway, 1985.

Cusic, Don. *The Sound of Light: A History of Gospel and Christian Music.* New York: Hal Leonard, 2002.

Gilmour, Michael J. ed. *Call Me the Seeker: Listening to Religion in Popular Music.* New York: Continuum, 2005.

Haynes, Michael K. *The God of Rock: A Christian Perspective of Rock Music.* Lindale, Tex.: Priority, 1982.

Howard, Jay R., and John M. Streck. *Apostles of Rock: The Splintered World of Contemporary Christian Music.* Lexington: The University Press of Kentucky, 1999.

Miller, Steve. *The Contemporary Christian Music Debate: Worldly Compromise or Agent of Change.* Wheaton, Ill.: Tyndale House Publishers, Inc. 1993.

Seay, Davin, and Mary Neely. *Stairway to Heaven.* New York: Ballantine, 1986.

Styll, John W. ed. *The Heart of the Matter: The Best of CCM Interviews, Volume 1.* Nashville, Tenn.: Star Song, 1991.

Thompson, John J. *Raised by Wolves: The Story of Christian Rock and Roll.* Toronto: ECW Press, 2000.

CHRISTIAN RADIO AND CONTEMPORARY CHRISTIAN MUSIC

For all of its history, defining the term "Christian radio" has been an elusive task. Christian radio has generally referred to radio stations—the number of which is quite significant—that have offered one or more forms of a wide variety of religious programming content and have generated operating revenue through a wide variety of methods. Some have programmed religious music, while some have offered a lineup of talk or "block" programming—usually 15-minute or 30-minute prerecorded segments featuring Bible teaching and preaching. The stations that have programmed music have chosen from a number of different music styles, including inspirational, gospel (black gospel or southern gospel), and more recently CCM (mainly in its contemporary hit radio and adult contemporary derivatives). Some Christian radio stations have generated revenue by selling advertising, while others, broadcasting as noncommercial licensees, have generated revenue through donations. Radio stations that schedule teaching and preaching programs have almost always generated their operating revenue from the sale of those blocks of time to ministries, who subsequently solicit donations from listeners "to keep this ministry on the air." Despite the explosive growth of CCM and the emergence of the CCM radio format, the diverse nature of Christian radio remains. Christian radio is still difficult to neatly define.

Christian Radio in the Pre-CCM Era

Christian radio programming did not begin with the dawn of contemporary Christian music. In fact, Christian radio programming has existed since the very birth of the aural medium. Noted radio scholar and historian Michael Keith's seminal work, *The Radio Station*, made the following observation:

"Live broadcasts of religious programming began while the medium was still in its experimental stage. In 1919 the U.S. Army Signal Corps aired a service from a chapel in Washington, D.C. Not long after that, KFSG in Los Angeles and WMBI in Chicago began to devote themselves to religious programming. Soon dozens of other radio outlets were broadcasting the message of God" (p. 94).

In the second edition of *Stay Tuned: A Concise History of American Broadcasting*, Christopher Sterling and John Kitross cited the same inaugural event with added color:

"Religious programming started when the U.S. Army Signal Corps (apparently unconcerned about separation of church and state) broadcast a church service in Washington, D.C., in August 1919. KDKA was probably the first private station to broadcast religious services when, on January 2, 1921, it transmitted an Episcopalian service, with microphones for organ,

choir, and clergyman and with two technicians (a Jew and a Catholic) dressed in choir robes, on standby in case anything went wrong" (78).

During the 1920s, several full-time Christian radio stations were started, mostly by churches, colleges, or other religious organizations. Although historians differ on the specifics of which stations were first (and even what defined "first"), some of the more prominent examples included WMBI-Chicago, owned by the Moody Bible Institute; KFSG-Los Angeles, owned by the International Church of the Foursquare Gospel; KTBI-Los Angeles, owned by the Bible Institute of Los Angeles (now Biola University); WCAL-Northfield, Minnesota, owned by Saint Olaf College; and WDM-Washington, DC, owned by the Church of the Covenant. Michael Keith's Radio Programming: Consultancy and Formatics included the following note regarding the earliest Christian radio stations:

"Stations began broadcasting religion in the 1920s. Among the first to do so were KFOU, Clayton, Missouri; WMBI (Moody Bible Institute), Chicago; and KPBC, Pasadena, California. All were affiliated with religious organizations. While many of the full-time religious stations today are owned and operated by fundamentalist Christian groups, others are the property of broadcasters who air religion primarily for its financial rewards" (172).

Potential financial rewards notwithstanding, these pioneering stations, and others like them, primarily used the new medium of radio for evangelistic purposes, combining preaching and teaching with brief segments of music to "proclaim the Gospel."

Through radio's golden age of the 1930s and 1940s, and even into the 1950s and 1960s, Christian radio broadened its scope as more stations began broadcasting Christian programming and as more media savvy ministries developed. In 1944, a group of Christian radio practitioners formed the National Religious Broadcasters (NRB) to provide mutual encouragement, support, and other benefits to its members and to advocate (if and when necessary) before Congress or the Federal Communications Commission (FCC). According to its website (www.nrb. org), the NRB currently claims more than 1,400 members. Another factor affecting the expansion of Christian radio during the pre-CCM era was an increase in the number of smaller, rural radio stations, many of which took advantage of the simultaneous emergence of southern gospel music as an art form.

Most of the Christian radio stations of the pre-CCM era were AM stations. That fact was of no great consequence at the time, because AM was the dominant radio band then—most radio stations were AM, and most radio listeners listened to AM radio. Later, however, as the FM broadcast band was developed and its superior fidelity made it the preferred band, a great number of Christian radio stations— especially those smaller, often rural operations—remained relegated to the AM dial. They have suffered from the sonic technical disadvantage ever since.

Most of the Christian radio stations of the pre-CCM era also delivered an older audience. The older makeup of the audience may have been the result of intentionality in targeting more mature listeners, who were considered more likely to be willing and able to support the station and its ministries financially. On the other hand, the older makeup of the audience may have been the result of the simple reality that younger listeners were not interested in the programming offered. Either way, a new "wave" in Christian music would soon reverse that trend for all time.

Christian Radio and the Jesus Music Movement

Several well-documented social and cultural changes during the 1960s set the stage for the advent of the CCM radio format. Rock music and its rebellious revolution matured. The anti-establishment mindset of American youth moved from being the domain of radical fringe elements of the population to become more mainstream. Ultimately, this "go-our-own-way" subculture found its way into Christianity and the church, music and all. Jesus music, however, was not so much about rebellion. Christian young people adapted the music of their culture as a means of expressing their faith and—at least early on—sharing their faith. Before long, the new genre of music— contemporary Christian music—was in the hands of disc jockeys and programmers at Christian radio stations, and the labor pains of birthing a new radio format began.

Early on, the presence of contemporary Christian music on the radio was sporadic at best. Christian radio stations that featured preaching and teaching programs avoided CCM at all costs. Many, in fact, described contemporary music as satanic, or "of the devil." On the other hand, Christian radio stations that featured music programming tended to take one of several types of hybrid approaches to content. One approach was to feature music for some of the broadcast day and block programming (preaching and teaching) for the rest of the broadcast day. Generally, the most attractive day parts, such as morning drive time and afternoon drive time, were devoted to block programming, paid for by the ministries who coveted premium access to the stations' listening audiences. The time that remained unsold—mostly evening and overnight—was given to music. Another hybrid approach to programming Christian music was to build a music playlist from a variety of Christian music genres. It was not uncommon for Christian radio stations to program a mix of inspirational music, CCM, and what was often referred to as lite contemporary—typically consisting of the trendy college-age minichoirs such as Truth, the Continental Singers, and Sound Generation. Some stations even mixed in a hint of southern gospel to fill out the playlist. Of course, in the early days of CCM, there was little music from which to choose. When the 2nd Chapter of Acts, or Phil Keaggy, or Evie Tornquist released an album, those Christian radio stations that wanted to play CCM music played the entire album "out of the box." But even then, it was impossible to program an entire broadcast day with contemporary Christian music. In the mid-1970s, however, a few brave pioneers would give it a try.

The birth of the contemporary Christian music radio format appears to have occurred in 1975. Although the details have been subject to debate, it is likely that the first attempt to program contemporary Christian music on a radio

station full time was a very brief episode in the storied history of KSON in San Diego. Since much of the Jesus music movement had its origin in Southern California (most notably through the ministry of Calvary Chapel in Costa Mesa), it was no surprise that CCM radio would begin there. If there was a potential audience for the new format anywhere, it would be in this geographic region where progressive churches were hosting Friday and Saturday evening concerts, and where evangelistically oriented rockers set up flatbed trailers on any beach or parking lot where a crowd might gather to hear the Good News like they had probably never heard it before. Unfortunately, while there may have been the beginnings of a modest—and loyal—radio audience in San Diego, advertisers were slow to bring the revenue necessary for the station's operation, and KSON abandoned the CCM format only a short time after launching it. One popular San Diego disc jockey who was part of the KSON experiment, however, was recruited to anchor another pioneering attempt in another part of the country. Not long after the demise of the CCM format on KSON, morning air personality Rod Hunter surfaced at Crawford Broadcasting Company's Houston, Texas, property, KFMK-FM.

KFMK-FM had been a moderately successful Christian radio station for a number of years, blending mostly southern gospel music with a full stable of local and national block programming under general manager Hardy Brundage. Not long after Brundage joined evangelist Jimmy Swaggart's broadcast ministry, executives at Crawford Broadcasting made the decision to re-brand KFMK as a full-time contemporary Christian music station. The decision was not an easy one to make. KFMK's previous success was not remarkable, but it was reasonably consistent. A rebranding with a new and unproven format was very risky. Don Crawford's commitment to the project was demonstrated when KFMK-FM's management assembled what had to have been considered an all-star lineup of that era's air personalities. In addition to Rod Hunter, the legendary Scott Campbell was hired as program director, and Seattle's Dewey Boynton was named music director. All had considerable mainstream radio experience, but like their musician counterparts, wanted to use their broadcasting skills to positively affect their culture. Within a few years, Hunter, Campbell, and Boynton were gone, replaced by the likes of Buddy Holiday and Mark Rider, and Crawford Broadcasting sold KFMK, but Houston would forever remain a key CCM radio market, with KXYZ, KGOL-FM, and KSBJ-FM building on, and benefiting from, the KFMK foundation.

At about the same time, in 1975, KYMS began broadcasting contemporary Christian music in suburban Los Angeles. Originating in Santa Ana, KYMS was geographically close to Calvary Chapel of Costa Mesa, the virtual epicenter of the Jesus music movement. In addition to programming the music of Calvary Chapel and the fledgling Maranatha record label, KYMS carried some block programming, still targeting the growing Jesus People subculture. KYMS continued as an important CCM radio station until the mid-1990s.

Other radio stations in other markets continued the pioneering efforts to establish the contemporary Christian music format. Before long, a trade paper had even surfaced, in an effort to bridge the gap between CCM radio programmers and the record ministries. Dan Hickling's *The Foreversong Journal* provided artist profiles, album reviews (called "disc-riptions"), and radio station and record company news, as well as rudimentary sales charts, presumably based on information from record labels. The March 1977 issue consisted of 12 letter-size pages of content, including the cover page. Its "Fine Tuning" page lists the following additions to the list of radio stations programming CCM for at least part of their broadcast schedules: WXRI-Norfolk, Virginia; WBIV-Buffalo, New York; WMIV-Rochester, New York; WEIV-Ithaca, New York; WCIV-Syracuse, New York; and WJIV-Albany, New York. Also noted on page 12 is a syndicated radio show, the "Maranatha! Music Show: #9," a 30-minute music and interview program featuring as its host a young John Styll, who would later publish *CCM Magazine* and serve as president and chairman of the board of the Gospel Music Association.

All these early CCM stations shared myriad challenges. There was neither enough music nor enough advertising revenue. Certainly, a solid group of core artists provided the "bread and butter" of the format. Some of these artists even had mainstream recognition and talent. Larry Norman was the front man for the 1960s band People, who charted with "I Love You." Norman is the probable originator of the popular Christian slogan, "one way," with its accompanying index finger toward the sky. Chuck Girard had enjoyed mainstream success with the studio group the Hondells, scoring a major hit during the cars and surf music era with "Little Honda." Girard became the driving force behind the CCM supergroup LoveSong before embarking on a prolific solo artist and songwriting ministry. Barry McGuire was a member of the 1960s folk group the New Christy Minstrels and recorded one of the biggest protest songs of the 1960s, "The Eve of Destruction." But by the end of the 1970s, he was better known in Christian music circles for "Cosmic Cowboy" and "Bullfrogs and Butterflies." Gary S. Paxton had several "novelty" hits during the 1960s, including "Monster Mash" and "Alley Oop." His effect on CCM during its infancy was significant, as an artist, writer, and producer. Despite this wealth of talent, as well as early CCM signature artists such as Dallas Holm, Andrae Crouch and the Disciples, the Imperials, Petra, and others, most radio playlists revealed how shallow the pool of CCM talent was by their ongoing inclusion of music from other Christian genres. To illustrate the point, consider the following anecdote: KFMK-FM in Houston maintained internal records documenting the most requested songs from the station's Request Line. For the month of July 1976, CCM artists on the Top 25 list included Daniel Amos, Chuck Girard, Hope of Glory, Andrae Crouch and the Disciples, the 2nd Chapter of Acts, Janny Grein, and others. Also included, however, were artists better known in inspirational or southern gospel music, including Marijohn Wilkin, the Downings, and the Rambos. In fact, KFMK's most requested song for July was "Brand New Touch" by a southern gospel group, the Lanny Wolfe Trio.

Virtually all of the advertising revenue in the early days of CCM radio came from what were termed "affinity" advertisers. Some were Christian proprietors who wanted to support the upstart Christian radio station. Some were businesses that specifically targeted the Christian audience, such as Christian bookstores. Some were employees of auto dealerships or insurance companies who purchased advertising out of their own pockets, always promising to do business "in a Christian manner." Most were loyal listeners to the CCM radio stations. At that time, however, there simply were not enough of them. Radio station employees often worked for minimal pay, usually with no fringe benefits. Stations owners sacrificed the potential for much greater profits to fulfill what most considered a mission. No one got rich as a CCM radio pioneer.

Christian Radio in Transition

As contemporary Christian music radio moved into the 1980s, it began to develop its own identity. Several important, even dramatic, programming developments occurred during this era. Perhaps the most significant development was the move toward a more homogenous sound. During the 1970s, most radio station playlists were unavoidably eclectic in sound. Still, much of what was considered contemporary Christian music in that era had a raw, "seventies rock" feel to it. But at the end of the decade, when mainstream music moved toward disco and then on to techno pop, CCM radio settled into a mellower, more pop-oriented adult contemporary style. Guitar driven, long-hair bands gave way to Amy Grant and Michael W. Smith.

Another significant development of this era was a change in the way song rotations were arranged. When playlists were more eclectic, it was not uncommon to rotate music based on style, or gender, or even genre. The first song at the top of the hour might be a contemporary Christian hit, followed by a male vocal, followed by an inspirational selection, with the ever-present—but never explained—rule against two female vocal cuts in a row. As the format began to mature, programmers relied more on record labels to provide current singles, and for the first time, music was rotated in a more traditional and typical way, based on a song's age and popularity. The first song at the top of the hour was now more likely to be a hot current or a power gold, followed by a recurrent or library gold (or whatever nomenclature the particular programmer might have used.) The rotations were more scientifically and mathematically organized, making it possible to control the number of spins each song would get in a day or week. Moreover, leading radio stations began to report their playlists to trade publications, such as Brad Burkhart's *Christian Research Report*. Burkhart, the son of legendary mainstream radio programmer Kent Burkhart, founded Brad Burkhart Christian Media and—in addition to providing CRR with its weekly charts, radio industry news, and radio programming tips—became one of Christian radio's first and most influential creative consultants, working with some of the best CCM radio stations and record labels alike. For the first time, Christian radio programmers contributed to, and relied on, airplay charts

that tracked which songs were hot and which ones were not. Eventually, the CCM radio format's cultural significance was validated—at least for a brief period of time—when the prestigious mainstream trade publication *Radio and Records* launched a contemporary Christian airplay chart for its weekly editions.

This period of growth for the CCM radio format was highlighted by the introduction of several radio stations that were crucial to that growth, including WWDJ in suburban New York City, KLTY in Dallas, Texas, and a group of noncommercial stations that were known individually and collectively as WAY-FM.

WWDJ featured mostly block programming or a blend of music and talk for much of its history, but at one key point in the 1980s, part of its broadcast day was devoted to contemporary Christian music, and its morning drive air personality was popular New York voice Frank Reed, who had previously been the midday announcer for WNBC, positioned between Don Imus (mornings) and Howard Stern (afternoons). For the first time, contemporary Christian music was heard on the radio in America's largest city. Another important figure in WWDJ's story was Joe Battaglia, who served for many years in a variety of roles, including general manager, as well as vice-president of WWDJ's parent company Communicom, which also owned WZZD in Philadelphia and KSLT in San Antonio.

Farther south, KLTY and its faithful Dallas-Fort Worth Metroplex audience spent years enduring changes in ownership, numerous changes in personnel, and even changes in dial position. But, perhaps more than any other CCM station, KLTY was certainly not without a steady stream of talented staff members. Several notable alumni that played pivotal roles in the station's success included Jon Rivers and David Pierce, in addition to Frank Reed, who moved to Dallas from New York in the early 1990s. Jon Rivers has long been one of the most recognized voices in Christian radio, having been—among other things—the host of the nationally syndicated *20 the Countdown Magazine* for years. David Pierce possessed a rich, smooth voice and was widely regarded for his programming intellect. Along with other brilliant and talented people, Rivers, Pierce, and Reed established KLTY as the standard by which all other Christian radio stations were measured. And the legacy continues. Despite all of its changes and incarnations, in any given Arbitron rating period, it is likely that KLTY remains the most-listened-to Christian radio station in America, reaching about half a million listeners each week. The KLTY website confirms that statement, expressing on its homepage "Thanks for listening to the #1 Christian Radio Station in America" (www.klty.com).

In Fort Meyers, Florida, Bob Augsburg envisioned a Christian music radio station that targeted a younger audience than most of the adult contemporary CCM stations that existed. In response to that vision, he built WAYJ-FM, referred to as WAY-FM, and that single station grew to a group of about 15 in markets such as Nashville, Tennessee; Huntsville, Alabama; Tallahassee, Florida; Louisville, Kentucky; Denver and Colorado Springs, Colorado; Charleston, South Carolina; and others. The WAY-FM organization also includes a number of low-power translators as well as the Christian Hit Radio Satellite Network (CHRSN).

This grand era for CCM radio also saw tremendous growth in terms of revenue generation. As the execution of the format and the quality of the music improved, the audience grew. As the audience grew, so did the viability of Christian radio as an advertising medium. Ad agencies started to notice. National advertisers started to notice. Stations were no longer solely dependent on affinity buys. They could sell "by the numbers." More sophisticated sales tools were developed, including an interesting publication from Gary Crossland's San Antonio-based SOMA Communications. Crossland was the first to incorporate formal research methods for Christian radio, providing extensive qualitative information about the Christian radio audience and its purchasing preferences.

It should be noted that this period of growth and maturity and homogeneity was not without its diversity of strategy, of methodology, and even of mission. Serious questions emerged during this era about the purpose of CCM radio. Who was the target audience—the Christian subculture for encouragement and support, or the unsaved for the opportunity to hear the Good News? Was Christian radio a ministry or a business, and how should it be funded? Was advertising an appropriate way to generate needed revenue, or should the listeners support the radio station? Should Christian radio stations be commercial or noncommercial? The debates surrounding these questions continue to this day. The explosive growth of CCM radio and particularly its participation in the creation of stars and celebrities generated a much more serious debate when scandal almost devastated the industry.

Christian Radio and Growing Pains

One of the "good news, bad news" phenomena of contemporary Christian music radio's maturing era was its contribution to the creation of Christian celebrities. The good news was that the creation of wholesome stars gave impressionable fans positive role models. The bad news was that it placed artists in increasingly vulnerable positions of self-importance, encouraged by adulation—perhaps even a form of worship—from those fans. Moreover, the star power became instantly more intense when mainstream record labels began to work in union with Christian record labels in an effort to help Christian artists cross over. Whether crossing over was an effort to reach a wider audience with the Christian message, or simply an effort to sell more units, it quickly raised the level of celebrity status for certain artists. Of course, Amy Grant was the most successful at crossing over. Michael W. Smith made a significant mark on popular culture as well. But for Christian radio, it added another question to the debate. Those (vocal) members of the radio audience who reacted negatively to a Christian artist crossing over also reacted negatively to the Christian radio station's continuing to play that artist's music.

The real test for Christian radio programmers came when the vague fear of potential moral compromise gave way to actual moral failure involving too many of CCM's most prominent stars. From Scott Douglas of White Heart to Michael English to Sandi Patty to Amy Grant—the details of heroes fallen were widely circulated. And the repercussions for Christian radio were critical. Unlike radio stations in other music formats that only had an obligation to play the hits and keep their audiences entertained, CCM radio stations quickly discovered that some members of their audiences expected them to serve as moral gatekeepers. Others did not. The dilemma moved the task of building a playlist beyond the simple matter of choosing to play a song based on its musical and lyrical appeal. Artist conduct became a factor in programming decisions as well. Although few Christian radio programmers treasured this role of "behavior police," none could risk alienating the audience. The debates intensified.

Christian Radio and Technology

Leading up to the close of the 20th century, rapid technological changes dominated popular culture. CCM radio was not immune from the effect—both positive and negative—of these changes.

Rapid expansion of satellite technology led to the establishment of several contemporary Christian music radio networks. Former KFMK and KSBJ executive Burt Perrault and his wife, Patsy, founded the Morningstar Radio Network in 1992. Morningstar was the first organization to offer live CCM radio programming delivered 24 hours a day by satellite from its studios in Houston, at its peak serving about 200 affiliates nationwide. The network was purchased by Bible publisher Thomas Nelson and moved to Nashville in the mid-1990s, and then by Salem Communications, which has continued to market the service under its on-air brand,

Today's Christian Music. Other satellite-delivered networks followed, including the Word in Music, CHRSN (owned by the Way-FM group of stations), and California-based K-Love, which was programmed by Jon Rivers and David Pierce, and which through its network of affiliates and owned stations successfully built the largest cumulative audience of any Christian music radio entity in America.

Another positive effect of technology on CCM radio was the growth of the Internet and the added connectivity of people and organizations. One important example was the creation of a Christian radio programmer virtual community known as the PD Forum. The brainchild of veteran CCM programmer Bob Thornton, the PD Forum connected programmers, managers, and other interested parties to each other for the purpose of mutual support, encouragement, and advice. Not only was the actual content helpful for both new and seasoned practitioners, but the sense of community gave participants a sense of belonging, even if they had never met other members of the community. It was contemporary Christian radio's own version of an online social network.

Not every aspect of technological change, however, was friendly to CCM radio. Like its mainstream counterparts, Christian radio stations broadcasting on the AM and FM radio bands (terrestrial radio) faced increasing competition from emerging technologies and alternative media options, including MP3 players, internet radio, and satellite radio. As media consumers were given more options for accessing entertainment, they chose to assume more control over the content to which they were exposed, and they became more

discriminating in their preferences. The best CCM radio programmers realized quickly that a business-as-usual approach to Christian radio would be catastrophic.

Christian Radio and the Modern Praise and Worship Movement

The beginning of the new century witnessed yet another shift in the sound and style of contemporary Christian music radio. The CCM radio format had been dominated by 70s-style, guitar-driven rock in its infancy. In the 1980s and 1990s, the music preferred by Christian radio programmers (and presumably their audiences) seemed to shift toward a more pop-oriented style referred to as adult contemporary. Early in the new century, another significant shift occurred when playlists became heavily loaded with music from the budding modern praise and worship movement. Lyrics tended to be more vertical (sung to God) than horizontal (sung to other people). Many songs were Psalms and other scripture verses set to modern rock influenced music. An odd consequence of this phenomenon was that it was very common for several artists to include some of the same songs on their respective recording projects. This presented Christian radio programmers with yet another dilemma in the decision-making process. Which artist's version of a particular song was added to the station's playlist?

Oddly enough, one of contemporary Christian music's biggest crossover songs has been credited with starting the praise and worship development in CCM radio. In an interview with EMI Christian Music Group Vice President

Grant Hubbard, the longtime CCM record label executive recounted the difficulty of getting Christian radio stations to play contemporary praise and worship music until popular band MercyMe scored a surprise mainstream hit with "I Can Only Imagine." Since then, worship leaders like Chris Tomlin and Darlene Zschech are as likely to be heard on Christian radio as Steven Curtis Chapman. Another unusual outcome of the stylistic shift toward modern praise and worship music was that for the first time, the music played on Christian radio stations closely resembled the music sung in many church worship services.

Christian Radio and the Future

Obviously, it is difficult to predict what the future holds for Christian radio. Cultural changes are occurring at such a rapid pace, and it is risky to speculate about the future of AM and FM (terrestrial) radio, recorded music styles and business models, or the tastes and preferences of the Christian subculture. It is likely the debates will continue about the purpose—and perhaps even the validity—of contemporary Christian music radio. But it is also likely the next generation of Christians—musicians and those who enjoy the music—will continue to seek cultural relevance in expressing and sharing their faith.

Rich Tiner

Works Cited

Boynton, Dewey. "KFMK's 25 Most Requested Songs for the Month of July." Internal station document dated July 1976.

Hubbard, Grant. Personal interview, June 2008.

Humphries, Rick. "KFMK Meets the Needs of Houston." *New Jerusalem Magazine* 1:1, June, 1976.

Keith, Michael C. *Radio Programming: Consultancy and Formatics*. Boston: Focal Press, 1987.

Keith, Michael C. *The Radio Station*. 6th ed. Boston: Focal Press, 2004.

Sterling, Christopher, and John M. Kitross. *Stay Tuned: A Concise History of American Broadcasting*. 2nd ed. Belmont, Calif.: Wadsworth, 1990.

For Further Reading

Berkman, Dave. "Long Before Falwell: Early Radio and Religion—as Reported by the Nation's Periodical Press." *Journal of Popular Culture* 21 (1988): 1–11.

Cusic, Don. *The Sound of Light: A History of Gospel and Christian Music*. New York: Hal Leonard, 2002.

CLARK, PAUL

Paul Clark was one of the pioneers of the Jesus movement. Born in Kansas City, Missouri, Clark formed Kommotions, a rock band with friends. In April 1970, he dropped out of college after his freshman year and moved to Colorado, where he lived in an isolated log cabin. He experimented with drugs and a variety of spiritual searches during these early years and was the lead singer and songwriter for the Rocky Mountain Goldrush. During this period he received some Christian books from his grandmother and read one that asked him to pray for Jesus to enter his life. He did, and after this dramatic conversion in May 1970 he spent the next eight days writing songs, which all appeared on his first album, *Songs from the Savior*. The financing for that first album came from a 65-year-old man who came to the coffee house where Clark performed, asked if there were any albums available of his songs, and when Clark said "no," wrote him a check for $3,000 to record the album and press up 1,000 copies.

Clark formed Seed Records and released his following product on that label. Later, he moved to Kansas City and became worship leader at a church there; he is also chaplain to the Kansas City Royals baseball team and Kansas City Chiefs football team.

Don Cusic

For Further Reading

Cusic, Don. *The Sound of Light: A History of Gospel and Christian Music.* New York: Hal Leonard, 2002.

Powell, Mark Allen. *Encyclopedia of Contemporary Christian Music.* Peabody, Mass.: Hendrickson Publishers, Inc., 2002.

CLAWSON, CYNTHIA

Cynthia Clawson (b. October 11, 1948, in Houston, Texas) was one of the most popular singers of contemporary Christian music, winning the Dove Award for Female Vocalist in 1980 and 1981. Clawson is a classically trained singer with a four octave range, the daughter of a Southern Baptist minister; she graduated from Howard Payne University in Brownwood, Texas, with a major in vocal performance and minor in piano. During her senior year in college she won the Arthur Godfrey Talent Show. Influenced by Julie London and Julie Andrews, Clawson was signed to a recording contract by Red Buryl and released her first album in 1975.

Clawson has also had roles as an actress in "Newcomers" on CBS, which was the summer replacement for "The Carol Burnett Show." She cowrote the musical *Bright New Wings* and the children's musical, *Angels*, with her husband, Ragan Courtney. Her recording of "Softly and Tenderly" was featured in the movie *The Trip to Bountiful*.

Clawson and her husband are copastors of the Sanctuary in Austin, Texas, where they use theatrical arts and musical expression to communicate the gospel.

Don Cusic

For Further Reading

Cusic, Don. *The Sound of Light: A History of Gospel and Christian Music.* New York: Hal Leonard, 2002.

McNeil, W. K., ed. *Encyclopedia of American Gospel Music.* New York: Routledge, 2005.

Powell, Mark Allen. *Encyclopedia of Contemporary Christian Music.* Peabody, Mass.: Hendrickson Publishers, Inc., 2002.

COCKBURN, BRUCE

Canadian singer/songwriter Bruce Cockburn (b. May 27, 1945, in Ottawa, Canada) is an example of a Christian who writes and performs music rather than someone who writes and performs Christian music. Although his songs often contain spiritual and Christian themes, the songs cover a wide range of topics and are aimed at the general—or secular—audience. Cockburn has a long list of albums he has released but is best known for his hit single, "Wondering Where the Lions Are," which reached number 21 on the American pop charts in 1980. That song came from Cockburn's album, *Dancing in the Dragon's Jaws*, released in the United States on the Millennium label in 1979.

Cockburn does not fit the stereotype of the right-wing Republican Christian; he has criticized American foreign policy, he has been a spokesperson for social justice and the poor, and his social and political beliefs are decidedly liberal. Cockburn supports abortion rights, smokes, drinks, and has used language not associated with mainstream Christianity in his songs and speech. He is more popular in his native Canada, and his songs have been recorded by Chet Atkins, Barenaked Ladies, Jimmy Buffett, Dan Fogelberg, Jerry Garcia, Maria Muldaur, and Anne Murray.

Cockburn attended the Berklee School of Music in Boston and received an honorary doctorate from that institution in 1977.

Don Cusic

For Further Reading

Alfonso, Barry. *The Billboard Guide to Contemporary Christian Music*. New York: Billboard Books/Watson-Guptill, 2002.

McNeil, W. K., ed. *Encyclopedia of American Gospel Music*. New York: Routledge, 2005.

Powell, Mark Allen. *Encyclopedia of Contemporary Christian Music*. Peabody, Mass.: Hendrickson Publishers, Inc., 2002.

CONTEMPORARY CHRISTIAN MUSIC

Contemporary Christian music is popular music with Christian lyrics. Musically, contemporary Christian music encompasses a number of genres. It comes under the general umbrella of gospel music, which includes everything from black gospel, spirituals, southern gospel, and contemporary hymns to the secular sounds of rap, hip-hop, rock, heavy metal, and any other musical genre. In fact, it may be argued that there is no such thing as gospel music, although there are gospel songs, and these are defined by the lyrics rather than by the music. These lyrics express the Christian faith, from personal journeys to biblical stories to songs to God thanking and praising Him.

Christian music is the term applied to white gospel music; gospel is the term generally applied to the music of African Americans whose songs and performers embrace the Christian message. This Christian message is based on (1) belief that the Bible is the unerring word of God; (2) belief in the divinity of Jesus Christ; and (3) belief in Jesus and his resurrection as the salvation of a person's soul.

Don Cusic

For Further Reading

Cusic, Don. *The Sound of Light: A History of Gospel and Christian Music*. New York: Hal Leonard, 2002.

CONTEMPORARY CHRISTIAN MUSIC, A HISTORY

Contemporary Christian music emerged when Jesus music became part of the music business; this began around 1977–1978.

The early Jesus music was a product of mostly live performances by young believers during the counterculture days of the 1960s. There was an innocence and naiveté in the early Jesus music; it was composed and sung by those who had fervently "discovered" Jesus—and He had "discovered" them—to the point where they were excited about their faith and wanted to share it with others. It was a group of spiritual seekers who had found "the Answer" and wanted to show others that they, too, could find the answer to their spiritual search by accepting that Jesus is a personal savior who could change their life if they became "born again" and saw the world with new eyes and a new faith that embraced Jesus as Lord of All.

Some of these early converts made records expressing this faith, but these records were not financed by the large multinational recording companies and were not made with the intention of selling millions of copies and getting on mainstream radio. These records were made either by established gospel record companies who had a relationship with a Christian subculture that included Christian bookstores and churches or by start-up labels created by a Christian—or group of Christians—intent on sharing the Christian message. As this Jesus music grew—a result of it becoming more popular with baby boomers who comprised the emerging Christian audience—some of these small labels contracted with major record labels for distribution agreements to get the records into mainstream record stores or were even bought by major labels who wanted a piece of the action. Eventually, the three major Christian labels—in 1977 they were Word, Benson, and Sparrow—were purchased by major multinational corporations who owned major record labels and incorporated under the corporate umbrella.

In 1977 Jimmy Carter was sworn in as president—the first born again president—and his Christian faith brought a public spotlight on the born again movement. That year Debby Boone released "You Light Up My Life," which became the most popular song of the 1970s as measured by radio airplay on the *Billboard* charts. The song seemed to be a Christian song, although the singer sang "you" instead of "Jesus," but the line in the song, "It can't be wrong if it feels so right," disturbed Christian audiences. This line seemed to embrace the "if it feels good do it" philosophy that seemed to lead so many youth astray. But Debby Boone was undeniably a Christian, the daughter of the undeniably Christian Pat Boone who had made his Christian faith public since the 1950s. Also in 1977 B. J. Thomas, a pop star whose hit "Raindrops Keep Falling on My Head" was a major hit in 1969, released an album, *Home Where I Belong*, on Word, a

Christian label. Thomas was a celebrity convert and his album sold well and brought attention to Christian music. Further, the album *Alleluia, a Praise Gathering for Believers* by the Bill Gaither Trio received a gold album award, the first release from a Christian label to do so.

The following year, 1978, *Contemporary Christian Music* magazine published its first issue and the name of the magazine gave the genre a name: contemporary Christian music. Also that year Amy Grant, who would become the first Christian artist to cross over into the pop world, released her first album.

Historical eras don't usually begin or end in neat time frames; the period 1977–1978 was preceded by a wealth of young performers idealistically doing Jesus music for the love of Jesus and not musical stardom, and the same was true after those years. But increasingly, the contemporary Christian music that evolved after this period was recorded and marketed by Word, Benson, and Sparrow. The artists and recordings were documented by *CCM* magazine, which established charts for airplay and sales and featured stories on the major performers of contemporary Christian music.

The Gospel Music Association, a trade organization for gospel music established in 1969, which awarded Dove Awards for gospel recordings, noted the growth of Jesus music in their 1978 awards. The organization began as an outgrowth of the Southern Gospel Quartet Convention and represented southern gospel music solely during its first eight years, but in 1977 it named Evie Tornquist as the "Female Vocalist of the Year" and Andraé Crouch won

the "Soul/Black Gospel Album" Dove in the first year of that award.

In 1978 the song "Rise Again" won the "Song of the Year" Dove and Dallas Holm, the writer and performer of that song, received the "Male Vocalist" and "Songwriter of the Year" honors. Evie Tornquist again won "Female Vocalist" awards and Bob Dylan's first Christian album, *Slow Train Coming*, won the Dove for "Album by a Secular Artist," the first time that award was given. During the 1980s the Gospel Music Association's Dove Awards increasingly reflected the top artists and songs in contemporary Christian music.

In the mid-1960s the church had been on the decline, with attendance decreasing and interest from the youth waning. The Jesus revolution of the late 60s and early 70s took the gospel back to the street, largely via music. For a number of years, the established churches resisted the music from the Jesus movement and contemporary Christian music. Because the major gospel record companies and Christian radio stations generally sided with the conservative churches and Christian bookstores, the result was a stifling of Christian music by the Christian culture itself.

By the mid-1970s, that began to change as churches realized that contemporary music was a way to reach the youth and the record companies and radio realized there was a demand for this music. Too, the musicians and others involved in the Jesus movement proved themselves to be sincere, dedicated Christians who involved themselves in local churches, so the fears of conservative church members were generally quieted as they realized this movement was not just wild hippies on the loose. As a matter of fact, churches realized that the audience for contemporary Christian music was sitting in their pews.

America underwent a spiritual awakening, and Christianity that was fundamental in its beliefs, active in its faith, and in touch with the contemporary culture became acceptable. The term "born again" became known, accepted, and practiced, with many Americans undergoing a rebirth in their spiritual lives. This was highlighted in 1977 by the publication of the book *Born Again* by Nixon's former hatchet man, Chuck Colson, and the beginning of Jimmy Carter's presidency.

By 1976 there was an infrastructure in place for contemporary Christian music to grow. A marketing network of Christian bookstores, represented by a trade organization, the Christian Booksellers Association, was firmly in place. Religious radio, Christian periodicals, and television evangelists were also an established part of the media landscape.

The first star in contemporary Christian music was Evie Tornquist. A small, blond-haired, blue-eyed young lady from New Jersey, Evie was pert and pretty. Vocally, her style was reminiscent of a trained voice that fit nicely into a church choir. Evie was the darling of the gospel world both in the United States and Europe, where she was "discovered." Her album sales were well over the 100,000 mark for each release, and many felt she would be the one to carry the banner of contemporary Christian music to the secular world. Gospel music was struggling for recognition and acceptance and many in the gospel industry felt the key was to find someone who could be a gospel artist yet successful in the pop field.

However, Evie married and stopped recording and touring for awhile and devoted herself to being a wife and mother for a number of years.

B. J. Thomas had a celebrated conversion in the mid-70s that took him away from drug addiction into a born-again experience. Thomas had been a pop star before his conversion (he had reportedly sold 32 million records with hits such as "Raindrops Keep Falling On My Head," "Somebody Done Somebody Wrong Song," and others) and afterward began recording Christian music for Word Records. He, too, was a bright star in this arena but soon developed problems with his concerts when two sets of fans showed up—one wanting the old pop hits and the other wanting just Christian music. Thomas tried to reconcile the two, singing all of his old hits while closing with his testimony, but the conflict proved too much and he moved out of gospel again. Somehow, the Christian audiences could not accept B. J. Thomas as a Christian entertainer; they wanted him all or nothing, so Thomas stopped recording Christian music on gospel labels and began recording country music.

In 1977 Debby Boone had one of the biggest hits of the year—"You Light Up My Life"—and was on her way to being the star who could bridge the gospel and secular worlds. Debby brought attention to Christian music because of her overt Christian beliefs. She won a Grammy for "Best New Artist" and followed this with a number one song on the country music charts but, again, a husband and family took precedence as she withdrew from her performing career to a more low-key life with occasional performances and recordings.

In contrast to those leading contenders, Amy Grant became the first artist to be comfortable as a Christian entertainer who achieved success in the mainstream secular field. In 1977, when she released her debut album, she was a young high school student.

With the release of her first album, her songs "Old Man's Rubble," "What a Difference You've Made in My Life," and "Beautiful Music" immediately received radio airplay.

Before Amy Grant appeared, few if any Christian artists had achieved popularity primarily through radio airplay. The others usually did it through extensive touring over a long period of time. So for Amy Grant to have three hit songs on gospel radio was a remarkable achievement and one that propelled her from oblivion to an almost overnight success.

The second album had attractive pictures of Amy on the front and back covers and was filled with excellent songs. Titled *My Father's Eyes*, the album had great production. On the second album, Amy emerged as a songwriter, writing four of the songs herself and cowriting another four with producer Brown Bannister.

During the time that Amy Grant released her first albums, the major artists in gospel music were the Bill Gaither Trio, B. J. Thomas, Evie Tornquist, Andrae Crouch, Jimmy Swaggart, Reba Rambo Gardner, the Downings, Dallas Holm, Walter Hawkins and the Love Center Choir, James Cleveland, Jessy Dixon, and Danniebelle.

In 1977 another artist became a major figure in contemporary Christian music when he released his debut album. More than any other artist, Keith Green provided the example of ministry over everything else in his career and inspired, encouraged, frustrated, and questioned record executives and recording artists in the field of gospel music.

Keith Green personified radical Christianity; he stood out for his beliefs, even within the Christian culture, and became a light to follow, an inspiration for others involved in gospel music, and an example of the Christian as radical.

Green's debut album, *For Him Who Has Ears*, released on the Sparrow label, was an immediate, overwhelming success. After his initial success, Green went to the Sparrow executives and told them he did not want to be on the label and in the Christian bookstores because he wanted to distribute the records himself. He said he wanted to make his records available directly to consumers, and free if they could not afford to pay. He felt the marketing system did not allow people to receive a free album and wanted his message available to all. Too, Green abhorred the business side of the music industry; he felt business people were, on the whole, standing in the way of him doing the Lord's work.

In July 1978, a new magazine geared to contemporary Christian music appeared. *Contemporary Christian Music* emerged as the leading voice for and about contemporary Christian music. It began as a tabloid music trade, based in Santa Ana, California, and during the first year 12,000 copies of each issue were mailed monthly free to those involved in the gospel music industry. On that first cover were the Boone Girls, who had recorded an album for their father, Pat Boone's, label, Lamb and Lion Records. This magazine dominated the contemporary Christian field and became the most popular and influential magazine in that area. Within that first year, in fact, it became for contemporary Christian music what *Rolling Stone* was for rock—the publication that defined a music culture and identified who's in and who's not.

The charts of *CCM* were a major contribution to contemporary Christian music because no other publication compiled charts from Christian bookstores about music, which is where most of the Christian buyers bought their records. The only other gospel music charts during this time were in *Record World*, a secular music trade magazine, and these were compiled primarily from secular distributors who handled some gospel product as part of their normal business. Their charts showed more sales on southern gospel, which sold primarily through regular retail outlets, and black gospel, which sold to the record stores in the black sections of a city, rather than the Christian bookstores.

Perhaps the most newsworthy event for Christian music in the secular world in 1979 was the arrival of Bob Dylan's Christian album, *Slow Train Coming*. The Christian music industry had long been infatuated with the pop world. The conversion of major celebrities and artists had always been seen as an affirmation of the appeal of Christianity; perhaps the most prized catch of all was Bob Dylan, and his conversion was expected to change American pop music. The theory was that someone of Dylan's magnitude—the "voice of a generation" who had the ears of almost every major rock artist, critic, and follower—would cause massive conversions from the rock 'n' roll world and the gospel fold would be multiplied mightily. Alas, it would not be so.

Dylan's conversion caused more celebration in the Christian world than it did in the rock world, which regarded it primarily as an aberration and viewed it with alarm. Those who followed wherever Dylan led found they could not bring themselves to follow him into Christianity, and the gospel world came face to face with a reality: the growth of Christian music in the future would not come from acceptance by the secular, or nongospel, music world, but from better marketing within its own ranks. The infatuation with secular success and the strategies of marketing to the rock 'n' roll world—so much a part of the contemporary Christian mentality at the end of the 1970s—gave way to the realization that gospel music's immediate future was with the true believers. The key to big sales would be saturating the Christian marketplace through the Christian bookstores rather than becoming the darling of the pop music world, which is always looking for "the next big thing."

During the 1980s, a shift occurred in the Christian music industry as contemporary Christian music began to dominate the field. Aimed at young people coming of age during the 1980s, it developed along the lines of pop and rock music, copying the sounds from pop radio and fitting Christian lyrics to them. But while rock fed on the rebellion inherent in the teenage years and directed it to a radical lifestyle away from the "norms" of societal expectations, contemporary Christian music led a generation toward being fans of Christianity. The commercial success of contemporary

Christian artists, and the growth in contemporary Christian music, depended on reaching these young Christians who were enthused about their faith.

For contemporary Christian music there were two links to the past: the Jesus revolution and Bill Gaither. In 1980 Gaither and his group began performing concerts "in the round" because audiences of up to 15,000 wanted to see them. Bill Gaither showed the way that gospel acts could have major success on tour within the Christian world.

The year 1981 was a landmark year for American Christianity in general and gospel music in particular. It is the year when two major secular record labels—CBS and MCA—began gospel divisions, when Bob Dylan released his third gospel-influenced album (*Shot of Love*), and former top pop acts Al Green, Richie Furay, Maria Muldaur, and Bonnie Bramlett released gospel albums. On television, Barbara Mandrell featured a special segment on gospel (with contemporary Christian artists) on her weekly NBC show.

In the gospel industry, Christian labels were busy announcing they had signed agreements with major secular labels for distribution, while Word, the label that dominated Christian music, celebrated its 30th birthday. The Imperials were the major group that linked southern gospel with contemporary Christian music, gospel artist Andrae Crouch released an album on Warner Brothers, and the contemporary Christian world received a gold album. *Music Machine* by Candle was revolutionary because it showed the Christian market the tremendous appeal of children's music to the Christian culture, which was filled with young born-again parents wanting to raise their children to accept the Christian message. It was the forerunner for an onslaught of children's albums that Christian labels released in the 1980s.

Singles were a hot issue in gospel music during the early 1980s. Secular record labels had long sent out 45 rpm singles before an album was released—in some cases not even releasing an album until or unless a single was a hit—but gospel radio was accustomed to receiving an entire album and programming whichever cuts it felt appropriate for its audience. Because Christian radio viewed itself as a ministry, the programmers felt they should be allowed to choose the cut on an album they programmed. The record companies, wanting to sell albums, knew that the success of a song (and album) depended on people hearing a single song over and over.

Christian companies sent out singles to focus attention on a particular song on an album and radio stations either had to play the single or refuse the act until the album came along. Since the single airplay charts were coming into their own, the success of a song could be measured and the success in one radio market meant it would probably be successful in other radio markets. The labels, knowing that radio stations often looked to the charts to help make their decisions about which records to program, knew if they got a song on the charts, the chances were much better that radio stations would play it and thus there would be a hit single to spur sales of the album.

In the end, the record companies won—the sheer economic factor alone dictated this path—and singles came to increasingly dominate Christian radio airplay.

The other issue contemporary Christian music had to face was the power of the National Religious Broadcaster's Association, the most powerful group representing religion on the airwaves. For years, the NRB had represented the "preaching and teaching" programs, the nonprofit stations, and the programs headed by a preacher whose main thrust was "spreading the gospel" over the airwaves. But as contemporary Christian music progressed and young listeners attracted to this music wanted radio to play music rather than preaching, the NRB looked dangerously out of step. The dilemma was solved over a period of years as more radio stations programmed a larger portion of their day with music.

The single most important album released in contemporary Christian music during the 1980s was Amy Grant's *Age to Age*, released in 1982, which dominated the Christian music industry that year and achieved gold status within a year after its release. No other Christian album had ever done that; *Alleluia* by the Gaithers and *Music Machine* by Candle both took several years to reach the gold plateau in sales.

That same year. Sandi Patti became the major artist within the Christian world as Amy Grant increasingly headed in the direction of pop music. Although Amy Grant still kept her base of support, she ran into a lot of flack because the Christian audience is very possessive and demanding: they want their artists to show a total commitment to Christian music at all times. Taking Christianity to the secular marketplace is an anathema in the view of many Christians, who hold that it must keep itself separate to remain "pure."

No other singer filled that void in 1982, and the marketing of Amy Grant's *Age to Age* album showed the Christian culture how an album and artist could achieve huge sales through exposure and saturation of the Christian marketplace. All the pieces of the puzzle came together—the puzzle of contemporary Christian music and how it could create a star who sold lots of records and attracted lots of concert-goers but did not dilute the Christian message or compromise Christian music.

The church openly embraced Sandi Patti during the 1980s, when she became the artist most honored within the gospel world. Her concerts (often at large churches) were more like a worship service as she stood on stage, leading the service, accepting that each member of the audience believed what she believed, accepted what she accepted. Sandi Patti did nothing to challenge the faith of her audience; she accepted and encouraged it.

At the end of 1982 contemporary Christian music was dominated by two artists who continued to dominate the field throughout the 1980s. Amy Grant had the hit singles "Sing Your Praise to the Lord" and "El Shaddai" from her *Age to Age* album, while Sandi Patti's hit singles were "We Shall Behold Him" and "How Majestic is Your Name."

Another artist emerged during the early 1980s who had a major impact on contemporary Christian music. Michael W. Smith became a teen idol and one-man boy band for many young Christians through his recordings and concerts. On stage he ran, danced, jumped, paced, and led the band and audience in concert aerobics, pouring his all into a concert until audience excitement was raised to a fever pitch. There were a few older people in his audience—probably because the kids were too young to drive and because the older generation wanted to check out all the hullabaloo their children were raving about—but, for the most part, the concert halls were filled with 13- to 20-year-olds, some of whom remained standing in front of the stage the entire concert, offering up shrieks and screams throughout the whole performance.

His first album, titled simply *Michael W. Smith*, was geared to young people—high energy techno-pop rock 'n' roll. It was a natural extension of Michael, who enjoyed communicating with high school students and had been part of church groups working with them. Now his recordings were another part of his appeal to Christian youth, and they bought them like they'd never bought any other new artist; his first two albums combined to sell almost half a million units.

Smith's audience was mostly church-going, clean-cut, well-scrubbed kids who kept the energy but discarded the rebellion of rock 'n' roll; the result was wholesome rock 'n' roll.

By this point there was a noticeable difference between the early followers of Jesus music and those who followed contemporary Christian music. Many of the early Jesus movement converts came from the counterculture of the 1960s; often they had been involved in drugs and spiritual searches that encompassed eastern religions and philosophical wanderings before they embraced Christianity. Those who emerged as followers of contemporary Christian music came primarily from

church backgrounds; they grew up in Christian homes but found in contemporary Christian music—and the emerging Christian culture—a new life in an old faith. Like those in the Jesus movement, they experienced a spiritual rebirth and were born again, but instead of a radical 180 degree turn in their life, it was often a bend in the road.

Because rock music was part of their growing up years, it was easy for this group to embrace Christian rock, and one of the early groups they embraced was Petra, who were dedicated evangelistic Christians in a rock band.

Petra felt they should aim for the un-Christian, unchurched, diehard rock fan, so they recorded loud and powerful. Feeling their competition was the reigning royalty of rock—REO Speedwagon, Rush, Styx—Petra went after a comparable sound. The Christian bookstores initially did not embrace Christian rock or Petra, but their fourth album, *Never Say Die*, yielded a number one song on Christian radio, "The Coloring Song," which was rather mellow by rock standards but which won them a new audience.

Still, Petra was unable to tour during their early years because of resistance from Christian concert promoters; however, the Christian rock group Servant invited Petra to join them on a national tour, which opened the door for them to become a touring band.

Petra blazed the trail for gospel rock for a number of other acts. Although this group was not the first Christian rock act, they were the first act to sell large numbers of records and have large, successful tours that attracted thousands of kids to Christian concerts.

The years 1976 to 1986 are key to understanding the Christian music industry; during this period contemporary Christian music came of age, defined itself, and became the major force in gospel music. Through its commercial success, it influenced southern gospel and black gospel, leading them to move toward a more contemporary sound. It also made them see a large potential market for those singing gospel and Christian music. This is proven by a simple fact: between 1985 and 1995, the sales of Christian recordings grew by $298 million.

In the late 20th and early 21st centuries, Christian music has proven itself to be a resounding success in the commercial market. This has allowed it to continue to pursue its goals of saving souls and changing lives.

The Christian music industry is both hit driven and star driven, and both gospel and Christian music produced a number of hits and stars from the late 1980s onward. Amy Grant and Sandi Patti were pioneers in the contemporary Christian field, soon joined by Michael W. Smith, Petra, and the Imperials. In the late 1980s, Steven Curtis Chapman began to dominate the field. The musical trends of rap and hip hop saw DC Talk emerge. Hits by Sixpence None the Richer, Jars of Clay, Bob Carlisle, Audio Adrenaline, Third Day, Point of Grace, Newsboys, and others created consumer demand. Although Christian artists are uncomfortable with the idea of stardom, these artists were indeed stars as measured by record sales, concert audiences, radio airplay, and exposure in the Christian media.

One of the most powerful musical trends in both gospel and Christian music was praise and worship—music in the church for the churched. It is music sung to God by believers. Both white and black churches increasingly used contemporary music in their services during the late 1980s and throughout the 1990s until it was difficult to find vibrant, growing churches who sang old hymns.

Another trend was the sale of black gospel to the contemporary Christian music audience. Kirk Franklin, along with BeBe and CeCe Winans, Tramaine Hawkins, Yolanda Adams, and others, proved that gospel music could sell in big numbers. The biggest trailblazer was Kirk Franklin, whose release, *God's Property from Kirk Franklin's Nu Nation*, sold 117,000 units the first week it was released, and, spurred by the hit single, "Stomp," and a video on MTV, landed at number three on *Billboard*'s top album charts. His Tour of Life was successful at selling tickets.

There was also a new kind of music—hip hop—which came out of the African American community. As hip hop came to dominate the tastes of young music lovers, contemporary Christian and gospel, which generally follow secular trends, embraced hip hop as it moved into the Christian world during the 1990s, initially through the success of the group DC Talk.

The emergence of contemporary Christian music was a result of the three major Christian labels recording and marketing this music. Word, Benson, and Sparrow with their spin-off labels such as Myrrh, Dayspring, Greentree, Birdwing, and others as well as distribution agreements with other labels dominated the Christian music industry. Their relationship with Christian bookstores made them trusted gatekeepers, so Christian bookstores felt comfortable stocking contemporary Christian music.

Another factor in the growth of Christian music was the consolidation of Christian bookstores, which led to several chains dominating this field. Corporate offices demanded they stocked what sold—so if it sold, then it was stocked. There was also consolidation of recording labels, usually becoming partners within a much larger organization.

In 1980 The Benson Company was sold to the Zondervan Corporation, a Christian company known for publishing Bibles and its chain of Family Bookstores. In 1992 Word was sold to Thomas Nelson and EMI purchased Sparrow. In 1994 the Music Entertainment Group bought the Benson Music Group, along with Tribute/Diadem. At the end of 1996, Thomas Nelson sold Word to Gaylord Entertainment, which also owned the Grand Ole Opry and the Nashville Network. Gaylord also purchased Blanton/Harrell Entertainment, which managed Amy Grant and Michael W. Smith.

In 1996 Warner Brothers created Warner Alliance, which marketed to the Christian booksellers market, then created Warner Resound, which marketed gospel to the secular market. By 1996 Word used Epic Records and the Sony Music Distribution system to reach the secular market while its own distribution system marketed to Christian bookstores.

In 1997 EMI bought the label Fore-Front, which they added to Sparrow and Star Song to create EMI Christian. In 1997 the Zomba Music Group announced the formation of Provident Music Group by combining Brentwood Music and Reunion; Provident then purchased the Benson Music Group from the Music Entertainment Group.

By the end of 1997, the major players were no longer Word, Benson, and Sparrow, the big three a decade earlier, but EMI Christian, Provident, and Word, which was owned by Gaylord. All were headquartered in Nashville, which became the center for contemporary Christian music. In 2001 Warner Brothers bought Word Records and in 2003 Curb bought 20 percent of Word, so the label became Word/Curb.

The corporations that owned these labels kept the distribution system that serviced Christian bookstores but also allowed the labels to distribute to secular outlets and receive shelf space in mainstream stores such as Wal-Mart, Target, Kmart, Blockbuster, Music-Land, and Sam Goody.

Another factor in the success of gospel and Christian music during the 1990s came from the fact that *Billboard*, the leading trade magazine in the music industry, began to compile its charts based on SoundScan, a computer technology based on bar codes. This reporting of raw numbers without prejudice to genre allowed Christian recordings to appear on pop charts and gain more shelf space in mainstream stores.

Between 1985 and 1995 Christian recordings grew by $298 million, or a 290 percent increase in sales. In 1995 the SoundScan technology began to be used to compile *Billboard*'s religious music charts; the next year, sales of recordings reached $538 million (or a 30 percent increase in one year), placing it sixth in popularity of all music genres, behind rock, country, urban contemporary, pop, and rap, but ahead of classical, jazz, oldies, and new age.

When concert ticket sales and merchandising were added, religious music generated an estimated $750–$900 million in revenue.

Christian music has succeeded in selling recordings because it is music by Christians, for Christians, about Christians and Christianity. Although many claim their intent is to reach the "lost," their commercial success comes by reaching the "found." It is an insular world, distrusting of and distrusted by the secular world. It is a subculture with its own traditions, language, and rules that has succeeded because it has established an alternative world to the mainstream popular culture. This world is filled with Christian media and marketed by Christian organizations. In many ways, a "Christian" is defined by what he or she buys and the purchase of contemporary Christian music is a "proof" of one's Christianity.

In the end, contemporary Christian music, while claiming to serve as a tool for evangelism, is more often a tool for Christian identity. It is a music that serves Christians in a variety of ways, but the most important is that it is part of the unifying force that holds Christians together, sets them apart, and gives them a music that strengthens, consoles, supports, and affirms their faith. It succeeds in the capitalist, open market system when its success is determined and defined by the capitalist, open market system of popular culture—selling recordings, selling tickets to personal appearances by artists, and acceptance by the mass media. Although Christian music wants to define its success in terms of souls saved and individual lives changed, it must incorporate these latter goals with the commercial market.

In the late 20th and early 21st centuries, Christian music has proven itself to be a resounding success in the commercial market. This has allowed it to continue to pursue its goals of saving souls and changing lives. In the future, these last two goals that Christian music sets for itself can be pursued only if it continues to achieve commercial success. Ironically, that commercial success rests on Christian music reaching those whose souls have already been saved and whose lives have already accepted Christianity as a way of life and who demand a music that strengthens, consoles, supports, and affirms that life.

Just as the secular music industry produces stars, so does the gospel music industry. The essential difference is that secular stars view themselves as entertainers with music being the most important thing in their lives while the Christian music stars generally view themselves as ministers with music secondary to their relationship with God. Their role is to convey the gospel message to those who don't believe or encourage those who do believe to keep the faith.

The Christian artist must be sincere, must truly believe what he or she is singing. They may acknowledge the troubles of life, but never doubt the great truth; may sometimes question aspects of the Christian faith but never abandon that faith. The gospel artist is more gospel than artist, a conduit for God's voice in the world, a spiritual salesman, and an example that God is alive and working within an individual's life. A concert performance is not just a show, it is a service too, and the recordings are not just to listen to—they are to be accepted and agreed with.

There are, of course, a wide range of possibilities and diversions within Christian music. There are those who prefer to be Christian entertainers, or entertainers with a Christian message, or entertainers who serve the saints—providing the church with entertainment that celebrates a total acceptance of the faith. There are also those who preach as much as they sing, who witness to the unbeliever, intent on conversion. It would be foolish to state that all motives are totally pure, but at least it must be acknowledged that at the core of all Christian artists is a firm commitment to live a Godly life and have a close relationship with God.

Those outside the Christian industry often don't see this and cast a jaundiced eye at the gospel world, viewing those involved as hypocrites or frauds. But that hypocrisy usually comes from trying to serve both man and God, and the fraud comes when a Christian artist deceives himself. It is more than a music, it is a way of life, and the Christian artist must live it as well as believe it. It is not an easy life, but the Christian artist is driven to use music as a function of the gospel. It is this higher calling that sustains him or her.

Within the world of Christian music there are questions for debate: Is the purpose of Christian music to convert nonbelievers to the faith? Or is it to encourage and support current believers as they live their faith day to day? Is it entertainment for Christians or a ministry to support Christians? Does it matter if the artist or songwriter is a Christian if the song itself delivers a Christian message? And does a Christian singing about loving a husband or wife or even a song addressing social justice or political issues make this a Christian song?

All of these questions are debated in the world of Christian music; indeed, the Christian music world is known for agonizing endlessly over what is or is not Christian. However, when all is said and done, Christian music, like other forms of music, is defined by its audience. If the Christian audience accepts a song as Christian, then it is; if the Christian audience accepts a performer as Christian, then that performer is Christian. The Christian audience is influenced by the gatekeepers of Christian music from Christian bookstore owners and managers to Christian radio stations to leaders in the Christian world such as influential pastors and business leaders.

At its most basic level, contemporary Christian music is popular music with Christian lyrics. If a performer has established himself or herself with the Christian audience, they will probably be given some leeway and their songs that are "marginal"—that don't mention Jesus or God and talk about marital love or other issues—will be accepted as Christian by the Christian audience.

And who is the Christian audience? By and large it is white, and its religious views may be characterized as fundamentalist Christian. "Fundamentalist" covers four major beliefs: (1) belief that Jesus is the son of God; (2) belief that Jesus rose from the dead after dying to forgive the sins of mankind; (3) belief that the Bible is the Word of God and is the means God uses to communicate with people; and (4) belief that the Holy Spirit is the way God and Jesus communicate with believers today. This Holy Spirit is the voice of God received by believers which guides them in their day-to-day life; it is usually soundless and wordless but convinces believers about their life and convinces them to follow a way that is not understood or even accepted by those who believe that the only wisdom is earthly wisdom.

This causes conflicts within the world of Christian music. The Christian audience wants to hear Christian music for religious reasons—to affirm, comfort, and strengthen their faith. Christian artists, on the other hand, sometimes want to challenge their audience to question their faith such as in the realm of social justice, political beliefs, or musically with lyrics that afflict the comforted rather than comfort the afflicted. Although a young audience may sometimes be willing to accept a challenge to their belief if the music is good, in general the Christian audience as a whole does not want their faith questioned; in fact, they feel the primary purpose of Christian music is to affirm their faith, not challenge or question it.

Don Cusic

For Further Reading

Baker, Paul. *Contemporary Christian Music: Where It Came from, What It Is, Where It's Going.* Westchester, Ill.: Crossway, 1985.

Brothers, Jeffrey Lee. *CCM Magazine Hot Hits: Adult Contemporary Charts 1978–2001.* Bloomington, Ind.: 1stBooks Library, 2003.

Cusic, Don. *The Sound of Light: A History of Gospel and Christian Music.* New York: Hal Leonard, 2002.

Ellwood, Robert S. Jr. *One Way: The Jesus Movement and Its Meaning.* Englewood Cliffs, N.J.: Prentice-Hall, 1973.

Enroth, Ronald M., Edward E. Ericson, Jr., and C. Breckinridge Peters. *The Jesus People: Old-Time Religion in the Age of Aquarius.* Grand Rapids, Mich.: Eerdmans, 1972.

Gilmour, Michael J., ed. *Call Me the Seeker: Listening to Religion in Popular Music.* New York: Continuum, 2005.

Granger, Thom, ed. *CCM Presents the 100 Greatest Albums in Christian Music.* Eugene, Ore.: Harvest House, 2001.

Haynes, Michael K. *The God of Rock: A Christian Perspective of Rock Music.* Lindale, Tex.: Priority, 1982.

Henderson, Stewart. *Greenbelt—Since the Beginning.* Ipswich, U.K.: Ancient House Press, 1983.

Howard, Jay R., and John M. Streck. *Apostles of Rock: The Splintered World of Contemporary Christian Music.* Lexington: The University Press of Kentucky 1999.

Landy, Elliott. *Woodstock Vision: The Spirit of a Generation.* New York: Landyvision, 1996.

Larson, Bob. *Rock and Roll: The Devil's Diversion.* McCook, Neb.: Larson, 1967.

Martin, Linda, and Kerry Segrave. *Anti-Rock: The Opposition to Rock 'n' Roll.* Hamden, Conn.: Archon Books, 1988.

Miller, Steve. *The Contemporary Christian Music Debate: Worldly Compromise or Agent of Change.* Wheaton, Ill.: Tyndale House Publishers, Inc. 1993.

Seay, Davin, and Mary Neely. *Stairway to Heaven.* New York: Ballantine, 1986.

Styll, John W., ed. *The Heart of the Matter: The Best of CCM Interviews, Volume 1.* Nashville, Tenn.,: Star Song, 1991.

Thompson, John J. *Raised by Wolves: The Story of Christian Rock and Roll.* Toronto, Ontario: ECW Press, 2000.

COOMES, TOMMY

Tommy Coomes (b. May 19, 1946) was a founding member of Love Song, the most influential early band in Jesus music; after the group disbanded in 1974, Coomes joined another group, Wing and a Prayer, then became an executive and producer for Maranatha Music where he led the trend toward praise and worship music with a series of albums released by Maranatha. He is known as the "father of modern praise and worship music."

The Jesus movement's focus was on evangelism, but as that movement evolved into contemporary Christian music—and the believers matured—the focus shifted to worship music, geared for a new, contemporary church whose members were often led by a rock band singing songs to God and Jesus. The songs are known for being relatively simple and easily remembered, although as praise and worship music progressed congregants found themselves singing rock and pop songs rather than praise songs that were patterned on the old hymns but updated musically. *See also* Love Song

Don Cusic

Discography

Love Is the Key (Maranatha, 1981)

CREED

Scott Stapp, vocals
Mark Tremonti, guitar
Scott Philips, drums
Brian Marshall, bass (until 2001)

Although Creed has never claimed to be a Christian band—and in fact denies a connection to any religious view—the audience for contemporary Christian music accepted them as a Christian band because they found a spiritual message in their lyrics, which often questioned faith and spiritual messages.

The group was formed in 1995 in Tallahassee, Florida, where lead singer Scott Stapp studied pre-law. Stapp grew up in a strict Pentecostal household (his father was a preacher) and was forbidden to listen to rock music; after a brief stint at a Bible college he moved to Tallahassee and enrolled at Florida State University, where he discovered Jim Morrison and the Doors. He began writing songs with guitarist Mark Tremonti; the two added bassist Brian Marshall and drummer Scott Phillips and began performing in northern Florida as Naked Toddler, influenced by bands such as Led Zeppelin, King's X, Bad Company, and Pearl Jam. They changed their name to Creed at the suggestion of bassist Brian Marshall, whose former band was Mattox Creed.

The group released its first album, *My Own Prison*, in 1997; the custom album cost only $6,000 to produce and was distributed to radio stations in Florida. It came to the attention of several major labels, who passed on the band, before Diana Meltzer with New York-based Wind-Up Records, which had major label distribution through BMG, signed the act. The label remixed the album and rereleased it and it caught on quickly with fans, selling over five million units. Four of the songs on that album, "My Own Prison," "Torn," "What's This Life For," and "One," reached the top of

Billboard's rock chart. Their success caused *Billboard* to name the group "Rock Artist of the Year" in 1998.

Their second album, *Human Clay*, debuted at number one on *Billboard*'s pop album chart and the single "Higher" was a hit on both rock and pop radio. During the tour to support the second album, bassist Brian Marshall criticized Pearl Jam and, because of the uproar, left the band. He was replaced as touring bassist by Brett Hestla, although guitarist Mark Tremonti doubled on bass for their third album, *Weathered*, which was released in 2001. That album sold more than six million copies.

Creed disbanded in June 2004, and lead singer Scott Stapp recorded a solo album while the other band members (including bassist Brian Marshall) formed Alter Bridge with Myles Kennedy.

The question of who or what is a Christian band has perplexed the Christian community. Is it a band that performs overtly Christian songs or can it be a band made up of Christians who perform songs that cover a wide variety of topics and issues? Ultimately, the audience decides whether or not a band is a Christian band, and the Christian audience latched onto Creed because their songs spoke to young Christians, even though Creed did not perform overtly Christian songs. The secular rock audience also related to Creed's songs, and the group reached both Christians and non-Christians, selling more than 25 million albums of their first three releases.

Don Cusic

For Further Reading

Alfonso, Barry. *The Billboard Guide to Contemporary Christian Music*. New York: Billboard Books/Watson-Guptill, 2002.

Powell, Mark Allen. *Encyclopedia of Contemporary Christian Music*. Peabody, Mass.: Hendrickson Publishers, Inc., 2002.

Discography

My Own Prison (1997)

Human Clay (1999)

Weathered (2001)

Greatest Hits (2004)

CROUCH, ANDRAE, AND THE DISCIPLES

Andrae Crouch, vocals and keyboard
Bili Thedford, vocals
Sherman Andrus, vocals (until 1971)
Ruben Fernandez, vocals (until 1971)
Perry Morgan, vocals (until 1971)
Sandra Crouch, vocals (since 1971)
Tramaine Davis, vocals (1971–1972)
Bill Maxwell, drums (since 1972)
Danniebell Hall, vocals (since 1973)
Fletch Wiley, trumpet (1973–1976)
Bea Carr, vocals (1976–1978)
Jimmie Davis, guitar (1976–1978)
Mike Escalante, keyboards (1976–1978)
James Felix, bass (1976–1978)

Andrae Crouch (b. July 1, 1942, in Los Angeles) is one of the most important artists in the history of contemporary Christian music. Crouch combined the sounds of black gospel and rhythm and blues with pop and rock music to create some of the most influential albums in early contemporary Christian music. He became the first African American to attract a large white following in early

CCM, which was dominated by a folk/pop sound and 1960s rock.

The son of Benjamin and Catherine Crouch, who owned a dry cleaning business in Los Angeles, Crouch's father preached in various churches and, according to Andrae, when he was 11 his father preached at a church in Val Verde, California and invited him to play the piano to accompany the choir on the hymn "What a Friend We Have in Jesus." Crouch accompanied the choir although he claimed he'd never played piano previously.

In high school Crouch formed the COGICS, named for Church of God in Christ Singers, with Billy Preston. He attended Valley Junior College and Life Bible College in Los Angeles and worked with recovering drug addicts but continued to pursue music. In the mid-1960s he formed the Disciples with his twin sister, Sandra (who had been a member of Janis Joplin's Full Tilt Boogie Band), Perry Morgan, and Bili Thedford, and in 1968 signed with Light Records, a label formed by Ralph Carmichael and released his first album *Take the Message Everywhere*.

Crouch is a prolific songwriter who began composing songs when he was 14. Among his major compositions are "Through It All," "Soon and Very Soon," "My Tribute," and "I've Got Confidence," which was recorded by Elvis Presley.

Andrae Crouch and the Disciples were the first contemporary Christian group to sell a million albums, the first to play Carnegie Hall and Royal Albert Hall, and the first to perform on "Saturday Night Live" and "The Tonight Show" starring Johnny Carson. They toured as an opening act for Santana and headlined major concerts until 1978, when they officially disbanded.

Crouch continued to record solo albums and write songs; his songs have been recorded by Bob Dylan, Elton John, Barbara Mandrell, Little Richard, Elvis Presley, and Paul Simon. Crouch worked with Quincy Jones on the music for the movie *The Color Purple* and performed and cowrote "Maybe God Is Trying to Tell You Something" on the soundtrack. Crouch also arranged the choir segments on that soundtrack.

Crouch suffered public embarrassment in 1982 when he was arrested for possession of cocaine; traces of the drug were found in a pipe in the pocket of his sweatsuit after a traffic stop. Crouch insisted the pipe had been used by a friend and he had found the pipe in his car and was driving to confront his friend with this. However, the arrest caused Crouch to shun the public spotlight for a decade.

Andrae Crouch displays his two Grammys backstage at the 37th annual Grammy Awards on March 1, 1995, at the Shrine Auditorium in Los Angeles. (AP Photo/Kevork Djansezian)

In the early 1990s both his mother and father died of cancer and his brother also died of cancer. Crouch became senior pastor at Christ Memorial Church in Pacoima, California, where his father had formerly been pastor. He moved out of his mansion, moved into his parents' former two bedroom home in the neighborhood surrounding the church, refused a salary (he lived off the royalties from his music), and pastored the 1,000 member congregation with his sister, Sandra, who became assistant pastor in 1998. He changed the name of the church to the New Christ Memorial Church and continues as pastor there.

In 1998 Andrae Crouch was inducted into the Gospel Music Hall of Fame. He returned to the recording studio and formed his own label, Slave, in 2002.

Don Cusic

Discography

Andrae Crouch and the Disciples

Take the Message Everywhere (1968)

Keep on Singing (1971)

Soulfully (1972)

Live at Carnegie Hall (1973)

Take Me Back (1974)

This Is Another Day (1976)

Live in London (1978)

Andrae Crouch

Just Andrae (1973)

I'll Be Thinking of You (1979)

Don't Give Up (1981)

More of the Best (1981)

Finally (1982)

No Time to Lose (1984)

Autograph (1986)

Mercy (1994)

Pray (1997)

The Gift of Christmas (2000)

The Best of Andrae (1974)

Vol. I: The Classics (1991)

Vol. II: We Sing Praises (1991)

Vol. III: The Contemporary Man (1991)

The Light Years (1995)

Gospel Music Hall of Fame (1999)

Legends of Gospel (2002)

Kings of Gospel (2003)

He's Everywhere (2004)

Gospel Music Association Dove Awards

1977	Soul/Black Gospel Album: *This Is Another Day* (Producer: Bill Maxwell; Label: Light)
1978	Cover Photo or Cover Art: Robert August for *Live in London* by Andrae Crouch and the Disciples
1978	Soul/Black Gospel Album: *Live in London* (Producers: Bill Maxwell and Andrae Crouch; Label: Light)
1985	Contemporary Gospel Album: *No Time to Lose* (Producer: Bill Maxwell; Label: Light)
1993	Traditional Gospel Album: *With All of My Heart* by Sandra Crouch and Friends (Producers: Sandra Crouch and

Andrae Crouch; Label:
Sparrow)

1997 Choral Collection Album: *My Tribute—Celebrating the Songs of Andrae Crouch* (Producers: Dale Mathews and John DeVries; Publisher: Brentwood Music)

1997 Contemporary Gospel Recorded Song: "Take Me Back" Written by Andrae Crouch; recorded by CeCe Winans on the album *Tribute—the Songs of Andrae Crouch*; Label: Warner Alliance

1997 Special Event Album: *Tribute—the Songs of Andrae Crouch* by CeCe Winans, Michael W. Smith, Twila Paris, Bryan Duncan, Wayne Watson, the Winans, Clay Crosse, Take 6, the Brooklyn Tabernacle Choir, First Call, Andrae Crouch and the All Star Choir (Producers: Norman Miller and Neal Joseph; Label: Warner Alliance)

1998 Contemporary Gospel Album: *Pray* by Andrae Crouch (Producers: Andrae Crouch and Scott V. Smith; Label: Qwest/Warner Brothers)

2007 Traditional Gospel Album of the Year: *Mighty Wind* (Producers: Andrae Crouch and Luther "Mano" Hanes; Label: Verity Records)

2007 Traditional Gospel Recorded Song of the Year: "Can't Nobody Do Me Like Jesus" by Andrea Crouch; on album *Blur the Lines*; Artist: The Crabb Family.

Grammy Awards

1975 18th Grammy Awards: Best Soul Gospel Performance: Andrae Crouch and the Disciples: "Take Me Back"

1979 22nd Grammy Awards: Best Soul Gospel Performance, Contemporary: Andrae Crouch: "I'll Be Thinking of You"

1980 23rd Grammy Awards: Best Gospel Performance, Contemporary or Inspirational: Reba Rambo, Dony McGuire, B. J. Thomas, Andrae Crouch, Walter Hawkins, Tremaine Hawkins, Cynthia Clawson, the Archers: *The Lord's Prayer*

1981 24th Grammy Awards: Best Soul Gospel Performance, Contemporary: Andrae Crouch: "Don't Give Up"

1984 27th Grammy Awards: Best Soul Gospel Performance, Male: Andrae Crouch: "Always Remember"

1994 37th Grammy Awards: Best Pop/Contemporary Gospel Album: *Mercy* by Andrae Crouch

1996 39th Grammy Awards: Best Pop/Contemporary Gospel Album: *Tribute—The Songs of Andrae Crouch* by Various Artists; Producers: Neal Joseph and Norman Miller

For Further Reading

Crouch, Andrae, with Nina Bell. *Through It All*. Waco, Tex.: Word, 1974

Cusic, Don. *The Sound of Light: A History of Gospel and Christian Music.* New York: Hal Leonard, 2002.

McNeil, W. K., ed. *Encyclopedia of American Gospel Music.* New York: Routledge, 2005.

Powell, Mark Allen. *Encyclopedia of Contemporary Christian Music.* Peabody, Mass.: Hendrickson Publishers, Inc., 2002.

CUA, RICK

Rick Cua was best known as the bass player for the southern rock group the Outlaws before he left that group and devoted his career to contemporary Christian music.

Rick Cua (b. March 12, 1952, in Stockton, California) has a strong Italian heritage that included music at an early age; his father was a guitar teacher, and there was always music in the house. From his first instrument, the accordion, Cua moved on to play piano, trumpet, clarinet, and guitar. Eventually his instrument of choice became the bass, and by the age of 14 he was a welcome addition to bands playing the Syracuse, New York, music circuit.

Cua's first bands were garage versions of later, more popular area groups, including Those Guys, the Campus Walkers, and CRAC, an acronym made up from the band member's initials. The bands played everything from the Beatles to the Motown hits; later Cua became interested in jazz. After years of looking for a recording deal, Cua accepted that his career might not go that route so he continued working locally. It was at this point that he received a call from a former road manager asking if he would like to audition for the southern rock band the Outlaws, who were looking for a bass player. Cua flew to Tampa, played five songs with the band, and flew home. When he arrived back at his house he checked his messages and heard that he had been hired and needed to be in Tampa the following Monday. That was in 1980, and he remained with the band until 1983.

While with the Outlaws he was part of their mega-hit "Ghost Riders in the Sky" and recorded two gold albums with them, *Ghost Riders* and *Los Hombres Malo*. Toward the end of his tenure with the Outlaws, Cua recorded his first Christian music album. After leaving the band, Cua entered the realm of Christian music full time, taking his rock 'n' roll attitude with him. His early Christian music was heavy rock 'n' roll, making him one of the earlier proponents of that type of music in the Christian community. His first album, *Koo-Ah*, resulted in his first number one single, "You Can Still Rock and Roll."

Being a leader in the movement was not without its detractors; Cua remembers people picketing his band's shows and people saying they were praying for him because they thought the music he sang was not really Christian. Cua signed with Reunion Records in 1988, and his music took on a more pop sound. In 1992 Cua formed his own label, UCA Records, and in 1998 Cua took an executive position as vice president of the creative department at EMI Christian Music Publishing, remaining there until 2003. He then formed Rick Cua Entertainment, an umbrella company with interests in managing artists, music publishing, and film and TV licensing. Included in that company is All for the King Music, which has allowed him to have an impact in the praise and worship segment of Christian music.

Cua works with churches, offering coaching and advice to music ministers and other related positions through workshops and original worship music. Cua is an ordained minister who released his twelfth album in 2007, celebrating 25 years in Christian music. He has had six number one songs. Cua has been married to his childhood sweetheart, Diane, since 1970.

James Elliott

For Further Reading

Alfonso, Barry. *The Billboard Guide to Contemporary Christian Music*. New York: Billboard Books/Watson-Guptill, 2002.

Powell, Mark Allen. *Encyclopedia of Contemporary Christian Music*. Peabody, Mass.: Hendrickson Publishers, Inc., 2002.

CURB, MIKE

Mike Curb (b. December 24, 1944, in Savannah, Georgia) is the founder and owner of Curb Records, whose roster of Christian acts includes Natalie Grant, Selah, Fernando Ortego, and Michael English. Curb's involvement with contemporary Christian music goes back to when he was president of MGM Records in the early 1970s. During that period he signed the 2nd Chapter of Acts, and promoted their single "Jesus Is." Curb also signed Larry Norman, who released two albums, one on MGM (*Only Visiting This Planet*) and one on Verve, *In the Garden*.

Later, Curb and Pat Boone formed Lamb and Lion Records and that label signed DeGarmo and Key, Dan Peek, and the Boone Girls. Curb also signed Chris Christian as a member of the group Cotton, Lloyd and Christian through a production agreement.

Curb's background in gospel music goes back to his high school years when he played piano and sang in the choir of the First Baptist Church in Los Angeles. Curb formed the original Mike Curb Congregation from members of that choir and landed a spot on "The Glen Campbell Goodtime Hour" during the early 1970s; the group did an inspirational song on each nationally televised show and also recorded several gospel albums for Word Records.

In 1977 Curb's agreement with Warner Brothers Records led to the release of "You Light Up My Life" by Debby Boone, which some consider to be the first contemporary Christian hit single; the song stayed on the *Billboard* hot 100 chart for 10 weeks and, according to *Billboard* chart activity based on radio airplay, was the most popular song of the 1970s. Curb later released that song on LeAnn Rimes in 1996 and the album by that name became the first contemporary Christian album to debut simultaneously at number one on the *Billboard* contemporary Christian chart, the *Billboard* country chart and the *Billboard* hot 100 chart.

During the 1990s Curb Records began signing and promoting Christian acts for the Christian market. Among the acts they signed were Michael English, Patty Cabrera, Jonathan Pierce, Fernando Ortega, Nicol Sponberg, White Heart, Nate Sallie, Plumb, Natalie Grant, and Selah. In 2005 Curb entered into an agreement with INO

Records to promote "I Can Only Imagine" by MercyMe and led the effort that resulted in that song becoming a major pop hit.

In 2004 Curb Records purchased a partnership in Word Records from Warner Brothers and Mike Curb was named chairman of the board for Word/Curb, which was named the Top Christian Imprint by *Billboard* for 2006.

Don Cusic

D

DANIEL AMOS

Terry Taylor, guitar, vocals
Jerry Chamberlain, guitar, vocals
(until 1983, 1993–2001)
Marty Dieckmeyer, bass (until 1981)
Steve Baxter, guitar, vocals (until 1976)
Mark Cook, keyboard, vocals
(1977–1981)
Ed McTaggard, drums (from 1976)
Alex MacDougall, percussion (1981)
Tim Chandler, bass (until 1987)
Greg Flesch, guitar (from 1986)
Rob Watson, keyboard (1983–1987)

Daniel Amos has been one of the premier contemporary Christian music alternative rock bands with penetrating, visionary songs and a belief that Christian music can be "art." Although they have never been commercially successful—or even a consistent touring group—Daniel Amos has left their mark on the Christian industry as an influence for later bands who came after them.

Terry Taylor grew up in the San Jose area and while a sophomore at Los Gatos High School formed a rock band, the Scarlet Staircase, then joined the Cardboard Scheme with Tim Warner. In 1967 members of that group formed Copperplate Window; after Taylor graduated in 1969 he joined the band Pecos Bill, also known as Down Home. In 1971 Taylor and Warner both became Christians and formed an acoustic trio, Good Shepherd. Warner left that group and Taylor formed Jubal's Last Stand with Steve Baxter, Kenny Paxton, and Chuck Starnes, and that group opened for Calvary Chapel's Love Song, whose members encouraged them to move to Costa Mesa and become part of Calvary Chapel.

Jubal's Last Stand evolved into Daniel Amos, taking that name from two Old Testament prophets, because another Calvary Chapel group was named Jubal (that group later became Gentle Faith).

Terry Taylor has been the foundation of the revolving ensemble. In 1974 he and Steve Baxter from Jubal's Last Stand, along with Jerry Chamberlain and Marty Dieckmeyer joined to form Daniel Amos; in 1975 Baxter left the group but Mark Cook and Ed McTaggert joined. Like many of the earliest contemporary Christian music groups, they were mostly an acoustic ensemble.

In 1976 the group signed with the Calvary Chapel affiliated label

Maranatha and released their first album, *Daniel Amos*, which was primarily an acoustic album. Heavily influenced by the Eagles, they sounded similar to that popular L.A. country/rock group. Like many in the Jesus movement, their music was rooted in the urban folk revival and they were heavily influenced by the folk music of the 1960s. After that initial disc, Daniel Amos signed with the Solid Rock label, owned by Larry Norman, and recorded *Horrendous Disc* in 1978, which showed the band evolving into a rock act. Because of problems with their contract, this album was not released until 1981.

A series of concept albums followed: *Alarma!*, then *Doppelganger* as the group toured with a stage show that was theater rock; but the Christian audiences were not comfortable with a band that challenged rather than sweetly supported their faith.

For their next album, *Vox Humana*, Jerry Chamberlain left the group and keyboardist Rob Watson provided synthesizers, which was certainly the trend in 1980s music.

Daniel Amos are the angry young men of Christian music; their songs are challenging both lyrically and musically and their albums do not provide an easy listening experience. Still, they paved the way for other Christian groups who are disturbed by the complacency and comfort level of American Christianity and seek to use their musical platform to afflict the comfortable rather than comfort the afflicted.

Critics loved Daniel Amos, and many of their most devoted fans consider this group along with the Seventy Sevens to be the greatest Christian rock bands of all time.

Musically, they have followed a meandering path, from acoustic based to rock to synthesizer laden and on to new wave and punk, although the term "alternative" seems to fit them best. Their albums defy categorization, and they are a marketing department's nightmare because they fit into no single category. They have recorded for several different labels and finally formed their own labels, Brainstorm and Stunt, for their albums.

In addition to their music being hard to categorize, the group has used the name DA for some albums and the Swirling Eddies, made up of Daniel Amos members Terry Taylor, Jerry Chamberlain, Rob Watson, Tim Chandler, and Greg Flesch are on other works. In addition to the Swirling Eddies, Terry Taylor has recorded as a solo artist and has been a member of the groups the Lost Dogs and the Rap'-sures. Other members of Daniel Amos have been part of other groups.

Don Cusic

For Further Reading

Alfonso, Barry. *The Billboard Guide to Contemporary Christian Music*. New York: Billboard Books/Watson-Guptill, 2002.

Powell, Mark Allen. *Encyclopedia of Contemporary Christian Music*. Peabody, Mass.: Hendrickson Publishers, Inc., 2002.

Discography

Daniel Amos (1976)

Shotgun Angel (1977)

Horrendous Disc (1981)

Alarma! (1981)

Doppleganger (1983)

Vox Humana (1984)

Fearful Symmetry (1986)

The Revelation (1987)

Darn Floor, Big Bite (1987)

Live Bootleg '82 (1990)

Kalhoun (1991)

Motorcycle (1993)

Bibleland (1994)

Preachers from Outer Space (1994)

Live at the Anaheim Center, Easter Weekend 1978 (1995)

Songs of the Heart (1995)

Our Personal Favorite World Famous Hits (1998)

The Alarma Chronicles Book Set (2000)

Live at Cornerstone (2000)

Mr. Buechner's Dream (2001)

DAVID CROWDER BAND

David Crowder, vocals, guitar
Jack Parker, guitar, piano
Mike Dodson, bass (since 2000)
Jeremy Bush, drums, percussion
Mike Hogan, violin
Mark Waldrop, guitar (since 2007)
Jason Solley, guitar, vocals
(1996–2006)
Taylor Johnson, guitar (2006–2007)
Kevin Morris, bass (1996–2000)

The David Crowder Band was formed as an outreach of a church. David Crowder and Chris Seay founded the University Baptist Church in Waco, Texas, when they realized that about half the students at Baylor University— a Christian university—did not attend church. Crowder led worship in the fledgling church, which led to him forming a band and writing songs. Their debut albums, *Pour over Me* and *All I Can Say*, came from these church worship times. As their reputation spread, the David Crowder Band was invited to perform at Christian festivals and other events, which led to their signing with sixstepsrecords, a division of Sparrow. Although the band tours nationally, they usually return to University Baptist Church for Sunday morning worship.

The David Crowder Band performed a track on the album *Music Inspired by the Chronicles of Narnia*, which won a Dove Award, and they recorded the theme for "Walk in the Word," a radio program hosted by Dr. James Mac-Donald that is an outreach of Harvest Bible Chapel in Rolling Meadows, Illinois.

The group won three Dove Awards in 2006: their album *A Collision* won in the "Rock/Contemporary Album of the Year" category; their song "Here is Our King" won in the "Rock/Contemporary Recorded Song of the Year" category and they participated in the album *Music Inspired by the Chronicles of Narnia: The Lion, the Witch, and the Wardrobe*, which won a Dove for "Special Event Album of the Year." In 2008 their song "Everything Glorious" won a Dove for "Rock/Contemporary Recorded Song of the Year" and their album *Remedy* won the Dove for "Worship Album of the Year."

Don Cusic

For Further Reading

Crowder, David. *Praise Habit: Finding God in Sunsets and Sushi*. Colorado Springs, Colo.: NavPress, 2005.

Crowder, David, and Mike Hogan. *Everybody Wants to Go to Heaven but Nobody Wants to Die (or, The Eschatology of Bluegrass)*. Orlando, Fla.: Relevant Books, 2006.

DC TALK

Toby McKeehan
Michael Tait
Kevin "Max" Smith

DC Talk was the first contemporary Christian group to successful present rap and hip hop to the contemporary Christian audience; in doing so, they reinvented Christian music by infusing the major trend in popular music into the genre.

Toby McKeehan and Michael Tait are both from the Washington, D.C., area; hence "DC Talk." They met and formed a group in 1988 with Kevin "Max" Smith while attending Liberty University in Virginia (founded by evangelist Jerry Falwell). They called themselves One Way Crew before settling on DC Talk (which a publicist later said meant "Decent Christian Talk"). They recorded a two-song demo, "Christian Rhymes and Rhythm," and sold it door to door.

They were signed to Forefront Records and relocated to Nashville where they recorded their first album in 1989. They toured with Michael W. Smith after their second album was released and appeared on "The Arsenio Hall Show." They covered Larry Norman's "I Wish We'd All Been Ready" and the Doobie Brothers "Jesus Is Just Alright" and composed others like "Jesus Freak." Within a few years they were the most popular Christian act on the planet, a result of breaking new ground in contemporary Christian music, which had previously shunned rap and hip hop.

As their career progressed, DC Talk increasingly became more musical, incorporating singing into their recordings. With their third album, *Free at Last*, they came into their own; they toured with Audio Adrenaline and their album had six chart singles, sold double platinum, and won a Grammy. Their recording of "My Deliverer" was on the *Prince of Egypt* soundtrack (1998) and their cover of Norman Greenbaum's "Spirit in the Sky" was on the soundtrack to the TV movie *Jesus* (2000).

The group was a mixed race group (Tait is African American) breaking more new ground in CCM. McKeehan cofounded a foundation, E.R.A.C.E. (Eliminating Racism and Creating Equality). Although the group never

The group DC Talk led an upsurge in Christian music with their single "Jesus Freak." From left to right are Kevin Max Smith, Toby McKeehan, and Michael Tait. (AP Photo/HO)

officially broke up, the three members increasingly pursued solo ventures in the 21 century. In 2001 each released a solo album: *Empty* by Tait, *Stereotype Be* from Smith, and *Momentum* from McKeehan. McKeehan cofounded Gotee Records and records as a member of the Gotee Brothers.

Don Cusic

Discography

DC Talk (1989)

Nu Thang (1990)

Free at Last (1992)

Jesus Freak (1995)

Welcome to the Freak Show: Live in Concert (1997)

Supernatural (1998)

Intermission: The Greatest Hits (2000)

Solo (EP) (2001)

Gospel Music Association Dove Awards

1991   Rap/Hip Hop Album: *Nu Thang* by DC Talk (Producers: Toby McKeehan, Mark Heimermann and T. C.; Label: YO! ForeFront)

1992   Long Form Music Video: "Rap, Rock and Soul" by DC Talk; Director and Producer: Deaton-Flanigen; Label: Forefront

1992   Rap/Hip Hop Recorded Song: "I Love Rap Music" Writers: Toby McKeehan and Jackie Gore; Recorded by DC Talk; Label: YO! Forefront

1993   Rap/Hip Hop Recorded Song: "Can I Get a Witness?" Written by: Toby McKeehan; Recorded by DC Talk; Label: YO! ForeFront

1994   Rap/Hip Hop Recorded Song: "Socially Acceptable" Written by Toby McKeehan and Mark Heimermann; Recorded by DC Talk; Label: ForeFront

1994   Rock Recorded Song: "Jesus Is Just Alright" Written by Arthur Reynolds; Recorded by DC Talk; Label: ForeFront

1995   Rap/Hip Hop Recorded Song: "Luv Is a Verb" Written by Toby McKeehan, Mark Heimermann, George Cocchini; Recorded by DC Talk; Label: ForeFront

1996   Artist of the Year

1996   Rock Recorded Song: "Jesus Freak" Written by Toby McKeehan, Mark Heimermann; Recorded by DC Talk; Label: ForeFront

1996   Song of the Year: "Jesus Freak" Written by Mark Heimermann and Toby McKeehan; Publishers: Fun Attic Music ASCAP; Mupin the Mix Music, BMI

1997   Pop/Contemporary Recorded Song: "Between You and Me" Written by Toby McKeehan, Mark Heimermann; Recorded by DC Talk; Label: ForeFront

1997   Rock Album: *Jesus Freak* by DC Talk (Producers: Toby McKeehan, Mark Heimermann, and John Painter; Label: ForeFront)

1997   Rock Recorded Song: "Like It, Love It, Need It" Written by Toby McKeehan, Mark Heimermann, Kevin Smith, David Soldi, Jason Barrett; Recorded by DC Talk; Label: ForeFront

1998   Short Form Music Video: "Colored People" by DC Talk; Producer and Director: Mars Media and Lawrence Carroll; Label: ForeFront/Virgin

1999   Special Event Album: *Exodus* by DC Talk, Jars of Clay, Sixpence None the Richer, Cindy Morgan, Chris Rice, the Katinas, Third Day, Crystal Lewis, and Michael W. Smith (Producer: Michael W. Smith; Label: Rocketown Records)

2000   Long Form Music Video: *The Supernatural Experience* by DC Talk; Producers and Directors: Eric Welch, Dan Pitts and Eric Welch; Label: ForeFront

2001   Modern Rock/Alternative Recorded Song: "Dive" Written by Toby McKeehan, Michael Tait, Kevin Max and Mark Heimermann; Recorded by DC Talk; Label: Forefront Records

Grammy Awards

1993   36th Grammy Awards: Best Rock Gospel Album: *Free at Last*

1996   39th Grammy Awards: Best Rock Gospel Album: *Jesus Freak*

1997   40th Grammy Awards: Best Rock Gospel Album: *Welcome*

to the Freak Show: DC Talk Live in Concert

2001   44th Grammy Awards: Best Rock Gospel Album: *Solo*

For Further Reading

Alfonso, Barry. *The Billboard Guide to Contemporary Christian Music*. New York: Billboard Books/Watson-Guptill, 2002.

Cusic, Don. *The Sound of Light: A History of Gospel and Christian Music*. New York: Hal Leonard, 2002.

McNeil, W. K., ed. *Encyclopedia of American Gospel Music*. New York: Routledge, 2005.

Powell, Mark Allen. *Encyclopedia of Contemporary Christian Music*. Peabody, Mass.: Hendrickson Publishers, Inc., 2002.

DEGARMO AND KEY

DeGarmo and Key were pioneers in the world of Christian rock, but their early years were years of frustration with the lack of support from Christian radio and the church and the lack of professionalism in Christian music. However, the duo endured and prevailed; by the time they disbanded in 1995 they had an impressive list of achievements and were recognized as one of the groups who laid the groundwork for the explosion of contemporary Christian rock in the 1980s.

The group played power pop and were usually joined by Tommy Cathey on bass and Greg Morrow on drums. Part of their frustration stemmed from the fact that they came from Memphis, influenced by Elvis and the blues, and the early Christian music came out of Southern California, where there was a built-in support structure of coffee-houses, churches, and a Christian community tuned into pop and rock music. Memphis at that time was in the beginning of a decline in terms of the music industry; Stax Records folded in the mid-1970s, Elvis died in 1977, and the Memphis musicians increasingly moved to Nashville.

Eddie DeGarmo and Dana Key are lifelong friends who grew up together in Memphis (near Graceland) and formed their first band, the Sound Corporation, in the sixth grade. The two, who claim to be descendants of Davy Crockett (DeGarmo) and Francis Scott Key (Key) joined a band in high school, Globe, that signed with Hi/London Records in 1972; however, earlier that year DeGarmo answered an altar call at a Dallas Holm concert and became a Christian. The next day he led his best friend, Key, to Christ. Since both had become Christians they left Globe; instead, they put together a three-piece band, the Christian Band, opened a storefront coffeehouse, and began working for Youth for Christ, which loaned them the money to record a demo.

DeGarmo played keyboards and Key was the lead singer and guitarist; they changed the name of their group to DeGarmo and Key and signed with Pat Boone's record label, Lamb and Lion. Their debut album, *This Time Thru*, was released in 1977, followed by four more albums on Lamb and Lion before they signed with PowerDiscs and released eight albums for that label, beginning with *Mission of Mercy* in 1983.

They continued to record as a duo until the 1990s, but each produced several solo albums, an indication the group had reached the point where it had passed its prime. By the mid-1990s they had been nominated a number of times for Grammys and Dove Awards but had not won any; they were the first Christian group to have a video on MTV but their *Six, Six, Six* video was pulled because it was deemed too violent. Later, the duo edited the video and it went into MTV rotation. They pioneered a marketing technique of selling two cassettes for the price of one, encouraging those who bought the album to give the extra cassette to an unsaved friend.

They backed Amy Grant on her first major concert tour and were on her first two *In Concert* albums; their duet with Amy, "Nobody Loves Me," was a hit on Christian radio. As their career progressed, DeGarmo and Key adapted a militant Christian message, going so far as to dress as soldiers for a magazine cover story.

After the group disbanded, Dana Key became an executive with Ardent Records, in Memphis and then a pastor of a Memphis church; Eddie DeGarmo became a key executive in the Christian music industry in Nashville and was one of the founders of ForeFront Records then a key executive with EMI Music Publishing.

In spring 2007 Dana Key and Eddie DeGarmo received the ASCAP Vision Award; that fall they reunited for several concerts, one of which was held after the Gospel Music Association Dove Awards.

Don Cusic

Discography

This Time Thru (1977)

Straight On (1978)

This Ain't Hollywood (1980)

No Turning Back/Live (1982)

Mission of Mercy (1983)

Communication (1984)

Commander Sozo and the Charge of the Light Brigade (1985)

Street Light (1986)

Street Rock (1987)

DandK (1987)

Rock Solid: Absolutely Live (1988)

The Pledge (1989)

Go to the Top (1991)

Destined to Win: The Classic Rock Collection (1992)

Heat It Up (1993)

DeGarmo and Key's Greatest Hits, Vol. 1 (1994)

To Extremes (1994)

Eddie DeGarmo Solo Discography

Feels Good to Be Forgiven (1988)

Phase II (1990)

Dana Key Solo Discography

The Journey: Walking with Jesus (1990)

Part of the Mystery (1995)

Gospel Music Association Dove Awards

2004   Special Event Album of the Year: *!Hero the Rock Opera*; Artists: Michael Tait, Mark Stuart, Rebecca St. James, T-Bone, Pete Stewart, Grits, John Cooper, Bob Farrell, Matt Hamnitt, Nirva, Paul Wright, Quinlan, Donnie Lewis; Pete Stewart, Eddie DeGarmo, Meaux Records

For Further Reading

Alfonso, Barry. *The Billboard Guide to Contemporary Christian Music*. New York: Billboard Books/Watson-Guptill, 2002.

Cusic, Don. *The Sound of Light: A History of Gospel and Christian Music*. New York: Hal Leonard, 2002.

Key, Dana, with Steve Rabey. *Don't Stop the Music*. Grand Rapids, Mich.: Zondervan, 1989

McNeil, W. K., ed. *Encyclopedia of American Gospel Music*. New York: Routledge, 2005.

Powell, Mark Allen. *Encyclopedia of Contemporary Christian Music*. Peabody, Mass.: Hendrickson Publishers, Inc., 2002.

DELIRIOUS

The British have had a tremendous influence on American popular music since the Beatles came over in 1964; however, the same cannot be said for Christian music. British Christian acts, with a few exceptions, have not managed to break into the American Christian music market. However, one of those exceptions is the group Delirious, formed in Littlehampton, England, in 1992.

The early version of the group was known as Cutting Edge and was made up of singer/guitarist Martin Smith and his brother, drummer Stewart Smith, with Tim Jupp; they led monthly worship services at Arun Community

Church in Littlehampton. All three of these young men had married a daughter of church elder David Thatcher, whose son, Jon, joined the group on bass. The addition of lead guitarist Stuart Garrard rounded out the group. In April 1996 the group was involved in a car crash; that event led them to change their name to Deliriou5 and then Delirious. They recorded and released four albums on cassette.

Delirious had two songs on the British pop charts, "Deeper" and "Promise," and two of their songs have become classics in worship and praise: "I Could Sing of Your Love Forever" and "Did You Feel the Mountains Tremble."

Don Cusic

For Further Reading

Borlase, Craig. *Purepop: The Delirious Journey So Far.* Littlehampton, U.K.: Furoous Press, 1998.

Thompson, John J. *Raised by Wolves: The Story of Christian Rock and Roll.* Toronto, Ontario: ECW Press, 2000.

DICKERSON, DEZ

Dez Dickerson (b. Desmond D'andrea Dickerson, 1955) had played with a number of rock bands in Minneapolis before he joined Prince's band in 1979, after answering an ad in the *Twin Cities Reader* and an audition in the back of Del's Tire Mart. Dickerson toured with Prince for several years and performed in Prince's 1999 album and tour. His guitar solo on Prince's "Little Red Corvette" is considered one of the 100 greatest guitar solos. However, Dickerson had a Christian conversion in 1980 during a Christmas break from touring and became increasingly bothered by Prince's sexual themes in his songs. After the 1999 tour, Dickerson left Prince and formed the Modernaires, which supported Billy Idol on his Rebel Yell tour in 1984. Dickerson and the Modernaires were in the movie *Purple Rain.* In 1987 Dickerson moved to Nashville where he backed singer Judson Spence, then did session work for other artists. In 1990 he joined Starsong, a contemporary Christian music label, as vice president of A&R; in 1994 he founded Absolute Records.

Don Cusic

For Further Reading

Dickerson, Dez. *My Time with Prince—Confessions of a Former Revolutionary.* Philadelphia: Pavilion Press, 2003.

DIMUCCI, DION

During the late 1950s and early 1960s, Dion (b. Dion Francis DiMucci, July 18, 1939) was a rock star, first with his group the Belmonts and then as a solo artist. The Bronx, New York, native grew up in the doo-wop era and seemed to be on top of the world until drugs and show business excesses took their toll. After a long, downward spiral in his personal life, Dion came back with a defining hit of the 1960s, "Abraham, Martin and John" and then, some years later, became a born again Christian and joined the contemporary Christian music world.

Dion came from a show business family; his father was a vaudeville

Singer Dion DiMucci in 1993. (AP Images)

entertainer and Dion loved country music and the blues. He also loved doo-wop and sang on Crotona Avenue Street corners. He released his first record in 1957 when he recorded "The Chosen Few" with the Timberlanes; then, with friends Fred Milano, Angelo D'Aleo, and Carlo Mastrangelo, he returned to the studio to record "I Wonder Why" as Dion and the Belmonts (the group name came from Belmont Avenue). That record and two others hit the national charts; in 1959 he released two top five records: "A Teenager in Love" and "Where or When."

"A Teenager in Love" hit the charts after the fateful plane crash that killed Buddy Holly, Richie Valens, and J. P. Richardson (The Big Bopper). Dion had been invited to fly with them but had to pay $35 for a seat on the chartered plane; he decided against it and so was spared that tragedy.

In October 1960, Dion embarked on a solo career; he had conflicts over musical direction with the Belmonts and he was addicted to heroin. His solo career flourished; at the end of 1960 he released his first solo album, *Alone with Dion*, and the singles "Lonely Teenager," "Runaround Sue," "The Wanderer," and several others were big hits. Dion had been recording for Laurie, a small independent label, but at the end of 1962 became the first rock 'n' roll artist signed to Columbia; there he released hits "Ruby Baby," "Donna the Prima Donna," and "Drip Drop."

During this time his professional life was going well but Dion's personal life was a downward spiral of drugs and parties; he move to Miami in hopes of finding a fresh start, and in April 1968, after a prayer from his father-in-law, ended his addiction to drugs and alcohol. By this time, he no longer had a recording contract so he went back to

Laurie, his old label, and asked for a second chance; they agreed if he would record a song they had, "Abraham, Martin and John." Dion recorded that song, which entered the pop chart at the end of 1968 and rose to number four, an anthem for that year when Martin Luther King and Robert Kennedy were both assassinated. (The song title refers to Abraham Lincoln, Martin Luther King, and John Kennedy.)

Dion had a spiritual rebirth on December 14, 1979, while he was out jogging; he states he "was flooded with white light. It was everywhere, inside me, outside me—everywhere. . . . Ahead of me, I saw a man with his arms outstretched. 'I love you,' He said. 'Don't you know that? I'm your friend. I laid down My life for you. I'm here for you now.'" That marked the beginning of Dion as a Christian singer and his involvement in the contemporary Christian music culture.

Dion recorded contemporary Christian songs for several years but in 1987 did a concert in Radio City Music Hall in New York that featured his old hits. The concert, a fundraiser for medical help for the homeless, also featured Bruce Springsteen, Paul Simon, and Lou Reed. In 1988 he published his autobiography and in 1989 was inducted into the Rock and Roll Hall of Fame and recorded a secular album, *Yo Frankie.*

Dion returned to his rock roots with several more albums in the 21 century, including *Bronx in Blue*, an album of country and blues standards. He also returned to the Catholic church and is involved in a prison ministry that helps men going through addiction recovery.

Don Cusic

Selected Discography

Inside Job (1980)

Only Jesus (1981)

I Put Away My Idols (1983)

Seasons (1984)

Kingdom in the Streets (1985)

Velvet and Steel (1986)

Yo Frankie! (1989)

Dream on Fire (1992)

Best of the Gospel Years (1997)

Deja Nu (2000)

Bronx in Blue (2006)

Son of Skip James (2007)

For Further Reading

DiMucci, Dion, with Davin Seay. *The Wanderer: Dion's Story*. Minneapolis, Minn.: Quill House, 1989.

Powell, Mark Allen. *Encyclopedia of Contemporary Christian Music*. Peabody, Mass.: Hendrickson Publishers, Inc., 2002.

DIXON, JESSY

Jessy Dixon (b. March 12, 1938, in San Antonio, Texas) is best known for his work with Paul Simon. Dixon, an African American artist, was born in Texas but moved to Chicago when he was 12 and became organist with the True Light Baptist Church, where he played double keyboards with Billy Preston. A child prodigy, Dixon studied piano at St. Mary's College and became pianist for Clara Ward and the Clara Ward Singers, then for Dorothy Love Coates and the Original Gospel Harmonettes, and then for Brother Joe May. In 1960 he joined James Cleveland's Gospel

Chimes and became director and lead singer of the Thompson Community Singers; he recorded with them under the name the Chicago Community Choir. In the late 1960s Dixon formed the Jessy Dixon Singers with Ethel Holloway, Elsa Harris, and Aldrea Lennox, later replaced by Charlotte Davis.

In 1972 Dixon performed at the Newport Jazz Festival and in a concert at Radio City Music Hall, where he received four encores; Paul Simon was in the audience and called several days later and invited Dixon to tour and record with him. Jessy Dixon toured with Paul Simon for eight years and is featured on two of Simon's albums, *Live Rhymin'* and *Still Crazy after All These Years*.

During the period 1967–1971, Dixon recorded four albums a year for Savoy; in 1977 he signed with Light Records and his first release for that label, *It's All Right Now*, was produced by Andrae Crouch. Later, he toured with DeGarmo and Key and most recently has teamed with Bill Gaither and appeared on Gaither's "Homecoming" series of videos and concerts.

Dixon is a prolific songwriter and wrote "I Am Redeemed," "I Love to Praise His Name," "He Has Done Great Things for Me," "There Is No Failure in God," and "I'm Satisfied." His album *Satisfied/Live* was recorded at Calvary Chapel in Costa Mesa, California. He won the 2002 Dove Award for "Traditional Gospel Recorded Song of the Year" for his song "Hold On," recorded by Selah.

Don Cusic

For Further Reading

McNeil, W. K., ed. *Encyclopedia of American Gospel Music*. New York: Routledge, 2005.

Powell, Mark Allen. *Encyclopedia of Contemporary Christian Music*. Peabody, Mass.: Hendrickson Publishers, Inc., 2002.

DOGWOOD

Dogwood was a popular group during the late 1970s and early 1980s before Steve and Annie Chapman left for a career that saw them become involved with Focus on the Family and Promise Keepers. Ron Elder and Steve Chapman were childhood friends; both grew up in West Virginia, the sons of ministers. Their music was folk/country, and the duo moved to Nashville where they performed at Koinonia Coffee House, a ministry arm of Belmont Church on Music Row. Their first album, released in 1975, was produced by Chris Christian. On that first album was a background singer named Annie; she and Steve Chapman later married and she became a member of the group in 1977. In the early 1980s Dogwood disbanded and Steve and Annie Chapman embarked on a separate career where they worked with James Dobson's Focus on the Family, released more than 20 independent albums, and wrote a number of books.

There is another group named Dogwood; it is a hard core punk group from San Diego.

Don Cusic

For Further Reading

Powell, Mark Allen. *Encyclopedia of Contemporary Christian Music*. Peabody, Mass.: Hendrickson Publishers, Inc., 2002.

DOVE AWARD

The Dove Award is a statuette awarded by the Gospel Music Association each year for the top artists, songs, albums, and videos by gospel and Christian artists.

The idea of an awards ceremony honoring those in gospel music was first presented by Bill Gaither during a Gospel Music Association quarterly board meeting in 1968. The first ceremony was held on October 10, 1969, at the Peabody Hotel in Memphis. The name Dove came from Bill Gaither and the design came from Les Beasley, who worked with an artist on the concept. The winners that first year came from the southern gospel field; among those who won those first awards were the Oak Ridge Boys, J. G. Whitfield, Bill Gaither, Vestal Goodman, James Blackwood, the Imperials, and the Speers.

The next year the Doves were again held in Memphis and the winners came from the southern gospel world. In the third year, 1971, disaster struck when it was discovered the Blackwood Brothers had stuffed the ballot box. The result was that all awards were deemed invalid and that year was wiped off the slate. As a result, the Gospel Music Association does not count 1971 as a Dove year and the winners do not appear on any of the Gospel Music Association's official releases of past Dove winners.

The Dove Awards continued to grow and moved to Nashville, where the gospel music business was increasingly centered. In 1976 they added a category, "Pop/Contemporary Album," which acknowledged the importance of contemporary Christian music; that award was won by the Imperials for their album *No Shortage*. The award

for "Album by a Secular Artist," also instituted that year, was won by B. J. Thomas for his album *Home Where I Belong*.

In 1977 Evie Tornquist won for "Female Vocalist," the "Pop/Contemporary Album" award was won by Reba Rambo Gardner and "Album By a Secular Artist" was awarded to the Boones for their album *First Class*.

The Dove Awards in 1978 were a turning point for the Doves and contemporary Christian music. Held at the Opryland Hotel, the awards were hosted by Jerry and Sharalee Lucas and featured performances by Ralph Carmichael and his Orchestra, Evie, the Cathedral Quartet, Shirley Caesar, the Mighty Clouds of Joy, and the Couriers. Dallas Holm was the big winner that night, carrying home four Doves, including "Song of the Year" honors for "Rise Again." He also won the "Songwriter of the Year" award and became the first person other than Bill Gaither to win that honor since the inception of the Doves. Evie was "Female Vocalist" for the second year in a row and the Imperials were the top group. Other award winners were Dino Karstonakis, the Bill Gaither Trio, the Boones, Andrae Crouch, and the Blackwood Brothers.

This was a critical year for the Gospel Music Association and Dove Awards because new blood had arrived—in the form of Dallas Holm, Evie, and Dino. In June the Gospel Music Association had signed an agreement with a Hollywood-based production firm to televise the Doves for the first time, but no deal could be struck and so the show was not televised.

There was no Dove Awards show in 1979 because the Gospel Music

Association decided to shift the awards from the fall to the spring of the year, and since that transition meant a 1979 Dove Awards was just a few months after the 1978 event, it was decided to skip 1979 altogether and hold the next one in 1980, 17 months later. The move to shift the Dove Awards was the major break with the National Quartet Convention. The southern gospel contingent had begun the Gospel Music Association and the Doves, and the awards remained part of the Quartet Convention Week activities, although the Gospel Music Association had sought to include all facets of gospel music. With contemporary Christian music coming on strong, and the Gospel Music Association needing the support of that segment of the industry, a major move was necessary. It worked, and the Dove Awards increasingly became a showcase for contemporary Christian music in the 1980s.

The 11th Dove Awards were held in March, 1980 at the Opryland Hotel in Nashville and was hosted by three couples: Bill and Gloria Gaither, Walter and Tramaine Hawkins, and Paul and Kathie Lee Johnson. Performers that evening included Pat Boone, Cynthia Clawson, James Cleveland, Rusty Goodman, Dallas Holm, Honeytree, Phil Keaggy, the Kingsmen, Tom Netherton, and Grady Nutt.

The Dove Awards were a disappointment in one area for the Gospel Music Association—they had signed a contract with a Hollywood production firm to televise the event that year and expected this show to be their first national telecast. But the networks gave a thumbs down to gospel music—the market research people couldn't come up with enough "numbers" to placate executives nervous about the appeal of gospel—so the show's success was only covered in the print media.

There was no "Artist of the Year" award yet (the "top" award was for "Male Gospel Group of the Year"—a remnant from the southern gospel heritage). The top song that year was "He's Alive" and the writer, Don Francisco, captured the "Songwriter of the Year" honor. Other top winners were the Imperials, Bill Gaither Trio, Dallas Holm ("Male Vocalist" and "Contemporary Album"), Cynthia Clawson ("Female Vocalist"), Doug Oldham ("Inspirational Album"), Dino Kartsonakis, and Bob Dylan for "Gospel Album by a Secular Artist," awarded for his album *Slow Train Coming*.

The Dove Awards held in Nashville in 1981 came in for a bashing. Among the musicians and singers involved in the contemporary Christian movement who had come out of the Jesus revolution, there had always been a backlash against awards. The prevailing idea was that all rewards should be "heavenly" and that, somehow, giving awards to Christians from Christians for Christian endeavors was ungodly. After this self-examination and self-criticism about awards in general and Christian ones in particular, no one refused a nomination or an award.

Cynthia Clawson won the "Female Vocalist" award for the second year in a row, Gary Chapman won the "Songwriter of the Year" award, Russ Taff won the "Male Vocalist" award, and album awards were won by the Hemphills, Larnelle Harris, Shirley Caesar, Teddy Huffam and the Gems, the Bill Gaither Trio, Debby Boone, and the ten artists on the album *The Lord's Prayer*.

The biggest winners that evening were the Imperials, who won three Doves, including the one for the newly instituted "Artist of the Year" award. This award was created to replace the "Associates Award" and gave the Doves one major, overall top award for the event. The Gospel Music Association has two categories of membership—professionals (who work and receive income from gospel music) and associates (or fans). The associates were only allowed to vote on one award, which until 1981 was the "Associates" award and could be given to a person, group, song, or album. But from 1981 on, this group has been allowed to vote (with the professional group) on the "Artist of the Year" honor, so this award reflected the artist who appealed to professionals, amateurs, and fans in the gospel music industry.

In 1983, at the 14th Doves, it was clearly Amy Grant's year as the success of her *Age to Age* album (it was the fastest-selling Christian album for Word) led Amy to capture the "Artist of the Year" honor as well as generating three other Dove Awards (including "Song of the Year" for "El Shaddai"). Hosted by Pat Boone, the show was a special evening for Bill Gaither, who was inducted into the Gospel Music Hall of Fame.

The Dove Awards held in 1984 were the first gospel music awards ceremony to be televised. It aired on cable, over the Christian Broadcasting Network, and came after a number of years of concentrated effort by the board of the Gospel Music Association. Hosted by Glen Campbell, the show achieved a level of notoriety when cue cards were dropped and shuffled, resulting in a series of miscues and mistakes from the presenters and host.

Sandi Patti received "Artist of the Year" honors and two other Doves. Amy Grant, who many had predicted to be the big winner after her year-long success with her gold album, *Age to Age*, received only one Dove—for the "Design" of her Christmas album.

The 16th annual Dove Awards, again televised nationally over the Christian Broadcasting Network, was hosted by Pat Boone and a former Miss America, Cheryl Prewitt. Sandi Patti collected three Doves—including the top honor, "Artist of the Year." A fellow Anderson College alumni, Steve Green, received his first Dove that evening. Other Dove winners included Shirley Caesar, the Rex Nelon Singers, Lulu Roman, Michael W. Smith (for "Songwriter of the Year"), Phil Driscoll, Andrae Crouch, and Amy Grant, who received the Dove for "Contemporary" album for her *Straight Ahead* LP.

By this time the Gospel Music Association had 16 different categories for its Dove Awards, reflecting the wide variety of music under the "gospel" umbrella. In 1995 there were 32 categories, reflecting the addition of musical genres such as hard rock and rap/ hip hop" as well as videos in the awards. In 2008 there were more than 40 different categories for Doves, which continue to be the premier awards show for contemporary Christian music.

Don Cusic

For Further Reading

Cusic, Don. *The Sound of Light: A History of Gospel and Christian Music.* New York: Hal Leonard, 2002.

Dove Award Winners

1969: 1st Annual Dove Awards

Song of the Year: "Jesus Is Coming Soon" Written by R. E. Winsett; Publisher: R. E. Winsett Music, SESAC

Songwriter of the Year: Bill Gaither

Male Vocalist of the Year: James Blackwood

Female Vocalist of the Year: Vestal Goodman

Male Group of the Year: Imperials

Mixed Group of the Year: Speer Family

Album of the Year: *It's Happening* by the Oak Ridge Boys (Producer: Bob MacKenzie; Label: HeartWarming)

Instrumentalist: Dwayne Friend

Album Jacket: *It's Happening* by Oak Ridge Boys; Label: HeartWarming

Television Program: "Gospel Jubilee" hosted by Florida Boys

D.J. of the Year: J. G. Whitfield

1970: 2nd Annual Dove Awards

Song of the Year: "The Night Before Easter" Written by Don Sumner and Dwayne Friend; Publisher: Gospel Quartet Music, SESAC

Songwriter of the Year: Bill Gaither

Male Vocalist of the Year: James Blackwood

Female Vocalist of the Year: Ann Downing

Male Group of the Year: Oak Ridge Boys

Mixed Group of the Year: Speer Family

Most Promising New Gospel Talent: Four Galileans

Album of the Year: *Fill My Cup, Lord* by the Blackwood Brothers (Producer: Darol Rice; Label: RCA Victor)

Instrumentalist: Dwayne Friend

Backliner Notes: Mrs. Jake Hess on *Ain't That Beautiful Singing'* by Jake Hess

Cover Photo or Cover Art: Bill Grine for *This Is My Valley* by the Rambos

Graphic Layout and Design: Jerry Goff for *Thrasher Brothers at Fantastic Caverns* by the Thrasher Brothers

Television Program: "Gospel Jubilee" hosted by Florida Boys

D.J. of the Year: J. G. Whitfield

1971: 3rd Annual Dove Awards

no awards

1972: 4th Annual Dove Awards

Song of the Year: "The Lighthouse" Written by Ron Hinson; Publisher: Journey Music, BMI

Songwriter of the Year: Bill Gaither

Male Vocalist of the Year: James Blackwood

Female Vocalist of the Year: Sue Chenault

Male Group of the Year: Oak Ridge Boys

Mixed Group of the Year: Speer Family

Most Promising New Gospel Talent: London Paris and the Apostles

Album of the Year: *Light* by the Oak Ridge Boys (Producer: Bob MacKenzie; Label: HeartWarming)

Instrumentalist: Tony Brown

Backliner Notes: Johnny Cash on *Light* by the Oak Ridge Boys

Cover Photo or Cover Art: Bill Grine for *Street Gospel* by the Oak Ridge Boys

Graphic Layout and Design: Ace Lehman for *L-O-V-E Love* by the Blackwood Brothers

Television Program: "Gospel Jubilee" hosted by the Florida Boys

D.J. of the Year: J. G. Whitfield

1973: 5th Annual Dove Awards

Song of the Year: "Why Me, Lord?" Written by Kris Kristofferson; Publisher: Resaca Music, BMI

Songwriter of the Year: Bill Gaither

Male Vocalist of the Year: James Blackwood

Female Vocalist of the Year: Sue Chenault

Male Group of the Year: Blackwood Brothers

Mixed Group of the Year: Speer Family

Album of the Year: *Street Gospel* by the Oak Ridge Boys (Producer: Bob MacKenzie; Label: HeartWarming)

Instrumentalist: Henry Slaughter

Backliner Notes: Eddie Miller on *Release Me* by the Blackwood Brothers

Cover Photo or Cover Art: NO AWARD

Graphic Layout and Design: Bob McConnell for *Street Gospel* by the Oak Ridge Boys

Television Program: "Gospel Jubilee" hosted by the Florida Boys

D.J. of the Year: Sid Hughes

1974: 6th Annual Dove Awards

Song of the Year: "Because He Lives" Written by Bill Gaither; Publisher: Gaither Music, ASCAP

Songwriter of the Year: Bill Gaither

Male Vocalist of the Year: James Blackwood

Female Vocalist of the Year: Sue Chenault Dodge

Male Group of the Year: Blackwood Brothers

Mixed Group of the Year: Speer Family

Associate Membership Award: Group: Blackwood Brothers

Album of the Year: *Big and Live* by the Kingsmen Quartet (Producer: Marvin Norcross; Label: Canaan)

Instrumentalist: Henry Slaughter

Backliner Notes: Don Butler on *On Stage* by the Blackwood Brothers

Cover Photo or Cover Art: Hope Powell for *On Stage* by the Blackwood Brothers

Graphic Layout and Design: Charles Hooper for *On Stage* by the Blackwood Brothers

Television Program: "Gospel Jubilee" hosted by the Florida Boys

D.J. of the Year: Jim Black

1975: 7th Annual Dove Awards

Song of the Year: "One Day at a Time" Written by Marijohn Wilkin and Kris Kristofferson; Publisher: Buckhorn Music, BMI

Songwriter of the Year: Bill Gaither

Male Vocalist of the Year: James Blackwood

Female Vocalist of the Year: Jeanne Johnson

Male Group of the Year: Imperials

Mixed Group of the Year: Speer Family

Associate Membership Award: Song: "Statue of Liberty" by Neil Enloe (Publisher: Neil Enloe Music, BMI)

Album of the Year: *I Just Feel Like Something Good Is about to Happen* by the Speer Family, (Producer: Bob MacKenzie; Label: HeartWarming)

Instrumentalist: Henry Slaughter

Backliner Notes: Wendy Bagwell on *Bust out Laffin'* by Wendy Bagwell and the Sunliters

Cover Photo or Cover Art: Spears Photo for *There He Goes* by the Blackwood Brothers

Graphic Layout and Design: Bob McConnell for *Praise Him . . . Live* by the Downings

Album By a Secular Artist: *Sunday Morning with Charley Pride* by Charley Pride (Producer: Jerry Bradley; Label: RCA)

Television Program: "Gospel Jubilee" hosted by Florida Boys

D.J. of the Year: Jim Black

1976: 8th Annual Dove Awards

Song of the Year: "Statue of Liberty" Written by Neil Enloe; Publisher: Enloe Music, BMI

Songwriter of the Year: Bill Gaither

Male Vocalist of the Year: Johnny Cook

Female Vocalist of the Year: Joy McGuire

Male Group of the Year: Imperials

Mixed Group of the Year: Speer Family

Associate Membership Award: Group: Blackwood Brothers

Southern Gospel Album: *Between the Cross and Heaven* by the Speer Family (Producer: Joe Huffman; Label: HeartWarming)

Inspirational Album: *Jesus, We Just Want to Thank You* by the Bill Gaither Trio (Producer: Bob MacKenzie; Label: HeartWarming)

Pop/Contemporary Album: *No Shortage* by the Imperials (Producers: Bob MacKenzie and Gary Paxton; Label: Impact)

Instrumentalist: Henry Slaughter

Backliner Notes: Sylvia Mays on *Just a Little Talk with Jesus* by the Cleavant Derricks Family

Cover Photo or Cover Art: Bill Barnes for *Old Fashion, Down Home, Hand Clappin', Foot Stomping, Southern Style Gospel Quartet* by the Oak Ridge Boys

Graphic Layout and Design: Bob McConnell for *No Shortage* by the Imperials

Album by A Secular Artist: *Home Where I Belong* by B. J. Thomas (Producer: Chris Christian; Label: Myrrh)

Television Program: "PTL Club," hosted by Jim and Tammy Bakker

D.J. of the Year: Sid Hughes

1977: 9th Annual Dove Awards

Song of the Year: "Learning to Lean" Written by John Stallings; Publisher: HeartWarming Music, BMI

Songwriter of the Year: Bill Gaither

Male Vocalist of the Year: James Blackwood

Female Vocalist of the Year: Evie Tornquist

Male Group of the Year: Cathedral Quartet

Mixed Group of the Year: Speer Family

Associate Membership Award: Group: Blackwood Brothers

Southern Gospel Album: *Then . . . and Now* by the Cathedral Quartet (Producer: Ken Harding; Label: Canaan)

Inspirational Album: *Ovation* by the Couriers (Producer: Jesse Peterson; Label: Tempo)

Pop/Contemporary Album: *Reba . . . Lady* by Reba Rambo Gardner (Producer: Phil Johnson; Label: Greentree)

Soul/Black Gospel Album: *This Is Another Day* by Andrae Crouch and the Disciples (Producer: Bill Maxwell; Label: Light)

Instrumentalist: Henry Slaughter

Backliner Notes: Joe Huffman on *Cornerstone* by the Speers

Cover Photo or Cover Art: Roy Tremble for *Then . . . and Now* by the Cathedral Quartet

Graphic Layout and Design: Dennis Hill for *Then . . . and Now* by the Cathedral Quartet

Album by a Secular Artist: *First Class* by the Boones (Producer: Chris Christian; Label: Lamb and Lion)

Television Program: "Gospel Jubilee" hosted by the Florida Boys

D.J. of the Year: Sid Hughes

1978: 10th Annual Dove Awards

Song of the Year: "Rise Again" Written by Dallas Holm; Publisher: Dimension Music, SESAC

Songwriter of the Year: Dallas Holm

Male Vocalist of the Year: Dallas Holm

Female Vocalist of the Year: Evie Tornquist

Male Group of the Year: Imperials

Mixed Group of the Year: Dallas Holm and Praise

Associate Membership Award: Song: "Rise Again" by Dallas Holm (Dimension Music, SESAC)

Southern Gospel Album: *Kingsmen Live in Chattanooga* by the Kingsmen (Producers: Joe Huffman and Eldridge Fox; Label: HeartWarming)

Inspirational Album: *Pilgrim's Progress* by the Bill Gaither Trio (Producers: Bob MacKenzie and John W. Thompson; Label: Impact)

Pop/Contemporary Album: *Transformation* by the Cruse Family (Producer: Ken Harding; Label: Canaan)

Soul/Black Gospel Album: *Live in London* by Andrae Crouch and the Disciples (Producers: Bill Maxwell and Andrae Crouch; Label: Light)

Instrumentalist: Dino Kartsonakis

Backliner Notes: Joe and Nancy Cruse on *Transformation* by the Cruse Family

Cover Photo or Cover Art: Robert August for *Live in London* by Andrae Crouch and the Disciples

Graphic Layout and Design: Bob McConnell for *Grand Opening* by Andrus, Blackwood and Company

Album by a Secular Artist: *Slow Train Coming* by Bob Dylan (Producers: Jerry Wexler and Barry Beckett; Label: Columbia)

Television Program: "Hemphill Family Time" hosted by the Hemphills

D.J. of the Year: Sid Hughes

1979: none

1980: 11th Annual Dove Awards

Song of the Year: "He's Alive" Written by Don Francisco; Publisher: New Pax Music, BMI

Songwriter of the Year: Don Francisco

Male Vocalist of the Year: Dallas Holm

Female Vocalist of the Year: Cynthia Clawson

Male Group of the Year: Imperials

Mixed Group of the Year: Bill Gaither Trio

Southern Gospel Album: *From out of the Past* by the Kingsmen (Producers: Joe Huffman and Eldridge Fox; Label: HeartWarming)

Inspirational Album: *Special Delivery* by Doug Oldham (Producer: Joe Huffman; Label: Impact)

Pop/Contemporary Album: *All That Matters* by Dallas Holm and Praise (Producer: Phil Johnson; Label: Greentree)

Soul/Black Gospel Album: *Love Alive II* by Walter Hawkins and the Love Center Choir (Producer: Walter Hawkins; Label: Light)

Instrumentalist: Dino Kartsonakis

Backliner Notes: Merlin Littlefield on *Breakout* by the Mercy River Boys

Cover Photo or Cover Art: Mike Borum for *You Make It Rain for Me* by Rusty Goodman

Graphic Layout and Design: Bob McConnell for *Special Delivery* by Doug Oldham

Album by a Secular Artist: *With My Song* by Debby Boone (Producer: Brown Bannister; Label: Lamb and Lion)

1981: 12th Annual Dove Awards

Song of the Year: "Praise the Lord" Written by Brown Bannister and Mike Hudson; Publishers: Home Sweet Home Music, BMI and Bug and Bear Music ASCAP

Songwriter of the Year: Gary Chapman

Male Vocalist of the Year: Russ Taff

Female Vocalist of the Year: Cynthia Clawson

Male Group of the Year: Imperials

Artist of the Year: Imperials

Southern Gospel Album: *Workin'* by the Hemphills (Producer: Jerry Crutchfield; Label: HeartWarming)

Inspirational Album: *You're Welcome Here* by Cynthia Clawson (Producer: JEN Productions; Label: Triangle)

Pop/Contemporary Album: *One More Song for You* by the Imperials (Producer: Michael Omartian; Label: DaySpring)

Inspirational Black Gospel Album: *Rejoice* by Shirley Caesar (Producers: Tony Brown and Ken Harding; Label: Myrrh)

Contemporary Gospel Album: *Give Me More Love in My Heart* by Larnelle Harris (Producers: Howard McCrary and Paul Johnson; Label: Benson)

Traditional Gospel Album: *Incredible* by Teddy Huffam and the Gems (Producer: Ken Harding; Label: Canaan)

Instrumentalist: Dino Kartsonakis

Praise and Worship Album: *The Lord's Prayer* by Various Artists (Producer: Dony McGuire; Label: Light)

Children's Music Album: *Very Best of the Very Best for Kids* (Producer: Robert MacKenzie; Label: Word)

Musical Album: *The Messiah* by Billy Ray Hearn and Irving Martin; Label: Sparrow

Recorded Music Packaging: Bill Barnes and Clark Thomas for *You're Welcome Here* by Cynthia Clawson

Album by a Secular Artist: *Amazing Grace* by B. J. Thomas (Producer: Pete Drake; Label: Myrrh)

1982: 13th Annual Dove Awards

Song of the Year: "We Shall Behold Him" Written by Dottie Rambo; Publisher: John T. Benson Publishing, ASCAP

Songwriter of the Year: Dottie Rambo

Male Vocalist of the Year: Russ Taff

Female Vocalist of the Year: Sandi Patti

Group of the Year: Imperials

Artist of the Year: Sandi Patti

Southern Gospel Album: *One Step Closer* by the Rex Nelon Singers (Producer: Ken Harding; Label: Canaan)

Inspirational Album: *Joni's Song* by Joni Eareckson (Producer: Kurt Kaiser; Label: Word)

Pop/Contemporary Album: *Priority* by the Imperials (Producer: Michael Omartian; Label: DaySpring)

Inspirational Black Gospel Album: *Edwin Hawkins Live*; Oakland Symphony Orchestra and Edwin Hawkins (Producer: Gil Askey; Label: Myrrh)

Contemporary Gospel Album: *Walter Hawkins and Family Live* by the Walter Hawkins Family (Producer: Walter Hawkins; Label: Light)

Traditional Gospel Album: *Go* by Shirley Caesar (Producers: Tony Brown and Shirley Caesar; Label: Myrrh)

Instrumentalist: Dino Kartsonakis

Praise and Worship Album: *Exaltation* (Producer: Ronn Huff; Label: Benson)

Children's Music Album: *Kids under Construction* (Producers: Robert MacKenzie and Ronn Huff; Label: Paragon)

Musical Album: *The Love Story* by Phil Brower and Don Wyrtzen; Label: New Dawn

Recorded Music Packaging: Bill Barnes, Matt Barnes, Pat Barnes for *Finest Hour* by Cynthia Clawson

Album by a Secular Artist: *He Set My Life to Music* by Barbara Mandrell (Producer: Tom Collins; Label: MCA)

1983: 14th Annual Dove Awards

Song of the Year: "El Shaddai" Written by Michael Card and John Thompson; Publisher: Whole Armor Publishing, ASCAP

Songwriter of the Year: Michael Card

Male Vocalist of the Year: Larnelle Harris

Female Vocalist of the Year: Sandi Patti

Group of the Year: Imperials

Artist of the Year: Amy Grant

Southern Gospel Album: *Feeling at Home* by the Rex Nelon Singers (Producer: Ken Harding; Label: Canaan)

Inspirational Album: *Lift Up the Lord* by Sandi Patti (Producer: Greg Nelson; Label: Impact)

Pop/Contemporary Album: *Age to Age* by Amy Grant (Producer: Brown Bannister; Label: Myrrh)

Inspirational Black Gospel Album: *Touch Me Lord* by Larnelle Harris (Producer: Greg Nelson; Label: Impact)

Contemporary Gospel Album: *I'll Never Stop Loving You* by Leon Patillo (Producer: Skip Konte; Label: Myrrh)

Traditional Gospel Album: *Precious Lord* by Al Green (Producer: Al Green; Label: Myrrh)

Instrumentalist: Dino Kartsonakis

Praise and Worship Album: *Light Eternal* (Producer: Billy Ray Hearn; Label: Birdwing)

Children's Music Album: *Lullabies and Nursery Rhymes* (Producers: Tony Salerno and Fletch Wiley; Label: Birdwing)

Musical Album: *The Day He Wore My Crown* by David T. Clydesdale; Label: Impact

Recorded Music Packaging: Dennis Hill and Michael Borum for *Age to Age* by Amy Grant

Album by a Secular Artist: *Surrender* by Debby Boone (Producer: Brown Bannister; Label: Lamb and Lion)

1984: 15th: Annual Dove Awards

Song of the Year: "More than Wonderful" Written by Lanny Wolfe; Publisher: Lanny Wolfe Music, ASCAP

Songwriter of the Year: Lanny Wolfe

Male Vocalist of the Year: Russ Taff

Female Vocalist of the Year: Sandi Patti

Group of the Year: NO AWARD

Artist of the Year: Sandi Patti

Southern Gospel Album: *We Shall Behold the King* by the Rex Nelon Singers (Producer: Ken Harding; Label: Canaan)

Inspirational Album: *More than Wonderful* by Sandi Patti (Producers: David Clydesdale, Greg Nelson, and Sandi Patti Helvering; Label: Impact)

Pop/Contemporary Album: *Side by Side* by the Imperials (Producers: Keith Thomas and Neal Joseph; Label: DaySpring)

Contemporary Gospel Album: *Come Together* by Bobby Jones and New Life (Producer: Tony Brown; Label: Myrrh)

Traditional Gospel Album: *We Sing Praises* by Sandra Crouch (Producer: Sandra Crouch; Label: Light)

Instrumentalist: Phil Driscoll

Praise and Worship Album: *Celebrate the Joy* (Producer: David T. Clydesdale; Label: Impact)

Children's Music Album: *Music Machine II* (Producers: Fletch Wiley, Tony Salerno, and Ron Kreuger; Label: Birdwing)

Musical Album: *Dreamer* by Cam Floria (Label: Christian Artists)

Recorded Music Packaging: Dennis Hill, Bill Farrell, and Michael Borum for *A Christmas Album* by Amy Grant

Album by a Secular Artist: *You Were Loving Me* by Lulu Roman Smith (Producer: Gary McSpadden; Label: Canaan)

1985: 16th Annual Dove Awards

Song of the Year: "Upon This Rock" Written by Gloria Gaither and Dony

McGuire; Publishers: Gaither Music, It's-N-Me Music, and Lexicon Music; ASCAP

Songwriter of the Year: Michael W. Smith

Male Vocalist of the Year: Steve Green

Female Vocalist of the Year: Sandi Patti

Artist of the Year: Sandi Patti

Southern Gospel Album: *The Best Of and a Whole Lot More* by the Rex Nelon Singers (Producer: Ken Harding; Label: Canaan)

Inspirational Album: *Songs from the Heart* by Sandi Patti (Producers: Greg Nelson and Sandi Patti Helvering; Label: Impact)

Pop/Contemporary Album: *Straight Ahead* by Amy Grant (Producer: Brown Bannister; Label: Myrrh)

Contemporary Gospel Album: *No Time To Lose* by Andrae Crouch (Producer: Bill Maxwell; Label: Light)

Traditional Gospel Album: *Sailin'* by Shirley Caesar (Producers: Sanchez Harley, Shirley Caesar and David Lehman; Label: Myrrh)

Instrumentalist: Phil Driscoll

Praise and Worship Album: *The Praise in Us* (Producer: Neal Joseph; Label: Myrrh)

Children's Music Album: *The New Songs with Kids for Kids about Life* (Producer: Ron W. Griffin; Label: Word)

Musical Album: *The Race Is On* by Steve Taylor (Label: Word)

Recorded Music Packaging: Eddie Yip, Stan Evenson, and Don Putnam for *Kingdom of Love* by Scott Wesley Brown

Album by a Secular Artist: *No More Night* by Glen Campbell (Producers: Glen Campbell and Ken Harding; Label: Word)

1986: 17th Annual Dove Awards

Song of the Year: "Via Dolorosa" Written by Billy Sprague and Niles Borop; Publishers: Meadowgreen and Word Music, ASCAP

Songwriter of the Year: Gloria Gaither

Male Vocalist of the Year: Larnelle Harris

Female Vocalist of the Year: Sandi Patti

Artist of the Year: Amy Grant

Southern Gospel Album: *Excited* by the Hemphills (Producer: Wayne Hilton and Trent Hemphill; Label: HeartWarming)

Inspirational Album: *I've Just Seen Jesus* by Larnelle Harris (Producer: Greg Nelson; Label: Impact)

Pop/Contemporary Album: *Medals* by Russ Taff (Producers: Russ Taff and Jack Puig; Label: Myrrh)

Contemporary Gospel Album: *Let My People Go* by the Winans (Producer: Marvin Winans; Label: Qwest)

Traditional Gospel Album: *Celebration* by Shirley Caesar (Producers: Dave Lehman and Shirley Caesar; Label: Rejoice)

Instrumentalist: Dino Kartsonakis

Praise and Worship Album: *I've Just Seen Jesus* by William J. Gaither and Randy Vader (Label: Gaither Music Records)

Children's Music Album: *Bullfrogs and Butterflies Part II* (Producer: Tony Salerno; Label: Birdwing)

Musical Album: *Come Celebrate Jesus* by Neal Joseph and Don Marsh (Label: Word)

Recorded Music Packaging: Thomas Ryan, Kent Hunter, and Mark Tucker for *Unguarded* by Amy Grant

1987: 18th Annual Dove Awards

Song of the Year: "How Excellent Is Thy Name" Written by Dick and Melodie Tunney and Paul Smith; Publishers Word Music, Marquis III; Laurel Press, and Pamela Kay Music ASCAP

Songwriter of the Year: Dick and Melodie Tunney

Male Vocalist of the Year: Steve Green

Female Vocalist of the Year: Sandi Patti

Group of the Year: First Call

Artist of the Year: Sandi Patti

Southern Gospel Album: *The Master Builder* by the Cathedrals (Producers: Bill Gaither and Gary McSpadden; Label: RiverSong)

Inspirational Album: *Morning Like This* by Sandi Patti (Producers: Greg Nelson and Sandi Patti Helvering; Label: Word)

Pop/Contemporary Album: *The Big Picture* by Michael W. Smith; (Producers: Michael W. Smith and John Potoker; Label: Reunion)

Contemporary Gospel Album: *Heart and Soul* by the Clark Sisters (Producers: Norbert Putnam and Twinkie Clark; Label: Rejoice)

Traditional Gospel Album: *Christmasing* by Shirley Caesar (Producer: Norbert Putnam; Label: Rejoice)

Instrumental Album: *Instrument of Praise* by Phil Driscoll (Producers: Lari Goss, Phil Driscoll and Ken Pennel; Label: Benson)

Praise and Worship Album: *Hymns* by 2nd Chapter of Acts (Producer: Buck Herring; Label: Live Oak)

Children's Music Album: *God Likes Kids* by Joel and Labreeska Hemphill (Label: Benson)

Musical Album: *A Mighty Fortress* by Steve Green, Dwight Liles, and Niles Borop (Label: Sparrow)

Recorded Music Packaging: Buddy Jackson and Mark Tucker for *Don't Wait for the Movie* by White Heart

Short Form Music Video: *Famine in Their Land* by the Nelons (Directors: Robert Deaton and George Flanigen; Label: Word)

Long Form Music Video: *Limelight* by Steve Taylor (Producers and Directors: John Anneman and Steve Taylor; Label: Sparrow)

1988: 19th Annual Dove Awards

Song of the Year: "In the Name of the Lord" Written by Phil McHugh, Gloria Gaither, and Sandi Patti Helvering; Publishers River Oaks Music and Sandi's Songs BMI; Gaither Music, ASCAP

Songwriter of the Year: Larnelle Harris

Male Vocalist of the Year: Larnelle Harris

Female Vocalist of the Year: Sandi Patti

Group of the Year: First Call

Artist of the Year: Sandi Patti

Southern Gospel Album: *Symphony of Praise* by the Cathedrals (Producer: Lari Goss; Label: RiverSong)

Inspirational Album: *The Father Hath Provided* by Larnelle Harris (Producer: Greg Nelson; Label: Benson)

Pop/Contemporary Album: *Watercolour Ponies* by Wayne Watson (Producers: Wayne Watson and Paul Mills; Label: DaySpring)

Contemporary Gospel Album: *Decisions* by the Winans (Producers: Marvin Winans, Barry Hankerson, Carvin Winans, and Michael Winans; Label: Qwest)

Traditional Gospel Album: *One Lord, One Faith, One Baptism* by Aretha Franklin (Producer: Aretha Franklin; Label: Arista)

Country Album: *An Evening Together* by Steve and Annie Chapman (Producers: Ron Griffin and Steve Chapman; Label: Star Song)

Rock Album: *Crack the Sky* by Mylon LeFevre and Broken Heart (Producers: Joe Hardy and Mylon LeFevre; Label: Myrrh)

Instrumental Album: *The Wind and the Wheat* by Phil Keaggy (Producers: Phil Keaggy and Tom Coomes; Label: Colours)

Praise and Worship Album: *The Final Word* by Michael Card (Producer: Norbert Putnam; Label: Sparrow)

Children's Music Album: *Bullfrogs and Butterflies Part III* by the Agapeland Singers and Candle (Producer: Tony Salerno; Label: Sparrow)

Musical Album: *A Son! A Savior!* by Claire Cloninger, Gary Rhodes, and Bob Krogstad (Label: Word)

Recorded Music Packaging: John Summers and Erick Neuhaus for *Peaceful Meditation* by Greg Buchanan

Short Form Music Video: *Stay for a While* by Amy Grant (Directors: Marc Ball and Jack Cole; Label: Myrrh)

Long Form Music Video: *The Big Picture Tour Video* by Michael W. Smith (Directors: Brian Shipley and Stephen Bowlby; Label: Reunion)

1989: 20th Annual Dove Awards

Song of the Year: "Friend of a Wounded Heart" Written by Wayne Watson and Claire Cloninger; Publisher: Word, ASCAP

Songwriter of the Year: Steven Curtis Chapman

Male Vocalist of the Year: Wayne Watson

Female Vocalist of the Year: Sandi Patti

Group of the Year: Take 6

Artist of the Year: Amy Grant

New Artist of the Year: Take 6

Southern Gospel Album: *Goin' in Style* by the Cathedrals (Producer: Lari Goss; Label: Homeland)

Southern Gospel Recorded Song: "Champion of Love" (Writers: Phil Cross and Caroly Cross; Recorded by the Cathedrals; Label: RiverSong)

Inspirational Album: *Make His Praise Glorious* by Sandi Patti (Producers: Greg Nelson and Sandi Patti Helvering; Label: Word)

Inspirational Recorded Song: "In Heaven's Eyes" Written by Phil McHugh; Recorded by Sandi Patti; Label: Word

Pop/Contemporary Album: *Lead Me On* by Amy Grant (Producer: Brown Bannister; Label: Myrrh)

Pop/Contemporary Recorded Song: "His Eyes" Written by Steven Curtis Chapman; Recorded by Steven Curtis Chapman: Label: Sparrow

Contemporary Gospel Album: *Take 6* by Take 6 (Producers: Mark Kibble, Claude V. McKnight III, and Mervyn E. Warren; Label: Reunion)

Contemporary Gospel Recorded Song: "If We Ever" Writer: Public Domain; Recorded by Take 6; Label: Reunion

Traditional Gospel Album: *Live . . . in Chicago* by Shirley Caesar (Producers: Bubba Smith and Shirley Caesar; Label: Rejoice)

Traditional Gospel Recorded Song: "Hold My Mule" Written by Shirley Caesar Williams; Recorded by Shirley Caesar; Label: Word

Country Album: *Richest Man in Town* by Bruce Carroll (Producer: Bubba Smith; Label: New Canaan)

Country Recorded Song: "Above and Beyond" (Written by Bruce Carroll and Paul Smith; Recorded by Bruce Carroll; Label: Word)

Rock Album: *Russ Taff* by Russ Taff (Producer: Jack Joseph Puig; Label: Myrrh)

Rock Recorded Song: "Won by One" Written by Scot Allen, Trent Arganti, Kenneth Bentley, Ben Hewitt, Paul Joseph, Mylon LeFevre, and Joe Hardy; Recorded by Mylon and Broken Heart; Label: Myrrh

Hard Music Album: *In God We Trust* by Stryper (Producers: Stryper and Michael Lloyd; Label: Enigma)

Hard Music Recorded Song: "In God We Trust" Written by Stryper; Recorded by Stryper; Label: Benson

Instrumental Album: *A Symphony of Praise* by Sandi Patti (Producer: David T. Clydesdale; Label: Word)

Praise and Worship Album: *Praise 10* by the Maranatha! Singers (Producers: Smitty Price and Tom Coomes; Label: Maranatha!)

Children's Music Album: *Wise Guys and Starry Skies* by Kathie Hill (Producers: Kathie Hill and Randall Dennis; Label: Sparrow)

Musical Album: *In His Presence: The Risen King* by Dick and Melodie Tunney (Label: Genevox)

Choral Collection Album: *Sandi Patti Choral Praise* (Producer: Greg Nelson; Publisher: Word Music)

Recorded Music Packaging: Patrick Pollei, Joan Tankersley, and Phillip Dixon for *Russ Taff* by Russ Taff

Short Form Music Video: *Lead Me On* by Amy Grant; Directors: Tina Silvey and Andrew Doucette; Label: Myrrh

Long Form Music Video: *Carman Live . . . Radically Saved* by Carman; Producers and Directors: Cindy Dupree, George J. Flanigen IV and Robert Deaton; Label: Benson

1990: 21st Annual Dove Awards

Song of the Year: "Thank You" Written by Ray Boltz; Publishers: Gaither Music and Shepherd Boy Music, ASCAP

Songwriter of the Year: Steven Curtis Chapman

Male Vocalist of the Year: Steven Curtis Chapman

Female Vocalist of the Year: Sandi Patti

Group of the Year: BeBe and CeCe Winans

Artist of the Year: Steven Curtis Chapman

New Artist of the Year: David Mullen

Southern Gospel Album: *I Just Started Living* by the Cathedrals (Producer: Lari Goss; Label: Homeland)

Southern Gospel Recorded Song: "I Can See the Hand of God" Written by Steven Curtis Chapman and Jim Chapman III: Recorded by the Cathedrals; Label: Homeland

Inspirational Album: *The Mission* by Steve Green (Producer: Greg Nelson; Label: Sparrow)

Inspirational Recorded Song: "His Strength Is Perfect" Written by Steven Curtis Chapman and Jerry Salley; Recorded by Steven Curtis Chapman; Label: Sparrow

Pop/Contemporary Album: *Heaven* by BeBe and CeCe Winans (Producer: Keith Thomas; Label: Sparrow)

Pop/Contemporary Recorded Song: "Heaven" Written by Keith Thomas and Benjamin Winans; Recorded by BeBe and CeCe Winans; Label: Sparrow

Contemporary Gospel Album: *Will You Be Ready?* by Commissioned (Producers: Fred Hammon and Michael Brooks; Label: Light)

Contemporary Gospel Recorded Song: "With My Whole Heart" Written by Patrick Henderson and Louis Brown III; Recorded by BeBe and CeCe Winans; Label: Sparrow

Traditional Gospel Album: *Saints in Praise* by the West Angeles Church of God in Christ Mass Choir (Producer: Patrick Henderson; Label: Sparrow)

Traditional Gospel Recorded Song: "Wonderful" (Writers: Virginia Davis, Theodore Frye; Recorded by Beau Williams)

Country Album: *Heirloom by Heirloom*; (Producer: Michael Sykes and Trent Hemphill; Label: Benson)

Country Recorded Song: "Tis So Sweet to Trust in Jesus" (Writer: Public Domain; Recorded by Amy Grant; Label: Word)

Traditional Gospel Recorded Song: "Wonderful" (Writers: Virginia Davis, Theodore Frye; Recorded by Beau Williams)

Rock Album: *The Way Home* by Russ Taff (Producers: Russ Taff and James Hollihan; Label: Myrrh)

Rock Recorded Song: "The River Unbroken" Written by Darryl Brown and David Batteau; Recorded by Russ Taff; Label: Myrrh

Hard Music Album: *Triumphant Return* by White Cross; (Producers: Rex Carroll and Joey Powers; Label: Pure Metal)

Hard Music Recorded Song: "In Your Face" Written by Ken Tamplin; Recorded by Shout; Label: Intense

Instrumental Album: *One of Several Possible Musiks* by Kerry Livgren (Producer: Kerry Livgren; Label: Sparrow)

Praise and Worship Album: *Our Hymns* by Various Artists (Producers: Various; Label: Word)

Children's Music Album: *The Friendship Company* by Sandi Patti (Producer: Sandi Patti; Label: Word)

Musical Album: *Friends Forever/Part 2* by Billy Sprague Jim Weber, and Nan Gurley (Label: Word: Publisher: Meadowgreen)

Choral Collection Album: *The A Cappella Collection* Recorded by the Greg Nelson Singers (Producer: Greg Nelson; Label: Wordsong)

Recorded Music Packaging: Buddy Jackson and Mark Tucker for *Petra Praise* by Petra

Short Form Music Video: *I Miss the Way* by Michael W. Smith; Producer: Stephen Yake; Label: Reunion

Long Form Music Video: *On Fire* by Petra; Director: Stephen Yake

1991: 22nd Annual Dove Awards

Song of the Year: "Another Time, Another Place" Written by Gary Driskell; Publisher: Word Music, ASCAP

Songwriter of the Year: Steven Curtis Chapman

Male Vocalist of the Year: Steven Curtis Chapman

Female Vocalist of the Year: Sandi Patti

Group of the Year: Petra

Artist of the Year: Steven Curtis Chapman

New Artist of the Year: 4Him

Southern Gospel Album: *Climbing Higher and Higher* by the Cathedrals (Producers: Bill Gaither, Mark Trammel, and Lari Goss; Label: Homeland)

Southern Gospel Recorded Song: "He Is Here" Written by Kirk Talley; Recorded by the Talleys; Label: Word

Inspirational Album: *Another Time, Another Place* by Sandi Patti (Producer: Greg Nelson; Label: Word)

Inspirational Recorded Song: "Who Will Be Jesus?" Written by Bruce Carroll and C. Aaron Wilburn; Recorded by Bruce Carroll; Label: Word

Pop/Contemporary Album: *Go West Young Man* by Michael W. Smith (Producers: Michael W. Smith and Brian Lenox; Label: Reunion)

Pop/Contemporary Recorded Song: "Another Time, Another Place" Written by Gary Driskell; Recorded by Sandi Patti; Label: Word

Contemporary Gospel Album (formerly Contemporary Black Gospel): *So Much 2 Say* by Take 6 (Producer: Take 6; Label: Warner Alliance)

Contemporary Gospel Recorded Songs (formerly Contemporary Black Gospel): "I L-O-V-E- You" (Writers: Mervyn Warren and Mark Kibble; Recorded by Take 6; Label: Warner Alliance)

Country Album: *Sojourner's Song* by Buddy Green (Producer: Bubba Smith; Label: Word)

Country Recorded Song: "Seein' My Father in Me" (Writers: Paul Overstreet and Taylor Dunn; Recorded by Paul Overstreet; Label: Word)

Rock Album: *Beyond Belief* by Petra (Producers: John and Dino Elefante; Label: DaySpring)

Rock Recorded Song: "Beyond Belief" (Writer: Bob Hartman; Recorded by Petra; Label: DaySpring)

Hard Music Album: *Holy Soldier* by Holy Soldier (Producer: David Zaffiro; Label: Myrrh)

Hard Music Recorded Song: "Stranger" (Writer: David Zaffiro; Recorded by Holy Soldier; Label: Myrrh)

Rap/Hip Hop Album: *Nu Thang* by DC Talk (Producers: Toby McKeehan, Mark Heimermann and T. C.; Label: YO! ForeFront)

Rap/Hip Hop Recorded Song: "It's Time" (Writers: Marvin Winans, Carvin Winans, Teddy Riley and Bernard Bell; Recorded by the Winans; Label: Warner Alliance)

Instrumental Album: *Come Before Him* by Dick Tunney (Producer: Dick Tunney; Label: Word)

Praise and Worship Album: *Strong and Mighty Hands* by Voices of Praise (Producer: John G. Elliott; Label: Reunion)

Children's Music Album: *Hide 'Em in Your Heart Songs* by Steve Green (Producers: Frank and Betsy Hernandez; Label: Sparrow)

Musical Album: *Handel's Young Messiah* by Various Artists (Producers: Paul Mills, Don Hart and Norman Miller; Label: Word)

Choral Collection Album: *I Call You To Praise* by Steve Green (Producer: Music Sculptures; Label: Sparrow)

Recorded Music Packaging: Buddy Jackson and Mark Tucker for *Beyond Belief* by Petra

Short Form Music Video: *Revival in the Land* by Carman; Director: Stephen Yake; Label: Benson

Long Form Music Video: *Revival in the Land* by Carman; Director: Stephen Yake; Label: Benson

1992: 23rd Annual Dove Awards

Song of the Year: "Place in This World" Written by Amy Grant, Michael W. Smith, and Wayne

Kirkpatrick; Publishers: Age to Age Music, O'Ryan, Emily Boothe, ASCAP/BMI

Songwriter of the Year: Steven Curtis Chapman

Male Vocalist of the Year: Michael English

Female Vocalist of the Year: Sandi Patti

Group of the Year: BeBe and CeCe Winans

Artist of the Year: Amy Grant

New Artist of the Year: Michael English

Southern Gospel Album: *Homecoming* by the Gaither Vocal Band (Producers: Ken Mansfield and the Gaither Vocal Band; Label: Star Song)

Southern Gospel Recorded Song: "Where Shadows Never Fall" (Writers: Carl Jackson, Jim Weatherly; Recorded by: Glen Campbell; Label: New Haven)

Inspirational Album: *Larnelle Live . . . Psalms Hymns and Spiritual Songs* by Larnelle Harris (Producer: Lari Goss; Label: Benson)

Inspirational Recorded Song: "For All the World" Written by Greg Nelson and Bob Farrell; Recorded by Sandi Patti; Label: Word

Pop/Contemporary Album: *For the Sake of the Call* by Steven Curtis Chapman (Producer: Phil Naish; Label: Sparrow)

Pop/Contemporary Recorded Song: "Home Free" Written by Wayne Watson; Recorded by Wayne Watson; Label: DaySpring

Contemporary Gospel Album (formerly Contemporary Black Gospel): *He Is*

Christmas by Take 6 (Producer: Take 6; Label: Warner Alliance)

Contemporary Gospel Recorded Song (formerly Contemporary Black Gospel): "Addictive Love" (Writers: Keith Thomas, Benjamin Winans and CeCe Winans; Recorded by BeBe and CeCe Winans; Label: Sparrow)

Traditional Gospel Album (formerly Traditional Black Gospel): *Through the Storm* by Yolanda Adams (Producer V. M. McKay; Label: Tribute)

Traditional Gospel Recorded Song (formerly Traditional Black Gospel): "Through the Storm" (Writer: V. M. McKay; Recorded by Yolanda Adams: Label: Tribute)

Country Album: *Sometimes Miracles Hide* by Bruce Carroll (Producers: Brown Bannister and Tom Hemby; Label: Word)

Country Recorded Song: "Sometimes Miracles Hide" (Writers: Bruce Carroll and C. Aaron Wilburn; Recorded by Bruce Carroll; Label: Word)

Rock Album: *Simple House* by Margaret Becker (Producer: Charlie Peacock; Label: Sparrow)

Rock Recorded Song: "Simple House" (Writers: Margaret Becker and Charlie Peacock; Recorded by Margaret Becker; Label: Sparrow)

Hard Music Album: *In the Kingdom* by Whitecross (Producer: Simon Hanhard; Label: Star Song)

Hard Music Recorded Song: "Everybody Knows My Name" (Writers: Dale Thompson and Troy Thompson; Recorded by Bride; Label: Pure Metal)

Rap/Hip Hop Album: *Mike-E and the G-Rap Crew* by Mike-E (Producers: Mike-E, Jet Penix, and Cedric Caldwell; Label: Reunion)

Rap/Hip Hop Recorded Song: "I Love Rap Music" (Writers: Toby McKeehan and Jackie Gore; Recorded by DC Talk; Label: YO! Forefront)

Instrumental Album: *Beyond Nature* by Phil Keaggy (Producer: Phil Keaggy; Label: Myrrh)

Praise and Worship Album: *Sanctuary* by Twila Paris (Producer: Richard Souther; Label: Star Song)

Children's Music Album: *Open for Business* by Sandi Patti and the Friendship Company (Producers: Ron Krueger and Greg Nelson; Label: Everland)

Musical Album: *The Big Picture* by Michael W. Smith (Producers: Andy Stanley and Robert Sterling; Label: Word)

Choral Collection Album: *The Michael W. Smith Collection* (Producers: Robert Sterling and Dennis Worley; Label: Word)

Short Form Music Video: *Another Time, Another Place* by Sandi Patti and Wayne Watson; Director: Stephen Yake; Label: Word

Long Form Music Video: *Rap, Rock and Soul* by DC Talk; Director and Producer: Deaton-Flanigen; Label: Forefront

Recorded Music Packaging: Mark Tucker, Buddy Jackson and Beth Middleworth for *Brave Heart* by Kim Hill.

1993: 24th Annual Dove Awards

Song of the Year: "The Great Adventure" Written by Steven Curtis

Chapman and Geoff Moore; Publishers: Sparrow Song, Careers-BMG Music, and Peach Hill Songs, BMI; Starstruck Music ASCAP

Songwriter of the Year: Steven Curtis Chapman

Male Vocalist of the Year: Michael English

Female Vocalist of the Year: Twila Paris

Group of the Year: 4 HIM

Artist of the Year: Steven Curtis Chapman

New Artist of the Year: Cindy Morgan

Southern Gospel Album: *Reunion: A Gospel Homecoming Celebration* by Bill and Gloria Gaither (Producer: Bill Gaither; Label: Star Song)

Southern Gospel Recorded Song: "There Rose a Lamb" Written by Kyla Rowland; Recorded by Gold City; Label: RiverSong

Inspirational Album: *Generation 2 Generation* by Benson artists and their families (Larnelle Harris, Matthew Ward, Glad, Fred Hammond, 4HIM, Dallas Holm, Kelly Nelon Thompson, Billy and Sarah Gaines, Dana Key) (Producers: Don Koch, Ed Nalle, Fred Hammond, Joe Hogue, and Dana Key; Label: Benson)

Inspirational Recorded Song: "In Christ Alone" Written by Shawn Craig and Don Koch; Recorded by Michael English; Label: Warner Alliance

Pop/Contemporary Album: *The Great Adventure* by Steven Curtis Chapman (Producer: Phil Naish; Label: Sparrow)

Pop/Contemporary Recorded Song: "The Great Adventure" Written by

Steven Curtis Chapman and Geoff Moore; Recorded by Steven Curtis Chapman; Label: Sparrow

Contemporary Gospel Album: *Handel's Messiah—A Soulful Celebration*; by Various Artists (Mervyn Warren, George Duke, David Pack, Patti Austin, Take 6, Gary Hines, Robert Sadin, Richard Smallwood, the Yellowjackets, Fred Hammon; Label: Warner Alliance)

Contemporary Gospel Recorded Song: "Real" Written by Daryl Coley; Recorded by Rev. C. B. Rhone and the Band; Label: Sparrow

Traditional Gospel Album: *With All of My Heart* by Sandra Crouch and Friends (Producers: Sandra Crouch and Andrae Crouch; Label: Sparrow)

Traditional Gospel Recorded Song: "T'Will Be Sweet" Written by Richard Smallwood; Recorded by the Richard Smallwood Singers; Label: Sparrow

Country Album: *Love Is Strong* by Paul Overstreet (Producers: Paul Overstreet and Brown Bannister; Label: Word)

Country Recorded Song: "If We Only Had the Heart" (Written by Bruce Carroll, Michael Puryear, and Dwight Liles; Recorded by Bruce Carroll; Label: Word)

Rock Album: *Pray for Rain* by Pray for Rain (Producers: Jimmie Lee Sloas and Bobby Blazier; Label: Vireo)

Rock Recorded Song: "Destiny" Written by Bob Hartman, John Elefante; Recorded by Petra; Label: DaySpring)

Hard Music Album: insufficient amount of eligible entries

Hard Music Recorded Song: "Rattle-snake" Written by Dale Thompson, Troy Thompson, Rik Foley, and Jerry McBroom; Recorded by Bride; Label: Star Song

Rap/Hip Hop Album: *Good News for the Bad Timez* by Mike-E (Producers: Mike E and Jet Penix; Label: Reunion)

Rap/Hip Hop Recorded Song: "Can I Get a Witness?" Written by Toby McKeehan; Recorded by DC Talk; Label: YO! ForeFront

Inspirational Recorded Song: "In Christ Alone" Written by Shawn Craig and Don Koch; Recorded by Michael English; Label: Warner Alliance

Instrumental Album: *Somewhere in Time* by Dino (Producers: Dino Kartsonakis and David T. Clydesdale; Label: Benson)

Praise and Worship Album: *Coram Deo* by Michael Card, Charlie Peacock, Susan Ashton, Michael English, and Out of the Grey (Producer: Charlie Peacock; Label: Sparrow)

Children's Music Album: *YO! KIDZ!* by Carman (Producers: Chris Harris and Ron Krueger; Label: Everland)

Musical Album: *The Majesty and Glory of Christmas* by Billy Ray Hearn and Tom Fettke (Label: Sparrow)

Choral Collection Album: *Steven Curtis Chapman Choral Collection* (Producers: Tom Harley, Randy Smith; Label: Sparrow)

Recorded Music Packaging: Larry Vigon and Denise Milford for *Coram Deo* by Susan Ashton, Michael Card, Michael English, Out of the Grey, and Charlie Peacock (Label: Sparrow)

Short Form Music Video: *The Great Adventure* by Steven Curtis Chapman; Directors: Nancy Knox; Greg Crutcher; Label: Sparrow

Long Form Music Video: *Addicted to Jesus* by Carman; Director: Stephen Yake; Label: Benson

1994: 25th Annual Dove Awards

Song of the Year: "In Christ Alone" Written by Shawn Craig and Don Koch; Publisher: Paragon Music, ASCAP

Songwriter of the Year: Steven Curtis Chapman

Male Vocalist of the Year: Michael English

Female Vocalist of the Year: Twila Paris

Group of the Year: 4HIM

Artist of the Year: Michael English

New Artist of the Year: Point of Grace

Southern Gospel Album: *Southern Classics* by the Gaither Vocal Band (Producers: Bill Gaither, Michael Sykes, and Michael English; Label: Benson)

Southern Gospel Recorded Song: "Satisfied" Written by Public Domain; Recorded by the Gaither Vocal Band; Label: Benson

Inspirational Album: *The Season of Love* by 4HIM (Producer: Don Koch; Label: Benson)

Inspirational Recorded Song: "Holding out Hope to You" Written by Joe Beck, Brian White, and David Wills; Recorded by Michael English; Label: Warner Alliance

Pop/Contemporary Album:
Hope by Michael English (Producer:
Brown Bannister; Label: Warner
Alliance)

Pop/Contemporary Recorded Song:
"Go There with You" Written by Steven Curtis Chapman; Recorded by Steven Curtis Chapman; Label: Sparrow

Contemporary Gospel Album: *Start All Over* by Helen Baylor (Producer: Bill Maxwell; Label: Word)

Contemporary Gospel Recorded Song:
"Sold Out" Written by Helen Baylor
and Logan Reynolds; Recorded by
Helen Baylor; Label: Word

Traditional Gospel Album: *Kirk Franklin and the Family* by Kirk Franklin
(Producers: Rodney Fraziere and
Arthur Dyer; Label: Gospo Centric)

Traditional Gospel Recorded Song:
"Why We Sing" Written by Kirk
Franklin; Recorded by Kirk Franklin;
Label: Gospo Centric

Country Album: *Walk On* by Bruce
Carroll (Producers: Brown Bannister
and Tom Hemby; Label: Word)

Country Recorded Song: "There But for
the Grace of God" Written by Paul Overstreet and Taylor Dunn; Recorded by Paul
Overstreet; Label: Word

Rock Album: *Wake-Up Call* by Petra
(Producer: Brown Bannister; Label:
DaySpring)

Rock Recorded Song: "Jesus Is Just
Alright" Written by Arthur Reynolds;
Recorded by DC Talk; Label:
ForeFront

Hard Music Album: *Tamplin* by Ken
Tamplin (Producer: Ken Tamplin;
Label: Benson)

Hard Music Recorded Song: "Psychedelic Super Jesus" Written by Troy

Thompson, Dale Thompson, Jerry
McBroom, Rik Foley; Recorded by
Bride; Label: Star Song

Rap/Hip Hop Album: insufficient
amount of eligible entries

Rap/Hip Hop Recorded Song:
"Socially Acceptable" Written by
Toby McKeeham and Mark Heimermann; Recorded by DC Talk; Label:
ForeFront

Instrumental Album: *Psalms, Hymns and Spiritual Songs* by Kurt Kaiser (Producer: Kurt Kaiser; Label: Sparrow)

Praise and Worship Album:
Songs from the Loft by Susan Ashton,
Gary Chapman, Ashley Cleveland,
Amy Delaine, Amy Grant, Kim Hill,
Michael James, Wes King, Donna
McElroy, Michael W. Smith
(Producers: Gary Chapman and Jim
Dineen; Label: Reunion)

Children's Music Album: *Come to the Cradle* by Michael Card (Producer:
Phil Naish; Label: Sparrow)

Musical Album: *God with Us* by
Don Moen, Tom Fettke, Tom Harley,
Jack Hayford, Camp Kirkland;
(Label: Integrity Music)

Choral Collection Album:
*Al Denson Youth Chorus Book,
Vol. III* (Producers: Dave Spear and
Al Denson; Label: Benson)

Recorded Music Packaging: Buddy
Jackson, Beth Middleworth, Mark
Tucker, and D. Rhodes for *The Wonder
Years 1983–1993* by Michael W. Smith
(Label: Reunion)

Short Form Music Video: *Hand on My
Shoulder* Sandi Patti; Director: Stephen
Yake; Label: Word

Long Form Music Video: *The Live
Adventure* by Steven Curtis

Chapman; Producers and Directors:
Bret Wolcott, Douglas C.
Forbes and Michael Solomon;
Label: Sparrow

1995: 26th: Annual Dove Awards

Song of the Year: "God Is in Control"
Written by Twila Paris; Publishers:
Ariose Music and Mountain Spring
Music, ASCAP

Songwriter of the Year: Steven Curtis
Chapman

Male Vocalist of the Year: Steven Curtis Chapman

Female Vocalist of the Year: Twila
Paris

Group of the Year: 4HIM

Artist of the Year: Steven Curtis
Chapman

New Artist of the Year: Clay Crosse

Southern Gospel Album: *High and
Lifted Up* by the Cathedral Quartet
(Producer: Lari Goss; Label: Canaan)

Southern Gospel Recorded Song: "I
Bowed on My Knees" (Writer: Public
Domain; Recorded by: Gaither Vocal
Band; Public Domain; Label: Benson)

Inspirational Album: *Find It on the
Wings* by Sandi Patty (Producers: Greg
Nelson and Phil Ramone; Label: Word)

Inspirational Recorded Song: "I Pledge
Allegiance to the Lamb" Written by
Ray Boltz; Recorded by Roy Boltz;
Label: Word

Pop/Contemporary Album: *Heaven in
the Real World* by Steven Curtis Chapman (Producers: Phil Naish and Steven
Curtis Chapman; Label: Sparrow)

Pop/Contemporary Recorded Song:
"Heaven in the Real World" Written
by Steven Curtis Chapman; Recorded
by Steven Curtis Chapman; Label:
Sparrow

Contemporary Gospel Album: *Join the
Band* by Take 6 (Producers: Alvin
Chea, Cedric Dent, Joel Kibble, Mark
Kibble, Claude V. McKnight III, David
Thomas, Vincent Herbert, Les Pierce,
David Foster, Brian McKnight, and
Stevie Wonder; Label: Warner
Alliance)

Contemporary Gospel Recorded Song:
"God Knows" Written by Angelo and
Veronica Petrucci; Recorded by Angelo
and Veronica Petrucci; Label: Benson

Traditional Gospel Album: *Live at
GMWA*. Shirley Caesar, O'Landa
Draper and the Associates, Rev. Milton
Brunson and the Thompson Commu-
nity Singers (Producers: Bubba Smith
and John Stewart; Label: Word)

Country Album: *The Door* by Charlie
Daniels (Producer: Ron W. Griffin;
Label: Sparrow)

Country Recorded Song: "The Door"
Written by Ron W. Griffin; Recorded
by Charlie Daniels; Label: Sparrow

Rock Album: *Going Public* by the
Newsboys (Producers: Steve Taylor
and Peter Furler; Label: Star Song)

Rock Recorded Song: "Shine"
Written by Peter Furler, Steve Taylor;
Recorded by Newsboys;
Label: Star Song

Hard Music Album: *Scarecrow Messiah* by Bride (Producers: John and
Dino Elefante; Label: Star Song)

Hard Music Recorded Song: "Come unto the Light" Written by Scott Wenzel, David Zaffiro, Jimmy Lee Sloas; Recorded by Whitecross; Label: R.E.X.

Rap/Hip Hop Album: insufficient amount of eligible entries

Rap/Hip Hop Recorded Song: "Luv Is a Verb" Written by Toby McKeehan, Mark Heimermann, George Cocchini; Recorded by DC Talk; Label: ForeFront

Instrumental Album: *Strike Up the Band* by Ralph Carmichael's Big Band (Producers: Ralph Carmichael and Paul Stilwell; Label: Brentwood)

Praise and Worship Album: *Coram Deo II: Out of the Grey* by Steve Green, Margaret Becker, Charlie Peacock, Steven Curtis Chapman, CeCe Winans, and Bob Carlisle (Producer: Charlie Peacock; Label: Sparrow)

Children's Music Album: *YO! KIDZ!2 The Armor of God* by Carman (Producers: Chris Harris, Ron Krueger, and David Mullen; Label: Everland)

Musical Album: *Living on the Edge* by Michael W. Smith and Robert Sterling; Label: Word

Choral Collection Album: *A Christmas Suite* (Producer: David T. Clydesdale; Publisher: David T. Clydesdale Music)

Recorded Music Packaging: Karen Philpott, R. J. Lyons, Gerhart Yorkovic, and E. J. Carr for *Heaven in the Real World* by Steven Curtis Chapman; Sparrow

Short Form Music Video: *I Will Be Free* by Cindy Morgan; Producer and Director: Cindy Montano and Thom Oliphant; Label: Word

Long Form Music Video: *Mouth in Motion* by Mark Lowry; Producers and Directors: Jack Clark, Stephen Yake, and Corey Edwards; Label: Word

1996: 27th Annual Dove Awards

Song of the Year: "Jesus Freak" Written by Mark Heimermann and Toby McKeehan; Publishers: Fun Attic Music ASCAP; Mupin the Mix Music, BMI

Songwriter of the Year: Michael W. Smith

Male Vocalist of the Year: Gary Chapman

Female Vocalist of the Year: CeCe Winans

Group of the Year: Point of Grace

Artist of the Year: DC Talk

New Artist of the Year: Jars of Clay

Producer of the Year: Charlie Peacock

Southern Gospel Album: *The Martins* by the Martins (Producers: Michael Sykes and Michael English; Label: Chapel)

Inspirational Album: *Unbelievable Love* by Larnelle Harris (Producers: Bill Cuomo, Robert White Johnson, and Lari Goss; Label: Benson)

Inspirational Recorded Song: "Man After Your Own Heart" Written by Wayne Kirkpatrick, Billy Luz Sprague; Recorded by Gary Chapman; Label: Myrrh/Word

Pop/Contemporary Album: *The Whole Truth* by Point of Grace (Producer: Robert Sterling; Label: Word)

Pop/Contemporary Recorded Song: "The Great Divide" Written by Grant Cunningham, Matt Huesmann; Recorded by Point of Grace; Label: Word

Contemporary Gospel Album: *The Call* by Anointed (Producers: Cedric Caldwell, Victor Caldwell, Chris Harris, and Mark Heimermanm; Label: Myrrh)

Contemporary Gospel Recorded Song: "The Call" Written by Mary Tiller, Steve Crawford, Nee-C Walls, Da'Dra Crawford; Recorded by Anointed; Label: Myrrh

Traditional Gospel Album: *He Will Come: Live* by Shirley Caesar (Producers: Bubba Smith and Shirley Caesar; Label: Word Gospel)

Traditional Gospel Recorded Song: "Great Is Thy Faithfulness" Written by Thomas Chisholm; Recorded by CeCe Winans; Label: Sparrow

Urban Album: *Give Your Life* by Angelo and Veronica (Producers: Fred Hammond, Cliff Branch, Ted Tjornhom, and Angelo Petrucci; Label: Benson)

Urban Recorded Song: It's in God's Hands Now" Recorded by Anointed; Written by Madeline Stone, Allen Shamblin; Label: Myrrh

Country Album: *Where Loves Runs Deep* by Michael James (Producer: Michael James; Label: Reunion)

Country Recorded Song: "Without You (I Haven't Got a Prayer)" Written by Robby McGee, Scott Rath, Peter Jeffrey; Recorded by MidSouth; Label: Warner Alliance

Rock Album: *No Doubt* by Petra (Producers: John and Dino Elefante; Label: Word)

Rock Recorded Song: "Jesus Freak" Written by Toby McKeehan, Mark Heimermann; Recorded by DC Talk; Label: ForeFront

Hard Music Album: *Promise Man* by Holy Soldier (Producer: David Zaffiro; Label: ForeFront)

Hard Music Recorded Song: "Promise Man" Written by Michael Cutting, Andy Robbins, Scott Soderstrom, Eric Wayne, David Zaffiro, Michael Anderson; Recorded by Holy Soldier; Label: ForeFront

Rap/Hip Hop Album: *Church of Rhythm* by Church of Rhythm (Producer: Peter Bunetta, Rick Chudacoff; Label: Reunion)

Rap/Hip Hop Recorded Song: Take Back the Beat" Written by Max Hsu, Jason Gregory, Nathan Clair, Carlton Coleman; Recorded by Church of Rhythm; Label: Reunion

Rap/Hip Hop Recorded Song: "R.I.O.T. (Righteous Invasion of Truth)" Written by Carman and Tommy Sims; Recorded by Carman; Label: Sparrow

Alternative/Modern Rock Album: *This Beautiful Mess* by Sixpence None the Richer (Producer: Armand John Petri; Label: R.E.X.)

Alternative/Modern Rock Recorded Song: "Monkeys at the Zoo" from the album *Everything That's on My Mind* by Charlie Peacock; Producers: Charlie Peacock, Douglas Kaine McKelvey; Label: Sparrow

Urban Album: *Give Your Life* by Angelo and Veronica (Producers: Fred Hammond, Cliff Branch, Ted Tjornhom, and Angelo Petrucci; Label: Benson)

Instrumental Album: *Classical Peace* by Dino (Producer: Rolin R. Mains; Label: Benson)

Praise and Worship Album: *Promise Keepers: Raise the Standard* by Maranatha! Promise Band (Producer: Bill Schnee; Label: Word Maranatha!)

Children's Music Album: *School Days* (Produced by Mike Gay and Sue Gay; Label: Cedarmont Kids)

Musical Album: *Saviour* by Bob Farrell and Greg Nelson (Label: Word Music)

Youth/Children's Musical of the Year: *Salt and Light* (Featuring the Songs from the Loft) (Producer: Beverly Darnall; Publisher: Word Music)

Choral Collection Album: *Praise Him . . . Live* Recorded by the Brooklyn Tabernacle Choir (Producer: Carol Cymbala; Publisher: Word Music)

Special Event Album: *My Utmost for His Highest* by Amy Grant, Gary Chapman, Michael W. Smith, Point of Grace, 4HIM, Cindy Morgan, Sandi Patty, Bryan Duncan, Steven Curtis Chapman, Twila Paris, Phillips, and Craig and Dean (Producers: Loren Balman and Brown Bannister; Label: Myrrh/Word)

Recorded Music Packaging: Loren Balman, Diana Barnes, Jeff and Lisa Franke, and Mathew Barnes for *My Utmost for His Highest*; Recorded by Various Artists; Label: Myrrh/Word

Short Form Music Video: *Flood* by Jars of Clay; Producers and Directors: Ricky Blair, Michelle Weigle-Brown, Robert Beeson; Label: Essential

Long Form Music Video: *Big House* by Audio Adrenaline; Producers and

Directors: Clarke Gallivan, Cindy Montano, Kari Reeves; Jeffrey Phillips, Thom Olipahnt; Label: ForeFront

1997: 28th Annual Dove Awards

Song of the Year: "Butterfly Kisses" Written by Bob Carlisle and Randy Thomas; Publishers: DMG Music, SESAC; Polygram International, ASCAP)

Songwriter of the Year: Steven Curtis Chapman

Male Vocalist of the Year: Steven Curtis Chapman

Female Vocalist of the Year: CeCe Winans

Group of the Year: Jars of Clay

Artist of the Year: Steven Curtis Chapman

New Artist of the Year: Jaci Velasquez

Southern Gospel Album: *Wherever You Are* by the Martins (Producers: Michael Sykes and Michael English; Label: Spring Hill)

Southern Gospel Recorded Song: "Only God Knows" Written by Joyce Martin McCollough, Harrie McCollough, Joel Lindsey; Recorded by the Martins; Label: Spring Hill

Inspirational Album: *Quiet Prayers (My Utmost for His Highest)* (Producers: Bryan Duncan and Dan Posthuma; Label: Myrrh)

Inspirational Recorded Song: "Butterfly Kisses" Written by Bob Carlisle and Randy Thomas; Recorded by Bob Carlisle; Label: Diadem

Pop/Contemporary Album: *Signs of Life* by Steven Curtis Chapman

(Producers: Brown Bannister and Steven Curtis Chapman; Label: Sparrow)

Pop/Contemporary Recorded Song: "Between You and Me" Written by Toby McKeehan, Mark Heimermann; Recorded by DC Talk; Label: ForeFront

Contemporary Gospel Album: *Whatcha Lookin' 4* by Kirk Franklin and the Family (Producers: Kirk Franklin, Buster and Shavoni; Label: Gospo Centric)

Contemporary Gospel Recorded Song: "Take Me Back" Written by Andrae Crouch; Recorded by CeCe Winans on the album *Tribute—the Songs of Andrae Crouch*; Label: Warner Alliance

Traditional Gospel Album: *Just a Word* by Shirley Caesar's Outreach Convention Choir (Producers: Bubba Smith, Michael Mathis, and Shirley Caesar; Label: Word Gospel)

Traditional Gospel Recorded Song: "Stop by the Church" Written by Sullivan Pugh; Recorded by Babbie Mason; Label: Word

Urban Album: insufficent amount of eligible entries

Urban Recorded Song: "Under the Influence" Written by Mark Heimermann; Recorded by Anointed; Label: Myrrh

Country Album: *Little Bit of Faith* by Jeff Silvey (Producer: Randy Boudraux; Label: Ranson)

Country Recorded Song: "Somebody Was Prayin' for Me" Written by Charlie Daniels; Recorded by Charlie Daniels; Label: Sparrow

Rock Album: *Jesus Freak* by DC Talk (Producers: Toby McKeehan, Mark Heimermann, and John Painter; Label: ForeFront)

Rock Recorded Song: "Like It, Love It, Need It" Written by Toby McKeehan, Mark Heimermann, Kevin Smith, David Soldi, Jason Barrett; Recorded by DC Talk; Label: ForeFront

Hard Music Album: insufficent amount of eligible entries

Hard Music Recorded Song: insufficent amount of eligible entries

Rap/Hip Hop Album: *Erace* by the Gotee Brothers (Producers: The Gotee Brothers; Label: Gotee)

Alternative/Modern Rock Album: *Free Flying Soul* by the Choir (Producers: Steve Hindalong, and Derry Daugherty; Label: Tatoo)

Alternative/Modern Rock Song: "Epidermis Girl" from the album *Space by Bleach*; Producers: Brad Ford, Dave Baysinger, Matt Gingerich, Sam Barnhart, Todd Kirby; Label: ForeFront

Instrumental Album: *The Players* by Michael Omartian, Dann Huff, Tommy Sims, Tom Hemby, Terry McMillan, Chris Rodriguez, Shane Keister, Mark Douthit, and Eric Darken (Producers: The Players and Bobby Blazier; Label: Warner Alliance)

Praise and Worship Album: *Welcome Home* by Ron Kenoly (Producer: Tom Brooks; Integrity Music)

Children's Music Album: *A Very Veggie Christmas* by Veggie Tales (Producers: Phil Vischer, Kurt Heinecke, and Mike Nawrocki; Label: Everland)

Musical of the Year: *Make Us One* by Babbie Mason, Kenny Mann, David T.

Clydesdale; Publisher: David T. Clydesdale Music

Youth/Children's Musical of the Year: *Candy Cane Lane* (Producers: Celeste and David T. Clydesdale; Publisher: David T. Clydesdale Music)

Choral Collection Album: *My Tribute—Celebrating the Songs of Andrae Crouch* (Producers: Dale Mathews and John DeVries; Publisher: Brentwood Music)

Special Event Album: *Tribute—The Songs of Andrae Crouch* by CeCe Winans, Michael W. Smith, Twila Paris, Bryan Duncan, Wayne Watson, the Winans, Clay Crosse, Take 6, the Brooklyn Tabernacle Choir, First Call, Andrae Crouch and the All Star Choir (Producers: Norman Miller and Neal Joseph; Label: Warner Alliance)

Short Form Music Video: *Jesus Freak* by DC Talk; Producer and Director: Steve Strachen and Simon Maxwell; Label: ForeFront

Long Form Music Video: *Roadwork* by Geoff Moore and the Distance; Producers and Directors: Dalrene Brock, Gael Van Sant; Tom Bevins; Label: ForeFront

Recorded Music Packaging: Toni Fitzpenn, Michael Wilson, Norman Roy, George Barris, and Anderson Thomas for *Take Me to Your Leader* by the Newsboys; Label: Star Song

1998: 29th Annual Dove Awards

Song of the Year: "On My Knees" Written by David Mullen, Nicole Colerman-Mullen and Michael Ochs; Publishers: Seat of the Pants Music and Word Music, ASCAP; Ochsongs Music BMI

Songwriter of the Year: Steven Curtis Chapman

Male Vocalist of the Year: Steven Curtis Chapman

Female Vocalist of the Year: Crystal Lewis

Group of the Year: Jars of Clay

Artist of the Year: Rich Mullins

New Artist of the Year: Avalon

Producer of the Year: Brown Bannister

Southern Gospel Album: *Light of the World* by the Martins (Producers: Michael Sykes and Lari Gross; Label: Spring Hill)

Southern Gospel Recorded Song: "Butterfly Kisses" Written by Bob Carlisle and Randy Thomas: Recorded by Tim Greene; Label: New Haven

Inspirational Album: *Artist of My Soul* by Sandi Patty (Producer: Robbie Buchanan; Label: Word)

Inspirational Recorded Song: "A Baby's Prayer" Written by Kathy Troccoli and Scott Brasher; Recorded by Kathy Troccoli; Label: Reunion

Pop/Contemporary Album: *Behind the Eyes* by Amy Grant (Producers: Keith Thomas and Wayne Kirkpatrick; Label: Myrrh)

Pop/Contemporary Recorded Song: "Let Us Pray" Written by Steven Curtis Chapman; Recorded by Steven Curtis Chapman; Label: Sparrow

Contemporary Gospel Album: *Pray* by Andrae Crouch (Producers: Andrae Crouch and Scott V. Smith; Label: Qwest/Warner Brothers)

Contemporary Gospel Recorded Song: "Up Where I Belong" Written by Will Jennings, Jack Nitschi, and Buffy Sainte-Marie; Recorded by BeBe and CeCe Winans; Label: Sparrow

Traditional Gospel Album: *A Miracle in Harlem* by Shirley Caesar (Producers: Bubba Smith, Shirley Caesar, and Michael Mathis; Label: Word Gospel)

Traditional Gospel Recorded Song: "I Go to the Rock" Written by Dottie Rambo; Recorded by Whitney Houston; Label: Arista

Urban Album: *God's Property from Kirk Franklin's Nu Nation* by God's Property (Producer: Kirk Franklin; Label: B'Rite Music)

Urban Recorded Song: "Stomp" Recorded by: God's Property; Kirk Franklin, George Clinton, Jr., Gary Shider, Walter Morrison; Label: B'Rite Music

Country Album: *Hymns from the Ryman* by Gary Chapman (Producer: Gary Chapman, Label: Word Nashville)

Country Recorded Song: "The Gift" Written by Tom Douglas and Jim Brickman; Recorded by Collin Raye; Label: Word Nashville

Rock Album: *Conspiracy No. 5* by Third Day (Producer: by Sam Taylor; Label: Reunion)

Rock Recorded Song: "Alien" Written by Mark Lee, Tai Anderson, Brad Avery, David Carr; Recorded by Third Day; Label: Reunion

Hard Music Album: insufficent amount of eligible entries

Hard Music Recorded Song: insufficent amount of eligible entries

Rap/Hip Hop Album: *Revived* by World Wide Message Tribe (Producer: Zarc Porter; Label: Warner Alliance)

Alternative/Modern Rock Album: *Caedmon's Call* by Caedmon's Call (Producer: Don McCollister; Label: Warner Alliance)

Alternative/Modern Rock Recorded Song: "Some Kind of Zombie" Written by Mark Stuart; Barry Blair, Will McGinniss, Bob Herman; Recorded by Audio Adrenaline; Label: ForeFront

Instrumental Album: *Invention* by Phil Keaggy, Wes King, Scott Dente (Producer: R. S. Field; Label: Sparrow)

Rap/Hip Hop Recorded Song: "Jumping in the House of God" Written by Andy Hawthorne, Zarc Porter, Lee Jackson, Justin Thomas; Recorded by World Wide Message Tribe; Label: Warner Alliance

Bluegrass Album: *Bridges* by the Isaacs (Producer: Ben Isaacs; Label: Horizon)

Bluegrass Recorded Song of the Year: "Children of the Living God" by This Bright Hour Written by Fernando Ortega, Alison Krauss; Recorded by Fernado Ortega, Label: Myrrh

Praise and Worship Album: *Petra Praise 2: We Need Jesus* by Petra (Producers: John and Dino Elefante; Label: Word)

Children's Music Album: *Sing Me to Sleep Daddy* by Billy Gaines, Michael James, Phil Keaggy, Michael O'Brien, Guy Penrod, Peter Penrose, Angelo Petrucci, Michael W. Smith, Randy Stonehill, and Wayne Watson

(Producer: Nathan DiGesare; Label: Brentwood Kids Co.)

Musical of the Year: *My Utmost for His Highest . . . a Worship Musical* by Gary Ghodes and Claire Cloninger; Publisher: Word Music

Youth/Children's Musical of the Year: insufficient amount of eligible entries

Choral Collection Album: *Our Savior . . . Emmanuel* (Producers: Greg Nelson and Bob Farrell; Publisher: Word Music)

Spanish Language Album of the Year: *La Belleze de la Cruz* by Crystal Lewis (Producers: Brian Ray and Dan Posthuma; Label: Word International)

Enhanced CD of the Year: *Live the Life—Maxi Single* by Michael W. Smith (Producer: Craig A. Mason; Label: Reunion)

Special Event Album: *God with Us—a Celebration of Christmas Carols and Classics* by Anointed, Michael W. Smith, Twila Paris, Sandi Patty, Steven Curtis Chapman, Chris Willis, Steve Green, Cheri Keaggy, Avalon, Out of the Grey, Ray Boltz, Clay Crosse, CeCe Winans, and Larnelle Harris (Producer: Norman Miller; Label: Sparrow)

Short Form Music Video: *Colored People* by DC Talk; and Producer and Director: Mars Media and Lawrence Carroll; Label: ForeFront/Virgin

Long Form Music Video: *A Very Silly Sing Along* by Veggie Tales; Producers and Directors: Mike Nawrocki, Chris Olsen, Kurt Heinecke; Label: Everland Entertainment

Recorded Music Packaging: Beth Lee, Gina R. Brinkley, Janice Booker, Ben Pearson, D. L. Taylor for *Sixpence None the Richer*; Recorded by Sixpence None the Richer; Label: Squint Entertainment

1999: 30th Annual Dove Awards

Song of the Year: "My Deliverer" Written by Rich Mullins and Mitch McVicker; Publishers: Liturgy Legacy Music and Word Music, ASCAP; White Plastic Bag Music, SESAC

Songwriter of the Year: Rich Mullins

Male Vocalist of the Year: Chris Rice

Female Vocalist of the Year: Jaci Velasquez

Group of the Year: Point of the Grace

Artist of the Year: Michael W. Smith

New Artist of the Year: Jennifer Knap

Producer of the Year: Michael W. Smith

Southern Gospel Album: *Still the Greatest Story Ever Told* by the Gaither Vocal Band (Producers: Bill Gaither, Michael Sykes, and Guy Penrod; Label: Spring Hill)

Southern Gospel Recorded Song: "I Believe in a Hill Called Mount Calvary" Written by William J. Gaither, Gloria Gaither; Recorded by Gaither Vocal Band; Label: Spring Hill

Inspirational Album: *Corner of Eden* by Kathy Troccoli (Producer: Nathan DiGesare; Label: Reunion Records)

Inspirational Recorded Song: "Adonai" Written by Stephanie Lewis, Lorraine Ferro, and Don Koch; Recorded by Avalon; Label: Sparrow Records

Pop/Contemporary Album: *Live the Life* by Michael W. Smith

(Producers: Mark Heimermann, Michael W. Smith, and Stephen Lipson; Label: Reunion)

Pop/Contemporary Recorded Song: "Testify to Love" Written by Paul Field, Henk Pool, Ralph Van Manen, Robert Riekerk; Recorded by Avalon; Label: Sparrow Records

Contemporary Gospel Album: *Nu Nation Project* by Kirk Franklin (Producer: Kirk Franklin; Label: Gospo Centric)

Contemporary Gospel Recorded Song: "Let the Praise Begin" Written by Fred Hammond; Recorded by Fred Hammond and Radical For Christ; Label: Verity Records

Traditional Gospel Album: *Christmas with Shirley Caesar* by Shirley Caesar (Producers: Steven Ford and Shirley Caesar; Label: Myrrh Records Black Music Division)

Traditional Gospel Recorded Song: "Is Your All on the Altar?" Written by Elisha Hoffman and Percy Bady; Recorded by Yolanda Adams

Urban Album: insufficient amount of eligible entries

Urban Recorded Song: "Revolution" Written by Kirk Franklin and Rodney Jerkins; Recorded by Nu Nation Project; Kirk Franklin; Label: Gospo Centric

Country Album: *A Work in Progress* by Jeff and Sheri Easter (Producer: Michael Sykes; Label: Spring Hill)

Country Recorded Song: "Count Your Blessings" Written by Kim Patton Johnston and Joe Johnston; Recorded by the Martins; Label: Spring Hill

Rock Album: *Anybody out There?* by Burlap to Cashmere (Producers: Jay Healy and David Rolfe; Label: Squint Entertainment)

Rock Recorded Song: "Undo Me" Written by Jennifer Knapp; Recorded by Jennifer Knapp; Label: Gotee Records

Hard Music Album: *Brightblur* by Massivivid (Producers: Wally Shaw and Mark Nash; Label: Tattoo Records, Benson)

Hard Music Recorded Song: "Awesome God" Written by Rich Mullins with additional lyrics by Joe Yerke; Recorded by the Insyderz; Label: Squint Entertainment

Rap/Hip Hop Album: *Heatseeker* by the World Wide Message Tribe (Producer: Zarc Porter; Label: Warner Resound)

Rap/Hip Hop Recorded Song: "Plagiarism" Written by T. Carter, S. Jones, T. Collins, and R. Robbins; Recorded by Grits; Label: Gotee Records

Alternative/Modern Rock Album: *Fourth from the Last* by the W's, Masaki (Producer: 5 Minute Walk; Label: Sarabellum)

Alternative/Modern Rock Recorded Song: "The Devil Is Bad" from the album *Fourth from the Last* by the W's; Producers: Andrew Schar, Todd Gruener, James Carter, Brian Morris, Val Hellman, Bret Barker; Label: Sarabellum

Bluegrass Album: insufficient amount of eligible entries

Bluegrass Recorded Song of the Year: "He Still Looks over Me" Written by Mike Richards, Rodney Lay Jr.; Recorded by the Lewis Family; Label: Thoroughbred Records

Instrumental Album: *Acoustic Sketches* by Phil Keaggy (Producers: Phil Keaggy and John August Schroeter; Label: Sparrow Records)

Praise and Worship Album: *Focus on the Family Presents Renewing the Heart: Live Hymns and Songs of Worship* by Kim Hill (Producers: David Zaffiro and Kim Hill; Label: Star Song Records)

Children's Music Album: *Veggie Tunes 2* by Veggie Tales (Producers: Kurt Heinecke and David Mullen; Label: Big Idea Productions)

Musical of the Year: *Mary Did You Know?* by David Guthrie, Bruce Greer (Publisher: Word Music)

Youth/Children's Musical of the Year: *2 Extreme!* (Producer: Steven V. Taylor; Publisher: Brentwood-Benson Music Publishing)

Choral Collection of the Year: *Peace Speaker* (Producer: Geron Davis; Publisher: Brentwood-Benson Music Publishing)

Spanish Language Album of the Year: (Tie) *Libertad De Mas* by Sandi Patty (Producers: Isaac Hernandez and Greg Nelson; Label: Word International) and *ORO* by Crystal Lewis (Producers: Brian Ray and Dan Posthuma; Label: Metro One)

Special Event Album: *Exodus* by DC Talk, Jars of Clay, Sixpence None the Richer, Cindy Morgan, Chris Rice, the Katinas, Third Day, Crystal Lewis, and Michael W. Smith (Producer: Michael W. Smith; Label: Rocketown Records)

Recorded Music Packaging: Beth Lee, Jimmy Abegg, and Ben Pearson for *The Jesus Record*; Recorded by Rich Mullins and a Ragamuffin Band; Label: Myrrh

Enhanced CD of the Year: *Stead on Enhanced CD* by Point of Grace (Producers: Denise Niebisch and Rose Ireland; Label: Word Records)

Short Form Music Video: *Entertaining Angels* by Newsboys; Producers and Directors: Janet Eisner, Joel Newman; Eden, A+R; Label: StarSong, Virgin

Long Form Music Video: *My Utmost for His Highest—The Concert* by Cindy Morgan, Avalon, Twila Paris, Bryan Duncan, Sandi Patty, Steven Curtis Chapman, Nancy Knox; Producers and Directors: Clark Santee and Word Entertainment; Label: Myrrh Records

2000: 31st Annual Dove Awards

Song of the Year: "This Is Your Time" Written by Michael W. Smith and Wes King; Publishers: Milene Music and Deer Valley Music, ASCAP; Sparrow Song and Uncle Ivan Music, BMI

Songwriter of the Year: Michael W. Smith

Male Vocalist of the Year: Steven Curtis Chapman

Female Vocalist of the Year: Jaci Velasquez

Group of the Year: Sixpence None the Richer

Artist of the Year: Steven Curtis Chapman

New Artist of the Year: Ginny Owens

Producer of the Year: Brown Bannister

Southern Gospel Album: *God Is Good* by the Gaither Vocal Band (Producers: Bill

Gaither, Michael Sykes, and Guy Penrod; Label: Spring Hill)

Southern Gospel Recorded Song: "Healing" Written by Roger Bennett: Recorded by the Cathedrals; Producer: Roger Bennett; Label: Homeland

Inspirational Album: *Selah* by Selah (Producers: Jason Kyle, Todd Smith, and Allan Hall; Label: Curb)

Inspirational Recorded Song: "I Will Follow Christ" Written by Clay Crosse and Steve Siler; Recorded by Clay Crosse; Label: Reunion

Pop/Contemporary Album: *Speechless* by Steven Curtis Chapman (Producers: Brown Bannister and Steven Curtis Chapman; Label: Sparrow)

Pop/Contemporary Recorded Song: "Dive" Written by Steven Curtis Chapman; Recorded by Steven Curtis Chapman; Label: Sparrow

Contemporary Gospel Album: *Anointed* by Anointed (Producers: Keith Crouch, Tony Rich, Chris Harris, Mark Heimermann, Wayne Tester, and Kern Brantley; Label: Myrrh)

Contemporary Gospel Recorded Song: "Power" Written by Fred Hammond and Kim Rutherford; Recorded by Fred Hammond and Radical for Christ on *The Prince of Egypt* Soundtrack; Label: Dreamworks

Traditional Gospel Album: *Healing— Live in Detroit* by Richard Smallwood with Vision (Producers: Richard Smallwood and Steven Ford; Label: Verity)

Traditional Gospel Recorded Song: "God Can" Written by Dottie Peoples; Recorded by Dottie Peoples; Label: AIR Gospel

Urban Album: insufficent amount of eligible entries

Urban Recorded Song: "Anything Is Possible" Written by Nee-c Walls-Allen, Steve Crawford, Da'Dra Crawford Greathouse, Keith Crouch, John Smith, and Sherree Ford Payne; Recorded by Anointed; Label: Myrrh

Country Album: *A Glen Campbell Christmas* by Glen Campbell (Producers: Barry Beckett and Eddie Bayers; Label: Unison)

Country Recorded Song: "Angel Band" Written by Public Domain; Recorded by Vestal Goodman and George Jones; Label: Pamplin

Rock Album: *Time* by Third Day (Producers: Robert Beeson, Bob Wohler, Blaine Barcus, Monroe Jones, and Jim Dineen; Label: Essential)

Rock Recorded Song: "Get Down" Written by Mark Stuart, Bob Herdman, Will McGinniss, Ben Cissell, Tyler Burkum; Recorded by *Audio Adrenaline*; Label: ForeFront

Hard Music Album: *Point #1* by Chevelle (Producer: Steve Albini; Label: Squint)

Hard Music Recorded Song: "MIA"; Written by Pete Loeffler, Joe Loeffler, and Sam Loeffler; Recorded by Chevelle; Label: Squint

Rap/Hip Hop Album: *Power by Raze* (Producers: Tedd Tjornham, Quinlan, and Zarc Porter; Label: ForeFront)

Rap/Hip Hop Recorded Song: "They All Fall Down" Written by T. Carter, S. Jones, R. Robbins, and O. Price; Recorded by Grits; Label: Gotee

Alternative/Modern Rock Album: *Candy Coated Waterdrops* by Plumb (Producers: Bob Wohler, Glenn Rosenstein, and Matt Bronleewe; Label: Essential)

Alternative/Modern Rock Recorded Song: "Unforgetful You" Writers: Dan Haseltine, Matt Odmark, Steve Mason, and Charlie Lowell; by Recorded by Jars of Clay; Label: Essential

Bluegrass Album: *Kentucky Bluegrass* by the Bishops (Producer: Mark Bishop; Label: Homeland)

Bluegrass Recorded Song of the Year; "So Fine" Written by Wayne Haun and Joel Lindsey; Recorded by Lewis Family; Label: Thoroughbred

Instrumental Album: *Majesty and Wonder* by Phil Keaggy (Producers: Phil Keaggy and David Shober; Label: Myrrh)

Praise and Worship Album: *Sonicflood* by Sonicflood (Producers: Bryan Lenox, Jeff Deyo, Jason Halbert, Dwayne Larring, and Aaron Blanton; Label: Gotee)

Children's Music Album: *Larry Boy: The Soundtrack by Veggie Tales* (Producers: Kurt Heinecke, Mike Nawrocki, Masaki, and David Mullen; Label: Big Idea)

Spanish Language Album of the Year: *Llegar a Ti* by Jaci Velasquez (Producers: Rudy Perez and Mark Heimermann; Label: Myrrh)

Musical of the Year: *A Christmas to Remember* by Claire Cloninger and Gary Rhodes (Publisher: Word Music)

Youth/Children's Musical of the Year; *Lord, I Lift Your Name on High*

(Producers: Karla Worley and Steven V. Taylor; Publisher: Word Music)

Choral Collection of the Year: *High and Lifted Up* (Producer: Carol Cymbala; Publisher: Brooklyn Tabernacle Music)

Special Event Album: *Streams* by Cindy Morgan, Maire Brennan, Michael McDonald, Sixpence None the Richer, Chris Rodriguez, Michelle Tumes, 4HIM, Delirious, Amy Grant, Jaci Velasquez, Burlap to Cashmere, and Point of Grace (Producers: Brent Bourgeois and Loren Balman; Label: Word)

Recorded Music Packaging: Loren Balman, Chuck Hargett, and Robert M. Ascroft II for *Streams*; Recorded by Various Artists; Label: Word

Enhanced CD of the Year: *Without Condition* by Ginny Owens (Producer: Craig A. Mason; Label: Rocketown)

Short Form Music Video: *This is Your Time* by Michael W. Smith; Producers and Directors: Amy Marsh, Brandon Dickerson, and Ben Pearson; Label: Reunion

Long Form Music Video: *The Supernatural Experience* by DC Talk; Producers and Directors: Eric Welch, Dan Pitts, and Eric Welch; Label: ForeFront

2001: 32nd Annual Dove Awards

Song of the Year: "Redeemer" Written by Nichole C. Mullen; Publishers: Seat of the Pants Music, ASCAP; Wordspring Music and Lil' Jas' Music, SESAC

Artist of the Year: New Day

New Artist of the Year: Plus One

Male Vocalist of the Year: Steven Curtis Chapman

Female Vocalist: Nichole Nordeman

Group of the Year: Third Day

Songwriter of the Year: Nichole C. Mullen

Producer of the Year: Brown Bannister

Bluegrass Album: *Inspirational Journey* by Randy Travis (Producer: Kyle Lehning; Label: Atlantic)

Bluegrass Recorded Song: "Are You Afraid to Die?" Written by Ira Louvin, Charlie Louvin and Eddie Hill; Recorded by Ricky Skaggs and Kentucky Thunder; Label: for Skaggs Family

Children's Music Album: *A Queen, a King, and a Very Blue Berry* by Veggie Tunes (Producers: Kurt Heinecke and Mike Nawrocki; Label: Big Idea)

Contemporary Gospel Album: *Purpose by Design* by Fred Hammond and Radical for Christ (Producer: Fred Hammond; Label: Verity)

Contemporary Gospel Recorded Song: "Alabaster Box" Written by Janice Sjostran; Recorded by CeCe Winans; Label: Wellspring Gospel

Country Recorded Song: "Baptism" Written by Mickey Cates; Recorded by Randy Travis; Label: Atlantic

Hard Music Album: *Above* by Pillar (Producer: Travis Wyrick; Label: Flickerrecords)

Hard Music Recorded Song: "Point #1" Written by Pete Loeffler, Sam Loeffler, and Joe Loeffler; Recorded by Chevelle; Label: Squint

Inspirational Album: *Home* by Fernando Ortega (Producer: John Andrew Schreiner; Label: Myrrh)

Inspirational Recorded Song: "Blessed" Written by Ginny Owens and Cindy Morgan; Recorded by Rachael Lampa; Label: Word

Instrumental Album: *Lights of Madrid* by Phil Keaggy (Producer: Phil Keaggy; Label: Wordartisan)

Modern Rock/Alternative Album: *Jordan's Sister* by Kendall Payne (Producers: Ron Aniello and Glen Ballard; Label: Sparrow)

Modern Rock/Alternative Recorded Song: "Dive" Written by Toby McKeehan, Michael Tait, Kevin Max. and Mark Heimermann; Recorded by DC Talk; Label: Forefront Records

Pop/Contemporary Album: *This Is Your Time* by Michael W. Smith (Producers: Michael W. Smith and Bryan Lenox; Label: Reunion)

Pop/Contemporary Recorded Song: "Redeemer" Written by Nicole C. Mullen; Recorded by Nicole C. Mullen; Label: Word

Praise and Worship Album: *Offerings: A Worship Album* by Third Day (Producers: Monroe Jones, Mac Powell, Mark Lee, Tai Anderson, Brad Avery, David Carr, and Joey Canady; Label: Essential)

Rap/Hip Hop/Dance Album: *The Plan* by Raze (Producers: Michael Anthony Talyro and Tedd Tjornhom; Label: ForeFront)

Rap/Hip Hop/Dance Recorded Song: "All Around the World" Written by Ja'Marc Davis, Zarc Porter, and Mark Pennels; Recorded by Raze; Label: ForeFront Records

Rock Album: *Tree63* by Tree63 (Producers: Andrew Philip and E. H. Holden; Label: Inpop Records)

Rock Recorded Song: "Sky Falls Down" Written by Mac Powell, Mark Lee, Tai Anderson, Brad Avery and David Carr; Recorded by Third Day; Label: Essential

Southern Gospel Album: *I Do Believe* by the Gaither Vocal Band (Producers: Bill Gaither, Guy Penrod, and Michael Sykes; Label: Spring Hill)

Southern Gospel Recorded Song: "God Is Good All the Time" Written by Tina Sadler; Recorded by the Gaither Vocal Band; Label: Spring Hill

Spanish Language Album: *Solo el Amor* by Miguel Agnel Guerra (Producer: Hal S. Batt; Label: Word Latin)

Special Event Album: *City on a Hill—Songs of Worship and Praise* by Jars of Clay, Sixpence None the Richer, Third Day, Caedmon's Call, FFH, the Choir, Gene Eugene, Sonicflood, and Peter Furler (Producer: Steve Hindalong; Label: Essential)

Traditional Gospel Album: *You Can Make It* by Shirley Caesar (Producers: Bubba Smith, Shirley Caesar and Michael Mathis; Label: Myrrh)

Traditional Gospel Recorded Song: "We Fall Down" Written by Kyle Matthews; Recorded by Donnie McClurkin; Label: Verity

Urban Album: *Thankful* by Mary Mary (Producer: Warryn "Baby Dubb" Campbell; Label: Columbia)

Urban Recorded Song: "Shackles (Praise You)" Written by Erica Atkins and Trecina Atkins; Recorded by Mary Mary; Label: Columbia

Youth/Children's Musical: *Friends 4Ever* Created by Karla Worley, Steven V. Taylor, Seth Worley, Peter Kipley,

and Michael W. Smith (Publisher: Word Music)

Choral Collection of the Year: *God Is Working* (Producer: Carol Cymbala; Publisher: published by Brooklyn Tabernacle Music

Musical of the Year: (tie): *2,000 Decembers Ago* by Joel Lindsey, Russell Maultin (Publisher: Brentwood Music) and *Redeemer* by Claire Cloninger and Robert Sterling (Publisher: Word Music)

Short Form Music Video: *Rock the Party (Off the Hook)* by P.O.D.; Producers: Angela Jones and Marcos Siega; Label: Atlantic

Long Form Music Video: *A Farewell Celebration* by the Cathedrals; Producers and Directors: Bryan Bateman, Bill Gaither, and Dennis Glore; Label: Spring House

Recorded Music Packaging: Art Directors Buddy Jackson and Karinne Caulkins/Jackson and Photographer Ben Pearson for *Roaring Lambs*; Label: Squint Records

2002: 33rd Annual Dove Awards

Song of the Year: "I Can Only Imagine," by Bart Millard; Publisher: Simpleville Music (ASCAP)

Songwriter of the Year: Bart Millard

Male Vocalist of the Year: Mac Powell

Female Vocalist of the Year: Nicole Mullen

Group of the Year: Third Day

Artist of the Year: Michael W. Smith

New Artist of the Year: ZOEgirl

Producer of the Year: Toby McKeehan

Bluegrass Album of the Year: insufficient amount of eligible entries

Bluegrass Recorded Song of the Year: "Thank You, Lord, for Your Blessings on Me" Written by Russell Easter, James Easter, and Edd Easter; from album *By Request, Their Greatest Hits*; Artist: Easter Brothers; Label: Thoroughbred

Children's Music Album of the Year: *Bedtime Prayers, Lullabies and Peaceful Worship*; Artist: Twila Paris (Producers: John Hartley and Derald Dougherty Label: Sparrow)

Contemporary Gospel Album of the Year: *CeCe Winan*; Artist: CeCe Winan (Producers: Brown Bannister, Robbie Buchanon, and Tommy Sims; Label: Wellspring Gospel)

Contemporary Gospel Recorded Song of the Year: "Anybody Wanna Pray?" by CeCe Winans; from album *CeCe Winans*; Songwriters: Cedric Caldwell, Victor Caldwell, Margaret Bell, Tommy Sims; Label: Wellspring Gospel

Country Album of the Year: *From the Heart* by the Oak Ridge Boys (Producers: Michael Sykes, Duane Allen; Label: Spring Hill)

Country Recorded Song of the Year: "Goin' Away Party" by Bruce Haynes; from album *Ordinary Day*; Artist: Jeff and Sheri Easter; Label: Spring Hill

Hard Music Album of the Year: *The Light in Guinevere's Garden*; Artist: East West (Producer: Bob Burch; Label: Floodgate)

Hard Rock Recorded Song of the Year: "Live for Him" by Rob Beckley, Travis Jenkins, Brad Noone, Michael Wittig; from album *Above*; Artist: Pillar; Label: Flicker

Inspirational Album of the Year: *Press On*; Artist: Selah; Producers: Jason Kyle, Todd Smith, Alan Hall, Nicol Smith; Label: Curb

Inspirational Recorded Song of the Year: "Above All" by Lenny LeBlanc, Paul Baloche; from album *Worship*; Artist: Michael W. Smith; Label: Reunion

Instrumental Album of the Year: *Freedom*; Artist: Michael W. Smith; Producers: Michael W. Smith, Bryan Lenox; Label: Reunion

Modern Rock/Alternative Album of the Year: *Invade My Soul*; Artist: By the Tree; Producers: Steve Hindalong, Bob Wohler; Label: Fervent

Modern Rock/Alternative Recorded Song of the Year: "Invade My Soul" by Chuck Dennie; from album *Invade My Soul*; Artist: By the Tree; Label: Fervent

Pop/Contemporary Album of the Year: *Declaration*; Artist: Steven Curtis Chapman; Producers: Brown Bannister, Steven Curtis Chapman; Label: Sparrow

Pop/Contemporary Recorded Song of the Year: "I Can Only Imagine" by Bart Millard; from album *Almost There*; Artist: MercyMe; Label: INO

Praise and Worship Album of the Year: *Worship*; Artist: Michael W. Smith; Producers: Michael W. Smith, Tom Laune; Label: Reunion

Rap/Hip Hop Recorded Song of the Year: "Somebody's Watching Me"; by TobyMac; on album *Momentum*; Label: ForeFront

Rap/Hip Hop/Dance Album of the Year: *Momentum*; Artist: TobyMac; Producers: TobyMac, Michael Anthony Taylor, Pete Stewart, Jeff Savage,

Randy Crawford, Todd Collins; Label: ForeFront

Rock Album of the Year: *Come Together*; Artist: Third Day; Producer: Monroe Jones; Label: Essential

Rock Recorded Song of the Year: "Come Together" by Tai Anderson, Brad Avery, David Carr, Mark Lee, Mac Powell; from album *Come Together*; Artist: Third Day; Label: Essential

Southern Gospel Album of the Year: *Encore*; Artist: Old Friends Quartet; Producers: Bill Gaither, Wesley Pritchard, Ben Speer; Label: Spring House

Southern Gospel Recorded Song of the Year: "He's Watching Me" by Tina Sadler; from album *I Do Believe*; Artist: Gaither Vocal Band; Label: Spring Hill

Spanish Language Album of the Year: *Mi Corazon*; Artist: Jaci Velasquez; Producers: Emilio Estefan, Jr. Rudy Perez, Mark Heimermann, Alberto Gaitin, Ricardo Gaitin, Alejandro Jean, Freddy Pinero, Jr., Lewis Martinee, and Jose Miguel Velasquez; Label: Word

Special Event Album of the Year: *Prayer of Jabez*; Artists: Sarah Sadler, Margaret Becker, Geroff Moore, Steve Reischl, Erin O'Donnell, Adrienne Liesching, Jamie Rowe, Phil Keaggy, Rebecca St. James, Michael Tait, Jill Phillips, Kevin Max; John Hartley, and David Zaffiro; Label: ForeFront

Traditional Gospel Album of the Year: *Hymns*; Artist: Shirley Caesar; Producers: Bubba Smith, Shirley Caesar, and Michael Mathis; Label: Word

Traditional Gospel Recorded Song of the Year: "Hold On" by Jessy Dixon; from album *Press On*; Artist: Selah; Label: Curb

Urban Album of the Year: *Just Remember Christmas*; Artist: Fred Hammond; Producer: Fred Hammond; Label: Verity

Urban Recorded Song of the Year: "Thank You" by Kirk Franklin; from album *Kingdom Come: The Soundtrack*; Artists: Kirk Franklin and Mary Mary; Label: Gospo Centric

Youth/Children's Musical of the Year: *The Noise We Make*; Writers: Karla Worley and Robert Sterling; Label: Word

Choral Collection of the Year: *God of Wonders*; Writers: Steven V. Taylor, Johnathan Crumpton; Publisher: Brentwood

Musical of the Year: *He Chose the Nails*; Writers: Bryan Lenox, Glenn Wagner; Publisher: Here to Him

Short Form Music Video of the Year: *Call on Jesus*; Artist: Nicole C. Mullen; Video: Randy Brewer, Jeffrey Phillips; Label: Word

Long Form Music Video of the Year: *Third Day Live in Concert—The Offerings Experience*; Artist: Third Day; Video: Micahel Sacci, Ken Conrad, Carl Diebold, Company: CT Ventures

Recorded Music Packaging of the Year: Album: *Freedom*; Artist: Michael W. Smith; Graphics: Tim Parker; Tim Parker; Andrew Southam; Label: Reunion

2003: 34th Annual Dove Awards

Song of the Year: "Holy" by Nichole Nordeman, Mark Hammond;

Publishers: Ariose Music, Mark Hammond Music (ASCAP)

Songwriter of the Year: Nichole Nordeman

Male Vocalist of the Year: Michael W. Smith

Female Vocalist of the Year: Nichole Nordeman

Group of the Year: Third Day

Artist of the Year: Michael W. Smith

New Artist of the Year: Paul Colman Trio

Producer of the Year: Brown Bannister

Bluegrass Recorded Song of the Year: "Walkin' and Talkin'" by Wayne Haun, Joel Lindsey; from album: *50th Anniversary*; Artist: The Lewis Family; Label: Thoroughbred

Children's Music Album of the Year: *Jonah, A Veggie Tales Movie Original Soundtrack*; Producers: Kurt Heinecke, Phil Vischer, Mike Nawrocki, David Mullin, Steve Taylor, Monroe Jones; Label: Big Idea

Contemporary Gospel Album of the Year: *The Rebirth of Kirk Franklin*; Artist: Kirk Franklin; Producers: Sanchez Harley, Kirk Franklin; Label: Gospo Centric

Contemporary Gospel Recorded Song of the Year: "In the Morning" by Warryn Campbell, Tina Atkins-Campbell, Erica Atkins-Campbell, J. Campbell; from album *Incredible*; Artist: Mary Mary; Label: Integrity

Country Album of the Year: *Rise and Shine*; Artist: Randy Travis; Producer: Kyle Lehning; Label: Word

Country Recorded Song of the Year: "The River's Gonna Keep on Rolling" by Amy Grant; from album *Legacy . . . Hymns and Faith*; Producer: Vince Gill; Label: Word

Hard Music Album of the Year: *Fireproof*; Artist: Pillar; Producer: Travis Wyrick; Label: Flicker

Hard Music Recorded Song of the Year: "Boom" by P.O.D. (Traa, Sonny, Marcos, Wuv), Paul Sandoval, Marco Curiel, Mark Traa, Noah Bernardo, Satellite; Artist: P.O.D.; Label: Atlantic

Inspirational Album of the Year: *Legacy . . . Hymns and Faith*; Artist: Amy Grant; Producers: Brown Bannister, Vince Gill; Label: Word

Inspirational Recorded Song of the Year: "Here I Am to Worship" by Tim Hughes; from album *Here I Am to Worship*; Artist: Tim Hughes; Label: Worship Together

Instrumental Album of the Year: *Hymnsongs*; Artist: Phil Keaggy; Producers: Phil Keaggy, Ric Kardinski; Label: Word

Modern Rock/Alternative Album of the Year: *The Eleventh Hour*; Artist: Jars of Clay; Producers: Dan Haseltine, Charlie Lowell, Stephen Mason, Matt Odmark; Label: Essential

Modern Rock/Alternative Recorded Song of the Year: "Breathe Your Name" by Matt Slocum; from album *Divine Discontent*; Artist: Sixpence None the Richer; Label: Reprise

Pop/Contemporary Album of the Year: *Woven and Spun*; Artist: Nichole Nordeman; Producers: Charlie Peacock, Mark Hammond; Label: Sparrow

Pop/Contemporary Recorded Song of the Year: "Holy" by Nichole

Nordeman, Mark Hammond; from album *Woven and Spun*; Artist: Nichole Nordeman; Label: Sparrow

Praise and Worship Album of the Year: *Worship Again*; Artist: Michael W. Smith; Producer: Michael W. Smith; Label: Reunion

Rap/Hip Hop Recorded Song of the Year: "All Around the World" by Joshua Washington, Je'kob Washington and Rachel Washington, Chris Rodriquez; from album *Fault Is History*; Artist: Souljahz; Label: Warner Brothers

Rap/Hip Hop/Dance Album of the Year: *The Art of Translation*; Artist: GRITS; Producers: Teron Carter, Stacey Jones, Ric Robbins, Otto Price, Kennie Bell; Label: Gotee

Rock Album of the Year: *Lift*; Artist: Audio Adrenaline; Producers: Mark Stuart, Will McGinnis, Ben Cissell, Tyler Burkam; Label: ForeFront

Rock Recorded Song of the Year: "40 Days" by Mac Powell, Brad Avery, David Carr, Mark Lee, Tai Anderson; from album *Come Together*; Artist: Third Day; Label: Essential

Southern Gospel Album of the Year: *50th Anniversary Celebration*; Artist: Lewis Family; Producers: Wayne Haun, Buddy Spicher; Label: Thoroughbred

Southern Gospel Recorded Song of the Year: "Don't You Wanna Go?" by Gerald Crabb; from album *A Crabb Collection*; Artist: The Crabb Family; Label: Family Music Group

Spanish Language Album of the Year: *Navidad*; Artist: Jaci Velasquez; Producers: Chris Harris for Fun Attic Prod., Alejandro Jean; Label: Word

Special Event Album of the Year: *City on a Hill—Sing Alleluia*; Artists: Caedmon's Call, FFH, Jars of Clay, Jennifer Knapp, Phil Keaggy, Nichole Nordeman, Bebo Norman, Fernando Ortega, the Choir, Third Day; Producers: Steve Hindalong, Marc Byrd; Label: Essential

Traditional Gospel Album of the Year: *Higher Ground*; Artist: Blind Boys of Alabama; Producers: John Chelew; Label: Real World/EMI Gospel

Traditional Gospel Recorded Song of the Year: "Holding On" by Dorothy Love-Coates; from album *Amazing Love*; Artist: Mississippi Mass Choir; Label: Malaco

Urban Album of the Year: (Tie) *Fault Is History*; Artist: Souljahz; Producer: Tonex; Label: Warner Brothers; and *This Is Your Life*; Artist: Out of Eden; Producers: Lisa Kimmey, Donnie Scantz, Jaimie Portee, Nate Clemmons; Label: Gotee

Urban Recorded Song of the Year: "Meditate" by Lisa Kimmey, Michael Clemons, Nate Clemons, Eric Roberson; from album *This Is Your Life*; Artist: Out of Eden; Label: Gotee

Musical of the Year: *The Christmas Shoes*; Writers: Donna VanLiere, Eddie Carswell, J. Daniel Smith; Publisher: Brentwood Music Publications

Youth/Children's Musical of the Year: *Meet Me at the Manger*; Writer: Celeste Clydesdale; Publisher: Clydesdale and Clydesdale Music

Choral Collection of the Year: *More Songs for Praise and Worship 2*; Arrangers: Ken Barker, Keith Christopher; Label: Word Music

Long Form Music Video of the Year: *Worship*; Artist: Michael W. Smith; Producer: Michael W. Smith; Video: Michael Sacci, Ken Conrad; Carl Diebold; Label: Reunion

Short Form Music Video of the Year: *Irene*; Artist: TobyMac; Video: Alex Moon; Rick Kim; Label: ForeFront

Recorded Music Packaging of the Year: *Welcome to the Rock 'n' Roll Worship Circus: Rock 'n' Roll Worship*; Graphics: Sam Noerr, Matthew Lloyd; Karen Mason-Blair; Vertical

2004: 35th Annual Dove Awards

Song of the Year: "Word of God Speak" by Pete Kipley, Bart Millard; Publishers: Wordspring Music/Songs from the Indigo Room (SESAC), Simpleville Music (ASCAP)

Songwriter of the Year: Mark Hall

Male Vocalist of the Year: Jeremy Camp

Female Vocalist of the Year: Stacie Orrico

Group of the Year: MercyMe

Artist of the Year: MercyMe

New Artist of the Year: Jeremy Camp

Producer of the Year: Brown Bannister

Bluegrass Album of the Year: *Wondrous Love*; Artist: Blue Highway; Producer: Alan O'Bryant; Label: Rounder

Bluegrass Recorded Song of the Year: "So Many Years, So Many Blessings" by Wayne Haun, Cindi Ballard, Belinda Smith; on album *50th Anniversary*; Artist: The Lewis Family; Label: Thoroughbred Records

Children's Music Album of the Year: *Shout Praises Kids 3*; Artist: Jeff Sandstrom; Label: Integrity Music

Contemporary Gospel Album of the Year: *Limited Edition*; Artist: Smokie Norful; Producers: Smokie Norful, Myron Butler; Label: EMI Gospel

Contemporary Gospel Recorded Song of the Year: "Hallelujah Praise" by CeCe Winans, Cedric Caldwell, Victor Caldwell; from album *Throne Room*; Artist: CeCe Winans; Label: Pure Springs Gospel

Country Album of the Year: *Worship and Faith*; Artist: Randy Travis; Producer: Kyle Lehning; Label: Word Records

Country Recorded Song of the Year: "Three Wooden Crosses" by Doug Johnson, Kim Williams; from album *Rise and Shine*; Artist: Randy Travis; Label: Word Records

Inspirational Album of the Year: *Above It All*; Artist: The Martins; Producer: Phil Naish; Label: Spring Hill Music

Inspirational Recorded Song of the Year: "Everything to Me" by Chad Cates, Sue Smith; from album *Testify to Love: The Very Best of Avalon*; Artist: Avalon; Label: Sparrow Records

Instrumental Album of the Year: *An Acoustic Christmas*; Artist: Tom Hemby; Producer: Tom Hemby; Label: Integrity Music

Modern Rock Album of the Year: *Two Lefts Don't Make a Right . . . But Three Do*; Artist: Relient K; Producers: Mark Lee Townsend, Matthew Thiessen; Label: Gotee Records

Modern Rock Recorded Song of the Year: "Breaking Me Down" by Marc Martel, Jason Germain, Glen Lavender; from album *So Much for Substitutes*; Artist: Downhere; Label: Word Records

Pop/Contemporary Album of the Year: *Stacie Orrico*; Artist: Stacie Orrico; Producers: Dallas Austin, Tedd T., Anthony Dent, Harvey Mason Jr., Damon Thomas, Matt Serletic, Sean Hosein, Dane DeViller, Matt Rollings, Moodie; Label: ForeFront Records

Pop/Contemporary Recorded Song of the Year: "Word of God Speak" by Bart Millard, Pete Kipley; from album *Spoken For*; Artist: MercyMe; Label: INO

Praise and Worship Album of the Year: *Offerings II—All I Have to Give*; Artist: Third Day; Producers: Tai Anderson, Brad Avery, David Carr, Mark Lee, Mac Powell, Monroe Jones; Label: Essential Records

Rap/Hip Hop Album of the Year: *It's Pronounced Five Two*; Artist: KJ-52; Producer: Todd Collins; Label: Uprok Records

Rap/Hip Hop Recorded Song of the Year: "Believe" by Jennifer Knapp, Teron Carter, Stacy Jones, Kene Bell, Otto Price; from album *The Art of Translation*; Artist: Grits; Label: Gotee Records

Rock Album of the Year: *Lose This Life*; Artist: Tait; Producers: Mark Heimermann, Michael Tait, Matt Bronleewe, Chad Chapin; Label: ForeFront Records

Rock Recorded Song of the Year: "Ammunition" by Jonathan Foreman; from album *The Beautiful Letdown*; Artist: Switchfoot; Label: Sparrow Records

Rock/Contemporary Album of the Year: *The Beautiful Letdown*; Artist: Switchfoot; Producers: John Fields, Chad Butler, Jerome Fontamillas; Jonathan Foreman, Tim Foreman; Label: Sparrow Records

Rock/Contemporary Recorded Song of the Year: "Meant to Live" by Jonathan Foreman, Tim Foreman; from album *The Beautiful Letdown*; Artist: Switchfoot; Label: Sparrow Records

Southern Gospel Album of the Year: *The Walk*; Artist: The Crabb Family; Producers: Jason Crabb, Adam Crabb, Aaron Crabb; Label: Daywind Music Group

Southern Gospel Recorded Song of the Year: (Tie) "The Cross" by Gerald Crabb; from album *The Walk*; Artist: The Crabb Family; Label: Daywind Music Group; and "The Promise" by Brian White, Don Poythress; from album *Above It All*, Artist: The Martins; Label: Spring Hill Music

Spanish Language Album of the Year: *Con Poder*, Artist: Salvador; Producer: Carlos Sosa; Label: Word Records

Special Event Album of the Year: *!Hero the Rock Opera*; Artists: Michael Tait, Mark Stuart, Rebecca St. James, T-Bone, Pete Stewart, Grits, John Cooper, Bob Farrell, Matt Hamnitt, Nirva, Paul Wright, Quinlan, Donnie Lewis; Producers: Pete Stewart, Eddie DeGarmo; Label: Meaux Records

Traditional Gospel Album of the Year: *CeCe Winans Presents . . . The Born Again Church Choir*; Artist: The Born

Again Church Choir; Producers: Cedric and Victor Caldwell; Label: Pure Springs Gospel

Traditional Gospel Recorded Song of the Year: "Poor Man Lazarus" by Jester Hairston; from album *In Bright Mansions;* Artist: Fisk Jubilee Singers; Label: Curb Records

Urban Album of the Year: *Unclassified*; Artist: Robert Randolph and the Family Band; Producers: Robert Randolph, Danyel Morgan, Marcus Randolph, John Ginty, Jim Scott; Label: Warner Brothers

Urban Recorded Song of the Year: "Dance, Dance, Dance" by Mary Mary, Erica Atkins-Campbell, Trecina Atkins-Campbell, Warryn Campbell; from album *Gotta Have Gospel*; Label: Integrity Gospel

Musical of the Year: *The Wonderful Cross*; Writers: David Guthrie, Dave Williamson; Publisher: Word Music

Choral Collection of the Year: *High Praises*; Arrangers: Phil Barfoot, Lari Goss; Label: Word Music

Worship Song of the Year: "Here I Am to Worship" by Tim Hughes; Publisher: Kingsway's Thankyou Music

Youth/Children's Musical of the Year: *Noelle, The First*; Writers: Annette Oden, Dave Noel; Label: Integrity Music

Long Form Music Video of the Year: *Third Day Live in Concert, The Come Together Tour*; Artist: Third Day; Video: Carl Diebold; Michael Sacci, Ken Conrad, Brian Mitchell, Terria Saunders, Paul Kerby; Jupiter Project; Label: Essential Records

Short Form Music Video of the Year: *(There's Gotta Be) More to Life*;

Artist: Stacie Orrico; Video: Dave Meyers, Joseph Sassone; Radical Media; Label: ForeFront Records

Recorded Music Packaging of the Year: *!Hero the Rock Opera*; Graphics: Bethany Newman; Bethany Newman; Todd and Jess Ericson, Kenda Benward, Elton Sawyer, Meaux Records

2005: 36th Annual Dove Awards

Song of the Year: "Who Am I" by Mark Hall; Publishers: Club Zoo Music (BMI), SWECS Music (BMI)

Songwriter of the Year: Mark Hall

Male Vocalist of the Year: Jeremy Camp

Female Vocalist of the Year: Nicole C. Mullen

Group of the Year: Casting Crowns

Artist of the Year: Switchfoot

New Artist of the Year: Building 429

Producer of the Year: Ed Cash

Bluegrass Album of the Year: *Angels Gathering Flowers*; Artist: The Lewis Family; Producer: Wayne Haun; Label: Thoroughbred Records

Bluegrass Recorded Song of the Year: "Heroes" by Rebecca Isaacs Bowman, Sonya Isaacs; from album *Heroes*; Artist: The Isaacs; Publisher: Gaither Music

Children's Music Album of the Year: *Angel Alert!*; Artist: Various; Producers: Celeste Clydesdale, David T. Clydesdale; Label: Word Music

Contemporary Gospel Album of the Year: *Live from Another Level*; Artist: Israel and New Breed; Producers: Israel Houghton, Aaron W. Lindsey; Label: Integrity Gospel

Contemporary Gospel Recorded Song of the Year: "Again I Say Rejoice" by Israel Houghton, Aaron Lindsey; from album *Live from Another Level*; Artist: Israel and New Breed; Label: Integrity Gospel

Country Album of the Year: *Passing Through*; Artist: Randy Travis; Producer: Kyle Lehning; Label: Word Records

Country Recorded Song of the Year: "Forever" by Jason Crabb, Gerald Crabb; from album *Driven*; Artist: The Crabb Family; Label: Daywind Records

Inspirational Album of the Year: *Hiding Place*; Artist: Selah; Producers: Jason Kyle, Nicol Sponberg, Allan Hall, Todd Smith; Label: Curb Records

Inspirational Recorded Song of the Year: "Voice of Truth" by Mark Hall, Steven Curtis Chapman; from album *Casting Crowns*; Artist: Casting Crowns; Label: Beach Street Records/ Reunion Records

Instrumental Album of the Year: *The Passion of the Christ Original Motion Picture Soundtrack*; Artists: Various; Producers: John Debney, Mel Gibson; Label: Integrity Music/Sony

Modern Rock Album of the Year: *Fight the Tide*; Artist: Sanctus Real; Producer: Tedd T.; Artist: Sparrow Records

Modern Rock Recorded Song of the Year: "Control" by Paul Meany, Darren King, Adam LeClave; from album *Reset EP*; Artist: MuteMath; Label: Teleprompt Records/Word Records

Musical of the Year: *Emmanuel— Celebrating Heaven's Child*; Writers:

Joel Lindsey, Russell Mauldin; Publisher: Brentwood-Benson Music

Pop/Contemporary Album of the Year: *Undone*; Artist: MercyMe; Producer: Pete Kipley; Label: INO Records

Pop/Contemporary Recorded Song of the Year: "Who Am I" by Mark Hall; from album *Casting Crowns*; Artist: Casting Crowns; Label: Beach Street Records/Reunion Records

Praise and Worship Album of the Year: *Arriving*; Artist: Chris Tomlin; Producer: Ed Cash; Label: Sixstepsrecords

Rap/Hip Hop Album of the Year: *Welcome to Diverse City*; Artist: TobyMac; Producers: Toby McKeehan, Christopher Stevens, Paul Meany, Solomon Olds, Joe Baldridge, Jeff Savage, Robert Marvin, Josiah Bell, Max Hsu, Michael Linney; Label: ForeFront Records

Rap/Hip Hop Recorded Song of the Year: "Hittin' Curves" by Teron Carter, Stacy Jones, Otto Price, S. Moss; from album *Dichotomy A*; Artist: Grits; Label: Gotee Records

Rock Album of the Year: *Day of Fire*; Artist: Day of Fire; Producer: Scott Humphrey; Label: Essential Records

Rock Recorded Song of the Year: "Stay" by Jeremy Camp; from album *Stay*; Artist: Jeremy Camp; Label: BEC Records

Rock/Contemporary Album of the Year: *Wire*; Artist: Third Day; Producer: Paul Ebersold; Label: Essential Records

Rock/Contemporary Recorded Song of the Year: "Dare You to Move" by Jonathan Foreman; from album *The*

Beautiful Letdown; Artist: Switchfoot; Label: Sparrow Records

Southern Gospel Album of the Year: *Driven*; Artist: The Crabb Family; Producers: Jason Crabb, Adam Crabb, Aaron Crabb, Kelly Bowling, Jerry Yoder; Label: Daywind Records

Southern Gospel Recorded Song of the Year: "He Came Looking for Me" by Gerald Crabb; from album *Driven*; Artist: Crabb Family; Label: Daywind Records

Spanish Language Album of the Year: *Te Amo Dios*; Artist: Praise Street Worship Band; Producers: Dave Moody, James Cobble Jr., Wesley Pritchard, Eulises Canada, Nelson McSwain; Label: Lamon Records

Special Event Album of the Year: *The Passion of the Christ: Songs*; Artists: Third Day, Steven Curtis Chapman, MercyMe, Scott Stap, POD, Brad Paisley, Sara Evans, Big Dismal, Lauryn Hill, Kirk Franklin, Yolanda Adams, MxPx, Mark Hoppus, Charlotte Church, BeBe Winans, Angie Stone, Dan Lavery; Producers: Tim Cook, Mark Joseph, Gregg Wattenberg, Steven Lemer; Label: Lost Keyword Records/Wind-Up Records

Traditional Gospel Album of the Year: *A Tribute to Mahalia Jackson*; Artist: Lynda Randle; Producer: Barry Beckett; Label: Gaither Music

Traditional Gospel Recorded Song of the Year: "Through the Fire" by Gerald Cragg; from album *Driven*; Artist: The Crabb Family featuring Donnie McClurkin; Label: Daywind Records

Urban Album of the Year: *Everyday People*; Artist: Nicole C. Mullen; Producers: Nicole C. Mullen, David Mullen, Tommy Sims, James "Big Jim" Wright, Andrew Ramsey, Shannon Sanders; Label: Word Records

Urban Recorded Song of the Year: "You Don't Know" by Rodney Jenkins, Danny Nixon, Fred Jenkins, LaShawn Daniels, Delisha Thomas; from album *I Owe You*; Artist: Kierra Kiki Sheard; Label: EMI Gospel

Worship Song of the Year: "Blessed Be Your Name"; Writers: Matt Redman, Beth Redman; Publishers: Thankyou Music, Worshiptogether.com Songs

Youth/Children's Musical of the Year: *Fear Not Factor*; Producers: Dennis Allen, Nan Allen; Label: Brentwood-Benson Music

Choral Collection of the Year: *Live . . . This is Your House*; Arranger: Carol Cymbala; Publisher: Brooklyn Tabernacle Music

Long Form Music Video of the Year: *Switchfoot Live in San Diego*; Artist: Switchfoot; Video: Dwight Thompson; New Revolution Entertainment; Label: Sparrow Records

Short Form Music Video of the Year: *Dare You to Move*; Artist: Switchfoot; Video: Nina Grossman Warner; Robert Hales; HIS Entertainment; Label: Sparrow Records

Recorded Music Packaging of the Year: *Happy*. Graphics: Jan Cook, Tim Frank, Emily West, Clark Hook, Susan Levy; Clark Hook, Michael Lavine; Label: Universal South

2006: 37th Annual Dove Awards

Song of the Year: "How Great Is Our God" by Chris Tomlin, Jesse Reeves, Ed Cash; Publishers: Worshiptogether.

com Songs (ASCAP), sixsteps music (ASCAP), Alletrope Music (BMI)

Songwriter of the Year: Christa Wells

Male Vocalist of the Year: Chris Tomlin

Female Vocalist of the Year: Natalie Grant

Group of the Year: Casting Crowns

Artist of the Year: Chris Tomlin

New Artist of the Year: The Afters

Producer of the Year: Ed Cash

Bluegrass Album of the Year: *One Rose*; Artist: Lewis Family; Producer: Wayne Haun; Label: Thoroughbred Records

Bluegrass Recorded Song of the Year: "Living Prayer" by Ronald Block; on album *Lonely Runs Both Ways*; Artist: Alison Krauss and Union Station; Label: Rounder Records

Children's Music Album of the Year: *Absolute Modern Worship for Kids*; Artists: Various; Producer: Craig Adams; Label: Fervent Records

Contemporary Gospel Album of the Year: *Mary Mary*; Artist: Mary Mary; Producers: Warryn Campbell, Dontae Winslow, Nisan Stewart, Steve Huff, Charlie Beveal, Kenny Beveal, Jazz Nixon; Label: Sony Urban/Columbia/My Block

Contemporary Gospel Recorded Song of the Year: "Not Forgotten" by Israel Houghton and Aaron W. Lindsey; from album *Alive in South Africa*; Artist: Israel and New Breed; Label: Integrity Gospel

Country Album of the Year: *Glory Train*; Artist: Randy Travis; Producer: Kyle Lehning; Label: Word Records

Country Recorded Song of the Year: "Jesus, Take the Wheel" by Brett James, Hillary Lindsey, Gordie Sampson; from album *Some Hearts*; Artist: Carrie Underwood; Label: Arista/Arista Nashville/19 Recordings

Inspirational Album of the Year: (Tie) *Hymned*; Artist: Bart Millard; Producers: Brown Bannister and Bart Millard; Label: Simple Records/INO Records; and *Rock of Ages . . . Hymns and Faith*; Artist: Amy Grant; Producers: Brown Bannister and Vince Gill; Label: Word Records

Inspirational Recorded Song of the Year: "In Christ Alone" by Don Koch and Shawn Craig; on album *WOW #1's*; Artist: Brian Littrell; Label: Reunion Records

Instrumental Album of the Year: *Life;* Artist: Andy Hunter; Producers: Tedd T. and Andy Hunter; Label: Sparrow Records

Pop/Contemporary Album of the Year: *Lifesong*; Artist: Casting Crowns; Producer: Mark A. Miller; Label: Beachstreet Records/Reunion Records

Pop/Contemporary Recorded Song of the Year: "Cry out to Jesus" by Mac Powell, Mai Anderson, Brad Avery, David Carr, and Mark Lee; from album *Wherever You Are*; Artist: Third Day; Label: Essential Records

Praise and Worship Album of the Year: *Blessed Be Your Name: The Songs of Matt Redman, Vol. 1*; Producers: Matt Redman and Nathan Nockels; Label: Sparrow Records/sixstepsrecords

Rap/Hip Hop Album of the Year: *Behind the Musik*; Artist: KJ-52; Producers: Aaron Sprinkle, Todd Collins, Tedd T., and KJ-52; Label: BEC Recordings/Uprok Records

Rap/Hip Hop Recorded Song of the Year: "Trainwreck" by Mat Keamey and Robert Marvin; from album *Bullet*; Artist: Mat Keamey; Label: Inpop Records

Rock Album of the Year: *Mmhmm*; Artist: Relient K; Producers: Mark Lee Townsend and Matthew Theissen; Label: Gotee Records/Capitol Records

Rock Recorded Song of the Year: "The Slam" by Toby McKeehan, Christopher Stevens, Joe Weber, T-Bone; from album *Welcome to Diverse City*; Artist: TobyMac featuring T-Bone; Label: ForeFront Records

Rock/Contemporary Album of the Year: *A Collision*; Artist: David Crowder Band; Producers: David Crowder, Jason Solley, Mike Hogan, Jack Parker, Mike Dodson, Jeremy Bush, and Tedd T.; Label: sixstepsrecords/Sparrow Records

Rock/Contemporary Recorded Song of the Year: "Here is Our King" by David Crowder; from album *A Collision*; Artist: David Crowder Band; Label: sixstepsrecords/Sparrow Records

Southern Gospel Album of the Year: *Live at Brooklyn Tabernacle*; Artist: Crabb Family; Producers: Jason Crabb, Adam Crabb, Aaron Crabb, and Kelly Bowling; Label: Daywind Music Group

Southern Gospel Recorded Song of the Year: (Tie): "Long as I Got King Jesus" by James Cleveland; from album *Live in NYC*; Artist: Brian Free and Assurance; Label: DayWind Music Group; and "Through the Fire" by Gerald Crabb; from album *Live at Brooklyn Tabernacle*; Artist: Crabb Family featuring Brooklyn Tabernacle Choir; Label: Daywind Music Group

Spanish Language Album of the Year: *Leonardo*; Artist: Leonardo; Producers: Isaac Hernandez and Leonardo Villanueva; Label: Lamon Records

Special Event Album of the Year: *Music Inspired by the Chronicles of Narnia: The Lion, the Witch, and the Wardrobe*; Artists: Jeremy Camp, Steven Curtis Chapman, David Crowder Band, Delirious, Bethany Dillon, Jars of Clay, Kutless, Nichole Nordeman, Rebecca St. James, TobyMac, and Chris Tomlin; Producers: Ed Cash, Steven Curtis Chapman, David Crowder, Andy Dodd, Sam Gibson, Dan Haseltine, Charlie Lowell, Toby McKeehan, Adam Watts, Christopher Stevens, and Mitch Dane; Label: Sparrow Records

Traditional Gospel Album of the Year: *Atom Bomb*; Artist: Blind Boys of Alabama; Producer: John Chelew; Label: Narada/EMI Gospel

Traditional Gospel Recorded Song of the Year: "God Blocked It" by Kurt Carr; from album *One Church Project*; Artist: Kurt Carr; Label: Gospo Centric/Zomba

Urban Album of the Year: *Hero*; Artist: Kirk Franklin; Producers: Kirk Franklin, Chris Godbey, Shaun Martin; Label: Fo Yo Soul/Zomba

Urban Recorded Song of the Year: "Looking for You" by Kirk Franklin,

Patrice Rushen, Charles Mims, Sheree-lyn Brown, and Fred Washington; from album *Hero*; Artist: Kirk Franklin; Label: Fo Yo Soul/Zomba

Worship Song of the Year: "How Great Is Our God"; Writers: Chris Tomlin, Jesse Reeves, and Ed Cash; Publishers: Worshiptogether.com Songs, sixsteps Music, Alletrope Music

Choral Collection of the Year: *Seasons of Praise*; Arranger: Carol Cymbala; Publisher: Brooklyn Tabernacle Music

Musical of the Year: *Grace That Amazes*; Producers: Claire Cloninger and Lari Goss; Label: Word Music

Youth/Children's Musical of the Year: *His Renown*; Producers: Steven V. Taylor and Louie Giglio; Label: Word Music

Long Form Music Video of the Year: *A Night of Stories and Songs*; Artist: Mark Schultz; Video: Ken Carpenter and Franklin Films; Label: Word Records

Short Form Music Video of the Year: *Stars*; Artist: Switchfoot; Video: Coleen Haynes, Scott Speer, and HIS Productions; Label: Sparrow Records/ Columbia Records

Recorded Music Packaging of the Year: *Redemption Songs* (Jars of Clay); Graphics: Stephanie McBrayer, Tim Parker, and Jimmy Abegg; Label: Essential Records

2007: 38th Annual Dove Awards

Song of the Year: "My Savior My God" by Aaron Shust; Publishers: Bridge Building, Whitespot Publishing

Songwriter of the Year: Aaron Shust

Male Vocalist of the Year: Chris Tomlin

Female Vocalist of the Year: Natalie Grant

Group of the Year: Casting Crowns

Artist of the Year: Chris Tomlin

New Artist of the Year: Aaron Shust

Producer of the Year: Ed Cash

Bluegrass Album of the Year: *Flyin' High*; Artist: Lewis Family; Producers: Wayne Haun and Kevin Ward; Label: Mountain Home

Bluegrass Recorded Song of the Year: "My Cross" by Wayne Haun; from album *Flyin' High*; Label: Lewis Family; Label: Vine Records

Christmas Album of the Year: *Christmas Offerings*; Artist: Third Day; Producers: Mac Powell, Tai Anderson, Brad Avery, David Carr, Mark Lee, Don McCollister; Label: Essential Records

Contemporary Gospel Album of the Year: *It's Not Over*; Artist: Karen Clark Sheard; Producers: Otto Price, Israel Houghton, Aaron Lindsey, Karen Clark Sheard, PAJAM, and John Orew Sheard; Label: Word Records

Contemporary Gospel Recorded Song of the Year: "Turn It Around" by Israel Houghton and Aaron Lindsey; from album *Alive in South Africa*; Artist: Israel and New Breed; Label: Integrity Gospel

Country Album of the Year: *Precious Memories*; Artist: Alan Jackson; Producer: Keith Stegall; Label: Arista Records

Country Recorded Song of the Year: "Jonah, Job and Moses" by Tia Sillers and Bill Anderson; from album *Front Row Seats*; Artist: Oak Ridge Boys; Label: Spring Hill Music

Inspirational Album of the Year: *Bless the Broken Road: The Duets Album*; Artist: Selah; Producers: Jason Kyle, Allan Hall, and Todd Smith; Label: Curb Records

Inspirational Recorded Song of the Year: "Find Your Wings" by Mark Harris and Tony Wood; from album: *The Line Between the Two*; Artist: Mark Harris; Label: INO Records

Instrumental Album of the Year: *End of the Spear Soundtrack*; Producers: Ronald Owen, Howell Gibbens, Matt Cody, David Mullen, Jamie Moore, Steven Curtis Chapman, Brown Bannister, Otto Price; Label: Word Records

Pop/Contemporary Album of the Year: *See the Morning*; Artist: Chris Tomlin; Producer: Ed Cash; Label: Sparrow Records, sixstepsrecords

Pop/Contemporary Recorded Song of the Year: "Praise You in this Storm" by Mark Hall, Bernie Herms; from album *Lifesong*; Artist: Casting Crowns; Label: Beach Street Records/ Reunion Records

Praise and Worship Album of the Year: *See the Morning*; Artist: Chris Tomlin; Producer: Ed Cash; Label: Sparrow Records, sixstepsrecords

Rap/Hip Hop Album of the Year: *Remixed*; Artist: KJ-52; Producers: KJ-52, Aaron Sprinkle, Joseph A. Kisselburgh, and Funky DJ Pablo; Label: BEC Recordings

Rap/Hip Hop Recorded Song of the Year: "Never Look Away" by John Sorrentino and Aaron Sprinkle; from album *Behind the Musik* (a boy named Jonah); Artist: KJ-52 featuring Brynn Sanchez; Label: BEC Recordings

Rock Album of the Year: *DecembeRadio*; Artist: DecembeRadio; Producer: Scotty Wilbanks; Label: Slanted Records

Rock Recorded Song of the Year: "Breathe into Me" by Jasen Rauch, Anthony Armstrong, Rob Graves, and Jason McArthur; from album *End of Silence*; Artist: Red; Label: Essential Records

Rock/Contemporary Album of the Year: *Good Monsters*; Artist: Jars of Clay; Producers: Dan Hasletine, Steve Mason, Charlie Lowell, and Matt Odmark; Label: Essential Records

Rock/Contemporary Recorded Song of the Year: "Me and Jesus" by Adam Agee and Ian Eskelin; from album *We Can't Stand Sitting Down*; Artist: Stellar Kart; Label: Word Records

Southern Gospel Album of the Year: *Give It Away*; Artist: Gaither Vocal Band; Producers: Bill Gaither, Michael Sykes, Marshall Hall, Guy Penrod, and Wes Hampton; Label: Gaither Music Group

Southern Gospel Recorded Song of the Year: "Give It Away" by Gloria Gaither and Benjamin Gaither; from album *Give It Away*; Artist: Gaither Vocal Band; Label: Gaither Music Group

Spanish Language Album of the Year: *Si Alguna Vez*; Artist: Alejandra; Producer: Alex Orozco; Label: Integrity Music Latin

Special Event Album of the Year: *Passion: Everything Glorious*; Artists:

Chris Tomlin, Christy Nockels, Kristian Stanfill, Charlie Hall, Matt Redman, and David Crowder Band; Producer: Nathan Nockels; Label: Sparrow Records, sixstepsrecords

Traditional Gospel Album of the Year: *Mighty Wind*; Artist: Andrae Crouch; Producers: Andrae Crouch and Luther "Mano" Hanes; Label: Verity Records

Traditional Gospel Recorded Song of the Year: "Can't Nobody Do Me Like Jesus" by Andrae Crouch; from album *Blur the Lines*; Artist: The Crabb Family; Label: Clear Cool Music

Urban Album of the Year: *This Is Me*; Artist: Kierra Kiki Sheard; Producers: Fred Jerkins III, Warryn Campbell, J. Drew Sheard, Tommy Sims, PAJAM, PJ Morton, Antonio Neal, Dwayne Wright, Avriele Crandle, and Fred Jerkins IV; Label: EMI Gospel

Worship Song of the Year: "Holy Is the Lord" by Chris Tomlin and Louie Giglio; Publishers: worshiptogether. com Songs, sixsteps Music (ASCAP)

Musical of the Year: *Everything Glorious*; Writer: Travis Cottrell; Producers: Sue C. Smith, David Moffitt, and Travis Cottrell; Publisher: Brentwood-Benson Music Publishing

Choral Collection of the Year: *I'm Amazed*; Artist: Carol Cymbala; Arranger: Carol Cymbala; Publishers: Brooklyn Tabernacle Music, Word Music

Youth/Children's Musical of the Year: *A King Is Coming to Town*; Artist: Brentwood Kids Music Club; Producers: Geron Davis, Sue C. Smith, and Craig

Adams; Publishers: Brentwood-Benson Music Publishing

Children's Music Album of the Year: *VeggieTales Worship Songs*; Artists: Phil Vischer, Mike Nawrocki, Lisa Vischer, and Matt Redman; Producer: Steven V. Taylor; Label: Big Idea records

Long Form Music Video of the Year: *Time Again . . . Amy Grant Live*; Artist: Amy Grant; Video: Ken Carpenter and Rod Carpenter; Franklin Films; Label: Word Records

Short Form Music Video of the Year: *Work*; Artist: Jars of Clay; Video: Monica Ortiz; Jeff Stephenson; Wild Spirit Native Soul; Label: Essential Records

Recorded Music Packaging of the Year: *Beyond Measure*; Artist: Jeremy Camp; Graphics: Invisible Creature; Ryan Clark; Jeremy Cowart; Label: BEC Records

2008: 39th Annual Dove Awards

Song of the Year: "East to West" by Mark Hall and Bernie Herms; Publishers: My Refuge Music (BMI), Club Zoo Music (BMI), SWECS Music (BMI), Word Music LLC (ASCAP), Banahana Tunes (ASCAP)

Songwriter of the Year: Cindy Morgan

Male Vocalist of the Year: Chris Tomlin

Female Vocalist of the Year: Natalie Grant

Group of the Year: Casting Crowns

Producer of the Year: Ian Eskelin

Artist of the Year: TobyMac

New Artist of the Year: Brandon Heath

Bluegrass Album of the Year: *Salt of the Earth*; Artist: Ricky Skaggs and the Whites; Producers: Ricky Skaggs and the Whites; Label: Skaggs Family Records

Bluegrass Recorded Song of the Year: "He's in Control" by Austins Bridge, Justin Rivers, Mike Kofahl, John Ramsey; on album *Austins Bridge*; Label: Daywind Records

Children's Music Album of the Year: *Veggie Tales Christian Hit Music*; Artist: Veggie Tales; Producer: Christopher Davis, Label: Big Idea Records

Christmas Album of the Year: *It's a Wonderful Christmas*; Artist: Michael W. Smith; Producers: David Hamilton, Michael W. Smith; Label: Reunion Records

Contemporary Gospel Album of the Year: *A Deeper Level*, Artist: Israel and New Breed; Producers: Israel Houghton, Aaron Lindsey; Label: Integrity Music

Contemporary Gospel Recorded Song of the Year: "Say So" by Michael Gungor, Israel Houghton; on album *A Deeper Level*; Artist: Israel and New Breed; Label: Integrity Music

Country Album of the Year: *Big Sky*; Artist: The Isaacs; Producer: Mark Bright; Label: Gaither Music Group

Country Recorded Song of the Year: "How You Live (Turn Up the Music)" by Cindy Morgan; from album *How You Live*; Artist: Point of Grace; Label: Word Records

Inspirational Album of the Year: *I Love To Tell the Story, a Hymns Collection*;

Artist: Mark Lowry; Producer: Paul Johnson; Label: Gaither Music Group

Inspirational Recorded Song of the Year: "By His Wounds" by Steven Curtis Chapman, Mark Hall, Brian Littrell, Mac Powell, Davis Nasser, and Mac Powell; Artist: Glory Revealed; Label: Reunion Records

Instrumental Album of the Year: *Amazing Grace (Original Score)*; Artist: David Arnold; Label: Sparrow Records

Pop/Contemporary Album of the Year: *The Altar and the Door*; Artist: Casting Crowns; Producer: Mark A. Miller; Label: Beachstreet Records, Reunion Records

Pop/Contemporary Recorded Song of the Year: "East to West" by Mark Hall and Bernie Herms; on album *The Altar and the Door*; Artist: Casting Crowns; Label: Beach Street Records; Reunion Records

Rap/Hip Hop Album of the Year: (Tie) *Group 1 Crew*; Artist: Group 1 Crew; Producers: Christopher Stevens, Andy Anderson; Label: Fervent Records; and *Redemption*; Artist: Grits; Producers: Mario "Rio" Moore, Grits; Label: Gotee Records

Rap/Hip Hop Recorded Song of the Year: "Name Droppin" by T-Bone; Rene F. Sotomayor, Teak Underdue, Dee Underdue; from album: *Bone-Appetit Servin' Up tha Hits*; Label: Flicker Records

Rock Album of the Year: *Scars Remain*; Artist: Disciple; Producer: Travis Wyrick; Label: SRE Recordings

Rock Recorded Song of the Year: "Comatose" by John L. Cooper, Brian Howes; on album *Comatose*; Artist: Skillet; Label: Arden Records, Atlantic, Lava, SRE Recordings

Rock/Contemporary Album of the Year: *Portable Sounds*, Artist: TobyMac; Producers: Toby McKeehan, Christopher Stevens, David Wyatt; Label: Forefront Records

Rock/Contemporary Recorded Song of the Year: "Everything Glorious" by David Crowder Band; on album *Remedy*; Artist: David Crowder Band; Label: Sparrow Records, sixsteprecords

Southern Gospel Album of the Year: *Get Away, Jordan*; Artist: Ernie Haase and Signature Sound; Producers: Lari Goss, Michael English; Label: Gaither Music Group

Southern Gospel Recorded Song of the Year: "Get Away, Jordan"; Traditional; from album *Get Away, Jordan*; Artist: Ernie Haase and Signature Sound; Label: Gaither Music Group

Spanish Language Album of the Year: *De Corazon a Corazon*; Artist: Seth Condrey; Producers: Seth Condrey, Mark Balltzglier; Label: CanZion

Special Event Album of the Year: *Glory Revealed*; Artists: Josh Bates, Steven Curtis Chapman, David Crowder, Mark Hall, Shawn Lewis, Brian Littrell, Trevor Morgan, Paul Neufeld, Candi Pearson-Shelton, Mac Powell, Shane and Shane, Michael W. Smith; Producer: Mac Powell; Label: Reunion Records

Traditional Gospel Album of the Year: *Past and Present*; Artist: Lillie Knauls: Producers: Wayne Haun, Lillie Knauls; Label: Vine Records

Traditional Gospel Recorded Song of the Year: "Ready for a Miracle" by Bunny Hull, Art Reynolds; on album *Evan Almighty Soundtrack*; Artist: LeAnn Rimes; Label: Curb Records

Urban Album of the Year: *T57*; Artist: Trin-I-Tee 5:7; Producers: The Bama Boyz, Matthew Knowles, Solange Knowles, Malter W. Millsap III, DJ Statis; Label: Music World Entertainment

Urban Recorded Song of the Year: "Listen" by Chanelle Haynes, Adrian Anderson, Walter W. Millsap III, Angel Helaire, Candice Nelson, Lamar Van-Sciver, Charles Griffin III, Ryan Farish, Frank Greenfield, Tony Jones; on album: *T57*; Artist: Trin-I-Tee 5:7; Label: Music World Entertainment

Worship Album of the Year: *Remedy*; Artist: David Crowder Band

Worship Song of the Year: "How Great Is Our God" by Chris Tomlin, Jesse Reeves, Ed Cash; Publishers: worshiptogether.com Songs, sixsteps Music, Alletrop Music

Musical of the Year: *Amazing Grace—My Chains Are Gone*; Producers: Dennis and Nan Allen; Publishers: Pilot Point Music, Lillenas Publishing Company

Choral Collection of the Year: *Let the Redeemed Say So*; Arranger: Lari Goss; Publisher: Word Music

Youth/Children's Musical of the Year: *Praise Rocks*; Producers: Gina Boe, Barb Dorn, Sue C. Smith, Brian Green; Artist: Brentwood Kids Music Club; Publishers: Brentwood-Benson Music Publishing

Long Form Music Video of the Year: *Live from Hawaii*; Artist: Audio Adrenaline; Video: Mark McCallie, Audio Adrenaline; Audio Adrenaline; Label: Forefront Records

Short Form Music Video of the Year: *Boomin'*; Artist: TobyMac; Video: Scott Speer, Jason Peterson; Symbolic Entertainment, Label: Forefront Records

Recorded Music Packaging of the Year: *Remedy* by the David Crowder Band; Graphics: Gary Dorsey, Gary Dorsey, Gary Dorsey, Kaysie Dorsey; Label: Sparrow Records, sixstepsrecords

DUNCAN, BRYAN

Bryan Duncan (b. March 16, 1953, in Ogden, Utah) spent 12 years with Sweet Comfort Band before he embarked on a solo career. The son of a pastor, Duncan moved around as a youth before landing in North Carolina; he formed a folk/rock band, Second Timothy, while attending college in Florida, then moved to Southern California to pursue Christian music. He plugged into the scene at Calvary Chapel in Costa Mesa, then formed Sweet Comfort in 1972 with brothers Kevin and Rick Thompson. Sweet Comfort Band was one of the early, successful groups to emerge from Calvary Chapel and they toured heavily until 1984, when they broke up. Duncan, a blue-eyed soul singer, signed with Light Records the following year and began recording his southern rock and black gospel influenced material. His debut album, *Have Yourself Committed*, was released in 1985; this album was followed by *Holy Rollin'* (1986), *Now and Then* (1987), *Whistlin' in the Dark* (1987), *Strong Medicine* (1989), *Anonymous Confessions of a Lunatic Friend* (1990), *Mercy* (1992), and *Slow Revival* (1994). Later, he performed with Bob Carlisle as the Self Righteous Brothers and in 2001 pulled together Sweet Comfort Band for a reunion tour.

Don Cusic

For Further Reading

Powell, Mark Allen. *Encyclopedia of Contemporary Christian Music*. Peabody, Mass.: Hendrickson Publishers, Inc., 2002.

DYLAN, BOB

Most in the Christian music community during the 1970s felt that if a major rock superstar converted to Christianity then their fans and followers would also convert. Especially if it was someone like Bob Dylan (b. Robert Alan Zimmerman, May 24, 1941, in Duluth, Minnesota) the "voice of a generation," whose followers analyzed everything he did and said and who often viewed him as a prophet and oracle. Well, the big event happened—Bob Dylan became a Christian—but instead of his audience following him in Christianity, most just shook their heads and wondered what happened.

At the time of his conversion, Bob Dylan was more than a singer/songwriter; he was a cultural icon for the Woodstock generation, the baby boomers who came of age as Dylan went from singing folk songs to performing with electric guitars in a rock band. Before his conversion he had written classic songs such as "Blowing in the Wind," "The Times They Are a-Changin'," "Masters of War," "A Hard Rain's a-Gonna Fall," "Don't Think Twice," "Just Like a Woman," "Positively Fourth Street," "It Ain't Me, Babe," "Mr. Tambourine Man," "Knockin' on Heaven's Door," "Lay, Lady, Lay," "Like a Rolling Stone," "All along the Watchtower," and "Tangled Up in Blue." He used allusions from the Old Testament in his previous works, and there had been rumors of his involvement in the Jewish Lubavitch sect in Brooklyn, but his conversion to Christianity came as a total surprise to most of his fans and followers.

The world became aware of Dylan's conversion in 1979 when he released *Slow Train Coming*, an album that contained overtly Christian songs like "Gotta Serve Somebody."

Dylan's conversion apparently came through his girlfriend at the time, actress Mary Alice Artes, who attended services at the Vineyard in Malibu, which was an offshoot of Calvary Chapel. Artes asked Vineyard pastors Larry Myers and Paul Edmond to visit with Dylan and they discussed Christianity and the Bible with Dylan for several days. After these conversations, according to Dylan, "I just sat up in bed at seven in the morning and I was compelled to get dressed and drive over to the Bible school. I couldn't believe I was there." This is what he told the *Los Angeles Times* in 1981.

Dylan was baptized at the home of Vineyard pastor Bill Dwyer and enrolled in the School of Discipleship at the Vineyard, where he attended Bible classes five days a week for almost four months; he was in a class with about 20 students.

According to Dylan, "When I believe in something, I don't care what

anybody else thinks." He was enthused about his newfound religion and read the Bible daily. He gave several benefit concerts for World Vision and became friends with Keith and Melody Green, who he met at the Vineyard. Although Dylan did not give many interviews, he made no secret of his faith during his concerts, speaking boldly from the stage.

Kenn Gullicksen, pastor at the Vineyard, advised Dylan not to become part of the world of contemporary Christian music but instead to use his secular platform to spread the Christian message, which Dylan certainly did for several years as his concerts were devoted to evangelistic pronouncements. The CCM world, on the other hand, distrusted anyone who did not leave the secular world behind and devote himself fully to the Christian subculture.

Dylan's general audience did not want to hear him preach Christianity; after several years, Dylan began mixing his secular songs with gospel material. However, during this period he produced three gospel albums: *Slow Train Coming, Saved*, and *Shot of Love*. The *Slow Train Coming* sessions were produced in Muscle Shoals, Alabama, and had a bluesy feel; the single "Gotta Serve Somebody" won the Grammy for best male vocal performance in the rock field. *Saved* is made up of songs that Dylan wrote while on tour, using sound checks to develop the songs. *Shot of Love* integrated his gospel and secular sides; the hauntingly beautiful "Every Grain of Sand" and "Lenny Bruce" are both on the album.

Dylan's "gospel period" lasted from 1979 to 1981, when he returned to recording secular albums, although many

Bob Dylan performs as the opening act of the Pawtucket Arts Festival on August 24, 2006, at McCoy Stadium. (AP Photo/Stew Milne, File)

songs on these albums had a spiritual undertone. To those who say Christianity was just another phase in the quixotic and mystical life of Bob Dylan, one has to counter that a conversion experience that powerful doesn't just disappear; there is no doubt that a strong residue of Christian faith remains with Dylan. However, the singer/songwriter has kept his distance from the contemporary Christian music scene and Christian subculture.

Don Cusic

Discography

Slow Train Coming (1979)

Saved (1980)

Shot of Love (1981)

Infidels (1983)

Empire Burlesque (1985)

Biograph (3 CDs) (1985)

Knocked out Loaded (1986)

Down in the Groove (1988)

Oh Mercy (1989)

Under the Red Sky (1990)

The Bootleg Series (3 CDs), (1991)

Bob Dylan's Greatest Hits, Vol. 3 (1994)

MTV Unplugged (1995)

Time out of Mind (1997)

Love and Theft (2001)

Gospel Music Association Dove Award

1978   Album by a Secular Artist: *Slow Train Coming* by Bob Dylan (Producers: Jerry Wexler and Barry Beckett; Label: Columbia)

Grammy Awards

1972   15th Grammy Awards: Album of the Year: *The Concert for Bangla Desh*; Artists: George Harrison, Ravi Shankar, Bob Dylan, Leon Russell, Ringo Starr, Billy Preston, Eric Clapton, and Klaus Voormann; Producers: George Harrison and Phil Spector

1979   22nd Grammy Awards: Best Rock Vocal Performance, Male: "Gotta Serve Somebody."

1989   32nd Grammy Awards: Best Rock Performance by a Duo or Group with Vocal: *Traveling Wilburys Volume One*. Artists:

Bob Dylan, George Harrison, Jeff Lynne, Roy Orbison, and Tom Petty

1994 37th Grammy Awards: Best Traditional Folk Album: *World Gone Wrong*

1997 40th Grammy Awards: Best Contemporary Folk Album: *Time out of Mind*

1997 40th Grammy Awards: Best Male Rock Vocal Performance: "Cold Irons Bound"

1997 40th Grammy Awards: Album of the Year: *Time out of Mind*

2001 44th Grammy Awards: Best Contemporary Folk Album: *Love and Theft*

2006 49th Grammy Awards: Best Contemporary Folk/Americana Album: *Modern Times*

2006 49th Grammy Awards: Best Solo Rock Vocal Performance: "Someday Baby"

For Further Reading

Cusic, Don. *The Sound of Light: A History of Gospel and Christian Music.* New York: Hal Leonard, 2002.

Mellers, Wilfred. *A Darker Shade of Pale: A Backdrop to Bob Dylan.* New York: Oxford University Press, 1985.

Powell, Mark Allen. *Encyclopedia of Contemporary Christian Music.* Peabody, Mass.: Hendrickson Publishers, Inc., 2002.

Shelton, Robert. *No Direction Home: The Life and Music of Bob Dylan.* New York: Beech Tree/William Morrow, 1986.

E

ENGLISH, MICHAEL

Michael English has seen the highest of highs in the Christian music industry; he also suffered the lowest of lows. His career has gone from mountaintop to deep valley, from someone who had it all to someone who had nothing; however, through it all, English's talent and faith kept him coming back to Christian music, and many in the Christian music industry have accepted him through his faults and failures because his story may be viewed as the story of God's love and redemption of sinners.

At the 1993 Dove Awards, held in the spring of 1994, Michael English took home an armful of trophies. He won Doves for "Inspirational Recorded Song" for "In Christ Alone," for his work on *Coram Deo*, which was voted the "Praise and Worship Album" award, as "Male Vocalist of the Year," and the Dove's highest honor, "Artist of the Year." One week later he returned the Doves to the Gospel Music Association and was dropped from his label, Warner Alliance. English confessed to an extramarital affair with another married gospel artist, Marabeth

Jordan; further, Jordan was pregnant (she later miscarried). Warner Alliance pulled all promotion and marketing efforts from his projects and radio stations stopped playing his music as English announced his retirement. Although he did continue to perform, for a short time, as part of the Gaither Vocal Band, his marriage to Lisa Bailey ended.

With a distinctive musical style and powerful voice, Michael English has established a string of successful albums, awards, and a loyal fan base in contemporary Christian and southern gospel music. At the pinnacle of his career he lost it all and became fodder for the tabloids. Filled with highs and lows, English's journey has come full circle. In 2008 he released his ninth studio album, aptly titled *The Prodigal Comes Home*.

Michael English (b. Kenansville, North Carolina, on April 12, 1962) was raised in Wallace, North Carolina, with a strict Pentecostal upbringing. He performed with the Singing Samaritans, his family's vocal group, for eight years, 1972–1980. After high school graduation he joined the Singing

Michael English has been a member of several groups as well as a successful solo artist. (AP Photo/Mark Humphrey, File)

Americans, where he honed his vocal skills until the offer came to join the Goodmans. English continued to work with the Goodmans and other southern gospel singing groups, recording and performing and making his name known in the community throughout the early 1980s. During this time, English married for the first time, and he and wife Lisa Bailey had their only child, Megan, in 1984.

That same year English came to the attention of Bill Gaither and was offered the chance to join the famed Gaither Vocal Band, replacing Gary McSpadden as their lead vocalist. Gaither became both a friend and mentor to English and encouraged him to pursue a solo career. While continuing to sing with the Gaither Vocal Band, he

signed a recording contract in 1991 with Warner Alliance, a move that marketed him beyond his southern gospel roots in the world of mainstream contemporary music. His first release, the self-titled album, *Michael English*, put his solo career squarely on the map and fans embraced him. In 1992 he earned the first of several Gospel Music Association Dove Awards for New Artist and Male Vocalist. For the next few years English was the toast of the Christian music community. That came to an end when news of his extramarital affair became public and he became tabloid fodder.

Later that year, English signed a contract with Curb Records to record pop music, but his problems were far from over. English began to enjoy success in a new genre of music, including a critically acclaimed duet entitled "Healing" with country music superstar, Wynonna. During this time he moved away from his cleancut Gaither image, grew his hair long, and began dating again, although his name and picture remained in the tabloids, which documented his every move. English continued to pursue a mainstream music career, but each album included material that harkened back to his roots. The gospel music community had turned their back on him and it weighed heavily on his heart.

Slowly but surely, he began a comeback to his roots, testing the waters in his old format by producing other acts. In 1996 and again in 1997, albums that he coproduced for the Martins took home "Southern Gospel Album of the Year" Dove Awards. Other producing projects followed, but so did a stint in rehab for an addiction to prescription pain killers and legal troubles stemming from how he obtained his prescriptions. English, now married to second wife Marcie Stambaugh, again was forced to clean up his act and apologize to his fans and peers.

It was eight years before English released his next official studio CD, *The Prodigal Comes Home*, but the singer stayed focused, straight, and productive. English turned in holiday and greatest hits collections for Curb Records, continued performing in churches and concert halls, and became a popular host on the Trinity Broadcasting Network. In concert, English always performs "In Christ Alone," a song he first recorded in 1992; the ballad remains his signature song.

With a distinctive musical style and powerful voice, Michael English rebounded back into the world of contemporary Christian music. Filled with highs and lows, English's journey has come full circle. In 2008 he released his ninth studio album, aptly titled *"The Prodigal Comes Home."*

Liz Cavanaugh

For Further Reading

Alfonso, Barry. *The Billboard Guide to Contemporary Christian Music*. New York: Billboard Books/Watson-Guptill, 2002.

English, Michael. *The Prodigal Comes Home: My Story of Failure and God's Story of Redemption*. Nashville, Tenn.: Thomas Nelson, 2007.

Powell, Mark Allen. *Encyclopedia of Contemporary Christian Music*. Peabody, Mass.: Hendrickson Publishers, Inc., 2002.

F

FARNER, MARK

Before his Christian conversion and entry into the contemporary Christian music field, Mark Farner (b. September 29, 1948, in Flint, Michigan) was best known as the lead singer, guitarist, and principal songwriter for Grand Funk Railroad, later known simply as Grand Funk.

Farner had a rebellious childhood; he learned to play guitar when he was 15 and was expelled from high school during his senior year. He joined a band, Terry Knight and the Pack, but Knight decided to quit performing and go into artist management. Knight put Farner with two former members of Question Mark and the Mysterians, drummer Don Brewer and bassist Mel Schacher, to form Grand Funk Railroad. That group proved incredibly successful; in 1970 they were the top-selling music act in the United States, and their performance at Shea Stadium in 1971 sold more tickets than the Beatles' performance. Their two biggest hit singles were "We're an American Band" in 1973 and "The Loco-Motion" in 1974.

Grand Funk toured constantly and were known for their raucous stage shows. After they quit performing, Farner moved to a farm in upper Michigan and opened an alternative energy store. He recorded several solo projects then, during the early 1980s, recorded some more projects with Grand Funk. However, in 1983 he suffered a personal crisis when his wife, Lesia, left him; distraught, Farner went to a church, answered an altar call, and prayed for his wife to return. That same morning, his wife attended a different church and also answered an altar call; the next day they were reunited, joined an Assemblies of God church, and embarked on life as evangelical Christians.

Farner gave up playing for awhile, then joined Mylon LeFevre's band, Broken Heart, before getting on the oldies circuit with a band he formed, God's Rockers. Farner mixed his Grand Funk songs with Christian material and during the Super Seventies Fest tours performed along with Bachman Turner Overdrive, Dr. Hook, Rare Earth, and the Guess Who.

Disillusioned with the Christian music industry, Farner returned to making albums for the general audience in the early 1990s. In 1996 he toured with Ringo Starr's All Starr Band and reunited with Grand Funk in 1997 for a tour and album.

Don Cusic

For Further Reading

Powell, Mark Allen. *Encyclopedia of Contemporary Christian Music.* Peabody, Mass.: Hendrickson Publishers, Inc., 2002.

FARRELL AND FARRELL

Bob and Jayne Farrell are a husband-wife duo who were part of the original Jesus music movement; during the early 1970s they toured with Randy Matthews and Love Song and in 1973 recorded an album as members of the group Millennium. In 1973, Jayne recorded a solo album for Cam Records; in 1976 they moved to Edmond, Oklahoma, and began working as a duo. In 1978 they signed with New Pax and recorded several albums of synthesizer based pop. As a songwriter, Bob Farrell has written songs for Bob Carlisle, Code of Ethics, DeGarmo and Key, Bryan Duncan, Hope of Glory, the Imperials, Michael W. Smith, the Pat Terry Group, Jaci Velasquez, and Sandy Patty; in 1996 he wrote the musicals *Saviour* and, with Greg Nelson, *Emmanuel: A Musical Celebration of the Life of Christ.*

Don Cusic

For Further Reading

Powell, Mark Allen. *Encyclopedia of Contemporary Christian Music.*

Peabody, Mass.: Hendrickson Publishers, Inc., 2002.

FESTIVALS

Rock music festivals began to gain popularity during the 1960s among the beatnik and hippie countercultures as well as college students. From the Newport Folk Festivals in the early 1960s to the Monterey Pop Festival and ultimately Woodstock in the late 1960s, they increased in their impact and size. The ICHTHUS festival was the first major Christian music festival; it first took place in 1970, as a direct reaction to the Woodstock festival the year before. As of 2008, it's still going strong.

Over the years, scores of other Christian festivals have been held in every part of the globe. Some of these

Crowd at a Christian festival. Eight-year-old Diana Arroyo waves her hand to the music as she sits on the shoulders of her father, Mario Arroyo, at the DC Festival with Luis Palau on October 9, 2005, on the National Mall in Washington, D.C. (AP Photo/Kevin Wolf)

festivals are strictly musical and provide good, wholesome entertainment, while others concentrate on the worship side of music. There are festivals associated with outdoor activities like whitewater rafting in Arkansas, along with European Christian death metal music in Scandinavia. There is a festival celebrating Easter in Australia and traveling one day festivals in the United States, along with a southern gospel cruise ship music festival.

There is a Christian music festival going on somewhere in the world at every time of the year to suit every individual taste. This article presents more than 60 of the choices available, with pertinent details like location, dates, attendance, musical acts, speakers, activities, geography, and contact information. This list is not exhaustive, but includes all of the major ongoing festivals, as well as some of the now defunct ones, that had information available at the time of this writing.

A Closer Walk

A Closer Walk is a three-day festival held in the middle of July, beginning on Thursday afternoon, and concluding by noon Saturday. Its began in 2002 and its name came from James 4:8, which states, "Draw close to God, and God will draw close to you." It takes place in Wildwood, New Jersey, at Morey's Piers Beachfront Waterparks on the Atlantic Ocean. The event is designed to be a Christian teaching tool for youth who want to grow in their relationship with Jesus Christ and one another.

A Closer Walk includes guest speakers, praise and worship sessions led by Christian musicians, encounters with

God, fellowship with and testimonies of teen believers. Also included is overnight camping under the stars, on the beach, unlimited access to Morey's amusement rides and water parks, and a catered meal. Another popular feature is ocean baptism.

Adventure Fest

Adventure Fest combines outdoor fun and adventure using activities like hiking, paintball, rock climbing and rappelling, a rope course, swimming, tubing, volleyball, and whitewater rafting, along with a pizza blast and barbecue in addition to praise and worship concerts. Adventure Fest is presented by OAR (Outdoor Adventure Rafting), and takes place over four days and three nights in the Cherokee National Forest on the middle section of the Ocoee River where Class III-IV whitewater rapids plunge 269 feet over a five mile course. For the less adventurous, an easy hiking trip to Chilowee Mountain, where there is a breathtaking view of Benton Falls along with a sandy white beach for relaxing or swimming, is an option. Sleep in cabins, bunkhouses, or return to town to motels in Cleveland or Chattanooga, Tennessee, which are respectively, only a 15 or 40 minute drive from the outpost. This is not your typical Christian festival. It can be enjoyed by individuals, couples, groups, and families.

Agape Music Festival

The Agape Music Festival, which began in 1977, is now called Agape-Fest; it is held at Greenville College, in Greenville, Illinois. The event began when Chaz Corzine led a group of

Greenville College students who organized the festival. Over the years the festival has evolved into a teaching festival and continues to be coordinated by students with oversight by members of the faculty.

Acts that have played the festival over the years include Audio Adrenaline, David Crowder Band, Steven Curtis Chapman, DeGarmo and Key, TobyMac, Newsboys, Reliant K, Second Chapter of Acts, Michael W. Smith, Randy Stonehill, Switchfoot, Russ Taff, and White Heart.

The festival is an outdoor two day event, Friday and Saturday, held at the Bond County Fairgrounds, in Greenville, Illinois, during the first week of May. The average attendance is 5,000, with the 1990 festival holding the record attendance of 6,500 when Michael W. Smith made his Agape Fest debut.

Alive Festival

The first Alive Festival took place in 1988 and has continued for 21 years. Its mission has been to bring believers together, from a variety of churches, denominations, and backgrounds for four days of fellowship. During that time individuals and groups enjoy camping, music, recreational fun, swimming, teaching, and worship.

A dozen teachers, artists, entrepreneurs, ministers, and celebrities of various genres, such Louie Giglio, Phil Joel, Tony Nolan, Brady Quinn, Dr. Joe, Phil Savage, and Jason Wright have conducted seminars. More than 50 artists, including Casting Crowns, David Crowder Band, Eleventyseven, Parachute Band, Salvador, Skillet, Thousand Foot Crutch, TobyMac, and Jaci Velasquez have performed on the three stages, which feature music performances from morning until night.

The event takes place in the rolling hills of northeast Ohio in a 350-acre park that includes basketball courts, beach volleyball, hiking, miniature golf, and a lake with paddle boats, swimming, and waterslides.

Atlanta Fest

Atlanta Fest, which began in 1986, is held in June in Atlanta, Georgia, and is presented by Chick-fil-A. The 2008 festival featured more than 50 artists, including Casting Crowns, TobyMac, Big Daddy Weave, Day of Fire, Jeremy Camp, Shane and Shane, Barlow Girl, Phil Joel, Shawn McDonald, Seventh Day Slumber, Sanctus Real, Building 429, Echoing Angels, Downhere, Waverly, Grey Holiday, This Beautiful Republic, Tenth Avenue North, Matt Papa, Living Anthem, Jason Grey, House of Thomas, Special D, Nitengale, Nate Huss, Stephanie Smith, Brooke Barrettsmith, Jalel, Delorean Grey, John Cook, the Sum, United Pursuit, Mary-Kathryn, Johannes, and Jonny Diaz. The acts perform on four different stages over three days. Seminars for Christian living feature speakers such as Christopher Coleman, James Ryle, Justin Lookadoo, Nancy Thompson, and Will Penner.

The AtlantaFest is a Christian music festival for the entire family. There are rides and attractions, Bible studies, seminars for Christian living, a talent search, Christian karaoke, and nonstop music featuring some of contemporary Christian music's top names. Primitive and full service camping are available on the 3,200-acre wooded site.

The Big Boss Festival

The Big Boss Festival is named for the Big Boss—God—and is an open air European Christian music festival, held in the vicinity of Belfond farm, in Tavannes, Switzerland. It began with two bands in 1999; ten years later more than 4,000 people heard over 14 international bands play on two stages. The festival includes a battle of the bands. The festival, held in July, features concerts Friday and Saturday nights with a worship meeting on Sunday.

Bands who have played at the festival include Day by Day, 29th Chapter, Escorte, White Spirit, Vera Cruz, Modern Day Heroes, Karisma, Watchman, Volver, Triplet, Superhero, Rescate, Glenn Kaiser, Matt Redman, YFriday, October Light, Danny Fresh, Nannup, Gospelchor Gossau, 7th Element, Alive, the Listening, Chrysalide, Petolette, Dave Band, Shelomith, Alane and GodMode. There are vendor booths selling food and Christian merchandise.

Black Stump Music and Arts Festival

Black Stump Music and Arts Festival is a four day Christian gathering that takes place in the Greater Sydney Metropolitan region in Australia. The festival, usually held over the first weekend in October (coinciding with Australia's Labor Day weekend), has taken place annually since 1985, with the exception of three years (1987, 1995, and 2000).

The first two years (1985 and 1986) Black Stump was held in Cattai, a suburb of Sydney, at the former Paradise Gardens site. Beginning in 1988, the festival has been held at Cataract Scout Park. Headline and international acts appear at the main stage, called the Big Top, along with Bible studies and worship. There are other venues for festival goers, including Off Broadway for comedy; The Palladium for theater and dance; Sacred Space for worship; The Village for food, paraphernalia, and additional performance areas; and the Supper Club, which is café style tables and chairs in front of a small music stage with food and beverages available.

Artists who have appeared at the Stump include Anteskeptic, Sarah Blasko, Butterfly Boucher, David Butts, Paul Colman, Tim Harding, Hi-5, Hooley Dooleys, Newsboys, Outback Hippies, and Rebecca St. James. Speakers like Tony Campolo have also been featured.

Clover Festival

The word clover is an acronym for "Christ's Love Restores, Respects and Rejoices" as well as being a symbol for the triune nature of God. At the same time clover also represents biblical examples that Jesus Himself used in His parables. Just as a single clover planted in a field will eventually overtake the entire field, so will strategically planted Christians transform the world around them with their presence and example. The festival celebrates the ultimate potential that each believer has within themselves and its creative power.

The festival's mission is to provide a connection point to energize the spirits of young adults who are committed to Christ and share an interest in life-inspiring dance music and wholesome entertainment, along with art, electronics, fashion, and games.

The festival features performances from nearly a hundred of the world's top Christian DJs and dance artists using dance, drum and bass, electro-pop, hip-hop, house, and live electronic music. The festival is free and held the last weekend of August on the northwest tip of lower Michigan, in Traverse City, on the shores of Lake Michigan.

Collide Festival

The Collide Festival takes place the second week of June at Willowood Ranch near Sherman, Texas. The purpose of the festival is to bring people closer to God through a collision between heaven and earth. This is done through the messages of seminar speakers and performances by Christian musicians.

Artists who have performed there include Reliant K, David Crowder Band, Michael W. Smith, MercyMe, Skillet, Pocket Full of Rocks, Sanctus Real, Jars of Clay, Barlow Girl, the Afters, Derek Webb, Robert Pierre, Thousand Foot Crutch, Downhere, Family Force 5, Chris Rice, Building 429, and Ayiesha Woods. The performances are held on five different stages while seminars and talks to help build and edify attendees are held concurrently. Speakers who have appeared include David Nassar, James Ryle, Norman Flowers, Justin Lookadoo, and Scott Pierre, discussing topics from worship and prayer to finances and friends.

Cornerstone Festival

The Cornerstone Festival was first held in 1984, after Jesus People USA (JPUSA), the publishers of *Cornerstone*

magazine, saw the need for a Christian music festival in the Midwest. The festival takes place over four days on 500 acres of private land outside of Bushnell, a central Illinois city, and features about 300 musical artists playing every current genre on a dozen stages.

Artists who have appeared at Cornerstone include the 77's, Anberlin, the Burial, Charlie Peacock, Daniel Amos, David Crowder Band, Family Force 5, Glenn Kaiser Band, the Lost Dogs, Kerry Livgren, the Rez Band, Larry Norman, Our Corpse Destroyed, P.O.D., Joe English, Skillet, Randy Stonehill, Stryper, Third Day, and the Wayside, to name a few.

The festival offers nearly two dozen seminars dealing with a diversity of subjects, conducted by some of Christianity's leading thinkers and speakers, such as James Wall, Jackie Hudson, Terry Wandtke, William Spencer, Crystal Downing, Miroslav Volf, Shane Claiborne, Norm Geisler, Ron Enroth, and Karen Sloan, speaking on subjects as diverse as war, politics, monasticism, race, theology, and cults.

Cornerstone is a family event, attended by 25,000 people, and has something for every age group, from children to senior citizens, including a skate park and lake for water activities.

Cornerstone California Festival

In 2007 the Cornerstone California Festival held its first two day West Coast version of the Cornerstone festival at the end of September. The event was held at the Oak Canyon Ranch in Orange County. Performers included Anberlin, Dakoda Motor Company, Demon Hunter, Disciple, Emery, Falling Up, Firefight, Haste the Day, Joy

Electric, Maylene and the Sons of Disaster, Dizmas, the Myriad, Project 86, Seventh Day Slumber, Showbread, Thousand Foot Crutch, Transistor Radio, and Underoath.

Cornerstone Florida Festival

The first Cornerstone Florida festival was held in 2003 in Orlando, Florida; the 2008 event was cancelled. The two day event is held in mid-May, an outgrowth of the original Cornerstone festival in Bushnell, Illinois. Acts who have performed include Anberlin, Brimstone Flavored Candy, David Crowder Band, Family Force 5, John Fischer, Flowers for the Dead, Glenn Kaiser Band, Kids in the Way, Kutless, Red Letter Bullet, Relient K, Risen Above Ashes, and Underoath.

Crossover Christian Music Festival

The Crossover Festival, held over a three day period, began in 1998 in Camdenton, Missouri. The festival is held at Stoneridge Amphitheater with theater seating. The amphitheater is located at the Lake of the Ozarks, which has water parks, recreation areas, shopping, restaurants, and entertainment in a 40,000 square mile forest of oak and hickory. Acts who have appeared include Skillet, Remedy Drive, Barlow Girl, Building 429, Downhere, Ruth, Jeremy Camp, Jael, House of Thomas, Richie McDonald, Waverly, 33 Miles, Brooke Barrettsmith, KJ-52, and This Beautiful Republic. The event features a talent search sponsored by Essential Records and the Christian Festival Association, with the winners performing on the main stage.

Creation Fest

Creation Fest is a three day festival held in Woolacombe, Devon, England, the first weekend of August. The festival began in 2002 as a one day festival; starting in 2007 a roadshow version of the festival took place as a mini, one day event that travels around, hitting places like Barnstaple, Bideford and Exeter Cathedral Green, Braunton, Bratton Flemming, South Molton, and Ilfracombe. Creation Fest is produced by Calvary Chapel Woodacombe. Pastor Phil Pechonis is the director of the event. It's based on the Great Commission as given in Matthew 28:18–20, and its purpose is to unite churches for evangelistic involvement, and partner with them, both nationally and internationally.

Artists who have played Creation Fest include Four Kornerz, Superhero, Manafest, Jahaziel, Universal Royalty, Scott Cunningham, [dweeb], Philippa Hanna, MOD, Electralyte, Narrowpath, Transition, Erin Starnes, BOSH, Sonz 1, Amber Jane, John Procter, Finchley, Mat Giles, Erin Starnes, Glass Darkly, Transition, the Kry, Raymond and Co, Phil Wickham, and Grand Prize. Creation Fest is a family day out, which includes a skate park, Creation Kidz holiday club, bouncy castles, and sports activities. Speakers have included Brian Brodersen and Phil Pechonis.

Creation Festival East

Creation Festival East takes place over four days in the rolling mountains of Mt. Union, Pennsylvania, during the last Wednesday through Saturday in June. The event was founded by Tim Landis and Harry Thomas in 1979 after

Explo 72, in Dallas. The following year they organized their own festival called Jesus 73 and a few years later Jesus 77.

Landis and Thomas believed that Christian music with a positive message, and the uplifting sound of positive rock 'n' roll, could impact and change the lives of those who hear it. Artists and speakers such as Keith Green, Barry McGuire, and Winkey Pratney helped make the event a reality. In its first years the festival was located on land next to a nuclear power plant, but it eventually moved to the Agape Farm, located in Pennsylvania's Allegheny Mountain range just off the Pennsylvania Turnpike between Pittsburgh and Harrisburg. The event is attended by as many as 75,000 annually.

Artists who have performed at the festival include Petra, Newsboys, Switchfoot, TobyMac, Chris Tomlin, David Crowder Band, Jeremy Camp, Kutless, Skillet, Flyleaf, Hawk Nelson, Barlow Girl, Family Force 5, Phil Keaggy, Sanctus Real, Disciple, Phil Wickham, Steve Fee, Parachute Band, Eleventy Seven, KJ-52, Vigilantes of Love, and Ruth, to name a few. Speakers have included Ron Luce, Bob Lenz, Reggie Dabbs, Justin Lookadoo, Greg Laurie, and Rob Schenck; they have discussed a variety of subjects, including controversial topics such as gay marriage, human cloning, pornography, and Christian roles in the arts, to name some.

Creation Festival Northwest

Creation Festival Northwest, which began in 2007, is the younger counterpart to Creation Festival East. The celebrations take place at the Gorge Amphitheater, located in central Washington near the Columbia River. The amphitheater at the event has been voted the best major concert venue in North America nine times by *Pollstar* magazine. The location is compared to the Grand Canyon because of its magnificent view and scenic beauty, along with great weather and outstanding acoustics.

The festival takes place over four nights and three days during the last weekend of July. During that time there are nearly 50 artists performing, along with a dozen national caliber speakers.

Many of the same bands and speakers featured at Creation Festival East also perform and participate in the Northwest. Bands like the Newsboys, Switchfoot, and David Crowder as well as speakers such as David Nasser, Duffy Robbins, Jose Zayas, Rich Van Pelt, Jeremy Kingsley, Greg Steir, and Julie Laipply have appeared there.

A camping area is available along with a main stage, fringe stages, a prayer tent, modern worship tent, candlelight service, water baptism, late night café, exhibit area, youth leader seminars, youth leaders VIP area, food court, fun contests, musician seminars, comedy night, skateboard and BMX, X-games, huge video screen, and gear giveaway.

Easterfest

Easterfest was originally called the Australian Gospel Music Festival (AGMF). The Christian pop music festival began in 1999, and took place at multiple venues in Toowoomba, Queensland; by 2001 it was concentrated primarily in Queens Park.

Easterfest takes place annually from Good Friday until Easter Sunday and has been attended by more than 40,000 people annually. The organizers claim it to be Australia's largest alcohol and drug free event. The name communicates the festival's theme and time. Included in the program is a passion play, and one year it featured a showing of Mel Gibson's movie *The Passion of the Christ* on Good Friday. Acts who have performed there include Alabaster Box, Antiskeptic, Geoff Moore, Jars of Clay, the Lads, Matt Corby, MxPx, Newsboys, Newworldson, and the QLD Pops Orchestra.

Encounter Ontario Festival

Encounter Ontario Festival became Canada's first major Christian music festival when it debuted August 20, 2005, in Toronto. One Star Entertainment and FaithLife Financial hosted Encounter in an attempt to connect Canada with the Christian/gospel music scene. Acts who have performed there include Casting Crowns, Kurt Carr, Greg Sczebel, Manic Drive, Kevin Pauls, Titus, Hetti-Marie, Patricia Shirley, Rhema Worship Band, Gary Beals, and Starfield. The festival has featured speakers such as Phil Callaway, workshops, and a representation of a number of international ministries. Admission to the festival also included admission to Ontario Place amusements, water park rides, and the opening day of the Canadian National Exhibition.

Expo '72

Expo '72 was the first major mass gathering of the Jesus movement that came out of the 1960s counterculture. It took place for six days in a number of locations in Dallas, Texas, June 12–17, 1972. The event was planned as an evangelical conference and was directed by Paul Eshleman of Campus Crusade for Christ.

The goal was to draw high school and college youth for training in evangelism. Billy Graham was a nightly speaker and a diversity of Christian music was performed, including Johnny Cash, Armageddon Experience, the Archers, Kris Kristofferson, Rita Coolidge, Randy Matthews, Andrae Crouch and the Disciples, Larry Norman, Great Commission Company, Danny Lee and the Children of Truth, Connie Smith, Forerunners, Willa Dorsey, Love Song, and the Speer Family, to name some. It was estimated that nearly 100,000 participated in the week of training along with another 100,000 for the concert events, bringing the total to 200,000.

The event was controversial because of the ecumenical mixing of denominations, which allowed Roman Catholics to participate in promoting and marketing the event. It was criticized for its endorsement of rock music with an eight hour long Jesus rock concert. Billy Graham, who had previously condemned rock music, openly embraced the Jesus rock band Love Song.

Festival Con Dios

Festival Con Dios was a Christian version of secular mobile festivals such as Lollapalooza and Ozzfest and traveled to more than 30 cities all over the United States. The event began in 2001 and lasted until 2004. It was a completely portable multicity tour that occupied an area the size of a football field, with a 300 foot stage with

100,000 watts of sound and lights. The portable village included an inflatable archway entrance and 35 brightly colored tents containing a variety of attractions. The event was organized by Wes Campbell, president of First Company Management, and Pete Furler, lead singer of Christian band the Newsboys.

Crowds of 3,500 to 10,000 attended at each stop and the event featured ten different bands, including the Newsboys, Audio Adrenaline, O. C. Supertones, the Normals, Earthsuit, Superchick, Switchfoot, Pillar, PAX217, Tree 63, Plus One, Thousand Foot Crutch, Kutless, and Sanctus Real. Also included were speakers such as Ryan Dobson, comedian Bob Smiley, a Christian music talent search, extreme games, a motorcycle show, and a community cookoff. During its four years of existence, the festival was sponsored by World Vision and Food for the Hungry.

Festival of Faith

Festival of Faith and Music is a biannual event that was first held in 2003 with repeats in 2005 and 2007. The festival takes place for two days on the last weekend of March. Speakers have included Lauren Winner and David Dark, and performers include Emmylou Harris, Neko Case, Sufjan Stevens, Anathallo, Sarah Masen, Liz Janes, Son Lux, Greg Brown, Denison Witmer, Dave Zollo, Brother Danielson, Bill Mallonee, Ralston Bowles, Pow Navarro, Albert Pedulla, and Michael Van Houten, to name some.

The Student Activities Office at Calvin College, part of the Christian Reformed Church, organizes the event. The Festival of Faith and Music is intended to create an atmosphere where an artistic epiphany can be realized, because it brings together art forms. The goal is to discover and revel in the mystery of the art form, including stories, experiences, and music in order to impact the world through grace, love, compassion, and the Christian faith.

Flevo Festival

Flevo Festival is an open air festival that takes place in the Netherlands for four days in August. It was first organized in 1978 as the Kamperland Festival by the Dutch arm of Youth for Christ. The Xnoizz Flevo Festival, takes place in Bussloo, close to Apeldoorn, in the Province of Gelderland, at the recreation area near Voorst.

The festival has attracted as many as 10,000 people in their teens to twenties and became a private foundation in 2002. It's a very popular European Christian festival and highlights all musical genres. Headline bands have included Audio Adrenaline, DC Talk, Five Iron Frenzy, Jars of Clay, Sarah Kelly, MxPx, Ruth Salvador, Sixpence None the Richer, Starfield, Stryper, Switchfoot, and Tourniquet, to name some. Speakers such as Keith Bakker, Orlando Bottenbley, Arie van de Veer, Jan van der Stoep, Arenda Haasnoot, Nynke Dijkstra, Gert-Jan Segers, and Johan ter Beek have talked about faith, God, politics, and sexuality.

Freakfest

Freakfest began in 2006; the four day festival is an open air alternative Christian festival that takes place in Eastern Europe's Czech Republic. The event includes Christian rock bands, dance music, pantomimes, drama, recitals, and a variety of art forms. The festival's main purpose is for outreach to the unchurched. There have been seminars covering a variety of topics, including AIDS, relationships, and ecology. Acts who have appeared include the Violet Burning, Waiting for Steve, Blossom, Illuminandi, Suspekt, Manahem, Projevy Radosti, Raincoat34, Michael, Long Silent Day, Waylan Bram, Sunrise Swift, Marklish Recital, Freax Element, Rest-Art, Lajf, and Kopy Show.

Freakstock

Freakstock is an annual Christian music festival held in Gotha, Germany, the weekend that July turns into August. It has some of the top talent from Europe and around the world playing over a five day period beginning on Wednesday and ending the following Sunday. It was started in 1995 by members of the German Jesus Freak movement in Wiesbaden and moved to Gotha in 1997. More than 8,000 people have attended teaching sessions and enjoyed the music from acts such as Brian Houston, Horatio, Deuteronomium, Opposition of One, the Rodeo Five, Obadja, Pistis, In Him Alone, Obus Gottist hier, Raincoat 34, Rapid Rascals, and the Hope of a Blind Man.

Get Focused

Get Focused is a Christian youth festival begun in 2001; it is held the first weekend in November in Tonsberg, Norway, and is produced by a coalition of local youth groups in the Toonsberg area of Vestfold, Norway. About 2,000 people attend the event, and some of the artists who have performed include Delirious, the Dream Pilots, United Norway, Rudi Myntevik, and Paul Groonseth. The coalition also produces about half a dozen other smaller events throughout the year under the banner Get United.

Ghoti, Inc.

See Red Letter Rock Festival.

Greenbelt Festival

The first Greenbelt Festival took place in 1974 on Prospect Farm in Suffolk, outside of London, England. It began as a hippie Jesus freak event organized to provide a Godly alternative to secular festivals like Woodstock. Its purpose was to celebrate the arts, especially rock music, as influenced by the Gospel. The first year drew a little over 2,000 people, but by 1980 more than 20,000 attended. Over the decades, the festival has hosted myriad spiritual and socially conscious acts like Adrian Snell, Garth Hewitt, Honeytree, Larry Norman, Randy Stonehill, Cliff Richard, Alwyn Wall, John Pantry, Jessy Dixon, U2, Bonnie Bramlett, Jerusalem, Noel Paul Stookey, Servant, Resurrection Band, Mighty Clouds of Joy, Bob Geldof, Midnight Oil, Waterboys, Michael Franti and Spearhead, Martyn Joseph, and Billy Bragg, to name some.

Speakers like George Patterson, Vinay Samuel, Dr. John Stott, Malcolm Doney, Jim Punton, Garth Hewitt, Graham Cray, Gustavo Parajon, Caesar Molebatsi, Elias Chacour, Sally Vickers, Philip Yancy, Frank Schaeffer, Brian McLaren, Bev Thomas, Ruth Valerio, and Nick Davies are some of the names who have spoken words of inspiration to attendees.

By 1999 attendance was at a low point, so the festival moved from the traditional green field location to Cheltenham Racecourse the last weekend of August, and attendance increased to nearly 20,000 again.

Heartfest

Heartfest takes place in Kansas City, Missouri, at Worlds of Fun amusement park, on a Saturday in mid-July. The one day event is a result of the success of the early Jesus music festivals that took place at Knotts Berry Farm and Disneyland in Southern California during the peak of the Jesus movement. Over the years, the festival has featured acts such as MercyMe, David Crowder Band, Hawk Nelson, and Tenth Avenue North. Also featured were a BMX stunt bike team and speaker Mark Stewart, the former lead singer of Audio Adrenaline.

Hills Alive

Hills Alive is a free two day music festival that takes place in the middle of July in Memorial Park, Rapid City, South Dakota. Two stages feature artists such as Group 1 Crew, Brandon Heath, Tree 63, Superchic[k], Toby-Mac, JayMay, Sound Method, Angel Dean, Wavorly, Building 429, Matthew West, Mandisa, Switchfoot, Lightswitch, Kronicles, Rex Lex, Flatfoot 56, and Fireflight, to name some. Close to 20,000 people usually attend the family-oriented event, which began in 1988 in Spearfish City Park, until it moved to Memorial Park in 1998.

Ichthus Music Festival

The Ichthus Music Festival takes place in Wilmore, Kentucky, for four days beginning the second Wednesday in June. A crowd of 15,000 to 20,000 is served by 1,500 staff members; the purpose of the festival is to provide students with life-changing experiences and encounters with Jesus Christ through performance, teaching, and worship.

The festival is named after the fish symbol that 1st-century Christians used to identify their gathering places. The festival began in 1970 as a Christian reply and alternative to the Woodstock festival in 1969. It was founded by Asbury Theological Seminary professor Dr. Bob Lyon and a group of concerned students. The festival was held at the Wilmore Campground until 1999 when ICHTHUS Ministries Inc. purchased a 111-acre farm, where it is now held.

Three stages with more than 100 artists perform there; acts who have been at ICHTHUS include Casting Crowns, TobyMac, Jeremy Camp, Kutless, Skillet, David Crowder, Hawk Nelson, Family Force 5, Grits, Ruth, Eowyn, Haste the Day, Esterlyn, Gwen Stacy, Inhale Exhale, Maylene and the Sons of Disaster, As I Lay Dying, XROSS, Eleventyseven, Disciple, MxPx, Through a Glass, O Jerusalem, Saints Never Surrender, Nineball, This Beautiful Republic, Destination 7, Ashes Remain, and Psalters, to name some.

Evenings have worship sessions, led by people like Brenton Brown, Robbie Seay Band, and Matt Maher. On Friday and Saturday everything closes down for breakout sessions with speakers who offer a variety of topics; speakers have included Efrem Smith, Justin Lookadoo, Jon Weece, Johnny Vermilya, Caleb Bislow, and Charlie Alcock.

Ignite Chicago

Ignite Chicago is a one day Christian music festival that takes place the third Sunday of July at Alexian Field in Schaumburg, Illinois, a suburb of Chicago. The stadium, which is home to a minor league baseball team, the Schaumburg Flyers, has a capacity of 7,000. The scriptural basis for the festival is Jeremiah 20:9—believers should be on fire for God and spread that fire around. The event is family oriented and has something for all ages. Artists who have appeared there include Tenth Avenue North, John Reuben, Red, Todd Agnew, Superchic[k], Hawk Nelson, David Crowder Band, MercyMe, and the Newsboys.

Inspiration Cruises and Tours

Inspiration Cruises and Tours began in the 1980s when Dennis Klassen, Ron Fryer, and Steven Dick began working with Christian travel groups. The idea was to charter Alaska, Caribbean, and Holy Land cruises for large Christian organizations and groups. Some of the featured cruises have been a Women of Faith cruise with speakers like Sheila Walsh, Ayiesha Woods, Luci Swindoll, and Sandi Patti. The Stand to Reason cruise featured Josh and Sean McDowell, along with J. P. Moreland. Other cruises featured a musical Alaskan cruise with Bill and Gloria Gaither, the Gaither Vocal Band, Ernie Hass and Signature Sound, Gordon Mote, Jessy Dixon, Ben Speer, the Hoppers, and Jeff and Sheri Easter, as well as a CCM cruise with Aaron Shust, Bebo Norman, Phil Joel, Matthew West, and comedian Bob Smiley.

Jesus Northwest

Jesus Northwest was a Christian music festival held at the Clark County Fairgrounds, in Vancouver, Washington, for 21 years. The summer festival, which began in 1977 and ended in 1997, took place over a three day period in July and featured a number of contemporary Christian acts from Petra to Jars of Clay along with speakers, seminars, kids' activities, and camping. It was sponsored by Peoples Church, in Salem, Oregon.

Joshua Fest

Joshua Fest is a four day Christian festival held the last weekend of August at the Plumas-Sierra County Fairgrounds in Quincy, California, which is about a three hour drive from Sacramento in northeast California on the Nevada border. In addition to Christian performers there are also marriage and couples seminars. Performers who have appeared there include Hawk Nelson, 1000 Foot Crutch, Kutless, Run Kid Run, Stellar Kart, Disciple Spoken, Wavorly, John Reuben, Dizmas, Transistor Radio, Olivia the Band, Glorious Unseen, KJ-52, Sarah Kelly, and speaker Mark Stuart. A feature of the festival is the opportunity for unknown bands to perform on the independent stage.

Kingdom Bound Festival

The Kingdom Bound Festival takes place annually in western New York at the Darian Lake theme park, between Buffalo and Rochester. The festival was first held in October 1987, and the one day event was attended by 6,000 people. The festival has grown to become a four day event held in early August. The theology that supports Kingdom Bound Ministries Inc. is conservative in nature, but believes in the use of the arts for both salvation and Christian growth. Aspiring artists are given the opportunity to compete in a talent search for a slot at the festival. Artists who have appeared at the festival include Third Day, Hawk Nelson, Delirious, Leeland, Mylon Lefevre, Seventh Day Slumber, Sheila Walsh, Matthew West, Russ Taff, Salvador, Skillet, This Beautiful Republic, Disciple, and Vicky Beeching. Speakers have included Justin Lookadoo, Bob Lenz, James Ryle, and Keith Davis.

Kings Fest

Kings Fest takes is held in Doswell, Virginia, at Paramount's King's Dominion; the event uses the entire amusement park in the tradition of Disneyland's or Knotts Berry Farm's Nights of Joy. Performers who have appeared at the three day event include Casting Crowns, David Crowder Band, Falling Up, Hawk Nelson, Jeremy Camp, Kutless, Newsboys, Third Day, TobyMac, Breathe Deep, Pocket Full of Rocks, Hyperstatic Union, Jackson Waters, Dizmas, the Send, Thousand Foot Crutch, Barlow Girl, Family Force 5, and Group 1 Crew. It includes speakers like Josh Finklea, David Edwards, Brad Duncan, and Justin Lookadoo.

Life Light Festival

The Life Light Festival is a free three day musical event held on Labor Day weekend in Sioux Falls, South Dakota. It began in 1997, and is based on Jesus'

words in John 8:12 about being the light of the world. Life Light is the name of the nonprofit organization that sponsors the festival and has been in existence for more than 10 years. Attendance began at 2,000, and in 2007 approximately 320,000 people attended. Artists who have appeared at the event include Family Force 5, Go Fish, Leeland, the Lighthouse, the Master's Heirs, Grits, Michael W. Smith, Switchfoot, Larry Gatlin, TobyMac, Jars of Clay, Barlow Girl, and Building 429, as well as speakers like Luis Palau, Stephen Baldwin, Ron Luce, and dozens of others.

Lifefest

The Lifefest Festival is an annual five day event that has taken place since 1998 at the Sunnyview Fairgrounds in Oshkosh, Wisconsin. Its purpose is to celebrate faith in Jesus Christ, along with thousands of other believers, while having a great time. It is held the second week of July. Artists who have appeared at the festival include Switchfoot, Newsboys, Casting Crowns, Steven Curtis Chapman, Delirious, Natalie Grant, Rebecca St. James, Superchic[k], Run Kid Run, Keith L. Cooper, Peder Eide, Rachel Kurtz, Lynn Stoneking, Stellar Kart, and scores of others. A variety of speakers like Bill Yonker, Tiffany Thompson, Daren Streblow, Reggie Dabbs, Bob Lenz, Joseph Rojas, and many others communicating relevant issues have also appeared.

New Song

The New Song Christian Music Festival was first held in 1985 and lasted until 2006. Nearly 8,000 people met for fellowship, ministry, music, and teaching while they camped in the hills in Leitchfield, Kentucky. Festival attendees were inspired and challenged by Bible studies, music, and seminars, where they were encouraged in their faith and commitment to serve Jesus Christ. Each year, a 72 hour prayer vigil was the foundational base for the event. Featured artists included Jeff Calhoun, the Afters, Superchic[k], Jeremy Camp, Andrew Peterson, Grits, Seventh Day Slumber, Krystal Meyers, and Building 429, to name some.

Night of Joy at Disneyland

The first Night of Joy at Disneyland, in Anaheim, California, was held on a Friday night in December 1976. Eventually the event expanded in 1983 to Disneyworld in Orlando, Florida, during the second week of September. In 2008 the festival was moved to Disney's Hollywood Studios, in Orlando. Some of the artists that have performed over the years are the Archers, Andrae Crouch and the Disciples, Larry Norman, Randy Stonehill, Petra, DC Talk, the Winans, Steven Curtis Chapman, Geoff Moore and the Distance, Cindy Morgan, Michael W. Smith, Delirious, Audio Adrenaline, Out of Eden, MercyMe, Rebecca St. James, Barlow Girl, Mandisa, Casting Crowns, Matthew West, Jeremy Camp, and Pure NRG, to name some.

Night of Praise

After the success of Explo 72 in Dallas, Texas, and the popular tour of Love Song in the Philippines, contemporary Christian music came into its own as a genre. In 1973 Knotts Berry Farm—located about ten minutes from Disneyland—held its first Night of Praise, featuring Love Song, Mustard Seed Faith, and other Maranatha Artists from nearby Calvary Chapel. After it attracted the largest capacity crowd that the struggling park had thus far experienced, it became a regular event. Artists who have performed at Knotts's Night of Joy concerts in the 21st century include Barlow Girl, Tree63, Sanctus Real, Aaron Shust, Stellar Kart, Telecast, Hawk Nelson, Leeland, Phil Joel, and comedian Bob Smiley. The park also began a separate event called the Gospel Showcase, featuring Marvin Sapp, Mary Mary, Dietrick Haddon, Kierra "Kiki" Sheard, Brent Jones, and the TP Mobb.

Parachute Music Festival

The Parachute Music Festival takes place in Mystery Creek, Hamilton, New Zealand, for four days on the last weekend of January. It was founded by Mark de Jong in 1989, when he was working with Youth for Christ. The goal of the festival is to use music to bring people to Jesus and improve the quality of Christian music in New Zealand. In 2008, 25,000 attended the event with 6,000 who were not Christians; during the event, 2,000 committed their lives to Christ. The World Vision sponsored event raised $60,000 to build classrooms in Rwanda. More than 100 bands like Switchfoot, Powhiri, Third Day, Lieutenant Funk, Thousand Foot Crutch, Hawk Nelson, Matt Chapman, Antiskeptic, Zebulun, DC Talk, Newsboys, Vince Harder, Rebecca St. James, Spacifix, and Woo'en have appeared at the festival as well as seminar speakers such as Joyce Meyer, Christine Caine, and Jurgen Matthesius.

Portland City Fest

Portland City Fest began after Jesus Northwest discontinued in the late 1990s to fill the void left in the Portland/Vancouver area. The Luis Palau Evangelistic Association organizes the free festival in Portland, Oregon's Waterfront Park on the banks of the Willamette River. The funds to produce the event are raised through donations and sponsors. The festival takes place in the middle of August and involves many local churches. Citywide projects ranging from painting schools to siding houses to cleaning up yards where the needy are ministered to by 15,000 volunteers make this a unique event of service. The festival itself is a party culminating a week of these activities. Artists like Matt Redman, Third Day, and Kutless have performed. In addition to this event, Luis Palau Ministries produces City Fest events in other worldwide cities as well, like Houston, Dallas; Lima, Peru; Manchester, England; and Bucharest, Romania, to name some.

Purple Door Festival

The Purple Door Festival is a two-day event held in Lewisberry, Pennsylvania, at the Roundtop Ski Resort in the middle of August. It was named after a purple door in the house that one of the founders saw during a Bible study. The event was first held in 1996, and an average of 10,000 attend it each year. Some of the artists who have performed include Skillet, Disciple, Supertones, August Burns Red, Wavorly, John

Rueben, Seabird, Spoken, Jars of Clay, POD, the Glorious Unseen, Gwen Stacy, and many others. Speakers like Bob Lenz and Kurt Weaver have given messages.

Red Letter Rock Fest

The Red Letter Rock Fest takes place the first Saturday in June at the Scurry County Coliseum in Snyder, Texas. Red Letter Rock began as a weekly Christian radio top 20 countdown show in 2003 hosted by Reid Johnson and Cody Christopher and syndicated on over 60 radio stations around the world. The first concert was held in 2006 under the umbrella of Ghoti Inc., a Christian concert production company based in Austin, Texas, and was attended by more than 3,000. The all-day event has featured bands such as Skillet, Pillar, Seventh Day Slumber, Michael Tait, Thousand Foot Crutch, Salvador, Falling Up, Fireflight, Crimson Soul, Jeremy Camp, Skillet, and Wavorly, along with speakers like Stephen Baldwin and Reid Johnson.

Revelation Generation Music Festival

The Revelation Generation Music Festival is a two-day music festival that takes place at Revelation Farms in Frenchtown, New Jersey. A variety of activities are available, including volleyball, skateboard demonstrations, and camping in addition to children's activities, including a puppet ministry, face painting, and games. The festival was started in 2005 by a team of local pastors, parents, and community leaders who wanted to present the gospel through music to a new generation. Simultaneous concerts also take place in

New York City, Philadelphia, and Nashville on Friday night.

Artists who have appeared at the event include KJ-52, Brian Littrell, Newsboys, Robbie Seay Band, Kutless, Matt Wertz, Sixpence None the Richer, TobyMac, As I Lay Dying, Skillet, Leeland, Mandisa, Flyleaf, Norma Jean, and Phil Keaggy.

Rock the Coast

The Rock the Coast festival at Michigan's Adventure Amusement Park in Muskegon began in 2004 as a one day festival sponsored by Grace Bible College and Alive on the Lakeshore. "Ride all day, rock all night" is the catch phrase. It takes place the third weekend of May on Saturday and Sunday with a worship service on Sunday. Nearly 4,000 people attend the annual event, with proceeds donated to Youth for Christ and First Priority Ministries. Bands who have appeared include Run Kid Run, Hawk Nelson, Secondhand, Good Luck Varsity, the Pete Cornelius Band, and Group 1 Crew.

Rock the Desert

Rock the Desert began in a church parking lot in Texas in 2000 with an attendance of 4,000. It was a free event intended to be an outreach and was supported by individual and corporate donors. The event grew to an attendance of more than 100,000, and a nominal fee was charged when it moved to an encampment between Midland and Odessa the second weekend of August. A battle of the bands is featured along with a new artist contest. Skateboarding is allowed and the King of Kings skateboarding ministry has given

demonstrations. Some of the bands featured have been Audio Adrenaline, David Crowder Band, Disciple, Brock Gill, Group 1 Crew, Family Force 5, Hawk Nelson, Need to Breathe, the Newsboys, Chris Tomlin, TobyMac, and the Paul Wright Group. One year Crystal Miller, a survivor of the Columbine massacre, was a featured speaker.

Rock the Light

Rock the Light is a two day festival attended annually by approximately 15,000 people on the last weekend of August in Kansas City, Missouri, at the Starlight theater complex. The festival features a main stage, two satellite stages, a talent search, a leadership oasis, a prayer path, street teams, meet and greets, a fun zone, and vendor alley. Acts who have performed there include Casting Crowns, Jeremy Camp, Chris Tomlin, Barlow Girl, Leeland, Decemberadio, Robert Pierre, Pillar, This Beautiful Republic, Derek Webb, and Roads to Rome, to name some. The festival is sponsored by Salvation Army, World Vision, and others.

Rock the Universe

The Rock the Universe festival takes place at Universal Studios in Orlando, Florida, in September, the first weekend after Labor Day. The event began in 1999 and some of the acts who have appeared include Switchfoot, Reliant K, David Crowder Band, Earthsuit, the Newsboys, Skillet, Grits, Group 1 Crew, New Method, Third Day, Jeremy Camp, Jars of Clay, Family Force 5, Stellar Kart, Leeland, Rebecca St. James, This Beautiful Republic, TobyMac, Third Day, and Special D, to name some. Featured speakers have included TNA wrestling superstar A. J. Styles, HEAD (former Korn founding member), and Dr. Jay Strack.

Seminole Sing, Singfest, and Songfest

Seminole Sing, Singfest, and Songfest events are southern gospel festivals produced by Frank Arnold Ministries; they take place over a three day period, Thursday, Friday, and Saturday evenings. Arnold and his wife, Vickie, are members of the southern gospel trio the Arnolds. Seminole Sing takes place in the middle of August in Seminole Music Park in Seminole, Oklahoma. Singfest takes place in the middle of April at Oral Roberts University in Tulsa, Oklahoma, at the Mabee Center; and Songfest takes place during the third week of July at the Jackson Civic Center in Jackson, Tennessee. The festivals all feature acts such as the Booth Brothers, Ivan Parker, the Isaacs, Legacy Five, Gold City, Jason Crabb, Aaron Wilburn, the Hoppers, the McKameys, the Talleys, the Dove Brothers, Mark Bishop, Jeff and Sheri Easter, Brian Free and Assurance, Karen Peck and New River, the Perrys, and the Arnolds.

Shout Fest

Shout Fest is a mobile one day Christian festival that appears for nearly two dozen dates annually. It is similar in concept to the traveling secular concerts like the Lollapalooza, Ozzfest, and H.O.R.D.E. Festivals. Two performance stages feature 18 bands who travel to 24 cities all over the eastern half of the United States. Proceeds from the festival are used to help feed people around the world through the Food for the Hungry project. Shout Fest features extreme games, a talent contest, and guest speakers like Tony Nolanand and Brad Duncan. Some of the bands that have played are Roads to Rome, Jessie Daniels, Fireflight, Flatfoot 56, Nevertheless, Eleventyseven, Detour 180, Pillar, Skillet, Jars of Clay, Superchic[k], Kevin Max, Rebecca St. James, and many others.

Sonfest

Sonfest was an annual Christian music festival that took place over three to four days in Boonah, Queensland, Australia. It featured some of the top Christian bands in the world, including Reliant K, Jars of Clay, Pillar, the Newsboys, Third Day, Audio Adrenaline, FIDO, the Spertones, and Wishful Thinking. It drew thousands of people from all over Australia and New Zealand but was cancelled in 2006 after operating for five years. The Sonfest organization still exists and promotes concerts in Brisbane, Melbourne, and Sydney.

Sonshine Festival

The Sonshine Festival has taken place in Wilmar, Minnesota, since 1982 when it was founded by local youth pastor Bob Poe. The attendance grew from 1,800 that first year to more than 20,000 in 2007. It takes place over four days from Wednesday through Saturday and features half a dozen stages, with everything from World Impact Wrestling and the Power Team to Chaos on Wheels and Sonshine for Kids. The music stages provide hip hop and a variety of other genres. Performers who have played there include

Sandi Patti, Jars of Clay, Pillar, Thousand Foot Crutch, Skillet, Sweet Comfort Band, Third Day, Russ Taff, Superchic[k], Leon Patillo, Stellar Kart, Hawk Nelson, and Barlow Girl, to name a few. Speakers have included Rosie Greer and Bob Lenz.

Soulfest

Soulfest, which began in 1998, is a four day festival held during the first weekend in August in Gilford, New Hampshire. It is geared for the entire family. The "soul" of its name refers to each person's inner self. It is held in the New Hampshire Lakes region at the Gunstock Mountain Resort. More than 13,000 people attend the annual festival. Activities include a skate park, kayaking, mini-golf, paddle boats, and biking. Soulfest is concerned with social justice, and is involved with issues like the AIDS epidemic in Africa, modern slavery, and extreme poverty. It is a music and teaching event that features five stages. Artists who have appeared include TobyMac, Jars of Clay, Kevin Max, Kutless, Superchic[k], Barlow Girl, KJ-52, Run Kid Run, Third Day, and Rebecca St. James, to name a few.

Spirit Song Festival

The Spirit Song Festival is a three day event, from Wednesday through Saturday on Kings Island in Mason, Ohio, that has taken place annually since 1995. The 10,000 seat Timberwolf Amphitheater has hosted acts such as the Newsboys, Kutless, Hawk Nelson, Barlow Girl, Casting Crowns, David Crowder Band, Pillar, and TobyMac; speakers have included Matt Pitt, Mark Stuart, and Tom Richter.

Spirit West Coast Monterey

Spirit West Coast Monterey began in 1997 and since then has grown into an annual attendance of more than 20,000 people. The purpose is to glorify the Lord Jesus Christ through music, teaching, fellowship, and encouragement. The location is Laguna Seca, a short 10 km run from the Pacific Ocean at Monterey Bay. It takes place Thursday through Sunday on the first weekend of August. More than 100 concerts take place; acts who have performed include the Newsboys, Michael W. Smith, Third Day, Hawk Nelson, Delirious, TobyMac, Jars of Clay, Skillet, Matthew West, Phil Joel, Group 1 Crew, and Run Kid Run. Also featured are seminars and workshops with people like Charles Stanley, Greg Laurie, Luis Palau, Tony Campolo, Frank Peretti, Miles McPherson, Ron Luce, and Louie Giglio, to name some. Also included are kids' shows and a petting zoo, along with comedians like Bob Smiley and Taylor Mason.

Spirit West Coast Del Mar

In 2004 the Del Mar edition of the Spirit West festival was held for the first time. Attendance was double that of its Monterey parent, and the combined total of all those attending both is more than 100,000. The festival is held at the Del Mar Fairgrounds in San Diego County Friday through Sunday on Memorial Day weekend in May.

Tom Fest

In 1994 Tom Fest, the Northwest's premier Christian indie-music festival, took place in Camas, Washington, for the first time. The purpose of the festival is to meet new friends, hear new music, and grow in the Lord, through worship, the word, and fellowship. More than 130 regional and national bands play on four stages for four days, beginning on Wednesday and ending Saturday on the second weekend of August. The acts range in style from acoustic to punk, indie pop to hardcore, along with movies, art, merchandise, and food vendors. Some of the bands who have performed include Athens, Cavalier, Rite of Redemption, Claira's Daze, the Undeserving, Broken, Rheanna Downey, Stillvoice, Ruth, Falling Up, Pacifico, Alitheia, Behold, the Martyrs, Show Bread, Gayle Skidmore, and Dogs of War.

Unity Music Festival

Alive on the Lakeshore is an all-volunteer organization that produced the Unity Music Festival for the first time in 2007. It is a four-day festival held the second weekend of August beginning on Wednesday. The festival site is at 7th Street and Shoreline Drive in Muskegon, Michigan. Artists who have appeared include TobyMac, Grits, Third Day, Yancy, Big Daddy Weave, Joel Weldon, Fee, 33 Miles, and the Stand Strength Team. Its purpose is to bring Christians together for praise, worship, and fellowship, while providing wholesome entertainment for the entire family.

Winterfest

Winterfest takes place for three days during Christmas break, ending on New Years Day, at Liberty University in Lynchburg, Virginia. The age groups that attend are sixth grade through college. Performers have included Jeremy Camp, Stellar Kart, Kutless, Hawk Nelson, December Radio, Aliesha Woods, Disciple, the Send, Downhere, Charles Billingsley, and KJ-52. The event is held in the Vines Center, a 10,000 seat arena. Speakers have included Clayton King, Ergun Caner, David Nassar, and Rev. Eric Timm. Other features of the festival include freestyle skateboarding, stage magic, and a ventriloquist. Tickets with and without lodging are available.

X Fest

X Fest takes place on Labor Day weekend in Stevenson, Washington, in the Columbia River Gorge at the Skamania County fairgrounds. The basic philosophy of the festival springs from the idea that this is God's will, because he created us and gave us these gifts to share with others, by being in community to develop relationships. From Friday until Sunday festival attendees watch stages with regional bands playing a variety of genres, including DJ, folk, hardcore, hip hop, and industrial. Bands who have performed include Insomniac Folklore, Destroy Nate Allen, Hyper Static Union, Dark Field Illuminator, Nevia Nevi, Jericho, Armchair Cartel, Ruth, Soul Junk, and the Skeleton Crew. There are also spoken-word poetry and films.

Bob Gersztyn

For Further Reading

Henderson, Stewart. *Greenbelt—Since the Beginning*. Ipswich, U.K.: Ancient House Press, 1983.

Landy, Elliott. *Woodstock Vision: The Spirit of a Generation*. New York: Landyvision, 1996.

Thompson, John J. *Raised by Wolves: The Story of Christian Rock and Roll*. Toronto, Ontario: ECW Press, 2000.

FIREWORKS

Marty McCall, vocals, keyboards
Lance Avery, bass (until 1981)
Chris Harris, drums (until 1979)
Gary Pigg, vocals (until 1979)
Cindy Lipford, vocals (until 1979)
Jerry Gaston (from 1979)
Bob Sinkovic (1979–1981)
Dave Curfman, guitar, bass
(from 1981)
Louie Weaver, drums (from 1982)

Marty McCall was the key figure in the formation of two contemporary Christian groups, Fireworks and First Call. A classically trained musician, McCall had studied medieval and renaissance music. Fireworks began as a trio of studio backup singers (Marty McCall, Gary Pigg, and Gwen Moore) who worked with Chris Christian on albums by B. J. Thomas and Amy Grant. When 2nd Chapter of Acts left Myrrh Records to join Billy Ray Hearn at Sparrow, the Word executives looked for a group to replace them and signed Fireworks, but Cindy Lipford replaced Gwen Moore for their first album, *Fireworks* (1977), which shows the influence of 2nd Chapter. Their second album, *Shatter the Darkness* (1979), was on Myrrh and then the group switched to MCA, where they did their final three albums, *Live Fireworks* (1980), *Up* (1981), and *Sightseeing at Night* (1982).

Don Cusic

For Further Reading

Powell, Mark Allen. *Encyclopedia of Contemporary Christian Music*. Peabody, Mass.: Hendrickson Publishers, Inc., 2002.

Thompson, John J. *Raised by Wolves: The Story of Christian Rock and Roll*. Toronto, Ontario: ECW Press, 2000.

FIRST CALL

Marty McCall, vocals
Bonnie Keen, vocals
Mel Tunney, vocals (until 1989)
Marabeth Jordon (1989–1995)

First Call was originally formed to replace Marty McCall's previous group, Fireworks, who disbanded. The members had worked as studio singers and toured as backup singers for Sandi Patty. The group was influenced by jazz and pop and did a cappella numbers that showcased their tight harmonies. They appealed to fans of groups like Manhattan Transfer, and their greatest success came for their Evening in December Christmas projects, which featured performances by Amy Grant, Russ Taff, Ashley Cleveland, and Melodie Tunney.

First Call won the 1987 and 1988 Dove Awards for "Group of the Year." The group suffered a setback in 1994 when Marabeth Jordon was forced to leave the group after an extramarital affair with Christian singer Michael English became public. First Call then continued as a duet with Marty McCall and Bonnie Keen.

Don Cusic

For Further Reading

Alfonso, Barry. *The Billboard Guide to Contemporary Christian Music.* New York: Billboard Books/Watson-Guptill, 2002.

Powell, Mark Allen. *Encyclopedia of Contemporary Christian Music.* Peabody, Mass.: Hendrickson Publishers, Inc., 2002.

FISCHER, JOHN

There is an ongoing debate about the roots of contemporary Christian music and the "first" contemporary Christian album. Larry Norman's album *Upon This Rock* generally gets the nod because it was widely distributed as a secular release on Capitol Records and because it was an extension of the California rock scene that was so influential in pop and rock music. However, several other albums predated Norman's; *Mass for Young People* by Ray Repp and *The Cold Cathedral* by John Fischer (b. May 17, 1947) were released before Norman's—although Fisher's was released just a few months before *Upon This Rock*—and both lay claim to being important first steps in Jesus music and, ultimately, contemporary Christian music. Both Repp's and Fischer's work were folk based; they came out of the Vatican II changes in Catholic churches and had their initial impact on the Catholic community. Still, it must be noted that the Jesus movement was not a single river flowing into contemporary Christian music but, instead, a number of musical tributaries that emptied into a great river of Christian music in the late 1970s. Since John Fischer has been an active voice in the contemporary Christian culture since that time, he must be acknowledged as a senior statesman for those in contemporary Christian music.

John Fischer grew up in the San Francisco Bay area where his father was a church music director; Fischer attended Wheaton College in Illinois, where he began writing songs and released his debut album, *The Cold Cathedral*, in his junior year. After graduating in 1969 he toured with musician Leighton Ford. During the 1970s he released a series of albums on Light Records and toured as a CCM act; however, his heart was in pastoral counseling and his urge to write reflected that.

In 1982 Fischer released an album and novel by the same title, *Dark Horse*. Since that time he has released albums as well as a series of books—both novels and works of nonfiction—and had a regular column in *Contemporary Christian Music* magazine that counseled Christian musicians and songwriters.

During the 1970s Fisher founded the Discovery Arts Guild as a ministry of Peninsula Bible Church in Palo Alto, California; later, he became artist in residence at Gordon College in Massachusetts.

Fischer hosted the Wild Angle Radio Show and is currently the senior writer with PurposeDrivenLife.com, a daily devotional that is an outreach of Pastor Rick Warren's Saddleback Church and book, *The Purpose Driven Life*.

Discography

The Cold Cathedral (1969)

Have You Seen Jesus My Lord? (1970)

Still Life (1972)

The New Covenant (1974)

Naphtali (1976)

Inside (1977)

Johnny's Café (1979)

Dark Horse (1982)

Between the Answers (1985)

Casual Crimes (1986)

Wide Angle (1992)

Some Folks' World (1999)

For Further Reading

Alfonso, Barry. *The Billboard Guide to Contemporary Christian Music.* New York: Billboard Books/Watson-Guptill, 2002.

Cusic, Don. *The Sound of Light: A History of Gospel and Christian Music.* New York: Hal Leonard, 2002.

Fischer, John. *Ashes on the Wind.* Grand Rapids, Mich.: Bethany House, 1998.

Fischer, John. *Be Thou My Vision.* Grand Rapids, Mich.: Bethany House, 1995.

Fischer, John. *Dark Horse.* Old Tappan, N.J.: Fleming H. Revell, 1983.

Fischer, John. *Fearless Faith.* Grand Rapids, Mich.: Bethany House, 2002.

Fischer, John. *Making Real What I Already Believe.* Grand Rapids, Mich.: Bethany House, 1991.

Fischer, John. *On a Hill Too Far Away.* Grand Rapids, Mich.: Bethany House, 1994.

Fischer, John. *Real Christians Don't Dance.* Grand Rapids, Mich.: Bethany House, 1988.

Fischer, John. *Saint Ben.* Grand Rapids, Mich.: Bethany House, 1993.

Fischer, John. *The Saints and Angels' Song.* Grand Rapids, Mich.: Bethany House, 1994.

Fischer, John. *True Believers Don't Ask Why.* Grand Rapids, Mich.: Bethany House, 1989.

Fischer, John. *12 Steps for the Recovering Pharisee (Like Me).* Grand Rapids, Mich.: Bethany House, 2000.

Fischer, John. *What on Earth Are We Doing?* Grand Rapids, Mich.: Bethany House, 1997.

McNeil, W. K., ed. *Encyclopedia of American Gospel Music.* New York: Routledge, 2005.

Powell, Mark Allen. *Encyclopedia of Contemporary Christian Music.* Peabody, Mass.: Hendrickson Publishers, Inc., 2002.

FLORIA, CAM

Cam Floria (b. September 22, 1937) is known as the founder and director of the Continental Singers, a Christian group of young people who perform and evangelize, primarily before church audiences, all over the world.

Floria graduated from Northwestern College in Minneapolis and then joined the Lansing Youth for Christ as music leader, although he had shown no interest or aptitude for music in his early life. In 1962 he joined the Portland (Oregon) Youth for Christ as music director and from this group formed the first Continental Singers in 1963. Following a five week tour, Floria conducted the first Continental Singers recording using the top youth choruses gathered at a Youth for Christ chorale competition in Winona Lake, Indiana.

Floria formed the Continental Singers, but each member had to raise money for their living expenses during the tours. During this period he completed a master's degree at Lewis and Clark College in Portland, Oregon.

In 1975 Floria formed the Christian Artists Seminar in the Rockies, which became an annual event for those involved in contemporary Christian music. Through the talent contests there, a number of Christian artists came to the attention of the Christian music industry, including Point of Grace, Mark Lowry, Jaci Valesquez, Michael W. Smith, Staci Orico, Rachel Lampa, Babbie Mason, Carman, and others. In Spring 2000, Floria sold the Christian Artists Seminar to the Gospel Music Association.

Floria's vision for the Continental Singers, a group of young Christians who traveled to various churches to perform uplifting, Christian songs, led to the creation of a number of other traveling groups, such as Renaissance, New Hope, Act One Company, Intermission, Realities, Donny Monk and Friends, and Wings of Light. Among those who have been a member of the Continentals are Dennis and Carla Worley, Steve Taylor, Don Cason, Robert Sterling, Don Hart, Phil Perkins, Jon Stemkoski, Chuck Bolte, John B. Lee, Wayne Watson, and Jim Chaffee.

Gospel Music Association Dove Award

1984   Musical Album: *Dreamer* by Cam Floria; Label: Christian Artists

Don Cusic

4HIM

Andy Chrisman, vocals
Mark Harris, vocals
Marty Magehee, vocals
Kris Sullivan, vocals

Formed in 1989 by four members of the group Truth, 4Him, based in Daphne, Alabama, is a vocal harmony group that was extremely popular in the 1990s, with numerous songs on the Christian adult contemporary charts. Patterned after boy groups like N'Sync, Backstreet Boys, and 98 Degrees, the group had strong southern gospel roots but was popular with the contemporary church audience.

4Him won the Dove for "New Artist of the Year" in 1991 and was voted "Group of the Year" from 1993 to 1995. Their album, *The Season of Love,* won the Dove for "Inspirational Album of the Year" in 1994.

In 1994 the group traveled to Russia as representatives of the American Bible Society and distributed Bibles. The group disbanded in 2005 after recording their last album. Andy Chrisman became worship leader at a church in Celebration, Florida; Mark Harris embarked on a solo career; and Kris Sullivan and Marty Magehee were involved in studio production and songwriting.

The group was involved with World Vision and performed on the World Vision 2003 Spring Tour. They also performed at Promise Keepers rallies.

Don Cusic

For Further Reading

Powell, Mark Allen. *Encyclopedia of Contemporary Christian Music.*

Peabody, Mass.: Hendrickson Publishers, Inc., 2002.

FRANCISCO, DON

Don Francisco (b. February 28, 1946) is best known for his song, "He's Alive," which was released in 1978. That song, along with "Rise Again" by Dallas Holm, were landmarks in the first wave of contemporary Christian music as it evolved from Jesus music. Contemporary Christian radio was in its infancy when those two songs were released and their popularity on radio marked a turning point in Christian music as that music began to reach large numbers of people through the electronic media; before that time, Jesus music reached people primarily through live performances.

Although best known for "He's Alive" (which was covered by Johnny Cash and Dolly Parton, among others), Don Francisco released several albums of story songs that illustrated the gospel story, using biblical stories written in a narrative fashion that brought to life the gospel message.

Don Francisco is the son of a Baptist minister and seminary professor; he bought his first guitar at 14 with winnings from a poker game. The young man joined the hippie culture in Southern California during the early 1970s and then moved to Decatur, Georgia, where he led a rock band. In 1974 he experienced a transcendent moment when, he claimed, he heard God speak to him in an audible voice. Francisco enrolled in Belmont University in Nashville and connected with noted producer Gary Paxton, who produced Francisco's first albums for NewPax.

Francisco moved to Colorado in 1982, where he formed Rocky Mountain Ministries, and then left his story songs for praise and worship songs as well as meditative pieces during the mid-1980s.

Like many other young Christian artists, Francisco struggled with the fact that contemporary Christian music was both a ministry and part of the music business. Although many Christian artists wanted their music and ministry to be free of business issues in their decisions, the recording industry demanded that artists pay attention to promotion, publicity, marketing, and other activities that make the ministry widely available while it makes the recording business profitable. Christian artists preferred to think of prophets rather than profits, but in the music industry they are linked.

This struggle caused Francisco to leave Nashville and, although he continued to record, his folk-based music was not embraced by a contemporary Christian music culture that increasingly mimicked the pop/rock music of the day.

Don Cusic

Discography

Brother of the Son (1976)

Forgiven (1977)

Got to Tell Somebody (1979)

The Traveler (1981)

The Live Concert (1982)

Holiness (1984)

The Poet: A Collection of the Best (1984)

One Heart at a Time (1985)

The Power (1987)

High Praise (1988)

Live in the U.K. (1989)

The Early Works (1991)

Vision of the Valley (1991)

Come Away (1992)

Songs of the Spirit, Vol. 1: Genesis and Job (1994)

He's Alive, Collection Vol. 1 (1997)

Beautiful to Me, Collection Vol. 2 (1992)

Word Pictures (1996)

Grace on Grace (1998)

Balladeer Tales (1999)

Only Love Is Spoken Here (2001)

The Package, Collection Vol. 3 (2004)

The Promises (2003)

That I May Know You (2005)

The Sower (2007)

For Further Reading

Alfonso, Barry. *The Billboard Guide to Contemporary Christian Music.* New York: Billboard Books/Watson-Guptill, 2002.

Cusic, Don. *The Sound of Light: A History of Gospel and Christian Music.* New York: Hal Leonard, 2002.

McNeil, W. K., ed. *Encyclopedia of American Gospel Music.* New York: Routledge, 2005.

Powell, Mark Allen. *Encyclopedia of Contemporary Christian Music.* Peabody, Mass.: Hendrickson Publishers, Inc., 2002.

FRANKLIN, ARETHA

Aretha Franklin (b. March 25, 1942, in Memphis, Tennessee) was never part of contemporary Christian music, and yet no book about gospel or Christian music can ignore her. Franklin's roots go long and deep into the church and gospel music; the "Queen of Soul" is the daughter of Reverend C. L. Franklin, a legendary evangelist with the New Bethel Baptist Church in Detroit. Rev. Franklin's sermons were recorded for several labels and sold well; Aretha was a soloist in the choir and by the age of 18 had released several gospel albums. She signed with Columbia Records and then moved to Atlantic where producer Jerry Wexler guided her career into soul music, beginning with "I Never Loved a Man" in 1967 and continuing through "Respect," "A Natural Woman," and "Chain of Fools," all in 1967.

In 1970 Aretha and James Cleveland recorded *Amazing Grace*, a double album that became one of the top-selling gospel albums of all time. Although this album was released as contemporary Christian music gained attention, it was largely ignored within the contemporary Christian community, primarily because Aretha was regarded with suspicion; she had run-ins with the law and continued with her secular career. Also, the black gospel tradition was not influential with early contemporary Christian music performers. Later, individual members of the contemporary Christian music community acknowledged how important and talented Aretha Franklin is in gospel music.

Don Cusic

For Further Reading

Carpenter, Bil. *Uncloudy Days: The Gospel Music Encyclopedia.* San Francisco: Backbeat, 2005.

Cusic, Don. *The Sound of Light: A History of Gospel and Christian Music*. New York: Hal Leonard, 2002.

Darden, Bob. *People Get Ready!: A New History of Black Gospel Music*. New York: Continuum, 2005.

Franklin, Aretha, and David Ritz. *Aretha from These Roots*. New York: Villard, 1999.

Jackson, Jerma A. *Singing in My Soul: Black Gospel Music in a Secular Age*. Chapel Hill: University of North Carolina Press, 2004.

McNeil, W. K., ed. *Encyclopedia of American Gospel Music*. New York: Routledge, 2005.

Powell, Mark Allen. *Encyclopedia of Contemporary Christian Music*. Peabody, Mass.: Hendrickson Publishers, Inc., 2002.

Young, Alan. *Woke Me Up This Morning: Black Gospel Singers and the Gospel Life*. Jackson: University Press of Mississippi, 1997.

Zolten, Jerry. *Great God A'Mighty: The Dixie Hummingbirds: Celebrating the Rise of Soul Gospel Music*. New York: Oxford University Press, 2003.

Aretha Franklin sings at the McDonald's Gospelfest on June 4, 2005, in New York. (AP Photo/Diane Bondareff)

FRANKLIN, KIRK

Since the 1990s, Kirk Franklin (b. January 26, 1970, in Fort Worth, Texas) has been one of the most influential African American artists in contemporary Christian music. Franklin's music and his performances have appealed to both contemporary Christian and black gospel audiences, a rare achievement for any artist.

Kirk Franklin launched his gospel music career in 1993 with the release of his debut album, *Kirk Franklin and the Family*. The album spent nearly two years on *Billboard* magazine's gospel charts. The collection included the number one Christian music radio single "Why We Sing," which also became a top 40 single on the R&B radio charts. The album became the first of Franklin's many million-selling albums and led to a number of Dove Awards; the album received the "Traditional Gospel Album" award and "Why We Sing" received the "Traditional Gospel Song" award.

The success of his debut album helped Franklin fulfill his goal of breaking "down the walls between black and white people, and between gospel and contemporary Christian music" (Franklin 1998, 11). In addition to his work with the Family, Franklin

Gospel singer Kirk Franklin responds during an interview on October 26, 1996, in Dallas. (AP Photo/Jon Freilich)

has recorded with God's Property and 1NC (One Nation Crew)

Franklin had a difficult childhood. Abandoned by his young mother, Franklin went to live with his 64-year-old Aunt Gertrude, who took him to church several times a week and recognized Kirk's musical talent at an early age. When he began to play the piano at four years old, his aunt collected and sold aluminum cans to help pay for piano lessons. By the time he was 11 years old, Franklin was earning $100 a month as the music director of the Mount Rose Baptist Church.

Although he began to stray from his Christian roots as a teenager, the shooting death of a close friend when he was 15 set him back on a course to pursue his musical talents. Franklin began writing and recording his songs and put together a gospel group with some friends called Humble Hearts. He also had the opportunity to attend the Professional Youth Conservatory, a performing arts high school on the campus of Texas Wesleyan University in Fort Worth. When he wasn't studying, Franklin spent much of his time leading music at various Fort Worth churches.

Franklin came to the attention of gospel music icon Milton Biggham when the Dallas/Fort Worth Mass Choir recorded his composition, "Every Day with Jesus." Biggham was so impressed with Franklin's talent that he invited him to direct the song for the choir at the 1990 Gospel Music Workshop of America Convention in Washington, D.C. Franklin went on to record the song with the Georgia Mass Choir, and it was later included on the soundtrack of the film *The Preacher's Wife*, starring Denzel Washington and Whitney Houston.

With a desire to chart his own musical course, Franklin put a group of friends together in 1992 to perform his songs and blend a variety of music styles. He decided to call the group of close friends the Family, and soon they came to the attention of record executive Vickie Lataillade. She had started her Gospo Centric label with a $6,000 loan and bought the tape that became Franklin's first radio hit, "Why We Sing," for $5,000.

Kirk Franklin and the Family's sophomore release, *Whatcha Lookin' 4,* earned platinum status with sales of over one million copies and earned Franklin his first Grammy award for "Best Contemporary Soul Gospel Album." His next project featured a different ensemble on *God's Property from Kirk Franklin's Nu Nation.* The album was propelled to multi-platinum sales with the help of the radio and video hit, "Stomp." That single rose to the number one spot on the *Billboard* R&B singles chart and became a top 40 hit on pop radio. The album spent more than a month atop the *Billboard* R&B album chart and earned Franklin his second Grammy award for "Best Gospel Choir or Chorus Album."

Kirk Franklin's next project brought him even more fame but also created controversy when he included several mainstream artists on the record. Released in 1998, *The Nu Nation Project* included the popular single "Lean on Me," which featured the vocals of Mary J. Blige, R. Kelly, and Bono of U2. The album topped both the contemporary Christian albums and gospel albums charts in *Billboard* for several months and brought Franklin his third Grammy award in the "Best Contemporary Soul Gospel Album" category.

Franklin launched his solo career in 2002 with the release of the platinum selling *The Rebirth of Kirk Franklin*. The project quickly rose to the top of the *Billboard* gospel and hot R&B/hip hop albums charts and featured collaborations with Yolanda Adams, Toby-Mac, Shirley Caesar, Bishop T. D. Jakes, and others. Although the album did not win a Grammy award, Franklin's 2005 release, *Hero*, brought him his fourth win in the "Best Contemporary R&B Gospel Album" in 2006 and earned platinum status. He also picked up a songwriting Grammy in the "Best Gospel Song" category for "Imagine Me."

In 2007 Kirk Franklin returned to the top of the gospel and Christian music charts with *The Fight of My Life*. He also teamed with the BET cable network to host the talent search show "Sunday Best." Franklin recruited friends BeBe Winans and gospel duo Mary Mary as celebrity judges. In 2008 Lionsgate Films optioned the rights to bring Franklin's 1998 autobiography, *Church Boy*, with Franklin writing and producing the film's soundtrack.

James Elliott

For Further Reading

Franklin, Kirk. *Church Boy*. Nashville, Tenn.: Word Publishing, 1998.

FURAY, RICHIE

During the 1960s in Southern California, Richie Furay (b. Paul Richard Furay on May 9, 1944, in Yellow Springs, Ohio) was a key component in the group Buffalo Springfield, which also included Stephen Stills, Neil Young, and Jim Messina. Out of this group, Stills and Young went onto successful solo careers after forming Crosby, Stills, and Nash and, later, Crosby, Stills, Nash, and Young. Furay and Messina formed Poco, which included bassists Randy Meisner and Timothy Schmitt (Schmitt succeeded Meisner); Furay then formed the Souther Hillman Furay Band with Chris Hillman and J. D. Souther. These were legendary musicians who went on to perform in a number of influential groups: Loggins and Messina, the Eagles, and the Desert Rose Band.

The Souther Hillman Furay Band was expected to be a "supergroup" like Crosby, Stills, Nash, and Young, but their albums were not commercially successful and they had no hit singles on the radio. In that band was steel guitarist Al Perkins, who witnessed to Furay until Furay committed his life to Jesus. A separation from his wife of seven years followed before they reconciled. Furay formed the Richie Furay Band after he was a Christian but had no commercial success with this secular release; finally, he recorded his debut Christian album for Myrrh in 1982, *Seasons of Change*. In the Richie Furay

Band were Tom Stipe, formerly of Country Faith, and Jay Truax and John Meler, formerly of Love Song—all part of the Jesus movement that came from Calvary Chapel in Costa Mesa, California.

Superstardom eluded Richie Furay as a solo artist, although Buffalo Springfield is now in the Rock and Roll Hall of Fame (inducted in 1997) and Poco has now reached nea-rlegendary status. Instead, Furay dedicated himself to a life of ministry, serving as senior pastor at Calvary Chapel in Broomfield, Colorado. Furay continues to perform with Poco on occasion and occasionally performs as a solo act.

Don Cusic

For Further Reading

Furay, Richie. *There's Something Happening Here: The Story of Buffalo Springfield for What It's Worth.* Dallas: Quarry Press, 1997.

Powell, Mark Allen. *Encyclopedia of Contemporary Christian Music.* Peabody, Mass.: Hendrickson Publishers, Inc., 2002.

G

GAITHER, BILL AND GLORIA

Bill and Gloria Gaither are a husband and wife team who have written more than 700 songs together, including songs that have become standards in the Christian community and appear in church hymnals across the country. Additionally, Bill Gaither is the one of the most important people in the history of white gospel and contemporary Christian music during the second half of the 20th and early 21rst centuries. As a songwriter he wrote classics such as "Because He Lives," "He Touched Me," and "I Am a Promise"; as a performer he organized a series of groups, beginning with the Bill Gaither Trio and including the Gaither Vocal Band, that have been commercially successful; as a mentor he has helped artists such as Sandi Patty, Michael English, Mark Lowry, Steve Green, Cynthia Clawson, Amy Grant, and Don Francisco; as a businessman he has founded a complex in Alexandria, Indiana, the Gaither Resource Center that includes a publishing company, studio, distribution company, record company, television production, and a telemarketing firm;

Gaither was born, grew up, and still resides in Alexandria, Indiana, the son of George and Lela Gaither. In the summer of 1953, after his junior year in high school, Gaither attended the Stamps School of Music in Dallas and the following summer, after his high school graduation, attended again where he met Charlie Hodge; they formed a quartet with Bill's brother, Danny, and a friend of Hodges. The group performed for eight months before they called it quits because they were unable to make a living.

Bill Gaither enrolled at Taylor University in Fort Wayne, Indiana, in Fall 1954 but transferred to Anderson College the following year, where he graduated with a major in English and minor in music in 1959.

In 1956 he first formed the Bill Gaither Trio with his brother Danny and sister Mary Ann while attending Anderson College. After graduation he taught English at a junior high school and earned a master's degree in guidance and counseling. He then taught

201

Gospel music singers Bill and Gloria Gaither speak after being presented with the 2008 Sachem by Indiana governor Mitch Daniels during a ceremony on April 2, 2008, at the Indiana State Museum in Indianapolis. (AP Photo/Michael Conroy)

English at Alexander High School where he met French teacher Gloria Sickal; they were married on December 22, 1962.

While in college, Gaither worked at a supermarket and convinced the owner to sponsor a daily radio broadcast of his family trio performing songs; the broadcast was successful to the point that the trio earned enough money for Gaither to quit working at the supermarket. However, after college the trio disbanded and Gaither directed a local church choir while teaching school. He wrote a song, "I've Been to Calvary," which was recorded by the Golden Keys; this was his entry into songwriting and his wife Gloria soon joined him, writing lyrics. The trio re-formed but in 1964 his sister Mary Ann dropped out when she married and Gloria replaced her.

In 1964 the Bill Gaither Trio opened for the Imperials on a concert that Bill booked, and came to the attention of the Benson Company, a gospel music label based in Nashville. The trio signed with Benson and their first album, *Sincerely*, was successful, selling thousands of albums, which led to a series of albums. In 1967 Bill Gaither quit his job teaching high school English and devoted himself full time to his music career.

Bill Gaither was entrepreneurial and had a strong business sense. He formed a publishing company so he could control the copyright of his songs at the beginning of his career. Bill and Gloria Gaither have written a number of songs that have become standards in the Christian field; these include "The Longer I Serve Him," "Because He Lives," "The King Is Coming," "Something Beautiful," "He Touched Me," "It Is Finished," "There's Something about That Name," "Let's Just Praise the Lord," and "I Am a Promise." The songwriting and publishing laid the foundation for a business empire that was built by Gaither in the years that followed.

In 1975 Gaither and Bob MacKenzie formed Paragon Associates, a gospel firm that had a record and publishing company; that same year he and Gloria compiled a hymnal, *Hymns for the Family of God*, that sold well.

In 1976 Danny Gaither left the trio and was replaced by Gary McSpadden, who remained with the group until 1988, when he was replaced by Michael English. In 1977 the trio's album *Alleluia: A Praise Gathering for Believers* was certified gold, the first album from a Christian record company to achieve this honor. Bill Gaither organized Praise Gatherings in Indianapolis, which were also successful and became the forerunner to a number of other gatherings by Christian organizations and individuals.

In 1981, during a concert by the Gaither Trio, Bill and Gary McSpadden, along with two backup singers in his group, formed an impromptu quartet and sang several songs. This led to the formation of the Gaither Vocal Band. Through the years there have been a number of singers in the Gaither Vocal Band; members have included Guy Penrod, Wes Hampton, Marshall Hall, Mark Lowry, David Phelps, Steve

Green, Michael English, Russ Taff, and Jonathan Pierce.

Bill Gaither was 55 years old in 1991 and felt the contemporary Christian world was passing him by. That year he returned to his first love, southern gospel music, and formed a quartet with old friends Hovie Lister of Statesmen Quartet, Glen Payne and George Younce of the Cathedrals, the Speer Family, and Jake Hess, founder of the Imperials and recorded for three hours with a video camera recording the event. He took this video to the Family Channel where it was broadcast as "Homecoming" and launched a series of videos and concerts under the title "Homecoming." Gaither produced more than 100 videos of classic southern gospel and contemporary Christian artists singing together and talking about their lives; they were enormously successful not just commercially but because they revitalized the world of southern gospel music, which had been struggling because the popularity of contemporary Christian music had overshadowed this field.

In 1996 the "Homecoming" series began performing concerts and these led to a TV show, "The Gaither Music Hour," which was broadcast on several cable outlets.

The Gaithers have received a plethora of awards; in addition to Dove and Grammy Awards, Bill was elected to the Gospel Music Hall of Fame in 1982 and Gloria was elected in 1996. They were inducted into the Christian Bookseller Association's Hall of Fame in 1996, in 2000 the two were named Gospel Songwriters of the Century by ASCAP, and in 2002 they were inducted into the International Gospel Music Hall of Fame.

There are not many who have become wealthy through gospel music, but Bill Gaither is one of those rare individuals; *Rolling Stone* named him one of the 50 richest musicians in the world. He has won more honors and awards than anyone in gospel or Christian music, but his greatest impact on the Christian world has been his songs, which are sung regularly in churches all over the world, and the example he set as an individual who has promoted not only his own career but the careers of a number of other Christian artists as well as the field of gospel and Christian music itself.

Besides the more than 700 songs Bill and Gloria wrote together, Gloria has written over 40 books. In addition to the honors she has received as part of the Bill and Gloria Gaither "team," she has been awarded six honorary doctorates and has served on the board of directors for the Council for Christian Colleges and Universities and the United Christian College Fund. Gloria is an active speaker at numerous Christian conferences and played a key role in the formation of the Gaither Family Resources gathering place, which markets gifts, books, recordings, videos, DVDs, and life-issues resources.

Don Cusic

For Further Reading

Cusic, Don. *The Sound of Light: A History of Gospel and Christian Music.* New York: Hal Leonard, 2002.

Gaither, Bill, and Ken Abraham. *It's More Than Music: Life Lessons on Friends, Faith and What Matters Most.* New York: Warner Faith, 2003.

Gaither, Bill, and Gloria Gaither. *God Gave Song.* Grand Rapids, Mich.: Zondervan, 2000.

Gaither, Bill, and Jerry Jerkins. *Homecoming.* Grand Rapids, Mich.: Zondervan, 1997.

Gaither, Bill, and Jerry Jerkins. *I Almost Missed the Sunset.* Nashville, Tenn.: Thomas Nelson, 1992.

Powell, Mark Allen. *Encyclopedia of Contemporary Christian Music.* Peabody, Mass.: Hendrickson Publishers, Inc., 2002.

Discography
The Bill Gaither Trio

Sincerely (1964)

Live (double LP) (1972)

Christmas . . . Back Home in Indiana (1972)

My Faith Still Holds (1972)

Especially for Children of All Ages (1973)

Let's Just Praise the Lord (1973)

Something Beautiful: An Evening with the Bill Gaither Trio (1974)

Because He Lives (1974)

Thanks for Sunshine (1974)

I Am a Promise (1975)

Jesus, We Just Want to Thank You (1975)

Praise (1976)

My Heart Can Sing: The Inspiring Songs of Stuart Hamblen (1977)

Alleluia: A Praise Gathering for Believers (1977)

Pilgrim's Progress (1978)

The Very Best of the Very Best (1978)

We Are Persuaded (1979)

He Touched Me (1979)

The Very Best of the Very Best . . . for Kids (1980)

Bless the Lord Who Reigns in Beauty (1981)

He Started the Whole World Singing (1982)

Fully Alive (1983)

Ten New Songs with Kids . . . for Kids about Life (1984)

Then He Said Sing (1985)

Welcome Back Home (1987)

Hymn Classics (1990)

Best of the Gaithers . . . Live! (1992)

Old Friends (1993)

Oh Happy Day, Vol. 1 and 2 (1994)

Precious Memories (1994)

Our Recollections (1996)

Bill Gaither Trio, Vol. 1 (2000)

Bill Gaither Trio, Vol. 2 (2000)

Bill Gaither Trio, Vol. 3 (2000)

Bill Gaither Trio, Vol. 4 (2000)

Solo

Bill Gaither (2005)

Gaither Vocal Band

The New Gaither Vocal Band (1981)

Passin' the Faith Along (1983)

New Point of View (1984)

One X 1 (1986)

Wings (1988)

The Best from the Beginning (1989)

A Few Good Men (1990)

Homecoming (1991)

Southern Classics (1993)

Peace of the Rock (1993)

Testify (1994)

I Bowed on My Knees (1994)

The King Is Coming (1994)

Reunion Precious Memories (1995)

Can't Stop Talking about Him (1995)

Southern Classics: Volume 2 (1996)

Back Home in Indiana (1997)

Lovin' God and Lovin' Each Other (1997)

Joy to the World: Gaither Gospel Series (1997)

Still the Greatest Story Ever Told (1998)

God Is Good (1999)

I Do Believe (2000)

Everything Good (2002)

A Cappella (2003)

8 Great Hits (2003)

Best of the Gaither Vocal Band (2004)

Give It Away (2006)

Together (with Ernie Haase and Signature Sound) (2007)

Gospel Music Association Dove Awards: Bill Gaither

1969	Songwriter of the Year
1970	Songwriter of the Year
1972	Songwriter of the Year
1973	Songwriter of the Year
1974	Song of the Year: "Because He Lives" Written by Bill Gaither; Publisher: Gaither Music, ASCAP
1974	Songwriter of the Year
1975	Songwriter of the Year
1976	Songwriter of the Year
1977	Songwriter of the Year

1986   Praise and Worship Album: *I've Just Seen Jesus* by William J. Gaither and Randy Vader; Label: Gaither Music Records

1987   Southern Gospel Album: *The Master Builder* by the Cathedrals; Producers: Bill Gaither and Gary McSpadden; Label: RiverSong

1991   Southern Gospel Album: *Climbing Higher and Higher* by the Cathedrals; Producers: Bill Gaither, Mark Trammel, and Lari Goss; Label: Homeland

2001   Long Form Music Video: *A Farewell Celebration* by the Cathedrals; Producers and Directors: Bryan Bateman, Bill Gaither and Dennis Glore; Label: Spring House

2002   Southern Gospel Album of the Year: *Encore; Old Friends Quartet*; Bill Gaither, Wesley Pritchard, Ben Speer; Spring House

Gospel Music Association Dove Awards: Bill and Gloria Gaither

1993   Southern Gospel Album: *Reunion: A Gospel Homecoming Celebration* by Bill and Gloria Gaither; Producer: Bill Gaither; Label: Star Song

1999   Southern Gospel Recorded Song: "I Believe in a Hill Called Mount Calvary"; Writers: William J. Gaither and Gloria Gaither; Recorded by: Gaither Vocal Band; Label: Spring Hill

Gospel Music Association Dove Awards: Gloria Gaither

1985   Song of the Year: "Upon This Rock" Written by Gloria Gaither and Dony McGuire; Publishers: Gaither Music, It's-N-Me Music, and Lexicon Music; ASCAP

1986   Songwriter of the Year: Gloria Gaither

1988   Song of the Year: "In the Name of the Lord" Written by Phil McHugh, Gloria Gaither, and Sandi Patti Helvering; Publishers River Oaks Music and Sandi's Songs BMI; Gaither Music, ASCAP

2007   Southern Gospel Recorded Song of the Year: "Give It Away"; Gaither Vocal Band; Gloria Gaither, Benjamin Gaither; Gaither Music Group

Gospel Music Association Dove Awards: The Bill Gaither Trio

1976   Inspirational Album: *Jesus, We Just Want to Thank You* by the Bill Gaither Trio; Producer: Bob MacKenzie; Label: HeartWarming

1978   Inspirational Album: *Pilgrim's Progress* by the Bill Gaither Trio; Producers: Bob MacKenzie and John W. Thompson; Label: Impact

1980   Mixed Group of the Year: Bill Gaither Trio

Gospel Music Association Dove Awards: The Gaither Vocal Band

1992   Southern Gospel Album: *Homecoming* by the Gaither Vocal Band; Producers: Ken Mansfield and the Gaither Vocal Band; Label: Star Song

1994   Southern Gospel Album: *Southern Classics* by the Gaither Vocal Band; Producers: Bill Gaither, Michael Sykes, and Michael English; Label: Benson

1994   Southern Gospel Recorded Song: "Satisfied"; Public Domain; Recorded by the Gaither Vocal Band; Label: Benson

1995   Southern Gospel Recorded Song: "I Bowed on My Knees"; Public Domain; Recorded by: Gaither Vocal Band; Public Domain; Label: Benson

1999   Southern Gospel Album: *Still the Greatest Story Ever Told* by the Gaither Vocal Band; Producers: Bill Gaither, Michael Sykes, and Guy Penrod; Label: Spring Hill

2000   Southern Gospel Album: *God Is Good* by the Gaither Vocal Band; Producers: Bill Gaither, Michael Sykes, and Guy Penrod; Label: Spring Hill)

2001   Southern Gospel Album: *I Do Believe* by the Gaither Vocal Band; Producers: Bill Gaither, Guy Penrod and Michael Sykes; Label: Spring Hill

2007   Southern Gospel Album of the Year: *Give It Away*; The Gaither Vocal Band; Bill Gaither, Michael Sykes, Marshall Hall, Guy Penrold, Wes Hampton; Gaither Music Group

Grammy Awards: Bill Gaither Trio

1973   16th Grammy Awards: Best Inspirational Performance: Bill Gaither Trio: "Let's Just Praise the Lord"

1975   18th Grammy Awards: Best Inspirational Performance (Non-Classical): Bill Gaither Trio: "Jesus, We Just Want to Thank You"

Grammy Awards: Bill and Gloria Gaither

1999   42nd Grammy Awards: Best Southern, Country, or Bluegrass Gospel Album: *Kennedy Center Homecoming* by Bill and Gloria Gaither and Their Homecoming Friends

2001   44th Grammy Awards: Best Southern, Country or Bluegrass Gospel Album: *Bill and Gloria Gaither Present a Billy Graham Music Homecoming*; Bill and Gloria Gaither and the Homecoming Friends

Grammy Awards: The Gaither Vocal Band

1991   34th Grammy Awards: Best Southern Gospel Album: *Homecoming* by the Gaither Vocal Band

GENTLE FAITH

The importance and influence of Gentle Faith (Paul Angers, Henry Cutrona, Don Gerber, Steve Kara, and Darrell Mansfield) goes beyond their only album, released in 1976. The group, formed by Darrell Mansfield, was the beginning of Mansfield's career in contemporary Christian music. The group, originally named Jubal, was part of the early group of musicians at Calvary Chapel in Costa Mesa, California; at a meeting with pastor Chuck Smith, the group discovered there was another group also named Jubal. That other group changed their name to Daniel Amos, and Mansfield chose the name Gentle Faith. The first album from Maranatha Records, based at Calvary Chapel, was *The Everlastin' Living Jesus Music Concert* (1971) and Gentle Faith recorded a song, "The Shepherd" for that album. On "The Shepherd" Gentle Faith was just Henry Cutrona and two others—Larry Needham and John Wilson.

Mansfield, a blues singer and legendary harmonica player, went on to a distinguished solo career and to minister at Calvary Chapel. Mansfield's album, *Get Ready*, released in 1980, was considered one of the best Christian albums released that year. On his album *Blues with a Feelin'*, he recorded the standards "People Get Ready," "Stand by Me," and "Nobody's Fault But Mine." Mansfield later was part of the duo Kaiser/Mansfield, the trio Mansfield, Howard, and Kaiser, and the group Shack of Peasants, which recorded several albums.

Don Cusic

For Further Reading

Powell, Mark Allen. *Encyclopedia of Contemporary Christian Music.* Peabody, Mass.: Hendrickson Publishers, Inc., 2002.

Thompson, John J. *Raised by Wolves: The Story of Christian Rock and Roll.* Toronto, Ontario: ECW Press, 2000.

GIANT

Studio musician and former White Heart member Dann Huff led Giant, a group composed of Nashville musicians. Dann's brother, drummer David Huff, bass player Mike Brignardello, and keyboard player Alan Pasqua were also in the group. Dann Huff later joined the Front and then the Players, a supergroup of session musicians. Giant released two albums, *Last of the Runaways* on A&M in 1989 and *Time to Burn* on Epic in 1991.

Don Cusic

For Further Reading

Powell, Mark Allen. *Encyclopedia of Contemporary Christian Music.* Peabody, Mass.: Hendrickson Publishers, Inc., 2002.

Thompson, John J. *Raised by Wolves: The Story of Christian Rock and Roll.* Toronto, Ontario: ECW Press, 2000.

GIRARD, CHUCK

Chuck Girard (b. August 27, 1943, in Los Angeles, California) became one of the leading architects of contemporary Christian music when he formed the group Love Song in 1970 with Tommy Coomes, Jay Truax, and Fred Fields. Guitarist Bob Wall later joined the group for the recording of the self-titled debut album *Love Song* in 1972. Distributed by the major United Artists Records label, the album quickly became the best-selling gospel album in America. Girard wrote or cowrote many songs on the album. including the popular "A Love Song," "Two Hands," and "Little Country Church."

Growing up in Southern California, Chuck Girard found success early in the music business as a member of the Casteels, who scored top 20 hits with "Sacred" and "So I Love You." Later he became the lead singer for the Hondells and recorded two albums for Mercury Records, yielding the radio hits "A Younger Girl," and "Little Honda."

Following his early success in Hollywood, Girard moved to Las Vegas, performing with various groups on the Vegas strip. Returning to Orange County, California, Girard joined the group Bigfoot and performed regularly at the Gold Street Club. During that time he attended a small church led by Pastor Chuck Smith called Calvary Chapel and was converted to Christianity. Quickly turning his musical gifts to his newfound faith, Girard formed the group Love Song and began performing at Calvary Chapel Bible studies.

When Love Song broke up in 1974, Chuck Girard launched a solo career, releasing the self-titled *Chuck Girard* in 1975 that included the popular songs "Rock 'N' Roll Preacher" and "Sometimes Alleluia."

In 2006 Girard reunited with fellow CCM pioneers Don Francisco, Barry McGuire, Dallas Holm, Leon Patillo, and others to perform in the Beginnings Concert in San Antonio, Texas, which was released on CD and DVD in 2008.

James Elliott

For Further Reading

Alfonso, Barry. *The Billboard Guide to Contemporary Christian Music*. New York: Billboard Books/Watson-Guptill, 2002.

Cusic, Don. *The Sound of Light: A History of Gospel and Christian Music*. New York: Hal Leonard, 2002.

McNeil, W. K., ed. *Encyclopedia of American Gospel Music*. New York: Routledge, 2005.

Powell, Mark Allen. *Encyclopedia of Contemporary Christian Music*. Peabody, Mass.: Hendrickson Publishers, Inc., 2002.

GLASS HARP

Glass Harp, a three member power trio, was Phil Keaggy's first band. The Youngstown, Ohio, band was formed in 1968 when Keaggy and John Sferra were both 17-year-old high school students. They were joined by bassist Dan Pecchio. The group opened for such acts as Traffic, Yes, the Kinks, Humble Pie, Alice Cooper, Iron Butterfly, Ted Nugent, and Grand Funk Railroad and were never known as a Christian group. Their debut album, released in 1970, was recorded at Jimi Hendrix's Electric Ladyland studios; Hendrix died the day before it was completed. Earlier that year Keaggy's mother, who served as the bookkeeper for the band, died, which led to Keaggy's Christian conversion after his sister witnessed to him.

The band recorded three albums for Decca before Keaggy left the group, intending to give up rock 'n' roll for the Lord. Keaggy moved to California where he became part of Love Song, then moved to upstate New York where he embarked on his career as a solo artist.

Glass Harp had reunion tours in 1981, 1987, and 1993.

Don Cusic

For Further Reading

Powell, Mark Allen. *Encyclopedia of Contemporary Christian Music.* Peabody, Mass.: Hendrickson Publishers, Inc., 2002.

Thompson, John J. *Raised by Wolves: The Story of Christian Rock and Roll.* Toronto, Ontario: ECW Press, 2000.

GODSPELL

In 1971 the musical *Godspell*, written by Stephen Schwartz and John-Michael Tebelak, opened in New York off Broadway. The story line comes from the Gospel of Matthew and, like Jesus Christ Superstar, which was produced around the same time, presented the gospel with rock music and made Jesus a contemporary, countercultural figure. The musical began as a master's thesis for John-Michael Tebelak at Carnegie Mellon University in Pittsburgh; the music was written by students in the music department. The musical then moved to La Mama in Greenwich Village, where a score was written by Stephen Schwartz; many of the lyrics came from the Episcopal Hymnal. The musical opened at the off-Broadway theaters Cherry Lane and Promenade in the summer of 1971 and then went to Broadway, where it ran from June 1976 until September 1977. The film of *Godspell* was released in 1973; it was set in contemporary New York and Tebelak cowrote the screenplay. Like *Jesus Christ Superstar, Godspell* presented Jesus as a man and omitted the Resurrection. A song from the musical, "Day by Day," sung by original cast member Robin Lamont, reached number 13 on the pop chart in the summer of 1972.

Don Cusic

For Further Reading

Cusic, Don. *The Sound of Light: A History of Gospel and Christian Music.* New York: Hal Leonard, 2002.

GOOD NEWS

Good News served originally as a backup band for Erick Nelson; the group was made up of Billy Batstone, bass, vocals; Bob Carlisle, vocals (from 1977), David Diggs, guitar, drums; John Hernandez and Yvonne Lewis, vocals; and Nelson. During the sessions for their first album *Good News* for Maranatha, Bob Carlisle left to join Psalm 150; the group disbanded after that debut album but then reunited for a second album, *Good News 2,* released on Sonrise in 1977, and Keith Green joined on piano. The group was a studio group; they never toured or performed together in public.

Don Cusic

For Further Reading

Powell, Mark Allen. *Encyclopedia of Contemporary Christian Music.*

Peabody, Mass.: Hendrickson Publishers, Inc., 2002.

Thompson, John J. *Raised by Wolves: The Story of Christian Rock and Roll.* Toronto, Ontario: ECW Press, 2000.

GOSPEL GRAMMY AWARDS

In the field of music, the most prestigious awards are the Grammys, given each year in honor of the top recordings and artists of the previous year. Although gospel was not initially included in the Grammy Awards, that award has come to acknowledge and reward the top performers in contemporary Christian music.

The National Academy of Recording Arts and Sciences (NARAS) was formed in 1957 as the debate over rock 'n' roll versus "good music" was raging. It was a reaction against Elvis and rock 'n' roll that inspired the organizers of NARAS to create an award to honor artistry and excellence rather than sales and mass popularity.

Representatives from the major labels formed NARAS at the Brown Derby Restaurant in Hollywood and appointed Jim Conkling, former president of Columbia Records, as its chairman. Membership in the organization was limited to members of the creative community—recording artists, songwriters, conductors, engineers, etc.—and only they could vote for award winners. The first Grammy Awards had 28 categories: six for classical, two for jazz, and one each for rhythm and blues, country, comedy, spoken word, movie sound track, Broadway, and children's recordings. Rock was not included and neither was gospel.

The first Grammy Awards banquet was held at the Beverly Hilton Hotel in Los Angeles on May 4, 1959; the second Grammy Awards was held six months later, on November 29, 1959, and, although there was no category for gospel, the Mormon Tabernacle Choir won the Grammy for "Battle Hymn of the Republic" in the "Best Performance by a Chorus" category.

The first category that acknowledged gospel, "Best Gospel or Other Religious Recording," was instituted in 1961 and Mahalia Jackson won that first award. Jackson also won in 1962, and in 1963 the Singing Nun won for "Dominique." There was only one category for gospel until 1967 when the 10th Grammy Awards had two awards: "Best Gospel Performance" and "Best Sacred Performance"; Elvis won the latter for "How Great Thou Art."

The Grammy Awards expanded to three gospel categories in 1967 and remained at three until 1977 when gospel expanded to include five categories.

The Grammy voters began looking to the Christian industry in 1973 when the Bill Gaither Trio won their first award; before this time award winners came from the black gospel field or from pop and country artists such as Elvis, Porter Wagoner, and Charlie Pride. In 1976 at the 19th Grammy Awards the first award given to what may be considered a contemporary Christian music artist was given to Gary S. Paxton for his album *The Astonishing, Outrageous, Amazing, Incredible, Unbelievable, Different World of Gary S. Paxton.*

The 1978 Grammy Awards produced both a surprise and a setback for contemporary Christian music. B. J. Thomas won for "Inspirational Performance," the Happy Goodman Family won for "Traditional Gospel Performance" and Larry Hart took home the Grammy for "Contemporary Gospel Performance." The Hart win shocked the gospel industry because he was a virtual unknown before the awards ceremony who had recorded a custom album, and his win became the basis for major changes in the Grammy voting process. Hart's victory came after he signed the members of the choir in his father's church in Detroit to NARAS membership and bloc-voted for the award. The scandal cast a dark cloud over the Grammys but, in the end, gospel music benefited from the increased attention as the Grammy telecast featured more performances by gospel artists.

The 1979 Grammy Awards, held in February 1980 in Los Angeles, featured a lot of gospel music; there were performances by Andrae Crouch and the Mighty Clouds of Joy as well as a tuxedo-clad Bob Dylan singing "Gotta Serve Somebody." Hosted by Andy Williams, the Grammy Awards featured five categories for gospel, with B. J. Thomas, the Imperials, the Blackwood Brothers, Andrae Crouch, and the Mighty Clouds of Joy all carrying home awards. In a *Billboard* article about the awards show, it was noted that "no less than seven times did Grammy recipients thank the Lord or God or Jesus for helping them achieve their coveted awards."

During the 23rd Grammy Awards held in 1981 there was a performance of "The Lord's Prayer," which had more major gospel entertainers on stage at one time than in any previous Grammy show. In addition to composers Dony McGuire and Reba Rambo, there were the Archers, Cynthia Clawson, Andrae Crouch, Walter and Tramaine Hawkins, and B. J. Thomas, who all performed on the album of the same title. This performance received one of the few standing ovations of that evening and that album won a Grammy. Other Grammy winners were Shirley Caesar, the Blackwood Brothers, James Cleveland, and Debby Boone.

Rev. James Cleveland and James Blackwood served as presenters during the evening while the show's host, Paul Simon, noted that "for years gospel music has been divided into two categories—inspirational and contemporary—which is essentially a euphemism for black gospel and white gospel music." After a brief pause for heavy applause, Simon continued that "of course, it seems God doesn't make the same distinction."

At the 24th Grammy Awards in 1982, gospel music took another step forward, featuring a lively performance by Al Green, the Archers, and the Crusaders with Joe Cocker on some gospel songs. Winning Grammys that year were B. J. Thomas, the Imperials, Al Green, Andrae Crouch, and the Masters V (J. D. Sumner, James Blackwood, Hovie Lister, and Jake Hess).

NARAS, composed primarily of people from the pop side of the music industry, had always tended to nominate and vote for gospel acts on major secular labels or who were best known to the secular world either because they had been around for so long (like the Blackwood Brothers) or because they had been secular stars before going gospel (like B. J. Thomas). But the gospel Grammy nominations that year were dominated by all-Christian labels. Christian record labels showed a real surge in voting strength as they captured 22 of the 28 nominations in the gospel categories.

The Grammys in 1983 were a disappointment for many contemporary Christian fans, who were getting accustomed to a healthy dose of their favorite music and artists on the network show. Gospel Grammy winners Al Green (with two), Barbara Mandrell, and the Blackwood Brothers were given their awards during the pretelecast ceremonies and, except for Ricky Skaggs and the Masters V singing "I'll Fly Away" and Little Richard rocking out with "Joy Joy Joy," there were no performances from contemporary Christian artists. Amy Grant picked up a Grammy for her *Age to Age* album.

The 26th Grammy Awards, held in Los Angeles in 1985 and hosted by John Denver, featured a barefoot Amy Grant performing "Angels." Approximately 140 million people saw a gospel medley, featuring performances by Andrae Crouch, Deniece Williams, the Clark Sisters, Pop Staples, and James Cleveland. Amy Grant and her song "Angels" won in the "Female" gospel category; other gospel winners included Michael W. Smith, Debby Boone, Phil Driscoll, and Donna Summer. By this time there were seven categories that honored gospel.

At this point, contemporary Christian music was accepted as a major force in the Grammy Awards. In the coming years the Grammy organization had to deal with the difference between black and white gospel for future awards, but it was obvious that contemporary Christian music was a major force in the Grammy Awards and contemporary Christian artists consistently won gospel Grammys.

Don Cusic

For Further Reading

O'Neil, Thomas. *The Grammy's for the Record.* New York: Penguin, 1993.

Schipper, Henry. *Broken Record: The Inside Story of the Grammy Awards.* New York: Birch Lane, 1992.

Grammy Gospel Award Winners

1958: 1st Grammy Awards: none

1959: 2nd Grammy Awards: none

1960: 3rd Grammy Awards: none

1961: 4th Grammy Awards

Best Gospel or Other Religious Recording: Mahalia Jackson: "Everytime I Feel the Spirit"

1962: 5th Grammy Awards

Best Gospel or Other Religious Recording: Mahalia Jackson: *Great Songs of Love and Faith*

1963: 6th Grammy Awards

Best Gospel or Other Religious Recording (Musical): Soeur Sourire (The Singing Nun): "Dominique"

1964: 7th Grammy Awards

Best Gospel or Other Religious Recording (Musical): Tennessee Ernie Ford: *Great Gospel Songs*

1965: 8th Grammy Awards

Best Gospel or Other Religious Recording (Musical): George Beverly Shea And the Anita Kerr Singers: *Southland Favorites*

1966: 9th Grammy Awards

Best Sacred Recording (Musical): Porter Wagoner–Blackwood Brothers: *Grand Old Gospel*

1967: 10th Grammy Awards

Best Gospel Performance: Porter Wagoner-Blackwood Brothers Quartet: *More Grand Old Gospel*

Best Sacred Performance: Elvis Presley: "How Great Thou Art"

1968: 11th Grammy Awards

Best Gospel Performance: Happy Goodman Family: *The Happy Gospel of the Happy Goodmans*

Best Sacred Performance: Jake Hess: *Beautiful Isle of Somewhere*

Best Soul Gospel Performance: Dottie Rambo: *The Soul of Me*

1969: 12th Grammy Awards

Best Soul Gospel Performance: Edwin Hawkins Singers: "Oh Happy Day"

Best Sacred Performance (Non-Classical): Jake Hess: *Ain't That Beautiful Singing*

Best Gospel Performance: Porter Wagoner, the Blackwood Brothers: *In Gospel Country*

1970: 13th Grammy Awards

Best Soul Gospel Performance: Edwin Hawkins Singers: "Every Man Wants to Be Free"

Best Sacred Performance (Musical): Jake Hess: "Everything Is Beautiful"

Best Gospel Performance (Other Than Soul Gospel): The Oak Ridge Boys: *Talk about the Good Times*

1971: 14th Grammy Awards

Best Soul Gospel Performance: Shirley Caesar: "Put Your Hand in the Hand of the Man from Galilee"

Best Sacred Performance: Charley Pride: *Did You Think to Pray*

Best Gospel Performance (Other Than Soul Gospel): Charley Pride: "Let Me Live"

1972: 15th Grammy Awards

Best Gospel Performance: Blackwood Brothers: *L-O-V-E*

Best Soul Gospel Performance: Aretha Franklin: "Amazing Grace"

Best Inspirational Performance: Elvis Presley: "He Touched Me"

1973: 16th Grammy Awards

Best Gospel Performance: Blackwood Brothers: "Release Me (from My Sin)"

Best Soul Gospel Performance: Dixie Hummingbirds: "Love Me Like a Rock"

Best Inspirational Performance: Bill Gaither Trio: "Let's Just Praise the Lord"

1974: 17th Grammy Awards

Best Gospel Performance: The Oak Ridge Boys "The Baptism of Jesse Taylor"

Best Soul Gospel Performance: James Cleveland with the Southern California Community Choir: "In the Ghetto"

Best Inspirational Performance (Non-Classical): Elvis Presley: "How Great Thou Art"

1975: 18th Grammy Awards

Best Gospel Performance (Other Than Soul Gospel): The Imperials: *No Shortage*

Best Soul Gospel Performance: Andrae Crouch and the Disciples: "Take Me Back"

Best Inspirational Performance (Non-Classical): Bill Gaither Trio: "Jesus, We Just Want to Thank You"

1976: 19th Grammy Awards

Best Gospel Performance (Other Than Soul Gospel): The Oak Ridge Boys: "Where the Soul Never Dies"

Best Soul Gospel Performance: Mahalia Jackson: "How I Got Over"

Best Inspirational Performance: Gary S. Paxton: *The Astonishing, Outrageous, Amazing, Incredible, Unbelievable, Different World of Gary S. Paxton*

1977: 20th Grammy Awards

Best Gospel Performance, Contemporary or Inspirational: The Imperials: "Sail On"

Best Soul Gospel Performance, Traditional: James Cleveland: *James Cleveland Live at Carnegie Hall*

Best Soul Gospel Performance, Contemporary: Edwin Hawkins and the Edwin Hawkins Singers: "Wonderful!"

Best Gospel Performance, Traditional: The Oak Ridge Boys: "Just a Little Talk with Jesus"

Best Inspirational Performance: B. J. Thomas: "Home Where I Belong"

1978: 21st Grammy Awards

Best Gospel Performance, Traditional: The Happy Goodman Family: "Refreshing"

Best Gospel Performance, Contemporary or Inspirational: Larry Hart: *What a Friend*

Best Soul Gospel Performance, Contemporary: Andrae Crouch And the Disciples: *Live in London*

Best Soul Gospel Performance, Traditional: Mighty Clouds of Joy: *Live and Direct*

Best Inspirational Performance: B. J. Thomas: "Happy Man"

1979: 22nd Grammy Awards

Best Gospel Performance, Traditional: The Blackwood Brothers: *Lift Up the Name of Jesus*

Best Gospel Performance, Contemporary or Inspirational: The Imperials: *Heed the Call*

Best Soul Gospel Performance, Traditional: Mighty Clouds of Joy: *Changing Times*

Best Soul Gospel Performance, Contemporary: Andrae Crouch: "I'll Be Thinking of You"

Best Inspirational Performance: B. J. Thomas: "You Gave Me Love (When Nobody Gave Me a Prayer)"

1980: 23rd Grammy Awards

Best Gospel Performance, Traditional: The Blackwood Brothers: *We Come to Worship*

Best Gospel Performance, Contemporary or Inspirational: Reba Rambo, Dony McGuire, B. J. Thomas, Andrae Crouch, Walter Hawkins, Tremaine Hawkins, Cynthia Clawson, the Archers: *The Lord's Prayer*

Best Soul Gospel Performance, Contemporary: Shirley Caesar: *Rejoice*

Best Soul Gospel Performance, Traditional: James Cleveland and the Charles Fold Singers: *Lord, Let Me Be an Instrument*

Best Inspirational Performance: Debby Boone: *With My Song I Will Praise Him*

1981: 24th Grammy Awards

Best Gospel Performance, Traditional: The Masters V (James Blackwood, J. D. Sumner, Hovie Lister, Rosie Rozell, and Jake Hess): *The Masters V*

Best Gospel Performance, Contemporary or Inspirational: The Imperials: *Priority*

Best Soul Gospel Performance, Contemporary: Andrae Crouch: *Don't Give Up*

Best Soul Gospel Performance, Traditional: Al Green: *The Lord Will Make a Way*

Best Inspirational Performance: B. J. Thomas: "Amazing Grace"

1982: 25th Grammy Awards

Best Gospel Performance, Traditional: The Blackwood Brothers: "I'm Following You"

Best Gospel Performance, Contemporary: Amy Grant: *Age to Age*

Best Soul Gospel Performance, Contemporary: Al Green: "Higher Plane"

Best Soul Gospel Performance, Traditional: Al Green: "Precious Lord"

Best Inspirational Performance: Barbara Mandrell: *He Set My Life to Music*

1983: 26th Grammy Awards

Best Gospel Performance, Female: Amy Grant: "Ageless Medley"

Best Gospel Performance, Male: Russ Taff: *Walls of Glass*

Best Soul Gospel Performance, Male: Al Green: "I'll Rise Again"

Best Soul Gospel Performance, Female: Sandra Crouch: "We Sing Praises"

Best Soul Gospel Performance by a Duo or Group: Barbara Mandrell and Bobby Jones: "I'm So Glad I'm Standing Here Today"

Best Gospel Performance by a Duo or Group: Sandi Patti and Larnelle Harris: "More Than Wonderful"

Best Inspirational Performance: Donna Summer: "He's a Rebel"

1984: 27th Grammy Awards

Best Gospel Performance, Female: Amy Grant: "Angels"

Best Gospel Performance, Male: Michael W. Smith: *Michael W. Smith*

Best Soul Gospel Performance, Male: Andrae Crouch: "Always Remember"

Best Soul Gospel Performance, Female: Shirley Caesar: "Sailin'"

Best Soul Gospel Performance by a Duo or Group: Shirley Caesar and Al Green: "Sailin' on the Sea of Your Love"

Best Gospel Performance by a Duo or Group: Debby Boone and Phil Driscoll "Keep the Flame Burning"

Best Inspirational Performance: Donna Summer: "Forgive Me"

1985: 28th Grammy Awards

Best Gospel Performance, Female: Amy Grant: *Unguarded*

Best Gospel Performance, Male: Larnelle Harris: "How Excellent Is Thy Name"

Best Soul Gospel Performance, Male: Marvin Winans: "Bring Back the Days of Yea and Nay"

Best Soul Gospel Performance, Female: Shirley Caesar: "Martin"

Best Soul Gospel Performance by a Duo or Group, Choir or Chorus: The Winans: "Tomorrow"

Best Gospel Performance by a Duo or Group, Choir or Chorus: Sandi Patti and Larnelle Harris: "I've Just Seen Jesus"

Best Inspirational Performance: Jennifer Holiday: "Come Sunday"

1986: 29th Grammy Awards

Best Gospel Performance, Female: Sandi Patti: "Morning Like This"

Best Gospel Performance, Male: Philip Bailey: "Triumph"

Best Soul Gospel Performance, Male: Al Green: "Going Away"

Best Soul Gospel Performance, Female: Deniece Williams: "I Surrender All"

Best Soul Gospel Performance by a Duo or Group, Choir or Chorus: The Winans: "Let My People Go"

Best Gospel Performance by a Duo or Group, Choir or Chorus: Sandi Patti and Deniece Williams: "They Say"

1987: 30th Grammy Awards

Best Gospel Performance, Female: Deniece Williams: "I Believe in You"

Best Gospel Performance, Male: Larnelle Harris: "The Father Hath Provided"

Best Soul Gospel Performance, Male: Al Green: "Everything's Gonna Be Alright"

Best Soul Gospel Performance, Female: CeCe Winans: "For Always"

Best Soul Gospel Performance by a Duo or Group, Choir or Chorus: Anita Baker and the Winans: "Ain't No Need to Worry"

Best Gospel Performance by a Duo or Group, Choir or Chorus: *Crack the Sky*; by Mylon LeFevre and Broken Heart; Producer: Greg Piccolo

1988: 31st Grammy Awards

Best Gospel Performance, Female: *Lead Me On* by Amy Grant

Best Gospel Performance, Male: *Christmas* by Larnelle Harris

Best Soul Gospel Performance, Male: *Abundant Life* by BeBe Winans

Best Soul Gospel Performance, Female: *One Lord, One Faith, One Baptism* by Aretha Franklin

Best Soul Gospel Performance by a Duo or Group, Choir or Chorus: *Take Six* by Take 6

Best Gospel Performance By a Duo or Group, Choir or Chorus: *The Winans Live at Carnegie Hall* by the Winans

1989: 32nd Grammy Awards

Best Gospel Vocal Performance, Female: *Don't Cry* by CeCe Winans

Best Gospel Vocal Performance, Male: *Meantime* by BeBe Winans

Best Soul Gospel Performance, Male or Female: *As Long As We're Together* by Al Green

Best Soul Gospel Performance by a Duo or Group, Choir or Chorus: *Let Brotherly Love Continue* by Daniel Winans

Best Gospel Performance by a Duo or Group, Choir or Chorus: *The Saviour Is Waiting* by Take 6

1990: 33rd Grammy Awards

Best Southern Gospel Album: *The Great Exchange* by Bruce Carroll

Best Gospel Album by a Choir or Chorus: *Dr. James Cleveland and the Southern California Community Choir*

Best Traditional Soul Gospel Performance: *Tramaine Hawkins Live* by Tramaine Hawkins

Best Gospel Pop Album: *Another Time . . . Another Place* by Sandi Patti

Best Rock/Contemporary Gospel Album: *Beyond Belief* by Petra

Best Contemporary Soul Gospel Album: *So Much 2 Say* by Take 6

1991: 34th Grammy Awards

Best Pop Gospel Album: *For the Sake of the Call* by Steven Curtis Chapman

Best Southern Gospel Album: *Homecoming* by the Gaither Vocal Band

Best Gospel Album by a Choir or Chorus: *The Evolution of Gospel* by Gary Hines

Best Traditional Soul Gospel Album: *Pray for Me* by Mighty Clouds of Joy

Best Rock/Contemporary Gospel Album: *Under Their Influence* by Russ Taff

Best Contemporary Soul Gospel Album: *Different Lifestyles* by CeCe and BeBe Winans

1992: 35th Grammy Awards

Best Traditional Soul Gospel Album: *He's Working It out for You* by Shirley Caesar

Best Southern Gospel Album: *Sometimes Miracles Hide* by Bruce Carroll

Best Pop Gospel Album: *The Great Adventure* by Steven Curtis Chapman

Best Gospel Album by a Choir or Chorus: *Edwin Hawkins Music and Arts Seminar Mass Choir—Recorded Live in Los Angeles*; Director: Edwin Hawkins

Best Rock/Contemporary Gospel Album: *Unseen Power* by Petra

Best Contemporary Soul Gospel Album: *Handel's Messiah—A Soulful Celebration* by Various Artists; Producer: Mervyn E. Warren

1993: 36th Grammy Awards

Best Traditional Soul Gospel Album: *Stand Still* by Shirley Caesar

Best Pop/Contemporary Gospel Album: *The Live Adventure* by Steven Curtis Chapman

Best Gospel Album by a Choir or Chorus: *Live . . . We Come Rejoicing* by the Brooklyn Tabernacle Choir; Director: Carol Cymbala

Best Rock Gospel Album: *Free at Last* by DC Talk

Best Southern Gospel, Country Gospel or Bluegrass Gospel Album: *Good News* by Kathy Mattea

Best Contemporary Soul Gospel Album: *All Out* by the Winans

1994: 37th Grammy Awards

Best Gospel Album by a Choir or Chorus: *Through God's Eyes* by Milton Brunson And Thompson Community Singers

Best Southern Gospel, Country Gospel or Bluegrass Gospel Album: *I Know Who Holds Tomorrow* by Alison Krauss and the Cox Family

Best Pop/Contemporary Gospel Album: *Mercy* by Andrae Crouch

Best Rock Gospel Album: *Wake-Up Call* by Petra

Best Contemporary Soul Gospel Album: *Join the Band* by Take 6

Best Traditional Soul Gospel Album: *Songs of the Church—Live in Memphis* by Albertina Walker

Best Gospel Album by a Choir or Chorus: *Live in Atlanta at Morehouse College* by the Love Fellowship Crusade Choir; Director: Hezakiah Walker

1995: 38th Grammy Awards

Best Traditional Soul Gospel Album: *Shirley Caesar Live . . . He Will Come* by Shirley Caesar

Best Rock Gospel Album: *Lesson of Love* by Ashley Cleveland

Best Gospel Album by a Choir or Chorus: *Praise Him . . . Live!* by the Brooklyn Tabernacle Choir; Choir Director: Carol Cymbala

Best Southern Gospel, Country Gospel or Bluegrass Gospel Album: *Amazing Grace—a Country Salute to Gospel* by Various Artists; Compilation Producer: Bill Hearn

Best Pop/Contemporary Gospel Album: *I'll Lead You Home* by Michael W. Smith

Best Contemporary Soul Gospel Album: *Alone in His Presence* by CeCe Winans

1996: 39th Grammy Awards

Best Gospel Album by a Choir or Chorus: *Just a Word* by Shirley Caesar's Outreach Convention Choir

Best Rock Gospel Album: *Jesus Freak* by DC Talk

Best Contemporary Soul Gospel Album: *Whatcha Lookin' 4* by Kirk Franklin and the Family

Best Southern Gospel, Country Gospel or Bluegrass Gospel Album: *I Love to Tell the Story—25 Timeless Hymns* by Andy Griffith

Best Traditional Soul Gospel Album: *Face to Face* by Cissy Houston

Best Pop/Contemporary Gospel Album: *Tribute—The Songs of Andrae Crouch* by Various Artists; Producers: Neal Joseph and Norman Miller

1997: 40th Grammy Awards

Best Gospel Choir or Chorus Album: *God's Property from Kirk Franklin's Nu Nation* by God's Property; Choir Directors: Kirk Franklin, Myron Butler and Robert Searight II

Best Southern, Country or Bluegrass Gospel Album: *Amazing Grace 2: A Country Salute to Gospel* by Various Artists; Producers: David Corlew and Peter York

Best Rock Gospel Album: *Welcome to the Freak Show: DC Talk Live in Concert* by DC Talk

Best Traditional Soul Gospel Album: *I Couldn't Hear Nobody Pray* by the Fairfield Four

Best Pop/Contemporary Gospel Album: *Much Afraid* by Jars of Clay

Best Contemporary Soul Gospel Album: *Brothers* by Take 6

1998: 41st Grammy Awards

Best Southern, Country, or Bluegrass Gospel Album: *The Apostle—Music from and Inspired by the Motion Picture* by Various Artists; Producers: Peter Afterman, John Huie, and Ken Levitan

Best Rock Gospel Album: *You Are There* by Ashley Cleveland

Best Gospel Choir or Chorus Album: *Reflections* by O'Landa Draper and the Associates Choir

Best Contemporary Soul Gospel Album: *The Nu Nation Project* by Kirk Franklin

Best Traditional Soul Gospel Album: *He Leadeth Me* by Cissy Houston

Best Pop/Contemporary Gospel Album: *This Is My Song* by Deniece Williams

1999: 42nd Grammy Awards

Best Contemporary Soul Gospel Album: *Mountain High . . . Valley Low* by Yolanda Adams

Best Traditional Soul Gospel Album: *Christmas with Shirley Caesar* by Shirley Caesar

Best Pop/Contemporary Gospel Album: *Speechless* by Steven Curtis Chapman

Best Gospel Choir or Chorus Album: *High and Lifted Up* by the Brooklyn Tabernacle Choir; Director: Carol Cymbala

Best Southern, Country, or Bluegrass Gospel Album: *Kennedy Center Homecoming* by Bill and Gloria Gaither and Their Homecoming Friends

Best Rock Gospel Album: *Pray* by Rebecca St. James

2000: 43rd Grammy Awards

Rock Gospel Album: *Double Take* by Petra

Pop/Contemporary Gospel Album: *If I Left the Zoo* by Jars of Clay

Best Southern, Country or Bluegrass Gospel Album: *Soldier of the Cross* by Ricky Skaggs and Kentucky Thunder

Traditional Soul Gospel Album: *You Can Make It* by Shirley Caesar

Contemporary Soul Gospel Album: *Thankful* by Mary Mary

Gospel Choir or Chorus Album: *Live—God Is Working* by the Brooklyn Tabernacle Choir; Director: Carol Cymbala

2001: 44th Grammy Awards

Best Rock Gospel Album: *Solo* by DC Talk

Best Pop/Contemporary Gospel Album: *CeCe Winans* by CeCe Winans

Best Southern, Country or Bluegrass Gospel Album: *Bill and Gloria Gaither Present a Billy Graham Music Homecoming* by Bill and Gloria Gaither and the Homecoming Friends

Best Traditional Soul Gospel Album: *Spirit of the Century* by the Blind Boys of Alabama

Best Contemporary Soul Gospel Album: *The Experience* by Yolanda Adams

Best Gospel Choir or Chorus Album; *Love Is Alive* by Hezekiah Walker and LFT Church Choir

2002: 45th Grammy Awards

Best Rock Gospel Album: *Come Together* by Third Day

Best Pop/Contemporary Gospel Album: *The Eleventh Hour* by Jars of Clay

Best Southern, Country or Bluegrass Gospel Album: *We Called Him*

Mr. Gospel Music—The James Blackwood Tribute Album by the Jordanaires, Larry Ford and the Light Crust Doughboys

Best Traditional Soul Gospel Album: *Higher Ground* by the Blind Boys of Alabama

Best Contemporary Soul Gospel Album: *Sidebars* by Eartha

Best Gospel Choir or Chorus Album: *Be Glad* by the Brooklyn Tabernacle Choir

2003: 46th Grammy Awards

Best Rock Gospel Album: *Worldwide* by Audio Adrenaline

Best Pop/Contemporary Gospel Album: *Worship Again* by Michael W. Smith

Best Southern, Country or Bluegrass Gospel Album: *Rise and Shine* by Randy Travis

Best Traditional Soul Gospel Album: *Go Tell It on the Mountain* by the Blind Boys of Alabama

Best Contemporary Soul Gospel Album: . . . *Again* by Donnie McClurkin

Best Gospel Choir or Chorus Album: *A Wing and a Prayer* by Bishop T. D. Jakes and the Potter's House Mass Choir

2004: 47th Grammy Awards

Best Gospel Performance: *Heaven Help Us All* by Ray Charles and Gladys Knight

Best Rock Gospel Album: *Wire* by Third Day

Best Pop/Contemporary Gospel Album: *All Things New* by Steven Curtis Chapman

Best Southern, Country or Bluegrass Gospel Album: *Worship and Faith* by Randy Travis

Best Traditional Gospel Album: *There Will Be a Light* by Ben Harper and the Blind Boys of Alabama

Best Contemporary Soul Gospel Album: *Nothing Without You* by Smokie Norful

Best Gospel Choir or Chorus Album: *Live . . . This Is Your House* by the Brooklyn Tabernacle Choir

2005: 48th Grammy Awards

Best Gospel Performance: *Pray* by CeCe Winans

Best Gospel Song: "Be Blessed" by Yolanda Adams

Best Rock or Rap Gospel Album: *Until My Heart Caves In* by Audio Adrenaline

Best Pop/Contemporary Gospel Album: *Lifesong* by Casting Crowns

Best Southern, Country or Bluegrass Gospel Album: *Rock of Ages . . . Hymns and Faith* by Amy Grant

Best Traditional Gospel Album: *Psalms, Hymns and Spiritual Songs* by Donnie McClurkin

Best Contemporary R&B Gospel Album: *Purified* by CeCe Winans

Best Gospel Choir or Chorus Album: *One Voice* by Gladys Knight and the Saints Unified Voices

2006: 49th Grammy Awards

Best Gospel Performance; *Victory* by Yolanda Adams

Best Gospel Song: "Imagine Me" by Kirk Franklin

Best Rock or Rap Gospel Album: *Turn Around* by Jonny Lang

Best Pop/Contemporary Gospel Album: *Wherever You Are* by Third Day

Best Southern, Country or Bluegrass Gospel Album; *Glory Train* by Randy Travis

Best Traditional Gospel Album: *Alive in South Africa* by Israel and New Breed

Best Contemporary R&B Gospel Album: *Here* by Kirk Franklin

2007: 50th Grammy Awards

Best Gospel Performance: *Blessed and Highly Favored* by the Clark Sisters (Elbernita "Twinkie" Clark, Dorina Clark-Cole, Jacky Clark-Chisholm, Karen Clark-Sheard)

Best Gospel Performance: *Never Gonna Break My Faith* by Aretha Franklin and Mary J. Blige (Featuring the Harlem Boys Choir)

Best Gospel Song: "Blessed and Highly Favored" by the Clark Sisters

Best Rock or Rap Gospel Album: *Before the Daylight's Shot* by Ashley Cleveland

Best Pop/Contemporary Gospel Album: *A Deeper Level* by Israel and New Breed

Best Southern, Country, or Bluegrass Gospel Album: *Salt of the Earth* by Ricky Skaggs and the Whites

Best Traditional Gospel Album; *Live One Last Time* by the Clark Sisters

Best Contemporary R&B Gospel Album; *Free to Worship* by Fred Hammond

GOSPEL MUSIC ASSOCIATION

The Gospel Music Association (GMA) was founded in 1964, with Tennessee Ernie Ford as its first president. Among the founding fathers were James Blackwood, J. D. Sumner, Cecil Blackwood, Don Light, and Don Butler.

Although the early success of the Country Music Association in Nashville served as the role model for the GMA, this organization was an outgrowth of the National Quartet Convention. This annual gathering of those involved in southern gospel music was first held in Memphis in 1956, where it grew from a 4-day to a 10-day event. The convention was a joint business venture of the Blackwoods and Statesman quartets. The Gospel Music Association created the Dove Award to honor the top artists in gospel music, and the first ceremony took place in Memphis on October 10, 1969, at the Peabody Hotel. By the end of the 1970s, contemporary Christian music artists began to dominate the Dove Awards, which moved away from the National Quartet Convention and established their ceremony in spring 1980 in Nashville.

The GMA's sister organization, the GMA Foundation, was established to recognize and preserve the history and legacy of all forms of gospel music and provide educational resources that encourage participation and appreciation by the general public. One of the key projects of the GMA Foundation is the Gospel Music Hall of Fame.

The GMA's other projects include GMA Week, a weeklong event held in Nashville that attracts more than 3,000 participants. The highlight of GMA Week is the annual GMA Awards ceremony where its members vote on the annual Dove Awards.

Another event sponsored by the GMA is GMA Music in the Rockies (formerly Seminar in the Rockies), a competition, gathering, and educational event in Christian music launched in 1984 by Cam Floria and purchased by the GMA in 2003. Beginning in 2009, that event is held in Nashville. In 1995, the GMA launched the GMA Academy to encourage and train musical talent interested in developing a ministry or a career in Christian music. The GMA Academy added a song critiquing service in 2004 to enable unsigned songwriters to have their songs evaluated by gospel music professionals.

Under the direction of the CMTA Anti-Piracy Task Force, the GMA launched the "Millions of Wrongs Don't Make It Right" project in 2004. This grassroots industry-wide campaign was designed to create education and awareness relating to illegal downloading, file sharing, and CD burning of Christian music.

In response to the 2004 tsunami, the GMA created Project Restore on January 11, 2005, in coordination with World Vision, an international Christian disaster relief agency. GMA worked previously with World Vision after September 11th.

Currently the GMA has 4,000 members who are involved in the gospel music ministry and business in a variety of capacities, including record company professionals, aspiring and established artists/writers/musicians, concert promoters, radio professionals, retailers, publishers, producers, booking agents, artist managers, and more.

Don Butler was the long-time executive director of the Gospel Music Association; the current head of the organization is John Styll.

Becky Garrison

For Further Reading

Cusic, Don. *The Sound of Light: A History of Gospel and Christian Music*. New York: Hal Leonard, 2002.

McNeil, W. K., ed. *Encyclopedia of American Gospel Music*. New York: Routledge, 2005.

GOSPEL MUSIC HALL OF FAME

The Gospel Music Hall of Fame is part of the Gospel Music Association Foundation; members of the Hall of Fame are elected by a select group of voters named by the Gospel Music Association. The Hall of Fame had its first inductees in 1971. Members of the Gospel Music Hall of Fame, in order of their year of induction, are:

1971	"Pappy" Jim Waites
1971	G. T. "Dad" Speer
1972	Albert E. Brumley
1972	James D. Vaughn
1972	Lena Brock "Mom" Speer
1973	Adger M. Pace
1973	Denver Crumpler
1973	E. M. Bartlett, Sr.
1973	Frank Stamps
1973	Homer Rodeheaver
1973	J. R. Baxter, Jr.
1973	John Daniel
1973	Robert E. Winsett
1973	W. B. Albert
1973	Lee Roy Abernathy
1973	Virgil Oliver Stamps
1974	Glenn Kieffer Vaughan
1974	James Blackwood
1975	Brock Speer
1975	Fanny Jane Crosby
1976	George Bernard
1976	Mosie Lister
1977	Eva Mae LeFevre
1977	James S. Wetherington
1978	George Beverly Shea
1978	Mahalia Jackson
1979	Connor Hall
1979	Ira D. Sankey
1981	Clarice Baxter
1981	Ira S. Stanphill
1981	John T. Benson, Jr.
1982	B. B. McKinney
1982	Charles H. Gabriel
1982	Dr. Lowell Mason
1982	Haldor Lillenas
1982	John Newton
1982	John T. Benson, Sr.
1982	Thomas A. Dorsey
1983	Bill Gaither
1983	Marvin Norcross
1984	Clara Ward
1984	Cleavant Derricks
1984	Ethel Waters
1984	J. D. Sumner
1984	James Cleveland
1984	Wally Fowler
1984	P. J. "Pat" Zondervan
1985	Ralph Carmichael

1985	Tim Spencer	1998	Andrae Crouch
1986	John W. Peterson	1998	Andrae Crouch and the Disciples
1986	Urias LeFevre		
1987	W. J. "Jake" Hess	1998	Hovie Lister and the Statesmen
1988	Cliff Barrows	1998	J. Bazzell Mull
1989	Les Beasley	1998	J. D. Sumner and the Stamps
1989	P. P. Bliss	1998	The Blackwood Brothers
1990	J. G. Whitfield	1998	The Chuck Wagon Gang
1991	Charles M. Alexander	1998	The Imperials
1991	Robert "Bob" Benson, Sr.	1998	The Jordanaires
1991	Sallie Martin	1998	The LeFevres
1991	Will M. Ramsey	1998	The Speer Family
1991	Bentley D. Ackley	1998	The Happy Goodman Family
1992	Dottie Rambo	1999	George Younce
1992	James B. Coates	1999	Mighty Clouds of Joy
1992	John Alexander "J. A." McClung	1999	2nd Chapter of Acts
1992	Oren A Parris	1999	The Cathedral Quartet
1992	W. Oliver Cooper	1999	The Fairfield Four
1993	Jarrell McCracken	1999	The Florida Boys
1993	Asa Brooks Everett	1999	The Gaither Trio
1993	Charles "Rusty" Goodman	1999	The Rev. Billy Graham
1993	Charles Albert Tindley	2000	Bob MacKenzie
1993	Charlie D. Tillman	2000	Edwin Hawkins
1993	James Edward Marsh	2000	Fisk Jubilee Singers
1993	James Rowe	2000	Petra
1993	W. F. "Jim" Myers	2000	Roger Breland
1994	Jimmie Davis	2000	Shirley Caesar
1994	Stuart Hamblen	2000	The Kingsmen
1994	Stuart K. Hine	2000	The Oak Ridge Boys
1994	Tennessee Ernie Ford	2001	Albertina Walker
1995	Ben Speer	2001	Elvis Presley
1995	Charles Wesley	2001	Keith Green
1995	Donald W. Butler, Sr.	2001	Kurt Kaiser
1995	Glen Payne	2001	Larry Norman
1996	Ray Herman Harper	2001	The Rambos
1997	Billy Ray Hearn	2001	Wendy Bagwell and the Sunliters
1997	Gloria Gaither		

2001	Doris Akers
2003	Amy Grant
2003	Pat Boone
2003	The Blind Boys of Alabama
2004	Al Green
2004	Frances Preston
2004	Sandi Patti
2004	Vestal Goodman
2005	Don Light
2005	Evie Tornquist
2005	Mylon LeFevre
2005	Ron Huff
2005	The Lewis Family
2005	Walter Hawkins
2006	Doug Oldham
2006	John T. Benson, III
2006	Richard Smallwood
2006	The Hinsons
2007	Joe Moscheo
2007	The Statler Brothers
2007	The Winans
2007	Phil Keaggy

Becky Garrison

For Further Reading

Cusic, Don. *The Sound of Light: A History of Gospel and Christian Music.* New York: Hal Leonard, 2002.

GRANT, AMY

Amy Grant (b. November 25, 1960) was the first superstar in contemporary Christian music and the first artist to be comfortable as a Christian entertainer, crossing over into the pop market. Her career began as the genre of contemporary Christian music was also beginning. Amy Grant was one of the first stars of contemporary Christian music as well as the first contemporary Christian artist to transcend the genre, becoming a pop star from the Christian field. She became a symbol of Christian music to the pop world and an icon in Christian music as she took her faith and her music into the world of popular culture. For those in Christian music, she became the example of how a Christian artist could fit into the world of popular culture. For those in secular music, she became the artist who brought legitimacy to the field of contemporary Christian music and made the pop world aware of this genre.

Amy Grant was raised in Nashville, the youngest of four daughters of Dr. Burton and Gloria Grant. She began attending Belmont Church in 1973, where a number of other musicians and singers also attended and where she was part of a high school Christian fellowship headed by Brown Bannister, who worked with Chris Christian at Home Sweet Home Productions. Christian's company had begun their association with Word Records by producing B. J. Thomas's first Christian album, *Home Where I Belong.* Amy had begun writing songs—she was influenced by singer-songwriters James Taylor, John Denver, and Carole King—and a family friend requested a tape of her songs, so she asked Brown, as a favor, if he would record them for her in the studio. He agreed and was impressed with the songs, so he played the tape for Chris Christian, who called the head of A&R at Word. Word had signed an agreement with Christian for him to bring three new acts to the label, so Amy became the first act in that deal, signed to the Myrrh label. The head of A&R agreed to sign her after hearing a tape played over the phone. At the time, Amy was 15 years old and attended Harpeth Hall School in Nashville; she had sung in public only once, at a high school chapel service.

Her first album, self-titled, was released in 1977 when she was 17 years old. Her first single, "Old Man's Rubble," was written by Brown Bannister and entered the *CCM* charts on July 11, 1978; it rose to number two and remained on the charts for 53 weeks. Her second single, "What a Difference You've Made in My Life" (a country hit for Ronnie Milsap), reached number five on the charts and remained for 31 weeks. The third single from that album, "Beautiful Music," reached number ten and stayed on the *CCM* chart for 21 weeks.

Amy Grant's timing was perfect; *Contemporary Christian Magazine* premiered in 1978, about the same time Amy Grant entered the Christian music industry. The first charts of contemporary Christian music were in this magazine, so her early success was quickly noted by the enthusiastic young readers of that magazine. By this time, Amy Grant was attending Furman University in Greenville, South Carolina, and had to juggle her studies with the increasing demands of her fledgling career as a Christian artist.

Amy's follow-up album was *My Father's Eyes*, released in 1979; the single "My Father's Eyes" reached number three on the *CCM* charts and remained there for 57 weeks. Like her previous singles, this song remained on radio playlists for a long time, so listeners had the opportunity to hear Grant for a long period, which is critical to building a base of fans and creating demand for an album. That song was written by Gary Chapman, and at the album premiere party Chapman and Grant met for the first time; he would become part of her tour and the two began a courtship that led to their marriage on June 19, 1982.

The second single from that album was "Faith Walkin' People" (written by Grant and Brown Bannister), which peaked at number ten but stayed on the charts for 30 weeks.

Amy's third album, *Never Alone*, was released in 1980. By this time, she had transferred to Vanderbilt University in Nashville where she majored in English and hoped to graduate; however, the demands of her career forced her to drop out before she finished her degree.

Amy Grant has been the most successful crossover artist in contemporary Christian music. (Andrew Southam)

During the winter of 1980–1981 Amy Grant performed on the Billy Graham Crusade and opened for the Bill Gaither Trio.

The next two albums from Amy were live albums: *Amy Grant in Concert* and *In Concert Volume Two*. The albums were recorded during her first national tour, appearing with DeGarmo and Key, and featured that group's band as a back-up group. The first album was a "Greatest Hits" up to that point, containing a medley of "Beautiful Music," "Giggle," "Old Man's Rubble," and "Never Give You Up" as well as "Father's Eyes" and "Faith Walkin' People."

"Singing a Love" was released as a single from the first live album and reached number 13 on the *CCM* adult contemporary charts. "I'm Gonna Fly," which led off the second LP, was a single that charted number ten on the *CCM* adult contemporary charts in the spring of 1982. In addition, Amy recorded a single with DeGarmo and Key, "Nobody Loves Me," which reached number six on the *CCM* adult contemporary charts and remained there for 23 weeks during the summer and fall of 1981.

In 1982 Amy Grant released *Age to Age*, one of the most significant albums in the history of contemporary Christian music. The first single, "Sing Your Praise to the Lord," written by Rich Mullins, was Amy's first number one single, staying in that position 15 weeks. Her next single, "El Shaddai," written by Michael Card and John Thompson, reached number two and remained on the charts for 35 weeks. Her third single from that album, "In a Little While," reached number five and stayed on the charts for 28 weeks,

which meant that 1982 ended with Amy Grant dominating the CCM charts, firmly established as a Christian star.

Age to Age was the first Christian album certified gold by a solo artist and the first to reach platinum status. It led to Amy winning her first Grammy (for "Best Contemporary Gospel Performance, Female") and two Dove Awards from the Gospel Music Association: "Gospel Artist of the Year" and "Pop/Contemporary Album of the Year." Both "Sing Your Praises to the Lord" and "El Shaddai" quickly became popular with churches, and congregations regularly sang them. *Age to Age* became the first of nine consecutive albums from Grant to be certified platinum.

The follow-up to the album *Age to Age* was *A Christmas Album* released in 1983, which contained "Tennessee Christmas," written by Amy and Gary Chapman. It became a Christmas standard, recorded by a wide variety of artists. Also on that album was "Emmanuel," written by Michael W. Smith, which became a favorite with church congregations and was a chart record on the *CCM* adult contemporary chart.

Unguarded saw Amy Grant moving in a pop direction. The album was released jointly by her Christian label, Myrrh, and the secular label A&M and resulted in a shift in direction from an emphasis on praise and worship music to pop material. One single, "Find a Way," cowritten with Michael W. Smith, became the first genuine contemporary Christian crossover hit. It reached number one on the *CCM* Christian chart, number two on the *CCM* adult contemporary chart and stayed on that chart for 26 weeks. The song crossed over to the *Billboard* Hot 100 chart, where it reached number 29, and the *Billboard* adult contemporary chart, where it reached number seven, becoming the first contemporary Christian crossover song. From this point forward until 2003, Grant's albums would be released in both the Christian and secular markets through a joint agreement between Word and A&M.

Straight Ahead was Grant's next album and contained the single, "Angels," which reached number one on the *CCM* adult contemporary chart and remained in that position for 13 weeks. "Thy Word," written by Amy and Michael W. Smith, became a favorite with church audiences and was a top five chart record from that album, as was "Jehovah," which reached the number two position. "The Now and the Not Yet" was the fourth single from that album, which became Amy Grant's third gold album.

The Collection was released on July 22, 1986, and the ten songs on the LP represented the most commercially successful recordings by Grant thus far in her career. The cassette version contained 15 songs and the CD version contained 17 songs, with songs released after the original LP. A new song, "Stay for Awhile," was released as a single and reached number one on *CCM's* Christian chart, number two on *CCM's* adult contemporary chart, and was number 18 on *Billboard's* adult contemporary chart.

In September 1986, Amy Grant's duet with Peter Cetera, "The Next Time I Fall," entered the *Billboard* Hot 100 chart; it reached the number one position and remained on that chart for 21 weeks. This was included on Cetera's album *Solitude/Solitaire* on the Full Moon label.

Grant's album *Lead Me On* was released on June 28, 1988, and was an overt attempt to extend Grant's fan base into the pop market. Produced by Brown Bannister, the album's title track was a number one *CCM* Christian hit, number five on the *CCM* adult contemporary Christian chart, number 96 on *Billboard's* Hot 100 and number 89 on the U.K. charts. "Saved by Love" was a number one Christian hit and number 32 on *Billboard's* adult contemporary chart. "1974" was number one on *CCM's* adult contemporary chart and "What about the Love," written by Kye Flemming and Janis Ian—whose pop hit "Seventeen" became a 1960s hit—reached number one on the *CCM* adult contemporary chart in 1989.

The album was criticized by some in the Christian community who felt Grant had strayed too far from Christian music with this release. However, in 2001 it was named the greatest album in the history of contemporary Christian music.

Heart in Motion, released in March 1991 was a further step away from an album geared specifically for the Christian market and an attempt to broaden Grant's pop appeal with songs about love and life issues. Brown Bannister, who had been Grant's producer since the beginning of her career, turned over most of the production duties to Keith Thomas for this project. Although many in the Christian community criticized the album because of a perceived lack of Christian content, the album did reach the top of the Christian album chart as well as top ten in the *Billboard* 200 album chart and sold more than five million copies. The first single, "Baby, Baby," was a number one pop hit on both the *Billboard* Hot 100 and the adult contemporary charts as well as number two in the U.K. Written by Grant and producer Keith Thomas, the song was inspired by Grant's young daughter. It was nominated for Grammys in the categories of "Best Female Pop Vocal," "Record of the Year," and "Song of the Year," but failed to win in any category.

There were five singles (out of eleven album cuts) from that album. The second single was "Every Heartbeat," which reached number two on the *Billboard* Hot 100; "That's What Love Is For" (number seven on the Hot 100 and number one on adult contemporary); "Good for Me" (number eight on the Hot 100 and number four on adult contemporary); and "I Will Remember You" (number 20 on the Hot 100 and number two on adult contemporary). On the Christian chart, "That's What Love is For" and "Every Heartbeat" both charted.

Home for Christmas contained a number of Christmas perennials, such as "Have Yourself a Merry Little Christmas," "It's the Most Wonderful Time of the Year," "Rockin' Around the Christmas Tree," "Winter Wonderland," and "I'll Be Home for Christmas," and some Christmas hymns—"O Come All Ye Faithful," "Joy to the World," and "Jesu, Joy of Man's Desiring"—as well as some originals, "Breath of Heaven (Mary's Song)," "Grown-Up Christmas List," and "Emmanuel, God with Us." The album reached number two on the *Billboard* 200 album chart and number one on the top contemporary Christian chart in that magazine.

House of Love was released in 1994 and contained five chart singles:

"House of Love" (number 37 on the *Billboard* Hot 100, number five on adult contemporary, and number 10 on Top 40 adult recurrents); " "Lucky One" (number 18 on the *Billboard* Hot 100, number two on adult contemporary and number 16 on Top 40 mainstream); "Helping Hand" (number one, Christian singles); a remake of Joni Mitchell's "Big Yellow Taxi" (number 67 on the *Billboard* Hot 100 and number 18 on adult contemporary); "Children of the World" (number one on Christian singles). In the U.K. "Lucky One," "Say You'll Be Mine," "Big Yellow Taxi," and "House of Love" all charted on the U.K. singles chart. Two songs on the album, "The Power" and "Oh, How the Years Go By," were covered by Cher and Vanessa Williams, respectively.

Amy Grant and Gary Chapman had marital woes, and her *Behind the Eyes* album reflected those marriage struggles. (Grant referred to the release as her "razor blades and Prozac" album.) The album was released in 1997 and reached number eight on the *Billboard* 200 album chart and number two on *Billboard*'s Christian album chart. Three singles from the album reached *Billboard* charts: "Take a Little Time" (21 on the *Billboard* Hot 100 and number four on adult contemporary); "I Will Be Your Friend" (number 27 on adult contemporary); and "Like I Love You" (number ten on adult contemporary). The album won a Gospel Music Association Dove Award for "Pop/Contemporary Album of the Year," and the single "Somewhere Down the Road" received extensive Christian airplay.

Behind the Eyes was Grant's first album since *Lead Me On* to not be certified platinum.

A Christmas to Remember, released in 1999, features Amy backed by the Patrick Williams Orchestra. The album was supported by a CBS-TV special, "Amy Grant: A Christmas to Remember," which was broadcast on December 15.

Amy Grant and Gary Chapman divorced in June 1999 after 16 years of marriage; she married country music superstar Vince Gill in March 2000. The divorce angered and upset many Christian fans, and a number of Christian radio stations boycotted her records. The Christian market generally reacts unfavorably to artists who do not live up to the exacting standards of what many believe the life of a Christian should be, and some Christian retail outlets refused to stock Grant's albums. Many former fans felt let down by Grant's divorce. Grant's personal life went through a difficult phase during her marital woes and then divorce from Chapman, but she found comfort and happiness with her marriage to Gill. The two had a daughter in March 2001.

Although personal happiness was a reward for her second marriage, Grant still had to cultivate former fans and supporters in the Christian market who felt abandoned. Her *Greatest Inspirational Songs* was released on March 19, 2002, and reconnected Amy to the Christian marketplace with an album of Christian favorites that spanned her career from 1977 to 1985.

Legacy: Hymns and Faith was a collection of mostly standards such as "Softly and Tenderly," "I Need Thee Every Hour," "Come, Thou Fount of Every Blessing," and "How Great Thou Art" as well as a few originals. Released May 21, 2002, the album

reached number 21 on the *Billboard* 200 album chart, number one on the top contemporary Christian chart and number 50 on the top internet albums chart. The album reconnected Amy to the Christian audience.

Simple Things, released August 19, 2003, was primarily a secular album, although some songs contained Christian themes, and the only single to chart, "Simple Things," reached number 23 on the *Billboard* adult contemporary, number six on the hot Christian adult contemporary, and number seven on the hot Christian singles and tracks charts. With this album the agreement to release Amy Grant's albums jointly on both Myrrh and A&M/Interscope ended, although *Greatest Hits 1986–2004*, released on October 12, 2004, was the last album released jointly by Word/Curb and A&M. The album contained 19 tracks including two previously unreleased songs, "The Water" and "Come Be with Me," and reflected Grant's secular success as a Christian artist.

20th Century Masters—The Christmas Collection: The Best of Amy Grant was a re-release of Amy Grant's second Christmas album, *Home for Christmas*, originally released on October 6, 1992. *Rock of Ages . . . Hymns of Faith,* released May 3, 2005, followed her *Legacy . . . Hymns of Faith* album and was filled with standards as well as some originals. The album was produced by Brown Bannister and Vince Gill and won a Grammy for "Best Southern, Country or Bluegrass Gospel Album" and a Gospel Music Association Dove Award for "Inspirational Album of the Year."

My Best Christmas was a compilation album, culling songs from Grant's three previous Christmas albums and released on YMC Records to take advantage of Grant's continuing appeal with Christmas songs. *Time Again . . . Amy Grant Live*, released on September 26, 2006, was recorded in Fort Worth, Texas, the same city where she recorded her first in concert albums 25 years before. The album contains 18 tracks and primarily reflects Amy's secular career, although the Christian standard "Thy Word" is included.

Amy Grant became the bridge between contemporary Christian music and pop music during the 1980s and 1990s. Her Christian faith was the key ingredient in her career as a Christian artist, and she became the leading star in that field through hit singles on radio, groundbreaking albums, and a genuine, transparent faith. Grant then moved into the pop world with a strong base of Christian album sales and showed that world a Christian artist could create hit singles for pop radio and be successful in pop music.

Contemporary Christian music is a relatively young genre and many in the pop music world were not aware of it or, if they were, disparaged it as second class. Amy Grant was a major factor in making contemporary Christian music a first class genre with a legitimate place in American popular music.

By 2007 Amy Grant's career had come full circle, from an artist whose music was intended primarily for the Christian artist to a pop artist with a Christian base and then back to an artist whose focus on her albums is the Christian market. However, the pop success Amy Grant achieved from the mid-1980s forward, when she began recording pop-oriented albums, meant the pop world had an awareness of her and she would always have a platform for her work in both the Christian and secular fields.

Although some in the Christian community criticized her pop-oriented albums and there was a backlash from her divorce, Amy Grant managed to maintain a solid base in the Christian market. On the 25th anniversary of *CCM*, the leading publication for contemporary Christian music, the magazine did a special "Amy Issue" because Grant had appeared on the cover more than any other CCM artist. For this issue she served as guest editor, chief writer, and primary subject.

Amy Grant showed that a Christian artist—or an artist who is a committed Christian—can succeed in American popular culture. In 1986 she collaborated with Art Garfunkel on a cantata written by Jimmy Webb, "The Animals Christmas," and released on Columbia. She sang "The Things We Do For Love," originally recorded by 10cc, for the movie *Mr. Wrong*. She recorded "You Didn't Have to Be So Nice" as a duet with Kevin Costner for the movie *The Postman*, which starred Costner.

Amy Grant raised or donated $1 million to the Schermerhorn Symphony Center, the major performance venue for classical music in Nashville, and a stage there is named in her honor. She is the first Christian artist to have a number one pop song and sell a platinum album, the first to perform a song live at the Grammys, and the first to receive a star on the Hollywood Walk of Fame. She performed at the Major League Baseball All Star game in 2003 and at the World Series in 2004 and has been a spokesperson for Target stores and Land O'Lakes butter.

Amy Grant was with Word Records (her albums were released on the Myrrh label) since she signed with them in 1976 and her first album was released in 1977. However, in 2007, 30 years later, she announced she would leave Word in August and sign with EMI Christian's Sparrow label, a label formed in 1976, the year she first signed with Word. She stated that she was more comfortable with the leadership at EMI Christian, citing a "comfort factor" with Bill Hearn, head of EMI Christian and son of the founder of Sparrow Records.

By 2007 Amy Grant was the best selling contemporary Christian artist of all time, having sold more than 25 million recordings worldwide. She had collected a number of awards from the Gospel Music Association and the Recording Academy and was elected to the Gospel Music Hall of Fame in 2003, her first year of eligibility. Her recording of "El Shaddai" was awarded one of the "Songs of the Century" by the RIAA in 2001. She had hosted a reality show on NBC, "Three Wishes," in the fall of 2006 and released a book in the fall of 2007.

The career of Amy Grant is more than the career of a single artist because she paved the way for other artists in this genre. Contemporary Christian music became a large part of the American music industry in the 1980s and 1990s, and Amy Grant led the way with her success in both the Christian and secular fields.

Don Cusic

Discography

Amy Grant (1977)

My Father's Eyes (1979)

Never Alone (1980)

Amy Grant in Concert (1981)

In Concert Volume Two (1981)

Age to Age (1982)

A Christmas Album (1983)

Straight Ahead (1984)

Unguarded (1985)

The Collection (1986)

Lead Me On (1988)

Heart in Motion (1991)

Home for Christmas (1992)

House of Love (1994)

Behind the Eyes (1997)

A Christmas to Remember (1999)

Legacy . . . Hymns and Faith (2002)

Her Greatest Inspirational Songs (2002)

Simple Things (2003)

20th Century Masters—The Christmas Collection: The Best of Amy Grant (re-mastered re-release of Home for Christmas) (2003)

Greatest Hits 1986–2004 (2004)

My Best Christmas (compilation of three Christmas albums) (2005)

Rock of Ages . . . Hymns of Faith (2005)

Time Again . . . Amy Grant Live (2006)

Gospel Music Association Dove Awards

1983	Artist of the Year
1983	Pop/Contemporary Album of the Year for *Age to Age*, Myrrh
1984	Recorded Music Packaging of the Year; *A Christmas Album*
1985	Pop/Contemporary Album of the Year for *Straight Ahead*, Myrrh

1986	Artist of the Year
1986	Recorded Music Packaging of the Year; *Unguarded*
1988	Short Form Music Video of the Year for *Stay for a While*
1989	Artist of the Year
1989	Pop Contemporary Album of the Year for *Lead Me On*, Myrrh
1989	Short Form Music Video of the Year for *Lead Me On*
1990	Country Recorded Song of the Year for "'Tis So Sweet to Trust in Jesus"
1992	Song of the Year for "Place in This World" Written by Amy Grant, Michael W. Smith and Wayne Kirkpatrick
1992	Artist of the Year
1994	Praise and Worship Album of the Year for *Songs from the Loft*; Reunion
1996	Special Event Album of the Year for *My Utmost for His Highest*; Myrrh/Word
1998	Pop/Contemporary Album of the Year for *Behind the Eyes*; Myrrh
2000	Special Event Album of the Year for *Streams*; Word
2003	Inspirational Album of the Year for *Legacy . . . Hymns and Faith*; Word
2003	Country Recorded Song of the Year for "The River's Gonna Keep on Rolling"
2006	Inspiration Album of the Year for *Rock of Ages . . . Hymns and Faith* (tied with Hymned by Bart Millard)

Grammys

1983	Best Gospel Performance, Female for "Ageless Medley"
1984	Best Gospel Performance, Female for "Angels"
1985	Best Gospel Performance, Female for *Unguarded*
1988	Best Gospel Performance, Female for "Lead Me On"
2005	Best Southern, Country or Bluegrass Gospel Album for *Rock of Ages . . . Hymns and Faith*

For Further Reading

Alfonso, Barry. *The Billboard Guide to Contemporary Christian Music*. New York: Billboard Books/Watson-Guptill, 2002.

Cusic, Don. *The Sound of Light: A History of Gospel and Christian Music*. New York: Hal Leonard, 2002.

McNeil, W. K., ed. *Encyclopedia of American Gospel Music*. New York: Routledge, 2005.

Millard, Bob. *Amy Grant: A Biography*. New York: Doubleday, 1986

Powell, Mark Allen. *Encyclopedia of Contemporary Christian Music*. Peabody, Mass.: Hendrickson Publishers, Inc., 2002.

GRANT, NATALIE

In a field filled with female singers, Natalie Grant (b. December 21, 1971) has managed to rise above that talented group to be awarded the Dove Award for "Female Vocalist of the Year" for three consecutive years: 2006, 2007, and 2008. However, it has not always been easy; despite movie star good looks and a powerful voice that reflects her love of gospel music, Natalie Grant's path to success has had its share of bumps in the road.

Grant is the youngest of five children who all attended the Assembly of God Church in Lynnwood, Washington, just outside Seattle. She enrolled at Northwest College in Kirkland, Washington, with the goal of becoming an elementary school teacher, and worked with the youth choir of the Shoreline Community Church, arranging music. During that period the Christian group Truth performed at the church, and Grant was immediately drawn in to their music; however, it was their message that left a lasting impression. Shortly after seeing them for the first time, she auditioned for the group and subsequently spent the next two years on the road, feeling as if she'd found her calling.

With road experience and a desire to pursue a solo career, Grant moved to Nashville and pursued her dream. She paid the bills by working as a worship leader at a local church and doing secretarial work. In 1997 she landed her first recording contract with Benson Records and released her self-titled debut album, *Natalie Grant*; however, Grant felt that Benson was not where she needed to be, so she left the label; two months after the release of her project the company closed their doors.

In 2001 she signed with the Pamplin music label and released her second solo project, *Stronger*. Although critically acclaimed, the album never had the chance to fulfill its potential when Pamplin folded shortly after its release. By 2003 she was back in the game and released her third album, *Deeper Life*, on Nashville-based Curb Records, where she found the support and freedom to develop her musical talents and ministry.

After an episode of NBC's *Law and Order* brought the tragedy of human trafficking to her attention, Grant researched the subject and was shocked and saddened by what she learned. In 2005 she traveled throughout the world to see the problem first hand, and while on a trip to the red-light district of Mumbai, India, saw young girls caught in sexual slavery. This moved Grant to create the Home Foundation, a non-profit charitable organization dedicated to the eradication of human trafficking both domestically and abroad. Through advocacy, education, and relief efforts, the Home Foundation is committed to end the suffering of women and children sold into sexual slavery. Grant's mission is simply to help those who may not otherwise be helped.

In October 2005, Grant added another accomplishment to her resume when the W Publishing Group released her first book, *The Real Me: Being the Girl God Sees*.

In 2006, Grant released her fourth album for Curb Records, *Awaken*. The album produced several successful radio singles, including the song "Held," which became her signature song and biggest selling record to date.

Grant's husband, Bernie Herms, is an accomplished songwriter and producer; he also travels with Natalie as her musical director and pianist.

In addition to her solo tours, Grant continues her association with Women of Faith as both a performer and speaker on the Revolve Tour, a

Natalie Grant performs at the Dove Awards show on April 23, 2008, in Nashville. (AP Photo/Mark Humphrey)

conference for teen girls. Her seventh album, *Relentless*, was released on Curb Records in February 2008.

Liz Cavanaugh

For Further Reading

Powell, Mark Allen. *Encyclopedia of Contemporary Christian Music.* Peabody, Mass.: Hendrickson Publishers, Inc., 2002.

GREEN, KEITH

It is difficult to imagine how revolutionary Keith Green's ministry was in the world of contemporary Christian music during the 1970s. Musically and lyrically he was a notch above most other CCM acts; his music, like the man himself, was demanding and deeper than most. Green was dogmatic in his faith and could be arrogant and obnoxious at times, but he demanded the same thing of himself as he demanded of others: a total, noncompromised life devoted to Jesus.

Keith Green (b. October 21, 1953; d. July 28, 1982) came from a musical family. His grandfather was a composer who worked for Warner Brothers and owned an early record company; his mother was a singer who turned down the opportunity to sing with Benny Goodman. Keith was born in New York but the family soon moved to the San Fernando Valley, California. He was a child actor; at 10 he had the role of one of the children in *The Sound of Music* in a major production. In 1965, at the age of 11, he signed with ASCAP and became the youngest person ever signed to that performing rights organization. He also signed a five-year contract with Decca Records, who intended to make him a teen idol, and he landed spots on "The Jack Benny Show," "The Joey Bishop Show," and Steve Allen's show.

During his teen years in California during the 1960s he embarked on a spiritual search that took him into drugs and Eastern religions before his first conversion to Christianity in late 1972 or early 1973. Green developed a go-it-alone Christianity during his early years, rejecting organized religion, but in 1975 had a "true conversion" that saw him become a demanding, difficult person who set high standards for himself and others in the Christian walk. It is appropriate that one of his first albums was titled *No Compromise* because that was the guiding philosophy in his Christian life.

Green's first album, *For Him Who Has Ears*, was released on Sparrow in 1977, and from the beginning it was obvious that this was an artist who was set apart. His piano-based songs, reminiscent of Elton John, sought a greater depth than other CCM songs at the time, and though the songs were lyrically challenging to the Christian audience they were also extremely commercial. From the very beginning, Green attracted a large following for his albums and concert appearances.

The concerts were more like worship experiences than musical concerts. In one concert, Green came out, played a few bars of the opening song, then said he was not prepared to perform yet so he immersed himself in prayer before the audience before he resumed. Each song was introduced with the intent to convert the nonbeliever and convince the believer whose faith was not as strong as it should be. At the end of his concerts, Green extended an altar call and had set up a support group for believers to plug into a Christian community.

Green was convinced that people should not pay to hear the gospel, so he made his concerts free, with only a "free will offering" taken from the audience. He informed his record company that he wanted to give away his records; they could not do this so he mortgaged his house and let his audience know that his third album, *So You Wanna Go Back to Egypt,* released on his own label, Pretty Good Records, in 1980 was free to those who wrote him requesting one. When critics asked, "What about those who don't have a record player to play it on?" Green responded that he would purchase those too. Green had become friends with Bob Dylan because both attended Kenn Gullicksen's Vineyard Church in Hollywood, and Dylan played harmonica on one of Green's album cuts, "Pledge My Head to Heaven."

Green established Last Days Ministries with his wife, Melody, who he had married in 1973. The two were songwriting partners as well as ministry partners. He sold his home in Los Angeles and relocated his ministry to Lindale, Texas, where he set up a compound that sponsored evangelistic crusades, operated an Intensive Christian Training Institute, and did social work.

On April 12, 1982, his fourth album, *Songs for the Shepherd*, was released. On July 28 of that year, he took his two children and nine others up in a plane he owned, and the plane—which was almost 500 pounds overweight with 12 passengers in six seats— crashed and killed everyone on board.

Keith Green was 28 years old when he died, but his impact belied his youth; at the time of his death he was one of the biggest stars in contemporary Christian music, although he rejected the very idea of "stardom" as well as the commercial aspects of Christianity. In the years following his death he became an icon in Christian music, the impact of his death was compared to that of John Lennon's, and a number of posthumous releases were culled from his released albums as well as from unreleased recordings and concerts.

Keith Green's death shocked the contemporary Christian community, which was mostly young men and women who had not yet faced the death of any of its members. Like the deaths of Jimi Hendrix, Janis Joplin, and Jim Morrison, which reminded the youth culture that they were not immortal, Green's death was a sobering reality to those in Christian music, reminding them that they, too, could encounter tragedy even though they believed strongly in a kind and loving God.

Keith Green was inducted into the Gospel Music Hall of Fame in 2001.

Don Cusic

For Further Reading

Alfonso, Barry. *The Billboard Guide to Contemporary Christian Music.* New York: Billboard Books/Watson-Guptill, 2002.

Cusic, Don. *The Sound of Light: A History of Gospel and Christian Music.* New York: Hal Leonard, 2002.

Green, Melody and David Hazard. *No Compromise: The Life Story of Keith Green.* Chatsworth Calif.: Sparrow, 1989.

McNeil, W. K., ed. *Encyclopedia of American Gospel Music.* New York: Routledge, 2005.

Powell, Mark Allen. *Encyclopedia of Contemporary Christian Music.* Peabody, Mass.: Hendrickson Publishers, Inc., 2002.

Discography

For Him Who Has Ears (1977)

No Compromise (1978)

So You Wanna Go Back to Egypt (1980)

The Keith Green Collection (1981)

Songs for the Shepherd (1982)

I Only Want to See You There (1983)

The Prodigal Son (1983)

Jesus Commands Us to Go (1984)

The Ministry Years 1977–1979 Vol. 1 (1987)

The Ministry Years 1980–1982 Vol. 2 (1988)

Early Years (1996)

Keith Green Live (His Incredible Youth) (1996)

Oh, Lord, You're So Beautiful: Songs of Worship (1998)

Make My Life a Prayer to You (1998)

Songs of Devotion (1998)

Because of You: Songs of Testimony (1998)

Here Am I Send Me (1998)

Songs of Evangelism (1998)

GREEN, STEVE

Steve Green (b. 1956) has had a long and successful career in contemporary Christian music; from being a member of groups to a solo artist, Green's career has evolved to the point where he is a consistent mainstay of the inspirational adult contemporary audience.

Green's parents were missionaries in Argentina; Green grew up there, and is fluent in Spanish. He became a member of the touring group Truth, where he met his wife, Marijean, then sang with the Gaither Vocal Band before becoming a founding member of the rock group White Heart. At the urging of Bill Gaither, Green embarked on a solo career that has seen him release children's albums and Spanish language albums, but he is most at home in praise and worship music.

Green's recordings have been produced by Greg Nelson, who also produced Larnelle Harris and Sandi Patti, a trio of church-oriented artists who are comfortable as worship leaders as well as solo performers.

Green received the Dove Award for "Male Vocalist of the Year" for 1985 and 1987 and his album *The Mission* won the Dove Award for 1990; his album *Hide 'Em in Your Heart Songs* won the Dove Award for "Children's Music Album" for 1991.

Don Cusic

For Further Reading

Alfonso, Barry. *The Billboard Guide to Contemporary Christian Music*. New York: Billboard Books/Watson-Guptill, 2002.

Powell, Mark Allen. *Encyclopedia of Contemporary Christian Music*. Peabody, Mass.: Hendrickson Publishers, Inc., 2002.

GREENBAUM, NORMAN

Norman Greenbaum (b. November 20, 1942) is best known for "Spirit in the Sky," which reached number three on the *Billboard* pop chart in 1970. The song was a surprise hit; Greenbaum was the founder of Dr. West's Medicine Show and Junk Band, an L.A. group that had a chart record with "The Eggplant That Ate Chicago" in 1966. The band broke up in 1967, and Greenbaum ran a dairy farm in Petaluma, California. "Spirit in the Sky" was released in 1970 and became a hit in the United States and number one on the British charts. The recording was later used in the movie *Apollo 13*, starring Tom Hanks. In 1986 the song was recorded by a British group, Doctor and the Medics, and again reached number one on the British charts. After "Spirit in the Sky," Greenbaum followed up with two minor hits, "Canned Ham" and "California Earthquake," then retired from the music business and became a short order cook.

The song came along when the Jesus movement was attracting notice; however, Greenbaum never claimed to be a Christian, and the Christian community had problems with the song being either gospel or Christian because of the line, "I never sinned." The pop audience saw it more as a Christian song than the Christian audience; still, its timing coincided perfectly with the emerging Jesus music being recorded.

Don Cusic

Discography

Spirit in the Sky (1969)

Back Home Again (1970)

Petaluma (1972)

For Further Reading

Hardy, Phil, and Dave Laing. *The Faber Companion to 20th Century Popular Music*. London: Faber and Faber, 1990.

Larkins, Colin, ed. *The Virgin Encyclopedia of Popular Music*. London: Virgin, 2002.

Powell, Mark Allen. *Encyclopedia of Contemporary Christian Music*. Peabody, Mass.: Hendrickson Publishers, Inc., 2002.

GRINE, JANNY

Janny Grine (aka Janny Grein) did not grow up in a Christian home and had virtually no knowledge of the Bible or Christianity until she saw the movie *King of Kings* in 1975 on television. She was led to her Christian faith by husband Bill Grein. Janny's first album, *Free Indeed*, was released on Sparrow in 1976, about a year after her conversion. This was followed by an album a year for the next four years: *Covenant Woman* (1977), *He Made Me Worthy* (1978), *Think on These Things* (1979), and *The Best of Janny* (1980).

A Nashville-based singer-songwriter, Grine's songs relied heavily on scripture. As the 1980s progressed she became involved in global missions, leading crusades to Mexico, South Africa, and Europe.

Don Cusic

For Further Reading

Grine, Janny. *Called, Appointed, Anointed*. Tulsa, Okla.: Harrison House, 1985.

H

HALL, DANNIEBELLE

Danniebelle Hall (b. Danniebelle Jones on October 6, 1938, in Pittsburgh, Pennsylvania; d. December 28, 2000, in Fremont, California) is best known for her lead vocal on the Andrae Crouch classic "Soon and Very Soon"; she also sang lead on Crouch's "Take Me Back." Danniebelle learned to play the piano at three years old and played in her hometown church; with two younger sisters she formed the trio the Jones Sisters. At 17 she moved to San Francisco, where she married Charles E. Hall in 1958; the couple had three children—Charlotte, Charles, and Cynthia. She formed the Danniebelles in 1969, and they toured with World Crusade Ministries, performing in Asia.

In 1969 she also joined Andrae Crouch and the Disciples and wrote songs recorded by Eartha Kitt, James Cleveland, and Pat Boone. After leaving Crouch, she embarked on a solo career.

Danniebelle had been an insulin dependent diabetic for a number of years, but in 1995 her case worsened; she was treated for hypertension, had a mastectomy from breast cancer, and her left leg was amputated below the knee. Her health deteriorated and she died three days after Christmas 2000; the Danniebelle Hall Diabetes Foundation was created after her death.

Danniebelle's first album was released in 1974; after her death several albums have been released that compile the best of her early work.

Don Cusic

For Further Reading

McNeil, W. K., ed. *Encyclopedia of American Gospel Music*. New York: Routledge, 2005.

Powell, Mark Allen. *Encyclopedia of Contemporary Christian Music*. Peabody, Mass.: Hendrickson Publishers, Inc., 2002.

HALL, PAM MARK

Pam Mark Hall's debut album *Flying* (Aslan, 1976) was released under her maiden name, Pam Mark; she was part of John Fischer's Discovery Arts Guild program at Peninsula Bible Church in

Palo Alto, California. After her second album, *This Is Not A Dream* (Aslan, 1977), she moved to Nashville and became part of the contemporary Christian music community there. Hall's acoustic folk sound is rooted in artists such as Joni Mitchell, and her songs have been recorded by Amy Grant ("The Now and the Not Yet"), Debby Boone, First Call, the Imperials, Noel Paul Stookey, Russ Taff, Kathy Troccoli, Rob Frazier, and Geoff Moore.

Don Cusic

For Further Reading

Powell, Mark Allen. *Encyclopedia of Contemporary Christian Music*. Peabody, Mass.: Hendrickson Publishers, Inc., 2002.

HARRIS, LARNELLE

Larnelle Harris (b. 1947, Danville, Kentucky) has been one of the most popular and successful singers of inspirational music in contemporary Christian music for more than a quarter of a century. An African American in a mostly white genre, Harris has had a string of number one hits on Christian radio, won numerous Dove and Grammy Awards, and was inducted into the Gospel Music Hall of Fame in 2007.

Harris grew up in Louisville and majored in voice at Western Kentucky University, toured as a drummer with the Spurrlows, and then performed with First Gear, a Christian rock band, as a drummer; they recorded two albums. Larnelle established himself as a major solo artist with his debut album *Tell It to Jesus* (1975), then recorded *Larnelle . . . More* (1977), *Free* (1978), *Give Me More Love in My Heart* (1981), and *Best of Larnelle* (1982).

Larnelle won "Male Vocalist of the Year" honors from the Gospel Music Association in 1983, 1986, and 1988 and "Songwriter of the Year" honor in 1988. His albums *Give Me More Love in My Heart* (1981), *Touch Me Lord* (1983), *I've Just Seen Jesus* (1986), *The Father Hath Provided* (1988), *Larnelle Live . . . Psalms Hymns and Spiritual Songs* (1992), and *Unbelievable Love* (1996) have all won Dove Awards.

Larnelle has won four Grammys: "Best Gospel Performance by a Duo or Group" for "More Than Wonderful," a duet with Sandi Patti, in 1983; "Best Gospel Performance by a Duo or Group, Choir or Chorus" for a duet with Sandi Patti on "I've Just Seen Jesus" in 1985; "Best Gospel Performance, Male" for "How Excellent Is Thy Name" in 1985; "Best Gospel Performance, Male" for "The Father Hath Provided" in 1987, and "Best Gospel Performance, Male" for his album *Christmas* in 1988.

During the period 1984–1987 Larnelle joined Bill Gaither and Gary McSpadden in the Gaither Vocal Band.

Don Cusic

For Further Reading

Alfonso, Barry. *The Billboard Guide to Contemporary Christian Music*. New York: Billboard Books/Watson-Guptill, 2002.

Cusic, Don. *The Sound of Light: A History of Gospel and Christian Music*. New York: Hal Leonard, 2002.

McNeil, W. K., ed. *Encyclopedia of American Gospel Music*. New York: Routledge, 2005.

Powell, Mark Allen. *Encyclopedia of Contemporary Christian Music*. Peabody, Mass.: Hendrickson Publishers, Inc., 2002.

HAWKINS FAMILY, THE

The Hawkins Family of Oakland, California, first achieved national fame when Edwin Hawkins (b. August 18, 1943) led a group that recorded the 1969 hit "Oh Happy Day," which reached number four on the American pop charts and became a world-wide hit that year. Hawkins grew up in the Ephesians Church of God in Christ (COGIC) in Berkeley, California, a Pentecostal church, and in 1967 he and Betty Watson formed the North California State Youth Choir, made up of the top soloists from other San Francisco-area choirs. The 50-voice choir—which included his brother Walter and Tramaine Davis—recorded an eight-song album, *Let Us Go into the House of the Lord*; "Oh, Happy Day" featured Dorothy Combs Morrison on lead vocal. The group pressed 500 copies of the album, and San Francisco disc jockey Tom "Big Daddy" Donahue, considered one of the founders of underground radio, which pioneered early FM broadcasting of rock music, began playing the song on his station. The record quickly caught on with other San Francisco stations, and Buddah Records signed the group and released their album nationally as *The Edwin Hawkins Singers*.

Gospel singer Walter Hawkins, of the Hawkins Family, performs during an event celebrating Black Music Month on June 17, 2008, in the East Room of the White House. (AP Photo/Haraz N. Ghanbari)

Gospel singer Edwin Hawkins, of the Hawkins Family, had a pop hit with "Oh Happy Day" in the 1960s. (AP Photo/Haraz N. Ghanbari)

The group did not have any other pop hits, although they provided background vocals to "Lay Down (Candles in the Rain)" by Melanie in 1970.

Walter Hawkins (b. May 18, 1949) began his career in the shadow of his younger brother; however, as their careers progressed, Walter often eclipsed his brother, particularly with his *Love Alive* albums in the late 1970s and early 1980s.

After "Oh Happy Day" became a hit, Walter toured with the Edwin Hawkins Singers, but during the early 1970s left to pursue his own career. In 1972 he released his first solo album, and in 1973 he founded the Love Center Church in Oakland, where he remains the pastor. His album *Love Alive I* by the Love Center Choir was released in 1975 and was the first in a string of hit albums by this group, based at his church.

Tramaine Davis (b. October 11, 1957), now known as Lady Tramaine, comes from a gospel family; her grandfather, Bishop E. E. Cleveland, was one of the founders of the Church of God in Christ. At the age of seven, she and Sly Stone's sister formed the Heavenly Tones; they later recorded an album. Right after graduation from high school she joined the choir led by Edwin Hawkins.

When Walter Hawkins founded Love Center Church in Oakland in 1973, Tramaine became a featured soprano soloist in the choir. When she was 19 she married Walter, and the couple had two children, Walter "Jamie" Hawkins, Jr. and Trystan Hawkins. Walter and Tramaine Hawkins divorced in 1985.

Tramaine was the leading voice in the *Love Center* albums by Walter Hawkins and Walter produced Tramaine's first two solo albums.

In 1986 Tramaine signed with A&M Records and released several dance-oriented gospel albums, which brought criticism from the gospel community. Her hit single, "Fall Down (Spirit of Love)," was a number one hit on the *Billboard* dance charts.

In 1988 Tramaine released an album on Sparrow Records, which brought her back into the gospel fold, although she continued to appeal to a mainstream audience. In 1994 she released an album on Columbia, then did not record an album again until her 2001 release on Gospo Centric.

Tramaine Hawkins sang at the funerals of Sammy Davis, Jr. and Rosa Parks. In 1993 she married Tommy Richardson, Jr.

Walter Hawkins has continued to work with his brother Edwin as well as Tramaine and his sister Lynette in the gospel field.

A dedicated pastor, Walter Hawkins earned a master of divinity degree from the University of California at Berkeley and cofounded the Edwin Hawkins and Walter Hawkins Music and Arts Seminar/Love Fellowship. In 1982 Edwin Hawkins founded the Edwin Hawkins Music and Arts Seminar, a week-long convention for church choirs, musicians, and soloists.

Don Cusic

Gospel Music Association Dove Awards: Edwin Hawkins

1982   Inspirational Black Gospel Album: *Edwin Hawkins Live: Oakland Symphony Orchestra and Edwin Hawkins* (Producer: Gil Askey; Label: Myrrh

Grammy Awards: Edwin Hawkins

1969   12th Grammy Awards: Best Soul Gospel Performance: Edwin Hawkins Singers: "Oh Happy Day"

1970   13th Grammy Awards: Best Soul Gospel Performance: Edwin Hawkins Singers: "Every Man Wants to Be Free"

1977   20th Grammy Awards: Best Soul Gospel Performance, Contemporary: Edwin Hawkins and the Edwin Hawkins Singers: "Wonderful!"

1992   35th Grammy Awards: Best Gospel Album by a Choir or Chorus: *Edwin Hawkins Music and Arts Seminar Mass Choir—Recorded Live in Los Angeles*; Director: Edwin Hawkins

Discography: Tramaine Hawkins

Tramaine (1981)

Determined (1983)

All My Best to You (1994)

The Search Is Over (1986)

Freedom (1987)

The Joy That Floods My Soul (1988)

Live (1990)

To a Higher Place (1994)

All My Best to You, Vol 2 (2001)

Still Tramaine (2001)

I Never Lost My Praise (2007)

Mega Collection (2002)

Discography: Tramaine Hawkins with Walter Hawkins

Live (1990)

Love Alive (1973)

Love Alive II (1978)

Love Alive V: 25th Anniversary Reunion (1998)

Grammy Awards: Tramaine Hawkins

1980   23rd Grammy Awards: Best Gospel Performance, Contemporary or Inspirational: Reba Rambo, Dony McGuire, B. J. Thomas, Andrae Crouch, Walter Hawkins, Tremaine Hawkins, Cynthia Clawson, the Archers: *The Lord's Prayer*

Discography: Walter Hawkins

Do Your Best (1972)

Love Alive I (1976)

Jesus Christ Is the Way (1977)

Love Alive 2 (1978)

The Walter Hawkins Family Live (1980)

I Feel Like Singing (1982)

Love Alive 3 (1984)

Love Alive Reunion (1987)

Special Gift: Hawkins Family (1988)

Love Alive 4 (1990)

The Light Years (1995)

The Hawkins Family Collection (1995)

Ooh Wee (1997)

Love Alive 5: 25th Anniversary Reunion (1998)

New Dawning (1998)

Take Courage (2000)

A Song in My Heart (2005)

Gospel Music Association Dove Awards: Walter Hawkins

1980 Soul/Black Gospel Album: *Love Alive II* by Walter Hawkins and the Love Center Choir (Producer: Walter Hawkins; Label: Light)

1982 Contemporary Gospel Album: *Walter Hawkins and Family Live* by the Walter Hawkins Family (Producer: Walter Hawkins; Label: Light)

Grammy Awards: Walter Hawkins

1980 23rd Grammy Awards: Best Gospel Performance, Contemporary or Inspirational: Reba Rambo, Dony McGuire, B. J. Thomas, Andrae Crouch, Walter Hawkins, Tremaine

Hawkins, Cynthia Clawson, the Archers: *The Lord's Prayer*

For Further Reading

Cusic, Don. *The Sound of Light: A History of Gospel and Christian Music.* New York: Hal Leonard, 2002.

McNeil, W. K., ed. *Encyclopedia of American Gospel Music.* New York: Routledge, 2005.

Powell, Mark Allen. *Encyclopedia of Contemporary Christian Music.* Peabody, Mass.: Hendrickson Publishers, Inc., 2002.

HEARD, MARK

Mark Heard (b. John Mark Heard on December 16, 1951; d. August 16, 1992) was a songwriter's songwriter in Christian music, a poet whose lyrics spoke of the triumphs and struggles of being a Christian in the everyday world. Although Heard was never commercially successful, he was influential as a songwriter and his lyric poetry inspired others and set the bar for what Christian songs could be.

Heard grew up in Georgia and graduated from the University of Georgia in 1974 with a degree in television journalism. After graduation he went to Christian theologian Francis Schaeffer's retreat in Switzerland, L'Abri in the Swiss Alps, where he met Larry Norman and Randy Stonehill. Norman was impressed with Heard's songs and signed him to his label, Solid Rock, and encouraged Heard and his wife to move to California, which they did in 1977.

Heard recorded his first album, *Setting Yesterday Free*, while in college; he recorded two other albums, *Mark Heard* and *On Turning to Dust*, but he recorded *Appalachian Melody* for Solid Rock. He recorded another album, *Fingerprint*, before he signed a recording and publishing contract with Chris Christian and Home Sweet Home. Heard released five albums for that label from 1981 to 1985: *Stop the Dominoes, Victims of the Age, Eye of the Storm, Ashes and Light,* and *Mosaics*. The label also released two compilation albums, *Best of Mark Heard: Acoustic* and *Best of Mark Heard: Electric*. Heard then recorded an album, *Tribal Opera*, under the name Ideola before he started his own label, Fingerprint, with Chuck Long and Dan Russell and released a series of albums, beginning with *Dry Bones Dance* in 1990.

Heard produced albums by John Austin, the Choir, John Fischer, Garth Hewitt, Jacob's Trouble, Pierce Pettis, Randy Stonehill, Pat Terry, and the Vigilantes of Love. He also worked with other artists as an engineer and studio musician. Although he was well-known in Christian music circles, Heard was a well-kept secret to the outside world. In a world filled with singer-songwriters, Heard's position in the Christian industry seemed like a barrier to widespread, secular success.

On July 4, 1992, Heard was performing on stage with Pierce Pettis and Kate Miner at the Cornerstone Festival near Chicago when he suffered a mild heart attack; he finished his performance then went to a hospital. Two weeks after his release from the hospital he was diagnosed with two blocked arteries. Heard decided to go home before he began treatment, but the afternoon he was released he had a heart attack and died; he was 40 years old.

After his death, Christian artists Victoria Williams, Chagall Guevara, Buddy Miller, Julie Miller, Daniel Amos, the Choir, Bruce Cockburn, and the Vigilantes of Love recorded a tribute album, *Strong Hand of Love*. In 2002 Cornerstone Music Festival initiated a songwriting contest in honor of Heard, and in 2005 Heard's song, "Worry Too Much," won "Song of the Year" honors from the Americana Music Association.

Don Cusic

Discography

Setting Yesterday Free (1972)

Mark Heard (1975)

On Turning to Dust (1978)

Appalachian Melody (1979)

Fingerprint (1980)

Stop the Dominoes (1981)

Victims of the Age (1982)

Eye of the Storm (1983)

Ashes and Light (1984)

Best of Mark Heard: Acoustic (1985)

Best of Mark Heard: Electric (1985)

Mosaics (1985)

Tribal Opera (as Ideola) (1987)

Dry Bones Dance (1990)

Second Hand (1991)

Satellite Sky (1992)

Reflections of a Former Life (1992)

High Noon (1993)

Mystery Mind (2000)

Millennium Archive Series (2000)

The Final Performance (2001)

Hammers and Nails (2003)

The Lost Artifacts of an American Poet (2007)

For Further Reading

Alfonso, Barry. *The Billboard Guide to Contemporary Christian Music*. New York: Billboard Books/Watson-Guptill, 2002.

McNeil, W. K., ed. *Encyclopedia of American Gospel Music*. New York: Routledge, 2005.

Powell, Mark Allen. *Encyclopedia of Contemporary Christian Music*. Peabody, Mass.: Hendrickson Publishers, Inc., 2002.

HEARN, BILLY RAY

Billy Ray Hearn (b. April 26, 1929) launched Myrrh Records, the first major label that recorded contemporary Christian music as a division of Word while he worked for the parent company. Later, he left that company and formed Sparrow Records in 1976, which became one of the three major contemporary Christian music labels.

Hearn grew up in Beaumont, Texas, where he received music lessons in both the church and school (he played violin at five). He spent two years in the Navy at Pensacola, Florida, after graduation and also worked in the music program of a local church. Later, he attended Baylor University in Waco, Texas, where he received a bachelor of music degree with a major in church music. He joined Trinity Baptist Church in San Antonio as youth and music director after graduation and

stayed there four years, then joined the Baptist Seminary in Fort Worth, where he taught music ministry and conducting. Hearn became minister of music at the First Baptist Church of Thomasville, Georgia, in 1960 and stayed there for eight years; there, he developed a large music program and booked contemporary music groups touring in the Southeast into his church. Working with young people and contemporary music, he developed the musical *Good News*, which debuted in 1968. He came to the attention of Word when the musical, a major success, toured throughout the United States and Europe. This led Word to invite Hearn to join its staff to help promote musicals that company had developed, including *Tell It Like It Is* by Kurt Kaiser and Ralph Carmichael.

After three years as a contemporary label, Myrrh came under increasing fire from Word executives who did not feel there was any future with contemporary Christian music and believed the new label was costing too much money while not generating enough income. But Jarrell McCracken, head of Word, stood behind Hearn and the label continued. However, Hearn grew increasingly frustrated and by 1975 looked for ways to begin his own label. That opportunity came when he received a phone call from Seth Baker, head of the CHC Corporation in Los Angeles.

On January 1, 1976, Sparrow opened its doors in Los Angeles with no artists. The first artist signed was Barry McGuire, whose contract was up with Myrrh and who wanted to go with Hearn. Then the Talbot brothers—John Michael and Terry—each signed for an album as did Janny Grein. Second Chapter of Acts—a group Hearn had signed to Myrrh and worked with extensively there—felt they should stay with the Word organization for one more album, but one of their members, Annie Herring, signed with Sparrow for a solo project. Those were the first acts with albums released in May 1976, when Sparrow presented its first product to the marketplace.

That first year, Sparrow sold about $700,000 worth of albums, but their big break came when they signed Candle, a group organized by Tony Salerno, who produced children's albums. Hearn was reluctant to sign the group—he did not feel their music fit with Sparrow—but finally became enthused after hearing some of the material; he then created a separate label, Birdwing, just for the group. The first album, *Chief Musician*, sold reasonably well; but the album that would turn the ears of Christian labels to children's music, *The Music Machine*, came out the following year, 1977, after it was previewed at the Christian Bookseller's Convention in July. That album became the biggest seller for Sparrow during their first five years in business and instigated an avalanche of children's product from Christian labels.

Sparrow became an independent company in August 1977 after the CHC Corporation was sold to ABC. CHC offered to sell the stock to Hearn, so he organized a group of investors who purchased Sparrow on August 31, 1977.

In 1992 Hearn moved Sparrow from Los Angeles to Nashville and sold it to EMI Music; Hearn was named chairman and CEO until 2001, when he stepped down and his son, Bill Hearn, took over as head of the label. In 1997 Billy Ray Hearn was elected to the Gospel Music Hall of Fame, and in 1999 the Gospel Music Association awarded Hearn and Sparrow a Lifetime Achievement Award. Billy Ray Hearn is the founder and sponsor of the biannual Hearn Symposium on Christian Music at Baylor University in Waco, Texas, and director of the Sparrow Foundation.

Don Cusic

For Further Reading

Cusic, Don. *The Sound of Light: A History of Gospel and Christian Music.* New York: Hal Leonard, 2002.

McNeil, W. K., ed. *Encyclopedia of American Gospel Music.* New York: Routledge, 2005.

HILL, KIM

During her growing up years, Kim Hill (b. December 30, 1963, in Starkville, Mississippi) attended only Christian schools and her parents would not allow her to listen to anything other than Christian music. She attended Mississippi State University in her hometown of Starkville before moving to Nashville to pursue a career in contemporary Christian music. Her first album, *Kim Hill* (1988), produced by Brown Bannister for Reunion Records, introduced her to the Blanton-Harrell group that managed Amy Grant, Michael W. Smith, and others; she later opened for Amy Grant during her Heart in Motion tour. In 1994, Hill tried a brief foray into country music with her album, *So Far So Good*, but soon returned to the contemporary Christian music fold.

Kim Hill has been associated with Focus on the Family as a worship leader in women's conferences they sponsored; she is also associated with Renewing the Heart, a national group similar to Promise Keepers that provides a ministry for women. She is also an advocate for chastity and has been active in the pro-life movement.

Don Cusic

For Further Reading

Alfonso, Barry. *The Billboard Guide to Contemporary Christian Music.* New York: Billboard Books/Watson-Guptill, 2002.

Powell, Mark Allen. *Encyclopedia of Contemporary Christian Music.* Peabody, Mass.: Hendrickson Publishers, Inc., 2002.

HOLM, DALLAS

Dallas Holm's song, "Rise Again," is tied with "He's Alive" by Don Francisco for most weeks spent on the Christian charts. Both songs came during the period when contemporary Christian music was evolving out of Jesus music and the Christian music industry was taking shape. Christian radio was in its infancy and young people wanted straightforward, unabashedly Christian songs that affirmed their faith. "Rise Again" is a song that cuts to the core of the Christian message: Jesus wasn't just a man who died; he was the Savior who rose from the dead.

Inspired by Elvis Presley, Dallas Holm (b. November 5, 1948) began playing in a rock band in high school. His Christian conversion came when he was 16, and Holm began to perform Christian songs at church, in jails, and during evangelistic outings on the street. During the late 1960s, Holm was a youth pastor at a church in the Dallas/Fort Worth area when evangelist David Wilkerson made him part of his crusades.

Holm formed the group Praise, made up of Randy Adams, bass; Ric Norris on drums, Tim Johnson on keyboards; and LaDonna Gatlin Johnson (sister of country singer Larry Gatlin) on vocals. The group recorded as "Dallas Holm and Praise" and the *Live* album went gold.

In 1980 Holm left Wilkerson and embarked on a ministry of his own. Holm's music is middle-of-the-road or adult contemporary. In addition to his regular albums, Holm and his group recorded *His Last Days*, the soundtrack for a musical, *Passion Play*, written by Holm. Active as a motorcyclist, Holm is director of Praise Ministries and participates in the Christian Motorcyclists Association.

Gospel Music Association Dove Awards

1978	Associate Membership Award: Song: "Rise Again" by Dallas Holm (Dimension Music, SESAC)
1978	Male Vocalist of the Year
1978	Mixed Group of the Year
1978	Song of the Year: "Rise Again" Written by Dallas Holm; Publisher: Dimension Music, SESAC
1978	Songwriter of the Year
1993	Inspirational Album: *Generation 2 Generation* by Benson

artists and their families (Lar-nelle Harris, Matthew Ward, Glad, Fred Hammond, 4HIM, Dallas Holm, Kelly Nelon Thompson, Billy and Sarah Gaines, Dana Key) (Producers: Don Koch, Ed Nalle, Fred Hammond, Joe Hogue, and Dana Key; Label: Benson)

Don Cusic

Discography

Dallas Holm (1970)

For Teens Only (1971)

Just the Way I Feel It (1971)

Looking Back (1972,)

Didn't He Shine (1973)

Peace, Joy and Love (1974)

Nothing But Praise (1975)

Just Right (1976)

Dallas Holm and Praise . . . Live (1977)

Tell 'Em Again (1979)

His Last Days (1979)

All That Matters (1979)

Looking Back at the Best of Dallas Holm (1980)

This is My Song (1980)

Holm, Sheppard and Johnson (with Tim Sheppard and Phil Johnson) (1981)

I Saw the Lord (1981)

Signal (1983)

Classics (1985)

Change the World (1985)

Praise and Worship (1986)

Against the Wind (1986)

Behind the Curtain (1988)

Soldiers Again (with Tim Sheppard and Phil Johnson) (1989)

Through the Flame (1990)

The Early Works (1991)

Chain of Grace (1992)

Mesa (with Dana Key and Jerry Williams) (1993)

Completely Taken In (1993)

Dallas Holm Live (1994)

Holm for Christmas (1994)

Face of Mercy (1995)

Before Your Throne (1999)

Signature Songs (2001)

Foundations (2002)

Good News Blues (2005)

For Further Reading

Alfonso, Barry. *The Billboard Guide to Contemporary Christian Music*. New York: Billboard Books/Watson-Guptill, 2002.

Cusic, Don. *The Sound of Light: A History of Gospel and Christian Music*. New York: Hal Leonard, 2002.

Holm, Dallas with Robert Paul Lamb. *This Is My Story*. Nashville, Tenn.: Impact, 1980.

McNeil, W. K., ed. *Encyclopedia of American Gospel Music*. New York: Routledge, 2005.

Powell, Mark Allen. *Encyclopedia of Contemporary Christian Music*. Peabody, Mass.: Hendrickson Publishers, Inc., 2002.

HONEYTREE

Honeytree (b. Nancy Heningbaum on April 11, 1952) was the "hippie chick" of early Jesus music. The name Honeytree was the English translation of her German last name, Heningbaum, and she acquired that nickname in high school in Davenport, Iowa, where she was attracted to the hippie culture and experimented with drugs as a high school senior. Honeytree came from a musical family; her parents were classical musicians and she studied cello, but her mother taught her to play guitar.

During her senior year in high school, on Easter break, 1970, Honeytree visited her sister, who was enrolled at the Fort Wayne Art School in Indiana. There, Honeytree met some "Jesus people" and was converted. One of those Jesus people was John Lloyd, a youth minister who operated the Adam's Apple, a Christian coffeehouse. After high school graduation, Honeytree moved to Fort Wayne and became secretary at the Adam's Apple, where she attended the Monday night Bible studies and began composing Christian songs. Influenced heavily by women folkie singer-songwriters such as Judy Collins, Joni Mitchell, and Carole King, Honeytree's songs sounded contemporary and led a minister to finance the recording of her first album, *Honeytree*, in 1973. The album was picked up by Myrrh, a division of Word Records, and given national distribution. The song "Clean Before My Lord" was later recorded by another Word artist, Evie Tornquist.

Honeytree's next album, *The Way I Feel*, featured two songs written by Phil Keaggy, a native of Youngstown, Ohio, who performed at the Adam's Apple during his tours. They became friends and Honeytree's third album, *Evergreen*, featured Keaggy on guitar and a more rock-oriented feel.

As Jesus music evolved into contemporary Christian music, a more pop-oriented sound emerged and Honeytree's 1978 album, *The Melodies in Me*, featured jazz and classical influences. She became fully involved in Calvary Temple in Fort Wayne, her home church, and in 1983 was formally ordained as a minister. She was over 30 and still single when she began a singles ministry, "Singles—A Challenge to Wholeheartedness" and also became involved with Chuck Colson's Prison Fellowship Ministry. By this point, Honeytree was known as Nancy Honeytree.

In June 1990, Nancy Honeytree married John Richard (J. R.) Miller, who owned a computer company and was also dedicated to ministry. The couple had a son, who died several hours after birth, but they adopted a son shortly afterward. She met Victor and Ruth Martinez, missionaries in Mexico, and this inspired her to learn Spanish in order to minister in Mexico and other Central American countries. Her album *Dios Ha Abierto la Puerta* (*God Has Opened the Door*) was released in 1994. She became involved in ministry in Pakistan and learned songs in the Urdu language; her album *Call of the Harvest*, released in 2005, featured songs in English, Spanish, and Urdu.

Don Cusic

Discography

Honeytree (1973)

The Way I Feel (1974)

Evergreen (1975)

Me and My Old Guitar (1977)

The Melodies in Me (1978)

Maranatha Marathon (1979)

Best of Growing Up (1981)

Honeytree's Best (1981)

Merry Christmas, Love Honeytree (1981)

Single Heart (1985)

Every Single Day (1987)

Best of Honeytree Classics (1989)

Resurrection Sunday (1991)

Pioneer: Twentieth Anniversary Recording (1994)

Dios Ha Abierto la Puerta (1994)

Change You Made in Me (2000)

Call of the Harvest (2005)

For Further Reading

Alfonso, Barry. *The Billboard Guide to Contemporary Christian Music.* New York: Billboard Books/Watson-Guptill, 2002.

Cusic, Don. *The Sound of Light: A History of Gospel and Christian Music.* New York: Hal Leonard, 2002.

McNeil, W. K., ed. *Encyclopedia of American Gospel Music.* New York: Routledge, 2005.

Powell, Mark Allen. *Encyclopedia of Contemporary Christian Music.* Peabody, Mass.: Hendrickson Publishers, Inc., 2002.

I

IMPERIALS, THE

Armand Morales
Jake Hess
Shaun Sherrill Nielsen
Gary McSpadden
Henry Slaughter

The history of the Imperials predates the Jesus movement and contemporary Christian music; their roots extend back to southern gospel during a time when that genre was the most commercially successful segment of white gospel music.

The Imperials were formed by Jake Hess, one of the greatest lead singers in the history of southern gospel; he had been with the Statesmen, which had been formed by Hovie Lister as a "super group," recruiting the top singers in southern gospel to form a top flight quartet. Jake Hess used that same philosophy when he formed the Imperials, which he envisioned as a "dream group" in December 1963.

In that first group, in addition to Hess, were Armand Morales, Shaun Sherrill Nielsen, Gary McSpadden, and pianist Henry Slaughter. The Imperials used a full production on their recordings—including electric guitars, bass, and drums—and were snappy dressers. The men were young and handsome; they soon attracted a large following and released four albums in 1964, their first full year.

Hess was plagued by health problems (heart trouble); he had to take a leave of absence from the Statesmen on several occasions and he left the Imperials in 1967. Nielsen had left the year before and was replaced by Jim Murray; Henry Slaughter also left, replaced by Joe Moscheo. When Hess left, Gary McSpadden also left and they were replaced by Roger Wiles and Terry Blackwood. The group continued their success, winning Dove Awards and from 1969 to 1972 sang with Elvis Presley during his concert appearances and recorded gospel material with him. They also sang and recorded with Jimmy Dean, performing in Las Vegas as well as other venues.

In 1972 Sherman Andrus, an African American and former member of Andrae Crouch and the Disciples, was hired, and the group became the first integrated group in southern gospel. In 1976 Blackwood and Andrus left the

Members of the Imperials—from left, Armond Morales, Jim Murray, David Will and Paul Smith—pose with their Grammy for gospel and soul at the 24th annual Grammy Awards on February 24, 1982, in Los Angeles. (AP Photo/Reed Saxon)

group to form Andrus, Blackwood and Company, which moved into contemporary Christian music.

The Imperials were successful in southern gospel at a time when most of those in the Jesus movement were not even aware of that genre; further, southern gospel had a less than sterling reputation because a number of men in the field had regularly succumbed to the temptations of the flesh and indulged in alcohol and drugs. For many who were aware of life off-stage, the world of southern gospel music was a den of sin and sinful activities. During the early days of contemporary Christian music, many of the young musicians who came out of the rock and folk fields looked down their noses at southern gospel music because of the genre's reputation and because they thought the music, stage shows, clothes,

and hair styles were tacky. It was a different generation and a different culture that followed southern gospel; the young hipsters who came out of the Jesus movement simply could not relate—and did not want to try.

Many of those in southern gospel music saw the increasing popularity of Jesus music as it evolved into contemporary Christian music but felt alienated; that generation and culture were alien to them. It was a classic case of a generation gap, akin to the cultural gap between the conservative country music establishment and the free-wheeling world of the anything-goes do-your-own-thing rock world. Unlike many others in southern gospel, the Imperials related to the Jesus movement's embrace of a personal Jesus and moved toward contemporary Christian music. Although they had to leave behind some of their fans in southern gospel, the Imperials decided to update their sound and join the contemporary Christian music world. It was a difficult time in southern gospel; the other top group in that field, the Oak Ridge Boys, elected to move into country music. Clearly, it was a time when southern gospel was at a crossroads, with some electing to embrace the genre more tightly while young people were increasingly attracted to CCM.

In 1976 David Will and Russ Taff joined the Imperials, and the first album with the new line-up, *Sail On*, was a step toward contemporary Christian music, albeit with a southern gospel line-up of four singers. That period, 1976–1982, was a transitional period from Jesus music to contemporary Christian music as well as a transitional period for the Imperials, who transitioned from southern gospel to CCM. They were successful and continued to be part of CCM although the group continued to change members. In 1982 Taff left for a solo career and was replaced by Paul Smith.

In southern gospel, a member—or perhaps several members—"own" the group, meaning they own the name and hire singers to fill out the group. Armand Morales was the owner of the Imperials, and he hired other singers to fill out the line-up when someone departed. Through the years, a number of singers have been in the Imperials, with Morales the only member who has remained since the beginning. Those who have been a member of the Imperials, in addition to those previously mentioned, include Larry Gatlin (1970), Greg Gordon (1970–1971), Randy Coryell (1975–1977), Danny Ward (1985–1986), Ron Hemby (1986–1990), Jimmie Lee Sloas (1986–1989), David Robertson (1989–1990), Jason Beddoe (1990), Jonathan (Hildreth) Pierce (1990–1993), Pam Morales (1991–1993), Steven Ferguson (1994–1999), Jeff Walker (1994–1996), Steve Shapiro (1996–1998), Barry Weeks (1998–1999), Jeremie Hudson (1999–), Jason Hallcox (1999–2000), Jason Morales (1999–), Richie Crook (2000–2002), Shannon Smith (2002–), and Ian Owens (2004).

Don Cusic

Selected Discography

Jake Hess and the Imperials (1964)

New Dimensions (1968)

Love Is the Thing (1969)

Gospel's Alive and Well (1970)

Time to Get It Together (1971)

Song of Love (1972)

A Thing Called Love (1973)

Live (1973)

Follow the Man with the Music (1974)

No Shortage (1975)

Just Because (1976)

The Best of the Imperials (1977)

Sail On (1977)

Live (1978)

Heed the Call (1979)

One More Song for You (1979)

Christmas with the Imperials (1980)

Very Best Of (1981)

Stand by the Power (1982)

Side by Side (1983)

Let the Wind Blow (1985)

This Year's Model (1987)

Free the Fire (1988)

Love's Still Changing Hearts (1990)

Big God (1991)

Stir It Up (1992)

Til He Comes (1994)

Treasures (1994)

Legacy (1996)

It's Still the Cross (1997)

I Was Made for This (2003)

For Further Reading

Hess, Jake, with Richard Hyatt. *Nothin' but Fine: The Music and the Gospel According to Jake Hess.* Columbus, Ga.: Buckland Press, 1996.

Taylor, David L. *Happy Rhythm: A Biography of Hovie Lister and the Statesmen Quartet.* Louisville, Ky.: Taylormade, 1998.

Gospel Music Association Dove Awards

1969	Male Group of the Year
1975	Male Group of the Year
1976	Graphic Layout and Design: Bob McConnell for *No Shortage* by the Imperials
1976	Male Group of the Year: Imperials
1976	Pop/Contemporary Album: *No Shortage* by the Imperials (Producers: Bob MacKenzie and Gary Paxton; Label: Impact)
1978	Male Group of the Year
1980	Male Group of the Year
1981	Artist of the Year
1981	Male Group of the Year
1981	Pop/Contemporary Album: *One More Song for You* by the Imperials (Producer: Michael Omartian; Label: DaySpring)
1982	Group of the Year
1982	Pop/Contemporary Album: *Priority* by the Imperials (Producer: Michael Omartian; Label: DaySpring)
1983	Group of the Year
1984	Pop/Contemporary Album: *Side by Side* by the Imperials (Producers: Keith Thomas and Neal Joseph; Label: DaySpring)

Grammy Awards

1975	18th Grammy Awards: Best Gospel Performance (Other Than Soul Gospel): The Imperials: *No Shortage*
1977	20th Grammy Awards: Best Gospel Performance, Contemporary or Inspirational: The Imperials: "Sail On"
1979	22nd Grammy Awards: Best Gospel Performance, Contemporary or Inspirational: The Imperials: *Heed the Call*
1981	24th Grammy Awards: Best Gospel Performance, Contemporary or Inspirational: The Imperials: *Priority*

For Further Reading

Cusic, Don. *The Sound of Light: A History of Gospel and Christian Music.* New York: Hal Leonard, 2002.

McNeil, W. K., ed. *Encyclopedia of American Gospel Music.* New York: Routledge, 2005.

Powell, Mark Allen. *Encyclopedia of Contemporary Christian Music.* Peabody, Mass.: Hendrickson Publishers, Inc., 2002.

INSTRUMENTALISTS IN CONTEMPORARY CHRISTIAN MUSIC

If Christian and gospel music is identified primarily by the lyrics, can an instrumental be a Christian song? And if Christian performers are known for presenting the gospel during their performances, can an instrumentalist be a Christian performer? The answer is, yes, an instrumental song can be "Christian" and a number of instrumentalists are Christian performers.

Perhaps the best known instrumentalist is Phil Keaggy. The guitarist has also done a number of songs and albums as a vocalist, so his instrumental numbers can be viewed as another aspect of his artistic endeavors.

Another well-known instrumentalist is Fletch Wiley, who introduced instrumental music to the genre of contemporary Christian music. Wiley plays the flute, trumpet, and flugelhorn and began his professional career as a member of the band for Andrae Crouch and the Disciples before he joined Sonlight. Wiley played easy listening jazz, and his first album, *Ballade*, was released in 1977. Wiley's second album was *Spirit of Elijah*, released in 1979. The instrumentalist was joined by the group Koinonia, and they performed with him on his third album, *Nightwatch*, released in 1981. Wiley followed these albums with *The Art of Praise* and *The Art of Praise 2*, released in 1986 and 1990,

respectively; all of these albums were on StarSong.

Wiley then joined Word and released *Repeat the Sounding Joy* (1990), *Lift High the Lord* (1993), and *Almighty God* (1996).

Sonlight was made up of Hadley Hockensmith, guitar, bass; Harlan Rogers, keyboard; Bill Maxwell, drums; and Fletch Wiley, flute, trumpet. They were a group of studio musicians who were the backing band for Andrae Crouch and the Disciples who formed a jazz-pop combo instrumental group that recorded a solo album, *Sonlight*, in 1972. Member Bill Maxwell produced Keith Green's albums. After their only album, the group evolved into Koinonia.

Koinonia included Alex Acuna, drums, percussion; Hadley Hockensmith, guitar; Abraham Laboriel, bass; Bill Maxwell, drums, percussion; Harlan Rogers, keyboards; Dean Parks, guitar (until 1984); John Phillips, guitar (until 1984); and Justo Almario, woodwinds (since 1984).

Koinonia was an instrumental group of star session players who were Christian. Group members Hadley Hockensmith, Bill Maxwell, and Harlan Rogers all played with Andrae Crouch, and Alex Acuna, Justo Almario, and Abe Laboriel were members of the Latin American All Stars jazz group. The group performed a jazz rock fusion and toured Scandinavia, where they recorded a live concert, which was released as *Celebration*.

The Christian audience was skeptical at first of an instrumental Christian group; after all, how can songs be "Christian" if there are no lyrics to make that clear? However, as groups and individuals identified themselves as

Christians, instrumentalists were accepted into the contemporary Christian music fold.

Koinonia recorded four albums for Sparrow: *More Than a Feeling* (1983), *Celebration* (1984), *Frontline* (1986), and *Compact Favorites* (1989).

Dino Kartsonakis (b. July 20, 1942, in New York), a classically trained pianist, has been called the Christian Liberace. He has been a fixture on the contemporary Christian music scene with his beautiful instrumentals of classic hymns as well as classical and contemporary songs.

Dino began playing piano when he was three; after high school he studied at the King's College, at the Julliard School of Music, and at music conservatories in Germany and France. He toured with Arthur Rubinstein; for seven years he was the pianist for evangelist Kathryn Khulman and was musical director of her TV show, "I Believe in Miracles."

Dino recorded his first album when he was 17; he served in the army and then moved to California, where he signed with Light Records in 1974.

In 1976 he married Debby Keener, who attended Oral Roberts University and sang with the World Action and Television Singers. He recorded and performed with her, and the two hosted "The Dino and Debby Show" on religious TV during the late 1970s. They were divorced, and in 1986 Dino married Cheryl McSpadden, sister of gospel singer Gary McSpadden.

Dino's appeal has been to adult contemporary fans who love the glitz and glamour that accompanies his Christian concerts; Dino dresses well and his stages are often elaborate sets. Since 2002 he has performed in Branson, Missouri, and his TV show, "The Dino Show," is broadcast on the Trinity Broadcasting Network.

Dino has recorded more than 50 albums and won the Dove Award for "Instrumentalist of the Year" annually from 1978 to 1983, then again in 1986, taking home that honor five times. In 1993 he won the Dove Award for "Instrumental Album," with *Somewhere in Time* and again in 1996 for his album *Classical Peace* (Producer: Rolin R. Mains; Label: Benson).

Phil Driscoll won the Dove Award for "Instrumentalist" in 1984 and 1985. In 1987 his album *Instrument of Praise* won the Dove Award for "Instrumental Album."

Driscoll had a storied history in rock music before he became a Christian. During the late 1960s he performed in Joe Cocker's band and also worked with Blood, Sweat and Tears and Stephen Stills. Cocker's influence can still be heard in Driscoll's gravelly vocals. A downward spiral from drugs and the rock 'n' roll lifestyle led Driscoll to a Christian conversion in 1977; since that time he has been one of the premier instrumentalists in contemporary Christian music through recordings of praise and worship music as well as patriotic songs.

Driscoll began trumpet lessons in the fifth grade at his school in Lancaster, Texas; in 1959 his family moved to Tulsa, Oklahoma, where he continued trumpet lessons. In addition to his work with rock acts, Driscoll also performed with the London Philharmonic Orchestra.

Driscoll was affiliated with the Kenneth Copeland ministry since the early 1980s, performing at many KCM Believers' Conventions. Driscoll has performed at Democratic party conventions and played during the dedication ceremony for Bill Clinton's presidential library.

Phil Driscoll was convicted in 2006 of using his ministry organization for tax evasion; he was sentenced to a year and a day in federal prison beginning March 2007.

Michael Omartian (b. November 26, 1945, in Evanston, Illinois) is best known as a producer, but his instrumental skills are evident in several of his albums. Fans of Jesus music first heard Omartian through his piano on "Easter Song" by 2nd Chapter of Acts; that intro is unforgettable for those who heard it and is a testament to the musical virtuosity of Omartian, who also played piano on Billy Joel's "Piano Man."

Michael Omartian had a long, successful history in secular music before turning his attention to contemporary Christian music and still works with secular artists, although he has tended to concentrate on CCM since the 1990s. He is one of the few figures in contemporary music who moves easily between the secular worlds of pop and country to contemporary Christian music.

Omartian grew up in Evanston and started playing the piano when he was four; later he studied at Tarkio College in Missouri and Northwestern University in Evanston. He became a Christian on Christmas Day 1965, He worked on the staff of Campus Crusade for Christ and led two ministry teams, Armageddon Experience and New Folk, before moving to Los Angeles to pursue songwriting in 1970s.

In L.A. Omartian soon became a sought-after session player, playing keyboards on sessions for Barbra Streisand, Steely Dan, Boz Scaggs, Michael Jackson, Julio Iglesias, John Lennon, Eric Clapton, and Al Jarreau. He produced the Grammy-winning album by Christopher Cross as well as albums by Donna Summer (he cowrote "She Works Hard for the Money"), Rod Stewart, and Whitney Houston, and coproduced the anthemic "We Are the World" with Quincy Jones. He was part of the studio group Rhythm Heritage that played "Baretta's Theme" for the TV show "S.W.A.T." and "Theme from Happy Days."

Omartian was involved in early Jesus music, playing on albums by Mike and Kathy Deasy, Richie Furay, Annie Herring, Phil Keaggy, Barry McGuire, Jamie Owens, and 2nd Chapter of Acts. As a member of Jack Hayford's Church on the Way, he performed with 2nd Chapter of Acts in a concert there that produced the album *Together Live.*

In contemporary Christian music, Omartian produced Amy Grant's album *Heart in Motion* and cowrote her hit single, "That's What Love Is For." Other CCM acts he produced include First Call, 4Him, Debby Boone, Steve Camp, Sandi Patti, Bob Carlisle, Jonathan Pierce, Michael W. Smith, Gary Chapman, the Imperials, Steven Curtis Chapman, Kathy Troccoli, Sheila Walsh, Crystal Lewis, and Wayne Watson.

In 1973 Michael married Stormie Sherric; she is a songwriter and singer who has written a number of best-selling books, including *The Power of a Praying Woman,* and released several best-selling exercise videos.

Dennis Agajanian's music leaned toward country and bluegrass; he is renowned for his flat-picking guitar instrumentals. Part of the early Jesus movement, Agajanian grew up on a small farm north of Los Angeles and first performed with his brother, then with the group Kentucky Faith. A flat picking guitar virtuoso, Agajanian is known for his patriotic songs and flat picking versions of a wide variety of music. He appears on behalf of Samaritan's Purse, a humanitarian organization headed by Franklin Graham and has performed at Promise Keepers rallies. From 2001 to 2003 Agajanian won the "Musician of the Year" award from the Christian Country Music Association and was named their "Entertainer of the Year" in 2002, 2003, 2005 and 2006.

Kerry Livgren, formerly of Kansas, is also a noted instrumentalist (see Kansas and Kerry Livgren), and Michael W. Smith has recorded a number of instrumental albums in addition to his pop/rock catalogue (see Smith, Michael W.)

Don Cusic

ISAACS, THE

Lily Fishman, the daughter of Jewish Holocaust survivors from Poland, loved Barbra Streisand; Joe Isaacs, raised poor in East Tennessee, grew up hearing bluegrass greats Ralph and Carter Stanley. Love knows no musical bounds, however, so after the two met at Gerdes Folk City in New York City, they fell in love. Joe was playing with the Greenbriar Boys at that time and Lily readily admits she'd never heard a banjo outside the theme song for "The Beverly Hillbillies" television show. She was more inclined to the theatre and had a record deal with Columbia in the late 1960s as part of the duo Lily and Maria.

Joe and Lily married in 1970; she converted to Christianity and Joe returned to his Christian faith attending a church service following the death of his brother. The two started singing together, performing Christian music, and left the nightclub circuit; Joe formed the Calvary Mountain Boys and performed in churches. The couple had three children soon after they were married: Ben, Sonya, and Becky. In 1975 Joe formed Joe Isaacs and the Sacred Bluegrass, which marked the first time the siblings performed with their parents. Harmonies came naturally, and they each learned to play a variety of instruments. The children joined their parents on the television show they had on the local access channel.

The family had a difficult time making ends meet with their music and Joe considered quitting, but Sonya, Ben, and Becky convinced their parents to let them become permanent members of the band; in 1986 they became the Isaacs. Relying on their Christian faith, the family bought a bus and began performing beyond the local churches where they had been playing. Their sound is based on bluegrass melodies and picking with vocals that draw on southern gospel harmonies. Infused in between are threads of Lily's folk heritage and her love for popular music like James Taylor and Eric Clapton. At first their sound was not readily accepted, but they persevered and soon became one of the top groups in bluegrass gospel.

In 1993 the Isaacs had their first top five hit, the a cappella tune "I Have a Father Who Can," in the *Singing News* gospel music magazine. Ironically, the song was never meant to be anything other than an album cut. The follow-up was "From the Depths of My Heart," which went to the top of the charts and was named "Song of the Year" by both *Gospel News* and *Gospel Voice*. Around this same time the Isaacs became a part of the Gaither Homecoming video series as it was being launched. The videos were a huge success and put them in front of thousands of new fans, both in their live performances and in the videos that were sold.

The Isaacs won the 1997 Dove Award for "Bluegrass Album of the Year" for their *Bridges and their Song* album; in 1997 "Man on a Mule" was nominated for "Bluegrass Song of the Year."

The group's thirtieth album, *Big Sky*, was produced by Mark Bright, who worked with Carrie Underwood and Rascal Flatts, and recorded the project at Reba McEntire's Starstruck Studio. The band members have ventured outside the family atmosphere on a few side trips. Ben has played with Tony Rice, Ralph Stanley, Aubrey Haynie, Rhonda Vincent, and many others. Sonya had a record deal as a solo artist, releasing several country singles. She also toured with Vince Gill and has recorded with Dolly Parton, Stanley, Reba McEntire, and Brad Paisley. Becky is an award-winning songwriter who made guest appearances as a vocalist with Parton, Bryan Sutton, Paul Simon, Stanley, Mark Lowry, and others. The Isaacs are now based out of Lafollette, Tennessee.

The Isaacs family members are Lily Isaacs (b. September 20, 1947, in Germany), Ben Isaacs (b. July 25, 1972, in Wilmington, Ohio), Sonya Isaacs, (b. July 22, 1974, in Wilmington), and Rebecca Isaacs Bowman (b. August 2, 1975, in Wilmington); their band members are Jesse Stockman, fiddle; Nathan Fauscett, drums and other percussion; and Troy Engle, guitar and banjo.

Vernell Hackett

For Further Reading

Powell, Mark Allen. *Encyclopedia of Contemporary Christian Music*. Peabody, Mass.: Hendrickson Publishers, Inc., 2002.

J

JARS OF CLAY

Dan Haseltine, lead vocals
Charlie Lowell, keyboards and
background vocals
Matt Odmark, guitars, background
vocals
Steve Mason, guitar, background vocals

Jars of Clay is a contemporary Christian group that has transcended the contemporary Christian genre and achieved success in the secular music industry without abandoning their Christian roots. Their career not only has embraced music but also has extended to international philanthropy with their Blood Water mission in Africa.

The members began as students at Greenville College in Greenville, Illinois, studying contemporary Christian music, when they entered a demo tape recorded originally for a class project for the Gospel Music Association's band competition in 1994. They won that competition and moved to Nashville in 1994 and signed with Essential Records.

The group originally consisted of Dan Haseltine, Matt Bronleewe on guitar, Mason on bass, and Lowell on keyboards. They jammed together in their dorm rooms; when Bronleewe left the group he was replaced by Odmark. The group's first album was one they recorded and released themselves in 1994; in May 1995 their first Essential album was released.

The group quickly became popular with some of their songs played on MTV, through constant touring, and through hits on Christian radio. The question of whether a band is a Christian band if the members are Christians but the group doesn't just record overtly Christian songs is answered with Jars of Clay because they embrace the contemporary Christian world and that audience embraces them. Their sound is reminiscent of the Crosby, Stills, Nash, and Young albums, and their albums have transcended the contemporary Christian music genre. They have performed with Billy Graham on his crusades and with pop acts Matchbox Twenty and Sting, and their music has been in the films *The Chamber, Crossroads, Jack Frost, The Prince of Egypt*, and *We Were Soldiers*. They have been the subject of features in *Rolling Stone, Entertainment Weekly, People*, and *Billboard*.

Jars of Clay—from left, Charlie Lowell, Steve Mason and Dan Haseltine—hold their Best Pop/ Contemporary Gospel Grammys at the 40th annual Grammy Awards on February 25, 1998, at New York's Radio City Music Hall. (AP Photo/Richard Drew)

Although Jars of Clay has toured the Christian circuit, they have not limited themselves to that circuit; during their career they have toured Europe, Australia, and Asia and performed in secular venues. Their albums have gone platinum.

In 2001 the group partnered with Amnesty International and performed a free concert to celebrate Amnesty International's 40th Anniversary. In 2002 Dan Haseltine visited Africa and was inspired to found a nonprofit organization, Blood Water Mission, which seeks to raise money and awareness of poverty and AIDS in Africa. Their mission began with the 1000 Wells project with a goal to dig a thousand new wells throughout Africa. According to the group, their organization hopes to help provide two of the things that Africa needs the most: clean blood and clean water.

Don Cusic

Discography

Frail (1994)

Jars of Clay (1995)

Much Afraid (1997)

If I Left the Zoo (1999)

The Eleventh Hour (2002)

Furthermore—From the Studio: From the Stage (2003)

Who We Are Instead (2003)

Redemption Songs (2005)

Good Monsters (2006)

The Essential Jars of Clay (2007)

Christmas Songs (2007)

Gospel Music Association Dove Awards

1996   New Artist of the Year

1996   Short Form Music Video: *Flood*; Producers and Directors: Ricky Blair, Michelle Weigle-Brown, Robert Beeson; Label: Essential

1997   Group of the Year

1998   Group of the Year

1999   Special Event Album: *Exodus* by DC Talk, Jars of Clay, Sixpence None the Richer, Cindy Morgan, Chris Rice, the Katinas, Third Day, Crystal Lewis, and Michael W. Smith (Producer: Michael W. Smith; Label: Rockettown Records)

2000   Alternative/Modern Rock Recorded Song: "Unforgetful You"; Writers: Dan Haseltine, Matt Odmark, Steve Mason, Charlie Lowell; by Recorded by Jars of Clay; Label: Essential

2001   Special Event Album: *City on a Hill—Songs of Worship and Praise* by Jars of Clay, Sixpence None the Richer, Third Day, Caedmon's Call, FFH, the Choir, Gene Eugene, Sonicflood, Peter Furler (Producer: Steve Hindalong; Label: Essential)

2003   Modern Rock/Alternative Album of the Year: *The Eleventh Hour*; Producers: Dan Haseltine, Charlie Lowell, Stephen Mason, Matt Odmark; Essential

2003   Special Event Album of the Year: *City On A Hill—Sing Alleluia*; Caedmon's Call, FFH, Jars of Clay, Jennifer Knapp, Phil Keaggy, Nichole Nordeman, Bebo Norman, Fernando Ortega, the Choir, Third Day, Steve Hindalong, Marc Byrd; Essential

2006   Recorded Music Packaging of the Year: *Redemption Songs* (Jars of Clay); Stephanie McBrayer, Tim Parker; Jimmy Abegg; Essential Records

2006   Special Event Album of the Year: *Music Inspired by the Chronicles of Narnia: The Lion, the Witch, and the Wardrobe*; Jeremy Camp, Steven Curtis Chapman, David Crowder Band, Delirious, Bethany Dillon, Jars of Clay, Kutless, Nichole Nordeman, Rebecca St. James, tobyMac, Chris Tomlin; Ed Cash, Steven Curtis Chapman, David Crowder, Andy Dodd, Sam Gibson, Dan Haseltine, Charlie Lowell, Toby McKeehan, Adam Watts, Christopher Stevens, Mitch Dane; Sparrow Records

2007   Rock/Contemporary Album of the Year: *Good Monsters*; Producers: Dan Haseltine, Steve Mason, Charlie Lowell, Matt Odmark; Essential Records

2007   Short Form Music Video of the Year: *Work*; Jars of Clay; Monica Ortiz; Jeff Stephenson; Wild Spirit Native Soul; Essential Records

Grammy Awards

1997   40th Grammy Awards: Best Pop/Contemporary Gospel Album: *Much Afraid*

2000   43rd Grammy Awards: Pop/
        Contemporary Gospel Album:
        If I Left the Zoo

2002   45th Grammy Awards: Best
        Pop/Contemporary Gospel
        Album: *The Eleventh Hour*

For Further Reading

Alfonso, Barry. *The Billboard Guide to Contemporary Christian Music*. New York: Billboard Books/Watson-Guptill, 2002.

McNeil, W. K., ed. *Encyclopedia of American Gospel Music*. New York: Routledge, 2005.

Powell, Mark Allen. *Encyclopedia of Contemporary Christian Music*. Peabody, Mass.: Hendrickson Publishers, Inc., 2002.

JESUS CHRIST SUPERSTAR

Jesus Christ Superstar was an album before it became a Broadway musical. Released in 1970, the concept album brought rock music to the gospel and the gospel to the masses. It was a controversial but highly influential work; the Christian world as a whole condemned it because the writers, Andrew Lloyd Webber and Tim Rice, did not even pretend to be evangelists and because Jesus was portrayed as a man, not God (there was no resurrection). However, it brought Jesus to life as a countercultural figure, and hippies related to him because he had long hair and a beard and wore sandals and was a revolutionary figure. It also made the Christian story into a rock opera and showed young Christians that the gospel message could be encased in contemporary culture with contemporary music and that there was an appeal to this story even to non-Christian audiences.

Jesus Christ Superstar was a double album that centered on the struggles between Jesus and Judas Iscariot; the story concentrates on the last weeks of Jesus' life and ends with the crucifixion. The role of Jesus was sung by Ian Gillan, lead singer for Deep Purple, and the role of Judas was sung by Murray Head whose recording of "Superstar" reached number 14 on the pop charts in early 1971. Yvonne Elliman sang "I Don't Know How to Love Him," which became a hit single in the spring of 1971. She also sang another song from the musical, "Everything's Alright," which charted in the fall of 1971.

The first staged production was in June 1971 at Southold High School in New York; this was one of several unauthorized productions before the official premiere on October 12, 1971, at the Mark Hellinger Theatre on Broadway. That original production starred Jeff Fenholt as Jesus and Ben Vereen as Judas with Yvonne Elliman as Mary Magdalene. Reviews were mixed; religious groups protested outside the theater and the musical ended after 18 months.

The musical opened in London in 1972 and ran for eight years; it became the longest running musical of all time at the time. It started its first American tour in 1976 and continued until 1980; in 1992 it was revived and ran for five years. Since that time, *Superstar* has toured regularly in the United States.

The film *Jesus Christ Superstar* was released in 1973; it was directed by Norman Jewison and filmed in Israel and other locations in the Middle East. The film generated less controversy from religious groups than the theatrical production; still, a number of Christians disliked the film and refused to see it.

Don Cusic

For Further Reading

Cusic, Don. *The Sound of Light: A History of Gospel and Christian Music.* New York: Hal Leonard, 2002.

JESUS MUSIC

Jesus music was born when the hippie counterculture of the 1960s merged with evangelical Protestant Christianity and converts combined the music of pop and rock with Bible based lyrics. Some pinpoint this first taking place in 1967 when a group of street Christians opened the Living Room, a storefront mission in the Haight Ashbury district of San Francisco. Early converts were primarily bikers, hippies, musicians, runaways, and students. One of them was an art student named Lonnie Frisbee.

In 1968 Frisbee moved to Southern California with his wife and became part of Calvary Chapel, Chuck Smith's small church in Costa Mesa. Soon Frisbee was running the House of Miracles, a communal house for Reverend Smith, and leading a Wednesday night Bible study where he taught new converts, some of whom were musicians. By the time the Woodstock festival was held in the summer of 1969, the Jesus movement was creating its own music.

By 1971 Frisbee and Smith had parted ways, but Calvary Chapel's attendance had outgrown its original sanctuary and was meeting in a large tent next to the construction site for the new sanctuary. It was here that Jesus music was regularly performed.

During the late 1960s the Zeitgeist was moving in a spiritual direction, as reflected in the music of that time. The Electric Prunes performed a Roman Catholic Mass in Latin using rock and roll instruments; Van Morrison released the introspective *Astral Weeks* the same year that Bob Dylan chronicled his spiritual journey on his album *John Wesley Harding*. Broadway had two plays about Jesus, *Jesus Christ Superstar* and *Godspell*, that each produced radio hits. By the time that Norman Greenbaum released his pop hit single "Spirit in the Sky" in 1970, Jesus music albums were being marketed.

By 1969 Southern California had become the epicenter for the Jesus movement, just as Haight Ashbury in San Francisco had been for the hippie counterculture. Artists such as Andrae Crouch, Chuck Girard, Barry McGuire, and Larry Norman were some of its first musical evangelists.

Andrae Crouch recorded his first album, *Take the Message Everywhere*, on Light Records, a subsidiary of gospel giant Word Records. Word emphasized traditional southern gospel recordings of the day while Light recorded new acts and was open to the new sound of the Jesus movement. Crouch, a minister's son, attended Bible college, performed in his father's church, at Teen Challenge events, and at coffee houses during the 1960s. By the 1970s he was the biggest gospel star in the world and his songs were covered and admired by secular artists.

Chuck Girard had been in the music business since he graduated from high school in 1960, at the end of the age of doo-wop. Girard was the lead singer of the Castells, whose hits included "Sacred." Girard worked in the studio with Beach Boy's insider Gary Usher, which led to Girard becoming the lead singer of the Hondells on their hit, "Little Honda."

With an established career in the music business, Girard was exposed to all the accoutrements associated with that lifestyle and was soon tripping on LSD; by his own estimate he had taken around 500 trips on the drug. But in 1969 Girard gave up the drug-fueled hippie counterculture and became a spirit-filled Jesus freak. His conversion took place at Calvary Chapel, where he and his friends began to compose and perform music expressing their newfound faith in the same contemporary music style they used to play at secular venues. Chuck formed the group Love Song with Tommy Coomes, Jay Truax, and Fred Field, but by the time they recorded their first album, Bob Wall had replaced Field and they added drummer John Mehler to become what some people called the Christian Beatles.

Love Song was the perfect personification of a Jesus freak band; they looked like hardcore hippies and had been until their conversion, yet sang about a fundamentalist evangelical religious experience. They were a message of hope to the Christian community who had been told during the 1960s that God was dead. When they appeared at Explo 72 in Dallas, Texas, which some refer to as the Christian Woodstock, they were embraced by Billy Graham and catapulted into Christian stardom. When the group returned to Southern California, they performed at Knott's Berry Farm for their first Night of Praise in 1973 and set a box office record, demonstrating the marketing potential of Jesus music. Around the same time, Disneyland began hosting their Night of Joy Christian music concerts.

Love Song's first recording was "Little Country Church," which appeared in 1971 on the first Maranatha record, *The Everlasting Living Jesus Music Concert*, a compilation album featuring eight of the new Maranatha artists. Their first solo album was released on the Good News label in 1972. Love Song produced only one other studio album, *Final Touch*, in 1974. After Bob Wall left the group, Phil Keaggy filled in during their remaining live gigs; by 1975 Girard was a solo artist and released his first self-titled album.

By 1971 Calvary Chapel had grown to the point where services were held in a large tent until a new sanctuary, large enough to hold the throngs of new converts, was constructed. Part of the regular weekly program at Calvary Chapel was a Saturday night concert where artists such as Love Song, Children of the Day, Gentle Faith, and Debbie Kerner performed. After the concert, one of Calvary Chapel's pastoral staff such as Greg Laurie or Tom Stipe gave a verse by verse Bible study and concluded with an altar call. By the end of the 1970s there were dozens of Calvary Chapels all over the country and the weekly attendance at Smith's church was around 25,000, making it the largest Protestant church in the country and the first mega-church, according to church growth expert Peter Wagner.

Sometimes Calvary Chapel invited Christian artists to perform who were not part of their fellowship, such as Larry Norman. Norman began his professional music career in 1965 when he became the lead singer of the secular band People in the San Francisco Bay area. In 1968 he left People for both religious and artistic reasons and began a solo career. He signed with Capitol Records and released *Upon This Rock* in 1969, often considered the first Jesus music album. Norman was featured in *Time* magazine and released a series of albums on his own record labels One Way and Solid Rock. His most ambitious and successful project was an album trilogy of *Only Visiting This Planet, So Long Ago in the Garden*, and *In Another Land*, all released in the early 1970s. He signed other artists to his label, such as Daniel Amos, Mark Heard, Randy Stonehill, and the JC Power Outlet, and produced their albums.

Another Jesus music pioneer was Barry McGuire, who began performing at local bars in Santa Monica, California, and eventually became the lead singer for the New Christy Minstrels. In January 1965, McGuire left the group and became a solo artist; he had a number one hit with "Eve of Destruction" but fell into a lifestyle of drug abuse. In 1971 he became a born-again Christian and released his first album of Jesus music, *Seeds*, on Myrrh Records in 1973. The recording engineer for McGuire's album was Buck Herring, whose wife Annie and her two siblings, Matthew and Nellie Ward, formed a singing trio that sang background vocals on *Seeds*. That trio became 2nd Chapter of Acts, another pioneer Jesus music group whose debut album, *With Footnotes,* contained "Easter Song," which became a Jesus music classic.

Many of the earliest Jesus music groups received exposure through a series of five albums that were produced and distributed by Maranatha, a label begun by Tom Coomes and Chuck Fromm at Calvary Chapel and initially financed by Chuck Smith and the church. The Maranatha series began in 1971 and ended in 1976. Their first release, *The Everlastin' Living Jesus Music Concert*, was not intended to be the start in a series, but the success of that album led to others. On that initial album, produced by Chuck Girard, were acts Love Song, Blessed Hope, Gentle Faith, Country Faith, the Way, Debby Kerner, and Children of the Day.

Children of the Day was the first Maranatha group to release an entire album of their work; it was produced by Buck Herring and the group had four members, sisters Marsha and Wendy Carter, Peter Jacobs, and Russ Stevens. The group played at churches and coffeehouses in the Southern California area and eventually released six albums during the 1970s. Their song, "For Those Tears I Died," written by Marsha Carter, was the first big hit from that group and became their signature song.

At this time there wasn't a contemporary Christian music top 40 because there were not enough albums that had been released in this new genre. However, "For Those Tears I Died" became one of the first CCM hits after it was included on *The Everlastin' Living Jesus Concert* album as well as *Come to the Waters,* the first album from Children of the Day. Religious radio stations were reluctant to play the new

Jesus music, but Children of the Day were a soft rock/folk group whose sound was similar to the popular group the Mamas and the Papas, so they received some airplay and performed at churches in the Los Angeles area.

Debby Kerner was the first female solo artist to release an entire album on the Maranatha label. In 1972, *Come Walk with Me* was released; it had some of the first new worship songs from the Jesus movement. One of those was the simple six stanzas of "Jesus" and another was "Amen, Praise the Lord," which often inspired congregations to leave their pews and dance in the aisles when that wasn't a normal part of the service.

The Way was made up of Dana Angle, Gary Arthur, Bruce Herring, and John Wickham, and they released a solo album in 1973. They had formed in 1971 and added Alex MacDougall on drums before they broke up in 1976. Many of the early Jesus groups, including Love Song, did not have drums in their live shows; the sound of most of these early groups was acoustic folk/country.

Maranatha 2, released in 1972, was produced and orchestrated by Children of the Day member Peter Jacobs, and the album featured artists Country Faith, the Way, Denny Stahl, Blessed Hope, Selah, Debby Kerner, Ken Gulliksen, and Children of the Day. One of the members of Country Faith was Tom Stipe, who was on Calvary Chapel's pastoral staff and was the Master of Ceremonies for the regular Saturday night Jesus music concerts in the big tent. Ken Gulliksen was a member of Calvary Chapel's staff and later founded an affiliate church, the Vineyard Christian Fellowship. In 1977 he

was joined by John Wimber, another Calvary Chapel pastor, after Wimber had a theological disagreement with Chuck Smith over the place that spiritual gifts had in church services.

Maranatha 3 was coproduced by Erick Nelson and Tom Stipe; it was released in 1973 and featured artists Blessed Hope, Karen Lafferty, Hosanna, Ernie Rettino, Bob and Steve, Country Faith, Becky, and Mustard Seed Faith. Karen Lafferty's song "Plan of Love" was featured on that album, and Lafferty soon released a solo album, *Bird in the Golden Sky*, produced by Peter Jacobs. Lafferty became known for her song, "Seek Ye First" (Matthew 6:33), which spread to a number of charismatic churches across the country.

Maranatha 4, released in 1974, was produced by Tom Stipe and leaned a little more toward rock 'n' roll than the previous folk-based albums. Artists on the album were Wing and a Prayer, Children of the Day, the Road Home, Mustard Seed Faith, Good News, Chuck Butler, Karen Lafferty, and Blessed Hope.

Although Blessed Hope was included on the first four Maranatha albums, they never produced their own album. They performed regularly at Southern California coffeehouses and were Bill Bradford (piano and lead vocals), Pat Patton (bass and vocals), Doug Krupinski (lead guitar), Don Kobayashi (drums), and David Rios (acoustic guitar and vocals). Wing and a Prayer also never released a solo project.

In 1974, the first *Praise Album* was released. Produced by Tom Coomes, it was the first album of worship music entirely created by the Jesus movement.

The songs contained on this and other Praise albums replaced the hymns in many churches or at least supplemented them as independent, nondenominational churches were formed as an outgrowth of the Jesus movement. Many of the songs were simply scripture set to a melody, such as "Seek Ye First" (Matthew 6:33) by Karen Lafferty. The songs were called choruses and many like "Praise the Lord," written by Chuck Girard and Tom Coomes, had been part of the worship service in a number of churches for a few years.

In 1975 *The Joy Album*, produced by Gary Arthur and Tom Coomes, contained more of the choruses that would soon be used in church worship services. The significance of these worship albums was that Maranatha music began to concentrate on these while the music groups at Calvary Chapel signed with Christian labels that were more rock oriented, like Solid Rock, Myrrh, Sparrow, Lion and Lamb, and Newpax, among others.

Maranatha 5 was the last of the Maranatha series. It was released in 1976 and had a harder, more rock-oriented sound. Artists on the album included Gentle Faith, Daniel Amos, Parable, Mustard Seed Faith, Fred Field, Erick Nelson, Bob Cull, Bethlehem, Sweet Comfort, and the Road Home.

The most successful band that debuted on *Maranatha 5* was Daniel Amos, which first formed at Calvary Chapel in 1975. The band members had played in a variety of other Jesus bands with names like Good Shepherd, Jubal's Last Band, and Judge Rainbow and the Prophetic Trumpets. The name Daniel Amos was chosen to avoid confusion with another band using the name Jubal, who changed their name to Gentle Faith. Daniel Amos, or DA as they were sometimes known, was originally Steve Baxter (vocals and acoustic guitar), Jerry Chamberlain (vocals and electric lead guitar), Marty Dieckmeyer (bass), and Terry Taylor (vocals and acoustic guitar). Their first release was "Ain't Gonna Fight It" on the *Maranatha 5* compilation album. Like many of the early Jesus bands that appeared on the Maranatha series, they did not have a drummer. Folk and country rock were popular genres and bands such as America, the Byrds, Crosby, Stills and Nash, the Eagles, and Poco were some of their most popular secular artists. DA's first two albums (the eponymous *Daniel Amos* and *Shotgun Angel*) had a distinctly country folk sound to them; however, by their second album Steve Baxter left the group and was replaced by Mark Cook (keyboards and vocals), and the group added Ed McTaggart (drums and vocals). For their third album, *That Horrendous Disc*, they changed record companies to Solid Rock (founded by Larry Norman) and the band's sound changed drastically to New Wave in the vein of Devo and the Talking Heads.

By the mid-1970s, Jesus music began to become more prolific as new artists produced albums for the growing market. Churches such as Hollywood Presbyterian and Highland Park Neighborhood Foursquare in Los Angeles offered Christian coffeehouse ministries with names like the Salt Company and Agape Inn in their basements where Jesus music groups performed for young people. A Christian night club opened on Sunset Strip in Hollywood where Christian acts like the Archers appeared, and many churches featured concerts of the new Jesus music.

A number of groups and individuals recorded Jesus music, and the musical palate of this new genre expanded. Agape was an early hippie-era psychedelic hard rock band started by Fred Caban, a young guitar player from Azusa, California. The band's sound was modeled after contemporary psychedelic hard rock bands like Cream and the Jimi Hendrix Experience. Their debut album, *Gospel Hard Rock*, was released in 1971 but, because their sound was a very raw blues based rock, most churches at that time would not allow them to perform. However, the group was committed to evangelizing their peers so they played whenever and wherever they could: on the beach, in parks, and at schools.

Bob Ayala was a popular singer-songwriter-performer during the early years of the Jesus movement who began losing his sight as a teenager; by the early 1970s he was legally blind. In 1969 he began performing at the Salt Company, a coffeehouse founded by youth pastor Don Williams, and by the mid-1970s was regularly playing at churches and coffeehouses all over the Southern California area. Ayala performed solo with an acoustic guitar with a sound that some compared to José Feliciano. In 1976 he released his first album, *Joy by Surprise*, on the Myrrh label.

Terry and John Michael Talbot were members of Mason Proffit, a secular country rock band during the late 1960s and early 1970s. By 1972, at the peak of the band's popularity, playing to audiences of up to 30,000, they left the group when they became born-again Christians. In 1974 they released *The Talbot Brothers* on Warner Brothers Records and, after meeting with Barry McGuire, joined Billy Ray Hearn's

new Christian record label, Sparrow. The duo recorded and released *Reborn* (as the Talbot Brothers); then John Michael Talbot became a Roman Catholic Franciscan monk, his brother Terry joined the Protestant arm of the Jesus movement, and each began solo careers. John Michael created contemporary Christian music for the Roman Catholic community while Terry did the same for the Protestant church and became a music director in the Foursquare church.

By this time—the early to mid-1970s—Christian artists like Michael Card, Paul and Terry Clark, John Fischer, Don Francisco, Lilly Green, Benny Hester, Pat Terry, Russ Taff, Evie Tornquist, Sandy Patti, the Wall Brothers, Randy Stonehill, John Pantano, and Ron Salsbury were regularly releasing albums. Artists who had established a career in the secular field such as Leon Patillo (Santana), Dan Peek (America), Noel Paul Stookey (Peter, Paul and Mary), B. J. Thomas, and Richie Furay (Buffalo Springfield and Poco) had a Christian conversion and released albums of Christian music.

Early Jesus rock pioneers like Randy Matthews and Larry Norman played at Calvary Chapel, and eventually the ultimate secular music conversion took place, through its influence, when Bob Dylan became a born-again Christian after attending Ken Gulliksen's Vineyard Fellowship in 1978. Gulliksen was a Maranatha musician and had been a pastor at Calvary Chapel.

Jesus music was blossoming in more areas than Southern California, and one of those places was Fort Wayne, Indiana, where Nancy Honeytree lived and was swept up by the Jesus movement in 1970. She began working at Adam's Apple, a Christian coffeehouse, and began writing and performing her own compositions; she recorded her debut self-titled album in 1973.

Fort Wayne is also where Bob Hartman founded Petra in 1972 at the Christian Training Center. In 1973 Petra signed with Myrrh Records; the band was Hartman, Greg Hough, John DeGroff, and Bill Glover; in 1974 they released their first eponymous album.

Since churches like Calvary Chapel in Costa Mesa paved the way for Christian rock bands, it was possible to do something that was previously unthinkable in the heartland like combine Christian lyrics with rock music. Even so, Petra struggled and went through numerous personnel changes until 1979, when they recorded the album *Washes Whiter Than*, which produced a Christian radio hit, "Why Should the Father Bother."

Mylon LeFevre came from a southern gospel music background; he was part of the Singing LeFevre family, a southern gospel group based in Atlanta, Georgia. After he went into the Army at the age of 17 in 1961, he wrote his first song, "Without Him," which was recorded by Elvis Presley in 1963. After his discharge he returned to his parents' home and became part of the Singing LeFevres, until 1969, when he formed Mylon, a country rock band that toured the counterculture hippie ballrooms and other venues where he played music that was a fusion between southern gospel and rock 'n' roll. During this time he played and hung out with the top musicians of that era, including former members of the Beatles, Eric Clapton, Elton John, Tina Turner, the Who, Steve Winwood, and ZZ Top, to name some.

Attending a concert where Mylon was performing was the equivalent of attending a church worship service. He and his band danced around the stage singing gospel lyrics to foot-stomping country rock. He had shoulder length hair and wore a leather vest with a cross on the back while a projector flashed a cross inside the star of David on a screen behind the band.

After heavy drug usage left him in a coma with brain damage, Mylon entered rehab and straightened out his life. By the end of the 1970s, at a 2nd Chapter of Acts concert, he recommitted his life to Jesus Christ, quit rock 'n' roll, and formed Broken Heart, a Christian rock group.

Phil Keaggy is another Jesus music pioneer who came out of the 1960s counterculture. A native of Ohio, he became the featured singer-songwriter-lead guitarist of Glass Harp. Keaggy has been acclaimed by both Christian and secular musicians for his guitar virtuosity. He became a born-again Christian while a member of Glass Harp, and when he left the group in 1972 he moved to New York and began work on his solo album, *What a Day,* in 1973.

Keaggy replaced Bob Wall in Love Song for the remainder of their tour before they broke up in the mid-1970s; in 1975 he appeared on the 2nd Chapter of Acts album *In the Volume of the Book,* which resulted in Buck Herring producing and engineering Keaggy's second solo album, *Love Broke Through.* He toured with 2nd Chapter of Acts and played lead guitar in a band called David.

Two of the most formidable new singer-songwriters to appear in the mid-1970s were Amy Grant and Keith Green. Green was 24 when he released *For Him Who Has Ears to Hear* on Sparrow. Green was a self-proclaimed Jesus freak who had a vision of Jesus while he was on LSD. In 1975 he became born again and began singing about his new experience. His performances consisted of sitting at the piano and preaching in between songs. By the time he was finished with his set he called the audience, usually in a church, to the altar for repentance and rededication to the Lord. The zeal and intensity with which he did this consistently offended many, since he even demanded that the pastor of the church where he was ministering come forward and repent.

Green and his wife Melody established Last Day's Ministries and moved their base from California to Texas at the end of the 1970s. In 1980, when he released his third album, *So You Wanna Go Back to Egypt*, he insisted that it be made available for whatever individuals could afford to pay. After releasing his fourth album in 1982, *Songs for the Shepherd*, Green was killed in an airplane crash.

Amy Grant was only 17 years old when her first album was produced by Chris Christian and Brown Bannister in 1977. She was a pioneer in bringing Christian music to the secular audience during the 1980s.

Bob Dylan had been the conscience and prophet of the counterculture since the early 1960s; he always sang about things that mattered, issues that were on the cutting edge, or on the distant horizon. What Dylan thought mattered, so when he became a born-again Christian, it made an impact.

Dylan had just concluded a divorce with his wife and was dating a woman who attended Ken Gulliksen's Vineyard Church. He accepted Jesus Christ into his heart, became a born-again Christian, and attended months of intense Bible training. *Slow Train Coming*, released in 1979, was the first of three albums dealing with the subject of religion from a evangelical fundamentalist perspective, and it won Dylan a Grammy.

The album wasn't religious enough for the diehards, so next came *Saved* in 1980, a full-blown gospel album influenced by black gospel music. Bob Dylan was so sanctified that for a series of concerts he didn't even play the songs that made him famous, which demonstrated the moral integrity demanded by his newfound faith. This angered and alienated his longtime fans but excited the former counterculture Christian audience who felt themselves in fellowship with the man who was their prophet so long ago. His third Christian album was *Shot of Love*.

One of the earliest Christian music pioneers outside the United States was Cliff Richard, who had his first releases in Great Britain in 1958. Richards was a rock star before and during the advent of the Beatles but never achieved stardom in the United States. In 1964 he gave his life to Christ and became a practicing Christian; from this point forward his music reflected his newfound faith, and he sometimes appeared at Billy Graham Crusades. He performed at the Greenbelt Festivals during the 1970s and influenced British artists Malcolm and Alwyn.

Malcolm Wild and Alwyn Wall were a singing duo from Nottinghamshire; in 1973 they released *Fools Wisdom* on Word's Myrrh label. In 1974, they released their second album,

WILDWALL, but soon afterward the duo split and the Alwyn Wall Band emerged, which played at the Greenbelt and other festivals. Malcolm Wild became the pastor of a Calvary Chapel at Merritt Island, Florida, and Alwyn Wall became the pastor of Calvary Chapel in Westminster, in central London.

Bruce Cockburn was part of a regional rock band from Canada who shared the stage with everyone from Jimi Hendrix to Wilson Pickett during the 1960s. By the early 1970s he turned to folk music, and by 1973 became a born-again Christian, writing songs that reflected his Christian faith.

His music embraced a social conscience, and by the end of the 1970s he became involved with Oxfam, a Christian relief organization based in Canada, and the Native American rights movement.

Van Morrison released *Astral Weeks* in 1968, the first of many albums where the veteran Irish rocker explored the mystical side of his Christian faith.

By the end of the 1970s, the hippie counterculture, and the Jesus movement fueled by it, had run out of gas, according to Jesus movement historians like Professor Larry Eskridge. Dylan's subsequent return to the secular recording world again initiated a new blending of rock and religion.

By 1980 the term "Jesus music" was used rarely; the term "contemporary Christian music" was the term that now defined the genre where the sounds of popular and rock music were wedded to Christian lyrics that expressed fundamental evangelical Christianity in songs.

Bob Gersztyn

For Further Reading

Cusic, Don. *The Sound of Light: A History of Gospel and Christian Music.* New York: Hal Leonard, 2002.

Eskridge, Larry. *Sweet, Sweet Song of Salvation: The Jesus People Movement and American Evangelicalism, 1967–1977.* New York: Oxford University Press, 2009.

Fahlbusch, Erwin. *The Encyclopedia of Christianity.* Grand Rapids, Mich.: Eerdmans, 1999.

McNeil, W. K., ed. *Encyclopedia of American Gospel Music.* New York: Routledge, 2005.

Shelton, Robert. *No Direction Home: The Life and Music of Bob Dylan.* New York: Beech Tree/William Morrow, 1986.

Thompson, John J. *Raised by Wolves: The Story of Christian Rock and Roll.* Toronto: ECW Press, 2000.

Whitaker, Beth. *The Calling of a Rock Star.* Mount Laurel, N.J.: Hawthorne Publishing Co., 1988.

JOHNSON, KATHIE LEE

Before Kathie Lee Gifford (b. Kathie Lee Epstein, 1954, Paris, France) became nationally known as the coanchor with Regis Philbin of "Live with Regis and Kathie Lee" and the wife of former football star Frank Gifford, she was a contemporary Christian artist. She grew up in Bowie, Maryland, just outside Washington, D.C., and performed with her sister Michie as Pennsylvania Next Right. Kathie Lee won the Junior Miss titles in Maryland and Alabama and attended Oral Roberts

University on a music scholarship she obtained through the efforts of Anita Bryant. After graduation, Kathie Lee was one of the singers on the "Oral Roberts TV Show."

In 1976 she married Paul Johnson and recorded an album with Michie. She had a role on the TV soap opera "Days of Our Lives" and was a featured singer on the TV show "Name That Tune." She recorded two solo albums, *Lovin' You* (1978) and *Finders Keepers* (Petra, 1979), produced and mostly written by her husband, noted songwriter, producer, and arranger Paul Johnson, but the two divorced in 1983. In 1986 she married Frank Gifford.

Don Cusic

For Further Reading

Powell, Mark Allen. *Encyclopedia of Contemporary Christian Music*. Peabody, Mass.: Hendrickson Publishers, Inc., 2002.

K

KAISER, KURT

Kurt Kaiser (b. December 17, 1934) is one of the most influential musicians, songwriters, and executives in gospel and contemporary Christian music. Kaiser had formal training as a musician; he studied at the American Conservatory of Music in Chicago, then attended Northwestern University's School of Music in Evanston, Illinois. He joined Word Records after his graduation in 1959 as director of artists and repertoire and later became a vice president and director of music for Word.

Kaiser worked as an arranger and producer in the pre-Jesus music and pre-contemporary Christian music days, working on albums by Kathleen Battle, Tennessee Ernie Ford, Larnelle Harris, Burl Ives, Ken Medema, Christopher Parkening, George Beverly Shea, Joni Eareckson Tada, Ethel Waters, and Anne Martindale Williams. He also recorded 16 solo albums of piano music and accompanied George Beverly Shea in concerts for more than 30 years.

His major influence on Jesus music and later contemporary Christian music came through his collaboration with Ralph Carmichael on the musicals *Tell It Like It Is, Natural High*, and *I'm Here, God's Here, Now We Can Start*, which were popular with church youth during the 1960s.

Kurt Kaiser was inducted into the Gospel Music Hall of Fame in 2001.

Gospel Music Association Dove Awards

1982   Inspirational Album: *Joni's Song* by Joni Eareckson (Producer: Kurt Kaiser; Label: Word)

1994   Instrumental Album: *Psalms, Hymns and Spiritual Song*s (Producer: Kurt Kaiser; Label: Sparrow)

Don Cusic

For Further Reading

Alfonso, Barry. *The Billboard Guide to Contemporary Christian Music*. New York: Billboard Books/Watson-Guptill, 2002.

279

Cusic, Don. *The Sound of Light: A History of Gospel and Christian Music.* New York: Hal Leonard, 2002.

McNeil, W. K., ed. *Encyclopedia of American Gospel Music.* New York: Routledge, 2005.

KANSAS AND KERRY LIVGREN

Phil Ehart, drums
Richard Williams, guitar
Kerry Livgren, guitar, keyboard
(until 1984; since 2000)
Robby Steinhardt violin, vocal
(until 1983; since 2000)
Dave Hope, bass (until 1984,
since 2000)
Steve Walsh vocals, keyboard
(until 1982, since 1986)
John Elefante, vocals, keyboards
(1982–1984)
Bill Gree, bass (1986–2000)
Steve Morse, guitar (1986–2000)

Kansas, one of the most popular bands of the 1970s with their progressive jazz-influenced sounds, was not originally a Christian band, although their spiritual lyrics led many in the Christian audience to embrace them. Then, in 1979, when leader Kerry Livgren became a Christian, the material of Kansas was overtly Christian until 1984, when label executives ordered the band to tone down their Christianity in order to appeal to a wider secular audience and Livgren left to pursue a solo career.

Kerry Livgren (b. September 18, 1949) and some high school friends in Topeka, Kansas, formed his first band, the Gimlets; he performed with them while attending Washburn University,

then joined the Mellotones, an R&B band. Livgren and Mellotones member Don Montre left that group and reformed the Gimlets, then renamed the band Saratoga. Phil Ehart, who was in Saratoga, was also in another band, White Clover; Ehart and Livgren decided to form a new band by combining the best elements of Saratoga with White Clover; the result was a band they named Kansas. This group would go through several permutations before they were signed to Kirshner Records in 1973.

Their first hit, "Carry on Wayward Son" in 1977, followed by "Dust in the Wind" in 1978, both written by Livgren, launched them into superstardom, where they performed to huge crowds in stadiums and sold millions of records. Their songs had deep, philosophical lyrics with spiritual themes while their shows were loaded with special effects. They were a thinking person's group, and their fans embraced the band's philosophical quests.

While touring with Kansas in 1979 to promote their *Monolith* album, Livgren, who studied *The Urantia Book*, became involved in a series of discussions with Jeff Pollard of Le Roux, the opening act for Kansas during this tour, about the validity of *The Urantia Book* versus the Bible. As a result of these discussions, Livgren rejected the beliefs of *The Urantia Book*, accepted the Bible, and became an evangelical Christian after a conversion experience in an Indianapolis hotel room at 3 A.M. in July 1979.

The next morning, Livgren heard "Joy to the World" in the hotel restaurant, a result of a Christmas in July celebration, then went to a Christian bookstore and bought an arm full of books to help him in his new faith.

Livgren did a solo album while he remained a member of Kansas. During their tour in support of their album, *Audio Vision*, bassist Dave Hope announced he was a Christian, and lead singer Steve Walsh walked out because he did not want to sing Livgren's overtly Christian lyrics. He was replaced by John Elefante, a devout evangelical Christian, as lead singer. The group then hired Warren Hamm, another Christian, who played saxophone, flute, and harmonica. The albums *Vinyl Confessions* and *Drastic Measure* were overtly Christian albums and Christian bookstores sold them.

This caused a conflict with members of the group who were not Christians as well as executives at the band's label, Kirshner Records, who saw album sales decline and insisted the band be a secular group with no Christian material. That caused Livgren, Hope, and Elefante to leave the group, which essentially ended the original Kansas. Lead singer Steve Walsh then reformed a "new" Kansas.

Livgren had released his first solo album, *Seeds of Change*, in 1980 along with his autobiography of the same title, but continued to record and tour with Kansas. However, his Christian faith came in conflict with the non-Christian members of the group.

Livgren formed a new group, AD, with former Kansas members Dave Hope and Warren Ham in addition to Michael Gleason and Dennis Holt. CBS Records, aware of Livgren's key role in Kansas, released the album as *Kerry Livgren AD*. Because of contractual obligations with Kansas, Livgren was unable to have albums by AD released on a secular label for the secular market; as a result, the AD albums were

released on Sparrow, a Christian label. The marketing of the AD product was split between trying to reach the old Kansas audience and the new Christian audience; the result was a difficult period for Livgren, who went from playing stadiums to clubs and churches. AD toured from 1983 to 1985.

Livgren did not totally sever his ties with Kansas; he appeared with them occasionally and contributed songs to several of their projects.

AD fell apart although the album *Prime Mover* recorded after the split is listed as *Kerry Livgren AD*. However, the album was recorded by former AD and Kansas member Warren Ham and Livgren in the studio.

During the period 1986 to 1995, Kansas was definitely not a Christian group. Meanwhile, Livgren and Elefante made solo albums, and Dave Hope became youth leader at St. Andrews by the Sea, a charismatic Episcopalian church in Destin, Florida. John Elefante and his brother, Dino, formed the group Mastedon, then became noted Christian music producers.

Kerry Livgren became a true solo artist with his instrumental album, *One of Several Possible Musiks*; Livgren played all the instruments on this album. In 1994 he moved back to Topeka from Atlanta and formed Numavox Records and GrandyZine Production Company. Livgren released his following projects through these companies.

In 2000 there was a reunion of the original Kansas lineup and they did a tour in support of a new album, *Somewhere to Everywhere,* which was written by Livgren. In 2003 some former members of Kansas joined Livgren to form Proto-Kaw, and they recorded several albums. Livgren also pursued solo work as a recording artist in addition to his involvement as a family man and Sunday School teacher at Topeka Bible Church.

Don Cusic

Discography: Kansas

Kansas (1974)

Masque (1975)

Song for America (1975)

Leftoverture (1976)

Point of Know Return (1977)

Two for the Show (1978)

Monolith (1979)

AudioVisions (1980)

Vinyl Confessions (1982)

Drastic Measure (1983)

The Best of Kansas (1984)

Power (1986)

In the Spirit of Things (1988)

The Kansas Box Set (1994)

Freaks of Nature (1995)

Kansas (1995)

Somewhere to Elsewhere (2000)

Discography: Kerry Livgren

Seeds of Change (1980)

One of Several Possible Musiks (1989)

Decade (1992)

When Things Get Electric (1994)

Odyssey into the Mind's Eye (1996)

Prime Mover II (1998)

Collector's Sedition, Vol. 1 (2000)

Best of Kerry Livgren (2002)

Discography: Kerry Livgren with A.D.

Time Line (1984)

Prime Mover (1988)

Reconstructions Reconstructed (1997)

Discography: A.D.

Art of the State (1985)

Reconstructions (1986)

Compact Favorites (1988)

AD Live (1998)

Discography: Proto-Kaw

Early Recordings from Kansas 1971–1973 (2003)

Before Became After (2004)

Wait of Glory (2006)

Gospel Music Association Dove Award

1990   Instrumental Album: *One of Several Possible Musiks* (Producer: Kerry Livgren; Label: Sparrow)

For Further Reading

Alfonso, Barry. *The Billboard Guide to Contemporary Christian Music*. New York: Billboard Books/Watson-Guptill, 2002.

Livgren, Kerry, with Kenneth Boa. *Seeds of Change*. Canoga Park, Calif.: Sparrow Books, 1983, 1991.

Powell, Mark Allen. *Encyclopedia of Contemporary Christian Music*.

Peabody, Mass.: Hendrickson Publishers, Inc., 2002.

KEAGGY, PHIL

Phil Keaggy is one of the premier instrumentalists in contemporary Christian music and as a guitarist holds his own with premier guitarists such as Eric Clapton and others at the top of the rock field. Keaggy has recorded numerous albums from the earliest days of contemporary Christian music, and his body of work is a definitive history of the evolution of contemporary Christian music.

Phil Keaggy (b. March 23, 1951, in Youngstown, Ohio) grew up in a large family in a small farmhouse in Hubbard, Ohio, that he shared with nine brothers and sisters. Keaggy took up guitar when he was 10, although he lost half of his middle finger on his right hand in an accident when he was four. Like most aspiring musicians, Keaggy played first in a garage band, the Squires, who made a recording for a compilation album, *Highs in the Mid-Sixties, Volume 9*. In 1968 he formed Glass Harp with drummer John Sferra and bassist Dan Pecchio. The trio won a Battle of the Bands contest, where one of the judges put them in touch with Lewis Merenstein, who was influential in getting Glass Harp signed to Decca Records. The band recorded its first album for the label in Greenwich Village at Jimi Hendrix's Electric Lady Studios with Merenstein producing. The trio opened shows for major artists such as Chicago, Iron Butterfly, Traffic, and Yes.

Keaggy became involved with drugs, including LSD, and on February 14, 1970, had a bad experience during a drug trip; on the same day he discovered his mother was in a fatal car accident. During this period his sister told him about Jesus and he changed his life, became a Christian, and left Glass Harp in 1972 when he released his first solo album, *What a Day*. Keaggy was married the following summer to Bernadette, then took time off from recording, although he continued to tour with acts such as Love Song, Paul Clark, 2nd Chapter of Acts, and Nancy Honeytree.

Keaggy spent time at the Love Inn community in upstate New York, where he recorded several albums for the New Song label. In 1976 he entered the studio and the following year released the only album by the Phil Keaggy Band. In 1979 Keaggy moved to Leawood, Kansas, then to Costa Mesa, California, in 1983, and finally to Nashville in 1988. He won his first Dove Award in 1988 for his second instrumental album, *The Wind and the Wheat*. He took home a second Dove the following year for *Beyond Nature*.

One of the highlights of Keaggy's career was jamming with former Beatle Paul McCartney when Keaggy was invited to play at McCartney's sister-in-law's wedding; after the ceremony he and McCartney played together. Keaggy had long revered McCartney and knew all the Beatles songs; and his vocals sounded eerily like McCartney's.

Keaggy has always walked both sides of the path by recording both Christian albums and secular music. Many of the musician's early albums such as *Love Broke Through*, *What a Day*, and *Emerging* helped define the concept of contemporary Christian music.

Vernell Hackett

Discography

What a Day (1974)

Love Broke Through (1976)

How the West Was One (1977)

Emerging (1977)

The Master and the Musician (1978)

Ph'lip Side (1980)

Town to Town (1981)

Play Thru Me (1982)

Underground (1983)

Getting Closer (1985)

Way Back Home (1986)

Prime Cuts (1987)

The Wind and the Wheat (1987)

Phil Keaggy and Sunday's Child (1988)

The Best of Keaggy/The Early Years 73–78 (1989)

Backroom Trax, Private Collection, Vol. 1 (1989)

Backroom Trax, Private Collection, Vol. 2 (1989)

Find Me in the Fields (1990)

Beyond Nature (1991)

Backroom Trax, Private Collection, Vol. 3 (1991)

Backroom Trax, Private Collection, Vol. 4 (1992)

Backroom Trax, Private Collection, Vol. 5 (1993)

Revelator (EP) (1993)

Crimson and Blue (1993)

Blue (1994)

Backroom Trax, Private Collection, Vol. 6 (1994)

Time (1995)

True Believer (1995)

220 (1996)

Acoustic Sketches (1996)

On the Fly (1997)

A Christmas Gift (1997)

Phil Keaggy (1997)

Premium Jams (1999)

Majesty and Wonder: An Instrumental Christmas (1999)

Music to Paint By: Brushstrokes (1999)

Music to Paint By: Splash (1999)

Music to Paint By: Electric Blue (1999)

Music to Paint By: Still Life (1999)

ReEmerging (2000)

Zion (2000)

Lights of Madrid (2000)

Inseparable (2000)

Uncle Duke (2000)

Gospel Music Association Dove Awards

1988   Instrumental Album: *The Wind and the Wheat* by Phil Keaggy (Producers: Phil Keaggy and Tom Coomes; Label: Colours)

1992   Instrumental Album: *Beyond Nature* by Phil Keaggy (Producer: Phil Keaggy; Label: Myrrh)

1998   Children's Music Album: *Sing Me to Sleep Daddy* by Billy Gaines, Michael James, Phil Keaggy, Michael O'Brien, Guy Penrod, Peter Penrose, Angelo Petrucci, Michael W. Smith, Randy Stonehill, and Wayne Watson (Producer: Nathan DiGesare; Label: Brentwood Kids Co.)

1998	Instrumental Album: *Invention* by Phil Keaggy, Wes King, and Scott Dente (Producer: R. S. Field; Label: Sparrow)
1999	Instrumental Album: *Acoustic Sketches* by Phil Keaggy (Producers: Phil Keaggy and John August Schroeter; Label: Sparrow Records)
2000	Instrumental Album: *Majesty and Wonder* by Phil Keaggy (Producers: Phil Keaggy and David Shober; Label: Myrrh)
2001	Instrumental Album: *Lights of Madrid* by Phil Keaggy (Producer: Phil Keaggy; Label: Wordartisan)
2002	Special Event Album of the Year: *Prayer of Jabez* by Sarah Sadler, Margaret Becker, Geoff Moore, Steve Reischl, Erin O'Donnell, Adrienne Liesching, Jamie Rowe, Phil Keaggy, Rebecca St. James, Michael Tait, Jill Phillips, and Kevin Max (Producers: John Hartley and David Zaffiro; Label: ForeFront)
2003	Instrumental Album of the Year: *Hymnsongs*; Phil Keaggy (Producers: Phil Keaggy and Ric Kardinski; Label: Word)

For Further Reading

Alfonso, Barry. *The Billboard Guide to Contemporary Christian Music*. New York: Billboard Books/Watson-Guptill, 2002.

Cusic, Don. *The Sound of Light: A History of Gospel and Christian Music*. New York: Hal Leonard, 2002.

Powell, Mark Allen. *Encyclopedia of Contemporary Christian Music*. Peabody, Mass.: Hendrickson Publishers, Inc., 2002.

KERNER, DEBBY

Debby Kerner is a pioneer female artist in contemporary Christian music; she was at Calvary Chapel as that church emerged as a leader in the Jesus music movement and recorded some of the earliest albums by a female artist. Kerner, Marsha Stevens, and Karen Lafferty all emerged out of Calvary Chapel as that church showed they were open to both men and women singing Christian music; Kerner and Lafferty were both ordained as music ministers at Calvary. With a soprano voice reminiscent of folk singers like Joan Baez, Kerner sang "Behold, I Stand at the Door" on Calvary Chapel's first album, *The Everlastin' Living Jesus Music Concert*. On the second Maranatha album she sang the ballad "The Peace That Passes Understanding." Kerner's debut album for Maranatha, *Come Walk with Me* (1972), contained both of those songs.

On the third Maranatha album she sang "I Will Never Leave" with Ernie Rettino; the duo released an album, *Friends* (1974), and later married. Their following three albums, *Joy in the Morning* (1975), *More Than Friends* (1977), and *Changin'* (1978), were all released on the Maranatha label.

Kerner and Rettino then moved into children's music and created the Psalty the Singing Songbook series for Maranatha, which was a pioneering venture into children's music for Calvary

Chapel. Kerner and Rettino also wrote the Christian musical *Hi Tops*.

Don Cusic

For Further Reading

Powell, Mark Allen. *Encyclopedia of Contemporary Christian Music*. Peabody, Mass.: Hendrickson Publishers, Inc., 2002.

KING'S X

Lead singer Doug Pinnick has led King's X, a "thinking man's heavy metal band" for more than 20 years. Despite a lack of success in mainstream contemporary Christian music—and even a backlash from some fans of CCM—King's X has thrived to become one of the premier bands in Christian rock.

Pinnick grew up in Joliet, Illinois, and joined a Christian community in Florida after college. He formed a community, Shiloh Fellowship, after he returned to Illinois, then moved to Springfield, Missouri, where he joined the group Servant. Drummer Jerry Gaskill, a former student at Evangel College in Springfield, and Pinnick began playing together and backed Phil Keaggy on a short tour.

In 1980 Pinnick, Gaskill, and guitarist Ty Tabor formed the Edge, a cover band who played rock and new wave on the rock club circuit for five years. In 1985 they moved to Houston, where they acquired a manager, Sam Taylor, who suggested they change their name to King's X.

King's X is a band of Christians but does not see itself as a Christian band.

They are one of the few interracial groups in Christian music (Pinnick is African American) and, although they are explicit in their faith, the Christian media has never really embraced them.

King's X has recorded for secular labels—they were initially turned down by Christian labels—and has toured with groups such as AC/DC, Living Colour, the Scorpions, and Pearl Jam.

The group's song "Junior's Gone Wild" was on the soundtrack of *Bill and Ted's Bogus Journey* in 1991.

In 1998 Pinnick released a solo album as Poundhound and created further controversy in Christian circles when he admitted he was gay.

Don Cusic

For Further Reading

Powell, Mark Allen. *Encyclopedia of Contemporary Christian Music*. Peabody, Mass.: Hendrickson Publishers, Inc., 2002.

Thompson, John J. *Raised by Wolves: The Story of Christian Rock and Roll*. Toronto, Ontario: ECW Press, 2000.

KNAPP, JENNIFER

Jennifer Knapp (b. April 12, 1974, in Chanute, Kansas) had a difficult childhood; she was raised by her divorced father and attended Pittsburg State University in Pittsburg, Kansas, on a trumpet scholarship where she studied music education. She was a "party hard wild child" until Christian dorm mates witnessed to her and she accepted Jesus in a grocery store parking lot at 3 A.M., which ended her partying lifestyle. Knapp began writing Christian personal confession songs in the folk/rock vein and released several self-produced CDs, one of which came to the attention of Toby McKeehan, who signed her to his label, Gotee Records. Her debut album with Gotee, *Kansas* (1997), was produced by Mark Stuart of Audio Adrenaline; Knapp was on the Lilith Fair concert tour with Sarah McLachlan, which allowed her to reach a wide audience and *Kansas* went gold. The Christian world loved her and the Christian media covered her extensively.

Knapp brought a Christian feminism into the genre and she opened for Audio Adrenaline, Big Tent Revival, DC Talk, Jars of Clay, and Third Day, which allowed the Christian audience to openly embrace her. In 1999 she sang for Pope John Paul II when he visited St. Louis and won the Dove Award for "New Artist of the Year." However, all was not well in the entire Body of Christ as Jerry Falwell attacked her for touring with Lilith Fair.

Jennifer Knapp is involved in the Ronald McDonald House, Mercy Ministries, and charities connected to children's hospitals and women's shelters.

Don Cusic

For Further Reading

Alfonso, Barry. *The Billboard Guide to Contemporary Christian Music*. New York: Billboard Books/Watson-Guptill, 2002.

Powell, Mark Allen. *Encyclopedia of Contemporary Christian Music*. Peabody, Mass.: Hendrickson Publishers, Inc., 2002.

L

LAFFERTY, KAREN

Karen Lafferty is best known for writing the song "Seek Ye First," which was on Maranatha's *Praise Album* (1974), and for founding Musicians for Missions, the European-based organization that sends contemporary Christian musicians to evangelize globally.

Lafferty grew up in Alamogordo, New Mexico, and majored in music education at Eastern New Mexico State University; she became a Christian after graduation and moved to Southern California to pursue a career in music. She joined Calvary Chapel as the Jesus movement was at its peak; her first three albums were all released on the Maranatha label: *Bird in a Golden Sky* (1975), *Sweet Communion* (1978), and *Life Pages* (1980).

Lafferty was among the first female contemporary Christian singers and, with Debby Kerner, was ordained as a minister of music by Calvary Chapel's Maranatha label—the first women to hold those positions.

Lafferty's first European tour was in 1973 when she opened for Children of the Day in Holland; in 1978 she headlined a tour in Europe and was amazed at the popularity of American music abroad. She was committed to bringing contemporary Christian music to Europe and formed Musicians for Missions in 1981 as an outreach of Youth With a Mission (YWAM). Lafferty moved to Amsterdam to head the project and set up seminars in addition to training Christian musicians and sending them into the musical mission field.

While in Amsterdam, Lafferty continued to record songs for Maranatha's praise albums and did an occasional album.

Don Cusic

For Further Reading

Cusic, Don. *The Sound of Light: A History of Gospel and Christian Music*. New York: Hal Leonard, 2002.

Powell, Mark Allen. *Encyclopedia of Contemporary Christian Music*. Peabody, Mass.: Hendrickson Publishers, Inc., 2002.

LAMB

Jews who convert to Christianity are known in Christian circles as "messianic Jews" or "completed Jews," the idea being that the acceptance of Christ "completes" the Jew who accepts Jesus as the Savior who was prophesized in the Old Testament. Although evangelical Christians feel the conversion of Jews is a high priority, non-Christian Jews tend to find this whole idea offensive.

Joel Chernoff is the son of Rabbi Martin Chernoff with the Beth Messiah Congregation in Philadelphia; Joel became a Christian and began writing songs using melodies from Jewish folk songs. Rick Coghill is a former Nashville session musician who played with James Brown and was a former member of the Lemon Pipers, whose "Green Tambourine" was a hit in 1968 (Coghill was not a member of that group when it recorded that song). Coghill was involved with drugs when the Lemon Pipers played American Bandstand and he ran into an old friend, Glenn Schwartz, who was with the group Pacific Gas and Electric (who had a top 15 hit with "Are You Ready" in 1970).

Schwartz witnessed to Coghill, who subsequently read the Bible and had a Christian conversion.

Coghill and Chernoff united as a Christian Simon and Garfunkel and aimed their material at the Jewish audience, hoping to convert them to Christianity.

In 1999 Joel Chernoff released a solo album, *The Restoration of Israel*.

Don Cusic

For Further Reading

Powell, Mark Allen. *Encyclopedia of Contemporary Christian Music*. Peabody, Mass.: Hendrickson Publishers, Inc., 2002.

LEFEVRE, MYLON

Mylon LeFevre (b. October 6, 1944, in Gulfport, Mississippi) has a long heritage in Christian and gospel music. The Singing LeFevres consisted of his mother and father, Urias and Eva Mae LeFevre, and various other members and friends throughout the group's 50-year history. The LeFevres were originally from east Tennessee but eventually moved to Atlanta, Georgia.

Mylon LeFevre grew up under the influence of gospel music, but during his teenage years he moved in the direction of rock 'n' roll. He eventually left home and joined the Army. He wrote his first song, "Without Him," when he was 17, and that song was recorded by Elvis Presley, which gave LeFevre his first major taste of success. Within the next year more than 126 recordings of the song were made, and his first royalty check was for $90,000.

After his discharge from the service, LeFevre began his recording career with his debut album *Mylon* (sometimes called *We Believe*). His popular song "Gospel Ship" was on this disc, which is often called one of the first Christian rock albums. However, as his career continued, the singer strayed from his Christian roots, recording highly acclaimed secular albums. His friends were those in the pop, country, and rock world—Eric Clapton, Elton John, Billy Joel, George Harrison, Paul McCartney, Willie Nelson, Charlie Daniels, ZZ Top, and others. He began using drugs and in 1973 almost lost his life from a heroin overdose. At that point he began to reflect on the Christian lifestyle he had been raised on.

In 1980 Mylon committed his life to Jesus and stopped performing secular music altogether. A year later he formed Mylon and Broken Heart and released *Brand New Start* on Songbird Records. In the next ten years he released a dozen albums and toured extensively. The group took a stab at mainstream rock after changing its name in 1987 to Look Up! That endeavor didn't work, but a year later the group won a Grammy for "Best Gospel Vocal Performance by a Duo, Group or Chorus" for the album *Crack the Sky*. The band received two Doves for 1988, one for "Rock Album" and the other for "Rock Record Song" for "Won by One" from the album *Crack the Sky*.

They continued to perform, but in 1989 LeFevre had a massive heart attack while touring with White Heart. Although he was advised to stop singing and touring, he released albums until 1992 when the group released a compilation album and disbanded. LeFevre then received a call to preach and formed Mylon LeFevre Ministries, based in Fort Worth, Texas.

Mylon LeFevre and his wife, Christi, are based in their church in Texas but continue to travel to worship seminars, motorcycle rallies, NASCAR, NFL, and NBA chapel services as well as to churches, revivals, and crusades to spread the gospel. They also team with Mike Barber Ministries to enter prisons and minister to the men and women housed there. In 2004 Mylon received an honorary doctorate from Life Christian University. The next year he was inducted into the Gospel Music Association Hall of Fame.

Vernell Hackett

For Further Reading

Alfonso, Barry. *The Billboard Guide to Contemporary Christian Music*. New York: Billboard Books/Watson-Guptill, 2002.

Cusic, Don. *The Sound of Light: A History of Gospel and Christian Music*. New York: Hal Leonard, 2002.

McNeil, W. K., ed. *Encyclopedia of American Gospel Music*. New York: Routledge, 2005.

Powell, Mark Allen. *Encyclopedia of Contemporary Christian Music*. Peabody, Mass.: Hendrickson Publishers, Inc., 2002.

LEWIS, CRYSTAL

Crystal Lewis (b. 1969 in Norco, California) is a powerful vocalist in the white soul tradition of Mariah Carey. An attractive fashion model, Lewis is the daughter of a Nazarene minister and began recording at 15 when she sang in the Christian musical *Hi Tops*, written by Debby Kerner and Ernie Rettino. In high school she sang lead in Wild Blue Yonder, a Christian band, and signed her first recording contract at 17.

Lewis's debut album, *Beyond the Charade*, was released on Frontline in 1987; she followed this with three more albums for that label, *Joy* (1989), *Let Love In* (1990), and *Simply the Best* (1991), before she and husband Brian Ray formed Metro One. Lewis's following album was released on that label as she worked with her producer/songwriter husband.

During 1993–1996 she was in the cast of the children's program

"Roundhouse," developed for Nickelodeon by Benny Hester, and in 1993 was a member of Shack of Peasants.

Don Cusic

For Further Reading

Alfonso, Barry. *The Billboard Guide to Contemporary Christian Music.* New York: Billboard Books/Watson-Guptill, 2002.

Powell, Mark Allen. *Encyclopedia of Contemporary Christian Music.* Peabody, Mass.: Hendrickson Publishers, Inc., 2002.

LOVE SONG

Tom Coomes
Chuck Girard
John Mehler
Jay Truax
Bob Wall

It is difficult to believe that the most influential—and popular—band in early Jesus music recorded only two studio albums, but Love Song's influence extends far beyond their recorded output. Sometimes described as the Christian Beatles, Love Song was the first band whose recordings sounded like they could be on top 40 radio.

A group of young men shared a house in Laguna Beach in the late 1960s; Chuck Girard, Jay Truax, Tommy Coomes, and Fred Field often explored spiritual ideas of philosophy and Eastern religions in conversations. Most had a background in music; Chuck Girard had been the lead singer of the Castelles, whose biggest hit was "Sacred" in 1961; later he was the lead singer for the Hondells, whose biggest hit, "Little Honda," was a top ten on the pop chart in 1964. Jay Truax had played with John Mehler in a Salt Lake City group, Spirit of Creation.

The young men began attending Calvary Chapel, where they entered a Bible study and played music. The first converts were Fred Field and Jay Truax, then Chuck Girard converted and the three gave a concert at the Orange County Fairground and invited Tom Coomes to join them to give them a better, fuller sound. Girard played keyboards, Truax played bass, and Field and Coomes played guitar. During that concert, Tom Coomes was converted to Jesus on stage. These were the original members of Love Song, which formed in 1970. They soon added drummer John Mehler.

The sounds of Crosby, Stills, and Nash were on the radio; they had hits with "Suite: Judy Blue Eyes," "Woodstock," "Teach Your Children," and "Ohio" during the 1969–1970 period. The Eagles had their first radio hits in 1972 with "Take It Easy" and "Witchy Woman;" America's first hits, "A Horse with No Name" and "Ventura Highway," came in 1972; and Bread had their first hits, "Make It with You" and "It Don't Matter to Me," in 1970. Of course, the Beach Boys and Beatles were popular throughout the 1960s and early 1970s. The sound of Love Song, with an eclectic mix of folk, acoustic rock, and country with blended harmonies reflected this musical stew in Southern California.

Calvary Chapel started a label, Maranatha, and released *The Everlastin' Living Jesus Music Concert*, a compilation album of Calvary Chapel artists in concert that was released in 1971. Love Song contributed a song to that album.

MGM executive Freddie Piro formed Good News Records and signed Love Song to his label.

Their first album, *Love Song*, was released in 1972, but there had been some personnel changes. Fred Field was on their cut on *The Everlastin' Living Jesus Music Concert* but was replaced by Bob Wall for the debut *Love Song* album. Field and John Mehler formed the group Noah, but Mehler returned to Love Song for their second album.

Their debut album sold 250,000 units, a huge amount for an unknown band. The group toured constantly and often performed at Knott's Berry Farm, where they drew huge crowds.

During the 1970–1974 period Love Song became the first stars of what later became known as contemporary Christian music. They were not the first Jesus music band—that honor belongs to Children of the Day—but Love Song played songs that sounded like some of the top radio hits of the day while Children of the Day were rooted in the folk sound of Peter, Paul and Mary, which had given way to a more rock-based sound by the early 1970s.

Their concerts were considered spiritual happenings, "anointed," and immersed in a warm feeling of Christian community rather than a "concert." Those who attended did not go to hear the music but rather to feel the presence of the Holy Spirit. There was a joy, a happiness, and a heart-filling emotional experience at a Love Song concert. The early converts during the Jesus movement felt an inner peace and joy when they accepted Jesus and embraced the Christian lifestyle as a reflection of that inner conversion. Most of the songs of the Jesus movement were personal and joyous, celebrating their discovery of the transformational power of Jesus and their discovery of a Christian community that shared their joy and beliefs.

The second album from Love Song, *Final Touch*, was released in 1974, and then the group broke up. By this time, Phil Keaggy had replaced Wall as the group's lead guitarist, although Keaggy did not play on their second album. A farewell tour followed and then, in 1977, a live album, *Feel the Love*, was released; it was recorded during a one-time reunion tour.

After the group disbanded, Coomes, Mehler, and Truax formed Wing and a Prayer with Tom Stipe of Country Faith and Al Perkins. Later, Truax and Mehler became part of Richie Furay's band and Coomes became an executive with Maranatha Music.

Many consider *Love Song* the *Sgt. Pepper's Lonely Hearts Club Band* of Christian music. Unlike Sgt. Pepper's, the Love Song album sounds a bit dated in the 21st century but brings those listeners who lived during that era and were part of the early Jesus movement back to that time and place. Young fans who grew up on synthesizer layered rock of the 1980s or rap and hip hop have a harder time relating to the album, but can generally relate to the music if they (or their parents) listen to oldies stations.

In 1995 Love Song was revived and produced a final album, *Welcome Back*.

Don Cusic

Discography

Love Song (1972)

Final Touch (1974)

Feel the Love (1977)

Welcome Back (1995)

For Further Reading

Alfonso, Barry. *The Billboard Guide to Contemporary Christian Music.* New York: Billboard Books/Watson-Guptill, 2002.

Baker, Paul. *Contemporary Christian Music: Where It Came from, What It Is, Where It's Going.* Westchester, Ill.: Crossway, 1985.

Brothers, Jeffrey Lee. *CCM Magazine Hot Hits: Adult Contemporary Charts 1978–2001.* Bloomington, Ind.: 1stBooks Library, 2003

Cusic, Don. *The Sound of Light: A History of Gospel and Christian Music.* New York: Hal Leonard, 2002.

Ellwood, Robert S., Jr. *One Way: The Jesus Movement and Its Meaning.* Englewood Cliffs, N.J.: Prentice-Hall, 1973

Enroth, Ronald M., Edward E. Ericson, Jr. and C. Breckinridge Peters. *The Jesus People: Old-Time Religion in the Age of Aquarius.* Grand Rapids, Mich.: Eerdmans, 1972.

Granger, Thom, ed. *CCM Presents the 100 Greatest Albums in Christian Music.* Eugene, Ore.: Harvest House, 2001.

McNeil, W. K., ed. *Encyclopedia of American Gospel Music.* New York: Routledge, 2005.

Powell, Mark Allen. *Encyclopedia of Contemporary Christian Music.* Peabody, Mass.: Hendrickson Publishers, Inc., 2002.

Styll, John W. ed. *The Heart of the Matter: The Best of CCM Interviews, Volume 1.* Nashville, Tenn.: Star Song, 1991.

Thompson, John J. *Raised by Wolves: The Story of Christian Rock and Roll.* Toronto: ECW Press, 2000.

M

MATTHEWS, RANDY

Randy Matthews is one of most important of the pioneering acts who was a bridge between the worlds of Jesus music and contemporary Christian music. Matthews is the son of Monty Matthews, one of founding members of the Jordanaires, who became the major backing group for Elvis Presley's recordings.

Matthews joined the Revelations, a southern gospel quartet, after high school and attended Ozark Bible College. After two years with the singing group, Matthews enrolled at Cincinnati Bible Seminary, where he began writing and singing folk songs during a period when folk music was popular.

Matthews's album, *I Wish We'd All Been Ready*, was the first Jesus music album released on Word Records; it was produced by Billy Ray Hearn, and Matthews had the opportunity because his father had recorded earlier for Word. The album was pretty tame by rock standards; still it raised some eyebrows in the traditional Christian community among those who were unsure about the Jesus movement.

Matthews and Arthur Blessit organized Spiritual Revolution Day in Cincinnati, and both young men carried large crosses through downtown that day. The Jesus House ministry center was formed after this event. Matthews second album, *All I Am Is What You See*, was initially rejected by Word, whose executives were nervous about upsetting their traditional audience. This led Matthews to suggest they form another label imprint for contemporary music, and Myrrh Records was formed with Billy Ray Hearn as label head; that label released his second album.

The third album from Matthews, *Son of Dust*, was folk rock with a blues influence, and it kicked up quite a bit of dust. The album was released after Matthews appeared on Explo '72; his performance of "Didn't He" was a defining moment in that concert. Matthews's following album, *Now Do You Understand?*, released in 1975, was a two-record live set with just Matthews and his guitar.

In 1974 Matthews toured with a rock band as the opening act for ZZ Top and Lynyrd Skynyrd; just before the tour he took his band to the Jesus '74 Festival in Pennsylvania, where concert organizers pulled the plug in the middle of his third song, claiming the music was "demonic." That event was a defining moment in Matthews's career; future bookings at Christian events were cancelled and his career in Christian music was basically over.

Matthews album *Eyes to the Sky* was released on Myrrh; he then joined a trio, Matthews, Taylor and Johnson, but Matthews was bitter at the Christian audience for the way he was treated during and after the Pennsylvania festival. He began using drugs before he recorded and released two albums on Spirit, *Plugged In* and *Edge of Flight*.

Matthews left Christian music, became an ordained Baptist minister in Florida, and opened a store that sold Native American art.

Don Cusic

For Further Reading

Alfonso, Barry. *The Billboard Guide to Contemporary Christian Music.* New York: Billboard Books/Watson-Guptill, 2002.

Cusic, Don. *The Sound of Light: A History of Gospel and Christian Music.* New York: Hal Leonard, 2002.

Powell, Mark Allen. *Encyclopedia of Contemporary Christian Music.* Peabody, Mass.: Hendrickson Publishers, Inc., 2002.

MCCRACKEN, JARRELL

Jarrell McCracken was the founder and head of the largest label for contemporary Christian music during the 1970s and early 1980s, when contemporary Christian music fully established itself as a genre.

McCracken (b. November 18, 1927) was the son of a Baptist minister who grew up in Dodge City, Kansas and graduated from Baylor University in Waco, Texas, with a degree in speech and religion; in 1953 he received a masters degree in religion in history.

During his college years, McCracken worked as a disc jockey at KWTX, a local radio station, and served as the announcer for Pittsburgh's Class B farm team, the Waco Pirates. In 1950 McCracken was approached by Ted Nichols, a Baptist youth minister from Hearne, Texas (about 60 miles south of Waco), to speak to a group on Christianity and football. An article by Jimmy Allen about a football game between the forces of good and evil inspired McCracken to compose "The Game of Life," where the opposing teams were coached by Jesus and Satan. McCracken recorded the play by play on tape and sent it to Nichols; he soon received requests for additional copies. McCracken paid for 100 discs of the 78 rpm record to be pressed and named the label Word after the fictional radio station in his presentation, WORD.

In 1974 McCracken and Marvin Norcross sold Word to the American Broadcasting Company for $7 million; McCracken remained president of the label until 1987. After leaving Word, McCracken bred and raised Egyptian Arabian horses at his farm; however, during the late 1980s his farm, Bentwood Farms, was forced to file Chapter 11 bankruptcy after an economic recession hit the oil, real estate, and banking markets. McCracken had Alzheimer's and died on November 7, 2007.

Don Cusic

For Further Reading

Cusic, Don. *The Sound of Light: A History of Gospel and Christian Music.* New York: Hal Leonard, 2002.

McNeil, W. K., ed. *Encyclopedia of American Gospel Music.* New York: Routledge, 2005.

MCGUIRE, BARRY

Barry McGuire (b. October 15, 1935) was an early celebrity convert to Christianity. As the lead singer for the New Christy Minstrels, a 1960s era folk group started by Randy Sparks, he wrote the biggest hit for that group, "Green Green" (1963), then embarked on a solo career. He had a number one pop hit with "Eve of Destruction" in 1965, but McGuire's life plunged into drug abuse and self-destruction before his conversion to Christianity. After that conversion McGuire turned his talents to contemporary Christian music and became a major force in that field during the 1970s and early 1980s.

Born in Oklahoma, McGuire moved to California with his mother after his parents divorced. After high school he enlisted in the Navy and purchased his first guitar when he was 25. He began performing in Santa Monica bars, where he was "discovered" by Peggy Lee and her producer, Fred Briskin. This led to a recording contract with Mosaic Records in 1961, but he had no hits on that label. In 1962 McGuire joined the New Christy Minstrels and remained with them three years; during that time they sang at the White House for President Lyndon Johnson and hosted a summer replacement TV show. In January 1965, McGuire left the New Christy Minstrels and began work with producer Lou Adler, who introduced him to P. F. Sloan, who wrote "Eve of Destruction." That song became a counterculture mainstay during the mid-1960s.

McGuire's success led him to several roles in movies and then as a lead in the original cast of *Hair*. However, by 1971 McGuire's health deteriorated, a result of extensive drug use. That year he met a member of Arthur Blessitt's outreach and was given a copy of *Good News for Modern Man*, a paperback edition of the New Testament. According to McGuire, "I was 35 years old and had never read the New Testament in my life. It blew me away! I discovered the truth I'd been looking for so many years. It was Jesus!" He was baptized on Father's Day in 1971.

McGuire became part of Agape Force, a Christian community in Sanger, California, and began singing Christian music. He met recording engineer Buck Herring and recorded his first Christian album, *Seeds*, for Myrrh in 1973. Singing back-up on McGuire's album was Herring's wife, Annie, and her two siblings, later known as 2nd Chapter of Acts.

In 1975 McGuire recorded *To the Bride*, a live album with 2nd Chapter of Acts and toured constantly. He became one of the first acts signed to Sparrow, a fledgling label started by Billy Ray Hearn, former head of McGuire's previous label, Myrrh.

His biggest hits in Christian music came in 1978 with the single "Cosmic Cowboy" and his recording of "Bullfrogs and Butterflies" on a children's album by Agape Force. McGuire toured for World Vision, and in 1979 he performed at the White House for President Jimmy Carter.

In 1984 McGuire became disillusioned with contemporary Christian music and moved to New Zealand, where his wife was from. McGuire worked full time for World Vision while in New Zealand and stayed there until 1990, when he moved back to the United States.

During the mid-1990s McGuire returned to performing, touring with Terry Talbot as Terry and Barry to support Mercy Corps, a Catholic relief organization. In 2004 McGuire and his wife moved back to New Zealand.

Don Cusic

Discography

The Barry McGuire Album (1963)

The New Christy Minstrels in Person (1963)

The New Christy Minstrels Tell Tall Tales, Legends and Nonsense (1963)

Merry Christmas (1963)

Ramblin' Featuring Green, Green (1963)

Land of Giants (1964)

Today (1964)

Barry McGuire, Featuring Eve of Destruction (1965)

Chim Chim Cheree (1965)

Cowboys and Indians (1965)

Star Folk with Barry McGuire (1965)

This Precious Time (1965)

Greatest Hits (1966)

Star Folk Vol. 2 with Barry McGuire (1966)

The World's Last Private Citizen (1967)

Barry McGuire and the Doctor (1971)

Seeds (1973)

Lighten Up (1974)

Jubilation (1975)

To the Bride (with 2nd Chapter of Acts) (1975)

C'mon Along (1976)

Anyone but Jesus (1976)

Firewind (1976)

Jubilation Too (1976)

Have You Heard (1977)

Bullfrogs and Butterflies (1978)

Cosmic Cowboy (1978)

The Witness (1978)

Inside Out (1979)

Best of Barry McGuire (1980)

Polka Dot Bear (1980)

Exaltation (1981)

Finer Than Gold (1981)

Pilgrim (1989)

El Dorado (1990)

Let's Tend God's Earth (1991)

Adventures on Son Mountain (1993)

When Dinosaurs Walked the Earth (1996)

Ancient Garden (1997)

Frost and Fire (1999)

Live (2000)

For Further Reading

Alfonso, Barry. *The Billboard Guide to Contemporary Christian Music*. New York: Billboard Books/Watson-Guptill, 2002.

Cusic, Don. *The Sound of Light: A History of Gospel and Christian Music*. New York: Hal Leonard, 2002.

McNeil, W. K., ed. *Encyclopedia of American Gospel Music*. New York: Routledge, 2005.

Powell, Mark Allen. *Encyclopedia of Contemporary Christian Music.* Peabody, Mass.: Hendrickson Publishers, Inc., 2002.

MEECE, DAVID

David Meece's (b. May 26, 1952, in Humble, Texas) background as a concert pianist is heard in his songs, which are often pop-flavored adult contemporary tunes with upbeat lyrics. As a child he was a prodigy on the piano; he performed classical works on the piano at ten and performed with the Houston Chamber Orchestra when he was 14; at 15 he toured Europe with Youth for Christ after winning a talent contest and was the featured soloist with the Houston Symphony under the direction of Andre Previn when he was 16. A scholarship to the Peabody Conservatory of Music in Baltimore, Maryland, led him to a serious study of classical piano as well as a Christian commitment. At Peabody he also met his future wife, Debbie, who majored in viola.

Meece's first album was released in 1976, and he released an album almost every year for more than a decade. After he was a successful contemporary Christian artist, established in the CCM world, he confronted the fact that his father was an abusive alcoholic and he made that public, encouraging others with abusive childhoods to confront those childhood demons. In 2003 he broadcast his story on a two-day broadcast on Focus on the Family the week before Father's Day.

Don Cusic

For Further Reading

Alfonso, Barry. *The Billboard Guide to Contemporary Christian Music.* New York: Billboard Books/Watson-Guptill, 2002.

Cusic, Don. *The Sound of Light: A History of Gospel and Christian Music.* New York: Hal Leonard, 2002.

McNeil, W. K., ed. *Encyclopedia of American Gospel Music.* New York: Routledge, 2005.

Powell, Mark Allen. *Encyclopedia of Contemporary Christian Music.* Peabody, Mass.: Hendrickson Publishers, Inc., 2002.

MERCYME

Bart Millard, vocals
Barry Graul, guitar
Mike Scheuchzer, guitar
Jim Bryson, keyboards
Nathan Cochran, bass
Robby Shaffer, drums

MercyMe is best known for their song, "I Can Only Imagine," written by group member Bart Millard when his father died of cancer. That song reached number one on the Christian charts in 2001, crossed over to the adult contemporary, pop, and country charts, and was voted "Song of the Year" at the Gospel Music Association Dove Awards in 2002.

Bart Millard grew up in Greenville, Texas, and had to enroll in chorus after he broke his ankles playing high school football. Encouraged by both his choral teacher and music minister at church, Millard began to sing more and do solos. During Millard's first year in college, his father died—a result of cancer he contracted five years before—and Millard felt like he needed a new start, so he moved to Lakeland, Florida, at the invitation of his youth pastor, who had moved there. The youth pastor invited Mark to sing with the church's praise band, which played for Wednesday evening services.

Millard met keyboard player Jim Bryson at a youth convention, and the two led a worship team that traveled to Europe in the summer of 1994. The two felt they were being led toward a full time music ministry, so when they returned, guitarist Mike Scheuchzer joined them and they moved to Oklahoma City, which was Bryson's home town. They performed in and around Oklahoma City and opened for Audio Adrenaline, which brought them to the attention of Audio's manager, Scott Brickell, who encouraged them to move to Nashville to pursue their career; they did, but after a year decided to move to Dallas, Texas. During their time in Nashville they performed at a showcase for label executives but realized they were drawn to praise and worship. With their new ministry focus, the group soon found themselves in demand for Christian youth conferences, churches, and youth gatherings; along the way the group added Barry Graul, Robby Shaffer, and Nathan Cochran.

MercyMe was soon overwhelmed by their success and demand for CDs; when they reached the point where they could no longer meet the business demands of their ministry, they signed with INO Records and Scott Brickell with Brickhouse Entertainment.

Don Cusic

Discography

Pleased to Meet You (1995)

Traces of Rain, Vol. 1 (1997)

Traces of Rain, Vol. 2 (1997)

The Worship Project (1999)

Look (2000)

The Need (2000)

Almost There (2001)

Spoken For (2002)

Undone (2004)

The Christmas Sessions (2005)

Coming Up to Breathe (2006)

All That Is Within Me (2007)

Gospel Music Association Dove Awards

2002	Pop/Contemporary Recorded Song of the Year: "I Can Only Imagine" from album *Almost There*; Artist: MercyMe; Songwriter: Bart Millard; Label: INO
2002	Song of the Year: "I Can Only Imagine," by Bart Millard; Publisher: Simpleville Music (ASCAP)
2002	Songwriter of the Year: Bart Millard
2004	Artist of the Year: MercyMe
2004	Group of the Year: MercyMe
2004	Pop/Contemporary Recorded Song of the Year: "Word of God Speak"; from the album *Spoken For*; Artist: MercyMe; Songwriters: Bart Millard, Pete Kipley; Label: INO
2004	Song of the Year: "Word of God Speak" by Pete Kipley, Bart Millard; Publishers:

Wordspring Music/Songs from the Indigo Room (SESAC), Simpleville Music (ASCAP)

2005 Pop/Contemporary Album of the Year: *Undone*; Artist: MercyMe; Producer: Pete Kipley; Label: INO Records

2005 Special Event Album of the Year: *The Passion of the Christ: Songs*; Artists: Third Day, Steven Curtis Chapman, MercyMe, Scott Stap, POD, Brad Paisley, Sara Evans, Big Dismal, Lauryn Hill, Kirk Franklin, Yolanda Adams, MxPx, Mark Hoppus, Charlotte Church, BeBe Winans, Angie Stone, Dan Lavery; Tim Cook, Mark Joseph, Gregg Wattenberg, Steven Lemer; Label: Lost Keyword Records/ Wind-Up Records

2006 Inspirational Album of the Year: (Tie) *Hymned*; Artist: Bart Millard; Producers: Brown Bannister, Bart Millard; Label: Simple Records/INO Records; *Rock of Ages . . . Hymns and Faith*; Artist: Amy Grant; Producers: Brown Bannister, Vince Gill; Label: Word Records

For Further Reading

Powell, Mark Allen. *Encyclopedia of Contemporary Christian Music*. Peabody, Mass.: Hendrickson Publishers, Inc., 2002.

MIGHTY CLOUDS OF JOY

Joe Ligon, vocals
Richard Wallace, vocals

Elmo Franklin, vocals (until 1999)
Johnny Martin (until 1987)
Ermant Franklin, vocals (until 1977)
David Walker, vocals (until 1977)
Paul Beasley (1980–1987)
Johnny Valentine, vocals (1980–1991; since 1999)
Michael McCowin, vocals (since 1991)
Ron Staples, vocals (since 1999)
Tim Woodson (since 1999)

The Mighty Clouds of Joy are a legendary black gospel group who have combined the sounds of contemporary Christian music with their traditional sound. They were originally formed in 1955 by Jimmy Jones, who was joined by Leon Polk around 1960, but both of these young men left the group before it made any recordings.

The founding members of the current group are considered to be Joe Ligon and Richard Wallace with Johnny Valentine, a long-time member of the group. Formed in Los Angeles, the group's first recording was "Steal Away to Jesus" in 1960 for Peacock Records; they recorded for that label for more than a decade and became one of the first black gospel groups to add drums and bass to their albums.

Although they were based in Los Angeles, they were not part of the contemporary Christian music scene that emerged around them; instead, they performed in clubs and concert halls, appeared on TV's "Soul Train" show, and opened shows for Earth, Wind and Fire, the Rolling Stones, and Paul Simon.

The group was not part of contemporary Christian music until they signed with Myrrh Records in 1980 and released their album *Cloudburst*. They recorded a string of albums for this Christian label, including *Miracle Man*

(1982), *Mighty Clouds Alive* (1982), *Sing and Shout* (1983), *Catching On* (1987), and *Night Song* (1989), before joining MCA Records.

Don Cusic

For Further Reading

Carpenter, Bil. *Uncloudy Days: The Gospel Music Encyclopedia*. San Francisco: Backbeat, 2005.

Cusic, Don. *The Sound of Light: A History of Gospel and Christian Music*. New York: Hal Leonard, 2002.

Darden, Bob. *People Get Ready!: A New History of Black Gospel Music*. New York: Continuum, 2005.

Jackson, Jerma A. *Singing in My Soul: Black Gospel Music in a Secular Age*. Chapel Hill: University of North Carolina Press, 2004.

McNeil, W. K., ed. *Encyclopedia of American Gospel Music*. New York: Routledge, 2005.

Powell, Mark Allen. *Encyclopedia of Contemporary Christian Music*. Peabody, Mass.: Hendrickson Publishers, Inc., 2002.

Young, Alan. *Woke Me Up This Morning: Black Gospel Singers and the Gospel Life*. Jackson: University Press of Mississippi, 1997.

Zolten, Jerry. *Great God A'Mighty: The Dixie Hummingbirds: Celebrating the Rise of Soul Gospel Music*. New York: Oxford University Press, 2003.

MILLER, BUDDY AND JULIE

The husband and wife team of Buddy (b. September 6, 1952, in Fairborn, Ohio) and Julie Miller (b. July 12, 1956, in Waxahachie, Texas) records a wide range of music with roots in country and gospel and lyrics with many spiritual overtones. They record separately and together, depending on the project that they are involved in. Buddy began his musical career in the late 1960s, playing upright bass in a high school bluegrass band. Julie lived in Waxahachie, Texas, for seven years before moving to Austin. That move set the stage for her later interest in music as the city was beginning to emerge as one of the most eclectic music towns in America: it birthed a combination of rock, blues, country, folk, and border styles that became known as Texas music. As Julie listened to music in this atmosphere she found herself wandering from the singer-songwriter influences of Jerry Jeff Walker to the blues of Muddy Waters and then on the folk/rock sounds of Emmylou Harris and Gram Parsons. She began singing professionally when she was 16 and soon became the girl singer in a band that included her future husband, Buddy Miller.

The two traveled to New York, Los Angeles, and finally on to Nashville, where they stopped in 1993. After moving to Nashville, Miller worked as a guitarist on records by country singer Trisha Yearwood and alt-country's Jim Lauderdale. He recorded his first album in 1983 and has also recorded with Julie, who cowrote several songs for the debut release, *Your Love and Other Lies*. He and Julie have similar themes to their music, writing what some have called gospel-country-protest songs. The tunes are socially conscious with definite word images of Buddy's interpretation of what he thinks God might observe on some of the things humanity is so caught up in today. This theme is evident on Julie's first recording, a mini-LP titled *Streetlight,* which included the original version of "Jesus in Your Eyes." The tune also appeared on her *Orphans and Angels* album.

The two teamed with Jim Lauderdale, Victoria Williams, and Mark Olson for a tour of Europe as the Rolling Creek Dippers. In 1997 and 1998 Julie joined her husband on tour with Emmylou Harris and Steve Earle in the United States and overseas. Julie got a break in her career when Sam Phillips found a demo tape of hers and gave it to friends at the Christian label Myrrh Records. Her first album for the label, *Meet Julie Miller,* was released in 1990 with background vocals by Amy Grant, Russ Taff, Shawn Colvin, Victoria Williams, and Kelly Willard. In 1999 Julie recorded her album *Broken Things* at their home studio. Buddy coproduced the album and played a number of different instruments on it. Julie wrote all the songs with the exception of the traditional "Two Soldiers." Emmylou Harris contributed background vocals and harmonies to the disc.

The songs of Julie and Buddy Miller are secular but ring with spiritual overtones. Many examine the battle of good and evil, things of this world, and things more spiritual. The 1992 release, *Cry of the Heart: Emily's Eyes*, was an album that sought to bring a focus on the victims of child abuse, and Julie wrote the title track. Buddy's 2004 album, *Universal House of Prayer,* with a guest appearance by Julie, is considered by some to be his most passionate gospel offering since 1995's *Sacred Cows: Man on the Moon.* The

album also features Emmylou Harris, Phil Madeira, and Regina and Ann McCrary.

Both Buddy and Julie have had songs cut by other artists; Julie has had songs recorded by the Dixie Chicks, Linda Ronstadt, Emmylou Harris, Brooks and Dunn, Jars of Clay, and Lee Ann Womack. Buddy's songwriting prowess was noticed by folks like country music's Dixie Chicks, Lee Ann Womack, and Brooks and Dunn. Buddy also wears the hat of producer, having worked with Solomon Burke, Jimmie Dale Gilmore, Jim Lauderdale, and Emmylou Harris. He toured with and played guitar for Emmylou's Spyboy Band, Steve Earle, Shawn Colvin, and Linda Ronstadt. He also toured with Robert Plant and Alison Krauss on their Raising Sand tour of the United States and Europe in 2008.

Vernell Hackett

For Further Reading

Alfonso, Barry. *The Billboard Guide to Contemporary Christian Music.* New York: Billboard Books/Watson-Guptill, 2002.

Powell, Mark Allen. *Encyclopedia of Contemporary Christian Music.* Peabody, Mass.: Hendrickson Publishers, Inc., 2002.

MOORE, GEOFF

Geoff Moore's (b. February 21, 1961, in Flint, Michigan) first three albums were released as a solo artist; however, when he signed with Sparrow Records, that label released his albums as Geoff Moore and the Distance, beginning with *A Place to Stand* in 1988. In the

Distance were Dale Oliver, guitar (1987–1990); Arlin Troyer, bass (1987–1990); Tom Reynolds, keyboards (1987–1989); Geoff Barkley, keyboards (1989–1998); Greg Herrington, drums (1989–1995); Roscoe Meek, guitar (1990–1995); Gary Mullett, bass (1990–1998); Chuck Conner, drums (1995–1998); Joel McCreight, guitars (1996–1998); Dale Oliver, guitars (1987–1989); and Lang Bliss, drums, 1987–1989).

In 1998 Moore disbanded the Distance and resumed a solo career.

An avid outdoorsman, Geoff Moore is the son of a former professional baseball player (with the Toledo Mud Hens) who ran a steel fabrication plant after his playing days. Moore studied business administration at Taylor University in Fort Wayne, Indiana, but dropped out after three years when his father died. Moore moved back to his hometown of Flint with the intention of taking up his father's business of steel fabrication but, after a short while, decided to pursue a career in contemporary Christian music because he felt God was calling him to do this.

In the early 1980s, Moore and his young wife moved to Nashville, where he landed a job in a men's clothing store; there, he met Michael W. Smith, who had come to purchase some clothes. Through Smith, Moore landed at Paragon Publishing, where he met Steven Curtis Chapman when he sang on the demo for one of Chapman's songs. The two hit it off and began writing together.

Geoff Moore released his first album, *Where Are the Other Nine?*, in 1984 on the Power Disc label; he recorded two others for that label, *Over the Edge* and *The Distance*. Moore then signed with Sparrow Records, and the label released his albums as Geoff Moore and the Distance, beginning with *A Place to Stand* in 1988.

In 1998 Moore disbanded the Distance and resumed a solo career; the follow year he released *Geoff Moore*. His album *A Beautiful Sound* moved away from the rock sound he had cultivated with the Distance and toward an acoustic sound.

Moore and his wife have two sons and have adopted two girls from China; Moore has been involved with Compassion International since 1995.

Don Cusic

For Further Reading

Alfonso, Barry. *The Billboard Guide to Contemporary Christian Music*. New York: Billboard Books/Watson-Guptill, 2002.

Powell, Mark Allen. *Encyclopedia of Contemporary Christian Music*. Peabody, Mass.: Hendrickson Publishers, Inc., 2002.

MULLEN, DAVID

David Mullen (b. 1964) grew up in Cullman, Alabama, and graduated from the University of Florida with a degree in biology. Playing a game of Trivial Pursuit with friends led to a discussion of the Bible, which, in turn, led Mullen to read the entire Bible in a month. Through this he came to Jesus. He moved to Nashville to be part of contemporary Christian music, toured with a band, One Blood, then met and married Nicole Coleman. David is involved in the Veggie Tales movies and songs, writing songs and producing sessions.

Mullen won the "New Artist of the Year" Dove Award for 1990 and his song, "On My Knees," cowritten with his wife, Nicole Coleman-Mullens, and Michael Ochs, won the Dove for "Song of the Year" in 1988.

Don Cusic

For Further Reading

Alfonso, Barry. *The Billboard Guide to Contemporary Christian Music*. New York: Billboard Books/Watson-Guptill, 2002.

Powell, Mark Allen. *Encyclopedia of Contemporary Christian Music*. Peabody, Mass.: Hendrickson Publishers, Inc., 2002.

MULLEN, NICOLE

Nicole Mullen (b. Nicole Coleman on June 26, 1967, in Cincinnati, Ohio) is an African American woman who has attracted primarily a white audience in contemporary Christian music; she is married to artist, songwriter, and producer David Mullen, and the two are one of the only interracial couples in that genre.

Both of Nicole's grandfathers were Pentecostal preachers; she grew up in Cincinnati but moved to Dallas in 1984 where she attended Bible college and sang with the group Living Praise. Her talent brought her to the attention of producer Tim Miner, who recorded her as a female rap artist; that album did not succeed.

She moved to Nashville and sang backup with Amy Grant and Michael W. Smith on their tours and also did choreography for Grant. She was an in-demand session singer and wrote the song "On My Knees" for Jaci Velasquez. In 1998 that song (cowritten with David Mullen and Michael Ochs) won "Song of the Year" honors from the Gospel Music Association. In 2001 she won two Doves for her song, "Redeemer": "Song of the Year" and "Pop/Contemporary Recording." That same year she won the Dove for "Songwriter of the Year" and the following year won the Dove for "Female Vocalist of the Year." In 2005 she was again awarded the "Female Vocalist" trophy by the Gospel Music Association.

Don Cusic

For Further Reading

Alfonso, Barry. *The Billboard Guide to Contemporary Christian Music*. New York: Billboard Books/Watson-Guptill, 2002.

Powell, Mark Allen. *Encyclopedia of Contemporary Christian Music*. Peabody, Mass.: Hendrickson Publishers, Inc., 2002.

MULLINS, RICH

In his short life, Rich Mullins (b. October 21, 1955, in Richmond, Indiana; d. September 19, 1997) had a tremendous impact on contemporary Christian music. He wrote "Awesome God," which became a hit for Amy Grant as well as a standard sung in churches.

Mullins was a man of great conviction who took to heart the Quaker principles of peace and social justice that he learned when attending the Arba Friends Meeting in Lynn, Indiana. The early guidance he received in those services served him throughout his short life. Mullins started playing piano when he was four, then went on to learn guitar, hammered dulcimer, and tin whistle. Mullins sang in his high school choir; he then attended Cincinnati Bible College from 1974 to 1978, where music was his focus.

Mullins formed his first band in college, and during his last three years there he was music and youth director at Erlanger United Methodist Church in Erlanger, Kentucky. In the late 1970s Mullins worked with Zion Ministries and performed during that time with Zion, a band that released one album, *Behold the Man*. While working for Zion Ministries, Mullins wrote "Sing Your Praise to the Lord," which became a hit for Amy Grant in 1982. A year later Debby Boone recorded Mullins's "O Come All Ye Faithful," which was later featured in a television movie, *Sins of the Past*.

Mullins moved to Nashville in the 1980s to hone his skills as a songwriter; in 1988 he moved to Wichita, Kansas; and in 1991 he became a student at Friends University, sharing a home with his best friend, Mark Hoffmann. Mullins received a B.A. in music education on May 14, 1995, and he and friend Mitch McVicker moved to the Tse Bonito Navajo reservation in New Mexico, where they taught music to Native American children. Mullins continued to record after leaving Nashville, and some of his best-known songs came after his Nashville years. His third album, *Winds of Heaven, Stuff of Earth*, produced the worship song "Awesome God," one of the best-known praise and worship songs of all time. His collaboration with other musicians resulted in *A Liturgy, A Legacy and A Ragamuffin Band* in 1993, after he was in New Mexico on the

reservation. Another of Mullins's projects was based on his interest in St. Francis of Assisi. Mullins, Beaker, and McVicker wrote a musical, *Canticle of the Plains*, which told the life of St. Francis set in America during the days of the old West.

Like St. Francis, Mullins lived a simple life. All the money he made from his tours and album sales was given to his church. The church paid Mullins the average salary in the United States for that year, and the rest of the money went to charity. Mullins was a supporter of Compassion International and Compassion USA.

Mullins continued to tour while living in New Mexico. As he and McVicker traveled to a benefit concert in Wichita, Kansas, on September 19, 1997, the Jeep they were riding in flipped over on I-39 just north of Bloomington, Illinois; Mullins died and was buried beside his baby brother, who died as an infant, and his father, in Hollansburg, Ohio. Interestingly, Mullins had been studying the Catholic faith and he was going to be baptized into the church the Monday after his death.

Not long before the accident, Mullins recorded a rough mix of a project he was working on called *Ten Songs about Jesus*. It was a concept album about the life of Christ. The rough mix was released as the first disc of the project *The Jesus Record*. A second disc, featuring the Ragamuffin Band along with Amy Grant, Michael W. Smith, Ashley Cleveland, and Phil Keaggy, was also released. In 1998, a tribute album, *Awesome God: A Tribute to Rich Mullins*, was released. Mullins's family founded a foundation, the Legacy of a Kid Brother of St. Frank, which continues his mission to develop programs of art, drama, and music camps for Native American youth. A collection of Rich's columns from his six years with *Release* magazine was published in 2004. Several books have been written about Mullins, including *An Arrow Pointing to Heaven* by his friend James Bryan Smith.

Vernell Hackett

For Further Reading

Alfonso, Barry. *The Billboard Guide to Contemporary Christian Music*. New York: Billboard Books/Watson-Guptill, 2002.

McNeil, W. K., ed. *Encyclopedia of American Gospel Music*. New York: Routledge, 2005.

Mullins, Rich. *Home*. Orlando, Fla.: Voxcorp, 1998.

Mullins, Rich. *Simply*. Orlando, Fla.: Voxcorp, 2005.

Mullins, Rich. *The World as I Remember It, Through the Eyes of a Ragamuffin*. Colorado Springs, Colo.: Multnomah, 2004.

Powell, Mark Allen. *Encyclopedia of Contemporary Christian Music*. Peabody, Mass.: Hendrickson Publishers, Inc., 2002.

MUSTARD SEED FAITH

Pedro Buford, keyboards, flute, vocals
Oden Fong, vocals, guitar
Wade Link, guitar, vocals (until 1975)
Lewis McVay, drums, vocals

Mustard Seed Faith came out of Calvary Chapel in the early 1970s after Love Song, Children of the Day, and the Way had paved the way for Jesus music bands. They came during a transitional period as Jesus music evolved into contemporary Christian music. Their songs were on several Maranatha compilation albums; "Happy in Jesus" was on *Maranatha Three*, released in 1973, and "All I Know" was on *Maranatha Four*, released in 1974. Their only album, *Sail on Sailor*, was released in 1975; most of the songs were written by Oden Fong. The group toured until 1977 when, burnt out from being on the road, they disbanded. Group members Oden Fong and Lewis McVay then released solo projects.

Don Cusic

For Further Reading

Powell, Mark Allen. *Encyclopedia of Contemporary Christian Music*. Peabody, Mass.: Hendrickson Publishers, Inc., 2002.

Thompson, John J. *Raised by Wolves: The Story of Christian Rock and Roll*. Toronto, Ontario: ECW Press, 2000.

N

NEWSBOYS, THE

Peter Furler, vocals, drums
(since 1985)
John James, vocals (1985–1998)
Sean Taylor, bass (1985–1994)
George Perdkis, guitar (1985–1990)
Jonathan Geange, guitar (1990–1991)
Corey Pryor, keyboards (1991–1994)
Vernon Bishop, guitar (1991–1992)
Kevin Mills, bass (1994–1996)
Jeff Frankenstein, keyboards
(since 1996)
Duncan Phillips, percussion
(since 1996)
Philip Urry, bass, vocals (1996–1998)
Phil Joel, bass (since 1998)
Jody Brian Davis, guitar

The Newsboys are an Australian band formed in 1985 in Mooloolaba; the founding members were vocalist John James, drummer Peter Furler, bassist Sean Taylor, and guitarist George Perdikis. The band was quite popular in Australia; since there weren't many Christian bands in that country, they often opened for American Christian bands touring Australia; during their time Down Under they opened for Phil Keaggy, David Meece, Petra, and White Heart.

The band was originally called the News and kept that name until they came to the United States in early 1988, when they changed to the Newsboys. They first moved to Los Angeles and played the church circuit of youth groups as well as the Atlanta Christian Music Festival.

The band's first three albums, *Read All about It* (Refuge, 1988), *Hell Is for Wimps* (StarSong, 1990), and *Boys Will Be Boyz* (StarSong, 1991), met with moderate success, but their fourth album, *Not Ashamed*, released in 1994 was produced by Steve Taylor and resulted in hit singles on Christian radio. Taylor was more than a producer; he wrote songs for the group and became a quasi-member. Since the band did not have a guitarist during this period, Dave Perkins played guitar on the album. The band added members Phillip Joel Urry and Jeff Frankenstein for their fifth album, *Take Me to Your Leader*, which was released in 1996.

The Newsboys made a movie with Steve Taylor in 1996, *Down under the*

Big Top, and performed at Pope John Paul II's World Youth Day in 1997. There were some more changes in the group in 2000 when bass player Kevin Mills was killed in a motorcycle accident.

During this period the Newsboys moved to the forefront of Christian pop music, crossing over to the secular audience as well as becoming favorites with Christian audiences. Although they have had a number of members during the years, they have maintained a level of professional and commercialism that has kept them one of the most popular bands in Christian music.

In 1997 John James left the band to become a pastor; James had been the front man for the band and Peter Furler had been the drummer; with the departure of James, Furler became the lead singer and Duncan Phillips switched from keyboard and percussion to drums.

The band moved into praise and worship with their 2003 release, *Adoration: The Worship Album*; however, during this year guitarist Jody David left the group and was replaced by Bryan Oleson. The band's next album, *Devotion*, was also a praise and worship album; Oleson left the group to concentrate on Casting Pearls, his own group, and Paul Colman replaced him on guitar.

The Newsboys received Doves for "Rock Album" and "Rock Recorded Song" in 1995 for their album *Going Public* and song, "Shine," written by Peter Furler and Steve Taylor.

The group came to the United States with manager Wes Campbell, who helped guide and shape the group but later became pastor at a Franklin, Tennessee, church.

Don Cusic

For Further Reading

Alfonso, Barry. *The Billboard Guide to Contemporary Christian Music*. New York: Billboard Books/Watson-Guptill, 2002.

Powell, Mark Allen. *Encyclopedia of Contemporary Christian Music*. Peabody, Mass.: Hendrickson Publishers, Inc., 2002.

Thompson, John J. *Raised by Wolves: The Story of Christian Rock and Roll*. Toronto, Ontario: ECW Press, 2000.

NORDEMAN, NICHOLE

Nichole Nordeman (b. January 3, 1972, in Victorville, California) became a contemporary Christian artist after she entered a songwriting contest sponsored by the Gospel Music Association and won first prize, which led to a recording contract with Sparrow Records. Nordeman, an attractive young lady with fashion model looks, grew up in Colorado, where she was raised in a Christian home, and then moved to Los Angeles. Her piano-based songs are introspective and her first two albums, *Wide Eyed* (1998) and *This Mystery* (2000), led to her Dove Awards in 2001 and 2003 for "Female Vocalist." In 2003 her album *Woven and Spun* was awarded the Dove for "Pop/Contemporary Album of the Year," her song, "Holy," was awarded the Dove for "Pop/Contemporary Song of the Year" and she received the "Songwriter of the Year" honor.

Don Cusic

For Further Reading

Alfonso, Barry. *The Billboard Guide to Contemporary Christian Music.* New York: Billboard Books/Watson-Guptill, 2002.

Powell, Mark Allen. *Encyclopedia of Contemporary Christian Music.* Peabody, Mass.: Hendrickson Publishers, Inc., 2002.

NORMAN, LARRY

In the world of Jesus music and contemporary Christian music, no one deserves the appellation of "pioneer" more than Larry Norman (b. April 8, 1947, in Corpus Christi, Texas; d. February 24, 2008, in Salem, Oregon). He was a son of the Jesus movement and the father of Jesus music, a child of rock 'n' roll who became the godfather of Christian rock. He was the leading spokesperson for Jesus music in the early days—the late 60s and early 70s—and his most lasting and influential work came out during the 60s and 70s, but by the 1980s he was a figure on the fringes of Christian music. He grew his hair long, wore old blue jeans, and looked like a hippie and his songs articulated important issues like religious hypocrisy, social justice, and racial harmony, but his Christian views were quite conservative, although they were perceived as radical because of his poetic genius and upfront insistent belief in Jesus as a radical figure.

Larry Norman was born in Texas but in 1950—when he was three—the family moved to San Francisco. In 1956 Elvis Presley exploded on the American musical landscape and sold 10 million records; nine-year-old Larry Norman became enamored with Elvis Presley, which led him to begin writing rock 'n' roll songs. At the age of 12 he was on Ted Mack's "The Original Amateur Hour."

After high school graduation, Norman moved to San Jose where he formed a band, People, with brothers Geoff and Robb Levin, drummer Dennis Fridkin, keyboardist Albert Ribisi, and Gene Mason, who shared lead vocals with Norman. They reportedly named the group People because there were so many other groups named after animals—The Beatles, the Turtles, the Byrds, and the Animals. The group signed with Capitol Records in 1966 and opened for acts such as the Doors, the Who, Janis Joplin, and Jimi Hendrix. Their first single did not chart, but their second single, a cover of the Zombies "I Love You," was a national hit and reached number 14 on the *Billboard* pop chart in the summer of 1968.

Norman had grown up a Christian but the other members, except fellow lead vocalist Gene Mason, were all in Scientology, which caused a conflict with the band. A further conflict came when Norman wanted to name their debut album *We Need a Whole Lot More of Jesus and a Lot Less Rock and Roll* with Christian imagery on the cover, but executives at Capitol decided to call it *I Love You* and put a picture of the band on the cover. These conflicts caused Norman to leave the group when the album was released, although his vocals are on several tracks of the group's second album.

After he left People, Norman wrote and staged two musicals, *The Epic* and *Lion's Breath*. He turned down the lead role in the Broadway cast of "Hair," which was taken by Barry McGuire. Norman signed with MGM and in 1969 released *Upon This Rock*, considered by many to be the first Jesus music album. The album contained a set of material that Norman would perform for the rest of his life, including "I Wish We'd All Been Ready," which became a classic in the early Jesus movement. Other songs on that album include "Sweet, Sweet Song of Salvation," "Moses in the Wilderness," "Nothing Really Changes," "You Can't Take Away the Lord," "Walking Backwards Down the Stairs," "Ha Ha World," "The Last Supper," and "Forget Your Hexagram." These songs tended to be darker than the early Christian cheerleader type of songs coming from other early Jesus music artists. Singing background on some of those songs were the three siblings who later became 2nd Chapter of Acts.

Pat Boone lent Norman $3,000 to start a record label, Solid Rock, and Norman recorded two albums of his own material, *Street Level* and *Bootleg*, released in 1970 and 1971, respectively, and produced Randy Stonehill's debut album, *Born Twice*.

The "One Way" sign, where a Christian pointed his or her index finger to the sky to indicate there was only "one way" to salvation, came from Norman's habit of pointing to the sky during concerts when he was applauded, signifying that God, not he, should get the applause. The term "Jesus freak" was reportedly coined to describe him.

Norman's next album for MGM, *Only Visiting This Planet*, featured arrangements by Beatles producer George Martin and contained the songs

"The Outlaw," "I've Got to Learn to Live Without You," "Righteous Rocker," "I Am the Six O'clock News" "The Great American Novel," "Readers' Digest," "Why Should the Devil Have All the Good Music?," "Why Don't You Look into Jesus," and "I Wish We'd All Been Ready." This was a strong line-up of songs, and Petula Clark, Gene Cotton, and Cliff Richard all covered songs from this album.

Only Visiting This Planet is considered the first of a trilogy from Larry Norman. The second album of that trilogy is *So Long Ago the Garden* and the third album is *In Another Land*, released in 1973, which contained the songs "One Way," "UFO," "Six Sixty Six," "Song for a Small Circle of Friends," "The Rock That Doesn't Roll," "I Love You," "I Am a Servant," and "Shot Down."

On Norman's next album, *Streams of White Light into Darkened Corners*, he recorded covers of "spiritual" songs such as "My Sweet Lord," "Spirit in the Sky," and "Bridge over Troubled Water." His next album, *Something New under the Sun*, was recorded in 1977 but not released until 1981. It contained blues-based material with Norman's piercing wit and genius lyrical turns.

This body of work was the apex of Norman's output; for the rest of his life he returned again and again to these songs during his live performances, his live albums, and even new recordings of these songs. He was a leading figure in contemporary Christian music up to this point, garnering a cult-like following and influential to the genre as well as individual artists, but after 1981 his star in the contemporary Christian music world faded and he increasingly became a figure on the fringes, an artist who became increasingly isolated from the mainstream of contemporary Christian music.

This may not have mattered much to Norman; he saw his work aimed at the rock 'n' roll audience—not those in contemporary Christian music—and he wanted his music to reach those who did not know the gospel. He succeeded to some degree; U2 members reportedly grew up listening to Larry Norman's albums and other rock acts were influenced by Norman's genius. But the contemporary Christian world headed in another direction—a mainstream pop type sound with personal "me and Jesus" songs or praise and worship material. Praise and worship was not what Larry Norman's music was about; instead, his songs could more accurately be considered "challenge and question" songs.

Norman remained active as an artist and producer; he eventually released almost 100 albums, mostly on his label Phydeaux, started with his father in 1981. He produced Randy Stonehill, Daniel Amos, Tom Howard, and Mark Heard, all of whom he signed to his Solid Rock label. He performed at the White House twice, at Moscow's Olympic Stadium, and at the Royal Albert Hall in London.

Norman's personal life suffered some setbacks; he was divorced in 1980, remarried, and divorced a second time by 1995. He wrote long liner notes on his albums released during the late 1980s and 1990s, rewriting his history, and seemed to be bitter with the press. In 1992 he had a massive heart attack and probably had another one before his heart attack in November 2001 led him to quadruple bypass heart surgery.

He moved from Los Angeles to Salem, Oregon, where he set up his record label and performed occasionally. However, there remained an intense, loyal following from Christians for Larry Norman, and his few concerts were well attended, with audience members sometimes traveling thousands of miles when they knew he was scheduled to perform.

Norman's health increasingly declined, his weak heart eventually giving out on February 24, 2008.

Don Cusic

Discography

I Love You (with People!) (1968)

Both Sides of People! (with People!) (1969)

Upon This Rock (1969)

Street Level (1970)

Bootleg (1971)

Only Visiting This Planet (1972)

So Long Ago the Garden (1973)

In Another Land (1976)

Streams of White Light into Darkened Corners (1977)

Starstorm (1977)

Live at the Mac (1979)

The Israel Tapes (with People) 1980)

Roll Away the Stone (with Mark Heard and Randy Stonehill) 1980)

Something New under the Son (1981)

The Tune (1981)

Letter of the Law (19834)

Labor of Love (1983)

The Story of the Tune (1983)

Come as a Child (with Barry McGuire) (1983)

Quiet Night (with the Young Lions)
1983)

A Chronological History (1966–1984)
(1984)

Stop This Flight (1984)

Back to America (EP) (1985)

Rehearsal for Reality (1986)

Down under but Not Out (1986)

White Blossoms from Black Roots
(1988)

The Best of the Second Trilogy
(1989)

Home at Last (1989)

Live at Flevo with Q-Stone (1989)

The Best of the 2nd Trilogy (1989)

The Best of Larry Norman (1990)

Rough Mix 3 (1990)

Stranded in Babylon (1993)

Omega Europa (Live) (1994)

Totally Unplugged: Alive and Kicking
(1994)

Children of Sorrow (1994)

Footprints in the Sand (1994)

A Moment in Time (1994)

Re-Mixing This Planet (1996)

*Gathered Moments (Somewhere in This
Lifetime)* (1998)

Shouting in the Storm (with Beam)
(1998)

Breathe in, Breathe Out (Live with
Beam) (1998)

Copper Wires (1998)

Live at the Mac (1999)

We Wish You a Larry Christmas (1999)

*When Worlds Collide: A Tribute to
Daniel Amos* (1999)

Rough Street Love Letter (1999)

The Vineyard (1999)

Father Touch (1999)

*The Cottage Tapes, Book One: Where
the Woodbine Twineth* (with Randy
Stonehill) (1999)

In the Beginning (2000)

Kiss the Blarney Stone (2000)

Sticks and Stones (2000)

Tourniquet (2001)

Rough Diamonds, Precious Jewels
(2001)

The Belfast Bootlegs (2001)

The Best of Larry Norman (2001)

Agitator (2002)

Collaborator (2002)

Survivor (2002)

Instigator (2002)

Rock, Scissors et Papier (2003)

Live at Cornerstone 2001 (2003)

Restless in Manhattan (2003)

Invitation Only (2003)

American Roots (2003)

The Very Best of Larry Norman
(2003)

Road Rage (2003)

Christmastime (2003)

The Six O'clock News (single) (2004)

Eve of Destruction (single) (2004)

Snowblind (2004)

Infiltrator (2004)

Liberator (2004)

The Final Concert (2004)

Sessions (2004)

Heartland Junction (2004)

The Norman Invasion (2004)

The Cottage Tapes—Book Two (featuring Randy Stonehill) (2004)

Emancipator (2004)

On the Prowl (2004)

70 Miles from Lebanon (2004)

Maximum Garden—The Anthology Series (2004)

Maximum Planet—The Anthology Series (2004)

The Very Best of Larry Norman—Vol 2 (2004)

Hattem (2005)

Face to Face (2005)

Siege at Elsinore (2005)

Frisbee (aka *Slinky*) (2005)

4 Track Motorola '66 Corolla (2005)

Live at the Elsinore (2005)

Dust on Rust (2006)

Maximum Son—The Anthology Series (2006)

Rebel Poet, Jukebox Balladeer: The Anthology (2008)

For Further Reading

Alfonso, Barry. *The Billboard Guide to Contemporary Christian Music*. New York: Billboard Books/Watson-Guptill, 2002.

Cusic, Don. *The Sound of Light: A History of Gospel and Christian Music*. New York: Hal Leonard, 2002.

McNeil, W. K., ed. *Encyclopedia of American Gospel Music*. New York: Routledge, 2005.

Powell, Mark Allen. *Encyclopedia of Contemporary Christian Music*. Peabody, Mass.: Hendrickson Publishers, Inc., 2002.

O

OMARTIAN, MICHAEL

Fans of Jesus music first heard Michael Omartian (b. November 26, 1945, in Evanston, Illinois) through his piano on "Easter Song" by 2nd Chapter of Acts; that intro is unforgettable for those who heard it and is a testament to the musical virtuosity of Omartian, who also played piano on Billy Joel's "Piano Man."

Michael Omartian had a long, successful history in secular music before turning his attention to contemporary Christian music; he still works with secular artists, although he has tended to concentrate on CCM since the 1990s. He is one of the few figures in contemporary music who moves easily between the secular worlds of pop and country to contemporary Christian music.

Omartian grew up in Evanston and started playing the piano when he was four; later he studied at Tarkio College in Missouri and Northwestern University in Evanston. He became a Christian on Christmas Day in 1965. He worked on the staff of Campus Crusade for Christ and led two ministry teams, Armageddon Experience and New Folk, before moving to Los Angeles to pursue songwriting in the 1970s.

In L.A., Omartian soon became a sought-after session player, playing keyboards on sessions for Barbra Streisand, Steely Dan, Boz Scaggs, Michael Jackson, Julio Iglesias, John Lennon, Eric Clapton, and Al Jarreau. He produced the Grammy-winning album by Christopher Cross as well as albums by Donna Summer (he cowrote "She Works Hard for the Money"), Rod Stewart, and Whitney Houston and coproduced the anthemic "We Are the World" with Quincy Jones. He was part of the studio group Rhythm Heritage that played "Baretta's Theme" for the TV show "S.W.A.T." and "Theme from Happy Days."

Omartian was involved in early Jesus music, playing on albums by Mike and Kathy Deasy, Richie Furay, Annie Herring, Phil Keaggy, Barry McGuire, Jamie Owens, and 2nd Chapter of Acts. As a member of Jack Hayford's Church on the Way, he performed with 2nd Chapter of Acts in a concert there that produced the album *Together Live*.

In contemporary Christian music, Omartian produced Amy Grant's album, *Heart in Motion*, and cowrote her hit single, "That's What Love Is For." Other CCM acts he produced include First Call, 4HIM, Debby Boone, Steve Camp, Sandi Patti, Bob Carlisle, Jonathan Pierce, Michael W. Smith, Gary Chapman, the Imperials, Steven Curtis Chapman, Kathy Troccoli, Sheila Walsh, Crystal Lewis, and Wayne Watson.

In 1973 Michael married Stormie Sherric, and they have three children. Stormie is a songwriter and singer who has written a number of best-selling books, including *The Power of a Praying Woman* and released several best-selling exercise videos.

Don Cusic

For Further Reading

Alfonso, Barry. *The Billboard Guide to Contemporary Christian Music*. New York: Billboard Books/Watson-Guptill, 2002.

Powell, Mark Allen. *Encyclopedia of Contemporary Christian Music*. Peabody, Mass.: Hendrickson Publishers, Inc., 2002.

ORTEGA, FERNANDO

The influence of Latin music and the Latin culture has come to contemporary Christian music through artists like Fernando Ortego, who records in both Spanish and English and whose audiences are both English and Spanish-speaking members.

Fernando Ortega (b. March 2, 1957) came from a long line of blanket weavers, but it would be his ability to weave together words and music that defined his artistic path. Best known for his unique interpretations of traditional hymns and songs, Ortega is a master songwriter, crafting passion and personal experience into his work. Growing up in Albuquerque, New Mexico, Ortega had the opportunity to experience and appreciate other cultures as he traveled with his father, whose work took him to places like Ecuador and Barbados. Later, his music reflected the influence of those places along with other types of music from around the world.

As a young man growing up, Ortega searched for his own spiritual path, eventually joining the extremist Children of God cult, lead by Moses David Berg. Berg called on his followers to devote their full time to spreading the message of Christ's love and salvation. Unfettered by convention or tradition, his focus was to teach others to do the same. He also condemned the de-Christianization and decay in moral values of western society. Berg openly viewed the trend toward a New World Order as setting the stage for the rise of the Antichrist.

Although a unique learning experience, Ortega remained with the group only a short time before becoming involved in a Pentecostal fellowship called the Answer. Again, the group failed to provide Ortega with the answers he was searching for. Disenchanted with the direction his life was taking, he enrolled in the University of New Mexico and pursued a music major. With classical training and a respect for his family's Hispanic heritage, Ortega began to compose his own creations infused with flavors of country, classical, Celtic, Latin, and folk music. Finding a new direction for his life in his music, he eventually returned to his Christian roots, and worked as a church pianist before landing a full-time position with Campus Crusade for Christ youth ministries.

Ortega began recording his own projects independently shortly after his college graduation, but it was 16 years before he landed his first major recording contract with Myrrh/Word Records in 1997.

Ortega recorded a string of critically and commercially successful albums; then, in 2004, Ortega signed with Curb Records and released his first project for the label, his self-titled *Fernando Ortega*. Ortega's album *The Shadow of Your Wings* was released in October 2006 and his first Christmas project was released in 2008.

Liz Cavanaugh

For Further Reading

Powell, Mark Allen. *Encyclopedia of Contemporary Christian Music*. Peabody, Mass.: Hendrickson Publishers, Inc., 2002.

OUT OF THE GREY

Scott and Christine Dente—a husband and wife team—are Out of the Grey; Scott plays guitar and does background vocals while Christine provides most of the lead vocals. Their name derives from the fact that they believe there are absolutes in life and not relativism. They met in 1985 when both attended Berklee School of Music in Boston and married in 1987; they moved to Nashville at the end of the 1980s and formed Out of the Grey in 1990. They

were "discovered" by Charlie Peacock, who produced and cowrote most of their first four albums; they toured with Steven Curtis Chapman in 1991. Since 2004 they have been inactive; Christine takes care of their three children and Scott pursues business ventures.

Don Cusic

For Further Reading

Alfonso, Barry. *The Billboard Guide to Contemporary Christian Music*. New York: Billboard Books/Watson-Guptill, 2002.

Powell, Mark Allen. *Encyclopedia of Contemporary Christian Music*. Peabody, Mass.: Hendrickson Publishers, Inc., 2002.

OWENS, GINNY

Ginny Owens (b. Virginia Leigh Owens, in Jackson, Mississippi) was born with poor eyesight and was blind by the age of two. She graduated from Belmont University in Nashville with a degree in music education but found limited opportunities to become a music teacher, so she concentrated on songwriting and signed with Final Four, a Nashville publishing company, where she met producer Monroe Jones, who had produced Third Day and Chris Rice. Jones produced Owens's debut album, *Without Condition*, for Rockettown Records. The album was an immediate hit and Owens won a Dove Award for "New Artist of the Year."

Owens toured with Sarah McLachlan's Lilith Fair, performed at the Sundance Film Festival in 2000, and was a guest on "Live! With Regis and

Kathie Lee." Her songs have been featured on the TV shows "Felicity," "Charmed," and "Roswell."

Don Cusic

For Further Reading

Powell, Mark Allen. *Encyclopedia of Contemporary Christian Music*. Peabody, Mass.: Hendrickson Publishers, Inc., 2002.

OWENS-COLLINS, JAMIE

Jamie Owens-Collins (b. 1954) grew up in contemporary Christian music; her parents, noted songwriters Jimmy and Carol Owens, wrote the popular and influential church musicals *Come Together* (1972) *Show Me* (1971), and *If My People* (1975). An Oakland, California, native, Jamie's earliest recording experience was on her parents' albums. Her first solo album, *Laughter in Your Soul* was released on Light Records in 1973, followed by *Growing Pains* in 1975; these were released under the name "Jamie Collins." She married Sparrow Records executive Dan Collins and released *Love Eyes* (1978) before she signed with Sparrow and released *Straight Ahead* (1980). Jamie and Dan Collins formed Live Oak Records, and she released her next two albums, *A Time for Courage* (1985) and *The Gift of Christmas* (1987), before they formed Newport Records, which released her album *Seasons* (1999).

Jamie Owens-Collins and the Talbot Brothers—John Michael and Terry—wrote the musical *Firewind* (1976). During the period 1989–1995 Jamie and Dan were members of the Maranatha Praise Band; her songs are praise and worship songs, and she has focused her music on the church.

Don Cusic

For Further Reading

Alfonso, Barry. *The Billboard Guide to Contemporary Christian Music*. New York: Billboard Books/Watson-Guptill, 2002.

Powell, Mark Allen. *Encyclopedia of Contemporary Christian Music*. Peabody, Mass.: Hendrickson Publishers, Inc., 2002.

P

PARABLE

Chuck Butler, vocals, guitar
Don Kobayashi, drums
Joy Strange, guitar, vocals
(until 1977)
Pat Patton, bass, vocals (until 1977)
Gary Arthur, bass, vocals
(since 1977)
Alan DiCato, keyboard, vocals
(since 1977)
Lisa Faye Irwin (Wickham),
vocals, percussion (since 1977)
John Wickham, guitar, vocals
(since 1977)

Calvary Chapel in Costa Mesa, California, was filled with talented Christian musicians; it became a hotbed for early Christian music because of the Southern California musical atmosphere and the encouragement from the leaders and members at Calvary Chapel. Parable followed in the wake of Children of the Day, Love Song, and the Way and emerged out of Country Faith, which was led by Chuck Butler. Butler, Pat Patton, and Joy Strange formed a folk trio and toured as Chuck, Pat and Joy; when they added drummer Don Kobayashi they renamed themselves Parable.

The group recorded two albums for Maranatha. *More Than Words* was released in 1975; after that album Joy Strange married Bob Cull and left the group, which added two former members of the Way: guitarist John Wickham and bassist Gary Arthur were members when Parable's second album, *Illustrations* was released in 1977.

Don Cusic

For Further Reading

Powell, Mark Allen. *Encyclopedia of Contemporary Christian Music*. Peabody, Mass.: Hendrickson Publishers, Inc., 2002.

PATILLO, LEON

Leon Patillo (b. January 1, 1947, in San Francisco, California) is an African American singer whose background included tours with Martha and the Vandellas, Funkadelic, and Santana—which lasted 1973 to 1979—and laid the groundwork for his dance-oriented Christian music in the late 1970s and early 1980s. Patillo actually began with a Sly and the Family Stone type group, Creation, which he formed after graduation from San Francisco City College before he moved to Los Angeles and worked as a background singer with the other acts.

Patillo met Carlos Santana after the guitarist called him and arranged a meeting; Patillo then joined Santana for his tours as vocalist and keyboards. Patillo left Santana when he signed with Word Records for his debut Christian album, *Dance, Children, Dance* in 1979.

Patillo became a Christian on July 4, 1974, during his time with Santana; while on a plane with Earth, Wind and Fire, who toured with Santana, EWF's lead singer Philip Bailey saw Patillo with a Bible and asked, "Do you know how that thing works?," and invited Patillo to teach from the Bible. Although Patillo was inexperienced as a teacher, these Bible studies led to Bailey accepting Christ.

During his time in Los Angeles, Patillo became involved with Calvary Chapel; later, he toured as a one-man electronic band and then with an all-female band. During 1986 Patillo worked as a stand-up comic but had some personal troubles in the late 1980s when he went through a divorce. During the 1990s he hosted a TV show, "Leon and Friends," on the Trinity Broadcasting Network and started a church in Long Beach, California. Patillo also started his own label, Power Pop, during the 1990s.

Leon Patillo serves as a church minister and works with Koinonia Foster Home to help homeless children.

Don Cusic

For Further Reading

Powell, Mark Allen. *Encyclopedia of Contemporary Christian Music*. Peabody, Mass.: Hendrickson Publishers, Inc., 2002.

PATTY, SANDI

Sandi Patty's (b. July 12, 1956) audience is the church world, and she became the preeminent female vocalist in the contemporary Christian music field during the 1980s by recording songs for the church. There was no attempt to cross over into the pop world from Patty; her concerts and recordings were aimed for those who were already Christians and who wanted a singer who affirmed their beliefs and provided an evening of comfortable Christian entertainment.

Her career was spectacular; by 2007 she had won 31 Dove Awards and five Grammys and sold 11 million albums, including three platinum and five gold albums. However, her divorce after an extramarital affair was revealed and remarriage alienated her from that church world who demanded a purity in her personal life. Her divorce in 1993 shocked the Christian audience, and many in that audience have never forgiven her for that indiscretion. Although Patty continues to record and tour, her career has never recovered and she no longer enjoys the heights of the success she attained before her divorce.

Born to parents who were touring with the Christian Brothers Quartet (her father was singing while her mother played the piano), Patty's family

Gospel music artist Sandi Patty presents an award at the annual Dove Awards on April 10, 2003, in Nashville. (AP Photo/Mark Humphrey)

moved to Phoenix, Arizona, when she was two and a half, where her father was a minister of music at a Church of God. After ten years in Arizona, the Patty family moved to San Diego, California, where her father again worked with a church and formed a family group, the Ron Patty Family. Heavily influenced by Karen Carpenter and Barbra Streisand, Patty entered Anderson College in Anderson, Indiana, the alma mater of her parents. There she became active in a student singing group called New Nature, where she met her first husband, John Helvering; they were married on November 17, 1978.

Before her marriage, Sandi had recorded a custom album, *For My Friends*, and the printer had misspelled her last name as "Patti." Rather than send the albums back, she went under the name Sandi Patti during the first decade of her professional career.

In 1979 she was signed to the Benson Company in Nashville and released *Sandi's Songs*. In 1981 she began touring with the Bill Gaither Trio as a backup singer and released her second album, *Love Overflowing*, which contained the song, "We Shall Behold Him." Because of the tremendous popularity of this song, written by Dottie Rambo, as well as her tours with Gaither, the top Christian touring act of that time, Sandi Patti won Dove Awards for "Artist of the Year" and "Female Vocalist" in 1982. In 1983, she released her third album, *Lift Up the Lord,* which contained "How Majestic Is Your Name," a song written by Michael W. Smith, which was also a tremendous hit for the church audience. This recording led to her second Dove for "Female Vocalist" as well as the Dove for "Inspirational Album of the Year."

In 1986 ABC television broadcast Sandi's recording of "The Star Spangled Banner" during its Fourth of July broadcast and this led to a number of patriotic appearances where she sang the national anthem as well as "God Bless America." Patti's career continued in an upward spiral because she was linked to the Christian movement in politics during the era when Republican politicians courted the evangelical Christian audience and contemporary Christian performers were often linked with Republican candidates for political office, including the office of president of the United States.

After she divorced her husband, it became public knowledge that she'd had an extramarital affair with one of her backup singers, Don Peslis. In August 1995 she married Peslis and they blended their families (she had four children, he had three, and they adopted one after their marriage).

The controversy over her affair erupted into a scandal that caused a number of Christian radio stations to stop playing her recordings, a number of Christian retailers to pull her recordings from their shelves, and a number of Christian buyers to quit purchasing her albums. She cut back on her public appearances, although she continued to appear with symphonies and in patriotic concerts.

After her divorce and remarriage, Sandi let her professional name revert to Patty instead of Patti and continued releasing albums, but the big sales were no longer there. Still, she remains a force in the Christian music world and her legacy is secure as the most awarded female artist in the history of the Dove Awards.

Don Cusic

Discography

For My Friends (1978)

Sandi's Song (1979)

Love Overflowing (1981)

Lift Up the Lord (1982)

The Gift Goes On (Christmas)(1983)

Live: More Than Wonderful (1983)

Songs from the Heart (1984)

Hymns Just for You (1985)

Morning Like This (1986)

Make His Praise Glorious (1988)

The Finest Moments (1989)

Sandi Patti and the Friendship Company (1989)

Another Time, Another Place (1990)

The Friendship Company: Open for Business (1991)

Hallmark Christmas: Celebrate Christmas! (1992)

Le Voyage (1993)

Quiet Reflections (compilation of songs from previous albums) (1994)

Find It on the Wings (1994)

Hallmark Christmas: It's Christmas! Sandi Patty and Peabo Bryson (1996)

An American Songbook (1996)

Artist of My Soul (1997)

Libertad de Mas (Spanish language recording) (1998)

Together: Sandi Patty and Kathy Troccoli (1999)

These Days (2000)

All the Best . . . Live! (2001)

Take Hold of Christ (2003)

Hymns of Faith . . . Songs of Inspiration (2004)

Yuletide Joy (Christmas) (2005)

Duets (compilation of duets through her career) (2005)

The Voice of Christmas (compilation of Christmas songs form Sandi's first three Christmas albums) (2006)

The Definitive Collection Presents Sandi Patty (2007)

Falling Forward: Songs of Worship (2007)

Gospel Music Association Dove Awards

1982	Artist of the Year
1982	Female Vocalist of the Year
1982	Song of the Year: "We Shall Behold Him" Written by Dottie Rambo; Publisher: John T. Benson Publishing, ASCAP
1983	Female Vocalist of the Year

1983 Inspirational Album: *Lift Up the Lord* (Producer: Greg Nelson; Label: Impact)

1984 Artist of the Year

1984 Female Vocalist of the Year

1984 Inspirational Album: *More Than Wonderful* (Producers: David Clydesdale, Greg Nelson, and Sandi Patti Helvering; Label: Impact)

1985 Artist of the Year

1985 Female Vocalist of the Year

1985 Inspirational Album: *Songs from the Heart* (Producers: Greg Nelson and Sandi Patti Helvering; Label: Impact)

1986 Female Vocalist of the Year

1986 Song of the Year: "Via Dolorosa" Written by Billy Sprague and Niles Borop; Publishers: Meadowgreen and Word Music, ASCAP

1987 Artist of the Year

1987 Female Vocalist of the Year

1987 Inspirational Album: *Morning Like This* (Producers: Greg Nelson and Sandi Patti Helvering; Label: Word)

1988 Artist of the Year

1988 Female Vocalist of the Year

1988 Song of the Year: "In the Name of the Lord" Written by Phil McHugh, Gloria Gaither, and Sandi Patti Helvering; Publishers River Oaks Music and Sandi's Songs BMI; Gaither Music, ASCAP

1989 Choral Collection Album: *Sandi Patti Choral Praise* (Producer: Greg Nelson; Publisher: Word Music)

1989 Female Vocalist of the Year

1989 Inspirational Album: *Make His Praise Glorious* (Producers: Greg Nelson and Sandi Patti Helvering; Label: Word)

1989 Inspirational Recorded Song: "In Heaven's Eyes" Written by Phil McHugh; Recorded by Sandi Patti; Label: Word

1989 Instrumental Album: *A Symphony of Praise* (Producer: David T. Clydesdale; Label: Word)

1990 Children's Music Album: *The Friendship Company* (Producer: Sandi Patti; Label: Word)

1990 Female Vocalist of the Year

1991 Inspirational Album: *Another Time, Another Place* (Producer: Greg Nelson; Label: Word)

1991 Pop/Contemporary Recorded Song: "Another Time, Another Place" Written by Gary Driskell; Recorded by Sandi Patti; Label: Word

1991 Song of the Year: "Another Time, Another Place" Written by Gary Driskell; Publisher: Word Music, ASCAP

1992 Children's Music Album: *Open for Business* by Sandi Patti and the Friendship Company (Producers: Ron Krueger and Greg Nelson; Label: Everland)

1992 Female Vocalist of the Year

1992 Inspirational Recorded Song: "For All the World" Written by Greg Nelson and Bob Farrell; recorded by Sandi Patti; Label: Word

1992 Short Form Music Video: *Another Time, Another Place* by Sandi Patti and Wayne Watson; Director: Stephen Yake; Label: Word

1994 Short Form Music Video: *Hand on My Shoulder* Sandi Patti; Director: Stephen Yake; Label: Word

1995 Inspirational Album: *Find It on the Wings* (Producers: Greg Nelson and Phil Ramone; Label: Word)

1996 Special Event Album: *My Utmost for His Highest*. Artists: Amy Grant, Gary Chapman, Michael W. Smith, Point of Grace, 4HIM, Cindy Morgan, Sandi Patti, Bryan Duncan, Steven Curtis Chapman, Twila Paris, Phillips, and Craig and Dean (Producers: Loren Balman and Brown Bannister; Label: Myrrh/Word)

1998 Inspirational Album: *Artist of My Soul* (Producer: Robbie Buchanan; Label: Word)

1998 Special Event Album: *God with Us—A Celebration of Christmas Carols and Classics* by Anointed, Michael W. Smith, Twila Paris, Sandi Patty, Steven Curtis Chapman, Chris Willis, Steve Green, Cheri Keaggy, Avalon, Out of the Grey, Ray Boltz, Clay Crosse, CeCe Winans, and Larnelle Harris (Producer: Norman Miller; Label: Sparrow)

1999 Long Form Music Video: *My Utmost For His Highest—The Concert* by Cindy Morgan, Avalon, Twila Paris, Bryan Duncan, Sandi Patty, Steven Curtis Chapman; Nancy Knox; Producers and Directors: Clark Santee and Word Entertainment; Label: Myrrh Records

1999 Spanish Language Album of the Year: (Tie) *Libertad de Mas* by Sandi Patty (Producers: Isaac Hernandez and Greg Nelson; Label: Word International) and *ORO* by Crystal Lewis (Producers: Brian Ray and Dan Posthuma; Label: Metro One)

Grammy Awards

1983 26th Grammy Awards: Best Gospel Performance by a Duo or Group: Sandi Patti, Larnelle Harris, "More Than Wonderful"

1985 28th Grammy Awards: Best Gospel Performance by a Duo or Group, Choir or Chorus: Sandi Patti, Larnelle Harris, "I've Just Seen Jesus"

1986 29th Grammy Awards: Best Gospel Performance, Female: "Morning Like This"

1990 33rd Grammy Awards: Best Gospel Pop Album: *Another Time . . . Another Place*

For Further Reading

Alfonso, Barry. *The Billboard Guide to Contemporary Christian Music*. New York: Billboard Books/Watson-Guptill, 2002.

Cusic, Don. *Sandi Patti: The Voice of Gospel*. New York: Dolphin/Doubleday, 1988.

Cusic, Don. *The Sound of Light: A History of Gospel and Christian Music.* New York: Hal Leonard, 2002.

McNeil, W. K., ed. *Encyclopedia of American Gospel Music.* New York: Routledge, 2005.

Powell, Mark Allen. *Encyclopedia of Contemporary Christian Music.* Peabody, Mass.: Hendrickson Publishers, Inc., 2002.

PAXTON, GARY

The blessing "May you lead an interesting life" was poured out in abundance on Gary S. Paxton (b. May 18, 1938). Paxton has written hit songs in the rock, country, and Christian genres, produced, engineered, and sung on numerous recordings, and has run afoul of drugs, booze, marriage, and business a number of times in his life and career.

"Alley Oop" was the first big hit associated with Paxton; it was recorded by his group, the Hollywood Argyles, in 1960, and in 1962 he produced "Monster Mash" for Bobby "Boris" Pickett, which was number one on his Garpax label. As a member of the duo Skip and Flip (Clyde Battin was "Skip") he recorded "Cherry Pie" in 1960.

In 1970 Paxton moved from Los Angeles to Nashville, where he wrote "Woman, Sensuous Woman," a number one hit for Don Gibson. In September 1971 Paxton, a habitual drug user and boozer, was "saved" and began writing and recording Christian music; he wrote "L-O-V-E" for the Blackwood Brothers, "No Shortage" for the Imperials, and "He Was There All the Time," which was initially on his album, *The Astonishing, Outrageous, Amazing, Incredible, Unbelievable, Different World of Gary S. Paxton*, which won a Grammy in 1976.

Paxton established a gospel label in Nashville, NewPax, and recorded Don Francisco, Scott Wesley Brown, Farrell and Farrell, Brown Bannister, and Tammy Faye Bakker. Paxton was close to Jim and Tammy Faye Bakker of the PTL Club and produced their recordings.

In a bizarre episode of Paxton's life, he was attacked and shot by hit men hired by a country singer he produced; they had come to his house under the ruse of needing help with their car and kidnapped him and put him in a van. Paxton survived and later visited the men in prison and forgave them.

In 1999 Paxton moved to Branson, Missouri, where he continues to write, record, and engage in various other entertainment projects.

Don Cusic

Selected Discography

The Astonishing, Outrageous, Amazing, Incredible, Unbelievable, Different World of Gary S. Paxton (1976)

More from the Astonishing, Outrageous, Amazing, Incredible, Unbelievable World of Gary S. Paxton (1977)

Anchored in the Rock of Ages (1978)

Terminally Weird But Godly Right (1978)

Gary Sanford Paxton (1979)

The Gospel According to Gary S. Paxton (by the Gary Paxton Singers) (1979)

(Some of) The Best of Gary S. Paxton (So Far) (1980)

Take Your Turf for Jesus (1981)

1976   19th Grammy Awards: Best Inspirational Performance: Gary S. Paxton: *The Astonishing, Outrageous, Amazing, Incredible, Unbelievable, Different World of Gary S. Paxton*

For Further Reading

Cusic, Don. *The Sound of Light: A History of Gospel and Christian Music.* New York: Hal Leonard, 2002.

Powell, Mark Allen. *Encyclopedia of Contemporary Christian Music.* Peabody, Mass.: Hendrickson Publishers, Inc., 2002.

PEACOCK, CHARLIE

Charlie Peacock (b. Charles Ashworth on August 10, 1956, in Yuba City, California) grew up in a musical family. His father, Bill Ashworth, was a teacher and trumpet player, and by his teenage years, Peacock was writing music. He quit high school when he was 16 and married his childhood sweetheart, Andrea Berrier, when he was 18. He later attended a semester of college at California State University in Sacramento, where he met the late Frank Kofsky, a journalist and drummer. Kofsky reviewed a Peacock performance in his *San Francisco Chronicle* column in 1976 and the two became friends, which led Kofsky to invite Peacock to go on interviews with him when he was interviewing jazz

musicians. It was a great history and music lesson for the budding musician.

The lure of the road pulled Peacock away from school and he joined a band, the Runners, where in 1978 he met engineer Stephen Holsapple, who began recording the young musician and writing songs with him. Holsapple helped Ashworth get a job at Maurice's American Bar, where the young man took the stage name Charlie Peacock. He merged jazz with pop for a sound that resulted in his placing his first song, "So Attractive," with major publisher Boyce and Hart.

In 1980 Peacock signed a demo deal with A&M Records but that did not lead to a recording contract; however, he continued to record while his personal life was beset with problems with drugs and alcohol abuse. A year later he cleaned up his personal life, formed the Charlie Peacock Group, and was again popular with fans in northern California.

In 1982 Peacock became immersed in Christianity through the 12-step recovery program he attended and began to meet other musicians in that community. These new friends encouraged him to leave secular music and record only Christian music. Peacock was unsure of making this decision until he read *Art and the Bible* by Francis Schaeffer, which confirmed to him that he could minister to people through his music. Around the same time Peacock met painter and guitarist Jimmy Abegg and through Abegg met other artists who felt the same way about their music. Peacock began producing bands, including the 77s and Steve Scott, and continued with his own recordings. His album *Lie Down in the Grass* garnered him touring gigs with the Fixx, General

Public, and Red Hot Chili Peppers. He recorded for Island Records but did not have any hits.

Peacock continued to play the circuit of venues in northern California and formed a jazz trio, Emperor Norton. Later he formed an acoustic duo and released a three-cassette series, *West Coast Diaries*. The success of these recordings took the trio on tour in the United States and Europe.

Christian singer Russ Taff recorded Peacock's song, "Down in the Lowlands," and Peacock sang background vocals. He also produced an alternative Christian band, the Choir, and then worked with Margaret Becker on her album, *Immigrant's Daughter*, which was nominated for a Grammy.

Peacock and Abegg moved to Nashville in 1989 and Peacock signed as an artist with Sparrow Records. Ironically he didn't produce his debut album for the label; Brown Bannister produced *The Secret of Time*, which was nominated for a Grammy in 1990. Peacock was in demand as a session musician, working with Amy Grant, Al Green, and Twila Paris. Although he enjoyed this work, Peacock felt that music with spiritual overtones didn't necessarily have to be labeled Christian, so in 1996 he formed a record label, re:think and signed Sarah Masen and Switchfoot. Peacock believed he could promote artists to both Christian and mainstream markets without compromising their music. His idea worked; Switchfoot became a major rock band that also had success in the Christian marketplace.

In 1989 Peacock wrote a book, *At the Crossroads*, which analyzed contemporary Christian music. In 2005 he released the album *Love Press Ex-Curio*, which is short for Loves

Pressure Exhibits Curiosity. Influences such as John Coltrane, Miles Davis, and Keith Jarrett permeate his jazz recordings. In 2007 he and Jeff Coffin released *Arc of the Circle*. The musician/producer was named one of the 500 most important record producers in music history in *Billboard's Encyclopedia of Record Producers*. He's worked with everyone from Grant and Becker to the South African group Ladysmith Black Mambazo, CeCe Winans, and Audio Adrenaline.

Peacock won Dove Awards as producer of Margaret Becker's album *Simple House* and song by the same title for 1992, as producer of *Coram Deo II*, the praise and worship album Dove winner in 1995, as "Producer of the Year" in 1996 and as coproducer for Nichole Nordeman's album, *Woven and Spun*, in the "Pop/Contemporary Album" category.

Vernell Hackett

For Further Reading

Alfonso, Barry. *The Billboard Guide to Contemporary Christian Music*. New York: Billboard Books/Watson-Guptill, 2002.

Peacock, Charlie, with Molly Nicholas. *At the Crossroads: Inside the Past, Present, and Future of Contemporary Christian Music*. Colorado Springs, Colo.: Shaw Books, 2004.

Powell, Mark Allen. *Encyclopedia of Contemporary Christian Music*. Peabody, Mass.: Hendrickson Publishers, Inc., 2002.

PEEK, DAN

Dan Peek (b. November 1, 1950, in Panama City, Florida) is best known as one of the founders of America, a group whose hits included "A Horse with No Name," "Ventura Highway," and "Sister Golden Hair." The group, Peek, Gerry Beckley, and Dewey Bunnell, met in Watford, England, where they attended Central High School while their fathers were in the Air Force. After high school, the trio formed several groups—Daze and Swallow the Buffalo—and signed with Jeff Dexter, who booked them in clubs and concerts. An audition with Ian Samwell at Warner Brothers led to them signing with that label in the U.K. and their first hit, "A Horse with No Name," was a hit in England before it was released in the United States.

The group's American release of the debut album and that song was in early 1972, and the song was number one on the pop chart for three weeks. Their succeeding singles, "I Need You," "Ventura Highway," "Tin Man," "Lonely People," and "Sister Golden Hair," all went into the top ten during the 1972–1975 period, and their albums sold gold and platinum.

In February 1977, America released *Harbor* and shortly afterward Peek, who had been raised in a Christian home but fell prey to the lifestyle of drugs and partying while in America, left the group to embark on a career in contemporary Christian music. He did so at a time when celebrity conversions attracted a lot of attention in the Christian world and as Christian pop succeeded the early Jesus music sound of raw, well-intentioned, but often not quite musically accomplished, recordings. It was a time when professionalism entered Christian music, and Peek had professional credentials.

Peek's first release, *All Things Are Possible*, was produced by Chris Christian for Pat Boone's Lamb and Lion label. Peek's next album was on Christian's label, *Home Sweet Home*, and then he recorded for Greentree, a division of the Benson Company. Peek later formed the group Peace, which recorded several albums

Don Cusic

For Further Reading

Powell, Mark Allen. *Encyclopedia of Contemporary Christian Music*. Peabody, Mass.: Hendrickson Publishers, Inc., 2002.

PETRA

Bob Hartman, guitars, vocals (1972–1995; 2001–2005)
John DeGroff, bass (1972–1979)
Greg Hough, guitar (1972–1979)
Bill Glover, drums (1972–1977)
Rob Frazier, guitar, keyboard, vocals (1979–1981)
Mark Kelly, bass (1981–1988)
John Slick, keyboard (1981–1985)
Greg Volz, vocals (1981–1986)
Louie Weaver, drums (1972–1982)
John Lawry, keyboard, vocals (1985–1995)
John Schlitt, vocals (1986–2005)
Ronny Cates, bass (1988–1998)
Jim Cooper, keyboard, vocals (1995–1998)
David Lichens, guitar, vocals (1995–1998)
Kevin Brandow, guitar (1998–2000)
Lonnie Chapin, bass (1998–2001)

"Petra" is the Greek word for "rock," and that was an appropriate name for the most successful, enduring rock band in Christian music. By the time they ended their career at the end of 2005, Christian rock was established as an important, accepted part of the genre; however, when they began in 1972, Christian rock was neither established nor accepted by those who led churches or ran Christian bookstores where most Christian albums were sold. It was a gigantic effort against long odds for Petra to break through into the mainstream contemporary Christian market. The fact that they did is a tribute to the band as well as an acknowledgment of how much the Christian market changed over 30 years.

The original group was formed by three young students at the Christian Training Center in Fort Wayne, Indiana. Bob Hartman, Greg Hough, and John DeGroff played folk-based music at the Adam's Apple, a Christian coffeehouse in Fort Wayne. Billy Ray Hearn, head of Myrrh Records at the time, signed the group and produced their first album, *Petra*, released in 1974.

The band's rock music was mild by later standards but faced immediate resistance from church leaders and Christian bookstore owners who felt that rock was the devil's music and wasn't appropriate or wanted in the Christian community. It was a clash of cultures; the church leaders and bookstore owners tended to be older and musically conservative. Also, Petra performed primarily in coffeehouses and church basements and never toured to support that album. The basic reason is that there wasn't a booking agency or business infrastructure that allowed Petra to tour.

Petra's first shake-up occurred after that first album. Hartman, Hough, and DeGross had added drummer Bill Glover before the first album was recorded; on that album Hartman and Hough did the singing. On their second album, Greg X. Volz was invited to join, and he sang some of the lead vocals, although Steve Camp and Austin Roberts also contributed vocals. They had a new label—StarSong—who saw the potential for a Christian rock band, and on that second album Petra moved away from a bluesy, southern rock sound into harder rock.

After the second album, original members Hough, DeGross, and Glover left the band and only Hartman and Volz remained. Volz, a drummer, shifted to lead vocals, although the group added Rob Frazier, who also did vocals as well as guitar and keyboards; Louis Weaver took over as drummer. The album, *Washes Whiter Than*, moved the group in a pop-oriented direction and they toured to support the album, but the album was difficult to find due to distribution problems.

Their fourth album, *Never Say Die*, released in 1981, was their breakthrough album. They were invited to tour as the opening act for Servant, another Christian rock band, and this launched their career as a full-blown touring rock band. They hired Mark Hollingsworth as manager, and he gave them the needed business support and direction. At this point the band consisted of Volz, the full-time lead singer; guitarist Hartman; bassist Mark Kelly; and keyboard player John Slick. Drummer Louis Weaver rounded out the group.

The next three albums, *More Power to Ya, Not of This World*, and *Beat the System*, saw the band build a solid fan base from touring full time and achieved significant album sales. But changes occurred; John Lawry replaced

John Slick on keyboards and, in 1985, Greg X. Volz left the group. This necessitated a major dilemma for Petra, who needed a strong singer to replace Volz, the lead voice of the band.

John Schlitt had been the lead vocalist for the rock group Head East; Hartman recruited him for the group, which also replaced producer Jonathan David Brown—who had produced the group's most successful albums—with brothers John and Dino Elefante. The sound of Petra moved toward a harder rock sound, bordering on heavy metal in some songs. The Elefante brothers brought the guitars out front as Petra's sound evolved into a stadium rock sound with the release of *Back to the Street*.

Petra's greatest commercial success came during the 1987–1994 period. Their success came from the group locking into a clearly defined sound and the fact that Christian bookstores stocked their albums and the resistance from church leaders and parents was muted; by this point, it was accepted that a Christian could like—and perform in—a rock band. Also, the group had proven itself through concerts and the media as a group of Christians filled with evangelical fervor to carry the gospel to the masses.

The band's albums during this period were *This Means War!*, *On Fire!*, *Petra Praise: The Rock Cries Out*, and *Beyond Belief*. The group adapted a militant view of Christianity—Christian faith was in an all-out ongoing war against the devil and the forces of evil. A Christian was a warrior, a soldier for Christ who, armed with his faith, did daily battle against the secular forces of the world. This militant imagery reflected the Christian subculture's embrace of this warrior mentality in fields as diverse as politics, education, and popular culture.

In 1995, founder, lead guitarist, and principal songwriter Bob Hartman decided to leave the band as a touring member, although he remained heavily involved, playing guitar on their albums, writing songs, and having a business interest in the group. John Lawry also left, and the band added David Lichens on guitar and Jim Cooper on keyboards. More changes occurred: Lonnie Chapin, Pete Orta, and Kevin Brandow joined the group, whose core now consisted of Schlitt and Weaver on the road with Hartman involved at home. By this point, Petra was floundering as a recording act; more members left and others joined while their long-time label dropped the group.

Their new label, Inpop, moved them toward praise and worship, which was the fastest growing segment of Christian music. In 2001 Hartman began touring with the band again for selected dates, and in 2003 he joined the touring group full time. However, long-time drummer Louis Weaver left the group under a cloud; a dispute between Schlitt and their manager left Weaver out in the cold.

In August 2003 Petra released its last studio album, *Jekyll and Hyde*. The group toured extensively in 2004, traveling to Europe, Australia, and India as well as numerous American dates. Petra had been a band, in one form or another, for 32 years by the end of 2004. Hartman and Schlitt decided to end the group at the end of 2005; the announcement was made by Hartman in May of that year and a farewell tour was organized.

Petra's concert in Franklin, Tennessee, in October 2005 was recorded and released as their last album, *Petra Farewell*. Former members of the group joined them for various concerts, and Petra performed its last concert on New Year's Eve of 2005 in Murphy, North Carolina, playing into the early hours of 2006 with former vocalist Greg X. Volz and current vocalist John Schlitt trading vocals on songs each had made famous.

Petra reunited for a concert in Buenos Aires, Argentina, in December 2007, and Schlitt and Harman produced a praise and worship album, *Vertical Expression*, after the band disbanded. (It was released as *II Guys From Petra*.)

Petra was never the critics' favorite; those in the Christian music industry as well as the secular industry often tended to dismiss the band as musical lightweights. But Petra was a long-haul group, and they endured. Their success owes as much to simply staying the course as it does to hit albums and a fan base. The group appealed to young people who yearned for an alternative to secular rock, and Petra provided that for them. They were not the only Christian rock band during the early days— Servant, the Resurrection Band, Agape, and Barnabas all evolved from the Jesus movement—but Petra outlasted them all.

Petra was an early and dedicated supporter of Compassion International and also signed on to promote a political campaign for a Constitutional amendment to legislate prayer in public schools.

In 2000 Petra became the first Christian rock band inducted into the Gospel Music Hall of Fame.

Don Cusic

Petra (1974)
Come and Join Us (1977)

Washes Whiter Than (1979)
Never Say Die (1981)
More Power to Ya (1982)
Not of This World (1983)
Beat the System (1985)
Captured in Time and Space (1986)
Back to the Street (1986)
This Means War (1987)
On Fire! (1988)
Petra Means Rock (1989)
Petra Praise (1989)
The Rock Cries Out (1989)
War and Remembrance: Fifteen Years of Rock (1990)
Beyond Belief (1990)
Unseen Power (1991)
Petrafied: The Very Best of Petra (1991)
Petraphonics (1992)
Wake-up Call (1993)
Petra Power Praise (1995)
The Rock Block (1995)
No Doubt (1995)
The Early Years (1996)
Petra Praise 2: We Need Jesus (1997)
God Fixation (1998)
Double Take (2000)
Revival (2001)
Jekyll and Hyde (2002)
Farewell (2005)

Gospel Music Association Dove Awards

1990   Long Form Music Video: *On Fire* by Petra; Director: Stephen Yake

1991   Group of the Year

1991   Rock Album: *Beyond Belief* by Petra (Producers: John and Dino Elefante; Label: DaySpring)

1991   Rock Recorded Song: "Beyond Belief" (Writer: Bob Hartman; Recorded by Petra; Label: DaySpring)

1993   Rock Recorded Song: "Destiny" (Writers: Bob Hartman, John Elefante; Recorded by Petra; Label: DaySpring)

1994   Rock Album: *Wake-Up Call* by Petra (Producer: Brown Bannister; Label: DaySpring)

1996   Rock Album: *No Doubt* by Petra (Producers: John and Dino Elefante; Label: Word)

1998   Praise and Worship Album: *Petra Praise 2: We Need Jesus* by Petra (Producers: John and Dino Elefante; Label: Word)

Grammy Awards

1990   33rd Grammy Awards: Best Rock/Contemporary Gospel Album: *Beyond Belief* by Petra

1992   35th Grammy Awards: Best Rock/Contemporary Gospel Album: *Unseen Power* by Petra

1994   37th Grammy Awards: Best Rock Gospel Album: *Wake-Up Call* by Petra

2000   43rd Grammy Awards: Best Rock Gospel Album: *Double Take* by Petra

For Further Reading

Alfonso, Barry. *The Billboard Guide to Contemporary Christian Music.* New York: Billboard Books/Watson-Guptill, 2002.

Cusic, Don. *The Sound of Light: A History of Gospel and Christian Music.* New York: Hal Leonard, 2002.

Hartman, Bob. *More Power to Ya.* Cincinnati, Ohio: Standard Publishing, 1997.

McNeil, W. K., ed. *Encyclopedia of American Gospel Music.* New York: Routledge, 2005.

Powell, Mark Allen. *Encyclopedia of Contemporary Christian Music.* Peabody, Mass.: Hendrickson Publishers, Inc., 2002.

PFR (PRAY FOR RAIN)

PFR, originally called Pray for Rain, was a group with strong Beatlesque melodies and smooth pop songs; the group was Patrick Andrew, bass, vocals; Joel Hanson, vocals, guitar; and Mark Nash, drums, vocals.

The group traces its origins back to Camp Shamineau in Minnesota: in the summer of 1987 music leader Joel Hanson met camp counselor Mark Nash and the two played some songs together. In the fall of 1988 Patrick Andrew began coming to the youth group pastored by Hanson; the three—Hanson on guitar, Nash on drums, and Andrew on bass—began playing songs for the worship services. The group was first called the Joel Hanson Band, then Inside Out. The band played for Christian youth groups in and around Minnesota and opened for several Christian acts coming through the area. They opened for Steve Camp, who was impressed and passed the word along about Inside Out to producer Jimmie

Lee Sloas, who brought them to the attention of producer Brown Bannister, who had just started a label, Vireo, as part of the Sparrow family.

Bannister signed the group and Sloas produced their first album; however, before the album was released, Andrew suggested they change their name to Pray for Rain because he had read that line in a poem. The group's debut album, *Pray for Rain*, caused a problem when it was discovered there was another group by that same name who threatened a lawsuit, so they changed their name to PFR.

The group has pop-type vocals and strong melodies with tight vocal harmonies; it is obvious that the Beatles were a strong influence, as well as singer-songwriters such as Dan Fogelberg. The group recorded "We Can Work It Out" with help from guitarist Phil Keaggy for an album, *Come Together: America Salutes the Beatles*, produced by Michael Omartian and released on Capitol, the Beatles label in 1995.

PFR won the 1993 Dove for "Rock Album" for their album, *Pray for Rain*.

The group recorded for five years, recording five albums, before they disbanded in 1997. Mark Nash married Leigh Nash with Sixpence None the Richer and became A&R director for Steve Taylor's Squint Records, then opened his own studio, Bookhouse. Hanson worked as a staff songwriter for a publishing company in Nashville, and Andrew formed the group Eager. Andrew recorded an album with Eager and then a solo album, *There* and *Then It's Gone*. Hanson recorded two solo projects, *Broken* and *Captured*. The group appeared together occasionally, usually for benefits or special concerts.

Later, Andrew moved to Scottsdale, Arizona, where he became worship leader at McDowell Mountain Community Church; Hanson moved to Minneapolis, where he works with Church of the Open Door.

In 2001, PFR reunited and recorded *Disappear* and in 2004 released *The Bookhouse Recordings*, recorded at Nash's studio and consisting of rerecordings of their previous hits with several new songs.

Don Cusic

For Further Reading

Powell, Mark Allen. *Encyclopedia of Contemporary Christian Music*. Peabody, Mass.: Hendrickson Publishers, Inc., 2002.

Thompson, John J. *Raised by Wolves: The Story of Christian Rock and Roll*. Toronto, Ontario: ECW Press, 2000.

PHILLIPS, SAM

Sam Phillips's (b. 1962) first contemporary Christian recording was the song "Bring Me Through" on Maranatha's *Back to the Rock* (1981) album. She then released four contemporary Christian music albums for Myrrh Records under the name Leslie Phillips, *Beyond Saturday Night* (1983), *Dancing with Danger* (1984), *Black and White in a Grey World* (1985), and *The Turning: Recollection* (1987), before she broke with the contemporary Christian culture. Phillips was critical of conservative Christianity, because "the fundamentalism I experienced in gospel music didn't hold up."

Phillips became a Christian when she was ten after her brother took her to the musical *Come Together*, written by Jimmy and Carol Owens. She then became involved in the Church on the Way, pastured by Jack Hayford in Van Nuys, California.

Phillips's fourth Christian album, *The Turning*, was produced by T Bone Burnett; they later married and she went into pop music and released a series of albums under the name "Sam Phillips" (a childhood nickname) on Virgin Records: *The Indescribable WOW* (1988), *Cruel Inventions* (1991), *Martinis and Bikinis* (1994), and *Omnipop (It's Only a Flesh Wound, Lambchop)* (1996).

Phillips has toured with Counting Crows, Cowboy Junkies, Elvis Costello, and Bruce Cockburn and made her acting debut in the movie *Die Hard With a Vengeance*, playing the wife of terrorist Jeremy Irons.

Don Cusic

For Further Reading

Alfonso, Barry. *The Billboard Guide to Contemporary Christian Music*. New York: Billboard Books/Watson-Guptill, 2002.

Powell, Mark Allen. *Encyclopedia of Contemporary Christian Music*. Peabody, Mass.: Hendrickson Publishers, Inc., 2002.

PILLAR, MICHELLE

Michele Pillar (nee Zarges) was raised in Long Beach, California, and was part of the Maranatha Music program at Calvary Chapel. Her first recording was the song "Thou Art Worthy" on Maranatha's *Praise Two* album (1976). Michelle and Erick Nelson performed as a duet and recorded *The Misfit* (1979), a concept album. She led Christian singles seminars as Michelle Zarges for seven years, then married Steve Pillar in 1979 and signed with Sparrow Records. Her first two albums, *Michele Pillar* (1982) and *Reign on Me* (1983), were recorded in Muscle Shoals, Alabama. Pillar was associated with James Dobson's Focus on the Family radio show and recorded the theme song for that show.

Pillar's fourth album, *Look Who Loves You Now* (1984), was produced by guitarist Larry Carlton; they later married and moved to Nashville.

Don Cusic

For Further Reading

Powell, Mark Allen. *Encyclopedia of Contemporary Christian Music*. Peabody, Mass.: Hendrickson Publishers, Inc., 2002.

PLUMB

Plumb was a group, but when the group disbanded, lead singer Tiffany Lee Arbuckle (b. March 9, 1975) decided to keep the name for herself. The name was chosen after Arbuckle first heard a song by Suzanne Vega called "My Favorite Plum." She later related it to the theme of a "plumb line" from the writings of the prophets. A plumb line is a simple but accurate tool used for determining whether or not something is perfectly vertical. It is believed that Jesus Christ owned a set of various plumb lines for use in his building trade as a carpenter. It is also believed that the Lord uses a plumb line to determine how upright his people are in his sight.

Born in Indianapolis, Indiana, and raised near Atlanta, Tiffany Arbuckle never imagined the path her life would take. With a lifelong love of music to her credit, at 19 she began working as a backup singer with the hope of putting away enough money for nursing school. She caught the attention of an area band called Benjamin and was invited to audition; that led to a stint of road travel with the group. She enjoyed the experience, but after a few years with Benjamin she decided it was time to move on to Nashville.

Her clear, expressive voice quickly made her in demand doing studio work. Nursing school was soon forgotten, and by the time she turned 21 she was living in Nashville and celebrating her first recording contract with Essential Records. After assembling a group of like-minded musicians, the group Plumb was born and hit the road with a unique blend of alternative Christian rock.

Encouraged by the label and frustrated with the material she was given to record, Plumb eagerly embraced writing her own material. She bought a used guitar from her next door neighbor, Matt Bronlewee, who is a founding member of the Christian rock band Jars Of Clay. Bronlewee and Arbuckle became fast friends and remain collaborators today.

In 1999 Plumb released their second album, *candycoatedwaterdrops* and it seemed like the group had found hit stride. The album received a Gospel Music Association Dove Award for "Alternative/Modern Rock Album" at the 2000 ceremony, but soon the relationship with her record label began to deteriorate and she made the decision to move on as a solo act. The group Plumb disbanded and the solo artist Plumb was born.

In 2003, Plumb signed a solo deal with Curb Records and released *Beautiful Lumps of Coal*. The album spawned several Christian radio hits and broadened her fan base. *Chaotic Resolve* followed in 2006 and, while awaiting the birth of her second son and unable to handle the rigors of road life, she wrote the material for what would be her third Curb studio album, *Blink*.

In 2008, the success of "In My Arms" from Plumb's *Blink* CD brought another first in her career when she became the first Christian artist to hit number 1 on the dance top 40 chart and the first artist (of any genre) to chart simultaneously on the dance, adult contemporary and Christian charts in *Billboard* with the same song.

Liz Cavanaugh

For Further Reading

Powell, Mark Allen. *Encyclopedia of Contemporary Christian Music*. Peabody, Mass.: Hendrickson Publishers, Inc., 2002.

PLUS ONE

The success of secular boy bands N'Sync and the Backstreet Boys led the Christian market to look for a Christian boy band; Plus One was formed by a major secular label—Atlantic—to fill this gap in the market. The five handsome young men all came from Assembly of God churches and three of the boys—Nathan Cole, Gabriel Combs, and Jason Perry—were the sons of preachers; the other two members were Jeremy Mhire and Nathan Walters. The group was formed after a series of national auditions to recruit a group.

Like N'Sync and the Backstreet Boys, Plus One had tight harmonies and stage moves choreographed to perfection; they had a gold album with their first release, produced by pop producer David Foster, and won a Dove for "New Artist of the Year" for 2001; but, like other boy bands, their audience of young teens grew older and left them. However, before the group disbanded in 2004, they had sung at the Democratic National Convention in 2004, appeared on an episode of the TV soap opera "Days of Our Lives," and enjoyed several successful tours.

In 2002 two members of the group—Jeremy Mhire and Jason Perry—left; the remaining three members of Plus One continued until 2004 when the remaining three dissolved the group. Nathan Cole and Gabe Combs formed Castledoor, a rock band, while Nathan Winters pursued a solo career.

Don Cusic

For Further Reading

Alfonso, Barry. *The Billboard Guide to Contemporary Christian Music*. New York: Billboard Books/Watson-Guptill, 2002.

Powell, Mark Allen. *Encyclopedia of Contemporary Christian Music*. Peabody, Mass.: Hendrickson Publishers, Inc., 2002.

POINT OF GRACE

Shelly Phillips Breen
Denise Jones
Terry Lang Jones
Heather Floyd Payne
Leigh Cappallino
Dana Cappallino, guitar
Tommy McGee, bass
Derek Wyatt, J. D. Blair, and Michael Passons have also performed with the group

The core audience for contemporary Christian music is females, so it is not surprising that a female group should become successful in Christian music. What is surprising is the level of success that Point of Grace has achieved, with gold and platinum albums, 24 consecutive number one singles, a string of Dove Awards and—outside the awards and hits—a profound connection with girls and women in the Christian audience.

The seeds of the group were planted when Heather Floyd, Denise Jones, and Terry Lang, who had been members of the same church in Norman, Oklahoma, found themselves at Ouachita Baptist University in Arkadelphia, Arkansas, in the early 1990s where the three were members of a 14-member vocal group, the Ouachitones. Shelly Phillips was a member of an eight-member mixed group (four guys and four girls) called the Praise Singers. Shelly and Denise Jones were roommates as well as sisters in Chi Delta, a social club.

The three young ladies from Norman, Oklahoma—Heather, Terry, and Denise—decided to form a trio and sing during the summer break from school. When Denise told her roommate, Shelly, about their plans, Shelly wanted in—so the trio became a quartet. They named the group Say So (from Psalm 107:2: "Let the redeemed of the Lord say so").

The group sang together in churches throughout the summer and fall; they recorded an independent album to sell at their concerts, and in the summer of 1992 entered the talent contest at the Music in the Rockies Christian Artists Seminar in Estes Park, Colorado, and won the grand prize in the group competition. This led to a contract with Word Records, and they moved to Nashville and recorded their first album.

The group was an immediate success: their first six singles—all from their debut album *Point of Grace*—went to number one on the Christian charts, they opened for Wayne Watson on a national tour (singing backup while he performed), and received a Dove Award for "New Artist of the Year."

Point of Grace were four attractive young women with tight vocal harmonies whose image was clean-cut and down to earth, so it is no surprise that they soon became role models for young female followers of contemporary Christian music.

Their second album, *The Whole Truth*, continued their streak of number one singles; five singles reached the number one position and the album was certified gold. They did a national tour, toured with the Young Messiah Farewell Tour, and contributed songs to various albums. In 1995 they signed a book deal and were the subject of features in *Time* magazine and *Ladies Home Journal*; their third album, *Life, Love and Other Mysteries*, was released the same day their book, *Advice and Inspiration from Christian Music's #1 Pop Group*, was also released. Their album was certified platinum and they co-headlined an arena tour with 4HIM.

As their career progressed the young ladies married and had children; Denise was the first, then Terry. In 1998 they headlined their first tour and hired their own band, led by guitarist Dana Cappillino. Brown Bannister became their producer beginning with their album *Steady On* and they followed that with a Christmas album. Heather was married in 1999 and Terry had a child.

Point of Grace became involved with the Women of Faith conferences during 2000, although they spent that year not touring. In 2002 they formed Girls of Grace, an organization for young girls that featured conferences, devotional books, and workbooks; the first conference was in October 2002. The group also became involved in Mercy Ministries, aimed at helping young women involved with abuse, depression, unplanned pregnancies, and eating disorders. The group has also been involved with Compassion International since 2006; this organization is a Christian group that sponsors children living in poverty.

The demands of a professional recording and touring act often conflicted with family demands of being a wife and mother; these conflicts led Terry Jones to announce her retirement from Point of Grace in November 2003. She was replaced by Leigh Cappillino, wife of band leader Dana Cappillino; her first concert with the group was on March 12, 2004.

In 2006 Heather gave birth to her third child; in 2008 she and her husband had their fourth child, which led her to resign from Point of Grace. The group—now Shelly Breen, Denise Jones, and Leigh Cappillino—decided to go forward as a trio, electing not to replace Heather.

The success of Point of Grace is due to a variety of factors; their tight harmonies, up-beat messages of joy and encouragement, and the fact that they relate well to the core female audience of contemporary Christian music—as well as their ability at finding and recording hit singles that speak to this audience—have enabled them to become the most successful group in contemporary Christian music since the mid-1990s.

Don Cusic

Discography

Point of Grace (1993)

The Whole Truth (1995)

Life, Love, and Other Mysteries (1996)

Steady On (1998)

A Christmas Story (1999)

Rarities and Remixes (2000)

Free to Fly (2001)

Girls of Grace (2002)

24 (2003)

I Choose You (2004)

Winter Wonderland (2005)

How You Live (2007)

Gospel Music Association Dove Awards

1994   New Artist of the Year

1996   Group of the Year

1996   Pop/Contemporary Album: *The Whole Truth* by Point of Grace (Producer: Robert Sterling; Label: Word)

1996   Pop/Contemporary Recorded Song: "The Great Divide" Written by Grant Cunningham, Matt Huesmann; Recorded by Point of Grace; Label: Word

1996   Special Event Album: *My Utmost for His Highest*; Artists: Amy Grant, Gary Chapman, Michael W. Smith, Point of Grace, 4HIM, Cindy Morgan, Sandi Patty, Bryan Duncan, Steven Curtis Chapman, Twila Paris, Phillips, and Craig and Dean (Producers: Loren Balman and Brown Bannister; Label: Myrrh/Word)

1999   Enhanced CD of the Year: *Stead on Enhanced CD* by Point of Grace (Producers: Denise Niebisch and Rose Irelan; Label: Word Records)

1999   Group of the Year

2000   Special Event Album: *Streams* by Cindy Morgan, Maire Brennan, Michael McDonald, Sixpence None the Richer, Chris Rodriguez, Michelle Tumes, 4HIM, Delirious, Amy Grant, Jaci Velasquez, Burlap to Cashmere, and Point of Grace (Producers: Brent Bourgeois and Loren Balman; Label: Word)

2008   Country Recorded Song of the Year: "How You Live (Turn Up the Music)"; on album *How You Live* by Point of Grace; Songwriter: Cindy Morgan; Label: Word Records

For Further Reading

Alfonso, Barry. *The Billboard Guide to Contemporary Christian Music*. New York: Billboard Books/Watson-Guptill, 2002.

McNeil, W. K., ed. *Encyclopedia of American Gospel Music*. New York: Routledge, 2005.

Point of Grace with Davin Seay. *Life, Love, and Other Mysteries*. New York: Pocket Books, 1996.

Point of Grace. *Circle of Friends*. West Monroe, La.: Howard Books, 1999.

Point of Grace. *Girls of Grace*. West Monroe, La.: Howard Books, 2002.

Point of Grace. *Girls of Grace: Make It Real*. West Monroe, La.: Howard Books, 2005.

Point of Grace. *Girls of Grace: Q&A with Point of Grace*. West Monroe, La.: Howard Books, 2004.

Point of Grace. *Keep the Candle Burning: Reflections from Our Favorite Songs*. West Monroe, La.: Howard Books, 2003.

Point of Grace. *Steady On . . . Secured by Love*. West Monroe, La.: Howard Books, 1998.

Point of Grace. *When Love Came Down at Christmas*. West Monroe, La.: Howard Books, 2000.

Powell, Mark Allen. *Encyclopedia of Contemporary Christian Music*. Peabody, Mass.: Hendrickson Publishers, Inc., 2002.

POLITICS AND CONTEMPORARY CHRISTIAN MUSIC

The Christian counterculture entered the mainstream in 1976 when Jimmy Carter, a born-again evangelical, was elected president. This brought an immense amount of media coverage to the evangelical movement in the United States. In a 1976 survey, the Gallup Poll found that one out of every three Americans considered themselves a born-again Christian; that same year, for the first time since World War II, church attendance increased rather than decreased.

America underwent a spiritual awakening, and Christianity that was fundamental in its beliefs, active in its faith, and in touch with the contemporary culture became acceptable. The term "born again" became known, accepted, and practiced, with many Americans undergoing a rebirth in their spiritual lives. This was highlighted in 1977 by the publication of the book *Born Again* by Nixon's former hatchet man, Chuck Colson, and the beginning of Jimmy Carter's presidency. Carter's campaign and presidency made the born-again movement known and accepted to a wide cross section of Americans who had looked with disfavor on the contemporary Christian culture. It also forced the press to seriously examine the Christian culture.

However, the greatest impact the political world made on contemporary Christian music came during the presidency of Ronald Reagan.

The Reagan revolution officially arrived on January 20, 1981, when Ronald Reagan was sworn in as the fortieth president of the United States. The Reagan revolution brought religion and politics together, and this had an immediate impact on politics (the born-again experience became a litmus test for candidates), social issues (such as abortion and school prayer), culture (it was a badge of honor to be considered "Christian" and a mark of disrepute to be labeled "liberal" in some circles), and religion (which received major news coverage on a regular basis).

The evangelical community had been disappointed with Jimmy Carter. First, his politics (and the politics of the Democratic party in general) were too liberal to suit their tastes; too, they felt he had let them down on issues like school prayer, abortion, and defense.

Reagan campaigned with the theme that "government isn't the solution, government is the problem" and held the view that less government is better, none is best. This fit perfectly with the evangelical right, who had an innate distrust of government institutions and generally felt a discomfort with some of the rules that governed them. The right, led by no less than the president himself, felt that government was not only too big and burdensome but that it was a moral evil infecting American society. They set about changing it, cleansing it, purifying it, and molding it to their own image.

Many of those in gospel music saw a battle raging between good and evil—the righteous and the ungodly—and believed that the force of righteousness would cleanse this country and lead it down the paths of righteousness. As musicians, they saw their position akin to the position of the musicians in Jehosophat's army from the Old Testament—as leaders who went before the army and won the battle before it could even be fought.

The Reagan revolution, which brought a number of evangelical Christians into the voting booths and got them involved in politics, had a direct influence on Christian music because people in the gospel music industry, inspired and influenced by the notion of activist voting, began to join the National Academy of Recording Arts and Sciences (NARAS) in larger numbers and to cast their votes for the Grammys. This represented a major change in attitude within the Christian community. Previously, evangelical Christians had generally shunned the political arena—many not even registering to vote or not voting if they were registered—because it was considered a worldly pursuit, had nothing to do with their faith, and was irrelevant to their salvation. A similar view was held in the gospel music community toward secular awards, so, until 1980, a large number of evangelical Christians did not bother joining NARAS because they felt it was irrelevant to their mission: to spread the gospel through music. That attitude changed dramatically in 1980, and the result was the election of Ronald Reagan as president and a much greater involvement from Christian labels and artists in the Grammy awards.

When Ronald Reagan captured 59 percent of the popular vote in the 1984 presidential election against Walter Mondale—capturing every state except Minnesota, the religious right looked at the outcome as a mandate for their ideas, views, and programs. Fundamentalists saw homosexuals, the Equal Rights Amendment, the legalization of abortion, sex education in public schools, and the absence of prayer in public schools as threats. These fundamentalists held traditional values, an absolute certainty about things temporal and eternal, and had an infectious enthusiasm for evangelism. They were also united in at least one mission: to rid America of secular humanism.

White evangelical Protestants accounted for about 20 percent of the U.S. population and, as evangelical leaders pushed voter registrations, 80 percent of these evangelicals voted for Reagan versus 20 percent for Mondale.

Blacks and Jews stayed predominantly Democratic in 1984 but mainline church attendees (who accounted for about 30 percent of the electorate) voted overwhelmingly for Reagan.

The embrace of cultural concerns by the Christian community meshed with the platform of the Republican Party beginning in the 1980s. Evangelical Christian leaders openly embraced the Republican Party, and the evangelical community became Republican voters because they felt this party reflected their Christian beliefs. Contemporary Christian artists embraced the Republican Party and a number of Christian acts—including Amy Grant, Michael W. Smith, Sandi Patti, and Steven Curtis Chapman—campaigned for Republican Presidents George H. W. Bush and George W. Bush and were invited to sing at the White House and socialize with presidents.

In many ways, the Jesus movement morphed into the religious right; their zeal for Jesus and the concept of the United States as a Christian nation found a home in the Republican Party beginning in the mid-1980s and the presidency of Ronald Reagan.

Don Cusic

For Further Reading

Cusic, Don. *The Sound of Light: A History of Gospel and Christian Music.* New York: Hal Leonard, 2002.

POPULAR MUSIC AND CONTEMPORARY CHRISTIAN MUSIC

Gospel and Christian songs—or songs that mentioned God or Jesus—were on the radio and pop charts since the 1950s, and served as a forerunner to contemporary Christian music, which was heavily influenced by pop and rock radio. Many of the songs on the charts during this period embraced a spirituality, although it was not always Christianity; still, this spiritual search manifested itself for many during the Jesus movement, when a number of young people came to embrace Jesus as the answer to their search.

The *Billboard* pop charts in 1955 had "Angels in the Sky" by the Crew Cuts, "The Bible Tells Me So" by Don Cornell, and two recordings of "He," one by Al Hibbler and the other by the McGuire Sisters, which all reached the top 15 that year. In 1956 "Every Time (I Feel His Spirit)" by Patti Page, "Give Us This Day" by Joni James, "The Good Book" by Kay Starr, and "Sinner Man" by Les Baxter all reached the charts. In 1957 "Peace in the Valley" by Elvis Presley and "There's a Gold Mine in the Sky" by Pat Boone charted. In 1958 "A Wonderful Time Up There" by Pat Boone as well as the two versions of "He's Got the Whole World in His Hands" were on the charts; "Battle Hymn of the Republic" by the Mormon Tabernacle Choir, "Deck of Cards" by Wink Martindale, and "When the Saints Go Marching In" by Fats Domino all charted in 1959.

As radio gave up live entertainment in favor of records in the 1950s because of economics (the advertisers shifted their ad buys to television), recordings achieved a new significance. Two single records, which each reached number one on the music trade charts, reflected large social movements that began in the 1950s. In 1955 Bill Haley and the Comets had a number one hit with "Rock Around the Clock," marking the official beginning of the rock 'n' roll era; in 1958 the Kingston Trio had a number one song with "Tom Dooley" ushering in the folk music movement.

Rock 'n' roll divided the generations because of its music while folk divided them because of the lyrics. As the Jesus movement developed and spread in the late 1960s, it was heavily influenced by both of these musical forms.

The Recording Industry Association of America (RIAA), the organization which monitors record sales and awards gold and platinum records, began awarding gold records in 1958, and that year "He's Got the Whole World in His Hands" by Laurie London achieved gold status. It also reached the number one position on the charts in April of that year. This was Laurie London's only success in the charts; ironically, Mahalia Jackson also recorded this old gospel song and released it at the same time, but Mahalia's version only reached number 60 on the charts.

In 1959 Tennessee Ernie Ford's album, *Hymns*, was awarded gold status, and in 1961 his *Spirituals* album achieved that summit. He had two other gold albums in 1962, *Nearer the Cross*, and a Christmas album, *Star Carol*. Ford hosted a popular weekly television show during this time.

The success of gospel songs on the pop charts in the late 50s and early 60s was an early indication of the spiritual revival that was to take place in the mid-to-late-60s. This spiritual revival preceded the Christian revival that took place at the end of that decade.

The 1960s began with Ferlin Huskey's "Wings of a Dove" reaching the number 12 position; in 1961 there was chart activity for "Child of God" by Bobby Darin and the number one song "Michael" by the Highwaymen; in 1963 the Singing Nun had a number one song with "Dominique" and Steve Alaimo reached the charts with his version of "Michael"; in 1964 "All My Trials" by Dick and Deedee, "Amen" by the Impressions, "I Believe" by the Bachelors, "Oh Rock My Soul" by Peter, Paul and Mary, "Michael" by Trini Lopez, "Tell It on the Mountain" by Peter, Paul and Mary, and "You'll Never Walk Alone" by Patti LaBelle and the Blue Belles all reached the charts. In 1963 *The Lord's Prayer* by the Mormon Tabernacle Choir was awarded a gold album.

In 1965 "Turn, Turn, Turn," a rewriting of the biblical Ecclesiastes, was a number one song for the Byrds, and "Eve of Destruction" by Barry McGuire also reached that spot. "People Get Ready" by the Impressions was a hit that year. "I'm a Believer" was not a song about Christianity, but that title reflected the religious undercurrent in 1966 when it became number one. "Crying in the Chapel" by Elvis reached number three in 1965, "Blowin' in the Wind" became a top ten song for Stevie Wonder in 1966, and "God Only Knows" was a chart record for the Beach Boys that same year.

In June 1967 the Beatles released their album *Sgt. Pepper's Lonely Hearts Club Band*, which ushered in the Summer of Love; at the end of 1967, the Beatles reached number one with "All You Need is Love" which also achieved gold status and personified that period. In 1968 Elvis Presley was awarded a gold record for his gospel album, *How Great Thou Art*, while

Simon and Garfunkel broke the invisible barrier pop radio had put up against the word "Jesus." That was the year of *The Graduate* soundtrack, and its number one single, "Mrs. Robinson" featured the line, "Jesus loves you more than you will know" in the chorus.

In addition to *The Graduate* at movie theaters, there was *Hair* on the Broadway stage, and Woodstock, the ultimate concert. And all of these were somehow "spiritual" experiences as well as entertainment for this generation. Perhaps this "spiritualness" was best expressed in the song "Abraham, Martin, and John" by Dion DiMucci.

In May 1969 "Oh Happy Day" reached the number four position on *Billboard*'s chart. The song was an old spiritual recorded by the Edwin Hawkins Singers, a black youth choir with a leader from Oakland. Outside of Mahalia Jackson, who reached the charts several times but never had a top ten single, the Edwin Hawkins Singers were the only genuine gospel artists to have a hit single on secular radio. All through this period of the late 60s, a number of spiritual and gospel-flavored songs were hits, but they would have to be done by secular artists. In 1969 came the anthem "Get Together" by the Youngbloods, which was a rock song ready-made for campfire gatherings, as well as "Jesus is a Soul Man" by Lawrence Reynolds, which put Jesus in the middle of the black movement.

The year 1969 is crucial in tracing the roots for contemporary Christian music because "Crystal Blue Persuasion" and "Sweet Cherry Wine," both by Tommy James and the Shondells, "Dammit Isn't God's Last Name" by Frankie Lane, "Kum Ba Ya" by Tommy Leonetti, "That's the Way God

Planned It" by Billy Preston, "Turn! Turn! Turn!" by Judy Collins, and "You'll Never Walk Alone" by the Brooklyn Bridge all reached the charts with a Christian message in the lyrics.

Writers Andrew Lloyd Webber and Tim Rice had written a 15-minute operetta titled *Joseph and the Amazing Technicolor Dreamcoat* in 1968 about the Joseph in Genesis. It was written for the schoolboy choir at Celet Court School in London and was well-received. Since they had done so well on their first project, the two decided to do another more elaborate rock operetta; the result was *Jesus Christ Superstar*. Two songs from *Jesus Christ Superstar* became hit singles—"I Don't Know How to Love Him," recorded originally by Yvonne Elliman and then by Helen Reddy, and "Superstar," by Murray Head, who was in the cast of the rock opera.

In addition to the songs previously mentioned, there was "Amazing Grace" by Judy Collins, "Are You Ready" by Pacific Gas and Electric, "Church Street Soul Revival" by Tommy James, "Holy Man" by Diane Kolby, "I Heard the Voice of Jesus" by Turley Richards, "Oh Happy Day" by Glen Campbell, "Spirit in the Sky" by Dorothy Morrison, "Stealing in the Name of the Lord" by Paul Kelly, "Stoned Love" by the Supremes, and versions of "Fire and Rain" by James Taylor, R. B. Greaves, and Johnny Rivers, which all reached the charts in 1970.

In 1971 there were two more gospel songs that were hits—"Put Your Hand in the Hand" by Ocean and "Amazing Grace" by Aretha Franklin. Both achieved gold status. Also on the charts in 1971 were "All My Trials" by Ray

Stevens, "Come Back Home" by Bobby Goldsboro, "Deep Enough for Me" by Ocean, "Mighty Clouds of Joy" by B. J. Thomas, "My Sweet Lord" by Billy Preston, "Take My Hand" by Kenny Rogers and the First Edition, "Life" by Elvis Presley, "Grandma's Hands" by Bill Withers, "Think His Name" by Johnny Rivers, "Top 40 of the Lordy" by Sha Na Na, "Turn Your Radio On" by Ray Stevens, and "Wedding Song (There is Love)" by Noel Paul Stookey.

Godspell, another rock opera based on the life of Jesus, appeared in 1972 and was also awarded gold status. "Day by Day" from the musical became a hit single. In 1972 "I'd Like to Teach the World to Sing," which began as a commercial for Coca-Cola, became another spiritual anthem for brotherhood. A country hit also reached the pop charts: "Me and Jesus," by Tom T. Hall provided a chorus that articulated the stand of defiance many were taking regarding Christianity: "Me and Jesus got our own thing going/ . . . got it all worked out/ . . . And we don't need anybody to tell us what it's all about."

Other gospel-related songs that reached the charts in 1972 were "Amazing Grace" by the Royal Scots Dragoon Guards, "I'll Take You There" by the Staple Singers, "Joy" by Apollo 100, "Jesus is Just Alright" by the Doobie Brothers, "Jubilation" by Paul Anka, "Morning Has Broken" by Cat Stevens, "Speak to the Sky" by Rick Springfield, "That's the Way God Planned It" by Billy Preston, "Wedding Song (There Is Love)" by Petula Clark, and "Wholly Holy" by Aretha Franklin.

The year 1973 brought a platinum album for the movie soundtrack of *Jesus Christ Superstar* as well as an answer from Glen Campbell: "I Knew Jesus Before He Was a Superstar." 1973 also saw an album by Kris Kristofferson, *Jesus Was a Capricorn*, that featured "Why Me, Lord," one of the most overt Christian songs ever to be a major hit. "Jesus is Just Alright," which was a top ten single for the Doobie Brothers, furthered the cause.

There was less gospel activity on the pop charts from 1974 through 1976, although gold records were awarded to "The Lord's Prayer" by Jim Nabors as well as another version of that song by Sister Janet Meade; "I Don't Know How to Love Him" by Helen Reddy and "Did You Think to Pray" by Charley Pride also went gold. But 1977 was a different story as Debby Boone had a number one single and platinum album with *You Light Up My Life*.

There were "celebrity conversions" that lent an air of respectability to contemporary Christian music. Paul Stookey and B. J. Thomas, then later Bob Dylan, B. W. Stevenson, Donna Summer, Philip Bailey, Deniece Williams, Johnny Rivers, Van Morrison, and U2 all made public confessions of their Christian faith.

In 1991 and again in 2001 Lee Greenwood had a hit with "God Bless the USA." Also in 2001 LeAnn Rimes had a pop chart record with "God Bless America." In 1992 Genesis had a chart record with "Jesus He Knows Me," and in 1996 George Michael had a top single with "Jesus to a Child."

Amy Grant is the contemporary Christian artist who has had the most success in the world of pop music; in 1985 she reached the pop charts with "Find a Way," followed by "Wise Up." In 1986 her duet with Peter

Cetera, "The Next Time I Fall," reached number one on the pop charts, and in 1991 "Baby Baby" was a number one pop hit followed by "Every Heartbeat," which reached number two and "That's What Love Is For," which reached number seven. In 1992 "Good for Me" was a top ten pop hit. Other songs from Grant that reached the pop charts in the 1990s were "I Will Remember You," "Lucky One," "House of Love," "Big Yellow Taxi," and "Takes a Little Time."

In 1991 Michael W. Smith had a top ten pop hit with "Place In This World." During the 1990s he had four more songs on the pop charts: "For You," "I Will Be Here for You," "Somebody Love Me," and "Love Me Good." In 1996 DC Talk was on the pop chart with "Just Between You and Me," and in 1997 Bob Carlisle had a top ten hit with "Butterfly Kisses."

Gospel has influenced the pop music world—and is influenced by the pop music world—yet the two remain mostly separate. There are few instances of musicians functioning in both worlds because, for the most part, it is an either/or situation and an artist must chose one side or the other.

Don Cusic

For Further Reading

Cusic, Don. *The Sound of Light: A History of Gospel and Christian Music*. New York: Hal Leonard, 2002.

Whitburn, Joel. *The Billboard Book of Top 40 Albums*. New York: Billboard Books, 1991.

Whitburn, Joel. *Pop Memories 1890– 1954*. Menomonee Falls, Wis.: Record Research, Inc., 1986.

Whitburn, Joel. *Top Pop Singles 1955– 2002*. Menomonee Falls, Wis.: Record Research, 2003.

PRAISE AND WORSHIP MUSIC

When those in the Jesus movement joined or founded churches, they wanted a music connected to popular culture rather than the traditional hymns and songs of the church. When these churches were founded, they generally began as small, independent, nondenominational "store-front" gatherings of believers who sang and worshiped with songs from the Jesus movement. Some of these churches grew to become major congregations, and church members often formed musical groups who performed at church services. There was usually a worship leader who led the congregation in songs with lyrics directed to God.

Praise and worship music evolved from the songs sung in the services of these nondenominational churches. They are songs that are musically more akin to pop and rock music (especially soft rock) than to traditional hymns. Churches often have a band comprising electric guitars, bass, keyboards, and drums playing behind a worship leader who serves as a lead singer for the congregation.

The songs are often simple, with few words and easy to remember melodies. These worship songs often come from scripture, taking a phrase from the Bible and setting it to a melody; other songs are written to praise and exalt God and Jesus.

The praise and worship genre first gained national attention in 1974 when

Maranatha, the label started by Calvary Church in Costa Mesa, California, released *The Praise Album*. This album featured songs originally sung at Calvary Chapel, but soon a number of other churches were singing these songs. In 1976 Maranatha released their second album, *Praise II*, and eventually released 20 volumes in this series.

Praise and worship songs were intended for church services but increasingly found favor with consumers who wished to celebrate praise and worship in their homes. As the genre became increasingly popular, a number of contemporary Christian artists devoted themselves to writing, recording, and performing praise and worship songs, which are used in concerts that often become a church-type service with the audience gathered not just to enjoy a concert but to worship God.

Don Cusic

For Further Reading

Alfonso, Barry. *The Billboard Guide to Contemporary Christian Music*. New York: Billboard Books/Watson-Guptill, 2002.

Cusic, Don. *The Sound of Light: A History of Gospel and Christian Music*. New York: Hal Leonard, 2002.

McNeil, W. K., ed. *Encyclopedia of American Gospel Music*. New York: Routledge, 2005.

Powell, Mark Allen. *Encyclopedia of Contemporary Christian Music*. Peabody, Mass.: Hendrickson Publishers, Inc., 2002.

Howard, Jay R., and John M. Streck. *Apostles of Rock: The Splintered World of Contemporary Christian Music*. Lexington: The University Press of Kentucky, 1999.

PRESLEY, ELVIS

Elvis Presley's (b. January 8, 1935; d. August 16, 1977) gospel roots—and his love of gospel music—make him a candidate for a pioneer in contemporary Christian music. However, his gospel roots are in southern gospel music, which the early Jesus music artists were not aware of or, if they were aware, did not trust this field as truly "Christian." Also, Elvis himself was never considered part of the contemporary Christian music field because his Christian convictions were always considered suspect.

In 1956 Elvis sold more than 10 million records and became a cultural phenomenon; not only did he dominate the music business that year, he also provided controversy as rock 'n' roll captured American youth. Preachers and parents preached against him, community leaders warned against him, and a significant portion of the adult middle class was against him, the music he sang, and his movements on stage, which were considered downright provocative and blatantly sexual.

On Elvis's third appearance on "The Ed Sullivan Show" he closed with the Thomas Dorsey hymn "Peace in the Valley" and in 1957, at the height of his early fame when many religious leaders accused him of being an instrument of the devil, Elvis released a four song EP *Peace in the Valley*, which contained that song as well as "It Is No Secret," "I Believe," and another Thomas Dorsey song, "Take My Hand,

Actor and singer Elvis Presley holds his semi-acoustic guitar during a December 1968 concert. (AP Photo)

Precious Lord." These were all gospel standards and came as a surprise to many of his fans who were not aware of Elvis's gospel roots or love of gospel music.

Elvis Presley had grown up listening to and singing gospel songs. He loved the Statesmen and the Blackwood Brothers, both southern gospel quartets, and initially wanted to be a gospel singer. His early success in rock 'n' roll changed his musical direction but he retained a love of gospel.

Elvis was born and grew up in Tupelo, Mississippi, and his parents attended a Pentecostal church and sang gospel music at home. When Elvis was 13 the family moved to Memphis, home of the Blackwoods, and Elvis was able to see gospel performers in concert as well as hear a lot of gospel music. Although he loved the southern gospel sound, Elvis also loved black

gospel and often attended the East Trigg Baptist Church to hear spirituals.

In 1960, after he was discharged from the Army, Elvis recorded his first full-length gospel album, *His Hand in Mine*. That album included the title song, "I'm Gonna Walk Dem Golden Stairs, "In My Father's House," "Milky White Way," "Known Only to Him," "I Believe in the Man in the Sky," "Joshua Fit the Battle," "He Knows Just What I Need," "Swing Down Sweet Chariot," and "Mansion over the Hilltop." Seven of those songs came from albums by the Statesmen that he owned.

In May 1966, he recorded the songs for his *How Great Thou Art* album. On that album were the title song, "In the Garden," "Somebody Bigger Than You and I," "Farther Along," "Stand by Me," "Without Him," "So High," "Where Could I Go But to the Lord," "By and By," "If the Lord Wasn't Walking by My Side," "Run On," "Where No One Stands Alone," and "Crying in the Chapel." That album was released in March 1967 and led to him receiving his first Grammy award for "Best Sacred Performance."

Elvis's next gospel album was *He Touched Me*, which featured the title song written by Bill Gaither in addition to "I've Got Confidence" (written by Andrae Crouch), "Amazing Grace," "Seeing Is Believing," "He Is My Everything," "Bosom of Abraham," "An Evening Prayer," "Lead Me, Guide Me," "There Is No God But God," "A Thing Called Love," "I John," and "Reach out to Jesus." This led to his second Grammy.

During the time when the Jesus movement was evolving, Elvis was certainly known to those in this movement—his movies were still playing and his "comeback special" on NBC at the end of 1968 reinvigorated his musical career—but was generally dismissed by the young Jesus music crowd. That audience was too young and immature to accept an artist such as Elvis, who never renounced his secular career or the wide range of American music he loved and sang. For the Jesus people, this was a sellout and a compromise; they believed that a true Christian could only sing Christian music. Also, the songs that Elvis sang were part of the past for the Jesus people and Elvis performed them with a southern gospel backing—the Jordanaires and later the Imperials, Stamps Quartet, and Sweet Inspirations gave him a full production backing. That was a far cry from the folk-based music of the early Jesus people or the later rock band sound that emanated from 60s groups such as the Beatles, Beach Boys, Buffalo Springfield, and other Southern California groups.

During Elvis's final years, as he performed in concerts with J. D. Sumner and the Stamps Quartet and regularly sang gospel during his shows as well as backstage and in hotel rooms when not in concert, there was a wide gulf between Elvis and the Jesus people. First, Elvis was a superstar who performed in Vegas and no longer connected with young performers other than those he met in recording studios or through his friends in southern gospel. Next, the Jesus people were young and Elvis was part of the past—not a contemporary influence or even someone that wanted to emulate. Finally, Elvis died in 1977 as Jesus music was evolving into contemporary Christian music. After his death, the public became aware of his final years when he became heavily dependent on drugs and his personal life unraveled, so the contemporary Christian world, who demanded their performers adhere to a lifestyle that was far removed from Elvis's life, simply dismissed him as not really "Christian."

The early Jesus music and contemporary Christian artists and audiences were ahistoric; they were not even aware of the history of gospel music or those who had gone before them. As they grew older and matured and became aware of history—because their generation and music were now part of music history—some came to appreciate the contributions Elvis made to gospel music. By 2001, when Elvis was inducted into the Gospel Music Hall of Fame, enough time had passed for some to acknowledge that Elvis was a pioneer to Jesus music because he showed the rock world that gospel was an important part of who he was and what he sang.

Don Cusic

Discography

Peace in the Valley (EP) (1957)

Elvis's Christmas Album (1957)

Elvis Sings Christmas Songs (EP) (1957)

Christmas with Elvis (EP) (1958)

His Hand in Mine (1960)

How Great Thou Art (1967)

Elvis Sings the Wonderful World of Christmas (1971)

He Touched Me (1972)

Amazing Grace: His Greatest Sacred Performances (1994)

If Every Day Was Like Christmas (1994)

Known Only to Him (1989, Elvis Gospel, 1957–1971)

Peace in the Valley: The Complete Gospel Recordings (2000)

Grammy Awards

1967	10th Grammy Awards: Best Sacred Performance: "How Great Thou Art"
1972	15th Grammy Awards: Best Inspirational Performance: "He Touched Me"
1974	17th Grammy Awards: Best Inspirational Performance (Non-Classical): "How Great Thou Art"

For Further Reading

Alfonso, Barry. *The Billboard Guide to Contemporary Christian Music*. New York: Billboard Books/Watson-Guptill, 2002.

Cusic, Don. *The Sound of Light: A History of Gospel and Christian Music*. New York: Hal Leonard, 2002.

Guralnick, Peter, and Ernst Jorgensen. *Elvis Day by Day: The Definitive Record of His Life and Music*. New York: Ballantine, 1999.

Guralnick, Peter. *Careless Love: The Unmaking of Elvis Presley*. Boston: Little, Brown and Co. 1999.

Guralnick, Peter. *Last Train to Memphis: The Rise of Elvis Presley*. Boston: Little, Brown, 1994.

Hopkins, Jerry. *Elvis: A Biography*. New York: Warner, 1971.

Hopkins, Jerry. *Elvis: The Final Years*. New York: Playboy, 1981.

McNeil, W. K., ed. *Encyclopedia of American Gospel Music*. New York: Routledge, 2005.

Moscheo, Joe. *The Gospel Side of Elvis*. New York: Center Street, 2007.

Powell, Mark Allen. *Encyclopedia of Contemporary Christian Music*. Peabody, Mass.: Hendrickson Publishers, Inc., 2002.

R

RAMBO, REBA

Those in contemporary Christian music were, for the most part, totally unaware of southern gospel music, while those in southern gospel were often aware of the Jesus movement but distant from it. The linking of the two came from southern gospel artists seeking to move toward a more pop or rock oriented sound as well as a spiritual revival amongst some young members of the southern gospel community.

Reba Rambo (b. October 17, 1951) was part of the Singing Rambos, a family group comprised of her, her mother Dottie, and father Buck; her mother was a legendary gospel songwriter who wrote classics such as "We Shall Behold Him."

Dottie Luttrell (b. March 2, 1934) grew up singing and started writing songs when she was eight; at 12 she left her home in Morganfield, Kentucky, to sing in church revivals and signed a publishing contract with Governor Jimmie Davis of Louisiana. In 1950, at the age of 16, Dottie married Buck Rambo (b. September 15, 1931) and the two called themselves the Singing Echoes. When Reba began singing with them they changed their name to the Singing Rambos and signed with the HeartWarming label, a division of the Benson Company, in 1964. The Singing Rambos were different from most southern gospel groups, who tended to be four males with a piano accompaniment; The Rambos were a mixed group with a guitar accompanist.

The group soon became popular and toured with the Stamps Quartet and the Oak Ridge Boys as Gospel Festival U.S.A. They made a number of recordings, usually recording Dottie's songs. During the 1970s, they stopped performing as a group when Reba embarked on her solo career.

Reba was the same age as many of those in the Jesus movement, but her background in southern gospel was entirely different; during the early 1970s, she began recording as a solo act, and when the Jesus movement began spreading, her label saw her as a way to bridge the southern gospel and Jesus music worlds. However, Reba was not a hippie; that is evident in her first major album, which is titled *Lady*.

That's how Reba saw herself and that's what she ascribed to be; still, she was young enough to be a contemporary Christian music artist, so she became part of that movement, although her singing was more like Barbra Streisand.

Reba toured with Andrae Crouch and the Disciples, sang at Explo '72, and had an early marriage that ended in divorce. She married Dony McGuire in 1980 and they wrote a concept album, *The Lord's Prayer*, that featured the Archers, Cynthia Clawson, Andrae Crouch, Walter and Tramaine Hawkins, and B. J. Thomas. It won both a Grammy and a Dove Award; the group performed this song in 1981 at the Grammys.

Don Cusic

For Further Reading

Alfonso, Barry. *The Billboard Guide to Contemporary Christian Music*. New York: Billboard Books/Watson-Guptill, 2002.

Cusic, Don. *The Sound of Light: A History of Gospel and Christian Music*. New York: Hal Leonard, 2002.

McNeil, W. K., ed. *Encyclopedia of American Gospel Music*. New York: Routledge, 2005.

Powell, Mark Allen. *Encyclopedia of Contemporary Christian Music*. Peabody, Mass.: Hendrickson Publishers, Inc., 2002.

RECORD LABELS

The pioneering record label for Jesus music was Maranatha, which began as an outreach of Calvary Chapel headed by Pastor Chuck Smith. Calvary Chapel, based in Costa Mesa, California, became a gathering place for many young converts to Christianity; Smith was open to these young men and women writing and performing songs about their faith. Music became an integral part of the services at Calvary Chapel, and at one point more than 15 different groups emerged from the church.

Tommy Coomes was one of the long-haired hippie converts attending Calvary Chapel and, like many other California teenagers, had played guitar in a rock 'n' roll bar band. Coomes and his bandmates became Christians, formed the group Love Song, and performed during the Saturday night services at Calvary Chapel. After about a year of performing at the church, Coomes and Chuck Fromm, nephew of Chuck Smith, formed Maranatha Music at the church. The first album, *The Everlastin' Living Jesus Concert*, was a compilation album of various artists that was financed by Pastor Smith and produced by Chuck Girard. The album was released in 1971 and featured cuts by Love Song, Gentle Faith, Selah, Debby Kerner, the Way, and Children of the Day.

An agreement was reached that each album had to pay for itself before another album was recorded. The success of that debut album led to a second album on Maranatha by the group Children of the Day, who had been singing at Calvary Chapel since 1969.

The first two albums released on the new label sold a combined total of more than 25,000 copies with no major distribution or marketing. During the 1970s the label released a number of albums by artists such as Country Faith, the Way, Blessed Hope, Good

News, Mustard Seed Faith, Karen Lafferty, Ernie Rettino and Debby Kerner, Ken Gulliksen, Daniel Amos, Kelly Willard, and the Sweet Comfort Band. Maranatha Music also released a number of compilation albums that featured cuts from various artists.

In addition to their pioneering efforts in recording and releasing Jesus music, Maranatha was a pioneer in the development of praise and worship music. *The Praise Album*, released in 1974, contained the popular praise choruses sung during worship services at Calvary Chapel. That became the first of a 20-volume *Praise Series*, with *Praise II* released in 1976, followed by an instrumental version titled *Praise Strings*. Maranatha Music also introduced the *Colours* series of instrumental collections that combined many of their popular songs with original versions of traditional hymns. Another expansion of their Praise franchise was the guitar-driven worship music collections dubbed *The Praise Band Series*.

Venturing into comedy in the late 1970s, Maranatha Music released two albums by the popular sketch team Isaac Air Freight, *Fun in the Sun* (1978) and *In the Air/on the Air* (1979). Other notable releases were *First Things First* by singer-songwriter Bob Bennett and *Dance Children Dance* by Leon Patillo, a former keyboard player and vocalist with the group Santana.

The executives in charge of Maranatha Music viewed the label as a ministry and made a decision at the end of the 1970s to focus exclusively on providing music for the church. The goal of the record company was to be a resource for churches in the United States and around the world by providing quality worship music.

Maranatha Music also believed there was a need for music that churches could use in children's ministry and released *The Kid's Praise Album* by the Kids Praise Singers in 1980. The album became a national bestseller and led to the first RIAA gold album for Maranatha Music. The popular album led to more *Kids Praise* albums and a series of videos.

By the mid-1980s the infrastructure was in place to make contemporary Christian music a major force in the world of music. Maranatha was an important label for praise and worship music, but three other labels dominated the Christian music field—and continued to dominate it in their various permutations—for the rest of the 20th century and into the 21st.

Those three labels all began as independent companies who recorded only gospel or Christian music but during the 1990s were purchased by major secular recording companies who integrated these artists and albums under their corporate umbrella while allowing the Christian divisions to be staffed separately. Those recording companies are now known as Word/Curb, EMI Christian, and Provident, and under each corporate umbrella are a number of label imprints.

The interest from secular labels came because contemporary Christian music was commercially successful. In mid-1978 the top sellers in contemporary Christian music were B. J. Thomas and Evie Tornquist; each was selling more than 100,000 units of each release, and some albums by these artists reached the 300,000–400,000 plateau. But for most acts, sales of 20,000 were considered good for a first album and 40,000 units was a hit. Ten years later there were gold and platinum albums (representing sales of 500,000 and 1 million, respectively) in contemporary Christian music.

Word Records was a major gospel and Christian label before contemporary Christian music arrived, and they were the first to sign contemporary Christian acts and market them. Word Records came to dominate the gospel music industry in the 20th century, becoming a total Christian communications company with book publishing, videotapes, and audio teaching cassettes in addition to its record labels during the 1980s. By the mid-1980s Word owned several labels and distributed a number of others, penetrating the Christian bookstores and the secular marketplace. Musically, they were diverse, recording and presenting southern gospel, inspirational choirs, black gospel, Jesus rock, contemporary Christian music, and great soloists to the Christian community.

Word Records was started in 1950 by Jarrell McCracken, a student at Baylor University in Waco, Texas. Their first release was "The Game of Life," a spoken word allegory of Christianity and a football game on a mythical radio station, WORD. McCracken decided to name the label Word.

Word's first artist was Frank Boggs, a baritone and old friend of McCracken's who first recorded for Word in 1951. Other early artists include Richard Baker, a song director from Ft. Worth, Billy Pearce, Dick Anthony, the White Sisters, the Melody Four Quartet, J. T. Adams, and some of the choirs at Baylor.

McCracken entered the wholesale distribution business for records in 1954; the company distributed a

progressive jazz label; classical product from Westminster Records; Cricket Records—a line of 25-cent children's records from Pickwick; and Angel Records, a division of EMI. Word stayed in the wholesale distribution business for four years. In 1957 Word began the Family Record Club with a record-of-the-month plan marketed by direct mail.

During its first decade, Word added some key personnel. In 1957, Kurt Kaiser, a pianist, composer, arranger, and conductor, joined Word as vice president and director of artists and repertoire. By 1960, the sale of Word Records was approximately $4 million annually.

The 1960s began for Word with the purchase of Sacred Records, which brought Ralph Carmichael into the Word organization. Carmichael was a noted West Coast writer, arranger, and producer who had been a pioneer innovator in the Christian music field since the late 1940s when he recorded religious music with the popular big band sound of the day. The purchase of Sacred Records also involved the purchase of half of Lexicon Music, a publishing operation owned and run by Carmichael. This involved Word in a total music publishing operation for the first time.

In the mid-1960s the Jesus movement led Word to hire Billy Ray Hearn in the A&R department. Because of his interest and involvement in contemporary Christian music, he was given approval to begin Myrrh Records, which would be their contemporary label while the more traditional artists remained on Word.

The first album on Myrrh was by Ray Hildebrand, who had two albums released on Word before his Myrrh release. Hildebrand was known for being the "Paul" of Paul and Paula, whose 1962 recording of "Hey, Hey Paula" sold close to three million records. The second album released by Myrrh was by an artist who had also had an album on Word. Randy Matthews's album, *Wish We'd All Been Ready*, was the first contemporary Christian release for that label, and he became the first Jesus rock artist to record for Word as Word joined the contemporary market.

Myrrh became the first commercially successful contemporary Christian label after they signed acts Barry McGuire (who had hit the pop charts with "Eve of Destruction" some years before), the 2nd Chapter of Acts, and others who were appealing to the youth with the gospel message. When Word put its muscle behind Myrrh and contemporary Christian music, this lent it a respectability and ensured it shelf space in Christian bookstores, which is where consumers bought most gospel music.

The 1970s brought more growth to Word as the Myrrh label grew with the contemporary Christian music field; at the end of 1979, Word, Inc. was grossing approximately $40 million in sales annually and employed 400 people—still based in Waco but with new offices established in Nashville and Los Angeles. The major signing for Word was Amy Grant on their Myrrh imprint in 1976; Grant emerged as the top-selling contemporary Christian artist with gold and platinum albums during the 1980s and 1990s.

In the mid-1970s Word began to distribute labels again, but it was small Christian labels such as Good News, Paragon, Solid Rock, Maranatha, Lamb and Lion, New Pax, and Image as well as Canaan, Myrrh, and Dayspring, which they owned, and Light, owned in partnership with Ralph Carmichael.

Carmichael formed Light Records and a publishing arm, Lexicon Publishing, as a joint venture with Word Records. Light provided the creative side—the recordings—and Word provided promotion and distribution. Among the early artists on Light were Richard and Patti Roberts, 102 Strings, the Continental Singers, Cliff Richard, the Archers, Children of the Day, Jamie Owens-Collins, the Jeremiah People, and an album of Jimmy Durante singing hymns.

In 1968 Carmichael signed Andrae Crouch and the Disciples to Light, and this led the label to become a powerhouse with black gospel for the contemporary Christian market. Crouch's breakthrough albums were *Keep on Singin'* (1971) and *Soulfully* (1972). Light also released successful albums by Walter Hawkins and the Love Alive choir.

In 1974 Word was sold to ABC; in 1980 Carmichael purchased Light and Lexicon, which were part of the Word agreement from ABC/Capitol Cities. In 1982 Light signed an agreement with Elektra for distribution but that same year almost went bankrupt despite having a number of strong selling acts.

Light was sold to CGI in the late 1980s, and in 1993 CGI/Light was purchased by Platinum Entertainment, Inc., which released albums from the Light catalog, including albums by Walter Hawkins, Vickie Winans, Danniebelle Hall, the New Jersey Mass Choir, and the Winans. In 1997 Platinum Entertainment acquired Intersound for $29 million and established a distribution agreement through Polygram. However, in 2001 Platinum Entertainment filed Chapter 11 bankruptcy; out of this reorganization, the Compendia Music Group emerged, which was operated by Dominion Resources, a financial firm. Compendia made Light their flagship label for black gospel artists, including Rizen, Bishop Paul S. Morton, Earl Bynum, and the Mighty Clouds of Joy as well as a Classic Gold Series from the Light catalog (Walter Hawkins, Sandra Crouch, Tramaine Hawkins, and Commissioned). In December 2004 Compendia was purchased by Sheridan Square Entertainment, a holding company based in New York that was controlled by Redux Records.

The move by Word to distribute other labels beginning in the mid-1970s was made because the contemporary Christian music field was growing at a phenomenal pace and these labels had the talent for the market.

Perhaps the biggest event that happened to Word was in 1976 when they were purchased by ABC Entertainment Corporation, making McCracken one of the principal stockholders in the corporation, which owned the ABC television network and the ABC Record label. In 1979, when ABC Records was sold to MCA Records, Word remained with ABC Entertainment Corporation.

Word dominated gospel music from the 1960s, and by the 1980s their acts accounted for 60 to 70 percent of all gospel music sold in America. In 1984 McCracken signed for secular distribution with A&M, which promoted Amy Grant to secular stardom. In March 1986, ABC merged with Capital Cities, Inc., and that September founder Jarrell McCracken, after 35 years at the helm,

left the company because of disagreements with the new owner. Still, Word remained the major Christian company marketing gospel music, with music accounting for about 50 to 60 percent of their $80 million annual income.

In 1992 Word was sold to Thomas Nelson for $72 million, and at the end of 1996, Thomas Nelson kept Word's book division and sold the recording label to Gaylord Entertainment, which also owned the Grand Ole Opry and the Nashville Network. Gaylord then purchased Blanton/Harrell Entertainment, which managed Amy Grant and Michael W. Smith. By 1996 Word was using Epic Records and the Sony Music Distribution system to reach the secular market; its own distribution system marketed to Christian bookstores.

In 1996 Warner Brothers created Warner Alliance, which marketed to the Christian Booksellers market, then created Warner Resound, which marketed gospel to the secular market. Warner Brothers wanted to be part of the Christian industry, but their labels were not successful, so in 2002 they purchased Word from Gaylord; then, in 2004, they sold a partnership of Word to Curb Records to create Word/Curb.

Curb Records is a major independent label based in Nashville with a country and pop roster that includes Tim McGraw, LeAnn Rimes, Wynonna Judd, and Jo Dee Messina; their contemporary Christian roster included Natalie Grant, Selah, and Michael English. Label owner Mike Curb recorded several albums for Word in the late 1960s and early 1970s with his group, the Mike Curb Congregation.

The Benson Company was another major label for contemporary Christian music with its two record divisions, HeartWarming and Impact. They added Greentree in 1976 just for contemporary music.

Founded in 1902 as a publishing company, it published its first songbook in 1904 but remained a small, local company until 1935, when John T. Benson, Jr. took over. In 1960 Bob Benson, the second son of John T. Benson, Jr., joined the organization and led the company into its first venture into the record business when HeartWarming Records was created. In 1969 John T. Benson III joined the organization after the company had been successful with its first artists, which included the Speer Family, the Rambos, and the Bill Gaither Trio; the company expanded into contemporary Christian music in the 1970s, moving away from the southern gospel quartet music they began with. The biggest signing was Sandi Patty, who emerged as one of the top-selling contemporary Christian music acts during the 1980s. Also on the roster was Dallas Holm and Praise.

The Benson Company was sold to the Zondervan Corporation, a Christian company known for its Bible publishing and chain of family bookstores, in 1980 for $3 million. In 1994 the Music Entertainment Group bought the Benson Music Group, along with Tribute/ Diadem. In June 1997 the Zomba Music Group announced the formation of Provident Music Group, by combining Brentwood Music, and Reunion— the label begun by Blanton and Harrell that had been sold to BMG before Zomba purchased it. Provident then purchased the Benson Music Group from the Music Entertainment Group. In 2003 Provident was purchased by the German-based major label BMG; in 2004 Sony and BMG merged, and in 2008 Sony purchased BMG's share of the music company. Provident is now under the umbrella of Sony Music.

Sparrow Records was formed on January 1, 1976, by Billy Ray Hearn, who left Myrrh to begin the new label. Financial support for the new start-up came from the CHC Corporation in Los Angeles, which owned *Los Angeles* magazine and a book publishing company, Acton House. In the following years, Sparrow became a leader in contemporary Christian music through its philosophy of signing acts who were committed to ministry and who used their music as part of that ministry to reach young people with the gospel.

Barry McGuire was the first artist signed to Sparrow, then the Talbot brothers—John Michael and Terry— each signed for an album, as did Janny Grein. Annie Herring with 2nd Chapter of Acts signed for a solo project before the group joined her on the label. The first albums by these acts were released in May 1976.

A commercial breakthrough came when Hearn signed Candle, a group organized by Tony Salerno, who produced children's albums and created a new label, Birdwing, to market the group. The first release on Birdwing was *To the Chief Musician* (1976) by Candle, and the second album was *Kids of the Kingdom* (1976) by Annie Herring, followed by three albums in 1977: *To the Chief Musician, Vol. 2, The Music Machine* by Candle, and *Sweeter Than Honey"* by the New Creation Singers. In 1978 they released *Bullfrogs and Butterflies* by Barry McGuire and Candle along with Annie Herring's *Kids of the Kingdom—Follow the Leader*. The first non-children's album released by Birdwing was *The Lord's Supper* by John Michael Talbot in 1979.

In 1977 Sparrow became an independent company after the CHC Corporation was sold to ABC; Hearn and a group of investors purchased the label from CHC. In 1992 EMI purchased Sparrow and the label moved to Nashville. In 1997 EMI bought ForeFront, adding that roster to Sparrow and Star Song to create EMI Christian, headed by Bill Hearn.

By the end of 2008, the major players were no longer Word, Benson, and Sparrow—the big three a decade earlier—but EMI Christian, Provident, and Word/Curb. All were headquartered in Nashville, which became the center for contemporary Christian music as well as country music. The corporations that owned these labels learned that Christian music needs to be controlled by those who know this business, so the top executives for these divisions were long-time Christian music executives. Next, the Christian distribution system that supplied product to Christian bookstores remained even though the major corporations had their own distribution network. Secular distribution allowed Christian music to get into the secular market, but the dual distribution system, and paying careful attention to the core Christian audience in the Christian bookstores, meant these labels could reach a much larger audience.

The major corporations provided immense capitalization. Those deep pockets helped ensure big sales when an artist had a hit. Small companies usually cannot afford to have a big hit because the costs of manufacturing, marketing, and promotion, which are incurred before the label has received income from sales, can break a small company.

By 1998 Wal-Mart, Kmart, Blockbuster, MusicLand, Target, and Sam Goody had all increased their stocks of gospel. Wal-Mart, which had 45 linear feet in its music department, had 8 linear feet for Christian music. This is where the major growth in religious music occurred; the sales at Christian bookstores increased 15–25 percent, but the mainstream market for religious music grew 70–80 percent.

Don Cusic

For Further Reading

Cusic, Don. *The Sound of Light: A History of Gospel and Christian Music.* New York: Hal Leonard, 2002.

McNeil, W. K., ed. *Encyclopedia of American Gospel Music.* New York: Routledge, 2005.

Powell, Mark Allen. *Encyclopedia of Contemporary Christian Music.* Peabody, Mass.: Hendrickson Publishers, Inc., 2002.

RELIGIOUS MUSIC IN AMERICA, A HISTORY

The story of contemporary Christian music is part of the story of Christianity in America. Although contemporary Christian music emerged during the 1960s and 1970s, a long history of religious music in America preceded it.

During the 17th century, the future United States was settled by Europeans, and each group of settlers brought new songs with them. There were songs from churches as well as secular songs, both traditional ballads and new songs composed by early songwriters. The Jamestown and Plymouth colonies were preceded by Spanish explorers who came through Mexico and the southwestern area of what is now the United States. The first religious songs sung in the new world were songs from the Roman Catholic church, and Catholic service books were published in Mexico as early as 1556. However, the settlement of what became identified as the United States came from the European settlers who settled the eastern seaboard and then moved westward.

To understand early American music, a knowledge of Europe and European music is necessary because the roots of America are embedded in the European culture these settlers left behind.

Roots of American Religious Music

The roots of contemporary American Christianity lie in the 16th century, particularly with three men: Martin Luther, John Calvin, and Henry VIII. Martin Luther, an Augustinian monk in Wittenberg, Germany, read about the "justification of faith" in the epistle to the Romans and became transformed by the concept of "grace." Luther's religious awakening led him to nail 95 theses to the door at Wittenberg protesting the selling of plenary indulgences by Catholic priests. This act marks the beginning of the Protestant Reformation.

Calvin's life provided Christianity with a book, *The Institutes of Christianity*, that defined and regulated Christianity for centuries. Henry VIII's reign produced a break with the Catholic church in England, creating a climate for religious dissent that led to the rise of Protestantism in England. This religious upheaval encompassed a spiritual awakening that resulted in the settling of America by religious dissenters who viewed the new land as a second Canaan and their mission akin to Moses leading chosen people to a chosen land for the creation of a new, God-ordained nation.

There was religious dissension in Europe before Martin Luther nailed his 95 theses on the Wittenberg door in 1516; however, it was this act—and the subsequent life and trials of Luther—that led to the Protestant Reformation in Europe and the rise of the Anglican church in England. The split with the Catholic church in England was a result of Henry VIII wanting a divorce from his wife, Catherine of Aragon, because he wanted a son as an heir to the throne and his wife had not produced one. The Pope refused to grant Henry a divorce, so the British Parliament created the Church of England. With this act, Henry VIII broke ties with Rome and ushered in the Protestant revolt in England, which set the stage for the settling of America as a "new Canaan."

Martin Luther as Songwriter

Martin Luther used music as a means of communicating with God, singing "psalms and hymns and spiritual songs" as a way of expressing prayer, love, and thanksgiving. From early in his life, Luther sang well and played the lute. Although Luther wrote only 37 songs, it is this body of work that has carried Luther's words and thoughts directly to people for more than five centuries. The legacy he left in song has lived longer and probably had as great an influence as any of the other works produced by this leader of the Reformation.

Martin Luther's greatest contribution to the music of the church was to return it to the people. For more than a millennium—from the Council of Laodicea in the 4th century until the Reformation in the 1520s—congregations had done no singing in church. Hymns were written, but their use was limited to special occasions such as processions, pilgrimages, and some major festivals, all held outside the sanctuary. Luther put music back into the church and in so doing made the congregation active participants rather than passive onlookers in the church service.

Luther wrote his first hymn, "Out of the Depths I Cry to Thee," in 1523 at the age of 40. He wrote 23 hymns that first year and a total of 37, which still survive. They were generally introduced as broadsheets at the church in Wittenberg and later collected into hymnals. Of the 37 he composed, 12 were translations from Latin hymns, 4 from German folk songs, and at least 5 were original.

The first hymnal from Luther was given to the congregation in 1524 to read while the choir was singing. However, the people were so unused to joining in the public service that it took four or five years before Luther taught the people of his own parish in Wittenberg to sing in church. After this, the custom spread swiftly. A major factor in Protestantism's appeal has been the songs it has inspired, and Luther's leadership in giving all people a chance to sing in church made that religion come alive, infused with joy, for centuries.

Isaac Watts and the Wesleys

The songs of Isaac Watts, an English clergyman, were a break from the Calvinist code, which insisted that songs should only come directly from scripture. Isaac Watts created a revolution in hymn writing by breaking the stranglehold of David's Psalms on the liturgy through the substitution of "hymns of composure." He was the first to thoughtfully develop a theory of congregational praise and provide a well-rounded body of material to be used in the church. Watts believed that religious songs are a human offering of praise to God, and therefore the words should be personal. This contrasted with the Calvinistic approach held by the Church that insisted the inspired words of the Bible, particularly the Psalms, were the only fit offerings of praise that man could make.

Isaac Watts wrote from both his head and his heart. He was an intelligent man who mastered the mechanics of writing what he fervently believed. This combination of a skillful writer writing songs from the heart, expressing his deep faith, is why the hymns of Watts remain so powerful today.

The Wesleys, like Isaac Watts, are known for their songs of personal experiences; however, while Watts lived amongst the rich, the Wesleys were involved with the poor as the Great Awakening brought a deep concern for the individual. Three great evangelists—John and Charles Wesley and George Whitefield—all confronted these societal problems during the Great Awakening.

John Wesley's major contribution to gospel music was editing, organizing, and publishing the hymns of his brother, Charles. This body of work became one of the most powerful evangelizing tools that England had ever known. Charles Wesley composed in his study, his garden, on horseback, anywhere. In the end, he composed 6,500 hymns of scripture texts on every conceivable phase of Christian experience and Methodist theology.

Religious Music in the American Colonies

The Reformation in Europe brought a new song, sung in the vernacular (not in Latin) by the entire congregation. When the settlers landed in Jamestown, Virginia, in 1607, they brought with them the Este Psalter (a psalter is a song book of the Psalms), with some evidence that they also had copies of the Sternhold and Hopkins (the Old Version) Psalter. The songbooks brought to the Plymouth colony were the Sternhold and Hopkins Psalter, the Scottish Psalter, and the Psalter by Ainsworth.

The Puritans of New England came from the Calvinist tradition and the transition in America from scriptural to devotional poems—psalms to hymns—was a long and gradual one, hindered by the Puritans' strict adherence to the psalms.

The first book published in America was *The Whole Booke of Psalmes Faithfully Translated into English Metre*, commonly known as *The Bay Psalm Book*. It appeared in 1640 in the Plymouth colony in Massachusetts and contained the first version of psalms made by Americans and used in American churches. The question of whether hymns ("Psalms invented by the gifts of godly men") were to be included in church services was raised in the preface (written by either Richard Mather or John Cotton), with the decision reached to sing only psalms or other paraphrases from passages in the Bible. Some hymns were added to the *Bay Psalm Book* in the 1647 edition.

The success of the *Bay Psalm Book* was immediate, with 1,700 copies in the first printing and 2,000 copies in a new edition in 1651. In all, there were 27 editions of this book printed in New England and at least 20 in England (the last in 1754), as well as 6 in Scotland. The ninth edition, published in 1698, was the first to contain music that accompanied the texts. Before that, only the words were printed, and these were sung to a known melody, with a handful of melodies serving a large number of songs.

In the 18th century, some changes evolved, basically reflecting the changes occurring in England. The Methodists and their Methodism brought the Wesley hymns to New Jersey, and the later comers to New England imported Isaac Watts. Ironically, the initial resistance Watts encountered to his hymns in America was the same he had encountered in England; his "hymns of human composure" were not literal renderings of the psalms but rather from the human heart. The psalm was still the predominant form of gospel music, sung in churches as well as in homes.

The Great Awakening was responsible for a large influx of hymns into church services, altering the traditional view of scriptural songs being the only acceptable music in church. Beginning in Wales under Howell Harris (c. 1730), the Great Awakening was a tremendous infusion of religion into society, producing laws that eliminated some of the exploitation and abuse of the poor as well as injecting a genuine spirit of revival into the souls of a great number of people, especially among the lower classes. It grew to epic proportions under George Whitefield (1736–1790) and the Wesleys (1739–1791). In America, the Great Awakening began with Jonathan Edwards in New England (c. 1734) and received an incredible boost under the leadership of George Whitefield, who came to America in 1740, met Edwards in Massachusetts, and traveled throughout the colonies preaching. Hymn singing caught fire in America about 1740 during Whitefield's visit.

During the 1600s and early 1700s, the New England congregations were noted for singing their psalm tunes at a very slow tempo, known as the "old way." Its adherents defended it as the "only proper mode" for performing music in church; however, this was challenged in the early part of the 18th century by advocates of the "new way," who encouraged singing by note instead of rote, briskly in harmony rather than slowly and in unison. The state of singing had sunk badly because of years of no formal music training for singers and psalm books with texts but no melodies to scan.

This problem was met with the rise of the singing school, which gave instruction and training to members of a church or community in the rudiments of music. The study of sight singing was enthusiastically taken up by Americans, and there was a singing school in Boston in 1717. This time was also marked by the rise of the singing master in the 18th and early 19th centuries. The impact of the singing master was greatest in the rural areas and small towns; the congregations in the coastal towns retained a closer tie with English tastes.

Although psalm singing dominated the 17th century and continued to prevail through the introduction of hymns in the 18th century, the 19th century was marked by the emergence of the denominational hymn. Although tenors generally sang the melody in earlier years, sopranos sang the melody in the 19th century.

As in the 18th century, the bass viol was often used as an accompanying instrument; it was basically a cello with a short neck. In Salem, Massachusetts, the clarinet and violin were first played in church on Christmas Day, 1792, and a flute was played there in 1795. In 1814, in Boston, the singing was accompanied by flute, bassoon, and cello. Gradually, the organ was accepted as a proper instrument for the church, with small pipe organs and melodeons. Still, the churches proved reluctant to adapt any musical adornment to the plain singing of the congregation during the first 200 years in America.

In the 17th century, one person "set the pitch," then the entire congregation sang the psalm. However, the 18th century saw the emergence of a musical elite—the choir—which changed the seating pattern (and architecture) within the church. A gallery was erected over the entrance vestibule and sometimes on three sides of the church, with the choir sitting apart from the congregation.

The influence of England remained strong throughout the 18th century in American churches. This was because

English tunes were republished in America and because many American composers were born and trained in England.

During the 18th century, the two most important psalters were those by Tate and Brady and by Isaac Watts. A major problem with the Watts Psalter was that Watts did not paraphrase all the psalms and did not repeat himself when the psalms did. Americans were accustomed to reading or singing all of the psalms in numerical order, sung at one standing, regardless of the subject of the sermon. The second major problem with the Watts Psalter was the laudatory lines to Great Britain and her ruler, which became increasingly unacceptable as America moved closer to its revolution and break with Great Britain.

The development of tune books (books that contained melodies) was due primarily to enterprising individuals who developed these books for singing school classes, church choirs, and, eventually, the organist. It was convenient to have the music associated with the words, although they were generally on opposite pages. After the mid-19th century, the congregation hymnal with words and music appeared. The words were generally under the tune on the same page, and sometimes several texts were given for one tune. The most convenient arrangement was where the words were printed between the staves, in upright form, a form still used today.

Sacred music had long felt the influence of secular music as congregations were exposed to both forms in their lives, and the 18th century saw a secularization of sacred music, which helped make that music more appealing to the masses of people and carried it beyond the church, where it stood alone outside of worship. The introduction of choirs led to more elaborate songs, with a tendency toward wide-ranging melodies, word repetitions, fuguing (imitative voice overlapping), fast tempos, and expressive treatment of text, which placed church music in a different musical environment and framework than that known to the New Englanders.

The evolution of sacred music from a part of the church service, integral but subordinate to the preaching, to a form of art that stood on its own is an important progression when looking at the history of religious music in America, especially the developments in the latter part of the 20th century. This affected audiences as well as musicians, and the secular influence was felt strongly in sacred music as the church began to be dominated by the culture, in much the same way that the Puritan church dominated the secular culture in early New England.

This influence of folk music, as well as the establishment of singing schools and the Great Revival of the 19th century, established the roots of the *Sacred Harp* and white spiritual traditions and paved the way for 20th-century southern gospel music.

The Secular Influence

During the nation's first 100 years, religious music dominated America; however, in the 18th century, popular music began to grow and blossom and establish itself, although the identity of American music remained an extension of Europe until the mid-19th century. There was, of course, secular music from the time of the first settlers, but it was frowned on by the religious leaders and churches that dominated early society, especially in New England.

The Puritan leaders were known to have spoken against ballad singing as well as "filthy songs," although some noted that a number of popular tunes were used with religious verses inserted, a practice that drew mixed responses but which seemed to be commonly accepted.

The Great Awakening, which began about 1734 in New England with Jonathan Edwards and gradually moved south and west, infused a new life into sacred music as it introduced hymns into religious music, which had been dominated by psalms taken directly from scripture and usually sung in a slow, drawn-out style. The hymns were more lively and, under the influence of Isaac Watts and the Wesleys, full of personal expressions of faith.

The rise of the singing schools, which began about 1717 in Boston, helped re-establish musical literacy and expanded the number of tunes that people knew, in addition to correcting the mistakes Americans had injected into the old ones. An early singing master, William Billings, is considered the first major composer in North America and his book, *New England Psalm Singer*, published in 1770, is one of the first books from a singing master. Credited with composing 263 hymns and psalms, Billings's best-known work is "Chester," a patriotic hymn that was the anthem for the Revolutionary War, and "Columbia," considered one of the "camp songs" of that period.

Two kinds of secular songs circulated in 18th-century England and the colonies. The oldest was the oral-tradition English and Scottish balladry, which was brought over by the earliest settlers and flourished primarily in the South, unaffected by topical currents. The other type was broadside ballads, which developed from Elizabethan times into the 18th century and were the earliest commercial popular music. The broadsides brought forth songs of news events, disasters, dying confessions, moralizing poems, and hymns.

Several different kinds of music-making flourished in the American colonies, but the most widespread creative response of America to the Revolutionary War lay in making verses to well-known tunes rather than in composing the tunes themselves. One of the earliest collections of secular songs in the colonies was the Mother Goose rhymes, which established a traditional set of songs that have remained an integral part of childhood since their publication. The book was assembled by Thomas Fleet, who had married Elizabeth Goose in 1715 and to whom a son was born the following year.

The period just before the Revolutionary War, beginning in the 1760s, marked the emergence of a society dominated by secularization. In terms of music, this meant the growing acceptance of musical instruments in homes as well as in churches, which had taken a stand against the use of instruments with sacred music. The acceptance and use of instruments for composing and performing music provided a striking difference between sacred and secular music.

After the Revolutionary War, Americans continued to look to Europe for their music and culture as immigrants came to the new country in large numbers and urban Americans grew wealthier and more desirous of luxury. European musicians took up residence in the major cities, and these professionals replaced the native amateur musicians who dominated the colonial period. With the establishment of the European professionals came the attitude that American musicians and music were not acceptable. The professionals were classically trained, and classical music had never been "popular music" in America like it had in Europe. Although the classically oriented music and musicians held a place in America, popular music gravitated toward a folk music that was brought over a century earlier and nurtured on native soil. These folk melodies influenced secular music as well as sacred music through the hymns of the Wesleys, Isaac Watts, and Bach as well as through the songs from native composers.

The beginning of the 19th century marked the end of the first two stages of American musical growth—the psalmody of the 17th century and the hymns and secular songs of the 18th century. The next era of American popular music began with Stephen Foster; he became the first major American composer with a distinctive American voice and an extensive body of musical work that changed America's music and set it apart from the music of the European heritage. His songs proved to be so popular that many of them were adapted for Sunday School use with the words changed to fit the Christian message but the same melodies retained. His material is an example of Christian churches taking advantage of popular music by incorporating revised tunes in the church.

Give Me That Old Time Religion

The revival that followed the Revolutionary War was not a highly organized affair and cannot be traced in a logical, sequential manner; rather, it was a number of religious freedom fires that seemed to ignite by spontaneous combustion. As the country pushed westward, these revivals sprang up in various areas of the country over several generations, offending established, organized religion because revival preachers paid no heed to denominational lines, preaching wherever they could gather a crowd.

The Revolutionary War had capped the great concept of freedom that had been raging in the colonies. For religion, this meant there was freedom of religion as well as freedom from religion. In the urban areas, the rationalism that fueled the French Revolution and provided new breakthroughs in science and philosophy caught hold. However, in the untamed parts of the country, this rationalism had little appeal—the settlers had neither the time nor the inclination to ponder intellectual enlightenment. These people needed a faith that was vibrant and alive, full of emotion and comfort, to help them relate to the lonely, danger-filled wilderness and a life steeped heavily in individualism. Thus, it was a "free" religion that took hold.

Socially, the new free religion was perfect for the common man, who was poor. The pursuits of the rich—drinking, gambling, and such—were quickly labeled as sinful and railed against. The large urban areas became dens of iniquity while rural America provided the most fertile soil for folk religion. Here, it grew and spread, watered by an emotional spirituality that provided a comfort to the lonely settlers. Although this folk religion came under no organizational guidelines, one basic tenet ran through it—all institutional mediacy between a man's soul and his redeemer must be rejected—every individual, no matter what his station in life, had direct access to God.

As the settlers moved westward, they moved beyond the influence of established churches and were served by a new kind of preacher, born on the frontier, or at least familiar with frontier life. Although they generally had little formal education, these preachers did have the ability to move audiences and preached wherever a group could be assembled. The camp meeting was born from the lack of a central church in the vast rural regions and because the settlers lived so far apart. Camp meetings brought people together for several days from a large area. Families brought food and lived in their wagons; the women slept inside and the men on the ground underneath or in improvised shelters.

The Baptists were a particularly free group, with dissension breaking out within their sect about predestination, grace, and a number of other theological questions. They were the folky sect of both Britain and America, never accepting a central church authority; in music this meant they were devoted to "free" singing rather than singing songs prescribed to them by a central authority. The spirit of the folk Baptists dominated this time of revivals after the Revolutionary War and the songs they chose to sing differed greatly from the psalms of the Puritans with their long texts. The revival spirituals, born from these mass meetings,

emphasized choruses, burdens, refrains, and repeated lines.

In the period 1780–1830, a great body of folk texts appeared in the country song tradition. Great Britain and the young United States were full of folk tunes, and religious folk often put religious verses to popular secular tunes. The wedding of religious lyrics and folk tunes probably began around 1770 and continued throughout this period. The composed tunes of the pre-Revolutionary War period in America remained unknown to the rural Americans who moved westward, so they used tunes from the folk tradition for their worship. The source for these American folk tunes was primarily British—England, Scotland, and Ireland—with only a handful from other sources.

The Kentucky Revival of 1800 established the revival spiritual in America. The Kentucky Revival was not the first and was similar to a number of other revivals that preceded it; however, the flames there seemed to burn higher and brighter because of a number of favorable conditions. One was the ethnic background of the population—primarily Gaels (Irish, Scots-Irish, Scottish, Welsh), who were known as highly emotional people. Another factor was climatic and geographic. The Kentucky farmers had a period of leisure during the summer from the time their crops were planted until harvesting time (as opposed to their New England counterparts who had a short summer), and the dry roads and trails invited long trips to big gatherings. Too, the dry hot summers lent themselves to meeting outdoors, thereby accommodating large numbers of people. The final factor was the lack of organized, established religion in that area, which meant no religious or civil authorities had to be battled for these revivals to occur.

The revivals were charged with spiritual emotionalism; the crowds at these gatherings sang from memory or learned songs that were repetitive and took little effort to learn because there were no song books. Here, the revival songs were in the hands of people as the real exhortational activity—praying, mourning, and other physical exercises—was by and for the crowd. The singers controlled the songs but the crowds joined in the chorus, on a short-phrase refrain or on a couplet. This led to the development of revival songs with repetitive passages.

The verse-with-chorus idea spread quickly, and some choruses proved so popular they were interjected into other songs with different verses. Two types of revival songs developed—the repetitive chorus and the call-and-response where a line was sung by the singer and the crowd sang the responding line, which always remained the same.

The folk tradition of song—an oral tradition that began in Britain and other parts of Europe—took over in religious music. The settlers moving west had little if any musical training and possessed neither song books nor established churches. When the revivals caught hold, music was returned to the people, who responded with a congregational type of singing reminiscent of the earliest Puritans, albeit much more emotional and active. They had to depend on tunes they already knew— much as the first Puritans did with their songs. But the nature of the revivals caused a major change—the melodies had to be altered to accommodate choruses that everyone could learn quickly. Thus the song leader knew the verses but everyone knew the chorus and joined on these choruses or on lines that repeated themselves.

This was democracy in action; everyone felt a part of religion and singing. Too, the choruses spoke the feelings of the settlers. The early religious folk-singing practice took hold in the period 1780–1830, when it enjoyed its greatest vigor. Everyday folk enjoyed the most control over their private and institutional affairs; there was wide participation by the "folk" and there was an interdependence of mass-controlled religion and mass-controlled song.

These songs reflected the oral tradition as well as the revival spirit of singing spontaneously, without books, led by a singer with the congregation joining on key lines, phrases, or the chorus. They are easily learned and easily remembered. They are also easily changed and adapted from singer to singer, and congregation to congregation, with the chorus or key lines remaining and the verse lyrics subject to individual changes. They are timeless songs because of their repetitiveness but also because of their emotional appeal—they can inspire joy or comfort in sorrow, verbalizing people's feelings and thoughts. Within these songs are the roots of blues, country, modern gospel, and rock 'n' roll. Musically and lyrically simple, their power rests in their emotional impact and their ability to be learned and sung easily.

The old-time religion was a personal, highly emotional relationship between an individual and God; the rise of modern Protestantism brought forth a social-ethical-esthetic gospel. The religions that were tribes of radicalism soon became cornerstones of the establishment. Methodists and Baptists, Mormons and Seventh-Day Adventists were no longer positioned outside mainstream society; they were now large denominations whose members occupied places of honor and respect and whose denominations spanned the globe.

As the first half of the 19th century ended, the old-time religion faded as the cultural environment gave way to the Industrial Revolution and the Civil War. The music from southern plantations—jig and cakewalk music, blues and spirituals—surfaced later in the 19th century as ragtime, jazz, popular blues, and the original spirituals from the church. However, for the 30 to 40 years following the Civil War there was a musical isolation imposed on both black and white cultures, with whites no longer exposed to music in the slave quarters and blacks excluded from white publishing houses. This period marks a sharp division in the church life of Americans as blacks established their own churches outside and away from white culture while white churches by and large developed unwritten codes and practices that effectively barred African Americans from their churches.

The folk hymns and Negro spirituals were the last gospel songs to be perpetuated solely via the oral tradition, although they survive now because they were collected in print and because folklorists collected them on tape. Although some were written by individuals, many of the hymns came from the broadside ballad tradition and folk songs brought to this country from Europe. The spirituals are often black adaptations of white songs, influenced heavily by the African origins of black Americans but also reflecting the culture of a people united and suppressed in America.

Black Gospel and the Fisk Jubilee Singers

The first slaves were brought to Virginia by Dutch traders in 1629. Soon, a whole economy and way of life was based on slavery, particularly in the South, where large plantations grew acres of cotton and relied on slave labor. During the early days of the freedom churches, there were militants who inspired slave revolts. These revolutionaries used biblical phrases learned on the plantations to inspire followers and often saw themselves as a Moses, leading the chosen and faithful to an exodus out of Egyptian slavery to the new Canaan, much in the same way that the early American Puritans visualized their flight to the new world. Slaves often combined Christianity with African folk religion to produce a hybrid religion. Two of the more famous—Denmark Vesey and Nat Turner—were killed in 1822 and 1831, respectively, for leading slave uprisings.

Slaves often communicated via a "grapevine" that let others know their movements. This was particularly needed on southern plantations, which were far apart and no blacks could effectively congregate outside their own plantations. Still, their mixture of African religion and Christianity continued to grow and helped them cope with their daily struggles. Their spirituals often had double meanings—the same songs spoke openly of eternal hope beyond the earthly life as well as underground railroads that could lead them to freedom.

The conversion of blacks was guided by the same principles as those for whites—each individual was expected to confront God and make his decision for Jesus, be "born-again" or "get religion." Many white settlers brought their slaves with them during the early camp meetings at the beginning of the 1800s, and there blacks heard psalms and camp meeting songs. The slaves made a number of conscious attempts to reproduce the songs they heard but often sang them in a different manner, affecting rhythms that were different from the original and, because of an insufficient vocabulary or inability to recall the words correctly, different lyrics or lyrics that have been published in collections as "Negro dialect," markedly different from white speech.

While early white settlers placed a heavy emphasis on the words, with the music being incidental—a handful of tunes were used, often interchangeable with different sets of lyrics—blacks felt a need to emphasize music over the words. But it was more than just a different melody—it was a whole new rhythm, an entirely new "feel" to the songs, which became defined as black gospel. Even though blacks and whites often sang the same words, learned from the same sources, the results were two entirely different songs, with the black gospel songs rhythmical in a way that white songs never were. These rhythms, often complex, are attributed to the African influence.

Spirituals were created by a people bound in slavery and were an integral part of the culture in the early 19th century. However, it was not until after the Civil War that the spiritual was first recorded. The first major book containing words and music of spirituals was *Slave Songs of the United States* in 1867, but the first real awareness of the spirituals came when the Fisk Jubilee Singers undertook a tour of northern cities to raise money for their financially strapped institution, the Fisk School. Still, black gospel music was virtually ignored by white Christians, and it was not until the 20th century that denominational hymnals included spirituals.

In January 1866, the Fisk School opened and suffered from a lack of funds from day one. As the years rolled by, its lone building fell into decay; meanwhile, money was hard to come by. The treasurer of the school was George W. White, who joined the Freedmen's Bureau in Nashville at the end of the war. He had a talent for teaching music and was especially known for his instruction in vocal music. White had the idea that a student group could travel in the North, performing for money, and this idea was discussed for several years. However, many at the school—and in the missionary organization—thought it was too risky. Finally, in 1871 White decided he had to take a chance on the idea.

When the group left Nashville, on October 6, 1871, they had barely enough money to get to Ohio. Billed as "a band of negro minstrels" and "colored Christian singers," the group's first appearance was at a Congregational church in Cincinnati. They struggled as they performed in Ohio, with receipts sometimes not covering expenses. After a concert in Columbus,

Ohio, White decided to name the group the Jubilee Singers after the year of Jubilee in the Old Testament, which had been a favorite figure of speech of the slaves. The group performed in several more concerts before they performed at the First Presbyterian Church in Elmira, New York, where Rev. T. K. Beecher preached. Beecher's brother was Rev. Henry Ward Beecher, the most famous preacher in the United States, and Beecher sent his brother a letter praising the Jubilee Singers.

Rev. Henry Ward Beecher welcomed the Fisk singers at his Plymouth Church in Brooklyn, and the *New York Herald* wrote an article titled "Beecher's Negro Minstrels," which publicized their work. This was a turning point for the group; concerts were organized and promoted by ministers at various churches. They toured New England to enthusiastic audiences, and President Ulysses S. Grant received them at the White House, where they sang "Go Down, Moses." At the concerts in Washington, the vice president and some members of Congress attended. That first tour of the Fisk Jubilee Singers lasted three months and raised $20,000.

The Jubilee Singers began their second tour in June 1872 at the second World's Peace Jubilee in Boston. They performed before large crowds, and by 1873 the Jubilee Singers had raised enough money for the school to purchase 25 acres for the permanent location of Fisk University. Here, they built Jubilee Hall, the first building on their campus.

In 1874 the Jubilee Singers expanded their vision to include England, and they spent three months in London. In 1875 they performed in Holland and Germany, and by the end of this tour the spirituals had become popular.

The Great Revival

The 19th century saw America expand geographically and politically, and its religion and politics reflected the country as the "land of the free and the home of the brave." Along with the political expansion came moralistic crusades, laissez-faire capitalism, the Industrial Revolution, and the Civil War. The two great forces of Christian revivalism and democratic nationalism set the stage for another great revival after the Civil War, which would center on the urban areas.

The second half of the 19th century witnessed the birth of this new religious trend in the white community as the wild, emotion-packed camp meeting style of religion gave way to a more solemn, sober movement, centered in the urban areas and accompanied by the music of the gospel hymns.

The Baptists and Methodists had been most active on the frontier, and the religious awakening of the settlers put the principle of voluntarism (churches being supported freely by their members) before liturgy, democracy before orthodoxy, and emotionalism before an intellectual, rational approach to religion. Denominational lines were broken and crossed as the church reached the masses. The camp meeting became a social institution that supported the politics of manifest destiny, while revivalism stressed the work of man in salvation as well as the sovereignty of God. There was a democratic character to the idea of a personal encounter with God as well as a linking of politics with religion through the belief that God was actively involved in American life.

The role of the evangelist during the rapidly changing times of the 19th century was to assure believers of the continuity of the ageless faith in a rapidly changing world. He had to convince believers that all good came from God, so the changes that advanced America were proof that God was smiling on the nation. The gap between modern science and old-time religion was seen as a bridge on which scriptural proofs were revealed and the great truth was again being confirmed.

The Salvation Army Band

In London, William Booth, an itinerant minister, found his calling in 1865, and the 19th century witnessed the birth of the Salvation Army. It began in London, amongst the poor and outcast who had no notion of religion. Although other movements sought to mobilize those asleep in church pews, Booth's movement brought religion to the streets, bringing church to the people instead of drawing people to church. Along the way, he revolutionized the use of instruments in religious music through the Salvation Army band.

Booth's intense devotion to the world's salvation gave him the strength to overcome adversity and immense odds to carry the gospel to the streets. Opposed by the churched as well as the unchurched, scorned by the respectable and the derelict, Booth nevertheless made an impact on London—and later the world—through his single-minded devotion to the gospel and his fervor for preaching this message to all listeners.

The Salvation Army band sprang from the same haphazard devotion that spread the Army's cause. In Salisbury, England, in 1879, a local builder named Charles William Fry offered Booth the services of himself and his three sons, Fred, Ernest, and Bertram. The Army was troubled by hooligans roughing up their members, and Fry and his sons stepped in as bodyguards, bringing along their instruments as an afterthought. As Fry and his sons played brass instruments while the Army marched through the streets, the first Salvation Army band was born. It brought attention to the Army's cause and attracted a crowd, which enlisted Booth's support. The instruments accompanied Army members when they sang their songs—Booth banned the word "hymns" because it sounded "too churchy"—using concertinas, tambourines, brass horns, and anything else that made music. The players were mostly spare-time musicians

Booth loved singing and was a maverick in his approach to evangelism as well as in his use of music. He regularly insisted that well-known secular tunes be used with Christian lyrics. Booth asked, "Why should the Devil have all the best tunes?" and regularly took the secular and made it sacred. Through songs like "There Are No Flies on Jesus," Booth brought Christianity to the street and made it a religion for the poor, the wretched, the socially undesirable, and the outcast. The Army's music reflected their tactics of spreading the gospel—loud, dramatic, and full of gusto.

Meanwhile, in America there arose two preachers in the 19th century who dominated evangelism on this continent—Henry Ward Beecher and Dwight Moody.

Beecher was a moderate, mainstream Protestant who attempted to prod Christianity toward modernity. For him, the good in the world was produced by a loving God and Christian thought should be flexible enough to pull in new ideas. From his platform at the Plymouth Church in Brooklyn, Beecher attracted a national following. He injected a healthy dose of humanism into the gospel, urging his members to seek perspiration as well as inspiration, a good day's work to go along with Divine grace. Ward Beecher appealed to the middle class who aspired to riches, arguing that poverty was a result of sin. This concept was applauded by Beecher's followers.

The concept of the religious leader as a spiritual salesman was refined by Dwight Moody, a former shoe salesman who used the pulpit to sell Christianity to the masses.

In 1865, Moody moved from Boston to Chicago and became a successful businessman, selling shoes, as well as an active member of the Plymouth Congregational church. Every Sunday Moody reportedly filled four pews he rented with those he had recruited and was so successful at recruiting members for Sunday School that at the age of 23 he founded his own Sunday School, where he served as administrator and recruiter. Moody was a forceful, though not grammatically elegant speaker, and was cautioned against speaking by members of his church. However, he began preaching one night after the scheduled speaker did not show up. Soon, he devoted himself full time to Christian work and spoke at Sunday School conventions and to troops, established a church of his own, and served as president of the Chicago YMCA.

Moody could not sing but knew the value of songs and singing in his evangelistic work. He enlisted the support of Ira Sankey in 1871 and together the two traveled to urban areas in the eastern United States as well as England. Moody was clearly the guiding light and visionary for the evangelistic endeavors, but he needed Sankey's songs to attract crowds and set the stage for his message. He let Sankey begin with songs, then he preached before letting Sankey conclude with a song as the sinners came forth. Moody viewed the Christian conversion as a successful sale—the set up, the hard pitch, and the closing or wrapping up where the convert made his decision and acted on it.

By the end of their careers, the names Moody and Sankey were linked and shared equal billing. A testament to the power of song is that the gospel singer Sankey was as important as the evangelist preacher Moody; their roles supplemented each other and each was indispensable to their cause.

Ira Sankey, as song leader for Dwight Moody's revivals, made the gospel hymn a popular song, presenting the format of verse-chorus-verse-chorus in a way that gave the songs emotional appeal and memorability. In making the hymn a popular song, Sankey evoked the charm of popular music and used the song as an instrument for religion to convict and convert people.

The camp meeting hymn was often the work of anonymous singers or the folk tradition, but the gospel hymn was created by individual writers and musicians. The camp meeting hymn was characteristic of the frontier and rural areas; the gospel hymn of the great cities. The gospel hymn is uniquely

American. It is evangelical in spirit and focuses on the winning of souls through conversion. Its primary use was in revivals, but it was gradually taken over by Sunday schools, Christian associations, and churches made up of less educated members, who preferred the appeals of emotion rather than literary form and quality.

The gospel hymn had certain characteristics that made it appealing to crowds. The mood might be optimistic or pleading, but the music was tuneful, melodic, and easy to grasp and learn. A march-like movement was typical, and the device of letting the lower parts echo rhythmically a line announced by the sopranos in a fuguing form became a mannerism.

The Pentecostal and Holiness Movements

A major religious movement began at the turn of the century that played an active role in guiding American Christianity throughout the 20th century. Pentecostalism had a major effect on religion in the United States as well as on music—particularly in the South—because a number of musicians came from this movement. This period also marked the beginnings of fundamentalism.

The roots of Pentecostalism are traced to two sources in the United States. Charles Fox Parnham began Bethel Bible School in Topeka, Kansas, in October 1900. In late December 1900, before he made a trip to Kansas City, Parnham instructed his students to study the Bible individually and learn about the baptism of the Holy Spirit. When he returned, the students told Parnham that in Apostolic times,

whenever believers were baptized with the Holy Spirit, there was speaking in tongues.

The source for this is Acts, Chapter Two, and after this meeting members of the college began to pray and seek for this baptism and gift of tongues. On New Year's Eve, as about 40 students and 70 others outside the student body gathered for the traditional "Watch Night" service, Miss Agnes Ozman requested that members lay hands on her so she might receive the Holy Spirit.

After only a few moments of prayer, Miss Ozman began to speak in Chinese and could not speak English for the next three days. The other believers accepted speaking in tongues, or glossolaia, as the outward sign that someone had received the gift of the Holy Spirit. The rest of the student body began to pray earnestly and soon most were speaking in tongues. This led to a major evangelistic effort by Parnham and his students that resulted in Pentecostalism spreading throughout the Midwest, South, and Southwest.

Parnham opened another school in Houston, Texas, in 1905. Like the one in Topeka, no tuition was charged (just "faith" offerings), the only textbook was the Bible, and the only lecturer was Parnham. One of his students was William J. Seymour, an African American preacher. Seymour was invited to preach at the Nazarene mission in Los Angeles after another student, Neely Terry, also an African American, received the Holy Spirit baptism in Houston and began speaking in tongues. She recommended Seymour to her home church after returning from Houston.

Parnham's first sermon offended a church member, and he found the doors barred to him after the first service. Invited to the home of Richard and Ruth Asberry (relatives of Neeley Terry), he conducted services there. On April 9, 1906, seven of the worshippers received this baptism of the Holy Spirit and began speaking in tongues, shouting and praising God for three days and nights. Soon, the small congregation moved into an old frame building, which once served as a Methodist Church, on Azusa Street and here the Apostolic Faith Gospel Mission, under the leadership of William J. Seymour, heralded in a revival whose effects were felt all over the world.

The Holiness movement's roots go back to the 1890s and the Latter Rain movement, which sought to "irrigate the dry bones" in churches. Holiness congregations, characterized by this intense emotionalism in the worship service, developed all over the country, especially among the poor and depressed. The term "holy rollers" came from this movement because people were liable to scream, shout, dance, jump, or roll on the floor for Jesus. These churches placed a heavy emphasis on "saved, sanctified, and filled with the Holy Spirit," which meant a possession by the spirit so the person is not chained to this world but free to act or say whatever God wants done or said, using the individual's voice and body. Speaking in tongues, or glossolalia (a fluent gibberish with a number of Hebrew-like sounds) is often practiced. Although the Pentecostal and Holiness movements began as an integrated movement, within a few years they became segregated, with whites becoming Pentecostal while African Americans used the term Holiness for their churches.

Both the Pentecostal and Holiness churches feature a great amount of singing and dancing in their services, with half of the service usually music. These churches were the first to use musical instruments in the service, instruments that churches had long considered "of the devil."

There are foot-stomping and hand-clapping up-tempo songs in Pentecostal and Holiness churches, but the Holiness songs tend to have more complex rhythms. The archetypal Holiness song is a slow chant, often begun as church starts or later, during a prolonged series of shouts and outbursts. The ministers, with their strong personal charisma and elaborate showmanship, are required to lead the church to a spiritual high during the service that enables the congregation to face six hard, troublesome weekdays.

Too, the Holiness church has encouraged and inspired African Americans to express their own culture rather than be black versions of white churches; therefore the evolution to a mainstream church has been much different from that of their white counterparts. With churches segregated, this served to divide Christianity and gospel music into two distinctive camps—black and white. Although each may borrow songs and musical influences from the other, and the performers watch the opposite race to incorporate ideas into their own performances, the congregations remain separate, often unaware of the music of their racial counterparts.

Fundamentalism is not unique to any one denomination but cuts across all denominational borders and represents an effort to establish doctrines and propositions that are universal and unchanging within the Christian faith.

The proper Christian doctrines and dogma are belief in the deity of Christ, the Virgin birth, bodily Resurrection of Christ, imminent Second Coming, substitutionary atonement, and the verbal inspiration and inerrancy of the entire Bible. These doctrines not only have come to define and dominate American Christianity, they are also the central themes of gospel songs throughout the century.

Fundamentalists generally see any deviation from essential doctrines as a compromise of the truth, a weakness of the faith, and a betrayal of the gospel. They often have difficulty accepting someone as a Christian if this person does not affirm the truth of a wide variety of necessary articles of faith or accept a common dogma of biblical authority. These dogma include an insistence on the Genesis account of creation, the acceptance of Adam and Eve as parents of the race of man, Christ's virgin birth, sacrificial atonement, bodily resurrection, the reality of his miracles, and a literal second coming. Fundamentalists are often rigidly secure in their faith, speaking unwaveringly on matters of faith and morals, with a tendency to distinguish between those whom are "true" Christians from those who they believe do not measure up because of ungenuine faith.

Billy Sunday and Homer Rodeheaver

One of the most famous people in America during the early 1900s was a baseball player turned preacher, Billy Sunday, who began working full time for the YMCA in the winter of 1890–1891, when he was made assistant secretary of the religious department. In 1893, he took a job with a well-known evangelist, J. Wilbur Chapman, and assisted with setting up revivals in the Midwest through the latter part of the 19th century. Sunday was the "advance man" for Chapman—who was considered the leading evangelist of his day—and worked for Chapman from 1893 to 1895. When Chapman quit holding revivals at the end of 1895 to pastor a church in Philadelphia, Sunday had a wife, two children, and no job. This was remedied when an offer came from the town of Garner, Iowa, for Sunday to conduct a revival campaign.

Sunday quickly became a successful evangelist, and a number of people were converted during his revivals. By 1900, Sunday was successful enough to hold revivals in large tents and hire a gospel singer, Fred Fischer, full time. Fischer sang familiar hymns and stayed with Sunday for ten years before he left.

Sunday's revivals were criticized because of their entertainment aspect. Like Dwight Moody, Sunday advertised his revivals in the entertainment section of the newspaper and, also like Moody, hired a handsome singer. He also sometimes employed a female singer, Miss Mamie Lorimer. But Moody was a man of proven devotion and his singer, Ira Sankey, always prefaced his songs with a prayer, which Fischer did not do, and accompanied himself on the reed organ. Fischer used a piano accompanist and encouraged local cornet and trombone players to join him on stage during the hymns. Encouraging audience members to compete with one another in singing (the men versus the women) and turning the music portion of the revival into a community songfest were techniques he used.

Billy Sunday conducted revivals that attracted larger and larger crowds. Musically, his revivals took a major turn when he hired Homer Alvin Rodeheaver to replace Fred Fischer in 1910. Rodeheaver revolutionized the musical portion of the revivals and began, in essence, the gospel music industry of the 20th century with his mixture of ministry and entertainment and his creation of an independent record company as well as publishing interests.

Rodeheaver was the perfect man for the job with Sunday. He was genial and created an atmosphere of enthusiasm and friendliness, which gave the revivals a tremendous popular appeal and made them entertaining. He had a rich baritone voice and incredible stage presence with his dark, wavy hair, moderately handsome face, and what has been described as his "ingratiating" personality. Always smiling, he was affable and mixed well socially with a wide range of people. But Rodeheaver had more than just flair and style—he soon proved to have skill as a singer and a trombonist, a talent for evangelistic speaking, and the ability to coordinate and direct both children's and adult choirs. Musically, he was more daring than his predecessor: he sought out new gospel songs instead of relying solely on old hymns, and experimented extensively with group singing.

A premier showman, Rodeheaver had the ability to win over a large crowd with a funny story or a magic trick; he produced various "noises" from his trombone and pulled practical jokes on other team members on the stage. He encouraged his choirs to be enthusiastic and advised them to "go at it like selling goods." A bachelor, Rodeheaver was the first chorister to

have an overt appeal as a "lady's man" or sex symbol. That, combined with a lively sense of humor, his musical ability, a thick southern accent, and his ability to catch the feeling of a crowd, made him an invaluable asset to Sunday. Rodeheaver became a major drawing card and source of appeal for Sunday's revivals. His polish and grace stood in marked contrast to Sunday's physical acrobatics and hoarse shouting and served to lend a tone of dignity to the meetings.

Rodeheaver went into the music publishing business in 1910. Inspired by the example of Ira Sankey, who published a successful series of books of hymns, it seemed natural for a chorister to compile songs, old and new, and sell them at revivals. Rodeheaver wrote a number of hymns and employed the services of such quality songwriters as B. D. Ackley and Charles Gabriel. In the 30-minute musical program before the sermon, designed to warm up the crowd and get them in the proper mood for Sunday, Rodeheaver generally began with some old hymns that the crowd knew and gradually introduced newer compositions. As a result, those newer gospel songs became popular and demand for the songbooks was created and sustained.

A major reason for the increasing popular appeal of gospel songs was phonograph records, and Homer Rodeheaver probably began the first gospel label, although there is other evidence that suggests James Vaughan in Lawrenceburg, Tennessee, may have been responsible for the first gospel recordings. At any rate, the time was ripe for gospel music to be marketed with the new technology and Rodeheaver's company, Rainbow Records, was instrumental in presenting many of the new gospel songs, actively competing with the secular labels for the consumer's dollar.

When Rodeheaver began with Sunday, the major source of revenue for music came from the copyrights in the songbooks; however, shortly after 1916, when he began his record company, the sales of records accounted for more income than sheet music sales. It was a sign of the times and the times to come that the new technology would dominate the music industry and records replaced songbooks and sheet music as the financial backbone of this industry. It was also a harbinger for the emergence of gospel music on independent labels later in the century, which ensured the development of the music for a Christian consumer rather than any attempt to appeal commercially to the culture at large. Rainbow Records was the first of a number of small labels that recorded only gospel music and which nurtured this music.

Because Sunday's services were not held in churches—they were generally held outdoors in a specially built "tabernacle"—Rodeheaver actively used all the tools of secular entertainment without any fear of disrupting the decorum of the sanctuary. The choirs between 1912 and 1918 were generally large, and this allowed Rodeheaver to popularize numerous new songs with them. With a large number of voices, the chorister created jazzy arrangements, did call and answer type numbers (often by placing some members of the choir in the back of an auditorium), and manipulated a song so that it contained many melodramatic flourishes and effects. Many people learned the new songs and often sang them after the revivals left town, ensuring their popularity.

Although local talent was encouraged to participate on the revival stage and Rodeheaver used large choirs during the services, it was he who provided the key thread that tied it all together. He served as host and master of ceremonies for the revivals in addition to his role as soloist and chorister. When Billy Sunday made his plea for converts, Rodeheaver was responsible for selecting the right song and leading it as people came forward as an act of faith.

During the early days of recording, many recording companies went into the field, recording singers in rural areas of the South, and collected a number of hymns. These were mostly old songs carried from the oral tradition or learned from songbooks. But it was the records produced by independent companies like Rodeheaver's that began to create the Christian culture in 20th-century America, as the gospel consumer became part of a segmented market. As radio and secular records created a national market for music, gospel music evolved from being a separately identifiable form of music-such as the hymns of Sankey or the spirituals-into songs that sounded much like their pop counterparts, the only difference being in the lyrics. Homer Rodeheaver was the first to bridge this musical gap and establish the trend of religious music mimicking pop music in an attempt to draw large audiences and appeal to those both in and outside of religion.

George Beverly Shea and Billy Graham

The conservative theology espoused after World War II tended to affirm traditional American culture, especially the values of patriotism, free enterprise, and the validity of financial rewards. During the period immediately after World War II, the evangelistic and fundamentalist movements embraced American culture while at the same time preaching a radical transformation for the individuals in this culture. For Christianity and gospel music, George Beverly Shea and Billy Graham are prime examples of an evangelical Christianity with mainstream appeal after World War II. Previously, the evangelicals and fundamentalists were on the fringes of American religion; Shea and Graham put evangelism in the mainstream.

Singers who appeared on evangelistic crusades with famous evangelists—like Rodeheaver and Sankey—were major stars in their own right. They brought the church to the public arena and, with their singing, put the crowd in the right spirit because they were great soloists and great song leaders who delivered songs of faith to audiences of both believers and nonbelievers. But George Beverly Shea became the first international singing star of the gospel world. He achieved this position from his solos on the Billy Graham Crusades and his exposure on television, radio, and records. His songs, delivered with reserved emotion and a controlled passion, have been assimilated into hymnals and choir books. Musically, he was not a trailblazer, but he achieved his fame and position of respect by providing audiences with messages carefully encased in the tradition of Protestant Christianity in America.

During his early life, George Beverly Shea worked for the Mutual Life Insurance Company but also sang on a local radio station, at churches, and in the community. In the late 1930s he joined the radio station at the Moody Bible Institute in Chicago. Billy Graham was a student at nearby Wheaton College, and one day he stopped by the station and told Shea how much he enjoyed hearing him sing on the program "Hymns from the Chapel."

In 1942 Shea joined evangelist Jack Wyrtzen for a summer of crusades in the New York area, singing at youth rallies. When he returned to Chicago he began singing at youth meetings in the area where Billy Graham spoke. In 1944 Shea joined WCFL for "Club Time," a 15-minute radio program broadcast weekdays; in 1945 this show was broadcast on the ABC network. When Billy Graham, then a young pastor at the Village Church in Western Springs, Illinois, took over the WCFL program "Songs in the Night" in 1944, he persuaded Shea to sing on the program. This led to a lifelong friendship and working relationship that was interrupted temporarily by World War II when Graham joined the Army for a year before being released because he contracted a severe case of mumps. After Graham was discharged from the Army, he began preaching at Youth for Christ rallies and traveled to Great Britain where he held meetings for six months.

When Graham returned to the States, he contacted Shea about singing for gospel meetings in Charlotte, North Carolina, which became the unofficial launching of his crusades in 1948. Billy Graham had to overcome a number of obstacles, mostly owing to the bad reputations of itinerant evangelists who had attempted to replicate the success of Billy Sunday in the 1920s and 1930s. His big break came in September 1949, when the troupe brought their campaign to Los Angeles and received international coverage from the Hearst newspapers. The conversion of some celebrities, chief among whom was Stuart Hamblen, a popular radio entertainer who later wrote "It Is No Secret" and a number of other gospel classics, as well as 1936 Olympic star Louis Zamperini and underworld figure Jim Vaus, helped propel Graham's career.

In 1951 Shea signed with RCA, where he enjoyed major recording success in the 1950s. Shea was the beneficiary of a big break received by Billy Graham after the evangelist was featured in *Life* magazine, which led to a White House visit with Harry Truman. A radio program, "Hour of Decision," began on December 5, 1950, from Atlanta and featured Graham preaching with Shea singing. By the fifth week, it had the largest audience of any religious program in history. In 1952 Shea resigned from other radio programs where he sang and devoted all his energies to the Billy Graham Evangelistic Association (BGEA).

During his first crusade abroad in 1954, Shea found a song that was linked with him throughout his career: "How Great Thou Art." Shea was given the sheet music to the song when he was in London; he performed it first on the Toronto Crusade in 1955 at the Maple Leaf Garden, and the song had an immediate impact.

"How Great Thou Art" became a standard during the 1957 Crusade in Madison Square Garden, where Shea performed it with the choir 99 times during the 16-week crusade.

The tall, genial Shea became a major star in the gospel world through singing this and other songs in his rich bass voice. The songs he sang fit perfectly in church—a key to their success—and Shea's voice is the epitome of the great choir soloist. His exposure on the Billy Graham Crusades and in the electronic media made him a household name in gospel circles as he became the first major gospel singing star to emerge in the second half of the 20th century, preceding and laying much of the groundwork for the commercial success of gospel music in that period. It was Shea who first proved that a religious artist could reach a sizeable market recording only gospel music directed at the Christian audience whose focal point is the church.

Don Cusic

For Further Reading

Anderson, Robert Mapes. *Vision of the Disinherited: The Making of American Pentecostalism.* New York: Oxford, 1979.

Blackwell, Lois S. *The Wings of the Dove.* Norfolk, Va.: The Donning Co., 1978.

Cusic, Don. *The Sound of Light: A History of Gospel and Christian Music.* New York: Hal Leonard, 2002.

Dowley, Tim, ed. *Eerdmans Handbook to the History of Christianity.* Grand Rapids, Mich.: Eerdmans, 1977.

Marsden, George M. *Fundamentalism and American Culture: The Shaping of Twentieth-Century Fundamentalism, 1870–1925.* Oxford: Oxford University Press, 1980.

Marsden, George M. *Understanding Fundamentalism and Evangelicalism.* Grand Rapids, Mich.: Eerdmans, 1991.

McLoughlin, William G., Jr. *Billy Sunday Was His Real Name.* Chicago: The University of Chicago Press, 1955.

Nichol, John Thomas. *Pentecostalism.* Plainfield, N.J.: Logos, 1966.

Shea, George Beverly, with Fred Bauer. *Songs That Lift the Heart.* Old Tappan, N.J.: Fleming H. Revell, 1972.

Shea, George Beverly, with Fred Bauer. *Then Sings My Soul.* Old Tappan, N.J.: Fleming H. Revell, 1968.

Synan, Vinson. *The Holiness Pentecostal Movement.* Grand Rapids, Mich.: Eerdmans, 1971.

REPP, RAY

For most of the 19th and 20th centuries there was an uneasy alliance between Catholics and Protestants; on one hand, both were Christian but neither felt the other was "truly Christian." In some fundamentalist circles, the Pope was considered to be the anti-Christ, while amongst Catholics the prevailing belief was that the Protestant Reformation was when Christianity lost its bearings and went astray. In fact, Catholics believed it was a sin to attend any church other than a Catholic church while most Protestants believed Catholicism was an old, dead religion that spoke a dead language (Latin) and was akin to still having a monarchy rule the country.

That began to change with Vatican II, when Pope John XXIII called the cardinals to the Vatican in Rome to overhaul the ancient faith. Out of that came the mass celebrated in everyday language and more participation from congregants in the mass.

Vatican II came when the urban folk music movement in America had peaked; still, a number of young people had grown up strumming guitars and singing folk songs like "Kumbaya," "Michael, Row the Boat Ashore," and "Blowin' in the Wind." One of the edicts from Vatican II was for Roman Catholic churches to develop materials relevant to their culture for the liturgy. Some of the first efforts involved introducing folk music into churches.

There was quite a bit of controversy involved; after all, the Roman Catholic church had followed its traditions for hundreds of years, so many members were upset to see any changes at all in the ancient traditions. Further, folk music was not only "new" but was often part of the liberal movement that sang about civil rights, social justice, and, increasingly, about the Vietnam War, which stirred debate and resistance amongst the generations.

Ray Repp (b. September 17, 1942) was a young seminarian, studying to be a priest at the time of Vatican II. In 1965 he wrote "Mass for Young Americans," which consisted of folk tunes to accompany the liturgy. It was a revolutionary work; not only did it bring the guitar into the church, it also invited young people to become actively involved in church services.

In 1963 Friends of the English Liturgy, better known as FEL, was founded by David Fitzpatrick. It was a publishing company dedicated to publishing works for the Catholic church. They published Repp's *Mass for Young Americans*, and in 1966 the album *Mass for Young Americans* was released on the FEL label.

Ray Repp is given credit for being "the one who started it all" because before there was Jesus music there was the folk music of the Roman Catholic Church; before there was a widespread Jesus movement of youth becoming Christians there was the movement within the Catholic church that brought contemporary music into the sanctuary and invited young people to participate in the service.

The music business wasn't even aware of this movement; the albums were not sold to consumers but were sold to those involved in church leadership positions who actively sought the involvement of youth in churches. The result was that the Catholic church was ahead of the Jesus movement in bringing young people to the faith through music.

The end result was a new Catholic service, spoken and sung in English in the United States with folk music accompanying the liturgy. And the key person who started this was Ray Repp.

Don Cusic

Discography

Mass for Young Americans (1966)

Allelu (1966)

Come Alive (1967)

Sing Praise (1968)

The Time Has Not Come True (1969)

Hear the Cryin' (1972)

Give Us Peace (1975)

Benedicamus (1978)

Sunrise, in the Dead of Winter (1980)

For Further Reading

Cusic, Don. *The Sound of Light: A History of Gospel and Christian Music.* New York: Hal Leonard, 2002.

Powell, Mark Allen. *Encyclopedia of Contemporary Christian Music.* Peabody, Mass.: Hendrickson Publishers, Inc., 2002.

RESURRECTION BAND

Glenn Kaiser, vocals, guitar
Wendi Kaiser, vocals
John Herrin, drums
Stu Heiss, guitar, keyboard
Tom Cameron, harmonic (until 1980)
Jim Denton, bass (until 1988)
Roger Heiss, percussion (1979–1980)
Steve Eisen, sax (1982–1984)
Roy Montroy, bass (since 1988)

Resurrection Band has been connected with the Jesus People U.S.A. (JPUSA) community. Their community, based in Chicago, is the oldest Christian commune still thriving. This community lives and works in inner city Chicago and is involved with social justice, helping to feed the poor and homeless.

The Jesus People U.S.A. community was started by Jim and Sue Palosaari in Milwaukee, where they established a Discipleship Training Center in 1973. From a core group of seven the community grew to 150 and bought a building, then divided into smaller groups for evangelization. The Palosaaris formed a musical group, the Sheep, and toured in Europe before returning to the United States. Another of the splinter groups, based in Milwaukee, was headed by John Herrin, Sr.

The group Charity was formed by John Herrin, Jr., Glenn and Wendi Kaiser (Wendi is Herrin Sr.'s daughter), and some other musicians. Glenn Kaiser (b. January 21, 1953) is the son of musical parents who were involved in jazz and pop; Kaiser's background included a series of teenage bands until he was 19, when his involvement with drugs ended his secular ambitions and led him to accept Christ.

Charity performed wherever they could attract a crowd—in parks, shopping centers, and community centers—for their evangelistic efforts. In 1972 Charity became the Resurrection Band. The band played "hard music for hard hearts," a no holds barred rock 'n' roll for no holds barred evangelism.

Some members of the Milwaukee community left to drive around the country, performing rock evangelism concerts; after a short stay in Florida they ended up in Chicago in 1972 where they settled. John Herrin, Sr. left the group and his wife, Dawn Herrin, assumed leadership. Through bassist Jim Denton, who studied at North Park Theological Seminary, the group became affiliated with the Evangelical Covenant Church, that seminary's sponsoring denomination. Members of the community, including Glenn Kaiser, became ordained ministers in that denomination.

The JPUSA group in Chicago lived together in the inner city and worked with the poor; all earnings (many had jobs in local and community-owned businesses) went into a common purse. This common purse not only supported the JPUSA group but also purchased meals for homeless and street people and offered Christian discipleship to those it attracted. Income from Resurrection Band's concerts and albums also went into this common purse.

The Resurrection Band began recording in 1974; their first two albums were self-produced and released on cassettes, but in 1978 they went to Pasadena, Texas, and recorded a hard rock album for Star Song Records. After two albums for that label, they were signed to Light Records and recorded several albums before moving to Sparrow, where they recorded as the Rez Band.

The Resurrection/Rez band played blues-based hard rock, which made it difficult to obtain radio airplay. Their lyrics are hard hitting, which made it difficult for the mainstream contemporary Christian gatekeepers to embrace them. Still, the band was committed to their music as well as their commune in Chicago and survived despite adversity.

In Chicago, the group built its own studio, Tone Zone, and during the 1990s reverted back to their original name, the Resurrection Band. Glenn Kaiser formed a record label, Grr, and released several solo albums; the band also released their product on this label.

Jesus People U.S.A. are pioneers in contemporary Christian music and Christian rock; they published *Cornerstone Magazine* and established the annual Cornerstone Christian Festival, originally in Bushnell, Illinois. This festival has become the leading festival for Christian rock performers.

JPUSA has had its share of criticism; they were criticized as being a cult, attacked in a book published by a leading Christian publisher (*Recovering from Churches that Abuse* by Ronald Enroth; published by Zondervan in 1994), and lambasted by Christian leaders Bob Larson, Jimmy Swaggart, and David Wilkerson for using "the devil's music."

Resurrection Band called it quits in July 2000, although they reunited for an appearance at the 25th Cornerstone Festival in July 2008. Still, the community has survived and is a living testament for those who desire to live a Christian life, living near poverty, pooling their resources, and committing each day to helping those who cannot help themselves while extending evangelistic efforts to their inner city community.

Don Cusic

Discography

Music to Raise the Dead (1974)

All Your Life (1974)

Awaiting Your Reply (1978)

Rainbow's End (1979)

Colours (1980)

Mommy Don't Love Daddy Anymore (1981)

D.M.Z. (1982)

As Rez

Best of Rez Music to Raise the Dead (1984)

Live Bootleg (1984)

Hostage (1984)

Between Heaven 'N Hell (1985)

Compact Favorites (1988)

Silence Screams (1988)

Innocent Blood (1989)

Civil Rites (1991)

20 Years (1992)

Reach of Love (1993)

Lament (1995)

The Light Years (1995)

Ampendectomy (1997)

Music to Raise the Dead 1972–1998 (2008)

For Further Reading

Alfonso, Barry. *The Billboard Guide to Contemporary Christian Music.* New York: Billboard Books/Watson-Guptill, 2002.

Powell, Mark Allen. *Encyclopedia of Contemporary Christian Music.* Peabody, Mass.: Hendrickson Publishers, Inc., 2002.

Thompson, John J. *Raised by Wolves: The Story of Christian Rock and Roll.* Toronto, Ontario: ECW Press, 2000.

RETAIL AND CONTEMPORARY CHRISTIAN MUSIC

The retail outlet for the Christian culture is the Christian bookstore. During the early 1950s, when the Christian Booksellers Association (CBA) was first formed to represent these stores as a trade organization, most of the stores were independently owned and saw themselves as a ministry first and a retail outlet second. The stores stocked Bibles and Christian books aimed to support Christians in their faith as well as encourage non-Christians to embrace the faith.

By the mid-1970s Christian bookstores had moved into malls. Christian books proliferated, and Christian music became widely accepted. Christian merchandise became big business as it moved into homes via recordings, books, jewelry, clothing, gifts, and assorted artifacts worn or hung on walls.

The infrastructure was in place for contemporary Christian music to grow through a marketing network of Christian bookstores, represented by a trade organization, the CBA. The CBA began in 1950 with about 25 stores; in 1976 they represented 2,800 members, who generated $500 million in sales, up from $100 million in 1971. Average annual revenue jumped 17.4 percent per year.

The Christian bookstores were mostly family owned, and most were initially started as a ministry that offered some religious books for sale. However, by the mid-1970s most were viewed as a family business, concerned deeply with ministry but also aware of the need to institute sound business practices in order to survive. Their growth came because they provided Christian product unavailable in other outlets.

In mid-1978 the top sellers in contemporary Christian music were B. J. Thomas and Evie Tornquist; each was selling more than 100,000 units of each release, and some albums by these artists reached the 300,000–400,000 plateau. But for most acts, sales of 20,000 were considered "good" for a first album and 40,000 units was a "hit."

The Christian Bookseller's 30th convention in 1980 was a five-day gathering attended by more than 8,000 with buyers from over 1,600 Christian bookstores placing orders. Built around the theme, "Making Christ Known," the convention featured seminars as well as sales pitches, with topics that included "How to Sell the Top Ten Bibles," "Increasing Sales with Specials and Promotions," "Displaying and Selling Music," "Store Personnel Management," and "Cash Flow Controls."

For recording artists, this was the single most important event of their year because of the necessity to establish good relations with Christian bookstore owners. Christian artists who appeared during that convention included Andrae Crouch, Kathie Lee Johnson, Candle, Johnny Zell, Jeremiah People, Christine Wyrtzen, Bridge, Cynthia Clawson, the Bill Gaither Trio, Pat Boone, Dan Peek, Chuck Girard, Rick Foster, David Meece, Truth, Fletch Wiley, Mike Warnke, Honeytree, Gary S. Paxton, Doug Oldham, and Sandi Patti. They all came to meet—and be met by—the Christian bookstore personnel who would, they hoped, stock and sell their music. It was a good way to be seen, heard, and noticed by the people who count in the Christian retailing industry.

During the 1980s, a shift occurred in the gospel music industry as contemporary Christian music began to dominate the field of gospel and Christian music as well as sales in Christian bookstores. There had always been a bit of conflict between books and music with retailers, and the name "Christian booksellers" and "Christian bookstores" indicates which side most stores chose to take. However, with sales of music accounting for 17 to 40 percent of a stores' revenue, the owners quickly saw they had to become more heavily involved and stock more of this inventory.

The early reluctance of Christian bookstores to stock contemporary Christian music was fading away. The store owners had looked on early gospel rock as music from the devil, unsuitable for their stores, and some customers—mostly older ones—had complained about rock 'n' gospel. However, as this segment of the culture grew and mainline Christians realized the sincerity and dedication of those in contemporary Christian music—and when they saw it as a wholesome alternative to real rock 'n' roll for their own children—some of the barriers began to fall away.

Research on the Christian market was released in mid-1983 and helped profile the Christian music consumer. The RIAA (Recording Industry Association of America), the organization representing record companies and which certifies gold and platinum albums, reported that gospel sales accounted for 6 percent of recorded product in the United States, up from the 4 percent retail and 5 percent direct marketing shares reported in 1981.

Gospel industry spokespersons indicated that gospel outsold jazz and classical; however, the RIAA disagreed, saying that classical outsold gospel in direct marketing (sales by mail) and its share of industry sales was larger. An inherent problem in measuring gospel sales against a music like jazz or classical was that the latter reached basically one audience with one kind of music (although there is, obviously, much variety within these musical genres) but gospel reaches a number of different audiences with an extremely wide range of music—from southern gospel quartets to black gospel choirs to heavy metal gospel and everything in between.

In secular music, radio airplay created a demand for album sales during the latter half of the 20th century; however, radio was not as large a factor in the sales of contemporary Christian music. Word Records commissioned a survey of Christian radio that showed Christian radio struggled for a tiny share of the radio audience. Of the contemporary Christian stations that did show up in surveys, most had shares in the 1.1 to 1.5 range. (Ratings are based on the percentage of those listening to a particular station measured against the total population of an area; share indicates the number listening to a particular station measured against the population listening to radio at that time.)

A major problem at contemporary Christian radio stations was music, or rather the lack of it. The survey reported that the average day at a Christian radio station was 18.2 hours, with music played an average of 8.2 hours and the bulk of the remaining 10 hours a day was taped programs, or "preaching and teaching" shows.

The Word report concluded that Christian radio was doing poorly, with about l.6 percent of the national marketplace, ahead only of Spanish-language programming, solid gold formats, and classical and jazz stations.

Contemporary Christian Music magazine surveyed their readers and discovered a music-loving group, with 59.4 percent of the respondents saying they bought 10 or more albums each year and 31.2 percent saying they purchased more than 16 albums a year. A large segment, 75.8 percent, said they listen to music more than 10 hours a week and 46.9 percent said what the artist was saying was more important than the quality of the recording (31.6 percent). The CCM survey also showed that 94.7 percent of respondents said they attended a concert in the past year,

47.6 percent said they attended more than 4, and 7 percent attended more than 11. Most (72.8 percent) listened to secular music and attended concerts by secular artists, but there was a "hardcore" group of Christian consumers (27.2 percent) who stated they listened to only Christian music. This survey also showed that 94.9 percent of those responding were under 34, with 57.6 percent under 25; 69.9 percent were male and most (61.6 percent) were single. Only 36.3 percent were married and only 56.7 percent of the readers were employed full time (reflecting a large number of students reading the magazine), although 35.5 percent of the respondents reported a family income exceeding $25,000 a year. Finally, those responding reported that *CCM* was the magazine they read most often (48.2 percent). All of these facts and figures helped clarify the Christian consumer in the marketplace and pointed out some interesting trends that the Christian music industry capitalized on in the future. First, there was a sizeable core of young Christians who liked contemporary Christian music and who were active buyers; second, there was a potential for Christian record companies to achieve big sales figures on albums if only they could convince radio to program singles in high rotation, like their secular counterparts.

The record companies began to release singles instead of just albums, and between 1985 and 1995 the sales of Christian recordings grew by $298 million. Surveys done during that period indicated that the buyers of contemporary Christian music were overwhelmingly white middle-class females in their 30s and 40s living in the suburbs and with some college education. Specifically, 76 percent of the music was purchased by females, and 59 percent of the buyers are in their 30s and 40s, with 85 percent of them white. About half of the buyers earned between $30,000 and $60,000 a year, with 77 percent having some college education and 43 percent a college degree.

This period of growth indicated that Christian music succeeded in selling recordings because it was music by Christians, for Christians, about Christians and Christianity, and it succeeded because it established an alternative world to the mainstream popular culture.

In the late 20th and early 21st centuries, Christian music proved itself to be a resounding success in the commercial market, primarily through sales in Christian bookstores. In 1976 music accounted for only 9 percent of sales in Christian bookstores, but in 1984 it accounted for 25 percent of gross sales in Christian bookstores.

By 1985 the Christian Bookseller's Association had 3,400 member stores out of the 5,200–5,500 that sold Christian products. The CBA stores generated $1.269 billion in sales in 1985, which meant the average store generated $235,000 in business. The Christian bookstores were mostly family owned, with about 56 percent in shopping or strip malls and about 5 percent in regional malls in 1985. The average owner was 37 years old (compared to a 59-year-old average owner in 1965) and often came armed with a degree in business. They saw themselves as retailers and businessmen, although they still acknowledged the ministry aspect of their business. This contrasted sharply with the Christian bookstores of the late-1960s, which saw themselves as primarily a ministry that offered some religious books for sale to support that ministry.

When the Christian Bookseller's Association began, it represented stores that sold books; however, by 1985 book sales accounted for 29 percent of sales and music accounted for 23 percent. Other items included Bibles, which accounted for 16 percent of sales; Sunday school curriculums, which accounted for 6 percent; greeting cards, 4 percent; jewelry, 2 percent; and gifts, 10 percent.

There were several reasons for the increase in sales in Christian and gospel music during the 1990s. First, there was consolidation. The Family Bookstore chain had expanded and corporate offices demanded they stock what sold—so if it sold, then it was stocked. Next, there was a consolidation of recording labels, usually becoming partners within a much larger organization.

The major corporations provided immense capitalization. Those deep pockets helped ensure big sales when an artist hit. Small companies usually could not afford to have a big hit because the costs of manufacturing, marketing, and promotion, which were incurred before the label has received income from sales, can break a small company.

Another factor in the success of gospel and Christian music during the 1990s came from the fact that *Billboard*, the leading trade magazine in the music industry, began to compile its charts based on SoundScan, a computer technology based on bar codes. This computer technology supplied the facts in raw numbers; if an album sold well—no matter what kind of music—it was reported by the computers. The fact that

gospel sold well became a proven fact, thus enticing retailers to expand their selection of gospel and stock more product, which led to more sales.

SoundScan also showed the recording labels where their albums were selling and which promotions worked, allowing marketers to make use of this information—which they received week by week—to maximize sales for a hot act.

Finally, the music industry is both hit-driven and star-driven, and both gospel and Christian music produced a number of hits and stars from the late 1980s onward. Amy Grant and Sandi Patti were pioneers in the contemporary Christian field, soon joined by Michael W. Smith, Petra, and the Imperials. In the late 1980s, Steven Curtis Chapman began to dominate the field. The musical trends of rap and hip hop saw DC Talk emerge. Hits by Sixpence None the Richer, Jars of Clay, Bob Carlisle, Audio Adrenaline, Third Day, Point of Grace, Newsboys, and others created consumer demand.

By 1995 the revenues from the Christian music industry were estimated to be as high as $750 million per year, with sales of recordings accounting for $381 million. In 1985, about 90 percent of all contemporary Christian music was sold in Christian bookstores; by 1995, 64 percent was sold in Christian bookstores, 21 percent in the general market, and 15 percent by direct mail.

Between 1985 and 1995 Christian recordings grew by $298 million, or a 290 percent increase in sales. In 1995 the SoundScan technology began to be used to compile *Billboard*'s religious music charts; the next year, sales of recordings reached $538 million (or a 30 percent increase in one year), placing it sixth in popularity of all music genres, behind rock, country, urban contemporary, pop, and rap, but ahead of classical, jazz, oldies, and new age. When concert ticket sales and merchandising were added, religious music generated an estimated $750 million to $900 million in revenue.

In 1996 gospel accounted for 4.3 percent of all music sales; that year there were 33.3 million scans of Christian/gospel product; in 1997 there were 44 million scans, or a 32 percent growth rate from the previous year. Between 1991 and 1996 Christian/gospel recordings averaged a 22 percent growth each year while other formats had an average growth rate of around 5 percent. In 1997 Christian/gospel recordings accounted for $550 million in sales; in 1987 that figure was $160 million.

By 1998 Wal-Mart, Kmart, Blockbuster, MusicLand, Target, and Sam Goody had all increased their stock of gospel. Wal-Mart, which had 45 linear feet in its music department, had 8 linear feet for Christian music. This is where the biggest growth in religious music occurred; while the sales at Christian bookstores increased 15–25 percent, the mainstream market for religious music grew 70–80 percent.

Don Cusic

For Further Reading

Cusic, Don. *The Sound of Light: A History of Gospel and Christian Music.* New York: Hal Leonard, 2002.

RICHARD, CLIFF

Cliff Richard (b. Harry Roger Webb, on October 14, 1940) is bigger than the Beatles in England; he is the most successful rock act in the history of rock in that country, surpassing the Beatles in longevity and number of hit records on the charts.

He began his career in 1957 as a member of the Dick Teague Skiffle Group. Inspired by Elvis, he formed the Drifters with drummer Terry Smart and guitarist Norman Mitham; in London they were joined by guitarist Ian Samwell. They were "discovered" by talent agent George Ganyou at a talent show; Ganyou financed a recording session that led to them being signed to EMI by producer Norrie Paramor. Richard's first release was "Move It," which was promoted heavily by TV producer Jack Good on whose show, "Oh Boy!," Richard appeared. Since the Drifters was the name of an American group, Richard changed his group's name to the Shadows.

British pop star Cliff Richard has also had a successful career in contemporary Christian music. (AP Photo/Lefteris Pitarakis)

Richard's performances inspired a backlash from adults; his gyrations were similar to Elvis Presley's, which outraged traditional music critics but screaming female fans assured him pop stardom.

Like Elvis, Richard starred in movies and had a string of hit singles and, also like Elvis, increasingly recorded adult contemporary pop and middle of the road songs throughout the 1960s.

In 1966 Richard announced his Christian conversion in London at a Billy Graham rally. He almost ended his pop career but decided instead to continue to record "positive pop." Richard performs gospel songs in his concerts and has recorded gospel albums but has generally kept his pop and Christian careers separate. He has shown longevity—his career spans 50 years—and he became Sir Cliff Richard when he was knighted in 1995.

Although he has never had a breakthrough hit single in the United States, Richard remains England's most successful and enduring pop star. He also became one of England's best known Christian figures (behind the Archbishop of Canterbury).

Don Cusic

Selected Discography

Good News (1967)

His Land (1970)

Two a Penny (1970)

About That Man (1970)

Now You See Me, Now You Don't (1982)

Walking in the Light (1984)

Carols (1988)

Songs of Life: Mission '89 (1989)

For Further Reading

Hardy, Phil, and Dave Laing. *The Faber Companion to 20th Century Popular Music*. London: Faber and Faber, 1990.

Larkins, Colin, ed. *The Virgin Encyclopedia of Popular Music*. London: Virgin, 2002.

Powell, Mark Allen. *Encyclopedia of Contemporary Christian Music*. Peabody, Mass.: Hendrickson Publishers, Inc., 2002.

Richard, Cliff. *Which One's Cliff?* London: Hodder and Stoughton, 1981.

Winter, David. *New Singer, New Song: The Cliff Richard Story*. Waco, Tex.: Word, 1967.

S

SCHULTZ, MARK

Mark Schultz (b. September 16, 1970, in Colby, Kansas) is one of contemporary Christian music's most popular singer-songwriters. His self-titled debut release, *Mark Schultz*, on Word Records in 2000 produced three number one singles, including "I Am the Way," that held the top chart position for four weeks. The *CCM Update* trade magazine named "I Am the Way" "Song of the Year 2000," and Schultz held the position of the longest-running debut single from a debut artist that year. Schultz continued to be a favorite on Christian radio with songs from his following five albums reaching the number one spot. He earned a certified platinum sales award from the Recording Industry Association of America (RIAA) for his live concert DVD/CD *Mark Schultz Live: A Night of Stories and Songs* for sales of 100,000 units. Schultz also received his first Dove Award for the project as "Long Form Music Video of the Year" in 2006.

Growing up in the small town of Colby, Kansas, Schultz developed a love for music at a young age and began singing in choirs and musicals in grade school. He continued to pursue his musical interest through high school and college at Kansas State University, where he earned a degree in marketing. With dreams of pursuing a musical career, Schultz moved to Nashville in 1994. He spent his early years there working as a waiter before landing a job as a youth pastor at First Presbyterian Church. Schultz wrote many of his songs on the piano in the chapel of the church, and the teenagers he worked with often became the focus of his writing.

"He's My Son," from Mark's debut album, was a song inspired by a member of Schultz's youth group who was battling cancer. The tender ballad with a plea from a parent to God for healing for a child was quickly embraced by Christian radio, rising to number one. The universal message of the song also reached the pop radio audience, and the song became a top 20 hit on the *Billboard* magazine adult contemporary chart.

Following the success of his debut album, Mark's sophomore release, *Song Cinema*, was released in 2002. He quickly returned to the top of the charts with "I Have Been There." A second single from the album, "Back in His Arms Again," quickly rose to number one on the Christian radio charts and held the top spot for seven weeks. Mark's third album, *Stories and Songs*, was released in 2003 and yielded another number one radio hit, "Letters from War." Mark made a video for the song and it was used as the theme for the U.S. Army's 2004 Be Safe—Make It Home campaign. The song and accompanying video were used as part of an awareness program designed to help reduce the occurrence of accidental death among soldiers. Schultz was also invited to perform the song at the Pentagon in Washington, D.C.

Mark Schultz became a favorite of concertgoers, and he decided to capture some live shows for this next project, an album and DVD titled *Mark Schultz Live: A Night of Stories and Songs*, released in 2005. The album produced the number one single, "I Am," and became a best seller. Returning to the studio, Schultz recorded *Broken and Beautiful*, which was released in 2006. The album included three more radio hits, "Broken and Beautiful," "Everything to Me," and "Walking Her Home." Mark added some new music and video to the project and released it as *Broken and Beautiful – Expanded Edition*, in 2007.

A mission trip Mark took with his wife Kate to orphanages in Mexico inspired him to make a cross-country bike trip to raise funds for the orphans. Calling his benefit bicycle ride Across America, Mark began his 3,500-mile trek in Newport Beach, California, on May 7, 2007 and completed the trip on July 6, 2007, in Portsmouth (Rye), New Hampshire. The trip raised more than $250,000 to benefit orphans and widows through the Family Christian Stores James Fund. One of the highlights of the trip was a stop at the Kansas Children's Service League, the agency from where Mark was adopted as a child.

James Elliott

For Further Reading

Powell, Mark Allen. *Encyclopedia of Contemporary Christian Music*. Peabody, Mass.: Hendrickson Publishers, Inc., 2002.

2ND CHAPTER OF ACTS

Annie Herring
Matthew Ward
Nelly Greisen

Most of the recordings of the early Jesus music groups sound dated in the 21 century, a part of late 1960s and early 1970s music rooted in that culture, but 2nd Chapter of Acts is a timeless group: their unique sound transcends that era and remains a shining example of the best of early contemporary Christian music.

The three members of 2nd Chapter—Annie Herring, Matthew Ward, and Nelly Greisen—are siblings. They grew up in North Dakota in a Catholic family of nine children. Annie Ward loved singing in the church choir and often sang at home with her siblings. In 1965 the family moved to the Sacramento area of California. Annie left home and sang in musical groups and acquired a boyfriend, Buck Herring, a recording engineer.

Tragedy struck the Ward family in 1968 when their mother, Elizabeth Ward, died of a brain tumor. Shortly after that Buck Herring became born again and shared his faith with Annie. He gave her a copy of *Good News for Modern Man*, the New Testament in plain English, and Annie too received Jesus. In early 1969 Buck and Annie were married.

A second tragedy struck the Ward family in the late summer of 1970 when their father, Walter Ward, died from leukemia. Nelly was 14 and Matthew was 12 at the time of their father's death, and the decision was made for them to live with Buck and Annie, who had been married less than two years. In the Herring home, Annie composed songs on the piano about Jesus; Nelly and Matthew both came to the faith and joined Annie in her songs, developing a tight, unique harmony sound.

On February 15, 1971—Matthew's 13th birthday—they recorded "Jesus Is," a song written by one of Buck's friends who wanted a recording of the song. It came to the attention of Pat Boone, who took the recording to Mike Curb at MGM Records and arranged for it to be released as a single. On that song, Matthew sang lead and his sisters and some friends sang background vocals. That was the beginning of 2nd Chapter of Acts. The group chose that name because they felt it captured the essence of the Christian faith and message. (Buck Herring said he heard the phrase "The 2nd Chapter of Acts" loudly in his mind one day while working in the studio and knew it was to be their name.)

The trio began singing locally at churches and coffeehouses. Their follow-up single, "I'm So Happy," did not chart, and MGM decided not to do an album. However, Buck Herring was working on Barry McGuire's first Christian album, *Seeds*, and asked McGuire to listen to the young singers; he did and agreed to include them on his album. The group began touring with Barry McGuire, and the singer whose secular success, including stints with the New Christy Minstrels as well as the counterculture hit "Eve of Destruction," attracted crowds who enjoyed the group as well as McGuire.

On McGuire's live album, *For the Bride*, the 2nd Chapter of Acts was prominently featured. The connection with McGuire led to the group signing with Myrrh Records and recording their first album, *With Footnotes*. On that album was "Easter Song," written by Annie Herring, with a distinctive piano intro played by Michael Omartian. That song soon caught the attention of the Jesus people, who began singing it in churches.

In 1977 they toured with Phil Keaggy and recorded an album with him, *How the West Was One*, which introduced the talented guitarist to the West Coast audience.

In 1978, convinced that no one should be required to purchase a ticket to one of their concerts, the 2nd Chapter of Acts decided to play only for "free will" offerings; instead of receiving a guaranteed amount for their appearances, the audience was invited to give whatever they felt was appropriate. That same year they released their first album on Sparrow, the label started by Billy Ray Hearn. Hearn had founded Myrrh Records for Word in Waco, Texas, and signed the 2nd Chapter to that label for their first three albums; however, in 1976 he started Sparrow Records in Los Angeles, where most of the Jesus music pioneers lived. The first album by 2nd Chapter of Acts on Sparrow was a classic, *Mansion Builder*; the title song soon became a classic in contemporary Christian music. Their follow-up album, *The Roar of Love*, was based on C. S. Lewis's classic set of children's stories, *Chronicles of Narnia*. (This was intended to be their first release on Sparrow, but problems with the C. S. Lewis estate held up its release for several years.)

The group believed in an uncompromised Christian faith and sought to sing to the Lord, not an audience, on their recordings and in their concerts. Although they were in the 1970s musical world, they were not "of" that world; their sound was unique and stood apart from other Christian and secular groups. In many ways, they defined early contemporary Christian music with not only their musical sound but also their public life. They were committed to Jesus, not the music business, and their songs were anthems of love and revelation of the power and love of Jesus. They did more than perform songs; they led worship before an audience so that each concert was essentially a church service unlike traditional church services, held outside of a church but in the presence of God.

The group attended Church on the Way in Van Nuys, California, and recruited musicians from that church for their tours; A Band of David continued to tour with them (Gene Gunnels, drums; Herb Melton, bass; Richard Souther, keyboard; Rick Azim, guitar (until 1977); Paul Offenbacker, guitar). Their strong Christian faith led to a conflict with their record labels, and the 2nd Chapter of Acts became uncomfortable with the business and promotional side of a career in music; they were uncomfortable with a commercial music industry, and their anticommercial attitude toward sharing the gospel through their music led them to move to Lindale, Texas (to a ranch next to Keith Green's Last Day's Ministries) in 1981 and start their own record label. Their first release on Live Oak Records was *Night Light*, released in 1985.

By 1988 the group was tired of touring; Nelly especially wanted to stay home and raise a family. Their Farewell Tour ended in Houston on August 12, 1988, where, after more than 1,500 concerts and 16 albums, the 2nd Chapter of Acts said good-bye to their audiences. However, Annie Herring and Matthew Ward, who had previously recorded solo projects, continued to record and perform before audiences.

Don Cusic

Discography

With Footnotes (1974)

In the Volume of the Book (1975)

To the Bride (with Barry McGuire and A Band Called David) (1976)

How the West Was One (with Phil Keaggy) (1977)

Mansion Builder (1978)

The Roar of Love (1980)

Rejoice (1981)

Encores (1981)

Together Live (with Michael and Stormie Omartian) (1983)

Singer Sower (1983)

Night Light (1985)

Hymns (1986)

Far Away Places (1987)

Hymns II (1988)

Hymns Instrumental (1989)

20 (1992)

Discography: Annie Herring Solo

Through a Child's Eyes (1976)

Search Deep Inside (1981)

Waiting for My Ride to Come (1990)

There's a Stirring (1992)

Glimpses (1997)

Wonder (1998)

Discography: Matthew Ward Solo

Toward Eternity (1979)

Armed and Dangerous (1987)

The Matthew Ward Collection (1992)

Point of View (1992)

My Redeemer (1997)

Even Now (2000)

For Further Reading

Alfonso, Barry. *The Billboard Guide to Contemporary Christian Music.* New York: Billboard Books/Watson-Guptill, 2002.

Cusic, Don. *The Sound of Light: A History of Gospel and Christian Music.* New York: Hal Leonard, 2002.

Herring, Annie. *Glimpses: Seeing God in Everyday Life.* Grand Rapids, Mich.: Bethany House, 1996.

McNeil, W. K., ed. *Encyclopedia of American Gospel Music.* New York: Routledge, 2005.

Powell, Mark Allen. *Encyclopedia of Contemporary Christian Music.* Peabody, Mass.: Hendrickson Publishers, Inc., 2002.

SELAH

Selah, originally Todd Smith, Nicol Smith, and Allan Hall, began singing together while attending Belmont University in Nashville, Tennessee. After graduation, all were in demand as session musicians and backup vocalists for artists such as Margaret Becker, Amy Grant, Wynonna, and Pam Tillis.

The trio came to the attention of Curb Records label owner Mike Curb when Nicol Smith, his favorite waitress at a local Nashville eatery, mentioned that she was a singer. Curb asked if she had a demo and, the next time he stopped in for dinner, Nicol presented one to him; Curb signed Nicol to her first recording contract the next day.

Todd Smith and Allan Hall became friends early in their Belmont student days, and Hall asked Smith to fill in for the music minister at the church where he played at. Although he had no professional training at the time, Smith agreed. The congregation liked him and asked if he would come back and put on a concert. Not wanting to sing alone, he convinced Nicol to sing with him; Hall accompanied them on the piano. With the show only a few weeks away there was no time to write original material; instead, they chose songs they all knew. Nicol and Todd added a few African songs (Nicol and Todd's parents were missionaries in Africa) and some worship songs from their own church.

After that youth concert, the three spent $2,000 to record a CD, *Be Still My Soul*. It took one week to complete the album; the finished project was a collection of hymns that included "Amazing Grace" and "When I Survey the Wondrous Cross" as well as a cover of the Beatles tune "In My Life."

Mike Curb allowed Nicol to sing on the independent project even though she was signed to his label. When Curb heard their project, he wanted to release it on Curb Records. In 2000, *Be Still My Soul* took home the Gospel Music Association's Dove Award for "Best Inspirational Album."

The name of the group came when one of Hall's roommates found the name "Selah" in the newspaper. It means "to lift the voices in praise," or "to pause and reflect." The group's sibling harmonies accompanied by Hall's piano prowess proved to be an irresistible combination.

In 2001 Selah released their second studio album, *Press On*, followed by a successful Christmas CD, *Rose of Bethlehem*, in 2002. In 2004, their album *Hiding Place* spawned their signature hit, "You Raise Me Up," and the album achieved gold status, selling more than 600,000 copies. The group recorded for eight years and four CDs before Nicol left to pursue a ministry with her new husband and seminary graduate, Greg Sponberg. In 2004, Curb allowed all three members to branch out and gave them each creative control of solo album projects: Allan Hall with *House of a Thousand Dreams*, Nicol Sponberg's *Resurrection*, and Todd Smith's *Alive*.

In 2005, Melanie Crittenden joined Selah for their *Greatest Hymns* CD and toured with the group for more than a year. In 2006 Crittenden left and was replaced by Amy Perry. In less than ten years, Selah has garnered six Dove Awards, including two consecutive nominations for "Group of the Year." The group has frequently appeared on respected television programs such as "The 700 Club" and the "Hour of Power," and has performed on the stage of New York's legendary Carnegie Hall.

Liz Cavanaugh

For Further Reading

Powell, Mark Allen. *Encyclopedia of Contemporary Christian Music.* Peabody, Mass.: Hendrickson Publishers, Inc., 2002.

SERVANT

During the 1970s there were two contemporary Christian groups named Servant. The group based in Joliet, Illinois, had Matt Spransy, keyboards and vocals, and Doug Pinnick, bass. The group based in Oregon had Owen Brock, guitar; Sandie Brock, vocals; David Holmes, drums; Rob Martens, bass; Bruce Wright, guitar; Bob Hardy, vocals (until 1985); Matt Spransy, keyboards and vocals (since 1981); and Eric Odell, vocals (since 1985).

The Oregon group named Servant was Bob Hardy, lead vocals (1979–1984); Eric Odell, lead vocals, guitar (1984–1986); Sandie Brock, lead vocals; Owen Brock, rhythm guitar, vocals; Bruce Wright, lead guitar, vocals (1977–1985); Rob Martens, bass, vocals; David Holmes, drums, vocals; Matt Spransy, keyboard (1981–1986); Tim Spransy, lead guitar (1985–1987).

Jim Palosaari was an evangelist in Victoria, British Columbia, who wanted to use musical groups as a key part of evangelistic outreach. He moved to Milwaukee where he and his wife Sue led a Christian community that divided into four smaller groups to proselytize more effectively. One of these groups became Jesus People U.S.A., out of which came the Resurrection Band. The Palosaaris led a group to Europe; in London they produced a multimedia rock opera, *Lonesome Stone*, in 1973 as an outreach of Jesus People Europe.

When the Palosaaris returned to the United States, they settled in southern Oregon where they established the Highway Missionary Society. Owen and Sandi Brock, who had been part of the *Lonesome Stone* cast, headed up their music program and formed Higher Ground, a Christian rock band, which then changed its name to Servant. This group believed in pooling all their resources in a communal setting, so all profits from ticket sales and albums were invested in supporting causes such as hunger relief, world missions, and refugee settlements.

Servant was involved in the Great American Album Giveaway campaign, where they gave hundreds of thousands of albums away to those who attended the group's concerts as a form of evangelical outreach. Those concerts featured laser shows, fog machines, extensive light shows, and everything a major rock concert would have. Servant was a pioneer Christian rock group, and among the acts who opened for them were Petra, DeGarmo and Key, the Joe English Band, Randy Matthews, Steve Camp and Jerusalem.

The group toured extensively, and when they performed in Chicago, Matt Spransy saw them and noticed they did not have a keyboard player, so he joined the group. Ironically, Spransy had also been in a group named Servant that was formed before the Oregon group. Spransy had been a member of the group the Sheep, which had gone to England in 1971; Spransy was involved in the formation of the Greenbelt Festival, an annual event for Christian music. When he returned to the States, Spransy formed a band with bass player Doug Pinnick called Servant in Chicago; however, that group disbanded in 1980.

The Highway Missionary Society evolved into the Servant Community, which moved to Cincinnati in 1984; that community lasted three years. Servant disbanded although a new lineup performed but did not record under that name. Later, Bob Hardy, who was the lead singer for Servant, embarked on a solo career and released an album, *Face the Distance*, and some former members of Servant formed Over the Rhine.

Don Cusic

For Further Reading

Powell, Mark Allen. *Encyclopedia of Contemporary Christian Music*. Peabody, Mass.: Hendrickson Publishers, Inc., 2002.

Thompson, John J. *Raised by Wolves: The Story of Christian Rock and Roll*. Toronto, Ontario: ECW Press, 2000.

SEVENTY SEVENS

Michael Roe, vocals, guitar
Mark Tootle, keyboard, guitar, vocals (until 1992)
Jan Eric Volz, bass (until 1992)
Mark Proctor, drums (until 1984)
Aaron Smith, drums (1984–1995)
David Leonhardt, guitar (1992–1995)
Mark Harmon, bass (since 1992)
Bruce Spencer, drums (since 1995)
Scott Reams, guitar, keyboard (since 2000)

Beginning in the 1970s, churches increasingly saw rock and pop music as a way to attract young people to their services, and young people often evaluated a church on whether or not it had contemporary Christian music in its worship services. This led many young pastors to actively seek out musicians to perform during their church services. One such pastor was Louis Neely, whose wanted his small church, Warehouse Ministries in Sacramento, California, to evangelize youth who were attracted to pop/rock music. The Scratch Band, so called because they were formed "from scratch" in 1979, consisted of Michael Roe, lead vocalist and guitarist, Mark Tootle on keyboards, Jan Eric Volz on bass, and drummer Mark Proctor.

The band's job was to lead worship and attract newcomers who would, hopefully, be converted to the Christian faith. Neely was ambitious in his evangelistic efforts; he sponsored "Rock and Religion," a radio show, built a recording studio devoted to creating Christian music (Sangre Studio), and formed a label, Exit Records. The Scratch Band was signed to that label,

although just before their album was released they changed their name to the 77s. That first album, *Ping Pong over the Abyss*, was released in 1983, and a second album, *All Fall Down*, followed the next year.

This second album was distributed in the secular market by A&M Records as the band progressed from worship leaders and tools of evangelism into a rock band who sought a wide audience of non-Christians. They received some sales and nice reviews on this album, and their third album, *The Seventy Sevens*, had secular distribution with Island Records. Also on Island was U2, who released *The Joshua Tree* during the same period of time. *The Joshua Tree* soared to the stratosphere of the rock world, bringing many Christians along; unfortunately, the Seventy Sevens' album did not achieve a comparable level of success. Part of the problem is that the promotional and marketing efforts of Island were focused on U2, leaving the Seventy Sevens to their own devices, and although their single "The Lust, the Flesh, the Eyes and the Pride of Life" attracted some attention, it did not chart nationally.

In 1988 there were some personnel changes in the band; keyboardist Tootle and bassist Volz left while Mike Roe worked on some solo projects and some tracks in the can were released.

The group, re-formed with the addition of David Leonhardt and Mark Harmon, were signed to Myrrh, a division of Word Records, and released an album they titled *Pray Naked*; however, because of negative feedback from Christian retailers and radio DJs, who took the title literally, the label changed the name of the album to *The Seventy*

Sevens, which was the same name of their 1987 release on Island.

The Seventy Sevens (or 77s) attracted a loyal core following of Christian fans but never captured a large audience in either the secular or Christian fields. They evolved into an experimental band with a variety of styles, although they remained true to their calling as a rock band. Some have called the Seventy Sevens one of the greatest bands in Christian music; others see them as a band who missed the large commercial market but have an influence that transcends their commercial lack of success.

The Seventy Sevens are loved by critics who lament their lack of commercial success. They are also loved by their coterie of die-hard fans for their talent, originality, and ability to survive against all odds. The band has survived because Michael Roe keeps returning to the Seventy Sevens even though he has developed a solo career and played with another Christian group, the Lost Dogs, since 1992.

Don Cusic

Discography

Ping Pong over the Abyss (1983)

All Fall Down (1984)

The Seventy Sevens (1987)

Sticks and Stones (1990)

More Miserable Than You'll Ever Be (sometimes listed as *7 by 7 Is*) (1990)

Eighty Eight (1991)

The Seventy Sevens (aka *Pray Naked*) (1992)

Drowning with Land in Sight (1994)

Tom Tom Blues (1995)

Echoes of Faith (aka *Played Naked*) (1996)

EP (EP) (1999)

Eighty-Eight/When Numbers Get Serious (2000)

Late (2000)

Daydream (2000)

A Golden Field of Radioactive Crows (2000)

Discography: Michael Roe Solo

More Miserable Than You'll Ever Be (sometimes listed as *7 by 7 Is*) (1990)

Safe as Milk (1995)

Michael Roe the Boat Ashore (1996)

For Further Reading

Alfonso, Barry. *The Billboard Guide to Contemporary Christian Music.* New York: Billboard Books/Watson-Guptill, 2002.

Powell, Mark Allen. *Encyclopedia of Contemporary Christian Music.* Peabody, Mass.: Hendrickson Publishers, Inc., 2002.

Thompson, John J. *Raised by Wolves: The Story of Christian Rock and Roll.* Toronto, Ontario: ECW Press, 2000.

SIXPENCE NONE THE RICHER

Sixpence None the Richer is best known for "Kiss Me," their hit single that was number one for two weeks in 1999 and featured in the movie *She's All That*, starring Freddie Prinze, Jr. That song was also featured in two TV shows, "Dawson's Creek" and "Party of Five."

The group was formed in New Braunfels, Texas, in 1992 by Matt Slocum and Leigh Bingham, two teenagers who took their name from a line in the book *Mere Christianity* by C. S. Lewis.

Leigh Bingham was 17 when their first album was recorded; Slocum, a guitarist for Love Coma, a group based in San Antonio, invited her to join a project he was working on, the Fatherless and the Widow. The first album was produced by Armand John Petri, who also managed the group, and released on R.E.X. Records; their second album saw the addition of Tess Wiley, guitar; Dale Baker, drums; and J. J. Plasencio on bass. The group toured with 10,000 Maniacs and the Smithereens, but problems arose when their label went bankrupt but would not release the group from its contract. Bassist Plasencio and guitarist Wiley both left for other groups.

The Austin-based group could not record for several years because of the contract dispute; however, Christian producer Steve Taylor agreed to work with them and the group added guitarist Sean Kelly, bassist Justin Cary, and drummer Dale Baker; singer Leigh Bingham married PFR member Mark Nash in 1996.

Their album *Sixpence None the Richer* was produced by Steve Taylor for Squint, a label founded by Taylor. The album was released in 1998, and the group toured as part of Lilith Fair in 1998 and 1999 and opened for acts such as Cher and the Wallflowers.

The group ran into label problems again when Squint folded in mid-2001, so their follow-up album was held up for over a year; however, *Divine Discontent* was released in the fall of 2002. After that album, drummer Baker left the group and was replaced by Rob Mitchell.

Sixpence None the Richer won the 1996 Dove Award for their album *This Beautiful Mess* in the "Alternative/Modern Rock Album" category; they were awarded the Dove for "Group of the Year" in 2000. Their song, "Breathe Your Name," was awarded the Dove for "Modern Rock/Alternative Recorded Song of the Year" for 2003.

The group disbanded in February 2004, and Slocam formed Astronaut Pusher with Lindsay Jamieson, Sam Ashworth, and Superdrag; Leigh Nash released an EP and album in the fall of 2005. At this point, it appears that Sixpence None the Richer may reunite.

Don Cusic

For Further Reading

Alfonso, Barry. *The Billboard Guide to Contemporary Christian Music*. New York: Billboard Books/Watson-Guptill, 2002.

Powell, Mark Allen. *Encyclopedia of Contemporary Christian Music*. Peabody, Mass.: Hendrickson Publishers, Inc., 2002.

Thompson, John J. *Raised by Wolves: The Story of Christian Rock and Roll*. Toronto, Ontario: ECW Press, 2000.

SMITH, MICHAEL W.

The career of Michael W. Smith (b. October 7, 1957, in Kenova, West Virginia) is more than gold and platinum

Michael W. Smith has been one of the most successful artists in the history of contemporary Christian music. (Harrell Cooke and Chaz Corzine)

albums and hit singles on the radio. During his career, Smith has become a spokesperson for contemporary Christian music through his personal appearances and active involvement in churches and communities. He has long been linked to the Republican Party through his friendships with both Presidents Bush and has actively worked for teenagers and youth, building Rockettown, a club for youth, and giving himself to causes encouraging Christian youth.

Michael W. Smith is one of the best-known singers, songwriters, and musicians in Christian music. He grew up in a middle class home where both parents held down jobs; his father worked in an oil refinery and his mother was a caterer. As Smith moved toward a career in music, his parents remained supportive of him and encouraged him to follow his heart. As is the case with most singers, Smith's first experience with music was in church. His love for music was instantaneous, and the youngster took up piano and sang in the church choir. His musical influences are diverse; he cites the Beatles, Elton John, Kansas, Andrae Crouch, the Evan Hoffman singers, Larry Norman, and Randy Stonehill as entertainers who had an impact on his own musical career.

Smith accepted Christ as his Savior when he was 10. He became involved with a group of students who were a little older, all of whom were devout Christians. When those friends moved on to college, Smith did not find a new group of friends with similar beliefs and went through bouts of loneliness. After graduation from high school, Smith turned to drugs and alcohol and became dependent on them. He attended Marshall University in West Virginia but was not concentrating on any career other than music.

A friend, Shane Keister, had moved to Nashville, and knowing of Smith's interest in music, encouraged him to move there too. Smith made the move in 1978, but success was not instantaneous; he had to take on other work to earn a living while he waited to have success with his music. He played with a few local bands but drifted into drugs and alcohol.

In November 1979 Smith had a spiritual awakening and made a recommitment to Christ. The next day he auditioned for Higher Ground, a Christian band. He got the job as their pianist and stopped using the drugs and alcohol that had plagued him. A few years later, some of the songs he had written were recorded by Bill Gaither, Amy Grant, Sandi Patty, and Kathy Troccoli. After meeting Grant, he accompanied her on the Age to Age tour, advancing from her keyboardist to her opening act. Smith gives a lot of credit for his success to Grant because she recorded his songs and took him out on tour with her. The two have remained friends over the years and continue to write together and share concert stages when possible.

Smith recorded his first album, *The Michael W. Smith Project*, in 1983. One of the songs he is most known for, "Friends," is on that debut disc. He wrote the song with his wife, Deborah, whom he says he fell instantly in love with when he saw her one day at a record company and knew instantly she was the woman he wanted to marry. The two wed four months after they met and have five children.

By 1984 Smith was headlining his own tour. He moved from pop to rock sounds with his 1986 project, *The Big Picture*. In the ensuing years Smith moved easily between pop, rock, and worship albums, finding acceptance for his music in all these genres of Christian music. As Smith expanded his musical horizons he also found success outside the Christian charts. In 1990 the crossover hit "Place in This World" went into the top ten on the *Billboard* hot 100 chart. A few years later he had a number one adult contemporary hit with "I Will Be Here for You." In 2004 he hit the *Billboard* hot 200 chart with his album *Healing Rain*.

The success outside Christian music came with some controversy. Once Smith had success in the pop and AC charts, VH-1 asked him to host a video show that had a beer company as a sponsor, and some Christian bookstores/record stores pulled his album from their shelves. In another instance, some Christians were offended by one of his songs, alleging that it needed to have more Christian overtones. These controversies ultimately did not negatively affect his career.

Smith gained national exposure after writing songs about two American tragedies. He released "This Is Your Time" about Cassie Bernall, a Columbine student who reportedly was killed after telling one of the shooters that she believed in God. He also wrote "There She Stands" after the 9/11 terrorist attacks on New York City and Washington, D.C.

Smith became a record executive in 1996, opening Rockettown Records and signing singer/songwriter Chris Rice. The label was named after his nightclub, Rockettown, which he had opened two years previously in Franklin, Tennessee. Later Smith moved the club to downtown Nashville so teenagers could have a place to hang out in a positive atmosphere.

Smith has a special place in his heart for children, working as a spokesperson for Compassion International. He and his wife have written the theme songs for Kanakuk Kamps for 20 years. Over the years, Smith became known as an excellent musician as well as a great singer-songwriter. In 2000 he released his first instrumental album, *Freedom*. A year later the singer-songwriter jumped into the worship music movement with *Worship*, followed in 2002 with *Worship Again*.

Smith's music has brought him in contact with other celebrities, including Bono of U2, and they have worked together on several projects. He performed at the 2004 Republican Convention and counts George W. Bush as a personal friend. Smith added the title actor to his resume in 2006 when he starred in the film *The Second Chance*. In 2008 Smith and friend Steven Curtis Chapman toured together for the first time, calling their effort the United Tour. That same year he released an album that once again showed his diversity. *A New Hallelujah* has a world-inspired sound, inspired by his travels to Europe, Israel, and Africa. The album was recorded at Lakewood Church in Houston, Texas, and features the African Children's Choir.

Smith has remained active in church over the years. A few years ago, he helped establish New River Fellowship Church in the Nashville area, where he served as copastor. Smith has had more than 30 number one singles and has sold more than 13 million albums. He has five platinum and 16 gold albums, an American Music Award, three Grammy Awards, and 40 Dove Awards.

Vernell Hackett

Discography

The Michael W. Smith Project (1983)

Michael W. Smith 2 (1984)

The Big Picture (1986)

The Live Set (1987)

I 2 (EYE) (1988)

Christmas (1989)

Go West Young Man (1990)

Change Your World (1992)

The Wonder Years (box set) (1993)

The First Decade (1983–1994) (1994)

I'll Lead You Home (1995)

Live the Life (1999)

Christmastime (1998)

Worship (2001)

Worship Again (2003)

The Second Decade (2003)

This Is Your Time (1999)

Freedom (2000)

Healing Rain (2004)

A New Hallelujah (2008)

Gospel Music Association Dove Awards

1985   Songwriter of the Year: Michael W. Smith

1987   Pop/Contemporary Album: *The Big Picture* by Michael W. Smith (Producers: Michael W. Smith and John Potoker; Label: Reunion)

1988   Long Form Music Video: *The Big Picture Tour Video* by Michael W. Smith; Directors: Brian Shipley and Stephen Bowlby; Label: Reunion

1990   Short Form Music Video: *I Miss the Way* by Michael W. Smith; Producer: Stephen Yake; Label: Reunion

1991   Pop/Contemporary Album: *Go West Young Man* by Michael W. Smith (Producers: Michael W. Smith and Brian Lenox; Label: Reunion)

1992   Choral Collection Album: *The Michael W. Smith Collection* (Producers: Robert Sterling and Dennis Worley; Label: Word)

1992   Musical Album: *The Big Picture* by Michael W. Smith (Producers: Andy Stanley and Robert Sterling; Label: Word)

1992   Song of the Year: "Place in This World" Written by Amy Grant, Michael W. Smith, and Wayne Kirkpatrick; Publishers: Age to Age Music, O'Ryan, Emily Boothe, ASCAP/BMI

1994   Praise and Worship Album: *Songs from the Loft* by Susan Ashton, Gary Chapman, Ashley Cleveland, Amy Delaine, Amy Grant, Kim Hill, Michael James, Wes King, Donna McElroy, and Michael W. Smith (Producers: Gary Chapman and Jim Dineen; Label: Reunion)

1994   Recorded Music Packaging: Buddy Jackson, Beth Middleworth, Mark Tucker, and D. Rhodes for *The Wonder Years 1983–1993* by Michael W. Smith; Label: Reunion

1995   Musical Album: *Living on the Edge* by Michael W. Smith and Robert Sterling; Label: Word

1996   Songwriter of the Year: Michael W. Smith

1996   Special Event Album: *My Utmost for His Highest* by Amy Grant, Gary Chapman, Michael W. Smith, Point of Grace, 4HIM, Cindy Morgan, Sandi Patty, Bryan Duncan, Steven Curtis Chapman, Twila Paris, Phillips, and Craig and Dean (Producers: Loren Balman and Brown Bannister; Label: Myrrh/Word)

1997   Special Event Album: *Tribute—The Songs of Andrae Crouch* by CeCe Winans, Michael W. Smith, Twila Paris, Bryan Duncan, Wayne Watson, the Winans, Clay Crosse, Take 6, the Brooklyn Tabernacle Choir, First Call, Andrae Crouch and the All Star Choir (Producers: Norman Miller and Neal Joseph; Label: Warner Alliance)

1998   Children's Music Album: *Sing Me to Sleep Daddy* by Billy Gaines, Michael James, Phil Keaggy, Michael O'Brien, Guy Penrod, Peter Penrose, Angelo Petrucci, Michael W. Smith, Randy Stonehill, and Wayne Watson (Producer: Nathan DiGesare; Label: Brentwood Kids Co.)

1998   Enhanced CD of the Year: *Live the Life—Maxi Single* by Michael W. Smith; (Producer: Craig A. Mason; Label: Reunion)

1998   Special Event Album: *God with Us—A Celebration of Christmas Carols and Classics* by Anointed, Michael W. Smith, Twila Paris, Sandi Patty, Steven Curtis Chapman, Chris Willis, Steve Green, Cheri Keaggy, Avalon, Out of the Grey, Ray Boltz, Clay Crosse, CeCe Winans, and Larnelle Harris (Producer: Norman Miller; Label: Sparrow)

1999   Artist of the Year: Michael W. Smith

1999   Pop/Contemporary Album: *Live the Life* by Michael W.

Smith (Producers: Mark Heimermann, Michael W. Smith,
and Stephen Lipson; Label:
Reunion)

1999 Producer of the Year: Michael
W. Smith

1999 Special Event Album: *Exo-
dus* by DC Talk, Jars of Clay,
Sixpence None the Richer,
Cindy Morgan, Chris Rice,
the Katinas, Third Day, Crys-
tal Lewis, and Michael W.
Smith (Producer: Michael W.
Smith; Label: Rockettown
Records)

2000 Short Form Music Video: *This
is Your Time* Michael W.
Smith; Producers and Direc-
tors: Amy Marsh; Brandon
Dickerson and Ben Pearson;
Label: Reunion

2000 Song of the Year: "This Is
Your Time" Written by
Michael W. Smith and Wes
King; Publishers: Milene
Music and Deer Valley Music,
ASCAP; Sparrow Song and
Uncle Ivan Music, BMI

2000 Songwriter of the Year: Michael W. Smith

2001 Pop/Contemporary Album:
This Is Your Time by Michael
W. Smith (Producers: Michael
W. Smith and Bryan Lenox;
Label: Reunion)

2001 Youth/Children's Musical:
Friends 4Ever Created by
Karla Worley, Steven V. Taylor, Seth Worley, Peter Kipley,
and Michael W. Smith; Publisher: Word Music

2002 Artist of the Year: Michael W.
Smith

2002 Inspirational Recorded Song of
the Year: "Above All" from
Worship; Michael W. Smith;
Producers: Lenny LeBlanc,
Paul Baloche; Label: Reunion)

2002 Instrumental Album of the
Year: *Freedom*; Michael W.
Smith (Producers: Michael W.
Smith and Bryan Lenox; Label:
Reunion)

2002 Praise and Worship Album of
the Year: *Worship*; Michael W.
Smith (Producers: Michael W.
Smith, Tom Laune; Label:
Reunion)

2002 Recorded Music Packaging of
the Year: *Freedom*; Artist:
Michael W. Smith; Tim
Parker; Tim Parker; Andrew
Southam; Label: Reunion

2003 Artist of the Year: Michael W.
Smith

2003 Long Form Music Video of the
Year: *Worship*; Michael W.
Smith; Michael Sacci, Ken
Conrad; Carl Diebold; Reunion

2003 Male Vocalist of the Year:
Michael W. Smith

2003 Praise and Worship Album of
the Year: *Worship Again*;
Michael W. Smith (Producer:
Michael W. Smith; Label:
Reunion)

2008 Christmas Album of the Year:
It's a Wonderful Christmas;
Michael W. Smith; (Producers:
David Hamilton, Michael W.
Smith; Label: Reunion
Records)

2008 Special Event Album of the
Year: *Glory Revealed* by Josh
Bates, Steven Curtis Chapman,
David Crowder, Mark Hall,

Shawn Lewis, Brian Littrell, Trevor Morgan, Paul Neufeld, Candi Pearson-Shelton, Mac Powell, Shane and Shane, Michael W. Smith, Mac Powell; Reunion Records

Grammy Awards

1984   27th Grammy Awards: Best Gospel Performance, Male: *Michael W. Smith*: Michael W. Smith

1995   38th Grammy Awards: Best Pop/Contemporary Gospel Album: *I'll Lead You Home* by Michael W. Smith

2003   46th Grammy Awards: Best Pop/Contemporary Gospel Album: *Worship Again*; Michael W. Smith

For Further Reading

Alfonso, Barry. *The Billboard Guide to Contemporary Christian Music*. New York: Billboard Books/Watson-Guptill, 2002.

Cusic, Don. *The Sound of Light: A History of Gospel and Christian Music*. New York: Hal Leonard, 2002.

McNeil, W. K., ed. *Encyclopedia of American Gospel Music*. New York: Routledge, 2005.

Powell, Mark Allen. *Encyclopedia of Contemporary Christian Music*. Peabody, Mass.: Hendrickson Publishers, Inc., 2002

Smith, Michael W., and Fritz Ridenour. *Old Enough to Know*. Waco, Tex.: Word, 1987.

SOUTHERN GOSPEL AND CONTEMPORARY CHRISTIAN MUSIC

The world of southern gospel music has a rich and storied history that, in many ways, laid the groundwork for the success of contemporary Christian music beginning in the mid-1970s.

The roots of southern gospel are traced back to the singing schools and shaped note song books, as well as to revivals in rural areas in America. The singing school attracted students from rural areas, where a "singing master" came for ten days to two weeks and taught students to sing using the shaped note system. This system used triangles, squares, and ovals instead of the traditional round notes so students learned a melody quickly by recognizing the shape of the note.

James D. Vaughan taught his first singing school in 1882 and, to publicize the school, created a family quartet that became the forerunner of all southern gospel quartets. This quartet demonstrated the songs and showed how a trained quartet could promote the selling of songbooks. Singing conventions, usually held annually, were social as well as musical events, and it didn't take song publishers long to realize this was fertile ground for songbook sales, and so shaped-note songbooks, singing conventions, and trained quartets performing new songs became widely accepted in the rural South. Young southern farm boys saw singing school teachers and traveling quartets as people they admired, respected and wanted to emulate; they were heroes and figures of renown to numerous young men who also wanted to stand in front of a crowd and lead them in singing.

In 1924 V. O. Stamps left the Vaughan Company, where he was the top salesman of song books, and formed his own firm, the Virgil O. Stamps Music Company; by 1926 Stamps acquired a partner, Jesse Randall (J. R.) Baxter, Jr., and this became the Stamps-Baxter Music Company. Frank Stamps, V. O.'s brother, had a quartet who hired pianist Dwight Brock as an accompanist. Before this, a quartet usually sang a cappella, although sometimes a member played piano, but the addition of the "fifth man" was a revolution in the quartet line-up.

By the end of the 1920s two major firms, the James D. Vaughan Music Company and Stamps-Baxter, stood at the forefront of shaped-note publishing, though there were numerous other companies vying for business. A number of well-known gospel groups worked for these firms, including the Blackwood Brothers, the Speer Family, and the Stamps Quartet.

The importance of the songbook publishers declined dramatically during the 20 years after World War II. As the quartets depended more on radio and recordings, they depended less on a single publisher to supply material.

The success of both black and southern gospel music after World War II was aided by the success of Pentecostalism in the second half of the century. Pentecostals accepted new musical styles much more quickly than mainline churches and were more open to new ways to spread the Christian message. Because Pentecostals were evangelistic, they embraced the idea that popular music with Christian lyrics could reach people that traditional music and church services could not. Most of the black and southern gospel performers after World War II were Holiness/Pentecostals who increasingly saw their shows as a ministry every bit as viable as that of a traditional pastor in a mainline church.

Some of the gospel groups still sang secular tunes as well as gospel; however, as the 1940s progressed, gospel groups had to face the decision of whether to be all-gospel or leave the field altogether. Increasingly, audiences demanded that groups make this choice.

After World War II the rural singing conventions began to die out. The inexpensive entertainment they provided was replaced by radio—and soon, by television—as well as by the touring gospel groups that appeared in their area. And, as the singing conventions died, the shaped-note publishing business began to die as well because these singing conventions were a major source of their income.

A number of new gospel groups were formed after World War II, including the Statesmen and the Blackwoods. Many southern gospel singers, whose roots ran back to those days, recalled that those times were marked by an emphasis on entertainment rather than ministry and that oftentimes many of the singers were not true believers but rather boys who had been raised in the church and in Christian homes and loved to sing. They looked on the quartets as a way to make a living doing something they enjoyed, feeling the lure of the spotlight much more intensely than any lure from the eternal light.

In 1948 Wally Fowler held the first All-Night Sing from the Ryman Auditorium, home of the Grand Ole Opry in Nashville. With the success of the

All-Night Sings at the Ryman, all-night shows soon spread to cities and towns throughout the South, often promoted by Fowler, who formed the Oak Ridge Quartet to sing gospel.

In Memphis the Blackwoods appeared on WMPS, and in 1951 they were signed to RCA Victor by Steve Sholes, the legendary A&R man, who contracted them to record singles. In 1952 the Blackwoods and Statesmen formed a partnership in which they toured together.

The biggest cultural force in music of the 1950s—indeed, of the entire 20th century—was Elvis Presley and rock 'n' roll. The rock 'n' roll revolution, led by Elvis, changed everything—music, language, and clothes—and created a new social revolution. Although religious leaders and parents railed against him, the roots of Elvis were firmly planted in gospel music. This was proven later when Elvis consistently recorded gospel albums and sang gospel songs in his performances throughout his career. All of Presley's gospel albums sold well—even the one recorded in 1957 when he was at the height of his notoriety as a rock 'n' roller, dangerous to youth's morals, and the perceived enemy of preachers who openly accused rock 'n' roll as being the devil's music.

Presley's first gospel recording came soon after he joined RCA, at the height of his rock 'n' roll popularity—after he had sold 10 million records in one year (1956) and presented himself to the nation on the major network television shows of the day. It came at a time when the younger generation was increasingly turning their backs on the religious heritage of their parents.

Many of the things that attracted so much initial attention to Elvis—like his long hair, flashy clothes, and flair for showmanship—came from the southern gospel world. During the 1950s, southern gospel singers wore flashy clothes and often had long hair combed back, before long hair came in style.

Elvis admitted to copying the singing style of Jake Hess. The source for so much of Elvis Presley's music and personal style came from the southern gospel world. The attitudes, tastes, and style in his dress and performances were then passed on to a whole generation of teenagers who had never heard of southern gospel or, if they had, probably despised it. Until his death in 1977, Elvis continued to sing gospel, followed the careers of gospel quartets, and featured some of those quartets on his records and shows.

It is difficult to gauge Presley's effect on southern gospel music except to note that by influencing popular music in general, he certainly had an effect on gospel, which often incorporates popular musical trends in songs and reflects those trends in recordings. The effect gospel music had on Presley is also difficult to ascertain, but by the end of his life, it was obvious that Presley kept in touch with his strong religious roots through gospel music. He seemed to find spiritual nourishment there and used the music as a way to keep in touch with his earlier days before he became the rich and famous rock 'n' roll star. It was through Elvis that so many rockers and rock writers learned about the gospel roots of early rock 'n' roll.

During the 1960s and 1970s, the southern gospel world seemed to be caught in a time warp, left behind by the flower children whose spiritual quest could not stomach such an outdated and outmoded form of rural religion. Even the Jesus music revolution could not relate to those in the southern gospel world—this was a music and culture of the past and the Jesus people wanted a current, hip Jesus, not an old-fashioned icon from history.

Still, it was a vibrant time for this music and several groups defined the era. The Florida Boys were formed in 1947 by J. G. Whitfield, who later left the group and formed *The Singing News*, the newspaper for southern gospel that he began in 1969. The idea came from *Good News*, a newsletter published by the Gospel Music Association, which was then headed by J. D. Sumner. In 1964 The Florida Boys began a television show, "The Gospel Singing Jubilee," one of the first gospel singing programs to be on Sunday mornings, and opened up Sunday morning television for southern gospel music. The show ran for 25 years, and during the late 1970s and early 1980s it had a better rating and larger audience than any of the high-profile televangelists.

In the mid-1960s there was no contemporary Christian music as it later became known; the Imperials and the Oak Ridge Boys, although part of the world of southern gospel music, were contemporary and Christian. The moves they made to contemporize were more than just changes in the music—they were also changes in attitudes and appearances.

The Oak Ridge Boys were pioneers in gospel fashion; they were the first to go on stage in sports coats and turtlenecks—not neckties—and were criticized for this. Some churches even forbade them to play in their sanctuaries. The group put an emphasis on "clean entertainment," not ministry. They performed some dates with Andrae Crouch and saw themselves as gospel entertainers, not gospel evangelists. They were criticized by other groups for their long hair, mod clothes, and contemporary sound. They were also the most successful gospel group on the road, attracting young and old to their shows.

In 1973 the Oaks left HeartWarming, a gospel label, and signed with Columbia Records. Columbia thought they could sell gospel to country audiences and had found some gospel rebels to attract young people. But Columbia did not service gospel stations and so the Oaks lost on two fronts—country radio would not and gospel stations could not play their recordings.

The idea that a top gospel group doing gospel songs could sell to the secular market was proving to be a bust; so was the idea that the most popular act in gospel music could have a secular appeal. The Oaks had fallen between the cracks; finally, they signed with a new record label, ABC/Dot, and in 1977 they recorded a country song, "Ya'll Come Back Saloon," that was a major country hit. From this point, they were country stars with a gospel heritage.

The Imperials are a different story. They were formed in 1964 by the hottest gospel singer of the day. Jake Hess wanted a super group and had his own theory of how a gospel group should look and perform. He handpicked who he felt were the best talents from other groups for the Imperials—Armand Morales (from the Weatherford Quartet), Shirl Neilson, Gary McSpadden, and pianist Henry Slaughter.

Hess required all group members to sign moral contracts. Because the other southern gospel groups dressed alike in matching suits, the Imperials dressed more casually, wearing sports coats of different colors while their vocal harmonies were smooth and tight. Because of the tremendous popularity of Hess, the group immediately had a full schedule of bookings, and because of the new look and sound, they took the southern gospel world by storm, ushering in a new era in this music.

Hess had health problems-a bad heart-and in 1965 he decided to quit the road, so the group re-formed. Their big break came when they were booked on an Elvis Presley session-the one that yielded the gospel album *How Great Thou Art*. The Imperials also recorded with Jimmy Dean, hot off his ABC-TV show, and then sang backup for Dean during his personal appearances and television show.

In 1969 Elvis called the Imperials to ask them to perform on his show, and soon the group was performing with Elvis as well as Dean. After several years of doing this, the conflict of performing with Dean and Elvis became so great that the Imperials had to reevaluate their position and decided to stay with Dean. After they left, Elvis hired J. D. Sumner and the Stamps Quartet to be part of his show; they remained with him until his death.

In 1975 the Imperials reached a crossroads: they had to decide whether to stay in gospel music or try for success in the secular world. The Imperials saw what happened when the Oaks tried to reach a secular audience with gospel music, and decided to stay with gospel and gave up performing in Las Vegas and other prestigious venues.

Too, they desired to be more heavily involved in the ministry, and less in entertainment.

The group proved their progressive thinking by hiring Sherman Andrus, an African American, to sing with the group in 1972. Andrus was the first black to enter the southern gospel world, and he paid a price; the Imperials had a number of dates cancelled and found themselves forbidden to play in a number of places where they had once performed.

The Imperials became accepted not only in the southern gospel world but also in the contemporary Christian world— two worlds that were not always compatible in the past. It was the bridge that the Imperials built between the contemporary and southern gospel worlds and even the secular world that was their greatest contribution. They showed there were no boundary lines because the worlds which were once so far apart had far more in common than either had originally thought. The Imperials proved their talent as well as their faith and priorities, arriving at a point where they were possibly the group who reached more people with more diverse tastes with the Christian message than any other musical ministry in Christian music.

The world of southern gospel went through difficult changes during the 1960s and 1970s; during the 1980s it tried to wrestle with a world that had left them behind. They were confronted by the Jesus revolution and contemporary Christian music, which captured a segment of their audience, then overshadowed them in the Gospel Music Association and Dove Awards, which they had founded. At least that's what it seemed like to those involved in southern gospel. To add insult to injury, the contemporary Christian music performers and audience were perceived as looking down their noses at southern gospel and wouldn't even acknowledge that genre for laying the groundwork for the Gospel Music Association and Dove Awards. It was a lot for the southern gospel groups to swallow. They hunkered down and dug in, but they did not change with the times, even when the times were changing rapidly all around them.

The 1980s were a period of struggles with a few high points for southern gospel. In 1985 Tennessee Ernie Ford hosted "The Great American Gospel Sound" for PBS television. This show was so popular that a follow-up, "More of That Great American Gospel," was also produced. But, by and large, the 1980s were a period when southern gospel music looked like a cultural artifact, a remnant of the past. Groups found it difficult to sell recordings or get bookings, and young people, who at one time might have been attracted to southern gospel, were now attracted to contemporary Christian music.

During the 1980s a number of new southern gospel groups formed, including the Singing Americans, Gold City, Dixie Melody Boys, Heaven Bound, and Kingdom Heirs as well as family groups such as the Hopper Brothers and Sister Connie, Hemphills, Nelons, Dixie Echoes, Bishops, McKameys, Talleys, Perrys, Greens, Paynes, and Jeff and Sheri Easter. There were even some African American groups in southern gospel: Teddy Huffam and the Gems, Charles Johnson and the Revivers, Don Degarte and Strong Tower, the Gospel Enforcers, Willis Canada, the Scotts, and the Reggie Saddler Family.

The most significant southern gospel group formed during the 1980s was the Gaither Vocal Band, created by Bill Gaither. With this group, Gaither returned to his first love—southern gospel. Because of his popularity and guidance, the Gaither Vocal Band was able to cross over into the larger world of contemporary Christian music.

In 1988 Charles Waller held a Grand Ole Gospel Reunion in Greenville, South Carolina, in which he brought together a number of the old-time southern gospel groups. This event inspired Bill Gaither to begin a video series called *Homecoming*, in which the older southern gospel performers came together, talked, reminisced, and sang. The videos were sold to southern gospel fans who had been having a hard time finding the kind of music they loved and admired. The series was incredibly successful and made Gaither millions of dollars. The southern gospel community was quite thankful. First, Bill Gaither was probably the only person in gospel music who had the finances to fund such a project. And second, this *Homecoming* series almost single-handedly revitalized southern gospel music and the careers of these southern gospel performers. Gaither also developed a show on southern gospel, based on this video series, for the Nashville Network. In short, Bill Gaither "saved" southern gospel by giving it national exposure, a new sense of pride, and elevating it when the field was at its lowest point.

Disenchanted with the direction the Gospel Music Association was headed, a new organization, the Southern Gospel Music Association, was formed by Charles Waller. But in June 1985 Les Beasley announced that the Gospel Music Association had purchased the Southern Gospel Music Association, which would now be under the Gospel

Music Association's umbrella. However, the next year another organization, the Southern Gospel Music Guild, was organized. Also, Maurice Templeton purchased *The Singing News* from J. G. Whitfield and made a decision that the publication would cover only southern gospel music. Before this time, *The Singing News* was known for its coverage of southern gospel, but gave space to contemporary Christian music as well.

Disenchanted with the treatment they perceived that the city of Nashville gave southern gospel, the National Quartet Convention moved its event to Louisville, Kentucky, in the 1990s, then established permanent headquarters in Louisville in 1994. In 1995 Maurice Templeton, owner of *The Singing News*, founded a new Southern Gospel Music Association. The field began to grow again and expanded to a Great Western Quartet Convention in Fresno, California, in 1997 and the Canadian Quartet Convention in Red Deer, Alberta, Canada, in 1999.

Southern gospel grew during the 1990s by reaching back to its roots in churches. During the 1970s, 17 percent of the concerts put on by southern gospel groups were in churches; by the mid-1990s, that figure was 65 percent. In their search for an audience through the 1970s and 1980s, it seems that they found it right back at home.

Don Cusic

For Further Reading

Blackwell, Lois S. *The Wings of the Dove*. Norfolk, Va.: The Donning Co., 1978.

Blackwood, James, with Dan Martin. *The James Blackwood Story*. Monroeville, Penn.: Whitaker House, 1975.

Cusic, Don. *The Sound of Light: A History of Gospel and Christian Music*. New York: Hal Leonard, 2002.

Eskew, Harry. "White Urban Hymnody." Jacket notes on *Brighten the Corner Where You Are*. South Weymouth, Mass.: New World, n.d.

Goff, James R., Jr. *Close Harmony: A History of Southern Gospel*. Chapel Hill: University of North Carolina Press, 2002.

Graves, Michael P., and David Fillingim, eds. *More Than Precious Memories: The Rhetoric of Southern Gospel Music*. Macon, Ga.: Mercer University Press, 2004.

Hess, Jake, with Richard Hyatt. *Nothin' but Fine: The Music and the Gospel According to Jake Hess*. Columbus, Ga.: Buckland Press, 1996.

Murray, David Bruce. *Murray's Encyclopedia of Southern Gospel Music*. Privately published, 2005.

Wolfe, Charles K. "Gospel Boogie: White Southern Gospel Music in Transition." *Popular Music* 1 (1981).

SPRAGUE, BILLY

Billy Sprague (b. 1952 in Tulsa, Oklahoma) was a member of Amy Grant's first backing band; a talented songwriter, he recorded a number of solo albums.

Sprague grew up in Borger, Texas, and learned to play the guitar during his senior year in high school when he was in a body cast and undergoing treatment for scoliosis. After high school, Sprague enrolled in Texas Christian University, where he played in a band, Jubal; after graduation in 1979 he enrolled in graduate school at the University of Texas, where he received a masters degree in English.

As a songwriter, Sprague has written songs recorded by Brown Bannister, Debby Boone, Sandi Patty ("Via Dolorosa"), Kathy Troccoli, and BeBe and CeCe Winans.

Tragedy struck Sprague's life in 1989 when his fiancée, Rosalynn Olivares, was killed in an auto accident on the way to see him perform in concert. Sprague took a three year break from recording and performing.

Don Cusic

For Further Reading

Powell, Mark Allen. *Encyclopedia of Contemporary Christian Music*. Peabody, Mass.: Hendrickson Publishers, Inc., 2002.

ST. JAMES, REBECCA

Rebecca St. James (b. Rebecca Jean Smallbone, on July 26, 1977, in Sydney, Australia) took her stage name at her label's request when she signed a recording contract in the United States. She is best known for her advocacy of teenage abstinence and remaining "pure" until marriage. She is consistently voted the favorite female singer with fans and has managed to live a model life in terms of being who she is, living what she preaches, and living out her public pronouncements in private.

St. James is the eldest of seven children and grew up in Sydney, Australia, where her father promoted Christian concerts. In 1990 Carman toured Australia and St. James was his opening act, which led to the release of her first album, *Refresh My Heart*, as Rebecca Jean. The Smallbone family had a serious financial setback when her father's concert promotion business went bust; in 1991 the family packed up, moved to Nashville, and landed jobs cleaning houses to make ends meet. Rebecca signed with ForeFront Records and released her debut for that label, *Rebecca St. James*, in 1994.

St. James's music has evolved from a high energy techno-pop dance sound to being influenced by hip hop and on to a more adult contemporary sound. Her tours are a family affair; her father, Thomas Smallbone, is her manager and her siblings help on the tour.

Rebecca St. James is as much an evangelist as she is an entertainer; she offers altar calls at her concerts and has written a number of devotionals as part of her ministry. Although she is in her 30s, she still vows to stay pure until marriage, wears a "purity ring" to affirm that vow, and does not smoke, drink, or date because she feels she is saving herself for her future husband and when he appears she will know it. She also claims to never listen to secular radio or be aware of secular pop and rock music.

St. James is involved as a spokesperson for Compassion International and has gone to Africa and worked with children in support of that organization. She was also a national spokesperson for the Center for Reclaiming America, organized to "take God back into schools" as a result of the shooting tragedies in American schools. St. James is also an advocate for the pro-life movement.

Her album *Pray* won the Grammy for "Best Rock Gospel Album" in 1999.

Don Cusic

For Further Reading

Alfonso, Barry. *The Billboard Guide to Contemporary Christian Music.* New York: Billboard Books/Watson-Guptill, 2002.

Powell, Mark Allen. *Encyclopedia of Contemporary Christian Music.* Peabody, Mass.: Hendrickson Publishers, Inc., 2002.

St. James, Rebecca. *40 Days with God: A Devotional Journey.* Cincinnati, Ohio: Standard Publishing, 1996.

St. James, Rebecca. *You're the Voice: Forty More Days with God—a Contemporary Devotional.* Nashville, Tenn.: Thomas Nelson Publishers, 1997.

STONEHILL, RANDY

Randy Stonehill (b. March 12, 1952, in Stockton, California) is one of the pioneers of early contemporary Christian music; he is often referred to as one of the "fathers of contemporary Christian music."

Stonehill brought rock music to the Christian marketplace, although the sounds of his early material seem more like soft rock now. However, when his albums were first released, critics deemed him and his music controversial. He worked closely with Larry Norman for a number of years, and Norman produced Stonehill's early works.

Stonehill released his first album, *Born Twice*, in 1971 and made his acting debut in *Beware! The Blob* in 1972. The singer-songwriter also began getting covers of his songs by other artists, including Russ Taff and Phil Keaggy. His 1976 recording *Welcome to Paradise* became the third most important contemporary Christian album, according to a poll of Christian music critics. Late in the 70s, Stonehill and rockers Daniel Amos joined together for the Amos n' Randy tour; subsequently Daniel Amos became Stonehill's band for his next two albums. Stonehill also did background vocals for several of Daniel Amos's projects.

Stonehill and friend Phil Keaggy have toured as the Keaggy/Stonehill Band, and he also recorded a duet with Amy Grant, "I Could Never Say Goodbye." On his twentieth anniversary in music, friends came together to offer special tributes with live music, including Amy Grant, Michael W. Smith, and Russ Taff. Stonehill's performance at that tribute was taped and released on VHS. In 1994 the singer started Street Level Records, releasing Julie Miller's "Invisible Girl." Stonehill took a shot at the children's market in 2001, releasing *Uncle Stonehill's Hat.* Stonehill continues to record and tour.

Vernell Hackett

For Further Reading

Alfonso, Barry. *The Billboard Guide to Contemporary Christian Music.* New York: Billboard Books/Watson-Guptill, 2002.

Cusic, Don. *The Sound of Light: A History of Gospel and Christian Music.* New York: Hal Leonard, 2002.

McNeil, W. K., ed. *Encyclopedia of American Gospel Music.* New York: Routledge, 2005.

Powell, Mark Allen. *Encyclopedia of Contemporary Christian Music.* Peabody, Mass.: Hendrickson Publishers, Inc., 2002.

STOOKEY, NOEL PAUL

One of the founding members of the popular folk group Peter, Paul and Mary, Noel Paul Stookey (b. December 30, 1937) was one of the first celebrity converts to Christianity.

Peter, Paul and Mary were formed by manager Albert Grossman in the spring of 1961 and released a string of hits, including "Blowin' in the Wind," "Don't Think Twice," "Puff the Magic Dragon" and "Leavin' on a Jet Plane."

Stookey had moved to New York in 1959 as a photographer and worked as a stand-up comic before joining Peter Yarrow and Mary Travers in Peter, Paul and Mary. The three were social activists, sang a number of topical songs, and were involved in a number of causes. In 1963 the group performed at the Lincoln Memorial before Martin Luther King Jr.'s "I Have a Dream" speech.

Peter, Paul and Mary disbanded in 1970, but Stookey had become disenchanted with life as a famous celebrity. Peter, Paul and Mary popularized a number of Bob Dylan's songs and Stookey had confided spiritual emptiness to Dylan, who advised him to take a long walk in the country the next

time he was in the Midwest and to read the Bible. Stookey did read the Bible but it was an encounter with someone backstage in 1968 who witnessed about Jesus to him that convinced Stookey to pray and ask Jesus into his life.

After Peter, Paul and Mary disbanded Stookey moved to South Blue Hill, Maine, joined a local Congregational church, sang in the choir, and took meals to the elderly. He also purchased an old hen house and converted it into a recording studio where he recorded his first solo album, *Paul and.* On that album was "Wedding Song (There Is Love)," which was written for Peter Yarrow's wedding, where Stookey was best man. Stookey refused to accept royalties for that song, stating that it came "through divine inspiration" and that he was only "a conduit." (He assigned the copyright to the Public Domain Foundation.) That song became a standard at weddings in the following years.

Although Peter, Paul and Mary broke up, they reunited for tours in 1972 and 1978 and often did fundraisers for PBS and humanitarian causes. Unlike many in the evangelical movement of the 1980s and 1990s, Stookey did not espouse anti-abortion, anti-gay, and school prayer issues; instead, he spoke out against apartheid, endorsed ecological programs, and worked for AIDS relief.

In 1979 Stookey recruited a local bar band called Star Song, renamed them Bodyworks, and recorded several albums with them. The group, which consisted of Denny Bouchard, keyboard; Jimmy Nails, guitar; Kent Palmer, percussion; and Karla Thibodeau, vocal, were not Christians when they began with Stookey but along the way they all became Christians, led to Jesus by Stookey.

In the late 1990s Stookey and his wife, Betty, moved to western Massachusetts where Betty was chaplain of the Northfield Mt. Hermon prep school. In 2005 they returned to Blue Hill, Maine. During their time in Massachusetts, Stookey was an artist in residence at the prep school, coproduced musical theater, edited and produced a series of Vesper Recordings, and taught a class in songwriting. He is active in Operation Respect, founded by Peter Yarrow, which advocates tolerance and a non-bullying curriculum.

Don Cusic

Discography

Paul and (1971)

One Night Stand (1973)

Real to Reel (1977)

Something New and Fresh (1978)

Band and Bodyworks (1979)

Wait'll You Hear This (1982)

There Is Love Anthology (1984)

State of the Heart (1985)

In Love Beyond Our Lives (1990)

There Is Love (with Michael Kelly Blanchard) (2001)

Circuit Rider (2002)

Virtual Party (2004)

Facets (2007)

For Further Reading

Powell, Mark Allen. *Encyclopedia of Contemporary Christian Music.* Peabody, Mass.: Hendrickson Publishers, Inc., 2002.

STRYPER

Michael Sweet
Robert Sweet
Tim Gains
Oz Fox

Big hair heavy metal entered contemporary Christian music when Stryper released their debut album, *The Yellow and Black Attack*, in 1984. The Christian community is usually reluctant to embrace new sounds from popular culture, and that was certainly true with Stryper; their album was released on a secular label, which made the Christian community doubly unsure whether Stryper was the real thing or bizarre devils in disguise. However, in the long term, Stryper turned out to be groundbreaking as well as earth-shattering; their music may not have pleased the ears of most of the CCM crowd, but the boys of Stryper proved themselves to be Christians and were accepted into the fold.

The origin of the group is Roxx Regime, a group formed by brothers Michael and Robert Sweet with guitarist Oz Fox (Richard Martinez) in Orange County, California, in 1983. Soon, they added bassist Tim Gaines (Tim Hagelganz). The Sweet brothers were raised in a Christian home, but fell away from the faith, then had a spiritual renewal in 1982. They took the name Stryper from Isaiah 53:5 "by His stripes we are healed" and say that Stryper stands for "Salvation Through Redemption Yielding Peace, Encouragement and Righteousness."

They played the heavy metal clubs in Southern California and were signed to Enigma Records; they wore bright yellow and black outfits and played heavy metal with Christian lyrics. During their concerts, Michael Sweet often threw Bibles into the audience.

Their first release was a mini-album, but *Soldiers under Command*, released in 1985, was a full-length album. This was followed by *To Hell with the Devil*, which produced the MTV hit video *Honestly*, then *In God We Trust* and *Against the Law* in 1990, which Benson refused to distribute to Christian bookstores.

At the height of their career they had two platinum and four gold records, and both Poison and Metallica opened for them; still, a number of Christians picketed Christian bookstores that carried their product, the Christian label (Benson) refused to distribute their product, and they were attacked in the Christian media by leading evangelicals. Jimmy Swaggart was particularly vehement in his attacks on Stryper; ironically, the Sweet brothers were "saved" through Swaggart's TV ministry.

In 1992 the band broke up when Michael Sweet left to pursue a solo career. The three remaining members, Robert Sweet, Oz Fox, and Tim Gaines, continued to tour but did not record. Later, Gaines and Robert Sweet were in the band King James; Oz Fox recorded with several Christian acts; then, in 1995 he formed Sin Dizzy with Tim Gaines. In 2000 Robert Sweet released a solo project, then formed Blissed with David Pearson, Trevor Barr, and Jeff Miller; they released one album, *Waking Up the Dead*, in 2003.

Stryper reunited in May 2000 at the first annual Stryper Expo in New Jersey; in December of that year they performed a full set in Costa Rica. At the second annual Stryper Expo, the group again performed a concert, then performed at Cornerstone in July 2001.

In 2003 Hollywood Records, which signed the group after Enigma went bankrupt, released a "best of" Stryper album, and the group did a 35 city tour that produced an album: *7 Weeks: Live in America*, released in 2003.

Don Cusic

Discography

The Yellow and Black Attack (1984)

Soldiers under Command (1985)

To Hell with the Devil (1986)

In God We Trust (1988)

Against the Law (1990)

Can't Stop the Rock: The Stryper Collection, 1984–1991 (1991)

Stryper-7: The Best of Stryper (2003)

7 Weeks: Live in America (2003)

Reborn (2005)

Discography: Michael Sweet Solo

Michael Sweet (1994)

Real (1995)

Truth (1998)

Unstryped (EP) (1999)

Discography: Robert Sweet Solo

Love Trash (2000)

Gospel Music Association Dove Awards

1989   Hard Music Album: *In God We Trust* by Stryper (Producers: Stryper and Michael Lloyd; Label: Enigma)

1989   Hard Music Recorded Song: "In God We Trust" Written by

Stryper; Recorded by Stryper; Label: Benson

For Further Reading

Alfonso, Barry. *The Billboard Guide to Contemporary Christian Music*. New York: Billboard Books/Watson-Guptill, 2002.

Erickson, Dale, and Jesse Sturdevant. *Stryper: Loud and Clear*. College Park, Md.: Classic CD Books, 2001.

McNeil, W. K., ed. *Encyclopedia of American Gospel Music*. New York: Routledge, 2005.

Powell, Mark Allen. *Encyclopedia of Contemporary Christian Music*. Peabody, Mass.: Hendrickson Publishers, Inc., 2002.

SWEET COMFORT BAND

The Sweet Comfort Band (Bryan Duncan, vocals, keyboard; Randy Thomas, guitar; Kevin Thomson, drums; Rick Thomson, bass) emerged as Jesus music was evolving into contemporary Christian music. The Sweet Comfort Band was in the second wave of the Jesus music groups, following Children of the Day and Love Song out of the Southern California music scene anchored at Calvary Chapel in Costa Mesa.

The group's first appearance was as a trio on New Year's Eve 1972, when brothers Rick and Kevin Thomson (drums and bass) joined Bryan Duncan, lead vocals and keyboard, to perform a high-powered concert. The group toured in the Southern California area and in 1976 added guitarist Randy Thomas, who had been a member of Jesus music groups Sonrise and Psalm 150. The group was popular in the area and opened for Three Dog Night.

The group began as a jazz-rock group but moved into straight-ahead rock by the time their first album, *Sweet Comfort*, was released on Calvary Chapel's Maranatha label. The group then signed with Light Records and released six more albums.

In 1983 Bryan Duncan left the group and Bob Carlisle was the lead vocalist during their final European tour. The group formally disbanded in 1984 and Bryan Duncan pursued a solo career while Randy Thomas formed the Allies with Bob Carlisle and later played with Identical Strangers. The Thomson brothers went into business in Riverside, California; Rick had a construction company and Kevin was in the insurance business.

In 2001 Sweet Comfort Band reunited for an appearance at Creation Fest.

Don Cusic

For Further Reading

Alfonso, Barry. *The Billboard Guide to Contemporary Christian Music*. New York: Billboard Books/Watson-Guptill, 2002.

Powell, Mark Allen. *Encyclopedia of Contemporary Christian Music*. Peabody, Mass.: Hendrickson Publishers, Inc., 2002.

Thompson, John J. *Raised by Wolves: The Story of Christian Rock and Roll*. Toronto, Ontario: ECW Press, 2000.

SWITCHFOOT

Jon Foreman, vocals, guitar
Tim Foreman, bass, backing vocals

Drew Shirley, guitar
Jerome Fontamillas, guitar, keyboard, backing vocals
Chad Butler, drums

Some acts feel hemmed in and limited in the genre of contemporary Christian music; they want their music to reach a wider audience—secular as well as Christian—and so they record songs that cross the borders the Christian music audience puts up around this genre. Such an act is Switchfoot.

The group began in 1996 when brothers Jon and Tim Foreman with Chad Butler formed Chin Up in San Diego; the following year they were signed to the independent label re: think by Charlie Peacock. The group added keyboardist Jerome Fontamillas to the group (he had been touring with them since 2000) and in 2005 added guitarist Drew Shirley to the group (he had been touring with them since 2003).

The group picked the name Switchfoot, a surfing term, because the members had been active surfers growing up in Southern California.

The group began as a Christian group on a Christian record label, but their songs transcended Christian music, and their big break came when four of their songs were included in the movie *A Walk to Remember* in 2002. These songs came from their third album, *Learning to Breathe*, and that album achieved gold status.

The success of their *Learning to Breathe* album led them to sign with a major secular label, Columbia, which released *The Beautiful Letdown*, which sold more than 2.5 million units. Columbia released their next two albums as the band's identity moved away from being a Christian band to being a band whose members are Christians but whose music seeks to reach a wide audience and whose lyrics embrace a wide variety of topics and issues.

The band felt hemmed in by the Christian market, locked in a box that caused them to defend their faith rather than discuss the life issues they preferred to discuss. For several years the band quit playing at Christian festivals and refused to do interviews with Christian-based media.

Their three guitar line-up and songs by Jon Foreman made them a popular band in both the Christian and secular markets. They toured constantly and obtained a loyal following. They became involved in several humanitarian causes, including Habitat for Humanity, the Keep A Breast Foundation, Invisible Children, the ONE Campaign, and To Write Love on Her Arms.

In 2007 Switchfoot announced the group had started a new record label, Lowercase People Records, and would record as an indie band from that point on. That same year they constructed their own studio to record future releases.

Don Cusic

Discography

The Legend of Chin (1997)

New Way to Be Human (1999)

Learning to Breathe (2000)

The Beautiful Letdown (2003)

Nothing Is Sound (2005)

Oh! Gravity (2006)

Gospel Music Association Dove Awards

2004   Rock Recorded Song of the Year: "Ammunition"; from

Jonathan Foreman, right, lead singer of Switchfoot, accepts the award for best rock/contemporary album for The Beautiful Letdown *with the rest of the band during the Gospel Music Association Awards on April 28, 2004 in Nashville. (AP Photo/Mark Humphrey)*

album *The Beautiful Letdown*; Songwriter: Jonathan Foreman; Sparrow Records

2004 Rock/Contemporary Album of the Year: *The Beautiful Letdown*; Producers: John Fields, Chad Butler, Jerome Fontamillas, Jonathan Foreman, Tim Foreman; Sparrow Records

2004 Rock/Contemporary Recorded Song of the Year: "Meant to Live"; *The Beautiful Letdown*; Switchfoot; Jonathan Foreman, Tim Foreman; Sparrow Records

2005 Artist of the Year: Switchfoot

2005 Long Form Music Video of the Year: *Switchfoot Live in San Diego*; Dwight Thompson; New Revolution Entertainment; Sparrow Records

2005 Rock/Contemporary Recorded Song of the Year: "Dare You to Move"; from album *The Beautiful Letdown*; Songwriter: Jonathan Foreman; Sparrow Records

2005 Short Form Music Video of the Year: *Dare You to Move*; Nina Grossman Warner; Robert

Hales; HIS Entertainment;
Sparrow Records

2006   Short Form Music Video of the
Year: *Stars*; Coleen Haynes;
Scott Speer; HIS Productions;
Sparrow Records/ Columbia
Records

For Further Reading

Powell, Mark Allen. *Encyclopedia of Contemporary Christian Music*. Peabody, Mass.: Hendrickson Publishers, Inc., 2002.

T

TADA, JONI EARECKSON

Joni Eareckson (b. October 15, 1949, in Baltimore, Maryland) was an athletic young lady when, at 17, she became a quadriplegic from a diving accident in the Chesapeake Bay. Since she could not use her hands, she learned to paint by holding the brush between her teeth and created inspirational artworks. This led a local TV station to air a feature on her, which, in turn, led "The Today Show" to feature her. A book publisher then invited her to write her autobiography, *Joni*, which was published in 1976. The film company owned by Billy Graham Ministries, World Wide Pictures, did a feature of her life, which was released in 1979.

These activities led Joni to become an author, recording artist, and advocate for the disabled. Her first two albums, *Joni's Song* (1981) and *Spirit Wings* (1982), were released on Word. She became a columnist for *Moody Monthly* and host of a five-minute radio show, and involved in issues and organizations related to those with disabilities, including a presidential appointment to the National Council on Disability.

Joni married Ken Tada on July 3, 1982, and became known as Joni Eareckson Tada. Ken, a former teacher, is active in Joni's ministry, Joni and Friends. She has received numerous awards and honors and has written more than 30 books.

Don Cusic

For Further Reading

Powell, Mark Allen. *Encyclopedia of Contemporary Christian Music*. Peabody, Mass.: Hendrickson Publishers, Inc., 2002.

TAFF, RUSS

Russ Taff (b. November 11, 1953, in Farmersville, California) is a blue-eyed soul artist who emerged from the southern gospel group the Imperials to become one of the top contemporary Christian rock and soul artists during the 1980s. Taff received the Dove Award for "Male Vocalist of the Year" in 1981, 1982, and 1984.

The fourth of five sons, Taff was raised in the Pentecostal church in central California; as a child he could not participate in nonchurch social functions, read newspapers or magazines, watch television, or listen to music that was not gospel. When Taff was 15 his family moved to Hot Springs, Arkansas, and there he formed his first band, the Sounds of Joy, with guitarist James Hollihan, Jr. Taff toured with evangelist Jerry Seville before he joined the Imperials in 1977; he was the lead singer on their albums *Sail On, Live, Heed the Call, One More Song for You, Christmas with the Imperials*, and *Priority*. He left the group in 1981 to embark on a solo career, and his first album was *Walls of Glass,* released on Myrrh in 1983. That album earned Taff a Grammy for "Best Gospel Performance, Male" in 1983.

Taff's album *Medals* won the Dove Award in 1986 in the "Pop/Contemporary Album" category; in 1989 his album *Russ Taff* won the Dove for "Rock Album," and in 1990 his album *The Way Home* was awarded a Dove in the "Rock Album" category. Taff's album *Under the Influence*, which was a tribute to artists such as Mahalia Jackson and others who influenced him, won a 1991 Grammy in the "Best Rock/Contemporary Gospel Album" category.

Don Cusic

For Further Reading

Alfonso, Barry. *The Billboard Guide to Contemporary Christian Music*. New York: Billboard Books/Watson-Guptill, 2002.

Cusic, Don. *The Sound of Light: A History of Gospel and Christian Music*. New York: Hal Leonard, 2002.

McNeil, W. K., ed. *Encyclopedia of American Gospel Music*. New York: Routledge, 2005.

Powell, Mark Allen. *Encyclopedia of Contemporary Christian Music*. Peabody, Mass.: Hendrickson Publishers, Inc., 2002.

TAKE 6

Take 6 is a talented, award winning a cappella group. At the Dove Awards for 1989, Take 6 won Doves for "Contemporary Gospel Album" for *Take 6*, "Contemporary Gospel Recorded Song" for "If We Ever," "Group of the Year," and "New Artist of the Year." In 1991 their album *So Much 2 Say* won the Dove for "Contemporary Gospel Album" and their song "I L-O-V-E You" won the Dove for "Contemporary Gospel Recorded Song." Their album *He Is Christmas* won the 1992 Dove for "Contemporary Gospel Album," and they won the "Contemporary Gospel Album" Dove for *Join the Band* in 1995. At the 1988 and 1989 Grammy Awards, Take 6 won "Best Soul Gospel Performance by a Duo or Group"; in 1990, 1994, and 1997 they won Grammys for "Best Contemporary Soul Gospel Album."

Take 6 is first tenor Claude V. McKnight III (b. October 2, 1962, in Brooklyn, New York), bass Alvin "Vinnie" Chea (b. November 2, 1967, in San Francisco, California), baritone Cedric Dent (b. September 24, 1963, in Detroit, Michigan), first tenor, Mark Kibble (b. April 7, 1964, in the Bronx, New York), second tenor David Thomas (b. October 23, 1967, in Brooklyn, New York), and second tenor Joey Kibble (b May 26, 1971, in Buffalo, New York); Mervyn Warren was an original member of the group and left in 1991.

Claude McKnight was born in Brooklyn but his family moved to Buffalo when he was a child. McKnight had three brothers: Fred, Mike, and Brian, who is an R&B singer. They grew up watching their grandfather, Fred Willis Sr., direct the choir at their church. McKnight often went with his mother to choir practice where he learned to do parts and harmonize. He also watched closely as his grandfather worked with the choir, observing what it was like to direct a group of voices. Although McKnight learned to play trombone in the fourth grade, it was the chorus that led him to his musical path. The family moved to Orlando, Florida, after McKnight graduated from high school, where he continued with his music. McKnight was also interested in sports and had to decide between that and music. After he enrolled at Oakwood College in Huntsville, Alabama, where his parents had gone to school, McKnight formed a quartet. Legend has it that the quartet was going through their routine for a show in a bathroom on campus when Mark Kibble walked by. He came in and started singing a fifth part and found himself singing with them that very night. Kibble is responsible for Mervyn Warren joining the group, which performed under the name Gentleman's Estate Quartet and then Alliance.

In 1991, Joey Kibble replaced Warren, who wished to pursue other avenues in the music industry, including working as a producer. The group performed locally while the men were in college, but after graduation in 1985 the bass, baritone, and second tenor left the group to continue other interests. It was at this time that current members Alvin Chea, Cedric Dent, and David Thomas joined them. Two years later the group signed to Warner Brothers, changing its name once again, this time to Take 6 after they discovered that Alliance was already in use.

Over the years Take 6 has worked with a number of pop and rock artists, including Stevie Wonder, Whitney Houston, Don Henley, Ray Charles, Queen Latifah, Quincy Jones, and Brian McNight, brother of Claude McKnight. All of the group's members are Seventh-Day Adventists; because of their strict religious beliefs, the group does not perform on Saturdays in order to observe the traditional Sabbath.

Vernell Hackett

For Further Reading

McNeil, W. K., ed. *Encyclopedia of American Gospel Music*. New York: Routledge, 2005.

Powell, Mark Allen. *Encyclopedia of Contemporary Christian Music*. Peabody, Mass.: Hendrickson Publishers, Inc., 2002.

TALBOT, JOHN MICHAEL

Brothers John Michael (b. May 8, 1954) and Terry Talbot were raised in Indianapolis and came from a musical family: their grandfather was a singing Methodist minister; their father, Dick, was a violinist in the Oklahoma City Orchestra; and their mother, Jimmie Margaret Talbot, a pianist. The brothers began their musical careers in 1962 when they formed the Quinchords; in 1969 they formed the country rock group Mason Proffit, recorded several albums for Warner Brothers, and toured 1975–1976 dressed in buckskin outfits that gave them the image of frontiersmen.

In 1971 John Michael, pursing a spiritual path that led him through Eastern religions and Native American practices, had a life-changing experience in a Holiday Inn hotel room. He claimed to see the image of Jesus in a man dressed in white robes with long hair and a beard lit up in brilliance; it changed his life. Talbot continued to record and tour with Mason Proffit but that experience prompted him to lead his brother, Terry, to a Christian commitment. The two recorded as the Talbot Brothers, and in 1976 the brothers cowrote the musical *Firewind*, with Jamie Owens.

John Michael Talbot was married when he was 17, but his dogmatic faith after his conversion caused his wife, Nancy, to divorce him, which precipitated a spiritual crisis in his life. This crisis led him to embrace the teaching of St. Francis of Assisi. He visited the Alverna Franciscan Retreat Center in Indiana where he found a mentor, Father Martin Wolter, and became a Roman Catholic. In 1978 Talbot sold most of his earthly possessions, created a monk's habit out of some old Army blankets, and set out on a path that led him to become a Third Order Franciscan and Lay Associate in the Catholic church. These Third Order monks take vows of poverty, chastity, and obedience but can marry, live with their families in outside homes, and work in regular jobs.

Talbot had recorded two albums for Sparrow, *John Michael Talbot*, released in 1976, and *The New Earth*, released in 1977, but his third album, *The Lord's Supper*, released in 1979, changed his life and his musical career. *The Lord's Supper* was an album of music that was embraced by the Catholic community; it embraced the liturgies of the historical Catholic church and led him to record a number of albums that also embraced ancient liturgies and Catholic worship. Although Talbot intended to spend his life as a celibate lay monk (he vowed he would remain chaste after his wife remarried), he found himself as the chief spokesman for the Catholic faith in the contemporary Christian community, the top-selling artist in the Christian community, and, after Ray Repp, the artist most closely identified with liturgical music in the world of CCM.

Talbot owned 25 acres of land in the Ozark Mountains that he was unable to sell; Father Wolter advised him to form a community and begin a music ministry. Talbot founded the Brothers and Sisters of Charity at Little Portion Hermitage, located near Eureka Springs, Arkansas. Approximately 40 residents live in this community comprising singles, families, and celibates; it is not officially part of the Franciscan order, although it embraces the Franciscan lifestyle of spiritual devotion. John Michael Talbot is the spiritual father of this community, which supports Mercy Corps, an international humanitarian agency. After wrestling with his vow to remain celibate, Talbot remarried in 1989.

Talbot is a prolific composer of worship songs and has recorded more than 40 albums and written a number of books. The income from these efforts helps fund his spiritual community.

Talbot, who refers to his music as "spiritual" rather than "Christian" or "gospel, formed his own label, Troubadour for the Lord, which is distributed by Sparrow. He has recorded some albums with his brother, Terry, and an album with Michael Card. In addition to his albums and books, Talbot is founder and president of the Catholic Association of Musicians and was elected to editorial board of *New Covenant* magazine in 1997.

Terry Talbot is a talented guitarist who has backed Glen Campbell, Chad Mitchell, and Sonny and Cher. Terry embarked on a solo career, and in 1995 he joined forces with Barry McGuire as Terry and Barry; they toured 1995–2000 and recorded several albums.

Don Cusic

Discography

John Michael Talbot (1976)

The New Earth (1977)

The Lord's Supper (1979)

Beginnings: The Early Years (1980)

Come to the Quiet (1980)

For the Bride (1981)

Troubadour of the Great King (1981)

Light Eternal (1982)

Songs for Worship, Vol. 1 (1983)

The God of Life (1984)

Songs for Worship, Vol. 2 (1985)

The Quiet (1985)

Empty Canvas (1986)

Be Exalted (1986)

Heart of the Shepherd (1987)

Quiet Reflections (1987)

The Regathering (1988)

The Lover and the Beloved (1989)

Master Collection (1989)

Hiding Place (1990)

Come Worship the Lord, Vol. 1 (1990)

Come Worship the Lord, Vol. 2 (1990)

The Quiet Side (1990)

The Birth of Jesus: A Celebration of Christmas (1990)

The Master Musician (1992)

Meditations in the Spirit (1993)

Meditation from Solitude (1994)

The John Michael Talbot Collection (1995)

Chant from the Hermitage (1995)

Brother to Brother (with Michael Card) (1996)

Troubadour for the Lord (1996)

Our Blessing Cup (1996)

The Early Years (1997)

Table of Plenty (1997)

Pathways of the Shepherd (1998)

Quiet Pathways (1998)

Spirit Pathways (1998)

Hidden Pathways (1998)

Pathways to Solitude (1998)

Pathways to Wisdom (1998)

Cave of the Heart (1999)

Simple Heart (2000)

Wisdom (2001)

Signatures (2003)

City of God (2005)

Monk Rock (2005)

The Beautiful City (2006)

Living Water (2007)

Discography: Talbot Brothers

Talbot Brothers (1974)

The Painter (1980)

No Longer Strangers (1983)

The Talbot Brothers Collection (1995)

Discography: Mason Proffit

Wanted (1969)

Movin' Toward Happiness (1970)

Last Night I Had the Strangest Dream (1971)

Bareback Rider (1973)

Come and Gone (1973)

Discography: Terry Talbot

No Longer Alone (1976)

Cradle of Love (1977)

A Time to Laugh . . . a Time to Sing (1978)

A Song Shall Rise (1981)

On Wings of the Wind (1982)

Sings the Stories of Jesus (1984)

Face to Face (1985)

The Teachings of Christ (1985)

Wake the Sleeping Giant (1987)

Terry Talbot (1988)

Steps of the Mission (2002)

Like I Am (2006)

Discography: Terry and Wendy Talbot

Concert of Praise (1989)

The Fullness of Times (1993)

Discography: Terry and Barry (McGuire)

When Dinosaurs Walked the Earth (1995)

Ancient Garden (1997)

Frost and Fire (1999)

Talbot McGuire Live (2000)

Trippin' the 60's Live (2007)

For Further Reading

Alfonso, Barry. *The Billboard Guide to Contemporary Christian Music*. New York: Billboard Books/Watson-Guptill, 2002.

Cusic, Don. *The Sound of Light: A History of Gospel and Christian Music*. New York: Hal Leonard, 2002.

McNeil, W. K., ed. *Encyclopedia of American Gospel Music*. New York: Routledge, 2005.

Powell, Mark Allen. *Encyclopedia of Contemporary Christian Music*. Peabody, Mass.: Hendrickson Publishers, Inc., 2002.

O'Neill, Dan. *Troubadour for the Lord: The Story of John Michael Talbot*. New York: Crossroad, 1983.

Talbot, John Michael. *Changes: A Spiritual Journey*. Chestnut Ridge, Ky.: Crossroad, 1984.

TAYLOR, STEVE

Steve Taylor (b. Roland Stephen Taylor, December 9, 1957) has been called "evangelical rock's court jester" for his brash wit satirizing Christian life. During his career Taylor has been influential as a recording artist, songwriter, producer, and executive, finding and producing Sixpence None the Richer, whose hit "Kiss Me" was on the soundtrack for the movie *She's All That* and was a hit on the secular charts.

Taylor is the son of a Baptist minister who forbid him to listen to secular

Steve Taylor has been a successful artist, producer, and film director in contemporary Christian music. (courtesy of Steve Taylor)

music while growing up in Denver. After high school he entered Biola University in Southern California, where he failed an audition to win a slot with the choir. In his teens Taylor became a fan of punk rock after hearing the album *London Calling* by the Clash. Taylor transferred to the University of Colorado in Boulder, where he received a degree in music in 1980.

Back in Denver he served as youth pastor for five years in his father's church, then toured as assistant director for the Continental Singers, headed by Cam Floria, followed by a job as director of Jeremiah People, headed by Chuck Bolte. That group did a variety show of skits and songs and performed at Youth for Christ rallies.

During the annual Christian Artists Retreat in 1982 held in Estes Park, Colorado, Taylor performed "I Want to Be a Clone," a song about Christian conformity. This led to a recording contract with Sparrow Records and his debut EP, *I Want to Be a Clone*, in 1983. On his first appearance as a solo artist, at the Cornerstone Festival, he broke his ankle when he leaped off the stage.

Taylor became controversial in contemporary Christian circles through songs like "We Don't Need No Color Code," which criticized the segregated dating policy at Bob Jones University.

In 1991 Taylor formed a secular band, Chagall Guevara, comprised of guitarists Dave Perkins and Lynn Nichols, bassist Wade Jaynes, and drummer Mike Mead; the group signed with MCA but was dropped from the label after one album.

Taylor produced albums by the Newsboys and Guardian, and in 1992 formed Squint Entertainment with funding from Gaylord Entertainment, parent company of Word/Myrrh Records at the time. Squint signed Sixpence None the Richer, Burlap to Cashmere, Chevelle, Waterdeep, PFR, and the Insyderz. In 2001 Word took over Squint and dismissed Taylor as the chief executive.

Taylor was active in video production and was the first Christian artist to make a long-form concept video to accompany an album. He directed music videos for Fleming and John, Rich Mullins, Sixpence None the Richer, Newsboys, and Guardian in addition to his own albums. He cowrote and directed the film *The Second Chance*, starring Michael W. Smith, and directed *Down under the Big Top*, starring the Newsboys.

Discography

I Want to Be a Clone (1983)

Meltdown (1984)

On the Fritz (1985)

Limelight: Live at Greenbelt (1986)

I Predict 1990 (1987)

The Best We Could Find (+3 That Never Escaped) (1988)

Squint (1994)

Now the Truth Can Be Told (1994)

Liver (1995)

Discography: with Chagall Guevara

Chagall Guevara (1991, MCA)

Gospel Music Association Dove Awards

1987   Long Form Music Video: *Limelight* by Steve Taylor; Producers and Directors: John Anneman and Steve Taylor; Label: Sparrow

1995   Rock Album: *Going Public* by the Newsboys (Producers: Steve Taylor and Peter Furler; Label: Star Song)

1995   Rock Recorded Song: "Shine" Written by Peter Furler, Steve Taylor; Recorded by Newsboys; Label: Star Song

For Further Reading

Alfonso, Barry. *The Billboard Guide to Contemporary Christian Music*. New York: Billboard Books/Watson-Guptill, 2002.

McNeil, W. K., ed. *Encyclopedia of American Gospel Music*. New York: Routledge, 2005.

Powell, Mark Allen. *Encyclopedia of Contemporary Christian Music*. Peabody, Mass.: Hendrickson Publishers, Inc., 2002.

TELEVISION AND CONTEMPORARY CHRISTIAN MUSIC

Television has generally not played a major role in the history of contemporary Christian music. The most popular religious shows are headed by an evangelist who controls the content, and the music performed is generally done at the beginning of the service, to set up the sermon, and after the sermon, when the evangelist gives an altar call or concludes his service. In that light, the music has always played a secondary role to the evangelist and his message.

During the 1950s network television dealt with mainline religious groups through established organizations: the National Council of Catholic Men represented Catholics, the Jewish Seminary of America represented Jews, and the Federal Council of Churches of Christ represented Protestants. The networks produced mainline religious programming: "Lamp unto My Feet" and "Look Up and Live" were on CBS, "Directions" was on ABC, and "Frontiers of Faith" was on NBC.

The most popular religious show was hosted by Bishop Fulton J. Sheen, who began broadcasting over WLWL in New York in 1928, doing "Catholic Hour." When he moved to TV, the production consisted of a speech or classroom lecture on a religious or moral subject; his only "prop" was a blackboard. The show was broadcast in the evening and quite popular; between 1952 and 1957 it drew competitive ratings.

The growth of independently syndicated evangelical or fundamentalist programs that purchased air time on

TV grew from 38 in 1972 to 72 in 1978. The major cause for the change was a Federal Communications Commission (FCC) ruling in 1960 that opened up the UHF frequency, allowing new TV stations to go on the air. These new UHF stations did not have a network affiliation, so there were no programs provided to them from the networks; instead, they had to either purchase or create their own programs. Many bought reruns from the networks or ran syndicated shows that were independently produced and contained time slots where the local station sold advertisements.

The FCC also stated, in essence, that there should be no difference in sustaining-time programs—those produced by the station and broadcast free—and commercially sponsored programs when the station's performance in the public interest was evaluated. This allowed stations to meet FCC regulations with religious programs for which airtime was provided as well as programs that paid for their airtime. It did not take television stations long to realize that running programs that paid them was more profitable than running programs that cost them money.

The FCC developed a "hands-off" approach to religious stations and programming; it did not enforce the noncommercial requirements of those holding educational or noncommercial licenses when it came to on-air fundraising, on-air solicitations, or the sale of religious items over the air.

Because they had to be profitable, the new UHF television stations soon discovered that selling time to religious broadcasters was a good way to fill up time and make money. It was especially appealing during the Sunday morning hours, the "broadcast ghetto" when the fewest number of people watch television. Because Sunday is a traditional day of worship, the reasoning ran, these shows provided a service for those who could not attend church.

As television stations came to receive this source of income from paid religious broadcasting, they shifted away from local programming—which cost them money—to paid programming, which made money. In 1959, 53 percent of all religious programs on TV purchased their own airtime; in 1977 the percentage was 92 percent. These paid programs virtually eliminated local religious programming. In 1979 this led CBS to cancel "Lamp unto My Feet" and "Look Up and Live," its two long-running religious shows.

Televangelists began appearing in the early 1950s. In 1953 Rex Humbard began his television ministry in Akron, Ohio; from 1953 to 1969 he purchased airtime regularly on 68 stations; in 1970 the show expanded to 110 stations, and over the next two years he added 100 stations each year. Oral Roberts began his television program in 1954, purchasing time on 16 stations; in 1967 he stopped for two years and, when he re-emerged, his show was more like a variety show. In 1956 Jerry Falwell began his church in Lynchburg, Virginia; his television program, "The Old Time Gospel Hour," was an edited version of one of his morning services at the Thomas Road Baptist Church. Pat Robertson purchased a television station in Virginia Beach in 1960 and began broadcasting in 1961 with his "700 Club," which led to the development of his Christian Broadcasting Network (CBN). In 1955 Robert Schuller, a minister with the Reformed Church of America, was sent to Orange County, California, to begin a new congregation; by 1980 his TV program, "Hour of Power," was broadcast from the Crystal Cathedral, a glass sanctuary.

Sophisticated computer technology, developed during the 1960s, provided a key element that televangelists needed to have successful programming. This technology allowed evangelical broadcasters to handle a large volume of incoming mail and develop mailing lists to solicit donations from their viewers. It also created money-generating organizations whose views had to be in tune with their audience to keep the funds rolling in. Although these religious broadcasters did not have to depend on Nielson ratings or the decision of network executives to stay on the air, the mail became a polling device and showed audience preferences.

Ten major evangelical programs accounted for more than half of all national airings of religious programs in 1979. The National Religious Broadcasters, formed in 1944, was a driving force behind these programs; most independent broadcasters were members of this organization.

The largest growth of TV evangelists on paid programs occurred from 1965 to 1975 and went virtually unnoticed; however, the election of Jimmy Carter to the presidency in November 1976 brought attention to the bornagain movement and religion in America. In 1977 the paid programs of televangelists were at their apex; ironically, because of their organizational and fund-raising abilities, and the fact they attracted the attention of the mass media, the period from 1980 to 1988 was the period when people perceived them to have the most power and influence.

In July 1980 the *Wall Street Journal* stated in an article that televangelists were reaching an estimated 128 million viewers each week. That same year, Jerry Falwell was claiming an audience of 20 million people for his show, and began organizing the "Moral Majority." Jim Bakker of "The PTL Club" also claimed 20 million viewers.

But, according to Nielsen ratings, in November 1980, Oral Roberts had 2.275 million viewers; the "Hour of Power" had 2 million; Rex Humbard had 1.9 million, Jimmy Swaggart had 1.6 million; "Day of Discovery" had 1.24 million; Falwell's "Old Time Gospel Hour" had 1.21 million, "Insight" had 790,000, the "PTL Club" had 621,000, and Pat Robertson's "700 Club" had 447,600 viewers. The Nielsen surveys showed a combined audience of 19.1 million for all the syndicated shows and, in 1981, only five syndicated programs received a rating of one or better: Oral Roberts, "Hour of Power," Rex Humbard, "Insight," and Jimmy Swaggart.

Ironically, the religious show with the highest rating and largest audience was "Gospel Singing Jubilee," a show hosted by the Florida Boys that featured southern gospel singing. This show had a 4.2 rating. During 1975 and 1976, "Gospel Singing Jubilee" had the largest audience of any religious program: 1.01 million and 1.09 million, respectively. During the 1977–1980 period, it was second, behind Falwell's "Old Time Gospel Hour" and in 1981 it was third, behind Falwell and "Insight." But the "Gospel Singing Jubilee" was never on as many stations as the other programs; also, it depended on advertising to stay on the air and subsequently vanished from the airwaves in 1981.

In November 1981, Nielsen estimated the religious programs audience at 21,751,000; other estimates went as high as 36 million but, since most religious program viewers watched several, it was estimated that the audience for religious broadcasts was actually 10 million to 15 million different people.

In 1981 independent evangelical groups accounted for 83.3 percent of the top syndicated religious programs on television; the Roman Catholic Church, which had 37.1 percent of the population in 1979, had only one major syndicated television program, "Insight." The National Council of Churches, which represented 30 percent of the church population in 1979 and 1981, had no major syndicated religious program.

Before cable television, most of the programs were broadcast on Sunday mornings in regions where church attendance was high. There were several reasons for this: (1) Sunday morning is the traditional day of worship; (2) time buys on Sunday were cheaper than almost any other time; (3) TV stations preferred selling Sunday morning time slots to religious broadcasters rather than prime time spots (in 1976 there was a potential national audience of 13 million adults on Sunday mornings; during prime time, the number was 70 million); and (4) the religious broadcasters realized their core audience watched during Sunday mornings. Therefore, to raise money, they had to appeal to a core audience—which they tended to find on Sunday mornings in areas that were already populated by churchgoers.

A breakdown of the audience watching religious programming showed that women outnumbered men about two to one. During the 1970s and 1980s the "Hour of Power" had 60.9 percent women, Oral Roberts had 59.8 percent, Jimmy Swaggart had 54.6 percent, and the "PTL Club" had 61.4 percent women. The "Gospel Singing Jubilee" had 55.3 percent women and 44.7 percent men.

The audience also tended to be older—half the regular viewers were over 60 years old. Surveys showed that as people age, particularly women, they tend to watch more religious television to the point that the core audience for religious programming is women over the age of 50.

The audience tended to have lower incomes, less education, and be employees in blue-collar occupations. Those in white-collar occupations, with higher incomes and more education, tended to watch less religious television. In terms of geography, those in the southern and midwestern states—where there was the highest church attendance—watched more than those in the West or East.

The world of TV evangelists has been dominated by a handful of men, 8 to 10 at most at any given time. Musically, these preachers rarely break any new ground, seeing music in the traditional role of "preparing the way" for the message. As the shows got slicker in the 70s and 80s and began adopting talk-show-type formats, music began to be featured more, with some Christian artists appearing on the shows. However, the urge for each preacher to dominate and control his own show prevailed, and the preachers all began to develop talent within their own organizations to appear on their programs. They usually controlled these singers, dictated which songs they sang and what music they played, and did not have to pay them much. Thus the medium with potentially the greatest influence had little, if any, influence on Christian music.

With the exception of Jimmy Swaggart, none of the televangelists has been particularly musical. Instead, they have seen themselves as preachers, and the thrust of their operations were themselves and their messages. Only Swaggart had a strong musical background, and he initially built his following on his ability to play and sing, becoming well known through his recordings. Along the way, he became the most successful artist in the southern gospel, or country gospel vein, dominating the airwaves and selling a large number of albums outside his own shows.

By 1976 Swaggart's radio program was on 550 stations, and he was selling over a million albums a year. By 1988 Swaggart was on television all over the world, broadcasting from the studios he had built in Baton Rouge, Louisiana. He founded the Jimmy Swaggart Bible College, planned a seminary, had 1,200 employees, and was head of an empire that was bringing in over $150 million annually. He was also the major spokesman against contemporary Christian music.

In 1988 Jimmy Swaggart achieved national notoriety for "moral failure" (he was caught with a prostitute) and was suspended for three months from preaching. Eventually, he resigned from the Assemblies of God Church to continue his TV shows, crusades, and worldwide evangelism.

For the televangelists in general, the 1980s and early 1990s proved to be their undoing; Swaggart's solicitation of a prostitute, Jim Bakker's extramarital affair, the exhortations of Oral Roberts about raising money or dying, and the Moral Majority of Jerry Falwell all caused many among the public to turn against these evangelical leaders.

Two developments kept two of these televangelists in the public spotlight: Jerry Falwell and Pat Robertson each established a university: Falwell's Liberty University in Lynchburg, Virginia, and Robertson's Regent University in Virginia Beach. Also, the Christian Coalition formed by Pat Robertson had a proven impact by raising money and support for Republican candidates.

As cable television became increasingly popular and more channels were made available, full-time Christian networks developed and it became possible to view TV evangelists seven days a week, 24 hours a day. Still, music was secondary to the evangelist. During the early 2000s, the most popular evangelist was Joel Osteen, who used a musical group at the beginning and end of his show. T. D. Jakes developed acts and marketed them through his television ministry, but the emphasis was on Jakes and his ministry.

Don Cusic

For Further Reading

Armstrong, Ben. *The Electric Church.* Nashville, Tenn.: Thomas Nelson, 1979.

Cusic, Don. *The Sound of Light: A History of Gospel and Christian Music.* New York: Hal Leonard, 2002.

Fishwick, Marshall, and Ray B. Browne, ed. *The God Pumpers: Religion in the Electronic Age.* Bowling Green, Ohio: Popular Press, 1987.

Horsfield, Peter G. *Religious Television: An American Experience*. New York: Longman, 1984.

Swaggart, Jimmy, with Robert Paul Lamb. *To Cross a River*. Plainfield, N.J.: Logos International, 1977.

THIRD DAY

Third Day is a Christian southern rock band from Atlanta that was formed in 1994 after Mac Powell and Mark Lee, who were playing in an acoustic group, met Tai Anderson and David Carr. A pastor put the four together and they added lead guitarist Brad Avery. Their line-up is Mac Powell, lead vocals, acoustic guitar; Mark Lee, guitar; Brad Avery, guitar; Tai Anderson, bass; and David Carr, drums

Their first album was initially released in 1995 on Gray Dot, an independent label, before they signed with Reunion and remixed that album for their first national release. After two albums with Reunion they signed with Essential. The band is known for presenting their blues-based southern rock sound as worship and praise music and for their constant touring. During the late 1990s they became one of contemporary Christian music's top drawing groups. In 1997 they recorded a commercial for Coca-Cola. The act has been popular in both the Christian and secular fields, evidenced by the large number of Dove and Grammy Awards they have won.

The band has been popular with contemporary Christian music fans as well as the Christian music industry. Their Dove Awards began with the "Rock Album" Dove for *Conspiracy No. 5* and "Rock Recorded Song" for "Alien" in 1998.

Third Day won the Dove for "Rock Album" in 2000 for *Time* and in 2001 was named "Group of the Year." That same year their album *Offerings: A Worship Album* won the Dove for "Praise and Worship Album," and "Sky Fall Down" won a Dove for "Rock Recorded Song." In addition, they received a Dove with a number of other groups for "Special Event Album" for their contribution to *City on a Hill—Songs of Worship and Praise*. In 2002 they again won "Group of the Year" honors and their album *Come Together* and song "Come Together" won "Rock Album of the Year" and "Rock Recorded Song of the Year."

In 2003 Third Day won the Dove for "Group of the Year" for the third consecutive year and their song, "40 Days" won "Rock Recorded Song of the Year." In 2004 they won the Dove for "Praise and Worship Album of the Year" with their album *Offerings II—All I Have to Give*. In 2005 their album *Wire* won "Rock/Contemporary Album of the Year." They won "Pop/Contemporary Recorded Song of the Year" for "Cry out to Jesus" in 2006, and in 2007 their album *Christmas Offerings* won "Christmas Album of the Year."

Third Day won Grammies for "Best Rock Gospel Album" for *Come Together* in 2002, "Best Rock Gospel Album" for *Wire* in 2004, and "Best Pop/Contemporary Gospel Album" for *Wherever You Are* in 2006.

Don Cusic

For Further Reading

Alfonso, Barry. *The Billboard Guide to Contemporary Christian Music*. New York: Billboard Books/Watson-Guptill, 2002.

The Atlanta-based Christian rock band Third Day, shown in a publicity photo from Reunion Records. The groups members are, from left, David Carr, Tai Anderson, Brad Avery, Mac Powell, and Mark Lee. (AP Photo/Reunion Records, James Blond)

Powell, Mark Allen. *Encyclopedia of Contemporary Christian Music*. Peabody, Mass.: Hendrickson Publishers, Inc., 2002.

Thompson, John J. *Raised by Wolves: The Story of Christian Rock and Roll*. Toronto, Ontario: ECW Press, 2000.

THOMAS, B. J.

B. J. Thomas (b. Billy Joe Thomas, August 7, 1942) had a string of pop hits in the 1960s and 1970s, beginning with "I'm So Lonesome I Could Cry" and continuing through "Billy and Sue," "Hooked on a Feeling," "I Just Can't Help Believing," and "(Hey, Won't You Play) Another Somebody Done Somebody Wrong Song." His recording of "Raindrops Keep Falling on My Head" in 1969 was the theme song for the movie *Butch Cassidy and the Sundance Kid*. Thomas descended into a spiral of drug abuse until his Christian conversion in 1976; after his conversion—one of the first celebrity conversions in Christian music—he recorded his first Christian album, *Home Where I Belong*, in 1977 for Myrrh. This period and this album were key factors in the evolution from Jesus music to contemporary Christian music, and the prevailing belief within the Christian world at that time was that a celebrity conversion would result in a singer's fans becoming Christians too. Unfortunately, what happened was a clash between Thomas's old fans, who just wanted to hear his old pop hits, and his Christian fans, who demanded that Thomas abandon those hit songs and just do Christian material. This resulted

B. J. Thomas poses at the Grammy Awards on February 24, 1982, in Los Angeles. (AP Photo/Reed Saxon)

in a great deal of conflict and frustration for Thomas, who felt he could please no one when he tried to present a concert of old hits and new Christian material.

Thomas grew up in Rosenberg, Texas, outside of Houston, and formed a band, the Triumphs, while in high school. He had a regional hit with "Billy and Sue" in 1964 before signing with Scepter Records and releasing his first national hit, a cover of the Hank Williams song "I'm So Lonesome I Could Cry" in 1966. According to his autobiography, Thomas's father was an alcoholic and he was an abused child; his success led him to a dependence on amphetamines and cocaine. Thomas had married when he was 26 and had a daughter, but his family left him because of his drug abuse. His wife and

daughter became born-again Christians, and during an attempt at reconciliation they led him to the Lord on January 28, 1976. Thomas's concerts soon became known for his Christian testimony, which led Word Records to offer him a contract to record Christian material with the intention he would record pop and country material for a secular label.

In 1981 Thomas became a member of the Grand Ole Opry and in 1983 had two country number one's: "Whatever Happened to Old Fashioned Love" and "New Looks from an Old Lover," both family-oriented songs, but the Christian audience demanded total allegiance to Christian music. His debut Christian album, *Home Where I Belong*, went platinum. His 1978 tour, featuring Andrae Crouch as the opening act, had him performing before hecklers who interrupted his performances, shouting verses of scripture at him and calling him an instrument of the devil for continuing to perform his pop and country hits. There were shouting matches between Thomas's old fans and the fundamentalist Christians who came to the concerts to heckle, with the result that he engaged in shouting matches with audience members, resulting in audiences walking out of his concerts. At this point Thomas decided to leave Christian music and concentrate on country. Later, he recorded several albums of hymns but the damage had been done: the career of B. J. Thomas at that point seemed to prove that an artist could not be both a Christian and secular artist.

Thomas sang the theme song to the TV show "Growing Pains" (with Jennifer Warren) and starred in the movie *Jory*. He continued to tour and some fans of contemporary Christian music, who were not as narrow-minded as the early group, seemed to accept the fact that a Christian could record secular material. Still, Thomas continued to be confronted with Christians who were dissatisfied with his conversion, which they deemed "inauthentic," and although he continued to record and tour, his audiences grew smaller, though more loyal.

Don Cusic

Selected Discography

Home Where I Belong (1977)

Happy Man (1978)

You Gave Me Love (When Nobody Gave Me a Prayer) (1979)

For the Best (1980)

The Best of B. J. Thomas (1980)

In Concert (1980)

What a Difference You Made in My Life (1981)

Amazing Grace (1981)

Peace in the Valley (1982)

Miracle (1982)

The Best of B. J. Thomas, Vol. 2 (1983)

Love Shines (1983)

Precious Memories (1995)

I Believe (1997)

The Inspirational Collection (1998)

You Call That a Mountain (2002)

Love to Burn (2007)

For Further Reading

Cusic, Don. *The Sound of Light: A History of Gospel and Christian Music.* New York: Hal Leonard, 2002.

Powell, Mark Allen. *Encyclopedia of Contemporary Christian Music.* Peabody, Mass.: Hendrickson Publishers, Inc., 2002.

Thomas, B. J., with Jerry B. Jenkins. *Home Where I Belong.* Waco, Tex.: Word, 1978.

Thomas, B. J., and Gloria Thomas. *In Tune.* Grand Rapids, Mich.: Fleming H. Revell, 1983.

TOBYMAC

Toby McKeehan (b. October 22, 1964) was a founding member of DC Talk; while a member of that group, he won Dove Awards as cowriter of the song "I Love Rap Music" (1992); writer of "Can I Get a Witness?" (1993); and cowriter of "Socially Acceptable" (1994); "Luv Is a Verb" (1995), "Jesus Freak (1996), "Between You and Me" (1997) "Like It, Love It, Need It" (1997), and "Dive" (2001).

In 1992, while still a member of DC Talk, McKeehan, Todd Collins, and Joey Elwood formed the Gotee Brothers and founded Gotee Records. In 1996 they released the album *ERACE*, which is an acronym for "Eliminating Racism And Creating Equality."

McKeehan coproduced the DC Talk albums, and in 2002 he struck out on his own with a solo album, *Momentum*, which won the Dove for "Rap/Hip Hop Dance" album; McKeehan won the Dove for "Producer of the Year."

Recording and producing under the name TobyMac, the singer and rapper has proved to be one of the most talented individuals in Christian music. His 2005 album, *Welcome to Diverse City*, won a Dove, and his song "The

TobyMac performs at the Dove Awards on April 25, 2007, in Nashville. (AP Photo/Mark Humphrey)

Slam" won the 2006 Dove for "Rock Recorded Song of the Year." In 2008 TobyMac won the top honor at the Dove Awards: "Artist of the Year." He also won "Rock/Contemporary Album of the Year" for his *Portable Sounds* product, and his song "Boomin'" was awarded the Dove for "Short Form Music Video of the Year."

Don Cusic

For Further Reading

Alfonso, Barry. *The Billboard Guide to Contemporary Christian Music.* New York: Billboard Books/Watson-Guptill, 2002.

McNeil, W. K., ed. *Encyclopedia of American Gospel Music.* New York: Routledge, 2005.

Powell, Mark Allen. *Encyclopedia of Contemporary Christian Music.*

Peabody, Mass.: Hendrickson Publishers, Inc., 2002.

TOMLIN, CHRIS

Chris Tomlin (b. May 4, 1972, in Grand Saline, Texas) emerged in the early 21st century as the premier leader in praise and worship music; according to a leading Christian copyright organization, Tomlin's songs and recordings are the most performed worship songs in the United States.

Tomlin is a founding member of the Passion worship team responsible for the One Day series of worship conferences and recordings. Passion Conferences began as Choice Ministries, founded by Louis Giglio in 1997. The conferences are geared for college students, known as the 268 Generation; the first was Passion 97 in Austin, Texas. The organization states its purpose is "uniting students in worship and prayer for spiritual awakening in this generation." The organization is headquartered in Alpharetta, Georgia.

Chris Tomlin leads worship at most Passion events. He was formerly a staff member at Austin Stone Community Church, and his first album, *Inside Your Love*, was released in 1995.

Chris Tomlin grew up in East Texas and attended Texas A&M University; after college he joined Louis Giglio with the Passion Conferences. He recorded a number of songs released on the Passion albums, including "How Great Is Our God." Other well-known songs written or cowritten by Tomlin include "Holy Is the Lord," "The Way I Was Made," "On Our Side," and "Mighty Is the Power of the Cross."

Chris Tomlin accepts the award for male vocalist of the year at the Dove Awards on April 23, 2008, in Nashville. (AP Photo/Mark Humphrey)

Tomlin performs with a band that includes Daniel Carson, guitar and backing vocals; Jesse Reeves, bass, harmonica, and backing vocals; Travis Nunn, drums; and Matt Gilder, keyboard. Tomlin and his band began working together while he was on the staff of the Woodlands United Methodist Church in Woodlands, Texas, during the late 1990s. Tomlin and pastor Matt Carter then founded the Austin Stone Community Church in Austin, Texas; in 2008 Tomlin and Louie Giglio founded a new church in Atlanta, Georgia.

Don Cusic

For Further Reading

Tomlin, Chris. *The Way I Was Made: Words and Music for an Unusual Life*. Colorado Springs, Colo.: Multnomah, 2004.

Discography

Inside Your Love (1995)

Authentic (1998)

Too Much Free Time (with Ross King) (1998)

The Noise We Make (Sixsteps, 2001)

Not to Us (2002)

Arriving (2004)

Live from Austin Music Hall (2005)

See the Morning (2006)

The Early Years (2006)

See the Morning Deluxe Edition (2007)

Arriving Platinum Edition (2008)

Hello Love (2008)

Discography: Passion Event Albums

Live Worship from the 268 Generation (1998)

Better Is One Day (1999)

The Road to One Day (2000)

One Day Live (2000)

Our Love Is Loud (2002)

Sacred Revolution: Songs from One Day 03 (2003)

Hymns: Ancient and Modern (2004)

How Great Is Our God (2005)

Everything Glorious (2006)

The Best of Passion (So Far) (2006)

Live From Passion 07: Pts. 1 and 3 (2007)

God of This City (2008)

Gospel Music Association Dove Awards

2005   Praise and Worship Album of the Year: *Arriving*; Chris

Tomlin (Producer: Ed Cash; Label: Sixsteps Records)

2006 Artist of the Year: Chris Tomlin

2006 Male Vocalist of the Year: Chris Tomlin

2006 Song of the Year: "How Great Is Our God" by Chris Tomlin, Jesse Reeves, Ed Cash; Publishers: Worshiptogether.com Songs (ASCAP), sixsteps music (ASCAP), Alletrope Music (BMI)

2006 Special Event Album of the Year: *Music Inspired by the Chronicles of Narnia: The Lion, the Witch, and the Wardrobe*; Artists: Jeremy Camp, Steven Curtis Chapman, David Crowder Band, Delirious, Bethany Dillon, Jars of Clay, Kutless, Nichole Nordeman, Rebecca St. James, TobyMac, Chris Tomlin; Producers: Ed Cash, Steven Curtis Chapman, David Crowder, Andy Dodd, Sam Gibson, Dan Haseltine, Charlie Lowell, Toby McKeehan, Adam Watts, Christopher Stevens, Mitch Dane; Label: Sparrow Records

2006 Worship Song of the Year: "How Great Is Our God" by Chris Tomlin, Jesse Reeves, Ed Cash; Publishers: Worshiptogether.com Songs, sixsteps Music, Alletrope Music

2007 Artist of the Year: Chris Tomlin

2007 Male Vocalist of the Year: Chris Tomlin

2007 Pop/Contemporary Album of the Year: *See the Morning* by Chris Tomlin; Producer: Ed Cash; Labels: Sparrow Records, sixstepsrecords

2007 Praise and Worship Album of the Year: *See the Morning* by Chris Tomlin; Producer: Ed Cash; Labels: Sparrow Records, sixstepsrecords

2007 Special Event Album of the Year: *Passion: Everything Glorious*; Artists: Chris Tomlin, Christy Nockels, Kristian Stanfill, Charlie Hall, Matt Redman, David Crowder Band; Producer: Nathan Nockels; Labels: Sparrow Records, sixstepsrecords

2007 Worship Song of the Year: "Holy Is the Lord" by Chris Tomlin, Louie Giglio; Publishers: worshiptogether.com Songs, sixsteps Music (ASCAP)

2008 Male Vocalist of the Year: Chris Tomlin

2008 Worship Song of the Year: "How Great Is Our God" by Chris Tomlin, Jesse Reeves, and Ed Cash; Publishers: worshiptogether.com Songs, sixsteps Music, Alletrope Music

TORNQUIST, EVIE

Evie Tornquist (b. March 1956) was the most popular female singer during the earliest days of contemporary Christian music. Recording under the name Evie, the attractive young blonde became the sweetheart of early CCM and had a strong following in the Christian community, who purchased her albums and attended her concerts. Her sound was a soft, middle-of-the road sound that was a contrast with the early Jesus music of either folk-based performers or rock acts. Her music is best labeled as inspirational because she recorded for the Christian audience with no attempt to water down her faith—or her songs—for a secular audience.

The Tornquist family was Norwegian, and her career began when the family returned to Norway for a visit. She was invited to perform at churches and at 14 was performing regularly on TV. She built a strong following in Norway before she recorded her first album for the American audience when she was 17. She soon became popular in the Christian adult contemporary market, appealing to older fans who were not comfortable with Jesus rock as well as young fans, particularly females, who saw her as a role model for young Christian girls.

During the 1970s she regularly sold out large venues, performed at Carnegie Hall and the White House. In 1979 she married Swedish pastor Pelle Karlsson, a former pop star in Sweden, and the two dedicated their lives to raising a family and Christian ministry. In 1981 she officially retired from touring to raise her family, which included a boy and a girl. She preferred to be known as Evie Tornquist Karlsson and continued to record, often with her husband, but her appearances were much more low key. She and her husband formed a company, White Field Music, which released their albums and the two became regulars on the Sky Angel Dominion Network. In 1980 the Karlssons moved to California and then in 1983 moved to Naples, Florida.

Evie's biggest hit is "Come on, Ring Those Bells" from her first Christmas album, which has become a standard in the Christian community.

Evie was inducted into the Gospel Music Hall of Fame in 2005.

Don Cusic

Discography

Evie (1974)

Evie Again (1975)

Gentle Moments (1976)

Mirror (1977)

Come on, Ring Those Bells (1977)

A Little Song of Joy for My Little Friends (1978)

Never the Same (1979)

Evie Favorites, Vol. 1 (1980)

Teach Us Your Way (with Pelle Karlsson) (1980)

Unfailing Love (1981)

Hymns (1983)

Restoration (with Pelle Karlsson) (1983)

When All Is Said and Done (1986)

Christmas Memories (1987)

Celebrate the Family (Evie and the Karlssons) (1980)

Our Recollections (1996, Word)

Songs for His Family (Evie and the Karlssons) (1997)

Day by Day (1998)

Kingdom Connection (2002)

Gospel Music Association Dove Awards

| 1977 | Female Vocalist of the Year |
| 1978 | Female Vocalist of the Year |

For Further Reading

Cusic, Don. *The Sound of Light: A History of Gospel and Christian Music.* New York: Hal Leonard, 2002.

Powell, Mark Allen. *Encyclopedia of Contemporary Christian Music.* Peabody, Mass.: Hendrickson Publishers, Inc., 2002.

TROCCOLI, KATHY

Kathy Troccoli (b. Kathleen Colleen Troccoli, June 24, 1958, in Brooklyn, New York) grew up in a Catholic family in East Islip on Long Island, New York. Her father died when she was a teenager, and she enrolled in Berklee College for a year before returning home and graduating from Suffolk County Community College. She sang in a nightclub with a jazz band and came to Jesus through a coworker. During a concert at church she met the group Glad, and Ed Nalle of that group was impressed with her powerful voice so he recorded a demo of her backed by Glad. Mike Blanton and Dan Harrell heard the tape, were impressed with her powerful, soulful voice, and invited her to move to Nashville; she came in 1982 and lived with Harrell's family and sang backup on Amy Grant's Age to Age tour. Unable to obtain a contract with a label for her, Blanton and Harrell launched Reunion Records and released her debut album, *Stubborn Love.* The album was produced by Brown Bannister, and the single by that title was written by Amy Grant, Gary Chapman, and Michael W. Smith.

In 1987 Troccoli moved back to Long Island and became the opening act for Jay Leno's Las Vegas shows; she also sang on sessions for Taylor Dayne. She released *Pure Attraction,* an album for the secular market, and toured with Michael Bolton, Boyz II Men, and Kenny Loggins. She recorded "I Can Hear Music" with the Beach Boys and had two singles on the pop charts, "Everything Changes" and "Tell Me Where It Hurts," in the early 1990s.

Troccoli returned to the Christian market and became a speaker at Christian women's events: Women of Faith, Time out for Women, and Heritage Keepers. Her song "Go Light Your World" was the theme song for the National Day of Prayer concert held in Washington, D.C., in 1999. She became the national spokesperson for Teen Life, a Catholic youth organization, and Chuck Colson's Prison Fellowship. She hosted a TV show with Mark Lowry ("The Mark and Kathy Show") on the Inspirational cable network and founded A Baby's Prayer Foundation to support pro-life causes.

In 1999 Troccoli and Sandi Patty did *Together,* an album of classic tunes from the American songbook; she also recorded "I Got It Bad (And That Ain't Good)" on the *Ultimate Ellington* album.

Don Cusic

For Further Reading

Alfonso, Barry. *The Billboard Guide to Contemporary Christian Music.* New York: Billboard Books/Watson-Guptill, 2002.

Powell, Mark Allen. *Encyclopedia of Contemporary Christian Music.* Peabody, Mass.: Hendrickson Publishers, Inc., 2002.

U

U2

Bono (b. Paul Hewson), vocals
Adam Clayton, bass
The Edge (b. David Evans), guitar, keyboard, vocals
Larry Mullen, Jr., drums

Is a rock band made up of Christians a Christian band? Is a rock band whose music and message are embraced by the contemporary Christian audience part of contemporary Christian music? The answers to those two questions determine whether or not someone believes that U2 belongs on a list of contemporary Christian music acts.

The group was formed in 1976 by students at Mount Temple High School and originally named Feedback, which played cover songs from rock acts such as the Rolling Stones and Beach Boys. They changed the name of the group to Hype before settling on U2 in 1978. That year they won a talent contest in Limerick, Ireland, and signed with manager Paul McGuiness, who negotiated a recording contract with CBS Records in Ireland. They released their debut EP, *Out of Control*, in 1979, which reached number one on the Irish pop chart.

The group was turned down by the U.K. office of CBS, so they signed with Island Records for the United States. The group was a critical success from their first album, *Boy*, released in 1980, although several previous singles had failed to chart. They toured the United States and then returned to Great Britain. In high school three members of the group were in Shalom, a Bible study group, and Bono, the son of a Catholic father and Protestant mother, was baptized in the Irish Sea. During their early tours the group—except bass player Adam Clayton—reportedly held Bible studies.

Their second album, *October*, was sold in Christian bookstores and reviewed in Christian periodicals. By their third album, *War*, the Christian audience was claiming them as their own, although they were signed to a secular label and pursued pop success. That album featured the hit single "Sunday, Bloody Sunday," about the Catholic-Protestant conflict in Northern Ireland.

Members of the rock group U2 pose for a studio portrait in April 1997. From left, guitarist Edge, drummer Larry Mullen, lead vocalist Bono, and bass player Adam Clayton. (AP Photo/Anton Corbijn, HO)

The *Joshua Tree* album, produced by Brian Eno and Daniel Lanois, contained their two biggest pop hits, "With or Without You" and "I Still Haven't Found What I'm Looking For." This was a breakthrough album, selling more than 15 million copies. This was also the beginning of Bono's public activism as he and his wife, Ali, went to Ethiopia, where they were involved in famine relief efforts.

U2 integrates their faith with their lives. American Christianity's emphasis on faith over works, and a "personal Savior" dedicated to making an individual's belief the center of their life, was not as appealing to Bono as reaching outward to the poor and disadvantaged in countries around the world. The group's secular fans did not really

acknowledge them as Christians, primarily because the image of Christians to many Americans was a narrow-minded isolated group whose leaders, such as Pat Robertson, James Dobson, Jerry Falwell and other members of the Religious Right, seemed to be intolerant of those who were not like them and aligned themselves with political conservatives who concentrated on issues such as abortion, gay marriage, and supporting the free market economics of the Republican party. The group did not perform at Christian festivals, did not do interviews with Christian periodicals, and did not see their music career as a ministry intent on converting nonbelievers. Instead, they were Christians as individuals who separated themselves from the American

Christian subculture; in essence, they were Christians outside of American Christianity. U2 supported Amnesty International, AIDS research, and the reduction of Third World debt—all considered "liberal" causes to the Christian Right.

Lyrically, the songs of U2 often emphasized the struggle between the forces of good and evil or light and dark. For *The Joshua Tree* album they embarked on a world tour and became one of the most popular acts in the world. Their double-live album, *Rattle and Hum*, reflected their crowd-pleasing live shows.

Although many in the Christian audience accepted them—primarily the children of those on the Religious Right who felt in U2 a breath of fresh air with the group's songs of social activism against a background of a personal struggle for salvation—the group caused controversy when Bono used the f-word a number of times when he accepted a Grammy in 1993. In 1995 at the MTV Awards in Paris, Bono took the opportunity to publicly criticize French President Jacques Chirac.

In 1999 Bono joined the Drop the Debt movement, originally named Jubilee 2000, which was dedicated to erasing the public debt of the world's poorest countries, many in Africa. Bono served as the ambassador for that movement.

In 2001 the song "Walk On" was dedicated to Burma's Nobel Peace Prize winner Aung San Suu Kyi, and in 2003 Bono and the Edge were part of a series of concerts hosted by Nelson Mandela in South Africa to promote HIV/AIDS awareness. In 2005 the band performed at the Live 8 concert in London, and that year U2 and their manager, Paul McGuinness, were awarded Amnesty International's Ambassador of Conscience Award. In 2006 the band raised money for the Global Fund and the American counterpart of Make Poverty History, the ONE Campaign, was promoted by Bono. The Edge promoted Music Rising in 2005 after Hurricanes Katrina and Rita to raise funds for musicians who lost their instruments during the storm.

In 2002 U2 performed at halftime of the Super Bowl, and in 2005 the group was inducted into the Rock and Roll Hall of Fame.

Don Cusic

Discography

Boy (1980)

October (1981)

War (1983)

Under a Blood Red Sky (EP) (1983)

The Unforgettable Fire (1984)

Wide Awake in America (EP) (1985)

The Joshua Tree (1987)

Rattle and Hum (1988)

Achtung Baby (1991)

Zooropa (1993)

Pop (1997)

The Best of 1980–1990 (1998)

The B-Sides (1998)

All That You Can't Leave Behind (2000)

The Best of 1990–2000 (2002)

How to Dismantle An Atomic Bomb (2004)

U2 18 Singles (2006)

Grammy Awards

1987   30th Grammy Awards: Album of the Year: *The Joshua Tree* (Producers: Brian Eno and Daniel Lanois)

1987   30th Grammy Awards: Best Rock Performance by a Duo or Group With Vocal. "The Joshua Tree"

1988   31st Grammy Awards: Best Performance Music Video: *Where the Streets Have No Name*

1988   31st Grammy Awards: Best Rock Performance by a Duo or Group with Vocal: "Desire"

1992   35th Grammy Awards: Best Rock Performance by a Duo or Group With Vocal: "Achtung Baby"

1993   36th Grammy Awards: Best Alternative Music Album: *Zooropa*

1984   37th Grammy Awards: Best Music Video, Long Form: *Zoo TV: Live from Sydney*

2000   43rd Grammy Awards: Best Rock Performance by a Duo or Group With Vocal: "Beautiful Day"

2000   43rd Grammy Awards: Song of the Year: "Beautiful Day." Songwriters: U2

2000   43rd Grammy Awards: Record of the Year: *Beautiful Day* (Producers: Brian Eno and Daniel Lanois)

2001   44th Grammy Awards: Best Rock Album: *All That You Can't Leave Behind* (Producers: Brian Eno and Daniel Lanois)

2001   44th Grammy Awards: Best Rock Performance by A Duo or Group With Vocal: "Elevation"

2001   44th Grammy Awards: Best Pop Performance by a Duo or Group With Vocal: "Stuck in a Moment You Can't Get out Of"

2001   44th Grammy Awards: Record of the Year: *Walk On*

2004   47th Grammy Awards: Best Short Form Music Video: *Vertigo*

2004   47th Grammy Awards: Best Rock Song: "Vertigo." Songwriters: U2

2004   47th Grammy Awards: Best Rock Performance by a Duo or Group With Vocal: "Vertigo"

2005   48th Grammy Awards: Album of the Year: *How to Dismantle an Atomic Bomb* (Producer: Steve Lillywhite)

2005   48th Grammy Awards: Song of the Year: "Sometimes You Can't Make It on Your Own." Songwriters: U2

2005   48th Grammy Awards: Best Rock Performance by a Duo or Group With Vocal: "Sometimes You Can't Make It on Your Own"

2005   48th Grammy Awards: Best Rock Song: "City of Blinding Lights." Songwriters: U2

2005   48th Grammy Awards: Best Rock Album: *How to Dismantle an Atomic Bomb* (Producer: Steve Lillywhite)

For Further Reading

Bordowitz, Hank, and U2. *The U2 Reader: A Quarter Century of Commentary, Criticism and Reviews.* New York: Hal Leonard, 2003.

Powell, Mark Allen. *Encyclopedia of Contemporary Christian Music*. Peabody, Mass.: Hendrickson Publishers, Inc., 2002.

Scharen, Christian. *One Step Closer: Why U2 Matters to Those Seeking God*. Ada, Mich.: Brazos Press, 2006.

Stockman, Steve. *Walk On: The Spiritual Journey of U2*. Orlando, Fla.: Relevant Books, 2005.

U2 and Neil McCormick. *U2 by U2*. New York: Harper, 2007.

Vagacs, Robert. *Religious Nuts, Political Fanatics: U2 in Theological Perspective*. Cascade, Iowa: Cascade Books, 2005.

V

VELASQUEZ, JACI

Jaci Velasquez (b. October 17, 1979) is the first full-fledged Hispanic superstar in contemporary Christian music; not only has she captured the Latino market but also she is a young female whose audience of young females see her as a role model.

Velasquez grew up in a musical home in Houston, Texas; her father, David Velasquez, was a member of a popular southern gospel group during the 1970s, the Four Galileans. That group disbanded before Jaci's birth, but her parents were musical missionaries and she first sang solos in church at three, then joined her parents on stage when she was ten. When she was 13 she sang at the White House. A performance in Houston in 1993, where the booking agent for Point of Grace was in attendance, led to a recording contract with Myrrh Records; her debut album, produced by Mark Heimermann, came in 1996 when she was 16 years old.

Jaci's debut and sophomore albums were both gold, and she signed with Sony Discos in 1999; ironically, she did not grow up speaking Spanish and only began speaking Spanish during her early teen years. Jaci became the first contemporary Christian artist to have a hit single on the Latin charts, and she developed a multicultural sound in her recordings. She became a national spokesperson for True Love Waits, a campaign that promises chastity until marriage, and wore a "purity ring" to symbolize her virginity before marriage.

Velasquez does not have deep family roots in the Hispanic community; her family is Protestant and most Latinos are Catholic and she did not grow up speaking Spanish; however, she soon became the leading Hispanic artist in contemporary Christian music, reaching both English and Spanish-speaking Americans. Velasquez became a columnist for *Campus Life* magazine and wrote a devotional book, *A Heavenly Place: Words of Inspiration to Bring a Little Bit of Peace and Paradise into Your Life* with Thom Granger.

Jaci Velasquez has had some heartbreaks during her life; her parents divorced and she was estranged from her father for awhile. (Ironically, her father won the Dove for "Best New Artist" in 1970 as member of the Four Galileans; Jaci won that same award 27 years later.)

In 2003 Jaci Velasquez married Darren Potluck; less than two years later she had a high profile divorce and moved to London for awhile. Then in December 2006, she married Nic Gonzales, leader of the group Salvador, and the two have a child.

Gospel Music Association Dove Awards

1997   New Artist of the Year: Jaci Velasquez

1999   Female Vocalist of the Year: Jaci Velasquez

2000   Female Vocalist of the Year: Jaci Velasquez

2000   Spanish Language Album of the Year: *Llegar a Ti Jaci Velasquez*; Producers: Rudy Perez and Mark Heimermann; Label: Myrrh

2000   Special Event Album: *Streams* by Cindy Morgan, Maire Brennan, Michael McDonald, Sixpence None the Richer, Chris Rodriguez, Michelle Tumes, 4HIM, Delirious, Amy Grant, Jaci Velasquez, Burlap to Cashmere, and Point of Grace; Producers: Brent Bourgeois, and Loren Balman; Label: Word)

2002   Spanish Language Album of the Year: *Mi Corazon*; Jaci Velasquez; Producers: Emilio Estefan, Jr. Rudy Perez, Mark Heimermann, Alberto Gaitin, Ricardo Gaitin, Alejandro

Jean, Freddy Pinero, Jr., Lewis Martinee, and Jose Miguel Velasquez; Label: Word

2003   Spanish Language Album of the Year: *Navidad*; Jaci Velasquez; Producer: Chris Harris for Fun Attic Prod. and Alejandro Jean; Label: Word

Don Cusic

Discography

Heavenly Place (1996)

Jaci Velasquez (1998)

Llegar a Ti (1999)

Crystal Clear (2000)

Mi Corazon (2001)

Christmas (2001)

Navidad (2001)

Milagro (2003)

Unspoken (2003)

Beauty Has Grace (2005)

On My Knees: The Best Of (2006)

Open House—Limited Edition Christmas EP (2007)

Love out Loud (2008)

For Further Reading

Alfonso, Barry. *The Billboard Guide to Contemporary Christian Music*. New York: Billboard Books/Watson-Guptill, 2002.

Powell, Mark Allen. *Encyclopedia of Contemporary Christian Music*. Peabody, Mass.: Hendrickson Publishers, Inc., 2002.

Velasquez, Jaci, with Thom Granger. *A Heavenly Place: Words of Inspiration to Bring a Little Bit of Peace and Paradise into Your Life.* Hoffman Estates, Ill.: Fireside, 1998.

VOLZ, GREG

Greg Volz (b. 1950) was the lead vocalist for Petra from 1980 to 1986, leading that group to the forefront of Christian rock. Volz grew up in Metamora, Illinois, and formed a rock band, the Wombats, when he was 13. He attended Illinois State University where he formed the group, Gideon's Bible; in 1970 he moved to Indianapolis where he formed another group, the E Band, a power trio featuring Dave Eden on drums, Greg Dunteman on bass, and Volz on guitar.

The E Band broke up in 1973, and Volz moved to Springfield, Missouri, where he worked with Phil Keaggy and played the lead role in *Ezekiel*, a Christian musical. Meanwhile, Petra had released their debut album with Bob Hartman handling lead vocals. For their second album, Petra recruited several vocalists, including Volz. After the album was released, Volz was invited to join Petra but he had a dilemma; REO Speedwagon also offered him the lead vocalist position. Volz chose Petra and was the lead singer for their albums *Never Say Die, More Power to Ya, Not of this World, Beat the System,* and *Captured in Time and Space.* Volz sang lead on Petra's hit single, "The Coloring Song," and on "Praise Ye the Lord," both songs from the E Band repertoire.

By 1986 the constant touring with Petra had taken a toll on his family, and personal clashes with Petra leader Bob Hartman led him to form a group, Piece of Eight, with former Wings drummer Joe England, and then embark on a solo career.

Volz released four solo albums for Myrrh between 1986 and 1991 and then formed his own label, River Records, where he continued to release product.

Don Cusic

For Further Reading

Alfonso, Barry. *The Billboard Guide to Contemporary Christian Music.* New York: Billboard Books/Watson-Guptill, 2002.

Cusic, Don. *The Sound of Light: A History of Gospel and Christian Music.* New York: Hal Leonard, 2002.

McNeil, W. K., ed. *Encyclopedia of American Gospel Music.* New York: Routledge, 2005.

Powell, Mark Allen. *Encyclopedia of Contemporary Christian Music.* Peabody, Mass.: Hendrickson Publishers, Inc., 2002.

W

WALSH, SHEILA

Sheila Walsh (b. in 1957 in Ayr, Scotland) was raised in a strict Baptist home in Ayr, the birthplace of poet and songwriter Robert Burns. She studied at the London Academy of Operatic Art, where she received training in classical music, and graduated from London Bible College in 1979. She became an associate evangelist with British Youth for Christ and sang with the Christian group the Oasis before she began her solo career in 1981. She toured with British pop star (and noted Christian) Cliff Richard and sang a punk-influenced music. In 1983 she made her first tour of the United States, opening for Phil Keaggy; she featured fireworks and smoke bombs in her concert, unaware that Christian music in the United States was more "tame" than it was in the U.K.

Her first album, *No One Loves Me Like You*, was released in the U.K. on a small label. Her second album, *Future Eyes*, produced by then-husband Norman Miller, who was president of Chapel Lane Records, and Larry Norman, became her first "official" release and the first to have distribution in the United States. Her follow-up, *War of Love*, was produced by Cliff Richard, and she sang a duet with Richard, "Jesus Call Your Lamb" on that release. As Walsh's career progressed, she moved toward an adult contemporary sound that was compatible with American audiences, and she became a top star in contemporary Christian music during the 1980s.

Walsh had hosted a BBC show, "The Gospel Rock Show," in the U.K. and during the period 1987–1992 became cohost of "The 700 Club" with Pat Robertson. In 1992 she was awarded the House of Hope Humanitarian Award and became a national spokesperson for that organization. That same year she was diagnosed with clinical depression and entered a psychiatric hospital. Her marriage dissolved and she left "The 700 Club," backing away from the public spotlight. This was a difficult period in Walsh's life, and she wrote about it in her book, *Honestly*, published by Zondervan in 1996.

After leaving "The 700 Club," Walsh earned a masters degree in theology and became affiliated with the Women of Faith organization. When she resumed her recording career she recorded a concept album, *Blue Waters*, which revealed her struggle with mental illness, then released *Love Falls Down*, an album of worship songs.

Walsh remarried, had a son, and resumed her career as an active speaker at women's conferences. She also wrote a number of books, including a series of children's books. She currently lives in Dallas.

Don Cusic

For Further Reading

Powell, Mark Allen. *Encyclopedia of Contemporary Christian Music*. Peabody, Mass.: Hendrickson Publishers, Inc., 2002.

WARNKE, MIKE

Mike Warnke was the top comedian in contemporary Christian music, wowing audiences with his humorous stories and ending each concert with a sermon and altar call until a scandal during the 1990s uncovered the fact that Warnke's claims of his past life as a Satanist priest were false.

Mike Warnke was a consummate performer who became famous after his book *The Satan Seller* (1972) was published. In the book Warnke claimed to have been a former high priest of Satanism who conducted satanic worship services; further, Warnke claimed he had also been a pimp and drug dealer before his conversion to Christianity.

Warnke's first album, *Mike Warnke Alive!* was released in 1976 on Myrrh as contemporary Christian music was gaining acceptance; his followup albums, *Jester in the King's Court* and *Hey, Doc!*, were released the following two years. Warnke developed a large following for his personal appearances and sold lots of records of his humorous routines where he told clean-cut mixed stories of his past life with a strong Christian message. In 1979 he released his second book, *Hitchhiking on Hope Street*, which was published by a mainstream publisher (Doubleday).

For 15 years Warnke was one of the top names in Christian entertainment; he not only appeared in Christian venues but also on "Larry King Live" and "The Oprah Winfrey Show" and was interviewed on "20/20." He presented himself as an expert on satanism and satanic worship and delivered a message of redemption from a sordid past.

Warnke's past caught up with him in June 1992 when *Cornerstone* magazine published an expose of Warnke's ministry, detailing that Warnke had simply made up the stories from his *Satan Seller* book. A full expose was published in a book by Mike Hertenstein and Jon Trott, *Selling Satan: The Tragic History of Mike Warnke*. It was revealed that Warnke had been a rather typical college student and never engaged in any of the satanist practices that he told about.

In 1991 Warnke and his wife, Rose, divorced; she had appeared with him on several of his albums, and after their divorce the two coauthored a book, *Recovering from Divorce* (1992). The *Cornerstone* article revealed that Rose was actually Warnke's third wife and that he had regularly engaged in sexual liaisons—and encouraged the musicians who traveled with him to do the same—during Christian concert tours.

He was also accused of drug abuse and drunkenness during his concert tours. Warnke was criticized for being overly concerned with money, accepting free will offerings at his concerts, but then badgering audiences to give more.

Warnke's comic routines consisted of exaggeration and embellishment with common, everyday stories, and after the exposure he admitted that he had exaggerated and embellished stories in his book *The Satan Seller*. Court records showed that he lived well; in 1991 he paid himself and ex-wife Rose, who continued to serve as codirector of his organization, a salary of $250,000 each. Their divorce showed that Warnke had extensive property holdings as well.

The Warnke scandal rocked the Christian world, and the contemporary Christian culture felt gullible and duped by Warnke. The secular world pointed a finger at the hypocrisy of a Christian world that allowed someone like a Mike Warnke to become a top Christian act.

Although Mike Warnke was "unmasked" during the 1990s and had to face a Christian media hostile to him, he continued to record with his fourth wife, Susan.

Don Cusic

Discography

Mike Warnke Alive! (1976)

Jester in the King's Court (1977)

Hey, Doc! (1978)

Coming Home (1981)

Higher Education (with Rose Warnke) (1982)

Growing Up (with Rose Warnke) (1983)

Stuff Happens (1985)

Good News Tonight (1986)

One in a Million (1988)

Live . . . Totally Weird (1989)

Out of my Mind (1991)

Full Speed Ahead (1992)

Jesus Loves Me (2001)

For Further Reading

Cusic, Don. *The Sound of Light: A History of Gospel and Christian Music*. New York: Hal Leonard, 2002.

Hertenstein, Mike, and Jon Trott. *Selling Satan: The Tragic History of Mike Warnke*. Chicago: Cornerstone Press, 1993.

Powell, Mark Allen. *Encyclopedia of Contemporary Christian Music*. Peabody, Mass.: Hendrickson Publishers, Inc., 2002.

Warnke, Mike. *Hitchhiking on Hope Street*. Garden City, N.Y.: Doubleday and Co., 1979.

Warnke, Mike. *The Satan Seller*. Bellingham, Wash.: Logos, 1972.

Warnke, Mike. *Schemes of Satan*. Old Hickory, Tenn.: Victory House, 1991.

Warnke, Mike, and Rose Warnke. *Recovering From Divorce*. Old Hickory, Tenn.: Victory House, 1992.

WATSON, WAYNE

Wayne Watson (b. 1955, in Wisner, Louisiana,) has a longevity in the field of contemporary Christian music rivaled by few others. Through his long recording career, which began with his album *Canvas for the Sun*, recorded for Archive in 1978, he has remained a steady presence on adult contemporary Christian radio.

Watson was raised a Southern Baptist in Louisiana and then Houston and attended Louisiana Tech University. He performed with the Continental Singers before he embarked on a solo career.

In 1980 he released his first album on Milk and Honey, *Workin' in the Final Hour* (1980), which was followed by *New Lives for Old* (1982), *Man in the Middle* (1984), and *Best of Wayne Watson* (1985), before he signed with Dayspring and released a series of albums on that label and Word.

Don Cusic

For Further Reading

Alfonso, Barry. *The Billboard Guide to Contemporary Christian Music*. New York: Billboard Books/Watson-Guptill, 2002.

Powell, Mark Allen. *Encyclopedia of Contemporary Christian Music*. Peabody, Mass.: Hendrickson Publishers, Inc., 2002.

Watson, Wayne. *Watercolor Ponies*. Waco, Tex.: Word, 1992.

WAY, THE

Dana Angle, guitars, vocals, bass
Gary Arthur, guitars, keyboards, bass
Bruce Herring, vocals
Ric Latendresse, guitars, vocals
(until 1973)
John Wickham, guitars, bass
(since 1973)
Alex MacDougall, drums, percussion
(since 1975)

The Way was in the first wave of Christian bands; like Love Song, they came from Calvary Chapel in Costa Mesa, California, and first appeared on the landmark *Everlastin' Living Jesus Music Concert* album released in 1971 by Maranatha, the church's label. The group sang "If You Will Believe" on that album and had two cuts on *Maranatha Two*, released the following year, and *Maranatha Four* in 1974.

The group's sound was reminiscent of the acoustic/folk sound popular in Southern California at the time, best demonstrated by the recordings of Crosby, Stills and Nash and other groups who played acoustic rock with a tinge of country.

Guitarist Jon Latendresse left the Way after their first album to become Maranatha's first accountant; drummer Alex McDougall later played with Daniel Amos and the Richie Furay Band; Gary Arthur and John Wickham joined Parable; and Bruce Herring was on a number of succeeding Maranatha releases.

Don Cusic

For Further Reading

Powell, Mark Allen. *Encyclopedia of Contemporary Christian Music*. Peabody, Mass.: Hendrickson Publishers, Inc., 2002.

WHITE HEART

White Heart was formed in Nashville in 1981 by two former members of the Bill Gaither Trio's touring band, guitarist Billy Smiley and keyboardist Mark

Gersmehl. Joining the duo were lead singer Steve Green (who gave the group its name after watching a video of Joan Jett and the Blackhearts), guitarist Dann Huff, bassist Gary Lunn, and drummer David Huff. The group changed personnel during its 17 years. In 1983, after their release of their debut album, *White Heart*, lead singer Green left and was replaced by Scott Douglas (real name: Scott Douglas Matthiesen); in 1985 Dann and David Huff left and were replaced by guitarist Gordon Kennedy and drummer Chris McHugh; in 1986 lead singer Scott Douglas left and was replaced by Ric Florian (who had been their bus driver); in 1988 Gary Lunn left and was replaced by Tommy Simms; in 1989 Sims, Kennedy, and McHugh left and were replaced by guitarist Brian Wooten, bassist Anthony Sallee, and drummer Mark Nemer; in 1992 Nemer left and was replaced by drummer Jon Knox; in 1995 Sallee left and was replaced by bassist John Thorn.

The group had great musicians; many of them played studio sessions in Nashville, and the talent of many of the individual members is evident from their post-White Heart success. Steve Green embarked on a successful solo career, Dann Huff played guitar for Michael Jackson and became an L.A. studio guitarist and producer of top acts, David Huff became the leader of David and the Giants, Tommy Simms joined Bruce Springsteen's touring band, Gordon Kennedy founded Dogs of Peace, and Gordon Kennedy and Simms wrote "Change Your World" for Eric Clapton.

The group played power pop, with most of their songs written by Billy Smiley and Mark Gersmehl. Their first single, "We Are His Hands," on Home Sweet Home Records, featured background vocals by Amy Grant and Russ Taff. The group toured constantly, and after their first three albums switched to Sparrow Records in 1986, then to Star Song in 1990, and finally to Curb Records in 1995, where they sought crossover success.

The group was touched by scandal when lead singer Scott Douglas was convicted of sex crimes and sentenced to prison in 1986; however, they continued with a strong dedication to ministry and held altar calls during their concerts.

The group disbanded in 1998.

Don Cusic

For Further Reading

Alfonso, Barry. *The Billboard Guide to Contemporary Christian Music.* New York: Billboard Books/Watson-Guptill, 2002.

Powell, Mark Allen. *Encyclopedia of Contemporary Christian Music.* Peabody, Mass.: Hendrickson Publishers, Inc., 2002.

Thompson, John J. *Raised by Wolves: The Story of Christian Rock and Roll.* Toronto, Ontario: ECW Press, 2000.

WILLARD, KELLY

Kelly Willard (nee Bagley, b. 1957) began her career in gospel music as a piano player for southern gospel groups; she performed with the Jake Hess Sound when she was 16, then played for the Oak Ridge Boys and the Archers. A native of Winter Haven,

Florida, Willard moved to Nashville when she became involved in southern gospel, and then moved to Oklahoma City where she was a founding member of the rock group Seth; also in that group was Jonathan David Brown. She married Maranatha engineer Dan Willard and left Seth to join Harlan Rogers and Friends, where she was first coaxed to sing lead vocals.

Willard's first contemporary Christian album, *Blame It on the One I Love,* was released on Maranatha in 1978; that album was produced by Jonathan David Brown. Her following two albums on Maranatha, *Psalms, Hymns, and Spiritual Songs* (1984) and *Message from a King* (1986), were produced by her husband.

In 1991, Willard announced her retirement from contemporary Christian music and dedicated her life to raising her family, singing background vocals in the studio, and writing songs.

Don Cusic

For Further Reading

Powell, Mark Allen. *Encyclopedia of Contemporary Christian Music*. Peabody, Mass.: Hendrickson Publishers, Inc., 2002.

WINANS, THE

The Winans are often called "the first family of gospel music." Mom and Pop Winans sang gospel music and raised their ten children in a Pentecostal Holiness church in Detroit; at home they sang only gospel. Nine of their ten children became recording artists: Carvin Jr., Marvin, Ronald, Angie, BeBe, CeCe, Daniel, Michael, and

Debbie; in addition, Vickie Winans, wife of Marvin, also records, and the group Winans Phase 2 is made up of the children of Carvin, Marvin, and Michael.

The first professional group from the Winans family, known as the Testimonial Singers, was a quartet, Carvin Jr., Marvin, Ronald, and a non-family member, Howard Smith, formed in 1975. They had a smooth, R&B sound with tight harmonies and released two albums. Howard Smith told Andrea Crouch about the group after Smith joined Crouch's group, and Crouch recruited them to tour with him, adding a fourth brother, Michael.

During the late 1970s the Winans toured with Andrea Crouch and Walter Hawkins; they sang on Crouch's records and Crouch produced their album *Introducing the Winans*. The group then signed with Qwest Records, the label owned and headed by Quincy Jones, and released albums for the secular market; they sang on Michael Jackson's *Bad* album, providing backing vocals on his song "Man in the Mirror."

The Winans used a number of top singers and musicians on their Qwest albums: Anita Baker, Michael McDonald, Kenny G., Stevie Wonder, Ricky Van Shelton, R. Kelly, and Kenny Loggins, and were widely criticized in the gospel community for using "worldly" sounds (like hip hop and rap) and secular musicians.

The Winans continued to perform, although Marvin became founder and pastor of a Detroit church, the Perfecting Church; Carvin recorded a children's album, and Ronald, Marvin, and Michael each recorded solo albums.

The most famous siblings in the Winans family are BeBe and CeCe

*Bebe, left, and Cece Winans pose during an August 1991 interview in New York City. (AP photo/
Dana Tynan)*

Winans (real names: Benjamin and
Priscilla); BeBe was the seventh child
and CeCe was the eighth and first girl
born to Pop and Mom Winans. The two
grew up singing together and, with
brothers Daniel and Michael, formed
the group Winans Part II.

In 1982 BeBe and CeCe Winans
joined the PTL Singers, which were featured on "The PTL Show" on TV hosted
by Jim and Tammy Bakker. They
recorded the album *Lord, Lift Us Up* as
part of that group. As their career progressed, BeBe and CeCe Winans caught
the attention of artists such as Anita
Baker, Natalie Cole, Freddie Jackson,
and Whitney Houston. They performed
with these artists and a number of others,
comfortable in an R&B styled gospel,
although their versatility enabled them to
cover a wide variety of material.

Their biggest album was *Different
Lifestyles*, which reached platinum status
and number one on the R&B charts. In
1995 CeCe began her solo career with a
duet with Whitney Houston on "Count
on Me," which was on the *Waiting to
Exhale* soundtrack. She hosted a TV program, "CeCe's Place," on the Odyssey
channel and endorsed Revlon cosmetics
and Crest toothpaste, becoming a
spokesperson for those products. CeCe
produced "Jesus Loves Me" for Whitney Houston on *The Bodyguard* soundtrack album and also produced Bobby
Brown, the Clark Sisters, Stephanie
Mills, and her sisters, Angie and Debbie
Winans. CeCe starred in *Your Arms Too
Short to Box with God* with Stephanie
Mills and appeared in the traveling musical *The Civil War*.

Don Cusic

Discography: The Winans

Introducing the Winans (1981)

Long Time Comin' (1983)

Tomorrow (1984)

Yesterday, Today and Tomorrow (1985)

Let My People Go (1985)

Decisions (1987)

Live at Carnegie Hall (1988)

Return (1990)

All Out (1993)

Heart and Soul (1995)

The Light Years (1995)

Discography: BeBe and CeCe Winans

Lord, Lift Us Up (1984)

BeBe and CeCe Winans (1987)

Heaven (1988)

Different Lifestyles (1992)

First Christmas (1992)

Relationships (1994)

Greatest Hits (1996)

Discography: BeBe Winans

BeBe Winans (1997)

Love and Freedom (2000)

Discography: CeCe Winans

Alone in his Presence (1995)

His Gift (1998)

Everlasting Love (1998)

Alabaster Box (1999)

CeCe Winans (2001)

Throne Room (2003)

Purified (2005)

Thy Kingdom Come (2008)

Gospel Music Association Dove Awards

The Winans

1986   Contemporary Gospel Album: *Let My People Go* by the Winans (Producer: Marvin Winans; Label: Qwest)

1988   Contemporary Gospel Album: *Decisions* by the Winans (Producers: Marvin Winans, Barry Hankerson, Carvin Winans, and Michael Winans; Label: Qwest)

1991   Rap/Hip Hop Recorded Song: "It's Time" (Writers: Marvin Winans, Carvin Winans, Teddy Riley, and Bernard Bell; Recorded by the Winans; Label: Warner Alliance)

1992   Contemporary Gospel Recorded Song (formerly Contemporary Black Gospel): "Addictive Love" (Writers: Keith Thomas, Benjamin Winans, and CeCe Winans; Recorded by BeBe and CeCe Winans; Label: Sparrow)

1997   Special Event Album: *Tribute—The Songs of Andrae Crouch* by CeCe Winans, Michael W. Smith, Twila Paris, Bryan Duncan, Wayne Watson, the Winans, Clay Crosse, Take 6, the Brooklyn Tabernacle Choir, First Call, Andrae Crouch, and the All Star Choir (Producers: Norman Miller and Neal Joseph; Label: Warner Alliance)

BeBe and CeCe Winans

1990 Contemporary Gospel Recorded Song: "With My Whole Heart" Written by Patrick Henderson and Louis Brown III; Recorded by BeBe and CeCe Winans; Label: Sparrow)

1990 Group of the Year: BeBe and CeCe Winans

1990 Pop/Contemporary Album: *Heaven* by BeBe and CeCe Winans (Producer: Keith Thomas; Label: Sparrow)

1990 Pop/Contemporary Recorded Song: "Heaven" Written by Keith Thomas and Benjamin Winans; Recorded by BeBe and CeCe Winans; Label: Sparrow

1992 Contemporary Gospel Recorded Song (formerly Contemporary Black Gospel): "Addictive Love" (Writers: Keith Thomas, Benjamin Winans, and CeCe Winans; Recorded by BeBe and CeCe Winans; Label: Sparrow)

1992 Group of the Year: BeBe and CeCe Winans

1998 Contemporary Gospel Recorded Song: "Up Where I Belong" Written by Will Jennings, Jack Nitschi, and Buffy Sainte-Marie; Recorded by BeBe and CeCe Winans; Label: Sparrow

BeBe Winans

2005 Special Event Album of the Year: *The Passion of the Christ*: Songs: Third Day, Steven Curtis Chapman, MercyMe, Scott Stap, POD, Brad Paisley, Sara Evans, Big Dismal, Lauryn Hill, Kirk Franklin, Yolanda Adams, MxPx, Mark Hoppus, Charlotte Church, BeBe Winans, Angie Stone, Dan Lavery; Tim Cook, Mark Joseph, Gregg Wattenberg, and Steven Lemer; Lost Keyword Records/Wind-Up Records

CeCe Winans

1992 Contemporary Gospel Recorded Song (formerly Contemporary Black Gospel): "Addictive Love" (Writers: Keith Thomas, Benjamin Winans, and CeCe Winans; Recorded by BeBe and CeCe Winans; Label: Sparrow)

1995 Praise and Worship Album: *Coram Deo II: Out of the Grey* by Steve Green, Margaret Becker, Charlie Peacock, Steven Curtis Chapman, CeCe Winans, and Bob Carlisle (Producer: Charlie Peacock; Label: Sparrow)

1996 Female Vocalist of the Year: CeCe Winans

1996 Traditional Gospel Recorded Song: "Great Is Thy Faithfulness" Written by Thomas Chisholm; Recorded by CeCe Winans; Label: Sparrow

1997 Contemporary Gospel Recorded Song: "Take Me Back" Written by Andrae Crouch; Recorded by CeCe Winans on the album *Tribute—*

the Songs of Andrae Crouch; Label: Warner Alliance

1997 Female Vocalist of the Year: CeCe Winans

1997 Special Event Album: *Tribute—the Songs of Andrae Crouch* by CeCe Winans, Michael W. Smith, Twila Paris, Bryan Duncan, Wayne Watson, the Winans, Clay Crosse, Take 6, the Brooklyn Tabernacle Choir, First Call, Andrae Crouch, and the All Star Choir (Producers: Norman Miller and Neal Joseph; Label: Warner Alliance)

1998 Special Event Album: *God with Us—a Celebration of Christmas Carols and Classics* by Anointed, Michael W. Smith, Twila Paris, Sandi Patty, Steven Curtis Chapman, Chris Willis, Steve Green, Cheri Keaggy, Avalon, Out of the Grey, Ray Boltz, Clay Crosse, CeCe Winans, and Larnelle Harris (Producer: Norman Miller; Label: Sparrow)

2001 Contemporary Gospel Recorded Song: "Alabaster Box" Written by Janice Sjostran; Recorded by CeCe Winans; Label: Wellspring Gospel

2002 Contemporary Gospel Album of the Year: *CeCe Winans*; CeCe Winans; Brown Bannister, Robbie Buchanon, Tommy Sims; Wellspring Gospel

2002 Contemporary Gospel Recorded Song of the Year: "Anybody Wanna Pray?" by CeCe Winans; CeCe Winans,

Cedric Caldwell, Victor Caldwell, Margaret Bell, Tommy Sims; Wellspring Gospel

2004 Contemporary Gospel Recorded Song of the Year: "Hallelujah Praise"; Throne Room; CeCe Winans; CeCe Winans, Cedric Caldwell, Victor Caldwell; Pure Springs Gospel

2004 Traditional Gospel Album of the Year: *CeCe Winans Present . . . The Born Again Church Choir*; The Born Again Church Choir; Cedric and Victor Caldwell; Pure Springs Gospel

Marvin Winans

1986 Contemporary Gospel Album: *Let My People Go* by the Winans (Producer: Marvin Winans; Label: Qwest)

1988 Contemporary Gospel Album: *Decisions* by the Winans (Producers: Marvin Winans, Barry Hankerson, Carvin Winans, and Michael Winans; Label: Qwest)

1991 Rap/Hip Hop Recorded Song: "It's Time" (Writers: Marvin Winans, Carvin Winans, Teddy Riley, and Bernard Bell; Recorded by the Winans; Label: Warner Alliance)

Grammy Awards
The Winans

1985 28th Grammy Awards: Best Soul Gospel Performance by a

Duo or Group, Choir or Chorus: The Winans: "Tomorrow"

1986 29th Grammy Awards: Best Soul Gospel Performance by a Duo or Group, Choir or Chorus: The Winans: "Let My People Go"

1987 30th Grammy Awards: Best Soul Gospel Performance by a Duo or Group, Choir or Chorus: Anita Baker, the Winans: "Ain't No Need to Worry"

1988 31st Grammy Awards: Best Gospel Performance by a Duo or Group, Choir or Chorus: *The Winans Live At Carnegie Hall* by the Winans

1989 32nd Grammy Awards: Best Gospel Vocal Performance, Female: "Don't Cry" by CeCe Winans

1993 36th Grammy Awards: Best Contemporary Soul Gospel Album: *All Out* by the Winans

BeBe and CeCe Winans

1991 34th Grammy Awards: Best Contemporary Soul Gospel Album: *Different Lifestyles* by CeCe and BeBe Winans

BeBe Winans

1988 31st Grammy Awards: Best Soul Gospel Performance, Male: "Abundant Life" by BeBe Winans

1989 32nd Grammy Awards: Best Gospel Vocal Performance, Male: "Meantime" by BeBe Winans

CeCe Winans

1987 30th Grammy Awards: Best Soul Gospel Performance, Female: CeCe Winans "For Always"

1995 38th Grammy Awards: Best Contemporary Soul Gospel Album: *Alone in His Presence* by CeCe Winans

2001 44th Grammy Awards: Best Pop/Contemporary Gospel Album: *CeCe Winans*; CeCe Winans

2005 48th Grammy Awards: Best Contemporary R&B Gospel Album: *Purified*; CeCe Winans

2005 48th Grammy Awards: Best Gospel Performance: "Pray"; CeCe Winans

Daniel Winans

1989 32nd Grammy Awards: Best Soul Gospel Performance by a Duo or Group, Choir or Chorus: "Let Brotherly Love Continue" by Daniel Winans

Martin Winans

1985 28th Grammy Awards: Best Soul Gospel Performance, Male: Marvin Winans: "Bring Back the Days of Yea and Nay"

For Further Reading

McNeil, W. K., ed. *Encyclopedia of American Gospel Music*. New York: Routledge, 2005.

Powell, Mark Allen. *Encyclopedia of Contemporary Christian Music*. Peabody, Mass.: Hendrickson Publishers, Inc., 2002.

Winans, CeCe, with Renita J. Weems. *On a Positive Note: CeCe Winans— Her Joyous Faith, Her Life in Music, and Her Everyday Blessings*. New York: Atria, 1999.

Z

ZOEGIRL

Zoe is Greek word for "life" or "eternal life" as used in the New Testament. ZOEgirl was formed by Chrissy Conway, Alisa Girard (daughter of Chuck Girard), and Kristin Swinford in 1999 as a Christian alternative to the young boy bands and girl singers (e.g., Backstreet Boys, N'Sync, Britney Spears) who were so successful in the late 1990s and early 2000s. They were an immediate hit with Christian teenagers (especially girls) because they used choreography in their Christian music shows. Their debut, released in 2000, was the fastest selling debut album in their label's history. They won the Dove for "New Artist of the Year" for 2002.

The group disbanded in late 2006 and Chrissy Conway formed a new group, ColemanBlue; Alisa (Girard) Childers released a solo album; and Kristin (Swinford) Schweain recorded a solo album.

Don Cusic

For Further Reading

Alfonso, Barry. *The Billboard Guide to Contemporary Christian Music.* New York: Billboard Books/Watson-Guptill, 2002.

Powell, Mark Allen. *Encyclopedia of Contemporary Christian Music.* Peabody, Mass.: Hendrickson Publishers, Inc., 2002.

ZONDERVAN

The Zondervan Corporation, based in Grand Rapids, Michigan, was a major Christian organization involved with contemporary Christian music during the 1970s and 1980s, when that genre experienced its greatest growth.

In 1931, P. J. (Pat) Zondervan (b. 1909) founded Zondervan Publishing House after his Uncle Bill Eerdmans fired him from Eerdmans Publishing Company. Initially, Pat and his brother Bernard (Bernie) Zondervan operated a direct mail religious bookselling company out of their mother's farmhouse in Grandville, Michigan. A bookstore was opened in Grand Rapids the following year. In 1933, they published their first book titled *Women of the Old Testament*.

The company expanded into religious music publishing when Zondervan bought Singspiration in 1959. The following year, the company assumed publication of *Halley's Bible Handbook* from a private firm. This title would go on to sell more than four million copies.

Zondervan expanded their production of Bibles and Bible related products when they purchased the Bible department from Harper and Row in 1966. Among the titles Zondervan assumed as a result of this acquisition included the popular *Harper Study Bible*. Also in this year Bernie died and his son, Bernie Jr., ascended to the position of vice-president of the company. Bernie Jr. died in 1970 at the age of 34.

In 1973, Zondervan formed a partnership with the International Bible Society to publish the *New International Version (NIV) New Testament*. The complete *NIV Bible* was first published in 1978. Zondervan has renewed its contract with the International Bible Society to continue publishing the *NIV* through 2023. As of 2005, the NIV Bibles have sold more than 150 million copies worldwide.

The TNIV, an updated and gender neutral version of *The NIV Bible*, made national news when Zondervan launched this version with a $1 million advertising "hip" campaign in 2005. *Rolling Stone* magazine initially refused to carry the ad on the grounds that their audience would rebel against a Bible advertisement. Following a slew of media coverage for this story, *Rolling Stone* decided to publish the TNIV ad.

Other Bibles published by Zondervan include the *New International Reader's Version* (NIrV), a Bible designed for those with reading difficulties, as well as the *New American Standard Bible, Amplified, The Good News Translation of the Bible*, the *African-American Devotional Bible*, and the *Collegiate Devotional Bible*.

Zondervan issued stock on the NASDAQ in 1976, thus becoming a publicly traded company. Accounting irregularities dating from 1979 through 1983 led to sanctions by the Securities and Exchange Commission. In the 1980s Zondervan sold off Revell and Chosen Books and acquired the John T. Benson Company, Chosen Books, Francis Asbury Press, Fleming H. Revell Company, and Tapley-Rutter Company.

Pat Zondervan retired from the Zondervan Corporation in 1984. That same year, he was inducted into the Gospel Music Association's Hall of Fame. He died in 1993.

In 1988, Zondervan became a division of HarperCollins Publishers, a publishing giant formed by the mergers of Harper and Row and Collins Publishing. The New Media division was formed the following year. The software, video, and audio product divisions merged in 1995 under the name ZPH New Media, marketing their products primarily to Christian bookstores. Zondervan's children line was renamed Zonderkidz in 1998. Big Idea partnered with Zonderkidz in 2002 to publish the popular VeggieTales books, videos, and other products.

Zondervan's gift category, Inspiro, was launched in 2000 to sell nonbook and music related products. The music division was sold in 1992. In the same year, the company split with

HarperCollins, assuming ownership of the bookstore division.

Their international offerings expanded in 1995 when Zondervan purchased Editorial Vida, a company that distributes Bibles in French, Spanish, and Portuguese. Then, in 2001, Zondervan assumed the publishing responsibilities for Marshall Pickering, a HarperCollins U.K. imprint that carries evangelical and Anglican titles.

In 2006, Zondervan began hosting the National Pastors Convention, an annual gathering for ordained and lay church leaders. Also in that year they acquired Youth Specialties, thus cementing a 30-year working relationship that produced products geared for youth workers.

Zondervan expanded their multicultural offerings by publishing *The Africa Bible Commentary* in 2005 and then releasing *Inspired By: The Bible Experience* audio bible in 2007. The *Inspired By: The Bible Experience* combined Old and New Testaments CDs that featured a star-studded cast of 400, including 3 Oscar winners, 5 Golden Globe winners, 7 Emmy winners, and 23 Grammy winners.

Currently, Zondervan lists more than 2,000 Bible, book, and other product titles in its catalog. They market approximately 60 Bible editions, 150 books, 80 gifts, and 50 new media products each year. These products are sold worldwide to more than 60 countries.

Zondervan's best-selling authors include Terri Blackstock, Ben Carson, Shane Claiborne, Henry Cloud, Charles Colson, Billy Graham, Bill Hybels, Karen Kingsbury, Ruth Graham Lott, Brian McLaren, John Otberg, Les and Leslie Parson, Lee Strobel, Joni Erickson Tada, John Townsend, Rick Warren, Philip Yancey, and Ravi Zacharias. In addition to traditional Christian authors, Zondervan publishes books with a broader mass appeal, such as Hal Lindsey's *The Late Great Planet Earth*, and authors that cross over to the secular market like Dave Dravecky, Oliver North, and Dan Quayle. Currently, Zondervan has 41 Bibles and books that have sold more than 500,000 copies in print as well as Rick Warren's international best seller, *The Purpose Driven Life,* which has sold more than 30 million copies to date.

Zondervan was named one of the top 40 Christian places to work in America by *Christianity Today* magazine. Finalists were selected based on employee surveys compiled by the Best Christian Workplaces Institute and published in the May 2005 issue.

As of 2007, Zondervan has earned a total of 80 Gold Medallion awards for its books and Bibles from the Evangelical Publishers Association. To date, Christian Bookseller's Association (CBA) awarded Zondervan the title Supplier of the Year seven times.

Becky Garrison

For Further Reading

Powell, Mark Allen. *Encyclopedia of Contemporary Christian Music.* Peabody, Mass.: Hendrickson Publishers, Inc., 2002.

Bibliography

Alfonso, Barry. *The Billboard Guide to Contemporary Christian Music.* New York: Billboard Books/Watson-Guptill, 2002.

Anderson, Robert, and Gail North. *Gospel Music Encyclopedia.* New York: Sterling, 1979.

Anderson, Robert Mapes. *Vision of the Disinherited: The Making of American Pentecostalism.* New York: Oxford, 1979.

Applebome, Peter. *Dixie Rising: How the South Is Shaping American Values, Politics, and Culture.* New York: Times Books, 1996.

Armstrong, Ben. *The Electric Church.* Nashville, Tenn.: Thomas Nelson, 1979.

Baer, Hans A. *The Black Spiritual Movement: A Religious Response to Racism.* Knoxville: University of Tennessee Press, 1974.

Bailey, Albert Edward. *The Gospel in Hymns.* New York: Charles Scribner's Sons, 1950.

Baker, Paul. *Contemporary Christian Music: Where It Came from, What It Is, Where It's Going.* Westchester, Ill.: Crossway, 1985.

Baker, Paul. *I've Got a New Song.* San Diego, Calif.: Scandinavia, 1983.

Baker, Paul. *Topical Index of Contemporary Christian Music.* Pinson, Ala.: Music Helps, 1987.

Baker, Paul. *Why Should the Devil Have All the Good Music.* Waco, Tex.: Word, 1979.

Balmer, Randall. *Mine Eyes Have Seen the Glory: A Journey into the Evangelical Subculture of America.* Oxford: Oxford University Press, 1989.

Becker, Margaret. *Coming Up for Air: Simple Acts to Redefine Your Life.* Irvine, Calif.: Harvest House, 2006.

Becker, Margaret. *Growing Up Together.* Eugene, Ore.: Harvest House, 2000.

Becker, Margaret. *With New Eyes: Fresh Vision for the Soul.* Eugene, Ore.: Harvest House, 1998.

Becker, Paula. *Let the Song Go On.* Nashville, Tenn.: Impact, 1971.

Berkman, Dave. "Long Before Falwell: Early Radio and Religion—as Reported by the Nation's Periodical Press." *Journal of Popular Culture* 21 (1988): 1–11.

Blackwell, Lois S. *The Wings of the Dove.* Norfolk, Va.: The Donning Co., 1978.

Blackwood, James, with Dan Martin. *The James Blackwood Story.* Monroeville, Penn.: Whitaker House, 1975.

Bonner, Clint. *A Hymn Is Born.* Nashville, Tenn.: Broadman Press, 1959.

Boone, Debby, and Dennis Baker. *Debby Boone So Far.* Nashville, Tenn.: Thomas Nelson, 1981.

Boone, Pat. *A New Song.* Peabody, Mass.: Charisma House, 1988.

Boone, Pat. *Pat Boone's America.* Nashville, Tenn.: B&H Publishing Group, 2006.

Bordowitz, Hank, and U2. *The U2 Reader: A Quarter Century of Commentary, Criticism and Reviews*. New York: Hal Leonard, 2003.

Borlase, Craig. *Purepop: The Delirious Journey So Far*. Littlehampton, U.K.: Furoous Press, 1998.

Boyer, Horace Clarence, text, Lloyd Yearwood, photography. *How Sweet the Sound: The Golden Age of Gospel*. Washington, D.C.: Elliott and Clark, 1995.

Bronson, Fred. *The Billboard Book of Number One Hits*. New York: Billboard Books, 1985.

Bronson, Fred. *Billboard's Hottest 100 Hits*. New York: Billboard Books, 1991.

Brothers, Jeffrey Lee. *CCM Magazine Hot Hits: Adult Contemporary Charts 1978–2001*. Bloomington, Ind.: 1stBooks Library, 2003.

Broughton, Viv. *Black Gospel*. Pool, U.K.: Blandford, 1985.

Brown, Scott Wesley. *Keeping the Gospel in Gospel Music*. Nashville, Tenn.: American Christian Writers, 1998.

Bruce, Dickson D., Jr. *And They All Sang Hallelujah*. Knoxville: University of Tennessee Press, 1974.

Burt, Jesse, and Duane Allen. *The History of Gospel Music*. Nashville, Tenn.: K&S Press, 1971.

Carmichael, Ralph. *He's Everything to Me*. Waco, Tex.: Word Books, 1986.

Carpenter, Bil. *Uncloudy Days: The Gospel Music Encyclopedia*. San Francisco: Backbeat, 2005.

Cash, Johnny. *Man in Black*. Grand Rapids, Mich.: Zondervan, 1975.

Cash, Johnny, with Patrick Carr. *Cash: The Autobiography*. San Francisco: HarperSanFrancisco, 1997.

Cash, June Carter. *Among My Klediments*. Grand Rapids, Mich.: Zondervan, 1979.

Cone, James H. *The Spirituals and the Blues: An Interpretation*. New York: Seabury, 1972.

Conn, Charles Paul. *The New Johnny Cash*. Old Tappan, N.J.: Spire, 1976.

Crouch, Andrae, with Nina Ball. *Through It All*. Waco, Tex.: Word, 1974.

Crowder, David. *Praise Habit: Finding God in Sunsets and Sushi*. Colorado Springs, Colo.: NavPress, 2005.

Crowder, David, and Mike Hogan. *Everybody Wants to Go to Heaven but Nobody Wants to Die (or, The Eschatology of Bluegrass)*. Orlando, Fla.: Relevant Books, 2006.

Cusic, Don. *Johnny Cash: The Songs*. New York: Thunder's Mouth, 2006.

Cusic, Don. *Sandi Patti: The Voice of Gospel*. New York: Dolphin/Doubleday, 1988.

Cusic, Don. *The Sound of Light: A History of Gospel and Christian Music*. New York: Hal Leonard, 2002.

Darden, Bob. *People Get Ready!: A New History of Black Gospel Music*. New York: Continuum, 2005.

Davis, Paul. *Pat Boone: The Authorized Biography: April Love: The Early Days of Rock 'n' Roll*. Grand Rapids, Mich.: Zondervan, 2001.

Dickerson, Dez. *My Time with Prince—Confessions of a Former Revolutionary*. Philadelphia: Pavilion Press, 2003.

DiMucci, Dion, with Davin Seay. *The Wanderer: Dion's Story*. Minneapolis, Minn.: Quill House, 1989.

Dowley, Tim, ed. *Eerdmans Handbook to the History of Christianity*. Grand Rapids, Mich.: Eerdmans, 1977.

Ellwood, Robert S., Jr. *One Way: The Jesus Movement and Its Meaning*. Englewood Cliffs, N.J.: Prentice-Hall, 1973.

English, Michael. *The Prodigal Comes Home: My Story of Failure and God's Story of Redemption*. Nashville, Tenn.: Thomas Nelson, 2007.

Enroth, Ronald M., Edward E. Ericson, Jr., and C. Breckinridge Peters. *The Jesus People: Old-Time Religion in the Age of Aquarius*. Grand Rapids, Mich.: Eerdmans, 1972.

Epstein, Dena J. *Sinful Tunes and Spirituals*. Urbana: University of Illinois Press, 1977.

Epstein, Jonathan S., ed. *Adolescents and Their Music: If It's Too Loud, You're Too Old*. New York: Garland, 1995.

Erickson, Dale, and Jesse Sturdevant. *Stryper: Loud and Clear*. College Park, Md.: Classic CD Books, 2001.

Eskew, Harry. "White Urban Hymnody." Jacket notes on *Brighten the Corner Where You Are*. South Weymouth, Mass.: New World, n.d.

Eskridge, Larry. *Sweet, Sweet Song of Salvation: The Jesus People Movement and American Evangelicalism, 1967–1977*. New York: Oxford University Press, 2009.

Fahlbusch, Erwin. *The Encyclopedia of Christianity*. Grand Rapids, Mich.: Eerdmans, 1999.

Fischer, John. *Ashes on the Wind*. Grand Rapids, Mich.: Bethany House, 1998.

Fischer, John. *Be Thou My Vision*. Grand Rapids, Mich.: Bethany House, 1995.

Fischer, John. *Dark Horse*. Old Tappan, N.J.: Fleming H. Revell, 1983.

Fischer, John. *Fearless Faith*. Grand Rapids, Mich.: Bethany House, 2002.

Fischer, John. *Making Real What I Already Believe*. Grand Rapids, Mich.: Bethany House, 1991.

Fischer, John. *On a Hill Too Far Away*. Grand Rapids, Mich.: Bethany House, 1994.

Fischer, John. *Real Christians Don't Dance*. Grand Rapids, Mich.: Bethany House, 1988.

Fischer, John. *Saint Ben*. Grand Rapids, Mich.: Bethany House, 1993.

Fischer, John. *The Saints and Angels' Song*. Grand Rapids, Mich.: Bethany House, 1994.

Fischer, John. *True Believers Don't Ask Why*. Grand Rapids, Mich.: Bethany House, 1989.

Fischer, John. *12 Steps for the Recovering Pharisee (Like Me)*. Grand Rapids, Mich.: Bethany House, 2000.

Fischer, John. *What on Earth Are We Doing?* Grand Rapids, Mich.: Bethany House, 1997.

Fishwick, Marshall, and Ray B. Browne, ed. *The God Pumpers: Religion in the Electronic Age*. Bowling Green, Ohio: Popular Press, 1987.

Flake, Carol. *Redemptorama: Culture, Politics and the New Evangelism*. Garden City, N.Y.: Anchor and Doubleday, 1984.

Flanagan, Bill. *U2: At the End of the World*. Concord, Calif.: Delta, 1996.

Ford, Tennessee Ernie. *This Is My Story, This Is My Song*. Englewood Cliffs, N.J.: Prentice-Hall, 1963.

Forntale, Peter, and Joshua E. Mills. *Radio in the Television Age*. Woodstock, N.Y.: The Overlook Press, 1980.

Franklin, Aretha, and David Ritz. *Aretha: From These Roots*. New York: Villard, 1999.

Frazier, E. Franklin. *The Negro Church in America, 1963*. Reprint. New York: Schocken Books, 1974.

Friedlander, Paul. *Rock and Roll: A Social History*. Boulder, Colo.: Westview, 1996.

Frith, Simon, ed. *Facing the Music: Essays on Pop, Rock, and Culture*. London: Mandarin, 1990.

Frith, Simon, ed. *Sound Effects: Youth, Leisure, and the Politics of Rock*. London: Constable and Company Ltd., 1983.

Furay, Richie. *There's Something Happening Here: The Story of Buffalo Springfield for What It's Worth*. Dallas: Quarry Press, 1997.

Gaither, Bill, and Ken Abraham. *It's More Than Music: Life Lessons on Friends, Faith and What Matters Most*. New York: Warner Faith, 2003.

Gaither, Bill, and Gloria Gaither. *God Gave Song*. Grand Rapids, Mich.: Zondervan, 2000.

Gaither, Bill, and Jerry Jerkins. *Homecoming*. Grand Rapids, Mich.: Zondervan, 1997.

Gaither, Bill, and Jerry Jerkins. *I Almost Missed the Sunset*. Nashville, Tenn.: Thomas Nelson, 1992.

Gallup, George, Jr., and David Poling. *The Search for America's Faith*. Nashville, Tenn.: Abingdon, 1980.

Gentry, Linnell. *A History and Encyclopedia of Country, Western, and Gospel Music*. Nashville, Tenn.: Clairmont Corp., 1969.

Gilmour, Michael J., ed. *Call Me the Seeker: Listening to Religion in Popular Music*. New York: Continuum, 2005.

Godwin, Jeff. *What's Wrong with Christian Rock?* Chino, Calif.: Chick, 1990.

Goff, James R., Jr. *Close Harmony: A History of Southern Gospel.* Chapel Hill: University of North Carolina Press, 2002.

Goreau, Laurraine. *Just Mahalia, Baby: The Mahalia Jackson Story.* Waco, Tex.: Word Books 1975.

Granger, Thom, ed. *CCM Presents the 100 Greatest Albums in Christian Music.* Eugene, Ore.: Harvest House, 2001.

Graves, Michael P., and David Fillingim, eds. *More Than Precious Memories: The Rhetoric of Southern Gospel Music.* Macon, Ga.: Mercer University Press, 2004.

Green, Melody, and David Hazard. *No Compromise: The Life Story of Keith Green.* Chatsworth Calif.: Sparrow, 1989.

Grine, Janny. *Called, Appointed, Anointed.* Tulsa, Okla.: Harrison House, 1985.

Guralnick, Peter. *Careless Love: The Unmaking of Elvis Presley.* Boston: Little, Brown, 1999.

Guralnick, Peter. *Last Train to Memphis: The Rise of Elvis Presley.* Boston: Little, Brown, 1994.

Guralnick, Peter. *Sweet Soul Music.* New York: Harper & Row, 1986.

Guralnick, Peter, and Ernst Jorgensen. *Elvis Day by Day: The Definitive Record of His Life and Music.* New York: Ballantine, 1999.

Hall, Mark. *Lifestories.* Nashville, Tenn.: Brentwood Music, 2006.

Hall, Sammy, with Charles Paul Conn. *Hooked on a Good Thing.* Old Tappan, N.J.: Fleming H. Revell, 1972.

Hardy, Phil, and Dave Laing. *The Faber Companion to 20th-Century Popular Music.* London: Faber and Faber, 1990.

Harris, Michael W. *The Rise of Gospel Blues: The Music of Thomas Andrew Dorsey in the Urban Church.* New York: Oxford University Press, 1992.

Hartman, Bob. *More Power to Ya.* Cincinnati, Ohio: Standard Publishing, 1997.

Haynes, Michael K. *The God of Rock: A Christian Perspective of Rock Music.* Lindale, Tex.: Priority, 1982.

Heilbut, Tony. *The Gospel Sound: Good News and Bad Times.* New York: Simon and Schuster, 1971.

Henderson, Stewart. *Greenbelt—Since the Beginning.* Ipswich, U.K.: Ancient House Press, 1983.

Henry, Carl F. *The Uneasy Conscience of Modern Fundamentalism.* Grand Rapids, Mich.: Eerdmans, 1947.

Herring, Annie. *Glimpses: Seeing God in Everyday Life.* Grand Rapids, Mich.: Bethany House, 1996.

Hertenstein, Mike, and Jon Trott. *Selling Satan: The Tragic History of Mike Warnke.* Chicago: Cornerstone Press, 1993.

Hess, Jake, with Richard Hyatt. *Nothin' but Fine: The Music and the Gospel According to Jake Hess.* Columbus, Ga.: Buckland Press, 1996.

Holm, Dallas, with Robert Paul Lamb. *This Is My Story.* Nashville, Tenn.: Impact, 1980.

Hopkins, Jerry. *Elvis: A Biography.* New York: Warner, 1971.

Hopkins, Jerry. *Elvis: The Final Years.* New York: Playboy, 1981.

Horsfield, Peter G. *Religious Television: An American Experience.* New York: Longman, 1984.

Horton, Michael S. *Made in America: The Shaping of Modern American Evangelicalism.* Grand Rapids, Mich.: Baker, 1991.

Howard, Jay R., and John M. Streck. *Apostles of Rock: The Splintered World of Contemporary Christian Music.* Lexington: University Press of Kentucky, 1999.

Humphries, Rick. "KFMK Meets the Needs of Houston." *New Jerusalem Magazine* 1 (1976).

Hunter, James Davison. *American Evangelicalism: Conservative Religion and the Quandary of Modernity.* New Brunswick, N.J.: Rutgers University Press, 1983.

Ingalls, Jeremiah. *The Christian Harmony.* New York: Da Capo, 1981.

Jackson, Irene. *Afro-American Religious Music.* Westport, Conn.: Greenwood Press, 1979.

Jackson, Jerma A. *Singing in My Soul: Black Gospel Music in a Secular Age.* Chapel Hill: University of North Carolina Press, 2004.

Johnson, James Weldon, ed. *The Second Book of Negro Spirituals.* New York: Viking, 1926.

Johnson, James Weldon, and J. Rosamond Johnson. *American Negro Spirituals.* New York: Viking, 1925.

Jorstad, Erling. *Popular Religion in America: The Evangelical Voice.* Westport, Conn.: Greenwood, 1993.

Keith, Michael C. *Radio Programming: Consultancy and Formatics.* Boston: Focal Press, 1987.

Keith, Michael C. *The Radio Station.* 6th ed. Boston: Focal Press, 2004.

Key, Dana, with Steve Rabey. *Don't Stop the Music.* Grand Rapids, Mich.: Zondervan, 1989.

Krasilovsky, M. William, and Sidney Shemel. *This Business of Music: The Definitive Guide to the Music Industry.* 8th ed. New York: Billboard Books, 2000.

Landy, Elliott. *Woodstock Vision: The Spirit of a Generation.* New York: Landyvision, 1996.

Larkins, Colin, ed. *The Virgin Encyclopedia of Popular Music.* London: Virgin, 2002.

Larson, Bob. *The Day the Music Died.* Carol Stream, Ill.: Creation House, 1972.

Larson, Bob. *Hippies, Hindus, and Rock & Roll.* McCook, Neb.: Larson, 1969.

Larson, Bob. *Rock.* Wheaton, Ill.: Tyndale House, 1980.

Larson, Bob. *Rock and Roll: The Devil's Diversion.* McCook, Neb.: Larson, 1967.

Larson, Bob. *Rock and the Church.* Carol Stream, Ill.: Creation House, 1971.

Liesch, Barry. *The New Worship: Straight Talk on Music and the Church.* Grand Rapids, Mich.: Baker, 1996.

Livgren, Kerry, with Kenneth Boa. *Seeds of Change.* Canoga Park, Calif.: Sparrow Books, 1983, 1991.

Lovell, John, Jr. *Black Song: The Forge and the Flame: The Story of How the Afro-American Spiritual Was Hammered Out.* New York: Macmillan, 1972.

Marsden, George M. *Fundamentalism and American Culture: The Shaping of Twentieth-Century Fundamentalism, 1870–1925.* Oxford: Oxford University Press, 1980.

Marsden, George M. *Reforming Fundamentalism.* Grand Rapids, Mich.: Eerdmans, 1987.

Marsden, George M. *Understanding Fundamentalism and Evangelicalism.* Grand Rapids, Mich.: Eerdmans, 1991.

Marsh, J. B. T. *The Story of the Jubilee Singers; with Their Songs.* Boston: Houghton, Mifflin and Company, 1881.

Martin, Linda, and Kerry Segrave. *Anti-Rock: The Opposition to Rock 'n' Roll.* Hamden, Conn.: Archon Books, 1988.

Mays, Benjamin E., and Joseph W. Nicholson. *The Negro's Church.* 1933. Reprint. New York: Arno Press, 1969.

McLoughlin, William G., Jr. *Billy Sunday Was His Real Name.* Chicago: University of Chicago Press, 1955.

McNeil, W. K., ed. *Encyclopedia of American Gospel Music.* New York: Routledge, 2005.

Medema, Ken, with Joyce Norman. *Come and See.* Waco, Tex.: Word, 1976.

Mellers, Wilfred. *A Darker Shade of Pale: A Backdrop to Bob Dylan.* New York: Oxford University Press, 1985.

Millard, Bob. *Amy Grant.* New York: Dolphin/Doubleday, 1986.

Miller, Steve. *The Contemporary Christian Music Debate: Worldly Compromise or Agent of Change.* Wheaton, Ill.: Tyndale House Publishers, Inc. 1993.

Moore, R. Lawrence. *Selling God: American Religion in the Marketplace of Culture.* New York: Oxford University Press, 1994.

Moscheo, Joe. *The Gospel Side of Elvis.* New York: Center Street, 2007.

Mullins, Rich. *Home.* Orlando, Fla.: Voxcorp, 1998.

Mullins, Rich. *Simply.* Orlando, Fla.: Voxcorp, 2005.

Mullins, Rich. *The World as I Remember It, Through the Eyes of a Ragamuffin.* Colorado Springs, Colo.: Multnomah, 2004.

Murray, David Bruce. *Murray's Encyclopedia of Southern Gospel Music*. Privately published, 2005.

Murrells, Joseph. *Million Selling Records*. New York: Arco, 1984.

Myers, Kenneth A. *All God's Children and Blue Suede Shoes: Christians and Popular Culture*. Wheaton, Ill.: Crossway, 1989.

Nichol, John Thomas. *Pentecostalism*. Plainfield, N.J.: Logos, 1966.

Nobel, E. Maron. *The Gospel of Music*. Washington, D.C.: MAR Press, 1971.

Nutt, Grady. *So Good, So Far.. . .* Nashville, Tenn.: Impact, 1979.

Oak Ridge Boys, with Ellis Widner and Walter Carter. *The Oak Ridge Boys: Our Story*. Chicago: Contemporary, 1987.

Odum, Howard W., and Guy B. Johnson. *The Negro and His Songs: A Study of Typical Negro Songs in the South*. Chapel Hill: University of North Carolina Press, 1925.

Oldham, Doug, with Fred Bauer. *I Don't Live There Anymore*. Nashville, Tenn.: Impact, 1973.

Oliver, Paul. *Blues off the Record*. Kent, U.K.: Baton Press, 1984.

Oliver, Paul. *Screening the Blues: Aspects of the Blues Tradition*. New York: Da Capo, 1968.

Oliver, Paul. *Songsters and Saints: Vocal Traditions on Race Records*. Cambridge: Cambridge University Press, 1984.

Oliver, Paul, Max Harrison, and William Bolcom. *The New Grove Gospel, Blues and Jazz*. New York: W. W. Norton, 1986.

O'Neil, Thomas. *The Grammys for the Record*. New York: Penguin, 1993.

O'Neill, Dan. *Troubadour for the Lord: The Story of John Michael Talbot*. New York: Crossroad, 1983.

Orgill, Michael. *Anchored in Love: The Carter Family*. Old Tappan, N.J.: Fleming H. Revell, 1975.

Owens, J. Garfield. *All God's Chillun*. New York: Abington, 1971.

Patti, Sandi. *The Book of Words*. Milwaukee, Wis.: Hal Leonard, 1986.

Peacock, Charlie, with Molly Nicholas. *At the Crossroads: Inside the Past, Present, and Future of Contemporary Christian Music*. Colorado Springs, Colo.: Shaw Books, 2004.

Peters, Dan, and Steve Peters with Cher Merrill. *Rock's Hidden Persuader: The Truth about Backmasking*. Minneapolis, Minn.: Bethany, 1985.

Peters, Dan, and Steve Peters with Cher Merrill. *What about Christian Rock?* Minneapolis, Minn.: Bethany House, 1986.

Peters, Dan, and Steve Peters with Cher Merrill. *Why Knock Rock?* Minneapolis, Minn.: Bethany, 1984.

Pike, G. D. *Jubilee Singers, and their Campaign for Twenty Thousand Dollars*. New York: AMS Press, Inc., 1974, reprinted from edition from Boston: Lee and Shepard, Publishers; New York: Lee, Shepard and Dillingham, 1873.

Point of Grace. *Circle of Friends*. West Monroe, La.: Howard Books, 1999.

Point of Grace. *Girls of Grace*. West Monroe, La.: Howard Books, 2002.

Point of Grace. *Girls of Grace: Make It Real*. West Monroe, La.: Howard Books, 2005.

Point of Grace. *Girls of Grace: Q&A with Point of Grace*. West Monroe, La.: Howard Books, 2004.

Point of Grace. *Keep the Candle Burning: Reflections from Our Favorite Songs*. West Monroe, La.: Howard Books, 2003.

Point of Grace. *Steady On . . . Secured by Love*. West Monroe, La.: Howard Books, 1998.

Point of Grace. *When Love Came Down at Christmas*. West Monroe, La.: Howard Books, 2000.

Point of Grace and Davin Seay. *Life, Love, and Other Mysteries*. New York: Pocket Books, 1996.

Powell, Mark Allen. *Encyclopedia of Contemporary Christian Music*. Peabody, Mass.: Hendrickson Publishers, Inc., 2002.

Quebedeaux, Richard. *The Heart of Rock 'n' Roll*. Old Tappan, N.J.: Fleming H. Revell, 1986.

Quebedeaux, Richard. *The Worldly Evangelicals*. San Francisco: Harper & Row, 1978.

Racine, Kree Jack. *Above All* (biography of the Blackwood Brothers). Memphis, Tenn.: Jarodoce, 1967.

Reagon, Bernice Johnson, and Linn Shapiro, eds. *Roberta Martin and the Roberta Martin Singers: The Legacy and The Music*. Washington, D.C.: Smithsonian, 1982.

Richard, Cliff. *Which One's Cliff?* London: Hodder and Stoughton, 1981.

Ricks, George Robinson. *Some Aspects of the Religious Music of the United States Negro*. New York: Arno Press, 1977.

Roach, Hildred. *Black American Music*. Boston: Crescendo, 1973.

Roell, Craig. *The Piano in America, 1890–1940*. Chapel Hill: University of North Carolina Press, 1989.

Rogal, Samuel J. *Sisters of Sacred Song*. New York: Garland, 1981.

Roland, Tom. *The Billboard Book of Number One Country Hits*. New York: Billboard Books, 1991.

Romanowski, Patricia, and Holly George-Warren, eds. *The New Rolling Stone Encyclopedia of Rock & Roll*. New York: Fireside, 1995.

Salvatore, Nick. *Singing in a Strange Land: C. L. Franklin, The Black Church, and the Transformation of America*. New York: Little, Brown and Company, 2005.

Schaeffer, Franky. *Addicted to Mediocrity: Twentieth Century Christians and the Arts*. Wheaton, Ill.: Crossway, 1985.

Scharen, Christian. *One Step Closer: Why U2 Matters to Those Seeking God*. Ada, Mich.: Brazos Press, 2006.

Schipper, Henry. *Broken Record: The Inside Story of the Grammy Awards*. New York: Birch Lane, 1992.

Schultze, Quentin. J. ed. *American Evangelicals and the Mass Media*. Grand Rapids, Mich.: Zondervan, 1990.

Seay, Davin, and Mary Neely. *Stairway to Heaven*. New York: Ballantine, 1986.

Shea, George Beverly, with Fred Bauer. *Songs That Lift the Heart*. Old Tappan, N.J.: Fleming H. Revell, 1972.

Shea, George Beverly, with Fred Bauer. *Then Sings My Soul*. Old Tappan, N.J.: Fleming H. Revell, 1968.

Shelton, Robert. *No Direction Home: The Life and Music of Bob Dylan*. New York: Beech Tree/William Morrow, 1986.

Smith, Anthony, ed. *Television: An International History*. New York: Oxford University Press, 1995.

Smith, Jane Stuard, and Betty Carlson. *A Gift of Music*. Chicago: Cornerstone Books, 1981.

Smith, Kevin. *At the Foot of Heaven*. Nashville, Tenn.: Star Song, 1994.

Smith, Michael W., and Fritz Ridenour. *Old Enough to Know*. Waco, Tex.: Word, 1987.

Southern, Eileen. *The Music of Black Americans: A History*. 2nd ed. New York: W. W. Norton, 1983.

Sterling, Christopher, and John M. Kitross. *Stay Tuned: A Concise History of American Broadcasting*. 2nd ed. Belmont, Calif.: Wadsworth, 1990.

St. James, Rebecca. *40 Days with God: A Devotional Journey*. Cincinnati, Ohio: Standard Publishing, 1996.

St. James, Rebecca. *You're the Voice: Forty More Days with God—a Contemporary Devotional*. Nashville, Tenn.: Thomas Nelson Publishers, 1997.

Stockman, Steve. *Walk On; The Spiritual Journey of U2*. Orlando, Fla.: Relevant Books, 2005.

Styll, John W. ed. *The Heart of the Matter: The Best of CCM Interviews, Volume 1*. Nashville, Tenn.: Star Song, 1991.

Swaggart, Jimmy, with Robert Paul Lamb. *Religious Rock 'n' Roll: A Wolf in Sheep's Clothing*. Baton Rouge, La.: Jimmy Swaggart Ministries, 1987.

Swaggart, Jimmy, with Robert Paul Lamb. *To Cross a River*. Plainfield, N.J.: Logos International, 1977.

Synan, Vinson. *The Holiness Pentecostal Movement*. Grand Rapids, Mich.: Eerdmans, 1971.

Talbot, John Michael. *Changes: A Spiritual Journey*. Chestnut Ridge, Ky.: Crossroad, 1984.

Tamke, Susan S. *Make a Joyful Noise unto the Lord.* N.p., 1978.

Thomas, B. J., with Jerry B. Jenkins. *Home Where I Belong.* Waco, Tex.: Word, 1978.

Thomas, B. J., and Gloria Thomas. *In Tune.* Grand Rapids, Mich.: Fleming H. Revell, 1983.

Thompson, John J. *Raised by Wolves: The Story of Christian Rock & Roll.* Toronto: ECW Press, 2000.

Tomlin, Chris. *The Way I Was Made: Words and Music for an Unusual Life.* Colorado Springs, Colo.: Multnomah, 2004.

U2 and Neil McCormick. *U2 by U2.* New York: Harper, 2007.

Vagacs, Robert. *Religious Nuts, Political Fanatics: U2 in Theological Perspective.* Cascade, Iowa: Cascade Books, 2005.

Van West, Carroll, ed. *The Tennessee Encyclopedia of History and Culture.* Nashville, Tenn.: Rutledge Hill, 1998.

Velasquez, Jaci, with Thom Granger. *A Heavenly Place: Words of Inspiration to Bring a Little Bit of Peace and Paradise into Your Life.* Hoffman Estates, Ill.: Fireside, 1998.

Wald, Gayle F. *Shout, Sister, Shout!: The Untold Story of Rock-and-Roll Trailblazer Sister Rosetta Tharpe.* Boston: Beacon Press, 2007.

Walsh, Sheila. *Never Give It Up.* Old Tappan, N.J.: Fleming H. Revell, 1986.

Ward, Andrew. *Dark Midnight When I Rise: The Story of the Jubilee Singers Who Introduced the World to the Music of Black America.* New York: Farrar, Straus and Giroux, 2000.

Warnke, Mike. *Hitchhiking on Hope Street.* Garden City, N.Y.: Doubleday, 1979.

Watson, Wayne. *Watercolor Ponies.* Waco, Tex.: Word, 1992.

Weber, Max. *The Protestant Ethic and the Spirit of Capitalism.* New York: Scribner, 1958.

Weill, Gus. *You Are My Sunshine: The Jimmie Davis Story.* Waco, Tex.: Word, 1977.

Whitaker, Beth. *The Calling of a Rock Star.* Mount Laurel, N.J.: Hawthorne Publishing Co., 1988.

Whitburn, Joel. *The Billboard Book of Top 40 Albums.* New York: Billboard Books, 1991.

Whitburn, Joel. *Pop Memories 1890–1954.* Menomonee Falls, Wis.: Record Research, Inc., 1986.

Whitburn, Joel. *Top 40 Hits.* New York: Billboard Publications, 1987.

Whitburn, Joel. *Top Pop Albums 1955–1985.* Menomonee Falls, Wis.: Record Research, 1985.

Whitburn, Joel. *Top Pop Singles 1955–2002.* Menomonee Falls, Wis.: Record Research, 2003.

White, A. and F. Bronson. *The Billboard Book of Number One Rhythm & Blues Hits.* New York: Billboard Books, 1993.

Wills, Garry. *Under God: Religion and American Politics.* New York: Simon and Schuster, 1990.

Winans, CeCe, with Renita J. Weems. *On a Positive Note: CeCe Winans—Her Joyous Faith, Her Life in Music, and Her Everyday Blessings.* New York: Atria, 1999.

Winter, David. *New Singer, New Song: The Cliff Richard Story.* Waco, Tex.: Word, 1967.

Witter, Evelyn. *Mahalia Jackson.* Milford, Mich.: Mott Media, 1985.

Wolfe, Charles K. "Gospel Boogie: White Southern Gospel Music in Transition." *Popular Music* 1 (1981).

Wolfe, Charles K. *Kentucky Country.* Lexington: University of Kentucky Press, 1982.

Wolfe, Charles K. *Tennessee Strings.* Knoxville: University of Tennessee Press, 1977.

Work, John W., ed. *American Negro Songs and Spirituals.* New York: Bonanza, 1940.

Work, John Wesley. *Folk Songs of the American Negro.* 1915. Reprint. New York: Negro Universities Press, 1969.

Young, Alan. *The Pilgrim Jubilees.* Jackson: University Press of Mississippi, 2001.

Young, Alan. *Woke Me Up This Morning: Black Gospel Singers and the Gospel Life.* Jackson: University Press of Mississippi, 1997.

Zolten, Jerry. *Great God A'Mighty: The Dixie Hummingbirds—Celebrating the Rise of Soul Gospel Music.* New York: Oxford University Press, 2003.

Index

About the Editor and Contributors

Don Cusic is professor of music business at Belmont University and the author of 18 books; these include *The Sound of Light: A History of Gospel and Christian Music*.

Liz Cavanaugh works for Curb Records and is actively involved in the promotion and marketing of Christian acts.

James Elliott is associate professor of music business at Belmont University; his songs have been recorded by a number of Christian artists, and he cowrote a song with Steven Curtis Chapman that was nominated for a Dove Award.

Becky Garrison is a New York-based religious satirist whose books include *The New Atheist Crusaders and Their Unholy Grail, Rising from the Ashes: Rethinking Church*, and *Red and Blue God, Black and White Church*.

Bob Gersztyn is a journalist based in Salem, Oregon, who was part of the early Jesus movement at Calvary Chapel and who regularly covers Christian music for Christian periodicals. He is writing a book on the history of contemporary Christian music.

Vernell Hackett is a well-known journalist who has covered both country and Christian music for more than 30 years and has been published in numerous publications.

Rich Tiner is professor of media studies at Belmont University and is considered one of the pioneers of contemporary Christian radio. His career highlights include programming KFMK, KXYZ, and KGOL in Houston; serving as vice president of programming and operations at the Morningstar Radio Network in Nashville; and owning a small group of radio stations in Texas and Washington State.